Freedom Rising

Human Empowerment and the Quest for Emancipation

This book presents a comprehensive theory of why human freedom gave way to increasing oppression since the invention of states – and why this trend began to reverse itself more recently, leading to a rapid expansion of universal freedoms and democracy. Drawing on a massive body of evidence, Christian Welzel tests various explanations of rising freedoms, providing convincing support for a well-reasoned theory of emancipation. The study demonstrates multiple trends toward human empowerment – a process through which people gain control over their lives. Most important among these trends is the spread of "emancipative values," which emphasize free choice and equal opportunities. The author identifies the desire for emancipation as the single source of the various human empowerment trends and shows when and why this desire grows strong; why it is the source of democracy; and how it vitalizes civil society, feeds humanitarian norms, enhances happiness, and helps redirect modern civilization toward sustainable development.

Christian Welzel is chair of political culture research at the Center for the Study of Democracy, Leuphana University Lüneberg, Germany, and president of the World Values Survey Association. He is also special foreign consultant to the Laboratory of Comparative Social Research at the Higher School of Economics, St. Petersburg, Russia, and a permanent affiliate of the Center for the Study of Democracy at the University of California, Irvine. A repeated recipient of large-scale grants from the German Science Foundation, Welzel is the author of more than one hundred scholarly publications in international peer-reviewed journals in sociology, political science, and psychology. His recent books include *Modernization, Cultural Change, and Democracy* (with Ronald Inglehart, Cambridge University Press, 2005); *Democratization* (with Christian Haerpfer, Patrick Bernhagen, and Ronald Inglehart, 2009); and *The Civic Culture Transformed* (with Russell J. Dalton, Cambridge University Press, forthcoming).

World Values Surveys Books from Cambridge University Press

Russell J. Dalton and Christian Welzel (eds.), *The Civic Culture Transformed: From Allegiant to Assertive Citizenries*, forthcoming.

Doh Chull Shin, *Confucianism and Democratization in East Asia*, 2012.

Pippa Norris and Ronald Inglehart, *Sacred and Secular: Politics and Religion Worldwide*, 2011.

Pippa Norris and Ronald Inglehart, *Cosmopolitan Communications: Cultural Diversity in a Globalized World*, 2009.

Ronald Inglehart and Christian Welzel, *Modernization, Cultural Change, and Democracy: The Human Development Sequence*, 2005.

Ronald Inglehart and Pippa Norris, *Rising Tide: Gender Equality and Cultural Change around the World*, 2003.

Freedom Rising

Human Empowerment and the Quest for Emancipation

CHRISTIAN WELZEL

Leuphana University, Lüneberg, Germany

CAMBRIDGE
UNIVERSITY PRESS

CAMBRIDGE
UNIVERSITY PRESS

32 Avenue of the Americas, New York NY 10013-2473, USA

Cambridge University Press is part of the University of Cambridge.

It furthers the University's mission by disseminating knowledge in the pursuit of education, learning and research at the highest international levels of excellence.

www.cambridge.org
Information on this title: www.cambridge.org/9781107664838

First published 2013

A catalogue record for this publication is available from the British Library

Library of Congress Cataloguing in Publication data
Welzel, Christian, 1964–
Human empowerment and the contemporary quest for emancipation / Christian Welzel.
    pages cm
ISBN 978-1-107-03470-9 (hardback)
1. Social values.   2. Liberty.   3. Democracy.   I. Title.
HM681.W453   2013
303.3′72–dc23   2013015876

ISBN 978-1-107-03470-9 Hardback
ISBN 978-1-107-66483-8 Paperback

To AMY,
the Love
and Inspiration
of My Life

Contents

Tables

Figures

Boxes

Abbreviations

CRI	Citizen Rights Index
CW	Cool Water
EV	Emancipative Values
EVI	Emancipative Values Index
EVS	European Values Study
GDP	Gross Domestic Product
LGBT	Lesbian, Gay, Bisexual, and Transgender
SMA	Social Movement Activity
SV	Secular Values
SVI	Secular Values Index
WA	Water Autonomy
WVS	World Values Surveys

Preface

This book is indebted to the lifetime work of Ronald Inglehart. Over the past fifteen years, I had the privilege of becoming one of Ron's closest collaborators and friends. Apart from our work on dozens of publications, Ron is a continuous source of inspiration in our frequent conversations about social change, human values, and the role of evolution in the civilization process. I know his work on postmaterialism since my days in college and followed the debate about this concept with fascination. Despite the criticism, I remain convinced that the basic logic holds: fading existential pressures open people's minds, making them prioritize freedom over security, autonomy over authority, diversity over uniformity, and creativity over discipline. By the same token, persistent existential pressures keep people's minds closed, in which case they emphasize the opposite priorities. I am equally convinced that the further implications of this logic hold as well: the existentially relieved state of mind is the source of tolerance and solidarity beyond one's in-group; the existentially stressed state of mind is the source of discrimination and hostility against out-groups.

These propositions assume a universal logic of how the human mind copes with existential conditions. This book describes this logic as the *utility ladder of freedoms*. The more existential pressures recede, the more does the nature of life shift from a source of threats into a source of opportunities. As this happens, societies ascend the utility ladder of freedoms: practicing and tolerating freedoms becomes increasingly useful to take advantage of what a more promising life offers. Since evolution favors utility-realizing capacities, it has "programmed" humans to seek freedoms – in as much as these are useful to thrive under given circumstances. Culture does not have the power to turn off this logic. Instead, the taboos that culture imposes and the choices that it tolerates are themselves selected by the utility of freedoms: when fading existential pressures make freedoms more useful, cultures shift from denying freedoms to guaranteeing them. This happens because people change their mind in this direction –

recognizing that improving living conditions move them up the utility ladder of freedoms. These individual adaptations reinforce each other through mutual recognition. Reciprocally reinforced adaptations generate mass trends that follow their own evolutionary logic; they are *not* the result of propaganda, indoctrination, and other elite-fabricated manipulations. As this book demonstrates, representative survey data from the World Values Surveys and European Values Study confirm an evolutionary logic of cultural change.

In a sense, this book is a sequel to my joint work with Ron in *Modernization, Cultural Change, and Democracy* (2005). The approach to analyze culture and development is basically the same, and various previous findings are updated with more recent data. Nevertheless, this book makes seven contributions that move our understanding of societal development ahead from where we were. To begin with, I explicate in a systematic way the *evolutionary theory of emancipation* that is implicit in our previous work (Chapter 1). Emancipation theory refers to everyone's freedoms; it is a theory of the utility of *universal* freedoms and the evolutionary origin of this utility. The theory explains when universal freedoms become useful and when people recognize this and begin to desire these freedoms, and when not. The logic behind this manifests itself in two opposing configurations, both of which shape the entire fabric of societies. Under existential pressures, universal freedoms have little utility, so people place little value on them. It is unlikely in this situation that elites would guarantee universal freedoms, and, when they do it against the odds, the guarantees are likely to be ineffective. This pattern describes where democracy does not take root or remains a façade of authoritarian practice. In contrast, fading existential pressures increase the utility of universal freedoms and people begin to value these freedoms accordingly. With the utility and value of freedoms rising, social pressures to guarantee them mount until the denial becomes too costly. Once guarantees are granted, pressures on elites to adhere to them continue, resulting in effective guarantees. This pattern describes where democracy emerges and thrives. Taken together, these propositions condense in the *sequence thesis* of emancipation theory: if freedoms grow, they grow in a chain of order from utilities to values to guarantees. Institutions that guarantee universal freedoms are the outcome, not the cause of this process – in contradiction to the prominent "institutions first" view.

Second, the theory of emancipation situates value change in a framework that focuses on human empowerment as the lead theme. In so doing, the theory rises to a higher level of generalization. What were separate fragments in our prior theorizing are now integrated into a coherent framework in which every aspect derives from a single root principle: the utility ladder of freedoms. The pervasiveness of this principle surfaces in juxtaposition of two opposing cycles that shape the entire fabric of societies. For one, when universal freedoms have little utility, low value, and no effective guarantee, a society is trapped in a cycle of human disempowerment: ordinary people have little control over their lives and their society's agenda. Conversely, when universal freedoms have great utility, a high value, and effective guarantees, a society thrives in a cycle of human empowerment: ordinary people are in control.

Third, I identify "emancipative values" as the mindset that arises as human empowerment proceeds. The major thrust of emancipative values is an emphasis on freedom of choice and equality of opportunities. Emancipative values are reminiscent of "self-expression values" in our prior work. However, as I show in Chapter 2, the concept of emancipative values is theoretically better grounded, and more consistently operationalized, and it has better measurement quality than its precursor self-expression values.

Fourth, I document in more nuanced ways and with broader evidence how emancipative values emerge. Generally speaking, these values grow as ordinary people gain control over *action resources*. Action resources include tools, skills, and opportunities that enable people to do things at will (Chapter 3). Furthermore, the action resources that people have in common with most other members of their society strengthen their emancipative values much more than the resources that people have on top of others. Hence, the utility of freedoms resides in *joint* utilities, creating solidarity in values and actions among those who share these utilities. And because action resources tend to become more widely shared in all of the world's culture zones, we see a ubiquitous rise of emancipative values over the generations (Chapter 4).

Fifth, this book demonstrates the consequences of emancipative values more broadly. As I show, emancipative values involve stronger intrinsic motivations (Chapter 5), nurture greater trust and humanism (Chapter 6), encourage social movement activity (Chapter 7), strengthen commitment to democratic norms (Chapter 10), and enhance environmental activism (Chapter 12). Quite naturally, values that radiate into so many domains have systemic consequences as well, most notably more extensive and effective guarantees of freedoms (Chapter 8), including those of specific subgroups such as women and homosexuals (Chapter 9). Moreover, the rise of emancipative values elevates a society's overall sense of well-being (Chapter 5). Finally, rising emancipative values contribute to better environmental quality (Chapter 12), helping to make societies more sustainable.

Sixth, this book develops a theory that is "complete" in the sense that it situates human empowerment and emancipative values in the entire process of civilization. In Chapter 11, I describe the Great Redirection through which the process of civilization has been diverted from perfecting human exploitation to advancing human empowerment. I show that this diversion happened recently on the time scale of history, and I explain both the redirection itself and its recentness by the utility ladder of freedoms. Urban civilization matured late in areas in which universal freedoms *naturally* have higher utility, due to an environment that harbors an original form of existential autonomy: easy and permanent access to water resources for everyone ("water autonomy"). This is what I call the *source thesis* of emancipation theory. According to the source thesis, water autonomy is an exceptional feature of areas characterized by moderately cold temperatures and continuous rainfall over all seasons: the "cool-water zones" (CW zones). Across the globe, the first civilization to reach urban maturity in a CW zone was Western Europe in about 1450–1500 CE. This is when and where the human empowerment process started and from where it diffused to the other CW areas of the world, most notably North America, the southeast of Australia, New Zealand, and Japan. These are still the areas that are most advanced in human empowerment. Yet, the era of globalization shows signs of decoupling human empowerment from its confinement to CW areas. As societies in Asia, Latin America, and – more recently – Africa are catching up, the human empowerment process is globalizing. This is the *contagion thesis* of emancipation theory.

Seventh, as this happens, human civilization faces the challenge of sustainability: the life improvements that come with human empowerment inflict unprecedented damage on the environment. But even though human empowerment causes the sustainability challenge, it also holds the key to its solution: emancipative values. As Chapter 12 demonstrates, these values stimulate environmental activism, which helps to redirect human empowerment to a path of "green" technologies. Sustainable human empowerment becomes a real possibility.

In light of these new explorations, I hope the scientific community will consider this book a useful theoretical, conceptual, and empirical extension of the work on which it builds.

Christian Welzel
Centers for the Study of Democracy
UC Irvine and Leuphana University
and
Laboratory for Comparative Social Research
Higher School of Economics, St. Petersburg
February 6, 2013

Acknowledgment

Over the past ten to fifteen years, I had the privilege of discussing my ideas with numerous colleagues, many of whom gave me important feedback. I am grateful for the time and energy that these colleagues have invested. These lines are written to acknowledge this.

The first person to be mentioned is Ronald Inglehart. I cooperated most intensely with Ron in the years leading up this book. The ways that he encouraged and helped me improve my ideas are invaluable. Thank you, Ron. Next, I must mention Hans-Dieter Klingemann, the former director of the department for Institutions and Social Change at the Science Center for Social Research Berlin (WZB). Hans-Dieter has been a mentor in various ways. His support of my scholarship brought me into contact with Ron and initiated my relationship with the Center for the Study of Democracy at the University of California (UC), Irvine. I received valuable feedback from the following former colleagues and guests at the WZB: Simon Bornschier, Thomas Cusack, David Easton, Sybille Frank, Dieter Fuchs, Philipp Harfst, Thomas Koenig, Hanspeter Kriesi, Annette Legutke, Seymour M. Lipset, Friedhelm Neidhardt, Kenneth Newton, Guillermo O'Donnell, Barbara Pfetsch, Edeltraud Roller, Kai-Uwe Schnapp, Carsten Schneider, Gunnar Folke Schuppert, Andrea Volkens, and Bernhard Wessels.

Among German colleagues, I received feedback from Jens Alber, Stefan Bergheim, Dirk Berg-Schlosser, Klaus von Beyme, Hermann Duelmer, Juergen Gerhards, Stefan Hradil, Wolfgang Jagodzinski, Werner Jann, Wolfgang Kersting, Helmut Klages, Markus Klein, Hans-Joachim Lauth, Steffen Mau, Wolfgang Merkel, Heiner Meulemann, Ekkehard Mochmann, Ingvill Mochmann, Gert Pickel, Susanne Pickel, Markus Quandt, Sigrid Rossteutscher, Friedbert Rueb, Fritz Scharpf, Wolfgang Schluchter, Rainer Schmalz-Bruns, Manfred G. Schmidt, Peter Schmidt, Siegmar Schmidt, Ruediger Schmidt-Beck, Hans-Juergen Schupp, Fritz Strack, and Jan van Deth.

Among international colleagues, I received input from Paul Abramson, Peter Anselm, Winton Bates, Jeannette Sinding Bentzen, Michael H. Bond, Dan Brandstrom, Michael Bratton, Renske Dorenspleet, Ronald Fischer, Joe Foweraker, Bruce Gilley, Herbert Ginthis, Gary Goertz, Axel Hadenius, Jacob Gerner Hariri, Soren Holmberg, Nicolai Kaarsen, Daniel Kahneman, Hans Keman, Odbjorn Knutsen, Todd Landman, Staffan Lindberg, Frederik Lundmark, Robert Matthes, Pippa Norris, Pamela Paxton, Anna Maria Pinna, Bo Rothstein, Jeffrey Sachs, Francesco Sarracino, Shalom Schwartz, Richard Sennett, Doh Chull Shin, Paul Sniderman, Dietlind Stolle, Roger Stough, Christian Thoeni, Jacques Thomassen, Nicolas Valentino, Evert van de Vliert, Peter Whybrow, and Asger Moll Wingender.

At my former workplace, Jacobs University Bremen, I repeatedly exchanged my ideas with Klaus Boehnke, Matthijs Bogaards, Hilke Brockmann, Jan Delhey, Juan Díez-Medrano, Jens Foerster, Freia Hardt, Max Kaase, Arvid Kappas, Ulrich Kuehnen, Marion Mueller, Klaus Schoemann, Ursula Staudinger, Marco Verweij, and Adalbert Wilhelm.

At the Institute for Future Studies, the host of the World Values Survey Association's secretariat, I had a particularly fruitful and intense exchange about my work with Peter Hedstrom, Bi Puranen, Victoria Spaiser, and David Sumpter.

I have had an especially intense exchange with people in the World Values Surveys network and the European Values Study. In this context, I received frequent comments from Fares al-Braizat, Marita Carballo, Jaime Díez-Nicolas, Juan Díez-Nicolas, Yilmaz Esmer, Christian W. Haerpfer, Jacques Hagenaars, Loek Halman, Ola Listhaug, Hennie Kotze, Martha Lagos, Bernhard Lategan, Ruud Luijx, Mansoor Moaddel, Alejandro Moreno, Neil Nevitte, Thorleif Pettersson, Catalina Romero, Ursula van Beeck, Birol Yesilada, and Ephraim Yuchtman-Yaar – as well as from Bi Puranen and her wonderful family who deserve special mention for all their encouragement in the past ten or so years.

As a regular visitor of the Center for the Study of Democracy (CSD) at UC Irvine, I had stimulating exchanges with Deborah Avant, Catherine Bolzendahl, Thomas Doyle, Wang Feng, Reuben Kline, David Meyer, Marc Petracca, Wayne Sandholtz, Willi Schonfeldt, David Snow, Rein Tagepeera, Yulia Tverdova, Carol Uhlaner, and Steven Weldon. Among the people at the CSD, former directors Russell J. Dalton, Bernie Grofman, and Willi Schonfeldt deserve special mention for their generous support during my regular visits. I am grateful in particular to Russell J. Dalton with whom I had the privilege to work on another book project that is close to completion (Dalton & Welzel).

I could not have finished this book without the support of the team of my chair at Leuphana University's Center for the Study of Democracy. Thus, I thank Dajana Badenhup, Bjoern Buss, Markus Kronfeldt, Stefan Kruse, Helen Ludwig, Jan Mueller, Nikolas Napierala, and Maren Wulff. Beyond my chair's team, I am grateful to comments from many other members of the center, including

Basil Bornemann, Sebastian Elischer, Dawid Friedrich, Florian Grotz, Ina Kubbe, Ferdinand Mueller-Rommel, Thomas Saretzki, Esther Seha, Charlotte Speth, and Ralf Tils.

In my role as a foreign advisor of the Laboratory for Comparative Social Research (LCSR) at the Higher School of Economics in St. Petersburg, I received intense and valuable feedback from Daniel Alexandrov, Evgenya Bystrov, Natalie Firsova, Olga Gryaznova, Ronald Charles Inglehart, Tatiana Karabchuk, Svitlana Khutka, Leonid Kosals, Veronika Kostenko, Anna Nemirenskova, Eduard Ponarin, Maria Ravlik, Andrey Sherback, Alexej Zakharov, Margarita Zavadskaya, Julia Zelikova, and Kyrill Zhirkov. Among these people, the director of the LCSR, Eduard Ponarin, and the assistant director, Tatiana Karabchuk, deserve special thanks for all their administrative and personal support during my stays in Russia.

The most intense exchange I had was with the people working in the DFG-funded project Drivers and Consequences of Postindustrial Value Change: Germany in Comparative Perspective. These people include, first of all, my associate project manager Franziska Deutsch, and our wonderful assistants: Jan Eichhorn, Eva Grzecznik, Maximilian Held, Jakob Hensing, and Julian Wucherpfennig.

Within this group, Stefanie Reher deserves her own thanks: she proofread an earlier version of the manuscript. Special thanks are also due to Roberto Foa, Chris Swader, Serban Tanasa, and Winton Bates who commented extensively on a draft version of the manuscript. Gary Goertz gave important feedback on some measurement issues. And I am indebted to Pippa Norris who shared with me her experience in preparing a book proposal and marketing information: thanks indeed.

Furthermore, I want to thank the German Science Foundation, the Alexander-von-Humboldt Foundation, the School of Humanities and Social Sciences at Jacobs University Bremen, the Centers for the Study of Democracy at UC Irvine and Leuphana University Lüneberg, and the Laboratory for Comparative Social Research at the Higher School of Economics in St. Petersburg, as well as the Institute for Future Studies in Stockholm for financial and administrative support. Special thanks indeed go to Lew Bateman, the chief social science editor of the U.S. branch of Cambridge University Press, and to Shaun Vigil, his associate. They did a formidable job in navigating me through the editing process. Their entire production team is just marvelous.

This book consumed a considerable proportion of my time and energy. Thus, I needed the sympathy of people in my personal environment, including my daughters (two real gems), Janika and Felipa Fe Welzel; my parents, Gisela and Peter Welzel; my parents- and brothers-in-law, Jeannette, Lynn, Sean, Mike, and Chris Alexander and their families; and my oldest and closest friend and his wife, Gert and Christine Schlossmacher. Thanks to all of you.

My last note of gratitude goes to Amy Alexander – my wife, friend, and colleague. From you, I received more feedback, inspiration, and encouragement than I could ever have hoped for. I dedicate this work to you.

Introduction

> There is greater dependence of governments on the governed who need to be highly motivated if a complex state-society is to function well. ... Even if the pressure is diffuse, the sentiment of the mass of the population ... is today a stronger factor in the power balance of a state society than ever before.
>
> – Norbert Elias 1984 [1939]: 229

I. THE THEME: FREEDOM RISING

From the dawn of our species until recently, most people lived in poverty and insecurity, and their lives were short. Worse, with the onset of civilization, people were subjected to overlords. Ever since, state organization was tailored to perfecting human exploitation and, for millennia, growing state capacities meant increasing oppression of freedoms (Diamond 1997; Nolan & Lenksi 1999). Indeed, abandoning original freedoms was the very definition of civilization (Elias 1984 [1939]). Only recently did this trend begin to reverse itself. The first signs occurred with the English, Dutch, American, and French revolutions of the seventeenth and eighteenth centuries (Grayling 2007). These liberal revolutions brought a game change in history: tyranny, although it continues to exist, is no longer safe; in fact, it is receding at an accelerating pace (Modelski & Gardner 2002).

That ordinary people stand up against oppression and enforce freedoms was initially an exclusive feature of the West. Yet, multiple failures of authoritarianism in other parts of the world encouraged several waves of democratization, the breakdown of communism, the Color Revolutions, and the Arab Spring (Huntington 1991; Markoff 1996; McFaul 2002; Weijnert 2005; Kalandadze & Orenstein 2009; Gause 2011). Mass pressures by people who claim freedoms were the driving force of all these revolutions (Karatnycky & Ackerman 2005; Schock 2005). Of course, as some striking cases of authoritarian resilience and revival remind us, people's freedoms do not always carry the day (Bunce & Wolchik 2010; Levitsky & Way 2010). Nevertheless, people's desire for freedoms has never been voiced so powerfully, so frequently, and in so many places as today – both inside and outside democracies (Clark 2009; Tilly & Wood 2009; Carter 2012).

This book is about the human quest for freedoms and its inspirational source – the desire for emancipation: an existence free from domination. Wherever and whenever this desire awakes, it is visible in what I call *emancipative values*. These values constitute the motivational source of a broad process of *human empowerment*. The human empowerment process is pervasive. It transforms the contemporary world in multiple and yet coherent ways, some of which will be outlined on the following pages. Since emancipative values represent the "spirit" of the human empowerment process, this book focuses on the rise of these values, examining their content, drivers, and consequences.

Emancipation, the idea of existing free from domination, is a universal desire (Sen 1999). As self-aware beings with the gift of imagination, humans have an inherent wish to live free from external constraints (Deci & Ryan 2000; Haller & Hadler 2004; Fischer & Boer 2011). Even if such a thing as "free will" does not exist in an absolute sense, as some authors suggest (Harris 2012), believing in free will is part of the human psychological makeup and when this belief is shattered, several negative consequences follow: people feel less happy, and they exert less control over their selfish impulses (Ryan & Deci 2000; Baumeister, Masicampo, & DeWall 2009).

The desire for freedoms is so fundamental that all major religions address it by advocating the idea of salvation. Salvation is an inherently emancipatory idea because it promises an existence free from domination in the afterlife (Dumont 1986; Lal 1998). The difference with emancipative values is that they aim at emancipation in *this* life. Emancipative values constitute a secular version of the desire for freedoms.

Emancipative values adapt to existential constraints beyond people's control. These values grow strong wherever external pressures on human life recede. Conversely, where existential pressures persist, emancipative values remain dormant. Hence, emancipative values develop in response to the variable utilities of freedoms. Where fading pressures increase the utility of freedoms, people begin to value freedoms accordingly. This utility-value link is instrumental to human livability: it keeps our values in touch with reality and helps people to adjust their life strategies to changing opportunities.

Over most of history, ordinary people's conditions were dire and miserable (Maddison 2007; Morris 2010; Galor 2011). As long as this was the case, there was no mass basis for emancipative values. Yet, since the Industrial Revolution growing proportions of humankind experience higher living standards, longer lives, and other improved conditions. With these improvements, life transforms from a source of threats into a source of opportunities, shifting from a struggle to survive to a drive to thrive. As life becomes more promising, how people act changes from what external pressures force them to do to what inner desires encourage them to do. Thus, entire populations ascend the *utility ladder of freedoms.* As this happens, practicing and tolerating freedoms becomes increasingly instrumental to taking advantage of the opportunities that a more promising life offers. This sea change in the nature of human lives does not only happen in rich Western societies. Millions of people in China, India, and other rapidly advancing societies are leaving behind poverty, oppression, and other miserable conditions (Simon 1996, 1998; Goklany 2007). As a result, the human quest for emancipation awakens; emancipative values grow strong.

This is not to deny that poverty and oppression continue to be real in parts of the world. But these parts are shrinking (Sachs 2005). Income, literacy, and longevity have never in history been at such high levels for so many people (Maddison 2007; Ridley 2010; Morris 2010). Indeed, living conditions are improving since the 1970s in most regions (Estes 1998, 2000a, 2000b, 2010; Moore & Simon 2000; Heylighen & Bernheim 2000; Lomborg 2001). Parts of sub-Saharan Africa are the exception, although recently the overall trend turns positive even there (Africa Progress Panel 2012). The same is true for the post-Soviet world: post-Soviet societies experienced deteriorating conditions after the breakdown of communism but are recovering. The three diagrams in Figure I.1 (p. 4) evidence these points with respect to ordinary people's longevity, education, and income in regions around the world.

The incidence of war, terror, torture, and other forms of physical violence is in decline in most places since the end of decolonization (Human Security Report Project 2006; Gat 2006; Nazaretyan 2009; Pinker 2011). The global spread of democracy and the increasing prominence of human rights norms help to reduce oppression on a global scale (Huntington 1991; Markoff 1996; Moravcsik 2000; McFaul 2002; Landman 2005; Pegram 2010). The female half of the human race profits in particular from receding oppression. Patriarchy, the most enduring form of human oppression, is declining, and the status of women is steadily improving in all but a handful of societies worldwide (Walter 2001; Inglehart & Norris 2003; Strom 2003; Alexander & Welzel 2010).[1]

The human condition improves even in a domain in which scholars considered such improvements impossible: subjective well-being (Easterlin 1995, 2005). As recent evidence suggests, life satisfaction and the number of "happy life years" have increased over the past thirty years in most societies for which data are available (Hagerty & Veenhoven 2006; Inglehart, Foa, Peterson, & Welzel 2008; Veenhoven 2010).[2]

Physical security, peace, prosperity, longevity, education, technology, democracy, rule of law, citizen rights, trust, tolerance, social movement activity, gender

---

[1] Evidence for this statement is available from the United Nations Development Program's (2011) *Gender Development Index* (GDI) and the *Gender Empowerment Measure* (GEM), which document continuous improvement in the living conditions and power sharing of women in all but a handful of societies worldwide.

[2] A study by Inglehart et al. (2008) shows that happiness has been increasing in fifty out of fifty-five societies worldwide for which a time series of at least fifteen years is available.

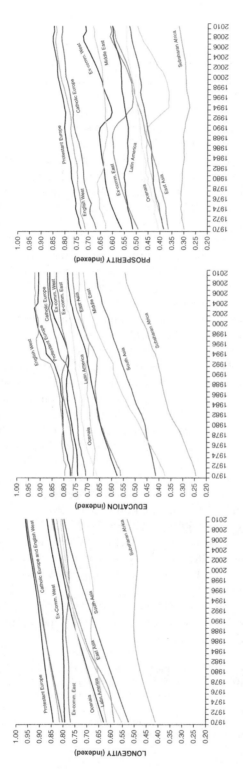

FIGURE I.1 Quality of Life Trends by Global Regions (1970–2010).

Trends are based on my own calculations from data for 136 countries published by the United Nations Development Program (2011). To see which country has been arranged into which region, see Appendix I (www.cambridge.org/welzel). Note that upward trends prevail throughout the past thirty years all over the world, with two exceptions: (1) longevity and prosperity in sub-Saharan Africa only rise recently; and (2) after the collapse of communism, ex-communist societies experienced a drop in quality of life, especially prosperity, but are on their way of recovery.

equality, social safety, environmental protection, and human happiness all are most advanced in postindustrial knowledge societies (Bell 1973; Toffler 1990; Drucker 1993; Florida 2002). These societies are at the forefront of the human empowerment process. People in knowledge societies experience weakening social control mechanisms, diminishing group norms, fading conformity pressures, and, more generally, individualization: a process that places behavioral control with people themselves (Wellman 1979, 2001; Beck 2002). As this happens, institutions increasingly need people's voluntary commitment in order to function (Coleman 1990). Individualization increases the importance of people's values as a guide for their actions. As this book demonstrates, emancipative values emerge as the psychological byproduct of individualization.

Emancipative values emphasize freedom of choice. However, the emphasis on freedom is not selfish but coupled with an emphasis on equality of opportunities. This directs people's attention to issues of social justice. As a consequence, people become more easily upset about incidents of discrimination. The relationship of emancipative values to tolerance cuts two ways for these reasons. On the one hand, emancipative values imply more tolerance of deviant behaviors that leave other people's personal integrity untouched. Homosexuality and other benign forms of norm deviation are more tolerated as emancipative values grow strong. On the other hand, emancipative values mean less tolerance of behaviors that violate other people's integrity. These values make Mill's harm principle real. Hence, sexual, racial, and other forms of discrimination are less tolerated as emancipative values grow strong. Emancipative values spawn a liberal type of tolerance. Liberal tolerance is intolerant of illiberal practices.

Understood as an orientation that emphasizes freedom of choice and equality of opportunities, emancipative values are not an entirely new phenomenon. Instead, emancipatory ideals were initially laid out in Enlightenment philosophy by authors like Kant, Mill, and Montesquieu (Grayling 2007). At the beginning of the early modern era, an ethos of emancipation inspired the liberal revolutions of the seventeenth and eighteenth centuries in Western Europe and North America (Chirot 1994). With these beginnings, the emancipatory surge focused on such things as the abolition of slavery and serfdom and the protection of people from tyranny. Since then, the spirit of emancipation has expanded on a mass basis and no field of group discrimination is left untouched – be it racism, sexism, ageism, or other forms of injustice. Most importantly, emancipative values are emerging outside the Western world. We see them grow in Latin America, the postcommunist world, Asia, the Middle East, and, more recently, in parts of Africa. At least, as we will see in Chapters 3 and 4, this is what data from the World Values Surveys (WVS) suggest.

As emancipative values grow, they motivate a multitude of equal opportunity movements, and they make antidiscrimination norms the prime evaluation standard of the critical media and a thriving industry of "watchdog" organizations (Keane 2009). Constant public pressures from social movements and critical media confine executive power over people. In knowledge societies, personal rights are massively expanding in what is labeled a "rights revolution" (Epp 1998; Ignatieff 2000; Franck 2001; Pinker 2011). Likewise, the protection of individuals against abuses of state and corporate power improves through a growing legislation of consumer protection, data protection, minority protection, and multiple other rights protections (Bainbridge 2000; Bagudu 2003; Freeman 2003; Switzer 2003; Carey 2004; Hibbert 2004; Long 2004; Kafka 2005; Keane 2009). At the same time, new channels of citizen participation in public policy and policy planning open up (Smith & Wales 2000; Petts 2001; Scarrow 2001; Ansell & Gingrich 2003; Cain, Egan, & Fabbrini 2003).

These trends are most advanced in knowledge societies, and the gap between them and the rest of the world is still wide. Nevertheless, other societies around the globe are catching up.

All the social changes alluded to have one thing in common: each of them, in one way or another, empowers people to exercise freedoms – including freedoms to guide their private lives and to participate in public life. But one of the most significant features of all of these changes is that their connecting theme is rarely noticed. Because of disciplinary specialization, different branches of the social sciences discuss pieces and bits of this broad change in isolation. The underlying theme that merges these multiple currents into a single stream is lost from sight. This unifying stream is a humanistic transformation of civilization that makes societies increasingly people-powered. It is best understood by what I call the *human empowerment* process.

Emancipative values are the inspirational source of the human empowerment process. For this reason, this book focuses on these values. The following section provides an overview of the various chapters. The subsequent section then presents a culture zone scheme and a categorization of societies along human empowerment criteria used throughout this book. The book is accompanied by an extensive Appendix, available online at www.cambridge.org/welzel. The Appendix documents every technical detail, especially as concerns measurement, and includes supplementary analyses. The Appendix also provides data for replication studies.

2. PLAN OF THE BOOK

The twelve chapters of this book are organized into four parts. Part A comprises four chapters and conveys a basic understanding of emancipative values. Part B consists of three chapters, each of which illuminates from a different angle how people's emancipative values merge into a civic force that recreates social capital. Part C includes three chapters. They focus on a major consequence of these values' civic force: the democratic impulse. Part D is composed of two chapters that place emancipative values in a broad civilizational perspective, examining their significance in history and their role in meeting the planetary sustainability challenge. What follows is a brief overview.

Chapter 1, A Theory of Emancipation, is conceptual. It situates emancipative values in the broader process of human empowerment. Building on Sen (1999) and Nussbaum (2000), the chapter describes human empowerment as a process that frees human lives from external domination. Emancipative values constitute the inspirational core of this process. They empower people *psychologically*, strengthening their motivations to exercise freedoms. As shown in Figure 1.1 (p. 44), emancipative values complement two other elements of human empowerment: action resources and civic entitlements. Action resources empower people *existentially*, enhancing their capabilities to exercise freedoms. Civic entitlements empower people *institutionally*, widening their guarantees to exercise freedoms. Linked by emancipative values, these three elements merge into human empowerment.

Chapter 1 posits that emancipative values rise as a psychological adaptation to receding pressures on life. As existential pressures fade, people control more action resources. Consequently, people can do more things at will: they become more capable. Hence, entitlements that guarantee freedoms become useful: capable people can do more things with entitlements; they ascend the utility ladder of freedoms. Because people are perceptive the ascension does not escape their attention and they begin to desire entitlements. Rising emancipative values are the manifestation of this desire. Since values direct people's actions toward desired outcomes, emancipative values encourage people to claim the entitlements they desire. Participation in voicing such claims expands as emancipative values become more widely shared. Shared values and joint actions among capable and motivated people create solidarity power that is difficult to resist. At some point, rulers are forced to concede the claimed entitlements and adhere to them.

If action resources are deficient, the same logic operates in the opposite direction: freedoms have lower utility for less capable people; as a consequence, people desire freedoms less and do not emphasize emancipative values as strongly; hence, little action to claim and safeguard entitlements takes place. In the absence of claims, rulers have no reason to grant entitlements; their self-interest in power maximization remains unchecked.

According to these propositions, the three elements of human empowerment – action resources, emancipative values, and civic entitlements – are connected by a single root principle: the *utility ladder of freedoms*. This principle refers to universal freedoms and explains when the guarantees for such freedoms become useful and desired and when they do not. The logic suggests that the three elements of human empowerment emerge sequentially: first, emancipative values emerge as a psychological reaction to grown action resources; second, civic entitlements are granted, extended, and respected in response to capable and motivated people's solidary action. The *sequence thesis* of my emancipation theory summarizes these ideas, suggesting that, if freedoms grow, they grow in a sequence from utilities to values to guarantees. Yet, as this thesis' emphasis on *universal* freedoms suggests, this is a *collective* sequence: universal freedoms grow from joint utilities to shared values to general guarantees.

All of the subsequent chapters are empirical. They test the propositions laid out in Chapter 1 using the extensive cross-national and longitudinal evidence from the WVS and the European Values Study (EVS). At the time of this writing, the sixth round of the WVS is still in the field but not yet completed, and the data will not be publically available for another two years. For this reason, I decided to take the last completed round of the WVS as the end point of investigation, which is round five conducted in 2005 to 2008.

Based on these data, Chapter 2, Mapping Differences, introduces a twelve-item index of emancipative values. The index is a conceptually more concise measure of Inglehart and Welzel's (2005) "survival versus self-expression values." In the context of a cross-cultural analysis, a key question is whether emancipative values measure a narrow Western construct that does not apply to non-Western cultures. Alternatively, emancipative values emerge as a result of expanding action resources wherever such expansions take place, regardless of cultural traditions. In testing these alternatives, I examine whether the emancipative values of people in ninety-five societies around the world are better explained by these societies' "Westernness" or their people's action resources. It turns out that action resources provide a much better explanation. Consequently, emancipative values are not a Western-bound concept but one induced by the expansion of people's action resources – as the utility ladder of freedoms suggests.

Further analyses show that people's emancipative values cluster nationwise, with great differences between the national clusters. The analysis also documents that, in each society, people's emancipative values distribute in a single-peaked bell curve around the mean. Hence, national scores in emancipative values indicate each society's *most common level* of emancipative values. They are a valid representation of a society's center of gravity as concerns emancipatory ideals.

Within-societal differences in emancipative values along the lines of generation, gender, education, income, occupation, religion, and ethnicity also exist. And they show a meaningful pattern: on each cleavage line, the group with greater action resources emphasizes emancipative values more than the one with fewer resources – again, as the utility ladder of freedoms suggests. Hence, we obtain a social profile of who typically emphasizes emancipative values. In each society, this profile is the same: it is people living in better material conditions and people who are more educated and more widely connected – attributes that dominate in urban settings, among younger cohorts, and in knowledge professions. However, these similarities do not homogenize the values of people across societies. On the contrary, national differences in emancipative values dwarf the within-societal differences. For instance, even though university graduates are, in every nation, somewhat more emancipatory than the median resident, we find the same cross-national differences among university graduates as we find among median residents. The reason for this pattern is that people's emancipative values take shape on the basis of the action resources that are most common in their country, and not so much on the basis of action resources that they have on top of what most others in their country have. These common action resources still differ enormously between countries.

Chapter 3, Multilevel Drivers, analyzes how individual- and societal-level characteristics interact in shaping emancipative values. Using multilevel models that cover approximately 150,000 individuals in more than ninety societies, I examine which type of action resources strengthens people's emancipative values more: *material, intellectual,* or *connective* resources. Moreover, I analyze whether action resources matter more for the part that (a) most people have in common or (b) for the part that is unique to each individual. I find two answers: (1) intellectual and connective resources strengthen emancipative values even more than do material resources; (2) for all three types of resources, it is the common part rather than the unique parts that strengthens emancipative values more. This pattern reflects an important principle: the utility ladder of freedoms is a ladder of socially shared utilities rather than individually unique utilities. There is a social dimension involved here, visible in the solidarities that surface when joint utilities nourish collective actions in pursuit of shared values.

The social dimension relates to a striking pattern that is generally neglected but reemerges throughout this book: *cross-fertilization.* Cross-fertilization means the amplification of a personal attribute's inherent impulse through the attribute's prevalence in the respective society. The emancipatory impulse of education is a case in point: education tends to make people more emancipatory in their orientations but when more people in a society are educated, this tendency becomes even stronger. Hence, highly educated people are more emancipatory when there are many of them than when there are few of them. This is a matter of social cross-fertilization: education's inherent tendency toward emancipation amplifies when more people with that tendency come in touch with each other.

The phenomenon of cross-fertilization provides an important insight: the social prevalence of values has consequences independent of individuals' preferences for these values. Prevalence patterns are worth their own consideration for this reason. Acknowledging this is paying tribute to culture because, as a collective phenomenon, culture is manifest precisely in the prevalence of values.

Chapter 4, Tracing Change, takes a dynamic perspective, documenting and explaining change in emancipative values across the world. Change in these values, when it occurs, is driven by two moments. First, as people's action resources grow over the generations, younger cohorts enter societies with stronger emancipative values than did older cohorts. This is true for all culture zones of the globe, including sub-Saharan, Islamic, and Confucian societies. Next, the continuing expansion of action resources elevates each cohort's emancipative values over time.

Building on this finding, a separate analysis examines the dominant direction of causality in the relationships among the three elements of human empowerment: action resources, emancipative values, and civic entitlements. For the first time, the societal-level relationships among these three elements are examined longitudinally and in opposite directions, using long-term temporal order models. Specifically, I examine for each element whether it affects the later presence of the two other elements – independent of the influence it obtains from these elements' earlier presence.

The results establish that there is a main direction of causality, operating from action resources to emancipative values to civic entitlements. Due to these results, action resources constitute the *founding* element, emancipative values the *linking* element, and civic entitlements the *completing* element of human empowerment. This causal order confirms the sequence thesis of emancipation theory: first, the value of freedoms grows because the utility of freedoms has grown; then, guarantees of freedoms are established, or more effectively instituted, because the utility and value of freedoms both have risen. In short, freedoms grow in a utility-value-guarantee sequence.

Parts B and C of the book reverse the perspective. We no longer look at how emancipative values emerge. Instead, we examine the impact of emancipative values. While Part B examines in broader terms how the emergence of emancipative values infuses societies with a "civic force" that builds new social capital, Part C focuses on one particular consequence: democracy.

Three things make emancipative values a groundbreaking civic force. First, emancipative values inspire people to follow their intrinsic motivations rather than being remotely controlled. Second, the intrinsic impulse comes with increased empathy for other people's legitimate concerns. This creates a prosocial form of individualism that sees even remote others as equals, which makes it easier for people to join forces for shared concerns. Third, emancipative values infuse people with a strong urge to take action for shared concerns. In that very sense, emancipative values create new social capital. Taken together, these facets make emancipative values a civic force that encourages people to take their lives into their own hands and to shape their societies' agenda. Chapters 5 to 7 highlight each of these facets separately.

Chapter 5, Intrinsic Qualities, examines how emancipative values affect people's life strategies. For this purpose, we look at how emancipative values vary the life domains that shape people's general sense of well-being. The assumption is that most people prefer to be better rather than worse off and therefore focus on those domains that have the strongest impact on their general well-being. Using multilevel models, I find that emancipative values vary these domains very strongly. Specifically, the satisfaction people obtain from their sense of material well-being drops rapidly with rising emancipative values. At the same time, the satisfaction people receive from their sense of emotional well-being increases just as sharply, leading to a complete turnover in the determination of general well-being. I interpret this turnover as a change in strategy from seeking better material conditions to seeking deeper emotional fulfillment. This signals a shift from *acquisition* strategies to *thriving* strategies. The strategy shift does not terminate people's search for material acquisitions, yet acquisitions are no longer an end in themselves; they are sought in as much as they serve the drive for emotional fulfillment.

Any strategy makes one more satisfied if it succeeds in obtaining its goal. However, apart from the success in obtaining the goal, the type of goal at which one aims matters. Holding success constant, thriving strategies yield more satisfaction than acquisition strategies. I demonstrate this in multilevel models in which a respondent's general sense of well-being is explained by his or her material and emotional well-being, as well as by the *priorities* placed on both types of well-being. As expected, both material and emotional well-being increase general well-being. But whereas prioritizing emotional well-being increases general well-being further, prioritizing material well-being actually diminishes general well-being. This diminishment almost cancels the satisfaction gained from material well-being itself.

From an evolutionary point of view, the reward advantage of thriving strategies is crucial. It means that there is an inherent drive in human existence to remove the obstacles that prevent us from prioritizing fulfillment. Acquisition strategies are – in an evolutionary sense – a transitory means to this end. Human existence is driven to ascend the utility ladder of freedoms.

The findings of Chapter 5 suggest that emancipative values encourage pro-social behavior. The reason is that thriving strategies aim at fulfillment – a feeling that resides in committing oneself to a higher purpose, to a goal bigger than oneself (Maslow 1988 [1954]). Arguably, such "self-transcendent commitments" are socially beneficial: they engage people in activities that generate added value for others and the wider society. However, emancipative values represent a strongly individualistic orientation, and individualism is often portrayed as an antisocial orientation. This suggests that emancipative values are antisocial too. Chapter 6, Benign Individualism, addresses these conflicting expectations, examining whether emancipative values are anti- or pro-social. The evidence is straightforward: emancipative values constitute a pro-social form of individualism.

Specifically, I demonstrate in multilevel models that both individual preferences for emancipative values and these values' social prevalence favor (a) *unselfish orientations* that involve a concern for others and the environment, (b) *bridging trust* that perforates the boundaries to outsiders, and (c) *humanistic orientations* that defy group discrimination. Again, there is a pronounced cross-fertilization of emancipative values' pro-social impulse: a person's emancipative values have a stronger pro-social impulse when these values are more prevalent in the society in which the person lives. Thus, emancipative values are a *reciprocal good* whose benefits surface through mutual recognition. The evidence in Chapter 6 qualifies emancipative values in unequivocal clarity as a pro-social set of values. This does not mean that egoistic versions of individualism won't exist. But this is not what emancipative values measure: they measure benign individualism.

Chapter 7, Collective Action, examines another idea implied by the findings of Chapter 5: emancipative values have a strongly expressive impulse, encouraging people to take action with others to voice shared claims. Again, I use multilevel models, analyzing the reported participation of several hundred thousand individuals from ninety societies in peaceful social movement activities, including petitions, boycotts, and demonstrations. These activities are a key manifestation of people power: they frequently help to impose democracy on autocratic regimes, and they establish popular pressure as an enduring source of influence in mature democracies. As the models show, both a person's own emphasis on emancipative values and the prevalence of these values in the person's society fuel social movement activity. Once more, we observe the phenomenon of cross-fertilization that is typical of reciprocal goods: the activating impulse of a person's emancipative values is stronger when emancipative values are more prevalent in that person's society. Other factors that previous research has identified as influential, including resources and entitlements, show only a weak impact on social movement activity once we take emancipative values into account.

The activating impulse of emancipative values dissolves collective action blockades. Participation in collective actions is usually instrumentally motivated: the reason to participate is the action's goal, not the action itself. With a purely instrumental motivation, the freerider problem is prominent: if the goal can also be achieved without one's participation, or if it cannot be achieved even with one's participation, one does not participate. But if the voicing of a jointly valued claim is itself a value, we face a different situation. The motivation to participate is *intrinsic* in this case, not instrumental. Consequently, the freerider problem dissolves because, if one obtains satisfaction from the joint expression of a valued claim, one participates even if one's participation is not necessary for the action's success and even if the action is not likely to be successful.

Testing these propositions, I examine whether a high risk of repression disrupts the link between emancipative values and social movement activity. I find that this is not at all the case. Instead, the solidarity effect of widely shared emancipative values is so strong that it leads people to raise their voices, even in high-risk situations. In fact, this explains why the risk of repression is usually low when emancipative values prevail. Prevalent emancipative values motivate widespread social movement activities – which create pressure for the guarantees that prevent repression. In short, emancipative values activate people to make their shared claims heard. This is a truly empowering feature.

The findings of Chapters 5 to 7 portray emancipative values as a groundbreaking civic force that unlocks a population's intrinsic qualities, vitalizes civil society, and recreates social capital. Clearly, the evidence implies that emancipative values are a major source of democratizing pressures from below. The three chapters in Part C examine this implication directly.

From the viewpoint of human empowerment, democracy is important because it provides the institutional element of people power. In this institutional function, democracy is linked to two preinstitutional elements of people power: action resources and emancipative values. Because these two elements are preinstitutional, I consider them as societal antecedents of democracy. Thus, Chapter 8, Entitling People, shows that democracy's dependence on its preinstitutional antecedents is more obvious the more sharply the measurement of democracy focuses on the institutions that actually empower people. Among the various institutional features that define democracy, I single out civic entitlements as the feature that empowers people most directly. I define civic entitlements as guarantees for private and public action, granted equally to all constituents of a society. Civic entitlements in this sense comprise both personal autonomy rights and political participation rights. The former allow people to shape their private lives as they prefer; the latter allow them to make their preferences heard and count in public life. I combine measures of personal autonomy rights and political participation rights into a *citizen rights index* (CRI), using data from Freedom House and the Cingranelli/Richards Human Rights Project.

Comparing the new index of citizen rights with the six most widely used measures of democracy, it turns out that the CRI is a more rigorous measure: most societies' democratic qualities show up much more modestly on this index than on the other measures. Linked with the rigor of the CRI are two insightful features. First, the global democratization trend is visible but appears less impressive on the CRI than when one uses other measures of democracy. Next, democracy's link with preinstitutional manifestations of human empowerment is more obvious with the CRI than with the alternative measures. Taken together, these findings illuminate something largely overlooked in the literature: institutionalizing people power is not easy because it requires empowering qualities in the social context of democracy – qualities that institutions themselves cannot create but on which they depend.

Chapter 8 implies that rising emancipative values are a motivating force behind the "rights revolution" of recent decades. Chapter 9, The Rights Revolution, tests this assumption. It examines whether emancipative values drive the expansion of citizen rights or the other way around, or whether both are driven by "third" causes – including economic development, exogenous contagion, and cultural globalization. The temporal order model in Chapter 4 already suggests that the causal arrow runs from values to rights, rather than the other way around. But, given the wide temporal scope of this model, I had to rely on proxy measures and could not include important controls. In Chapter 9, I focus on the rights expansions of the more recent period, use direct measures of values and rights, and include relevant controls. Moreover, the emphasis is on *dynamic* relationships, looking at whether change in emancipative values drives change in citizen rights or vice versa. Alternatively, I test whether both changes are driven by change in plausible third causes.

Holding other things constant, I find that rising emancipative values drive expanding rights. Expanding rights, in turn, have a much weaker effect on rising emancipative values than the rights obtain from values. This confirms in a dynamic perspective the sequence thesis of emancipation theory: guarantees of freedoms are a response to an increased value of freedoms.

This pattern is not only evident for citizen rights in general but also for group-specific rights, most notably the rights of women and those of lesbians, gays, bisexuals, and transgenders (LGBTs). These rights, too, have been expanding, and the analyses show that these rights expansions are also driven by a concurrent rise of emancipative values, rather than the rights causing emancipative values to grow. As concerns the values-rights nexus, these findings establish a causal priority of culture over institutions – disconfirming the prominent "institutions first" view in political economy.

Chapter 10, The Paradox of Democracy, addresses one of the great puzzles of democracy: the *coexistence paradox*. This paradox describes the fact that widespread popular desires for democracy frequently coexist with serious deficiencies and even with the entire absence of democracy. However, if we take into consideration how emancipative values shape people's desires for democracy, the coexistence paradox dissolves. To demonstrate this point, the analysis focuses on a new battery of democracy questions fielded for the first time in round five of the WVS. Using multilevel models to examine the combined individual- and societal-level effects of emancipative values, a first noteworthy finding is that these values hardly affect the strength of people's desire for democracy. The democratic desire seems to be strong everywhere, showing very little variation across the globe. But emancipative values do change the *nature* of people's democratic desires. And they do so in a double way.

First, with growing emancipative values, people define democracy more unequivocally in terms of the liberal features that guarantee universal freedoms. Thus, the desire for democracy becomes more liberal with emancipative values. The evidence disproves the widespread assumption that people's desire for democracy is rooted in a redistributive notion of democracy. In fact, the notion of democracy as a tool to redistribute income from the rich to the poor is the least popular notion of democracy and does not motivate people's desire for democracy at all. The strongest driver of people's desire for democracy is the liberal notion of democracy, and this notion is systematically strengthened by emancipative values.

Second, with growing emancipative values, people assess their society's democratic quality as more deficient. In other words, mass assessments of democracy become more critical. Thus, the invariance in the mere strength of people's democratic desires hides fundamental differences in people's democratic expectations – which rise with emancipative values.

Once more, we find the phenomenon of cross-fertilization by which the social prevalence of emancipative values enhances the inherent impulses of these values: the liberal and critical impulse of a person's own emancipative values is stronger when this person lives in a society in which emancipative values are more prevalent.

These findings hold when one controls for democratic socialization and cognitive mobilization. To be sure, both democratic socialization and cognitive mobilization also make people's democratic desires more liberal and more critical. But the effect of emancipative values exists independent from these factors and is considerably stronger. Since cognitive mobilization is itself a determinant of emancipative values, its effect on democratic orientations is mostly indirect: cognitive mobilization is a democratizing force insofar as it strengthens emancipatory orientations. In conclusion, the strength of the desire for democracy does not vary much. Yet, the nature of this desire varies profoundly, becoming more liberal and critical with rising emancipative values.

These findings dissolve the coexistence paradox: the frequent coexistence of strong desires for democracy with severe deficiencies and even the absence of democracy. In every instance of this seeming paradox, people's desire for democracy is detached from the critical-liberal orientation that emancipative values create. Such detached desires are no source of pressure to establish or improve democracy. Therefore, detached desires easily coexist with deficient and absent democracy.

The two chapters of Part D widen the perspective, illuminating the role of emancipative values from the broadest possible point of view: human civilization.

Chapter 11, The Redirection of Civilization, examines the role of people power and human emancipation in the civilization process. I argue that human empowerment became the lead theme of the civilization process very late in history, demarcating a striking discontinuity: the Great Redirection. The Great Redirection marks a sharp turn in the direction in which civilization was moving, from perfecting human exploitation to advancing human empowerment. This did not happen until the "Rise of the Atlantic West" to global dominance in about 1450–1500 CE. Compared to Mediterranean Europe, the Middle East, India, China, and the Amerindian civilizations, the Atlantic West was a belated civilization. Yet, it was the first civilization to reach the mature stage of urbanization while being situated in what I call a CW zone. The next civilization in a CW zone to reach mature urbanity was Japan: it reached this stage in about 1600 CE at the beginning of the Tokugawa period. Reaching the mature urban stage of civilization in a CW zone comes with a signature feature that every other urban civilization lacked: *water autonomy*, that is, easy, equal, and permanent access to water resources for every individual in a territory.

Water autonomy cancels a historic route to despotism in agrarian societies: centrally controlled water supply. Making constituents more independent from their overlords, water autonomy proliferates derivative autonomies once urban markets emerge – including autonomy in market access, property disposal, profit acquisition, and skill allocation. These existential autonomies place their beneficiaries higher up on the utility ladder of freedoms, focusing their attention on entitlements. Herein resides the seed of the emancipatory spirit. This proposition constitutes the *source thesis* of my theory of emancipation.

Using climate data from Gallup, Mellinger, and Sachs (2010), I create an index that measures the presence of the CW condition in each society of the world. The CW index (CWI) correlates very strongly with indicators of all three elements of human empowerment, from action resources to emancipative values to civic entitlements. Indeed, the populations of the most advanced societies on the globe concentrate in the areas with the world's highest scores on the CWI, including Northwestern Europe, the coastal areas of North America, Japan, Southeastern Australia, and New Zealand. However, these areas were not always more advanced. Quite the contrary, civilization matured especially late in areas with high CW scores, if it matured at all. Before that happened, human empowerment was by no means a feature of civilization, not even in the most advanced civilizations. Hence, before the rise of the Atlantic West in about 1500, there was no correlation between human empowerment and the CW condition among societies around the world. This is shown using historic estimates of per capita income from Maddison (2007) as a proxy for human empowerment.

As the Atlantic West reached preindustrial urbanization, it had by far the highest CWI scores among all mature urban civilizations of Eurasia and Amerindia, matched only by Japan – which was, by no coincidence, the first society to emulate the Western take off. Outside Eurasia, there were also areas with high CWI scores: the coastal regions of Northern America, the south of South America, Southeastern Australia, and New Zealand. However, because of their migratory distance from the origin of humanity in East Africa, these regions were among the latest to be populated by modern humans. Moreover, these populations were disconnected from each other and cut off from the pool of civilizations in Eurasia. This isolation shielded the non-Eurasian CW-areas from the diffusion of urban civilization. Indeed, urban civilization was imported by European settlement into all CW-areas *outside* Eurasia. Within Eurasia, Western Europe and Japan have the biggest migratory distances from the initial centers of civilization in the Middle East and India. Intensive agriculture and urbanity eventually arrived there but did so considerably later than in the early centers of civilization. Once that happened, however, the utilities that a high degree of water autonomy bestows on freedoms came quickly to fruition, and the human empowerment process began.

During the colonial period, Western societies erected a world order that preserved the gains of human empowerment for Western peoples. Since the decolonization period, however, the Western monopoly over human empowerment erodes. Ongoing globalization accelerates this erosion. The global pooling of human experiences and knowledge offers our species the opportunity to liberate intercultural learning from the confines of geography. Thus, my analysis shows that the correlations of human empowerment with the societies' CWI scores decline since 1980 and that progressing globalization is responsible for that. Globalization helps environmentally disadvantaged societies to overcome their disadvantage, and human empowerment itself begins to globalize.

This evidence supports the *contagion thesis* of my theory of emancipation. The thesis assumes that, if given the chance, human effort directs itself toward more rather than less empowerment. This is why globalization makes human empowerment contagious: perforating people's ignorance, it gives them a chance to see how prosperous and free people live elsewhere and to refer to these achievements as a justification to mobilize for change in their own places.

Ironically, at the moment when human empowerment begins to globalize, the very success of this process threatens to destroy its own fundament. Globalizing human empowerment pushes civilization to the planetary boundaries of its sustainability. However, as much as the human empowerment process poses the sustainability challenge, it also holds the key to its solution. This conclusion is true on two accounts. First, to cope with the sustainability challenge, more knowledge about sustainable technologies is needed and human empowerment is intimately linked with the advancement of technologies. Second, to mobilize mass support for sustainable policies, public awareness of the sustainability challenge and readiness to contribute to its solution is needed. This is where emancipative values are beneficial. As Chapter 12, The Sustainability Challenge, shows, emancipative values close the awareness-behavior gap: with stronger emancipative values, people's ecological awareness translates more easily into environmental activism. This allows for a relatively optimistic outlook concerning public support of an ecological policy turn. By and large, this last finding rounds up a rich body of evidence, demonstrating from a variety of angles the importance of emancipative values for the future of human civilization.

Finally, the Conclusion rounds up this study in five sections. Section 1 summarizes the key findings of the various chapters, illustrated by a synopsis in Figure C.1. Section 2 outlines the main findings' chief implications for democracy. Section 3 relates the utility ladder of freedoms on which my theory is built to other important concepts, including the human need hierarchy, existential security, and social capital. Section 4 argues that rising emancipative values indicate the moral progress of humanity. The last section provides a condensed restatement of the theory of emancipation.

I'd like to remind readers again that the book is accompanied by an extensive Appendix, available online at www.cambridge.org/welzel. The Appendix illustrates measurement procedures, includes supplementary analyses, and provides data for replication studies.

The last section of this Introduction describes the schemes that I use throughout the remainder of the book to categorize societies around the world.

3. SCHEMES TO CATEGORIZE SOCIETIES AROUND THE WORLD

The human empowerment framework focuses on three elements: action resources in the domain of people's capabilities, emancipative values in the domain of their motivations, and civic entitlements in the domain of their guarantees. Of these three elements, emancipative values are the most complicated to measure, although the effort is worth it, as we will see. For now, we focus on the more easily observable elements of human empowerment, action resources and civic entitlements, and classify societies along these lines. These classifications are useful in giving us some oversight when describing cross-country variation in emancipative values.

3.1 Stages of Human Empowerment

Today's technologically most advanced societies feed themselves from the intellectual input of wide segments of their population (Bell 1973; Toffler 1990; Florida 2002; Baker 2007). Thus, technological advancement on a mass scale[3] implies that ordinary people command *intellectual* resources. These are provided by widespread education and broad access to information. Technological advancement also implies that ordinary people possess *material* resources. Technologies provide tools and equipment that ease people's lives. They also enhance people's productivity, so their work yields higher incomes. Moreover, technological advancement implies that ordinary people have access to *connective* resources. Transportation and communication technologies allow people to connect with like-minded others and to coordinate their activities for a common purpose. All three types of resources – material, intellectual, connective – are *action resources*: their disposition widens the scope of activities that people can pursue at will. All three types of action resources expand with a society's technological advancement, proliferating societies with better equipped, skilled, and connected people.

To measure a society's technological advancement, I use the World Bank's *knowledge index* (KI), which is available online at http://info.worldbank.org/etools/kam2/KAM_page5.asp. For now, I use the measure from 1995 because this year is at the beginning of the period over which we will have a first look at emancipative values. The KI is a summary measure of a society's per capita scientific productivity, its information and communication technology, and its level of education as detailed in Appendix I (www.cambridge.org/welzel). I "normalize" the index scores into a scale range from minimum 0 to maximum 1.0 and label it the *technological advancement index* henceforth.

Using this index, I divide societies into three broad categories:

1. *Traditional Economies*: societies in this category score in the lower third of the technological advancement index, that is, below 0.33 index points. Societies at such a low level of technological advancement usually employ a plurality of the workforce in the agrarian sector. Where this is not the case, low-tech societies are mostly oil-exporting economies. They share with agrarian economies a focus on rents from fixed assets, namely land or oil, which preserves traditional socioeconomic structures.
2. *Industrial Economies*: societies in this category score in the middle section of the technological advancement index, that is, between 0.33 and 0.66 index points. Most societies at medium levels of technological advancement employ a plurality of the workforce in the industrial sector.
3. *Knowledge Economies*: societies in this category score in the upper third of the technological advancement index, that is, above 0.66 index points.

---

[3] The qualification "mass scale" is intended to indicate the development of technologies that are used by wide population segments, not just the elites.

All of these high-tech societies employ the plurality of the workforce in the knowledge sector.

Again, technological advancement involves more widespread intellectual, material, and connective resources. Together, these three types of action resources enhance people's capabilities to pursue their own and mutually agreed goals. Hence, people are more capable of exercising freedoms in industrial economies than in traditional economies and more capable in knowledge economies than in industrial economies.

Besides technological advancement, democratic achievement is another key element of human empowerment. Whereas technological advancement empowers people on the level of their *capabilities*, democratic achievement empowers them on the level of their *guarantees*. To measure democratic achievement, I use a new index of citizen rights, which is discussed and examined in detail in Chapter 8. The index uses Freedom House's ratings of a society's civil liberties and political rights (Freedom House 2012) but enriches this information with ratings of a society's human rights performance from the Human Rights Data Project (Cingranelli & Richards 1999, 2010). These ratings are combined into the citizens rights index (CRI) with a minimum of 0, when not a single right is guaranteed by either law or in practice, to a maximum of 1.0, when every right is guaranteed in both law and practice. Based on these data, I distinguish three levels of democratic achievement:

1. *Nondemocracies* score in the lower third of the CRI, from 0 to 0.33 scale points. Because these societies deny more citizen rights than they grant, they are rather undemocratic.
2. *Hybrid Regimes* score in the middle section of the index, from 0.33 to 0.66 scale points. Because these societies do not make it far into either the denial or the granting zone of the CRI, they are neither democratic nor undemocratic.
3. *Democracies* score in the upper third of the CRI, from 0.66 to 1.0 scale points. Because these societies grant more rights than they deny, they are rather democratic.

If human empowerment is a coherent phenomenon, it converges over the capabilities and guarantees domains. In this case, societies should match over the three categories of technological advancement and democratic achievement, showing equivalent progress over the capabilities and guarantees domains of human empowerment. Table I.1 depicts in conceptual terms how this correspondence would look like. Table I.2 shows how societies actually distribute over the categories in technological advancement and democratic achievement. The table is limited to the sample of ninety-five societies that were surveyed at least once by the WVS or EVS. I restrict the overview to these societies because my main object of study – emancipative values – is only measured in these ninety-five societies. However, this is not too much of a limitation because these ninety-five societies spread all around

TABLE I.1 *Stages of Human Empowerment over the Capability and Guarantee Domains.*

		GUARANTEES		
		Narrow (Nondemocracies)	*Modicum* (Hybrid Regimes)	*Wide* (Democracies)
CAPABILITIES	*Weak* (Traditional Economies)	Human **Suffering**	Intermediate-Low	[*Paradox*]
	Modicum (Industrial Economies)	Intermediate-Low	**Human Struggling**	Intermediate-High
	Strong (Knowledge Economies)	[*Paradox*]	Intermediate-High	**Human Thriving**

Shades of gray represent expected likelihoods of cases to be found, with the darker shade indicating a higher likelihood.

the globe, include the largest populations and biggest economies from each world region, and cover the entire variation that exists with respect to stages of human empowerment, spanning the whole range from Rwanda to Sweden.[4]

Table I.2 shows that technological advancement and democratic achievement do indeed correspond with each other, representing the same stage of human empowerment in the capability and guarantee domains. In the capability domain, traditional economies represent the low stage of human empowerment. In the guarantee domain, nondemocracies represent this stage. Hence, the two match closely: with the exception of India, Mali, and Zambia, all traditional economies are nondemocracies. Even taking these three exceptions into account, not a single traditional economy is a democracy in a genuine sense of the word, not even India.[5] A medium

---

[4] When we use the latest available survey from each of our ninety-five societies, we cover a survey period from 1995 to 2005. To place the measures of technological advancement and democratic achievement at the beginning of this period, I take measures from 1995. As concerns democratic achievement, I average the measure over five years before the survey period to even out fluctuations that are particular to the year 1995. This is not necessary in the case of technological advancement because it hardly ever happens that a society makes a categorical switch from one year to the next in technological advancement. With democratic achievement, this is more frequently the case: a regime change can switch democratic achievement literally overnight.

[5] Under a strictly electoral definition of democracy, one had to classify India as a democracy because it holds competitive elections in which the opposition has a chance to win. However, the viewpoint of human empowerment mandates a genuinely liberal instead of a merely electoral definition of democracy. Such a definition must take into account violations of citizen rights. If one does so, India scores in the middle range of effectively respected citizen rights, as Chapter 8 will document.

TABLE I.2 *Technological Advancement and Democratic Achievement in the Mid-1990s (ninety-five societies covered by the World Value Surveys/European Values Surveys).*

		Level of Democratic Achievement 1990–1995		
		Nondemocracies	Hybrid Regimes	Democracies
Level of Technological Advancement 1995	Traditional Economies	Algeria, Azerbaijan, Bangladesh, Burkina Faso, Ghana, Guatemala, Indonesia, Iran, Iraq, Nigeria, Pakistan, Rwanda, Saudi Arabia, Tanzania, Uganda, Venezuela, Vietnam, Zimbabwe (N = 18)	India, Mali, Zambia (N = 3)	(N = 0)
	Industrial Economies	Albania, Armenia, Belarus, Bosnia, China, Colombia, Egypt, Georgia, Jordan, Kyrgyzstan, Malaysia, Mexico, Morocco, Peru, Russia, Serbia, Turkey, Ukraine (N = 18)	Brazil, Chile, Dominican Republic, El Salvador, Latvia, Lithuania, Macedonia, Moldova, Philippines, Romania, Thailand (N = 11)	South Africa, Trinidad-Tobago (N = 2)
	Knowledge Economies	Singapore, Hong Kong (N = 2)	Argentina, Bulgaria, Croatia, Cyprus, Estonia, Greece, Israel, South Korea, Taiwan (N = 9)	Andorra, Australia, Austria, Belgium, Canada, Czech Republic, Denmark, Finland, France, Germany (East/West), Greece, Hungary, Iceland, Ireland, Italy, Japan, Luxemburg, Malta, Netherlands, New Zealand, Norway, Poland, Portugal, Slovakia, Slovenia, Spain, Sweden, Switzerland, United Kingdom, United States, Uruguay (N = 32)

Overlapping variation between technological advancement and democratic achievement is 52 percent. Sample from Ethiopia is excluded because of deficient data quality; for Northern Ireland and Montenegro, data on technological advancement are missing. The level of technological advancement of Andorra, Iraq, Malta, and Hong Kong for 1995 is estimated from later data.

stage of human empowerment in the capability domain is represented by industrial economies. In the guarantee domain, hybrid regimes represent this stage. Accordingly, we find the largest number of hybrid regimes in industrial economies. Finally, a high stage of human empowerment is represented by knowledge economies in the capability domain and by democracies in the guarantee domain. Thus, the two categories match: with the exception of Trinidad-Tobago and South Africa, all democracies are knowledge economies. Conversely, Singapore[6] and Hong Kong are the only knowledge economies that are nondemocratic. Of these two, Hong Kong would most likely be democratic if it had political autonomy.

The correspondence between technological advancement and democratic achievement suggests to integrate these two domains into a single scheme of human empowerment, as indicated in Table I.1. Accordingly, one can describe the human condition of societies as:

1. *Suffering* when people's capabilities are weak and their guarantees are narrow;
2. *Struggling* when capabilities and guarantees are mediocre; and
3. *Thriving* when capabilities are strong and guarantees are wide.

Inconsistent combinations of capabilities and guarantees represent intermediate conditions. Table I.3 shows which society falls into which category.

Table I.3 not only classifies societies on human empowerment criteria; it also arranges them into culture zones. Prominent scholars believe that a society's culture zone membership exerts a major influence on its development (Toynbee 1974 [1946]; Eisenstadt 2003 [1988]; Huntington 1996; Inglehart & Baker 2000). Culture zones are supranational entities. They group societies that are shaped by the same historic forces – most notably empires, religions, and migrations. Societies of the same culture zone often share similar economic, cultural, and institutional characteristics, and they perceive each other as members of the same "family of nations" (Castles 1993). Huntington (1996) characterizes culture zones as distinct "civilizations" that divide humanity into parallel universes with no identity bridges between them. If the imprint of culture zones is indeed as deep as many authors suggest, it should be visible in the societies' stages of human empowerment. Hence, we risk missing a chief force that shapes human empowerment if we do not use a reasonable categorization of global culture zones. The following paragraphs describe the culture zone scheme

This places India among regimes with serious deficiencies in qualities that are directly indicative of the extent to which formal democratic institutions meet their empowering purpose. Because of such deficiencies, *The Economist* (2007) classify India as a "flawed democracy" (for a more detailed discussion of cases like India and Singapore, see Alexander and Welzel 2010).

[6] Like the oil-exporting monarchies, Singapore is a striking outlier from the otherwise positive relationship between development and democracy. A commonality of these outliers is the fact that state revenues are not obtained as much as usual from taxing citizens and that tax rates are generally very low while state benefits are rather generous. This exempts these economies from the "no taxation without representation" logic that favors democracy (cf. Verweij & Pelizzo 2009; Conrad & DeMeritt 2013).

TABLE I.3 *Culture Zones and Stages of Human Empowerment (for ninety-five societies covered by the World Values Surveys/European Values Study.*

	STAGES OF HUMAN EMPOWERMENT					
	Suffering Stage		Struggling Stage			Thriving Stage
CULTURE ZONES	Low	Modicum-Low	Modicum	Modicum-High		
Islamic East	Algeria, Iran, Iraq, Saudi Arabia	Egypt, Jordan, Morocco, Turkey				
Indic East	Bangladesh, Indonesia, Pakistan	India, Malaysia	Philippines, Singapore, Thailand			
Sinic East	Vietnam	China	Hong Kong	S. Korea, Taiwan	Japan	
Orthodox East	Azerbaijan	Albania, Armenia, Belarus, Bosnia, Georgia, Kyrgyzstan, Russia, Serbia, Ukraine	Macedonia, Moldova, Romania	Bulgaria		
Old West				Cyprus, Greece, Israel		Andorra, Austria, Belgium, Estonia, France, Ireland Italy, Luxemburg, Malta, Portugal, Spain
Reformed West						Denmark, Finland, Germany (W.), Iceland, Netherlands, Norway, Sweden Switzerland, United Kingdom

TABLE I.3 (cont.)

STAGES OF HUMAN EMPOWERMENT

CULTURE ZONES	Suffering Stage		Struggling Stage		Thriving Stage
	Low	Modicum-Low	Modicum	Modicum-High	Thriving Stage
New West					Australia, Canada, New Zealand, United States
Returned West			Croatia, Latvia, Lithuania	Estonia	Czech Republic, Germany (E.), Hungary, Poland, Slovakia, Slovenia
sub-Saharan Africa	Burkina Faso, Ghana, Nigeria, Rwanda, Tanzania, Uganda, Zimbabwe	Mali, Zambia		South Africa	
Latin America	Guatemala, Venezuela	Colombia, Mexico, Peru	Brazil, Chile, Dominican Republic, El Salvador	Argentina, Trinidad-Tobago	Uruguay

Nonparametric correlations are 0.59 (Kendall's τ-B) and 0.72 (Spearman's ρ), both significant at p <.001. Overlapping variation between culture zones and stages of human empowerment is 46 percent.

used throughout this book. The scheme intends to pick up some of the most distinctive patterns of global state history.

3.2 Global Culture Zones

One of the deepest incisions in the history of civilizations was the rise of the West to global dominance in the era of colonialism and imperialism (McNeill 1990). Never before had one civilization risen to dominance over all others (Fernandez-Armesto 2002). In human history, this is a true singularity, and one whose consequences leave a deep imprint on the world until this day (Morris 2010).

There are many reasons to regret the global impact of the West. Western rule meant the humiliation, exploitation, and even the extinction of other cultures. Moreover, at the same time as the human empowerment process began to shape the West's identity, Western nations monopolized the benefits of this process for their own people. By exploiting overseas territories in colonial times and by backing up authoritarian regimes in post-colonial times, Western powers often denied other peoples the very freedoms that their own people had gained. Until today, this historic legacy is visible in the fact that human empowerment is most advanced in Western societies, even though many non-Western societies are catching up quickly. Recognizing the historic significance of the Western/non-Western division, I take this division as the starting point of my culture zone classification.

Western civilization began to take shape when the Latin strand of Christianity merged the legacy of the West Roman Empire with Germanic tribal traditions into medieval feudalism (Quigley 1979). For reasons outlined in Chapter 11, the Western form of feudalism was unique: it was a distinctively "contractual" version of feudalism that listed the farming households' duties but also their rights, however rudimentary (Powelson 1997). Early on, contractual feudalism oriented Western civilization toward emancipatory gains. Driven by this orientation, subsequent formative experiences of the West include the Reformation and Counter-Reformation and, most important, the emancipatory movements of Humanism and the Enlightenment. The emancipation of science from dogma that came with these movements laid the knowledge base for the Industrial Revolution through which the West rose to global dominance (Braudel 1993; Elias 2004 [1984]; Goldstone 2009; Ferguson 2011).

Despite these commonalities of the West, there is a differentiation within the West as to how early and how rapidly societies began to industrialize and when they were affected by the emancipatory consequences of industrialization, most notably democracy. The Industrial Revolution started where intellectual emancipation from the church was most decisive: in the Protestant areas of Northwestern Europe. In the Catholic south and center of Europe, industrialization and its emancipatory consequences set in later and caused greater tensions. These tensions hindered the smooth and early success of democracy. Only after painful authoritarian and fascist episodes did democracy succeed in Central and Southern Europe, although earlier than in non-Western civilizations.

Geographically, the West emerged at the Atlantic flank of the "axial belt" of Eurasian civilizations (Fernandez-Armesto 2002). By definition, then, all other Eurasian civilizations are Eastern relative to the West. The Eastern civilizations are at least four in number. To begin with, there is the Orthodox branch of Christianity based on Eastern Europe with Muscovite Russia as its historic center. Next, there is the vast Islamic civilization based on the Middle East and Northern Africa with the Arab nations, Persia, and Turkey as historic centers. Then, there is the Indic civilization spanning over South Asia with India as the center. Finally, there is the Sinic civilization in East Asia with China as its historic center.

Outside Eurasia, there are three culture zones: the Western offshoots in North America, Australia, and New Zealand; sub-Saharan Africa; and Latin America. North America, the Southeast of Australia, and New Zealand were populated by modern humans considerably later than Eurasia (Oppenheimer 2004). The populations in these areas remained isolated; they were shielded from the diffusion of agriculture and urbanization that happened among Eurasian civilizations. Hence, when Europeans discovered these areas, there were no densely populated urban civilizations. Instead, Europeans found wide, thinly inhabited territories with a climate similar to Northwestern Europe. These areas allowed for the same type of rain-fed family farming as that practiced in Northwestern Europe. This opportunity attracted land-hungry settlers who brought with them the emancipatory spirit from this part of Europe (McNeill 1990). Unhindered by a feudal legacy, this spirit came to fruition even more vigorously in the settler colonies than at their European origin. Consequently, the Western settler colonies followed the pathway to industrialization and democracy even more quickly than did Protestant Europe.

Until the onset of colonialism, the region where humanity originated – sub-Saharan Africa – was cut off from Eurasian developments by the barrier of the Sahara. Because of natural conditions unfavorable to intensive forms of agriculture (Masters & Wiebe 2000), sub-Saharan Africa did not produce enough agrarian surplus to form and sustain an encompassing urban civilization with a consistent historic center. Given its mostly tropical climate, sub-Saharan Africa did not attract Western settlement. Hence, its indigenous populations were not replaced by Europeans.[7] Yet Africa came under full control of the West's extractive colonial regime: the main purpose was to ship slaves to the plantation and mining colonies in the Americas and fruits and minerals to Europe. The decolonized sub-Saharan Africa of today is still the poorest region in the world, although since a decade or so growing parts experience increasing prosperity and democracy (Mahajan 2011; Africa Progress Panel 2012).

---

[7] The exception is South Africa's cape region whose mild climate attracted Western settlement.

Central and South America were the last continents to be populated by modern humans (Oppenheimer 2004). The arriving populations independently erected the Amerindian civilizations, of which the Aztec and Inca empires crumbled quickly under European conquest. Major parts of the Amerindian populations were wiped out on contact with European populations: because of their isolation from the Eurasian disease pool, Amerindians had no immunity from European germs (Diamond 1997). This opened Central and South America for European settlement. But, given the mostly tropical and subtropical conditions, it was not the North American type of free farmer settlement that attracted people to South America. Instead, Europeans came as rent-seekers to manage plantations and mines. Working on plantations and in mines under tropical conditions was insufferable to Europeans; hence, they imported slaves from Africa after most of the indigenous labor force had been wiped out (Engerman & Sokolov 1997). Thus, state organization was built around labor-repressive regimes that left Latin America with a legacy of extreme social inequality and a polarization between leftist guerilla warfare and rightist military oppression (Rueschemeyer, Stephens, & Stephens 1992).

There are reasons to consider Latin America as a branch of Western civilization, as well as reasons to consider it as a separate civilization. The same applies to the Orthodox East. One might consider Latin America a branch of Western civilization because the area became the new world extension of Catholic Southern Europe. But if we consider the emancipatory legacy of the Enlightenment as the signature feature of Western civilization, Latin America is distinct from the West. The region became the playground of Europe's most exploitative forms of plantation and mining colonialism and attracted reactionary segments of Catholic Europe. The weakness of the emancipatory tradition distinguishes Latin America from the other branches of Western civilization (Huntington 1996: 59).

The Orthodox East could also be considered a branch of Western civilization because it shares with the West a white ethnic origin and a Christian heritage. Yet, an unbroken legacy of despotism along the sequence of Byzantine-Muscovite-Mongol-Tsarist-Soviet empires separates the Orthodox East from the West's emancipatory tradition. For the same reason as Latin America – weakness of an emancipatory tradition – the Orthodox East is distinct from the West.[8]

These considerations support a threefold distinction of global culture zones, which differentiates (1) four distinct Eastern civilizations, (2) four intertwined branches of Western civilization, and (3) two areas, sub-Saharan Africa and

---

[8] The key manifestation of the emancipatory tradition is to entitle citizens with rights. Initially, the granting of rights was limited to Western nations' treatment of their own people. The people of other culture zones, by contrast, were suppressed by Western powers during the colonial era. Since the decolonization era, however, Western and non-Western representatives increasingly claim the universality of rights for all people.

Latin America, that do not fit into the East-West separation. I use this threefold structure to distinguish ten global culture zones (for a similar distinction, see Inglehart & Welzel 2005: 63).

3.2.1 Eastern Culture Zones

As Eastern, I consider all societies rooted in Eurasian civilizations that were located to the East of Western civilization. The cultural fault line is not between Europe and Asia; instead, it runs on a North-South axis through the middle of Europe, dividing Western Christianity (which includes both Catholicism and Protestantism) from Eastern Orthodox Christianity and Islam (Huntington 1996: 159). The Eastern civilizations are much older than the West, and they overshadowed the West for many centuries but then were impacted deeply by the West's sudden rise to global dominance beginning in the sixteenth century.

Compared to the New World, the Western impact on the East was limited in demographic and cultural terms. Western impact did not wipe out indigenous Eastern populations, nor did it destroy the cultural identities of Eastern societies. No Eastern society became a target of Western settler colonialism[9]: there already were dense urban populations that shared the same disease pool with Europeans, for which reason they did not die off on contact with Western visitors (McNeill 1990; Diamond 1997). But, except for the Orthodox East and Japan, Eastern economies from Northern Africa to China were rearranged to fit into a Western-dominated world order. Part of this rearrangement included the destruction of autonomous manufacturing facilities and the erection of extractive structures to capture natural products such as tea, spices, and silk (Jones 1987; Bairoch 1995). Western extraction colonialism aggravated indigenous Eastern traditions of despotism – a combination that hindered both economic and democratic development in the East for a long time. However, with the rise of Japan to an advanced postindustrial democracy and with the recent ascension of India, China, and other "Asian Tigers," this situation is changing dramatically: the East is rapidly catching up (Morris 2010). The following paragraphs briefly portray the four Eastern culture zones.

The *Islamic East* centers on the cradle of civilization in Mesopotamia and includes all Arab societies in the Middle East and Northern Africa, plus Iran and Turkey. This grouping reflects the fact that the Arab, Persian, and Ottoman empires have each been at some point the centers of Islam. A unifying commonality of the societies in the Islamic East is that these were the earliest areas into which Islam expanded. This happened mostly by military conquest. Societies in the Islamic East share some connection with the West because Islam in this zone

---

[9] Russian settlement in Siberia does not fall into the category of Western colonialism because Russia is not part of Western civilization. The fact that Russia's ethnic roots are Caucasian "white" does not make it a Western society when the definition of Western civilization is a *cultural* one, based on the emancipatory legacies of the Reformation, Humanism, and the Enlightenment.

followed a long period of Greco-Roman influence. Islamic societies in South and Central Asia do not share these characteristics of the Islamic East and are for this reason not ordered into this group. In alphabetic order, the WVS includes eight societies in the Islamic East: Algeria, Egypt, Iran, Iraq, Jordan, Morocco, Saudi Arabia, and Turkey.

The *Indic East* stretches over South Asia and comprises the second oldest area of human civilization (counting Mesopotamia and Egypt as one region, the Middle East). Since the beginning, India has been the major civilization of this area. Being the cradle of Buddhism and Hinduism, India's influence radiated throughout the region. In addition to the Islamic East, the Indic East is the culture zone that is most impacted by Islam. And even though India itself is not primarily Islamic, the Mughal Empire subdued India to Muslim rule for centuries. India, thus, hosts a sizeable Muslim population, and Muslims represent the vast majority in societies that branched off from India, notably Pakistan and Bangladesh. In fact, in the case of Indonesia, the Indic East includes the largest Muslim society worldwide. Yet, because of Islam's coexistence with Asian religions in the Indic East and because Islam was mostly imported by trade rather than conquest, Islam is not as predominant and not as rigid in the Indic East as in the Islamic East. The WVS covers eight societies in the Indic East: Bangladesh, India, Indonesia, Malaysia, Pakistan, the Philippines, Singapore, and Thailand.

The *Sinic East* represents a civilization about as old as the earliest European civilization in Crete. Much as India is the core society of the Indic East, China is the core society of the Sinic East. Like India, China is influenced by Buddhism but in neither area was Buddhism the formative belief system. As much as Hinduism is the formative belief system for India, it is Confucianism for China. And as much as Indian culture radiates into all of South Asia, Chinese culture radiates into all of East Asia. The area of Chinese influence included Japan for a long span of history, and even as Japan began to develop its own culture, China remained its key reference. Historically, societies of the Sinic East were not much affected by the major monotheistic religions. By tradition, religion is mostly a matter of the private sphere in Sinic cultures. Although not unimportant as a matter of spirituality, religion lacks political and ideological significance in the Sinic culture. The WVS includes six societies in the Sinic East: China, Hong Kong, Japan, South Korea, Taiwan, and Vietnam.

The *Orthodox East*: Diffusing from its Middle Eastern origin, civilization reached Europe first in the Southeastern Mediterranean, centering on Greece. Under the Roman Empire, a pan-Mediterranean culture emerged. Yet, ever since the division of the empire into Eastern and Western spheres, the two European parts developed along separate pathways. Whereas the Western part remained Latin, the Eastern part turned back to the Greek language and became the foundation of Orthodox Christianity under the Byzantine Empire. As Byzantium turned into an embodiment of Oriental despotism, this left a lasting imprint on Eastern Orthodoxy. After the downfall of the Byzantine Empire, the Orthodox legacy was taken over by Muscovite Russia, which became the leading civilization of Eastern Europe. Shaped by a long era of Mongol despotism, the Russian conception of rule was receptive of Byzantium's cesaropapism. The result was yet another version of despotism, framed as czarist autocracy. Under czarist autocracy, the Orthodox East was shielded from the West's emancipatory movements, including Humanism, the Reformation, and the Enlightenment. Even though Soviet communism remodeled societies economically, it continued the tradition of political despotism. With its expansion into Siberia and large parts of Central Asia, Islamic populations came under Russian dominance. Soviet imperialism cemented this fact. For this reason, I arrange not only Christian Orthodox societies into the Orthodox East but also Islamic societies that came under Russian dominance, the lead civilization of the Orthodox East. Neighbored by Orthodox societies and sharing a communist legacy with them, I also arrange Albania and Bosnia into this culture zone, although these societies are dominantly Islamic. Most of the societies of the Orthodox East were part of the Soviet Union, and all of them were under communist rule.[10] The WVS includes thirteen societies in the Orthodox East: Albania, Azerbaijan, Belarus, Bosnia-Herzegovina, Georgia, Kyrgyzstan, Macedonia, Moldova, Montenegro, Romania, Russia, Serbia, and Ukraine.

3.2.2 *Western Culture Zones*
Western societies share with the Islamic East and the Orthodox East common roots in the Greco-Roman tradition. In addition, they share Christianity and the dominantly "white" Caucasian ethnicity with the Orthodox East. But they are sharply separated from all other culture zones by the emancipatory imprint from Humanism, the Reformation, and the Enlightenment. Western societies industrialized and democratized early. Based on their suddenly achieved technological and military powers, Western societies became colonizers of the rest of the world.

The earliest parts of Western civilization originate in those regions of the Roman Empire in which the Latin version of Christendom withstood, first, the expansion of Islam and, second, the Reformation. Societies of the *Old West* are mostly located in Southern Europe and center on the Mediterranean. The two largest societies of the Catholic West are France and Italy. Since emancipatory movements were not quite as strong there as they were in the Reformed West (see below), societies in the Old West industrialized and democratized later and

---

[10] Because of their Christian-Orthodox tradition, one could group Cyprus and Greece into the Orthodox East. However, they did not come under Russian or communist rule, joined the Western community on their liberation from the Ottoman Empire in 1827, are part of the European Union, and belong in their self-conception to the West. Like Israel, I group these countries into the mostly Mediterranean-based Old West (see below).

under greater frictions than did those of the Reformed West. The WVS and EVS include twelve societies in the Old West: Andorra, Austria, Belgium, Cyprus, France, Greece, Israel, Italy, Luxemburg, Malta, Portugal, and Spain.

Societies of the *Reformed West* include the Protestant societies of Northern, Central, and Northwestern Europe. Most of these societies were only briefly part of the Roman Empire or neighbored it. Hence, they were not as strongly affected by the Roman tradition. Instead, they were shaped by a mixture of Roman traditions and Germanic tribalism. All societies of the Reformed West, except Ireland, became centers of the Reformation. The Enlightenment gained most momentum here. Societies of the Reformed West were the earliest to industrialize and democratize, and they were the major source of early emigration into the New West. The WVS and EVS cover ten societies in the Reformed West: Denmark, Finland, Germany (West), Great Britain, Iceland, Ireland, the Netherlands, Norway, Sweden, and Switzerland.

After the Great Discoveries, the *New West* in Northern America, Australia, and New Zealand emerged as the overseas extension of the Reformed West (even though waves of Catholic immigration from Ireland and Italy followed later). Lacking the abundance of silver and other mineral resources known from Latin America, the New West was not attractive to state-managed extraction colonialism and other rent-seeking activities. The exception were the plantations in the South of the United States – not by coincidence the area where the emancipation of slaves had to be enforced from outside during the American Civil War. Apart from that, North America embodies large areas with a cool, wet climate similar to Northwestern Europe. These areas are suitable for the type of independent family farming practiced in Northwestern Europe. This attracted independence-seeking farmers who were searching for a plot of land at the new frontier. The new frontier society favored an even more vigorous development of the features that distinguished the Reformed West, especially the libertarian-egalitarian ethos of emancipation. The New West, thus, also industrialized and democratized early and at times more quickly than the Reformed West. Tragically, the colonization of the New West was linked with wiping out the majority of Native Americans in North America and with the marginalization and uprooting of the Aborigines and Maoris in Australia and New Zealand. The WVS includes all four societies in the New West: Australia, Canada, New Zealand, and the United States.

A group of societies that are culturally Western on the basis of their Catholic and Protestant tradition were separated from the West against their will by four decades of Soviet communism. Compared to the other ex-communist culture zone, the Orthodox East, the rejection of communism and the quest for liberty and democracy was much more pronounced in these societies. As soon as communism fell, they quickly joined the European Union. As we will see, the value system of the societies of the *Returned West* is not very different from that of the Old West. The Returned West is located in Central and Eastern Europe, bordering the Orthodox East. The WVS and the EVS cover ten societies in the

Returned West: Croatia, the Czech Republic, Estonia, Germany (East), Hungary, Latvia, Lithuania, Poland, Slovakia, and Slovenia.

3.2.3 Neither East Nor West

The East-West division is mostly a distinction within Eurasia. Outside Eurasia, two culture zones do not fit the East-West division: sub-Saharan Africa and Latin America. These two zones, respectively, represent areas where human populations originate and where they last arrived.

Sub-Saharan Africa is the region where humankind originates, yet urban civilization did not manifest itself as strongly there as in the Eurasian belt from the Mediterranean to China. This made sub-Saharan Africa the region most devastatingly impacted by colonialism and slave trade. The indigenous roots of this region stem mostly from a precivilization era; the most lasting manifestations of civilization were imported through colonialism. In the shape of today's nation states, African societies have few precolonial antecedents, became independent late in the decolonization process, and continue to suffer from a heritage of extraction colonialism. One of the legacies consists in unabridged ethnic cleavages that fuel tribal conflict over state power, which is mostly treated as a source of revenue for the ruling group, not as a commitment to provide public goods. The WVS covers ten societies in sub-Saharan Africa: Burkina Faso, Ghana, Mali, Nigeria, Rwanda, South Africa, Tanzania, Uganda, Zambia, and Zimbabwe.

Societies in *Latin America* established themselves on the ruins of the wiped-out Amerindian civilizations. They share a Spanish or Portuguese colonial heritage, are predominantly and still strongly Catholic, and were early decolonizers, with national independence dating back to the 1820s and 1830s. Societies in Latin America suffered from extractive colonialism based on labor-repressive mining and plantation economies using masses of slaves imported from sub-Saharan Africa. This history left most societies with a legacy of extreme social inequalities, with the well-known consequence that, no matter what social alliance governs, its representatives consider state power as a source of revenue for the ruling coalition itself, not as a commitment to deliver goods for all. The WVS includes eleven Latin American societies: Argentina, Brazil, Chile, Colombia, Costa Rica, El Salvador, Guatemala, Mexico, Peru, Uruguay, and Venezuela.

As is obvious from this list of ninety-five societies, the WVS provides fair coverage of global culture zones and includes from each region in the world those societies with the biggest populations and largest economies, namely China and Japan in East Asia; India and Indonesia in South Asia; Iran and Turkey in the Middle East; Egypt in North Africa; Nigeria and South Africa in sub-Saharan Africa; Brazil and Argentina in South America; Mexico in Central America; the United States in North America; Russia in Eastern Europe; Poland in Central Europe; Germany, France, and the United Kingdom in Western Europe; Italy and Spain in Southern Europe; and Australia. The WVS thus represents almost 90 per cent of the world's population. For this reason, findings based on the WVS are unlikely to be affected by selection bias.

As is evident from Table I.3 (p. 23), the relationship between a society's stage of human empowerment and its culture zone is not arbitrary. Instead, a clear Western/non-Western dichotomy surfaces: except for a handful of societies of the Old West and the Returned West, all Western societies are located in the "thriving" stage of human empowerment. Among non-Western societies, only two – namely, Japan and Uruguay – are found in that stage, and not more than a handful come close, including Argentina, Bulgaria, South Korea, and Taiwan. Conversely, the large majority of non-Western societies is found in the "struggling" or "suffering" stages of human empowerment. The suffering stage does not include a single Western society.

Colonialism and its legacy of a Western-benefitting world are still visible in this pattern. The patternedness of human empowerment by culture zones is so apparent that it cannot be ignored. Considerable portions of this book are therefore dedicated to illuminating the sources of this culture zone pattern.

PART A

UNDERSTANDING EMANCIPATIVE VALUES

A Theory of Emancipation

The power of the people and the power of reason are one.

Georg Buechner

This chapter establishes the theoretical foundation of my study. I present a human empowerment framework based on an evolutionary theory of emancipation. This is a theory of "emancipation" because it centers on the human desire for an existence free from domination. The theory is "evolutionary" because it derives its description of the human empowerment framework from an evolutionary root principle: the *utility ladder of freedoms*. This principle starts from an evolved feature universal to our species: human agency – people's faculty to act with purpose.

Agency is an inherently emancipatory quality that has been selected for its power to shape reality. Agency makes guarantees for freedoms a useful good – to the extent to which people have the resources to access their agentic faculty. To the extent to which this is the case, people recognize the value of freedoms and take action for their guarantee. If this is a correct proposition, then the quest for freedoms is adaptive: it waxes and wanes in response to existential constraints on people's action resources. Once existential constraints recede, the quest for freedoms awakens and starts to spread, until it has spread wide enough so that people join actions on behalf of their commonly valued freedoms. As this happens, the power of solidarity grows irresistible at some point. Consequently, rulers are forced to guarantee freedoms and pressured to abide by these guarantees. Conversely, if existential constraints persist, the same logic works in the opposite direction: the quest for freedoms remains dormant, no actions in pursuit of freedoms occur, and rulers are unlikely to give guarantees or, if they do so against the odds, can easily circumvent them.

These ideas can be summarized in one proposition: if freedoms grow, they grow in a utility-value-guarantee sequence. This is what I call the *sequence thesis* of emancipation theory.

When freedoms grow, we observe human empowerment: people gain control over their lives and their society's agenda. As human empowerment advances, emancipative values emerge, providing the psychological link between freedoms' growing utilities and guarantees. Institutions that guarantee universal freedoms are the result, not the cause, of this process. This is an important stipulation because it defies the prominent view that institutions are the cause of all development (North, Wallis, & Weingast 2009; Acemoglu & Robinson 2012; Fukuyama 2012).

This chapter outlines these propositions in detail. Section 1 summarizes the epistemological premise of human empowerment theory: the universality of the human desire for emancipation and its adaptability to existential pressures. Section 2 describes the three elements of human empowerment, each of which covers a distinct domain of agency: action resources in the domain of capabilities, emancipative values in the domain of motivations, and civic entitlements in the domain of guarantees. Section 3 outlines how the sequence thesis views the causal connections among the three elements. Section 4 uses an evolutionary root principle, the utility ladder of freedoms, to explain why societies find themselves in opposing cycles of development: disempowering and empowering cycles. Societies in disempowering cycles are stable as long as they remain shielded from societies in empowering cycles but become unstable on confrontation with the latter – and herein lies the evolutionary advantage of human empowerment. I conclude the chapter with a summary of key points.

1. HUMANISTIC UNIVERSALISM

1.1 The Question of Human Nature

Human empowerment denotes the process by which people are freed from external constraints on pursuing their own and mutually shared values (Sen 1999). Thus, human empowerment is altogether an emancipatory process: it is the liberation of people's agency (Bates 2012). The human empowerment process would be complete if the *sole* remaining constraint on everyone's freedoms is everyone else's equal freedoms. This is, of course, an ideal state that might never be achieved. Yet, as we will see, reality shows different degrees of approximation to this ideal state.

The concept of human empowerment, as I see it, has no claim as to whether "free will" exists. From the viewpoint of human empowerment, the critical question is whether people are free from external constraints to act as agents of their values, not whether humans are internally free, in the sense of having full control over the values they prefer.[1] Regardless of how freely people choose their

---

[1] Ironically, people's freedom to value freedoms is limited. The adaptive quest for freedoms is an evolution-shaped coping mechanism; it predisposes people to value freedoms to the extent to which their action resources bestow utility on freedoms. The operation of this mechanism is *outside people's willing control*. In that sense, there is a limitation to "free will."

values, once these values are in place, being free to act in their pursuit is the chief criterion of judgment from the viewpoint of human empowerment.

With its emphasis on freedom from external domination, the concept of human empowerment evaluates every society against the same standard. A universal approach like this is defensible if – and only if – such a thing as human nature exists in a culture-invariant way. The reason is obvious: only if human nature exists, we can say what it means to be human in a general sense. Only then we can define human well-being and human utility in a universal way.[2] And only then it is appropriate to measure all societies against the same standard. The assumption of a human nature is constitutive for humanistic universalism – the normative position taken by the human empowerment approach (Anand & Sen 2000).

Humanistic universalism conflicts with cultural relativism (Kukathan 2006). Cultural relativism denies the existence of a universal human nature. As social beings, humans are seen entirely as the products of their specific cultures. Across cultures, humans have little in common except trivial biological properties. Thus, humans are divided by their cultures into separate species. Beyond biology, there is no common meaning of humanness, human well-being, and human utility. Consequently, humanistic universalism is flawed in applying the same standard across cultural boundaries (Wong 2006).

However, cultural relativism seems to be losing ground in the empirical sciences. New insights in evolutionary psychology (Brown 1991; Geary 2007), cross-cultural psychology (Ryan & Deci 2000; S. Schwartz 2004), evolutionary anthropology (Boyd & Richerson 2005; Turner & Maryanski 2008), comparative linguistics (Chomsky 2000; Pinker 2002), experimental economics (Fehr & Gaechter 2005; Gächter, Herrmann & Thöni 2010), and experimental philosophy (Guglielmo, Monroe, & Malle 2009) all point to the conclusion that there are meaningful human universals across cultures. One such universal consists of an evolutionary principle in the formation of human values.

This is not to deny cultural differences in human values. Quite the contrary, cultural differences are profound. In fact, they are measured with increasing precision. For instance, scholars measure to what extent cultures are "tight" or "loose," "collectivistic" or "individualistic," and "survival-oriented" versus "emancipation-oriented." However, the mechanisms that determine which of these cultural orientations dominate in a society derive from an evolutionary root principle that governs all cultures: the utility ladder of freedoms. The findings of three cross-cultural studies highlight the power of this principle. To

---

[2] To separate objective from subjective aspects of human existence, I use the term "utility" exclusively in the sense of *objective* utilities and the term "well-being" exclusively in the sense of *subjective* well-being. Maintaining this distinction is important for the argument that evolution has tied our subjective well-being to our objective utility. The utility–well-being link is central to our connection with reality.

begin with, Inglehart and Welzel (2005) show that, in societies in which most people live under existential stress, survival values dominate. These values place security over freedoms. The opposite orientation, emancipative values, dominates in societies with low existential pressures. Likewise, Triandis (1995) argues that existential pressures explain whether a culture is "collectivistic" or "individualistic." Fading pressures lower the need of collective discipline, which opens room for individual freedoms. In the same vein, Gelfand et al. (2011) find that existential pressures determine whether a culture is "tight" or "loose." Fading pressures reduce the need for rigid norms, making cultures looser and hence freer.

The root principle of these findings is, once again, the utility ladder of freedoms. In an objective sense, freedoms gain utility when existential pressures recede: lower pressures mean that people are less forced to do things over which they have no choice. The degree of freedom in their actions thus increases. Consequently, guarantees that entitle people to make their own choices become useful (Bates 2012). This does not remain unnoticed: evolution has led humans to the top of the food chain because it has equipped them with exceptional perceptive abilities, especially as regards life opportunities (Geary 2007; Kaplan, Gurven, & Lancaster 2007). For this reason, it does not escape people's attention when freedoms become more useful; they recognize this. Accordingly, people begin to value freedoms, and emancipative values emerge. These values shift cultures from a tighter to a looser and from a more collectivistic to a more individualistic outlook. These shifts are rooted in an adaptation mechanism of the human mind whose logic is a universal component of human nature. In a nutshell, people resist emancipative values when pressing conditions fix their lives at the low end of the utility ladder of freedoms. Conversely, people adopt emancipative values when permissive conditions move their lives up on the utility ladder of freedoms.

If the utility ladder of freedoms is indeed an evolutionary root principle that shapes cultural differences, a universal human nature obviously does exist. From this, it follows that human utility, well-being, and dignity have a culture-invariant meaning. And it follows that the human empowerment approach pinpoints that meaning.

The idea of human empowerment has been made prominent under the term "human development" by Sen (1999) and Nussbaum (2000, 2006). The term can refer to individuals or societies, and has an equivalent meaning for both entities. For individuals, human empowerment means the development of *personal agency* – that is, a stage of maturation at which one is conscious about one's values and chooses actions accordingly. For societies, human empowerment denotes the development of *civic agency* – that is, a stage of maturation in which all people are free, and equally so, to choose their actions in accordance with their own and mutually shared values. Human empowerment is, hence, the freedom to pursue valued utilities, including individually and commonly valued utilities (Nussbaum & Sen 1993; Anand & Sen 2000; Clark 2002, 2006).

These ideas are inspired by a specific notion of what defines a human being. The notion of humanness in turn determines what is understood as a humane life and a humane society. In a nutshell, the underlying notion of humanness can be described as follows: as a species, humans are distinct from other beings on this planet by possessing a higher degree of freedom in choosing their actions. Freedom of choice is, hence, a defining characteristic of what it means to be human.[3] This freedom roots in an evolution-shaped capacity of the human intellect: the capacity to imagine alternative courses of action and to anticipate their divergent outcomes. This capacity allows humans to choose an action for an anticipated outcome that one values (Miller 2001; Kaplan, Gurven, & Lancaster 2007; Mithen 2007). Now, if the potential for freedom defines humanness, then "human" development is the realization of this potential. Consequently, a humane life is a life that one lives in the freedom to act in accordance with one's own and mutually shared values (Bates 2012).

Since the potential for freedom is universally human, it is present in everyone. In that sense, every person is equally human and equally valuable for this reason. The humane society can therefore only be a society in which freedoms, and the things needed to realize them, are equally accessible to everyone.

This line of thought is inherently emancipatory: it idealizes a world in which people are free from external constraints, except for the same freedoms of everyone else. The emancipatory ideal is formulated most forcefully in Enlightenment philosophy, especially in the classic works of Kant and Mill and in the contemporary work of Popper (1971 [1962]), Rawls (1971), Dworkin (1988), Sen (1999) and Nussbaum (2000). The emancipatory spirit unifies republican, liberal, contractual, and democratic thought and continues into what Sunder (2003) calls the New Enlightenment: the infusion of the spark of emancipation into persisting domains of domination that the original Enlightenment left untouched – especially the family and religion. Most important, emancipatory ideals are advocated with increasing vigor in non-Western societies – by human rights activists in Asia, Africa, and the Middle East, including people of such moral stature as Nelson Mandela (1994), Aung San Suu Kyi (1995), the Dalai Lama (1999), Saad Eddin Ibrahim (2002), and Chaohua Wang (2005).

1.2 The Question of Western Centrism

It might seem that the emancipatory ideal of an unconstrained human existence is uniquely Western, but it is not. In every culture, one finds ideas about an

---

[3] Does this position deny or support the notion of a "free will"? I think the least we can say is that our intellectual ability to model alternative choices and evaluate their utility under a given value system extends the behavioral repertoire. In fact, the function of values is to equip us with a higher authority to overrule instinctive impulses. Hence, humans have some degrees of freedom to control instinctive impulses. The human ability for delay of gratification only exists because of that. In that sense, there is partly a free will.

existence in which humans are free from external constraints (Dumont 1986). All of the world's major religions advocate the realization of a free existence as salvation and thereby defer it to the afterlife. Yet, salvation is an inherently emancipatory concept that has nothing particularly Western about it (Valea 2010). What seems to be particularly Western – although increasingly less so – is the secular conception of emancipation: the idea that freedoms can be realized in *this* life.

The appeal of emancipation is rooted in a discrepancy that troubles human existence: the *imagination-realization discrepancy* (Bakan 1966). This discrepancy touches on the "mind-body problem" – a problem discussed in both Western and Eastern philosophy. In their minds, humans are free in the sense that there are few limits to the realities that they can imagine. However, of these imagined realities, humans can realize only a tiny portion. Given this discrepancy, our material existence is far from being as unconstrained as we imagine it could be. Still, precisely because humans can imagine an unconstrained existence, such an existence becomes an ultimate desire – a terminal value. The desire for immortality, which is addressed in all major religions by some conception of eternal afterlife, epitomizes this ultimate value (Valea 2010).

Until the dawn of the Industrial Age, life was "short, brutish, and nasty," as Hobbes suggested long ago. Until recently, the idea that a life free from misery could be possible in this world, and that a considerable amount of freedoms could be enjoyed in this life, seemed implausible. As long as misery was the prevailing human condition, the only way to cope with the imagination-realization discrepancy was to believe in a freed existence in an afterlife. This comforting function is one of religion's key purposes.

But with the scientific revolution in the forefield of industrialization, technological knowledge has been catapulted to unprecedented impact levels. This has widened human control over reality into new dimensions. Those societies at the forefront of these gains have used their increased technological capacities to make the lives of their people longer, more secure, more comfortable, more exciting, more purposeful – and freer (Ridley 2010; Morris 2010; Pinker 2011). The challenge today is to spread the emancipation of human existence to all those regions where people continue to suffer from oppression and poverty – without destroying the planet.

In contractual, liberal, democratic, and cosmopolitan thought, as well as in human empowerment theory, every person has the same right to live in freedom. Hence, opportunities to live in freedom must be equally available in a humane society. In that sense, human empowerment theory defies a contradiction between freedom and equality (Nussbaum 2006). In fact, equality is a key substantiating property of freedom; the issue is equal freedom for everyone. This position echoes Rawls's (1971: 53) *first principle of justice*: "Each person is to have an equal right to the most extensive scheme of equal basic liberties compatible with a similar scheme of liberties for others."

The emphasis on freedom of choice and equality of opportunities might be criticized as prescribing a Western view of the good life and the good society. But this criticism rests on two untenable premises, which can be phrased as follows:

1. Exercising freedoms is not a universal human *potential* but one that only Western people possess.
2. Exercising freedoms is not a universal human *value* but one that only Western people embrace.

Neither of these premises withstands closer scrutiny. The first is obviously absurd: the potential to exercise freedoms is rooted in a cognitive capacity of the human mind – the imagination of alternative courses of action. One cannot seriously suggest that this ability is the sole property of "Westerners."

What about the second premise: Are freedoms a valued feature of life only among "Westerners"? This claim has been put forward vigorously by advocates of the Asian Values Thesis (Yew 1994; cf. Thompson 2004). However, the claim that non-Western peoples do not share the West's valuation of freedoms has been more often postulated than evidenced. In fact, the few empirical investigations of the question indicate the opposite.

Whether people value freedoms is evident in whether feeling free enhances their life satisfaction. Inglehart and Welzel (2005: 140) examine this question based on evidence from seventy societies around the world. They find that feelings of freedom increase people's life satisfaction in every society, regardless of cultural background. Other studies, including a meta-analysis of all previously published work on this topic, support the same finding: the effect of feeling free on life satisfaction is universally positive (Fischer & Boer 2011). What varies is only the strength by which feeling free affects people's life satisfaction. Yet, the source of this variation is not culture but the severity of existential pressures: where life is easier, feeling free increases people's life satisfaction even more strongly (Delhey 2009; Welzel & Inglehart 2010). These insights testify to three things. First, the quest for freedoms is real. Second, it is adaptive. Third, the logic of its adaptation is culture-invariant.

Perhaps people in different cultures define freedoms in entirely different ways. But then it is a mysterious coincidence that these different definitions always line up so neatly with life satisfaction. Of course, coincidence is an inherently implausible explanation of the cross-cultural regularity of the freedom–wellbeing link. In fact, experimental research in the framework of self-determination theory confirms that the positive effect of feeling free on life satisfaction is a cross-cultural universal (Deci & Ryan 2000; Chirkov, Ryan, Kim, & Kaplan 2003; Haller & Hadler 2004). As Turner and Maryanski's (2008) work suggests, the satisfying benefits of feeling free derive from an emancipatory desire that evolution has hardwired into our minds.

In conclusion, the emphasis that the human empowerment concept places on freedoms does not prescribe a specifically Western view of the good life and the good society. It champions an inherently humane view.

2. THE THREE ELEMENTS OF HUMAN EMPOWERMENT

Sen's concept of human development focuses on capabilities that enable people to exercise freedoms. For this reason, the approach is often described as the "capability approach" (Clark 2002, 2006; Nussbaum 2000). Welzel, Inglehart, and Klingemann (2003) broaden the capability approach into a human empowerment framework by including emancipative values as an additional element.

Emancipative values emphasize freedom of choice and equality of opportunities. They operate as a meta-value that tolerates the pursuit of a great variety of specific values under its umbrella: emancipative values emphasize people's freedoms to pursue specific values of their choice.

Yet the diversity of tolerated specific values has limits. To protect emancipation from destruction by its own principles, not every specific value must be tolerated. To protect tolerance from self-destruction, one cannot tolerate intolerance. This is known as the "paradox of freedom": to sustain freedom, one cannot allow the freedom to choose unfreedom. For instance, the freedom to follow a cultural tradition of one's liking does not protect cultural traditions that violate freedoms. Under the primacy of emancipation, there are no sanctuaries from the claim to universal freedoms. In that sense, emancipative values spawn a liberally qualified tolerance that is intolerant of illiberal practices.

In the most general sense, human empowerment denotes the freedoms of people to act in accordance with their values – in as far as this does not violate everyone else's equal freedoms. To make freedoms practicable for as many people as possible, the lives of people must be enriched by three ingredients, as shown in Figure 1.1. These ingredients are discussed one by one in the following sections.

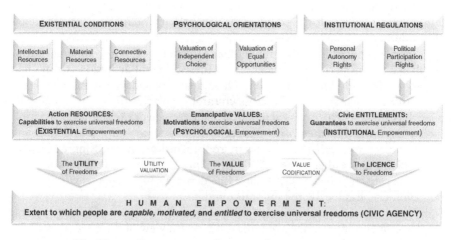

FIGURE 1.1 The Human Empowerment Framework

2.1 Empowerment through Guarantees: Civic Entitlements

To begin with the most obvious ingredient, ordinary people must be allowed to exercise freedoms. This allowance is endowed by legal guarantees for freedoms. Guarantees must be "democratic" in the sense that they entitle every constituent of a society equally.

In all state-organized societies one can distinguish two domains of life: a private domain in which matters are decided by personal choices and a public domain in which matters are decided by political choices. To empower people in both domains, civic entitlements must guarantee private and public freedoms (Beetham 1999; O'Donnell 2004; Saward 2006; Williams 2006). Private freedoms are guaranteed by *personal autonomy rights*; public freedoms are guaranteed by *political participation rights*. To institutionalize "people power" in a complete sense, both sets of rights must be guaranteed, and they must be guaranteed in even proportions so that no domain is neglected on behalf of the other.

To the extent that inherited disadvantages prevent the equal practice of autonomy rights and participation rights, compensation rights are needed as a third sphere of rights (Marshall 1950). Thus, the human empowerment concept provides no justification for pure market liberalism. Instead, human empowerment requires an organization of society that issues state intervention wherever markets fail to secure equality of opportunities. The guarantee of compensation rights for members of specifically disadvantaged groups is a means to this end. Hence, the concept of human empowerment champions autonomy rights and participation rights for all people, and compensation rights for people belonging to unduly disadvantaged groups. Human empowerment points to a unified concept of rights.

The often cited tensions among participation rights, autonomy rights, and compensation rights dissolves in the theory of human empowerment. As Brettschneider (2007: 8, fn. 4) notes, "democracy and rights are not in tension but part of a coherent, unified theory of self-government." In any case, civic entitlements empower people on the level of guarantees, contributing the institutional element to human empowerment.[4] Civic entitlements provide the license to freedoms.

2.2 Empowerment through Capabilities: Action Resources

People's power to exercise freedoms is not only a matter of guarantees. It is also a matter of capabilities, which are less easily established than guarantees. The reason is obvious: guarantees are directly accessible to human engineering

---

[4] I use the term "institutions" in an exclusively *formal* sense, referring to constitutions, laws, and other forms of official regulation. I refrain from extending the term to include "informal institutions" because doing so makes institutions indistinguishable from culture. Blurring this distinction would deprive us of the possibility to analyze the culture–institution nexus.

because they are declared and made binding by law. But capabilities cannot be put into place by law: laws can prescribe a preferred reality, but they cannot create it.

People's capability to exercise freedoms is a direct reflection of their available resources. People who command more resources are freer, in the sense that they can do more things to pursue what they value. This property qualifies resources as *action resources*. Action resources involve three distinctive types of resources:

1. *Intellectual resources*: knowledge, skills, and information
2. *Connective resources*: networks of exchange and contact interfaces
3. *Material resources*: equipment, tools, and income

No type of human activity comes entirely for free. To perform an activity, one usually needs some skill; many activities require some equipment or are otherwise costly; and some activities can only be performed jointly, requiring the possibility to connect with like-minded others.

Mass-scale[5] technological advancement increases all three types of resources (Bell 1973; Toffler 1990; Drucker 1993; Elias 2004 [1984]). Technologically advanced societies prolong human lives and equip people with tools that free up time from doing unpleasant work for doing more exciting things. As Veenhoven (2005) shows, longer lives with less time wasted for unpleasant things lead to a measurable increase in "happy life years." Technological progress also amplifies labor productivity, which enhances the value of our work hours, thus elevating incomes and purchasing power. Moreover, modern-day technological progress feeds itself from mobilizing intellectual capacities on a mass level, which involves expanding education and information. Finally, technological advancement interlinks people in wide-ranging webs of exchange. These tendencies enhance ordinary people's intellectual, connective, and material resources. These are resources of action because each of them widens the options of what people can do at will. Action resources unlock the gift of agency.

Action resources in this sense empower people on the level of capabilities, providing the existential element to human empowerment. Action resources increase people's utilities from freedoms. The more widespread action resources are, the larger are people's *joint* utilities from freedoms – the basis of solidarity.

2.3 Empowerment through Motivations: Emancipative Values

Even in combination, guarantees and capabilities do not complete human empowerment. People may be enabled and allowed to exercise freedoms, but if they are not eager to do so, they will not practice freedoms. Freedoms then remain an unrealized potential. Thus, besides guarantees and capabilities,

---

[5] The qualification "mass scale" is intended to indicate the development of technologies that are used by wide population segments, not just the elites.

motivations are another component of human empowerment. Motivations are a direct reflection of what people value in life. I label the values that constitute a strong motivation to exercise freedoms "emancipative values."

Emancipative values are an empowering motivation because they encourage people to become masters of their lives. This impetus activates people in at least two ways. First, the emphasis on equal opportunities inherent in emancipative values comes with an internalization of humanitarian norms; these norms make people sensitive to social injustice and more easily upset about its incidence. Second, emancipative values involve an appreciation of human self-expression; accordingly, the voicing of shared concerns becomes itself a value and thus a source of satisfaction. As a result, the utility calculus changes: utility no longer consists only in achieving a goal; it also consists in voicing it. "Expressive utility" diminishes action blockades that otherwise prevent people from voicing their concerns.

In summary, emancipative values empower people on the level of motivations, providing the psychological element to human empowerment. As much as action resources increase the utility of freedoms, and as much as civic entitlements provide the guarantee for freedoms, emancipative values establish the appreciation of freedoms. Together, these three elements of human empowerment define the status of freedoms in a society.

2.4 Human Empowerment as Civic Agency

To estimate an entire society's stage of human empowerment, the critical question is inclusion: What is the typical condition of *most* people in a society? The criterion of inclusion imposes requirements on the three elements of human empowerment. As concerns civic entitlements, these must be endowed equally to every resident if they are to promote inclusive empowerment.

With action resources and emancipative values, the situation is more complicated. The reason is that resources and values divide into *unique* parts and *common* parts. Unique are those parts of people's resources and values that divert from what is typical for most people in a society; common are those parts that coincide with what is typical for most people. As concerns resources, the unique part indicates to what extent a person's own utility from freedoms differs from most other people's utility. The common part indicates his or her joint utility with most others. As concerns values, the unique part indicates to what extent a person's own valuation of freedoms differs from most other people's valuation. The common part indicates his or her shared valuation with most other people. This distinction clarifies that human empowerment becomes more inclusive only as the *common* parts of people's action resources and emancipative values grow.

Inclusion is not only a normative qualification of human empowerment; it also has practical consequences. For inclusion provides the basis of solidarity. Solidarity, in turn, is the key ingredient of a population's capacity for collective action. When people use this capacity, they exert *civic agency* – the formula for a strong civil society. Hence, inclusive human empowerment is synonymous with civic agency.

3. THE SEQUENCE THESIS

3.1 Freedoms' Evolutionary Utility

The existence of culture does not shield human societies from evolution; culture shifts evolution onto a new level. Like its biological basis, culture is a system of inheritance, programmed to accumulate, store, and transmit tried-and-tested knowledge of how to manage reality (Avery 2003). In the biological realm, reality-managing knowledge is encoded in genes and transmitted through sexual reproduction. In the cultural realm, knowledge is embodied in shared memories, sometimes called "memes," and transmitted through learning (Dunbar, Knight, & Power 1999; Chattoe 2002; Boyd & Richerson 2005).

Any inheritance system – whether biological or cultural – is permanently subject to a reality check. Consequently, inheritance systems are continuously shaped by selection for reality-fitness (Distin 2011). The persistence of selection establishes a self-driven engine of progress (Roux 2010). Progress is obvious in both the biological and the cultural system of inheritance, even though progress in both domains is punctuated with phases of stagnation before major accelerations occur.

A major acceleration in biological evolution is the "cephalization" trend in the history of primates. Cephalization describes the trend toward larger and more complex brains with higher intellectual capacities (Flinn, Geary, & Ward 2005). About 150,000 years ago, cephalization culminated in the human brain – the most powerful device to handle knowledge on this planet (Alexander 1987; Ehrlich 2000). Selection operated toward the brain because the brain's intellectual capacities allow for unusual control over reality (Flinn, Geary, & Ward 2005; Geary 2007).

By shaping human intellect, evolution has invented its own accelerator: agency. Agency is the power to act with purpose. Agency allows for intentional experimentation, which accelerates the discovery of better working solutions. In biology, evolution works on genetic information. Here, evolution lacks agency. Natural improvements in a species' gene code occur randomly, through accidental errors in copying the DNA. This is a blind process of experimentation and hence a slow engine of progress. In culture, evolution works on learned information. Since the capability to think endows the learning actor with agency, learned information is open to systematic improvement through purposeful experimentation. This allows for intentional innovation, which is a fast engine of progress (Nolan & Lenski 1999; Avery 2003; Boyd & Richerson 2005).

Despite the difference in pace, in both biology and culture evolution shapes inheritance toward greater utility by deselecting what does not work and by favoring what does work better in coping with reality (Elias 1984 [1939]; Nolan & Lenski 1999; Rubin 2002; Popper 2009 [1987]). None of our social constructions is exempted from selection: technologies, ideologies, and institutions all are permanently subject to a reality check and deselected from the pool of viable models in case they fail (Runciman 1998; Chattoe 2002; Diamond 2005).

Sometimes, evolution "discovers" the most useful features late. But once a useful feature is found, evolution accelerates in perfecting this feature (Miller 2001). Brains, for instance, existed for a very long time before accelerated cephalization set in. Once it began, the advantages of greater brain power paid off so quickly that selection operated with increasing speed in favor of it.

The growth of technological knowledge in cultural evolution is a phenomenon comparable to the growth of intellectual capacities in biological evolution (Avery 2003). Both processes are targeted toward greater control over reality, and both illustrate the utility of freedoms. Human societies have always gathered and transmitted technological knowledge (Nolan & Lenski 1999). As a consequence, the stock of human knowledge has grown since the dawn of humanity and so has the reality control that human societies exert over their environments (Fernandez-Armesto 2002). Yet, as the record of technological innovations illustrates, the growth of knowledge was very slow over most of history (Spier 2010). Societies made no systematic effort to outperform each other by investing more than their neighbors into research and development until the emergence of modern science demonstrated the advantages of doing exactly this. Since the emergence of science, human knowledge grows exponentially and has elevated our reality control to levels that dwarfed, within a few centuries, all that has been achieved in more than 150 millennia of human existence. This is obvious from the sharp and sudden increase in the curve of knowledge growth starting around 1500 CE (Nolan & Lenski 1999; Oppenheimer 2004; Morris 2010).

Like brain growth in biological evolution, knowledge growth in cultural evolution accelerated so suddenly that, in both cases, this acceleration marks a sharp discontinuity from the previous pace of evolution. Interestingly, both accelerations are striking illustrations of the utility of freedoms.

The accelerated growth of intellectual capacities in biological evolution came with a powerful feature: imagination. Imagination grants the power of agency, and agency involves the freedoms to experiment and to learn on purpose. Humans owe to the handling of these intellectual freedoms their dominant status on this planet (Birch & Cobb 1981; Ehrlich 2000; Rubin 2002). In cultural evolution, the accelerated growth of technological knowledge set in with a powerful feature too: science (Elias 2004 [1984]). Research is a natural human activity but it was not institutionalized until science emerged as an independent social sector during Renaissance-Humanism. (Braudel 1993). The independence of science was safeguarded by guarantees for intellectual freedoms, followed by derivative freedoms in other spheres of life, including market access and political participation (Goldstone 2009). Liberal democracy is the product of these freedoms. Ever since, freedoms are the signature feature of societies with the most advanced technological knowledge (North, Wallis, & Weingast 2010; Acemoglu & Robinson 2012). Attempts by oppressive systems, such as Nazi Germany and Soviet Russia, to take the leadership in technological knowledge ended as crushing failures. The most plausible reason for these failures is oppression itself: oppressive systems are unable to harness people's intrinsic motivations, and this disables them to mobilize human intellect at its full scope (Popper 1971 [1962]; Fukuyama 1992). Against this backdrop, it is doubtful that China will advance to world leadership in technological knowledge without guaranteeing freedoms to its people.

At any rate, the most striking accelerations of biological evolution and cultural evolution are powerful illustrations of the utility of freedoms. On both accounts, evolution favors growth in the power to manage freedoms because this power involves greater control over reality. Freedoms embody evolutionary utility.

3.2 The Mind as a Utility-Pursuing Device

A defining characteristic of the human mind is its power to imagine better realities – realities in which our existence is less constrained. By endowing the mind with this power, evolution shaped a device for the intentional pursuit of valued goals. This is the source of the human quest for freedoms (Birch & Cobb 1981; Kaplan, Gurven, & Lancaster 2007; Turner & Maryanski 2008).

However, to be useful the quest for freedoms must not be static. Instead, it must adjust to external constraints that are beyond momentary control. Hence, the evolution of the mind selected an *adaptive* quest for freedoms.

To keep the quest for freedoms adaptive, the mind must stay in touch with reality. For this purpose, three psychological mechanisms must work. The first mechanism, *utility valuation*, means that humans recognize in roughly accurate ways what imaginable freedoms they can handle in practice. This mechanism works because evolution has shaped humans as perceptive beings who recognize what is within reach of their capabilities. If this were not the case, our species would have failed long since. But recognizing the useful freedoms would be irrelevant if the recognition did not trigger a corresponding valuation of the freedoms in question. Thus, recognition of objective utilities leads to their subjective valuation, creating a *utility-value* link.

The second mechanism, *value activation*, implies that humans have an urge to act in pursuit of what they value. It is only because of this value-action link that values matter. With respect to freedoms, the value-action link implies that people act for the freedoms they value. This includes actions to voice one's valued freedoms when they are denied or challenged and actions to exercise one's valued freedoms when they are guaranteed.

The third mechanism, *action satisfaction*, is the reason why the second works: when valued freedoms are claimed and practiced, this is inherently satisfying.

The reason for the reward is that claiming and practicing freedoms demonstrates to a person his or her agency. A sense of agency generates self-esteem – the ultimate source of satisfaction for a self-aware being (Deci & Ryan 2000; Wright 2004; Welzel & Inglehart 2010). Importantly, satisfaction feeds back to values: satisfaction with asserted and practiced freedoms reinforces the value placed on these freedoms. Because of this feedback loop, the mental processing of freedoms operates as a *self-sustaining cycle*.

The sequence of these mechanisms ties freedoms' satisfying reward to our capabilities. This keeps people's life strategies in touch with reality. The result is an adaptive quest for freedoms, one that adjusts to external constraints beyond our momentary control. This leads to an interesting paradox: although the quest for freedoms is an ineradicable part of human nature, it is so adaptable that it can hibernate throughout the ages, being unrecognizable for generations. Thus, people can live without freedoms if necessary. Otherwise, oppressive systems could not have dominated most of the history of civilization. If people live under constraints that they do not have the means to change, they see little utility in freedoms. Hence, they value freedoms less, take less action on their behalf, and partly decouple their satisfaction from the exercise of freedoms. This adjustment allows people to function in the absence of freedoms.

Still, eliminating freedoms as a source of satisfaction diminishes the amount of satisfaction people can obtain: there can be no inner fulfillment for a self-aware being without the mastery of freedoms. Consequently, demands to guarantee freedoms will always grow strong, to the extent that people acquire the resources to master freedoms. In other words, the quest for freedoms hibernates as long as necessary but awakes as soon as possible. The awakening often appears sudden and can lead to what Kuran (1991) described as the "element of surprise": the surprise striking observers when rapidly swelling masses of people who have shown hardly any sign of opposition for decades suddenly rise against oppression and demand freedoms.

The mechanisms shaping people's mentality with respect to freedoms do not operate among individually isolated minds. Humans evolved as a group animal (Bowles & Gintis 2011). For this reason, the human mind has been shaped as a social mind (Forgas, Williams, & Wheeler 2001; Wilson 2004; Dunbar & Shultz 2007a; 2007b; Flinn & Coe 2007; Kaplan, Gurven, & Lancaster 2007). One of the most remarkable social abilities of the mind is empathy. Empathy leads to the extension of one's ego into a "collective self" that includes others whom one considers equal. This is what I call the *solidarity mechanism*. The solidarity mechanism extends the pursuit of utilities to *joint* utilities with equals (Wilson 2004). How widely the recognition of joint utilities reaches depends on the social radius of people with similar resources. When action resources are so widespread that no group monopoly over freedoms can be established, then the recognition of freedoms' joint utilities transcends to large segments of a society. In this case, people's efforts aim at *universal* freedoms.

The joint valuation of freedoms motivates collective action to assert these freedoms. If such collective action is successful, as in the case of mass protests ousting a dictator, the satisfying reward is enhanced: socially shared success creates a solidarity experience that grants all participants a common sense of satisfaction (Forgas, Williams, & Wheeler 2003).

Summing up, I suggest that the mind operates four mechanisms to deal with freedoms: the valuation mechanism, the activation mechanism, the satisfaction mechanism, and the solidarity mechanism. The first three mechanisms operate in an order of sequence from valuation to activation to satisfaction, with a self-reinforcing feedback loop from satisfaction to valuation. The solidarity mechanism works on each of the first three, extending them into the social dimension. Solidarity with equals transcends the pursuit of individually unique utilities to the pursuit of socially shared utilities. Social alliances emerge from shared utilities. Utility pursuit thus becomes a group-embedded process.

Following these propositions, freedoms evolve in two consecutive steps, as suggested by the two horizontal arrows in Figure 1.1 (p. 44). In the first step, *utility valuation*, freedoms are valued subjectively to the extent that their objective utility has grown. In the second step, *value codification*, freedoms are guaranteed institutionally to the extent that their subjective value has increased. Hence, if they grow, freedoms grow in a utility-value-guarantee sequence. This is what the sequence thesis suggests.

4. THE CYCLES OF HUMAN (DIS)EMPOWERMENT

My evolutionary theory of emancipation links human well-being and human empowerment in ways that explain three striking features in the history of civilization:

1. societies are easily and often for long times trapped in a self-sustaining cycle of disempowerment;
2. a cycle of empowerment only emerges under demanding conditions but, once in motion, is self-sustaining as well;
3. societies in the disempowering cycle become unstable when confronted with societies in the empowering cycle.

Figure 1.2 schematizes the opposing cycles. Both cycles shape the entire fabric of societies. The disempowering cycle originates in pressing existential conditions. Existential pressures mean that ordinary people lack action resources. In this condition, emancipative values remain dormant. With dormant emancipative values, people take no action to assert and exercise freedoms. Consequently, people gain little satisfaction from freedoms. Low satisfaction from freedoms reinforces the weak valuation of freedoms, creating a self-sustaining cycle. Precisely because the cycle is self-sustaining, rulers do not need to exert much effort to keep it going. There is no pressure on them to guarantee freedoms. As a result, they either do not guarantee freedoms or, when they do so against the

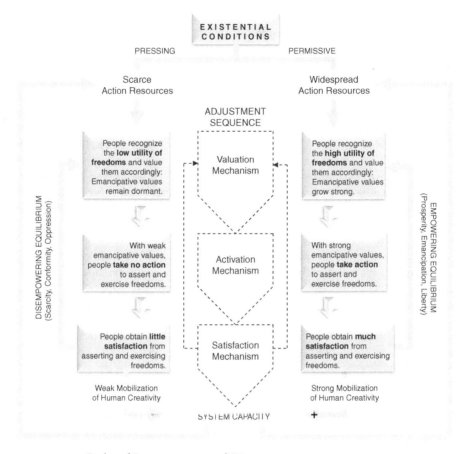

FIGURE I.2 Cycles of Empowerment and Disempowerment

odds, they ignore them in practice and get away with it. In the disempowering cycle, people suffer from deficient capabilities, motivations, and guarantees. They have little control over their lives and their society's agenda.

The empowering cycle is the exact opposite. It is rooted in permissive existential conditions that make action resources widely available. With widespread action resources, people emphasize emancipative values. Shared emancipative values create solidarities that encourage joint actions to assert and exercise freedoms. The solidarity experience generates common satisfaction. This reinforces the strong valuation of freedoms, creating another self-sustaining cycle. In this constellation, rulers are severely restricted in their institutional choices. They are under the pressure of public claims that are difficult to resist because these claims are put forward by capable and motivated people who act with the power of solidarity. Eventually, rulers must guarantee universal freedoms and are pressured to adhere to these guarantees. In the empowering cycle, people benefit from strong capabilities, motivations, and guarantees. People are in control of their lives and their society's agenda.

Obviously, people's lives differ drastically in the two opposing cycles. In the disempowering cycle, life is a source of constraints, and what people do is mostly enforced on them by external pressure. Driven by outside pressure, people's motivations are extrinsic. In the empowering cycle, life is a source of opportunities, and much of what people do is a matter of choice. Hence, what motivates people shifts from outside pressures to inner drives: motivations become intrinsic. I suggest that this difference in motivations has three fundamental consequences.

First, empowering societies generate higher levels of well-being because, for humans as a self-aware species, intrinsic motivations yield more satisfaction than do extrinsic motivations. Second, and for this reason, empowering societies receive more support from their constituents; they are more legitimate. Third, because human creativity resides in intrinsic motivations, empowering societies mobilize human creativity at a fuller scope. Consequently, empowering societies are more innovative, develop more knowledge, and acquire superior system capacities, including technological and organizational capacities. Hence, human empowerment creates societies with both higher legitimacy and higher capacity. Higher legitimacy makes societies more stable inside; higher capacity makes them more competitive with the outside world. Because of this double advantage, evolution favors human empowerment – once it started somewhere.

Arguably, disempowering societies do not make people happy, yet people do not need to be happy in order to function. For this reason, disempowering societies are internally stable – as long as ordinary people lack action resources. A millennia-long history of oppressive systems testifies to the internal stability of disempowering cycles. As long as disempowering societies are not confronted with empowering societies, disempowerment remains unchallenged.

Once that confrontation happens, however, the game changes. Empowering societies outperform disempowering societies in technological and organizing capacities. Eventually, this leads to the dominance of empowering over disempowering societies. Moreover, whereas legitimacy sustains the viability of empowering societies, disempowering societies now become unstable because their people see the better living conditions in empowering societies. In history, the advantage of empowering societies became obvious late because the empowering cycle requires demanding conditions that did not begin to take shape until the emergence of preindustrial capitalism and the Industrial Revolution (McNeill 1990). Chapter 11 discusses this point in detail.

Over the long preindustrial era, the evolution of state organization peaked in the erection of despotic empires in the Middle East, India, China, and pre-Columbian America. Even though despotism created marvelous architecture, fielded impressive armies, and invented important technologies, at some point it always ended up in development blockades (Goldstone 2009). Over millennia, the living conditions of ordinary people remained miserable: not even the oldest, most persistent, and most advanced civilizations achieved any significant improvement in people's living standards and life expectancies (Jones 1987; Hall 1989; Maddison 2007; Galor 2011). Despite this failure, despotism remained unchallenged as a way to organize civilized life until the contemporary confrontation with empowering societies. Upon this confrontation, traditional despotism crumbled. In the meanwhile, modern versions of despotism occurred – most notably in Nazi Germany and Soviet Russia. These systems can be seen as an experiment: Can one achieve technological leadership and global dominance while continuing people's disempowerment? With unfathomable human costs, the failure of both experiments suggests that one cannot. If this is an accurate lesson, China's ambition for technological leadership will not materialize unless it begins to empower its people.

KEY POINTS

Evolution has shaped the human mind as a device to pursue control over reality. Pursuing control over reality involves a quest for freedoms. For the power to control reality resides in the faculty to master freedoms. But to keep the quest for freedoms an efficient device to pursue utilities, the quest must adapt to circumstances beyond human control.

The adaptive quest for freedoms channels the human pursuit into a sequence of coping mechanisms. These are integrated into a self-regulating system through satisfying feedback. To begin with, the mind recognizes what has utility under given circumstances. Thus, we estimate with rough accuracy which freedoms are within reach of our capabilities, and we value freedoms according to their recognized utility (utility valuation). Then, we act to assert the freedoms that we value (value activation). Finally, the more freedoms we assert successfully, the more satisfaction we gain in the currency of self-esteem (action satisfaction).

Since the human mind evolved through a history of group life, it does not work in isolation; the mind operates as a socially embedded device. The social abilities of the mind – empathy in particular – assure that humans recognize the utilities they share with others. This brings jointly valued freedoms into focus: people value freedoms as the equal freedoms of all with whom they share the same utility (the solidarity mechanism). As a consequence, people ally to assert jointly valued freedoms. How wide the circle of solidarity reaches depends on the dispersal of the resources to handle freedoms. The less these resources are concentrated, the wider the circle of solidarity. The solidarity mechanism ensures that the human pursuit of utilities operates in a socially allied, not an individually isolated, way.

The adaptive quest for freedoms is the engine of the human empowerment process. This process includes three ingredients: action resources, emancipative values, and civic entitlements. Echoing the adaptive quest for freedoms, people's emancipative values wax and wane in response to their action resources, and people do or do not take action to assert civic entitlements depending on their emphasis on emancipative values. Pressures on rulers to enact and respect civic entitlements vary in response to people's actions, making effective guarantees more likely under broad and sustained popular pressure.

I believe that the adaptivity of the quest for freedoms explains some of the most striking features of the history of democracy. These features are four-fold, including, first, the absence of democracy throughout most of history; second, why democracy eventually did emerge at some places; third, why it has been successful since its emergence; and fourth, why it does not flourish yet everywhere. For most of the time, lack of development limited people's action resources so much so that the quest for freedoms remained dormant. Consequently, there was no pressure for democracy and hence no democracy. Only with the explosion of development in the modern era did the quest for freedoms awake, but then with a vengeance. Since then, we observe the Great Redirection of Civilization from perfecting human exploitation to advancing human empowerment. This Redirection started in the West, for reasons outlined in Chapter 11. But it has been and is continuing to spread elsewhere rapidly. Because the adaptivity of the quest for freedoms is a universal feature of human nature, the quest can awake everywhere. Where this happens, democracy is the likely outcome.

Together, these propositions form the evolutionary theory of emancipation – the basis of the human empowerment framework. Human empowerment is the process through which people acquire what is needed to be in control of their lives. All empowerment processes originate in an inherently emancipatory desire: the desire to exist free from external domination. This desire is engraved on human existence because it has evolutionary utility: it is the source of the intentional search for control over reality. Yet the utility principle also suggests that the desire for freedoms is adaptive: it drives our efforts only so far as existential constraints allow. How strongly the desire for freedoms drives people's efforts is evident in emancipative values – the central link between the utility of freedoms and their guarantee. To examine whether the evidence is in favor of this theory or not, we must measure emancipative values. This is the task of the following chapter.

2

Mapping Differences

Emancipation is people's liberation from external domination.

– Immanuel Kant, modified wording[1]

Chapter 1 presented a theory of the role of emancipative values in the human empowerment process: human empowerment advances as the utility, value, and guarantee of freedoms grow. In this process, emancipative values provide the psychological link between freedoms' growing utilities and guarantees. This chapter details how emancipative values are measured. The chapter is organized in three sections.

Section 1 portrays twelve items from the World Values Surveys and European Values Study suited to measure four domains of emancipative values. I explain why this combination of items is an improvement over Inglehart and Welzel's (2005) "self-expression values." I discuss different ways of combining the twelve items into an overall index of emancipative values and conclude that the most appropriate way to do so is to follow the logic of a so-called formative index.

Section 2 examines the quality of the emancipative values index (EVI) under reliability and validity criteria. Special emphasis is placed on whether the index represents a Western-specific concept. The analysis shows that this is not the case and that the index of emancipative values fares well in terms of cross-cultural validity.

Section 3 demonstrates that national mean scores on the EVI provide valid representations of each soctiety's center of cultural gravity. As we will see, the differences between national centers of gravity are pronounced. And even though within-societal value differences along the lines of gender, cohort,

---

[1] My own modification; the original quote reads: "Enlightenment is man's emergence from self-imposed immaturity" (Kant "What Is Enlightenment?").

income, education, religion, and ethnicity are sizeable, too, they are dwarfed by the cross-national differences. The chapter closes with a summary of key points.

I. MEASURING VALUES

According to Kluckhohn (1951) and Rokeach (1973), values represent utilities that people desire – so much that their actions are targeted toward pursuing them. From this premise follows that the social prevalence of values determines what kinds of actions dominate in a society. People's actions, in turn, decide how a society develops. Because of this, estimating how strongly given values prevail in a society is of inherent interest. As the works of Hofstede (1997), S. Schwartz (1992, 2004, 2006), and Inglehart (1990; 1997) demonstrate, it is indeed possible to estimate with decent accuracy how strongly given values prevail in different societies, using standardized population surveys (Fontaine, Poortinga, Delbeke, & Schwartz 2008).

To obtain an accurate estimate of a value's prevalence, one needs nationally representative survey data. Among the values surveys that use representative data, the World Values Surveys combined with the European Value Study (henceforth, WVS/EVS) have by far the widest country coverage and temporal scope. Since 1981, the WVS/EVS have surveyed almost a hundred societies worldwide in five different rounds, the last one having been finalized between 2005 and 2008. Surveys have been conducted on all inhabited continents. In each region of the world, those societies with the largest populations and biggest economies are covered. Altogether, the WVS represent almost 90 percent of the world population. For these reasons, I use the WVS as the prime data source throughout this book. Details on fieldwork, sampling, questionnaires, and data are available on the website of the WVS at www.worldvaluessurvey.org.

Scholars have long since recognized that social transformations come with profound changes in prevalent values (Inkeles & Smith 1974; Diamond & Inkeles 1980; Triandis 1995; Florida 2002; Bernstein 2004; Gelfand et al. 2011). The best documented theory about how values change in response to social transformations is the sequential modernization theory by Inglehart and Welzel (2005).

The authors argue that a first transformation – the transition from agrarian to industrial societies – accompanies increasing *bureaucratization*. Growing bureaucratization favors a mechanical worldview that gives rise to "secular-rational values." These values demystify quasi-divine sources of authority over people, including the authority of religion, the nation, the state, and conformity norms. The second transformation – the transition from industrial to knowledge societies – comes with increasing *individualization*. Growing individualization feeds an emancipative worldview that gives rise to "self-expression values." More than demystifying authority over people, self-expression values shift authority into the people themselves.

The human empowerment framework builds on these ideas but focuses more sharply on the desire for emancipation as a rising force in human history. From the emancipatory point of view, we need, on the one hand, a measure of values that indicates people's dissociation from external authority. For reasons of brevity, I call these values *secular values*. On the other hand, we need a measure of values that shows how strongly people claim authority over their lives for themselves. This would be a direct measure of *emancipative values*. The established measures of secular-rational values and self-expression values are too fuzzy in this perspective; they do not focus sharply enough on the themes of secularization and emancipation. Solving this problem requires modifications in item selection, item combination, and item scaling.

1.1 Item Combination

So far, items are included into the measure of secular-rational values and self-expression values primarily on empirical grounds. The logic of inclusion is a *dimensional* one: an item is included when – statistically speaking – it reflects the same dimension with other items. The logic that combines items because they represent a single dimension is known as the "reflective" logic, but I suggest that the term *dimensional* logic fits better what this approach means (see Box 2.1).

The alternative is known as the "formative" logic, which would be better characterized as the *compository* logic. In compository logic, one does not combine items into an overall measure because they reflect a single dimension. Instead, one combines items (1) because the very combination meets the meaning of a predefined umbrella concept and (2) because the combination is supposed to have consequences that reach beyond each constituent Item.

In this context, it is important to note that a combination can be meaningful and consequential even if the constituent parts are *entirely* uncorrelated. Thus, a combination does not need to reflect a single dimension in order to make sense and have an impact. For example, cultural theories of democracy – such as those of Almond and Verba (1963), Eckstein (1966, 1998) and Putnam (1993) – tell us that (1) interpersonal trust and voluntary engagement form a meaningful combination defined as the civic culture, and (2) that this combination is consequential for the functioning of democratic institutions. To test the theory, we must measure the civic culture as the combination of trust and engagement, *no matter* how closely the two correlate.[2] With this compository logic, inter-item correlation is not a criterion to judge the measurement quality of a construct. It is simply a description of inter-item overlap, which is allowed to be imperfect and even entirely absent in a compository concept. In fact, the compository logic mandates the non-overlapping variance between items to be quite sizeable. The reason is simple: the more variance the items share, the less do these items

---

[2] However, items should *not* have a strong *negative* correlation because then, in combination, they cancel each other out.

Box 2.1 Dimensional and Compository Index Construction

In *dimensional* logic, one combines single elements into a summary scale because one sees the elements as manifestations of an underlying dimension. The dimension is considered *existentially prior* to the elements: the elements "reflect" the dimension. In this perspective, unique variation in an element is to be treated as measurement error. This error should be eliminated from the measurement of the dimension; thus, an element is weighted down to the extent that its variation falls outside the shared variation. In dimensional logic, measurement quality is equivalent to *internal scale reliability*. This means that measurement quality increases with item interchangeability.

In *compository* logic, one summarizes single elements not because they overlap empirically but because they complement each other conceptually. Elements are seen in this perspective as "components" that cover separate domains in the definitional range of an overarching construct. The construct is seen as *existentially posterior* to the elements: the combination of elements "forms" the construct. Unique variation among elements is not defined as measurement error but simply as complementary parts of variation, each of which contributes to the completion of the construct. Accordingly, one does not use factor weights to downgrade an element's contribution to the overall index. Instead, each component is given equal weight. In compository logic, measurement quality is not equivalent to internal scale reliability.

What matters in compository logic is the *external index validity*. This means that measurement quality increases with an index's power to explain other phenomena. If the index indeed constitutes a consequential combination of elements, then the very combination should yield added value, showing higher explanatory power than each of its elements alone. Thus, the quality of a compository index is better, the more the explanatory power of the index exceeds that of each of its elements.

The guiding rationale in dimensional logic is to measure an *internally coherent syndrome*. In compository logic, the rationale is to measure an *externally consequential combination*. Dimensional logic is known in the literature as the "reflective" approach and compository logic as the "formative" approach (Bagozzi 1982; Bollen 1984; McCallum & Browne 1993; Edwards & Bagozzi 2000; Diamantopoulos & Winklhofer 2001; Coltman, Divenney, Midgley, & Venaik 2008). Goertz (2006) calls dimensional logic the "family resemblance model" and compository logic the "ontological model."

Sometimes, an assembly of elements has overlapping and complementary variance components that are both sizeable. In such cases, researchers have a choice according to which logic they summarize the elements. In this situation, whenever the research interest focuses on the external impact of the combination of elements, compository logic is to be preferred.

complement each other and the less does their combination make a difference to what each single item captures.

To measure secular values and emancipative values, the compository logic is more appropriate for two reasons. First, these two sets of values are indeed theoretically predefined. Second, as my theory posits, it is the very combination of their constituent parts that is supposed to have important consequences. For this to be true, there is absolutely no requirement that the constituent parts need to be interchangeable correlates of a single dimension. In fact, to assume that the combination matters, implies that the constituent parts are, at best, moderately correlated so that their variance components are more complementary than interchangeable. Complementarity among the components is the only reason why their combination can make a difference.

If the reasons to combine items change, the methods to calculate these combinations must change accordingly. So far, encompassing measures of secular-rational values and self-expression values are created by running a two-factor analysis over a selection of ten items. The estimation procedure calculates for each respondent two factor scores to measure her position on the two sets of values. Doing so has three undesirable properties.

First, items whose unique variance components are larger show lower factor loadings on the shared dimension; these loadings are used as weights to deter-mine to what extent an item is included in the measurement of the dimension. Effectively, this means to downgrade items for the unique parts of their variance: unique variance components are treated as measurement error. From the com-pository point of view, this is inappropriate: downgrading items is unjustified unless there are *theoretical* reasons why an item covers a less important domain of a concept. In fact, the compository view does not consider unique variance components as measurement error but as complementary parts that contribute to the overall construct's distinction from each constituent item. Hence, I leave items unweighted so that their unique variance components flow undiminished into the overarching construct.

Second, factor analyses yield so-called z-scores to measure people's value positions. These scores indicate where the value position of a respondent is relative to the mean position, which is standardized to zero. Thus, z-scores ignore whether the mean itself is high or low and where a respondent's absolute value position is located within the possible score range. The same z-score for respondents from two different samples hides substantial differences in these respondents' absolute value positions if the two samples have substantially different means. Because such differences are real and meaningful, one should not standardize them away. For this reason, I abstain from using z-scores. Instead, I measure value positions by their location within the possible score range.

Third, extracting scores from a two-factor analysis creates two value dimen-sions that are perfectly uncorrelated, even if the various items are strongly correlated across the two dimensions. Dimensional independence is thus imposed on the data.[3] This is undesirable, especially when the theory itself suggests that the two value constructs should be correlated. The human empowerment framework suggests exactly that for secular values and emancipative values. By dissociating people from sacred authority, secular values are a likely precursor of the internalization of authority that comes with emancipative values. This suggests a positive relationship between secular values and emancipative values. To see if this relationship exists, we must allow the two measures to be correlated. To do so, I calculate emancipative values and secular values separately, aggregating each from its own set of items. If these items correlate, the encompassing indices of emancipative values and secular values correlate as well.

Assuming we have identified a number of items that meet the definitions of secular values and emancipative values, the next question is how we calculate from single item scores the overall score on an index of secular values and an index of emancipative values. The first thing we need to do is to bring all items into the same polarity, so that the lowest score on each item always means the least secular or emancipative position, and the highest score always means the most secular or emancipative position. Next, we need to standardize the score ranges of all items, assigning every item the same theoretical minimum and maximum. Then we can think of how to combine the item scores. Several possibilities exist.

For one, we can apply the "weakest link approach" and take as the overall score the score of the lowest scoring item (Goertz 2006). Alternatively, we could follow the "best shot approach" and take as the overall score the score of the highest scoring item. Both approaches rely on a single item, discarding all other information. If measurement error was a negligible problem, either of these approaches might be appropriate. But with mass survey data, this is certainly not the case: these data contain a great deal of random noise (Page & Shapiro 1992).[4]

In contrast, taking the mean of all items does not discard any information, and it averages out measurement error that is specific to each item. Moreover, taking the mean of several items improves the scale level: the scale produced by the mean is more finely grained and thus comes closer to a continuum than do the scales of each single item. Among the different versions of the mean, the *arithmetic mean* treats items in a balanced way: there is no bias in favor of low-scoring or high-scoring items. By contrast, the *geometric mean* favors low-scoring items over high-scoring items, whereas the *quadratic mean* does the opposite.[5] In the absence of strong reasons to justify either bias, it is better to avoid it and go with the unbiased item treatment of the arithmetic mean.

---

[3] The exception is when one searches for a nonorthogonal factor solution, which is not done in the Inglehart/Welzel framework.

[4] The randomness of the error is fortunate because it leaves the validity of aggregate measures untouched.

[5] For any identical set of item scores, the geometric mean yields a lower score and the quadratic mean a higher score than the arithmetic mean.

An alternative to the mean is the cross-product of the items. Actually, I will use the cross-product sometimes – but only if I have reasons to assume that the items are of conditional quality to each other. This is a strong assumption that can lead to extreme results, and it requires clear reasoning because of that. In multiplication, the lowest scoring item decides where in the possible score range the resulting product is located. In the most extreme case, the lowest scoring item is zero; then the product is zero too, even if all other items score at the maximum. Multiplication resembles the "weakest link approach" in that it maximizes the impact of the lowest scoring item. In the absence of a clear reason for that, I go with the less rigid assumption and treat the single items in such a way that they complement each other. The mathematical expression of complementarity is the arithmetic mean (see Box 3.1, p. 110).

1.2 Item Scaling

Before one can combine items that are measured with different coding schemes, one must recode the items into the same polarity. In our case, the least secular and least emancipative position on all items obtains the lowest score, and the most secular and most emancipative position obtains the highest score. In addition, the coding schemes must all be in the same scale range: for every item, the possible minimum and maximum must be the same.

The coding scheme used throughout this book is a "normalized" scale with minimum 0, maximum 1.0, and fractions of 1.0 for intermediate positions. With a binary disagree–agree response scheme, normalization produces a 0–1 dummy variable. With a three-point response scheme,[6] normalization yields the score sequence 0, 0.50, 1.0. With a four-point response scheme, we obtain the score sequence 0, 0.33, 0.66, 1.0. With a five-point response scheme, it is the sequence 0, 0.25, 0.50, 0.75, 1.0. For a ten-point response scheme, normalization yields the score sequence 0, 0.11, 0.22, ... 1.0.

Calculating averages over variables in the normalized range always reproduces this range, yet with a more fine-grained division between 0 and 1.0 for every additional item covered. This would be true for any other standardized scale range (such as a 0–100 or 1–10 range), but standardization between 0 and 1.0 has several preferable properties (detailed in Box 2.2, p. 64).

1.3 Item Selection

1.3.1 Secular Values

The established measure of secular-rational values is based on five items. Specifically, secular-rational values involve (1) a low importance assigned to God in one's life, (2) no desire for greater respect for authority, (3) a weak sense of national pride, (4) an emphasis on independence and imagination instead of

---

[6] An example is a "disagree–neither disagree, nor agree–agree" response format.

Box 2.2   Advantages of 0–1.0 Score Normalization

Standardizing scores between minimum 0 and maximum 1.0 has various advantages. To begin with, a minimum of 0 is the "natural" expression of the complete absence of a property. Correspondingly, a maximum of 1.0 is the natural expression of the occurrence of an event or the completeness of a property. Accordingly, fractions of 1.0 are the numerical expression of the likelihood of an event or the degree of completeness of a property. Scores are easily interpretable as the partial completeness of a property, with meaningful endpoints and thresholds: 0 indicates that a property is completely absent, 0.25 and 0.33 that it is mostly but not completely absent, 0.50 that it is half-way present, 0.66 and 0.75 that it is mostly but not completely present, and 1.0 that it is completely present.

Normalized scales in a 0–1.0 range also have desirable properties in creating interaction terms to express mutual conditionality (see Box 8.1, p. 259). With 0–1.0 scales, multiplication is equivalent to weighting: one weighs down one component for deficiency in the other. Mathematically, this is a direct expression of the idea that one component loses substance through deficiency in the other or that one component conditions the other. Moreover, when creating interaction terms with 0–1.0 scales, we always remain within the 0–1.0 range and need no further mathematical operation to bring the product back into that range.

In regression analyses, coefficients are easily interpretable when all variables are normalized in a 0–1.0 range. In this case, the unstandardized regression coefficient tells us what fraction or multiple of its observed score an independent variable adds to or subtracts from the constant to obtain the expected score of the dependent variable.[7] By the same token, the unstandardized regression coefficient tells us in what ratio change within the theoretical range of an independent variable translates into change within the same range of the dependent variable.[8]

---

faith and obedience as qualities for children, and (5) a toleration of divorce as justifiable. Although one would agree that most of these items fit the definition of secularism, it does not seem that this selection is based on a systematic screening of the WVS questionnaire under a theoretical definition. So let's try another approach.

---

[7] For instance, an unstandardized coefficient of +0.33 tells us that we add a 0.33-fraction (i.e., a third) of the observed score in the independent variable to the constant to obtain the dependent variable's expected score. Alternatively, we can say that a 1-unit change in the independent variable yields a third of a 1-unit change in the dependent variable; this is equivalent to a change ratio of 3:1.

[8] An alternative form of standardization is the z-transformation. I reject this alternative because it discards all information on a variable's theoretical scale range, even though this information is often meaningful. For the same reason, I will not refer to standardized coefficients in interpreting regression results.

From the viewpoint of human empowerment, secularization is the demystification of sacrosanct sources of authority over people. The WVS covers four domains of such authority: (1) religious authority, (2) patrimonial authority, (3) state authority, and (4) the authority of conformity norms.[9] Screening the WVS questionnaire, I find three items in each of these domains that measure a secular distance from sacred authority. I select items under the restriction that they are available in consecutive rounds of the WVS, which is a necessary restriction to trace value change over time. A documentation of the measurements used in this chapter is included in Appendix 2 (www.cambridge.org/welzel).

To measure the distance from religious authority, I use items indicating (a) whether a person describes him- or herself as a "religious person," (b) whether a respondent mentions "faith" as an important child quality, and (c) how frequently a respondent attends religious service.[10] I consider refusal to describe oneself as a religious person, not mentioning faith, and abstention from religious service as secular positions in the domain of religious authority. I label secular values in this domain "agnosticism."

In the domain of patrimonial authority, I measure the distant orientation using items that indicate (a) how proud a respondent says he or she is of his or her nationality, (b) how much emphasis a respondent places on "making your parents proud," and (c) whether he or she thinks that greater respect for authority is needed for his or her country. I consider the absence of national pride, lacking orientation toward parental pride, and the rejection of a need of greater respect as secular positions in the domain of patrimonial authority. I label secular values in this domain "defiance."

As concerns state authority, I measure the distant orientation using items that indicate confidence in coercive state institutions, including (a) courts, (b) the police, and (c) the army. I follow Welzel (2006, 2007a) who presents evidence that reporting low confidence in these institutions indicates a distant orientation toward state authority.[11] I label secular values in this domain "skepticism."

---

[9] The demystification of these authorities' sacrosanctity does not mean that one questions the legitimacy of their existence but rather that an attitude of blind loyalty is replaced with a critical distance that reserves the right to express dissatisfaction in case of malperformance.

[10] I do not use the "importance of God" item because this item is unsuited to measure the importance of religion in cultures where monotheistic religions with a central God played a minor role in history. The best example is the Sinic East.

[11] Why are confidence ratings highest in the most authoritarian societies? One possibility is that respondents in authoritarian societies who desire democracy are critical of their regime's institutions but do not express this out of fear. However, these people have few opportunities to express their dissatisfaction and might be particularly eager to express it if given the chance. Now, if both impulses exist, they obviously conflict with each other. The easiest way out of this dissonance is nonresponse. Thus, if citizens in authoritarian regimes are dissatisfied and would like to express this, but fear sanctions for doing so, one would expect that nonresponse to delicate assessment questions is very high. But it is not. For instance, nonresponse to the question about confidence in government is a negligible 3.6 percent across the societies classified as nondemocracies in Table I.1 of the Introduction. This is more than in democracies (1.2 percent), but the point is that the

With respect to the authority of conformity norms, I measure the distant orientation by items indicating a certain resistance to saying what one is expected to say about freeriding behavior. The types of freeriding behavior include (a) cheating on a transport fare, (b) accepting a bribe, and (c) tax evasion. The respondent's stance to these behaviors is measured on a scale from 1 for "never justified" to 10 for "always justified." Distributions over these scales show for each national sample that the dividing line is between those opting for 1 (never justified) and those choosing any other number. This dichotomous response pattern suggests that people's answers are driven by social desirability: not opting for 1 already indicates that a person is less susceptible to the pressures of social desirability and, thus, is less prone to say what one is obviously expected to say (Welzel 2006, 2007a). Hence, I dichotomize responses and treat every response that is higher than 1 as an indication of "relativism," that is, secular values in the domain of conformity norms.

Considered in isolation, none of these items is a perfect measure of the authority distance implied by the concept of secular values. Yet, in combination with each other, the imperfections of each item are contextualized and weigh less. The combined measure of secular values should, hence, be more valid than each of its single items.

1.3.2 *Emancipative Values*

The established measure of self-expression values is also based on five items. They include (1) a feeling of happiness, (2) trust in other people, (3) signing petitions, (4) acceptance of homosexuality, and (5) a priority on freedom and participation.

Against the definition of emancipation, the assembly of orientations included in self-expression values is too broad. For instance, self-expression values include happiness, yet happiness is not a value orientation but an indication of emotional well-being. Likewise, trust in people and signing petitions do not measure value orientations. Trust in people reflects an assessment of other people's trustworthiness and is not a value. Signing a petition is not a value either but an action. Thus, to measure emancipative values, I exclude anything that does not indicate a value and concentrate on items that directly relate to the theme of emancipation.

proportion is very small. Hence, it is likely that people's high institutional confidence in authoritarian societies reflects a true belief in authority. This might, in many cases, explain the stability of authoritarian regimes: they have a legitimacy basis. This interpretation is supported by the fact that high institutional confidence in nondemocracies correlates positively with support of the idea of "having the army rule" ($r = 0.20$, $N = 88,573$). Moreover, citizens in nondemocracies often define as democratic how their regimes work. Asked about their understanding of democracy, 47.5 percent of the citizens in nondemocracies, compared to 17.6 percent in democracies, support the statement "The army takes over when government is incompetent" as the meaning of democracy. Likewise, 46.2 percent of the citizens in nondemocracies, compared to 11.2 percent in democracies, support the statement "Religious leaders ultimately interpret the laws" as the meaning of democracy. More evidence to this pattern is provided in Chapter 9 (p. 283).

Based on my understanding, emancipative values include a combination of two orientations:

1. A *liberating* orientation; namely, an emphasis on freedom of choice
2. An *egalitarian* qualification of this liberating orientation as *equal* freedom of choice or equality of opportunities.

Screening the WVS questionnaire for orientations that indicate an emphasis on freedom of choice or equality of opportunities and restricting the search to orientations that have been asked throughout various rounds of the WVS, I identify twelve items.

The twelve items group into four domains of emancipatory orientations, covering an emphasis on *autonomy, choice, equality,* and *voice.* Even though the distinction is not perfectly sharp, the emphases on autonomy and choice address more directly the liberating aspect of emancipation, whereas the emphases on equality and voice address more directly the egalitarian aspect.

Autonomy: To measure people's emphasis on autonomy, I use three items revealing whether respondents consider (a) independence and (b) imagination as desirable child qualities but do *not* consider (c) obedience as such a quality.

Choice: To measure how strongly people value freedom in their reproductive choices, I use three items indicating how acceptable respondents find (a) divorce, (b) abortion, and (c) homosexuality.

Equality: The most basic area of equality is gender equality. To measure a respondent's emphasis on gender equality, I use three items indicating how strongly they disagree with the statements that (a) "education is more important for a boy than a girl," (b) "when jobs are scarce, men should have priority over women to get a job," and (c) "men make better political leaders than women."

Voice: To measure how strongly the respondents value the voice of the people as a source of influence in their society, I use three items from Inglehart's (1977) materialism/postmaterialism batteries. These items indicate whether respondents assign first, second, or no priority to the goals of (a) "protecting freedom of speech," (b) "giving people more say in important government decisions," and (c) "giving people more say about how things are done at their jobs and in their communities."

1.4 Index Construction

To construct indices for secular and emancipative values, I normalize all twenty-four items into a scale range from a minimum of 0, for the least secular or emancipative position, to a maximum of 1.0, for the most secular or emancipative position. Intermediate positions are fractions of 1.0. Then I average item scores into more encompassing and fine-grained indices, according to the definition of secular and emancipative values and their respective domains. This is done in two steps and separately for secular values and emancipative values: in the first step, I average groups of three items into subindices for the domains of secular values and emancipative values; in the second step, I average the subindices into the overall indices of secular values and emancipative values. Table 2.1 shows the arrangement for secular values, Table 2.3 for emancipative values. At the subindex level, and even more so at the level of the encompassing indices, we obtain very fine-grained scales from 0 to 1.0.

Tables 2.1 and 2.3 also display the results of a dimensional analysis of the items and subindices. The results do not inform the index construction: in compository

TABLE 2.1 *Measuring Secular Values with World Values Surveys/European Value Study Data.*

SINGLE ITEMS	L1 Loadings	Level-1 CONSTRUCTS	L2 Loadings	Level-2 CONSTRUCT
Low Priority on Parents' Pride	0.68			
Low National Pride	0.68	Defiance	0.78	
Rejection of Respect for Authority	0.68			
Unimportance of Religion	0.84			
No Religious Practice	0.81	Agnosticism	0.69	
Not a Religious Person	0.79			SECULAR
Indifference about Bribery	0.86			VALUES
Indifference about Cheating	0.82	Relativism	0.60	
Indifference about Tax Evasion	0.80			
Distrust in Police	0.84			
Distrust in Courts	0.83	Skepticism	0.56	
Distrust in Army	0.73			
Kaiser-Meyer-Olkin Measure	0.73		0.64	
Cronbach's α	0.67		0.57	
Explained Variance	62%		44%	
N			147,871 respondents from 95 societies	

Results are from a hierarchical factor analysis with oblique rotation ("direct oblimin") at the first level (Δ: 0.20) and no rotation at level two. Factor analysis conducted with the country-pooled individual-level data of all ninety-five societies surveyed at least once by the WVS/EVS, using from each society the latest available survey (1995–2005). National surveys weighted to equal sample size. Number of extracted factors at both levels due to the Kaiser criterion. Pairwise exclusion of missing values.

TABLE 2.2 *Dimensional Uniformity of Secular Values (within-societal variance).*

COMPONENTS	SAMPLES	
	Non-Western Samples	Western Samples
Defiance Index	0.70	0.69
Skepticism Index	0.60	0.61
Agnosticism Index	0.50	0.60
Relativism Index	0.48	0.53
Kaiser-Meyer-Olkin Measure	0.57	0.62
Explained Variance	33%	37%
N	103,713	44,158

Entries are factor loadings on first-and-only dimension. Factor analysis conducted with the country-pooled individual-level data of all ninety-five societies surveyed at least once by the World Values Surveys/European Value Study (WVS/EVS), using from each society the latest available survey (1995–2005). National samples are weighted to equal size. Individual-level data are reduced to their within-societal variation by subtracting the country mean from each respondent's score on each variable. As Western, I categorize samples from societies grouped into one of the four Western culture zones in Table I.3 (p. 23) of the Introduction. Samples from all other societies are classified as non-Western.

index construction, there is no requirement of single dimensionality. The analysis is only shown out of curiosity about whether dimensional logic would support the same arrangement of items and subindices as compository logic.

I employ a two-step calculation procedure because it gives me more flexibility. For some questions, a specific subindex of secular or emancipative values might be of particular interest; for other questions, the overall indices of these values might be more interesting. In calculating both subindices and overall indices, I can change perspective whenever this seems appropriate.

Because the items used to build the various subindices employ response schemes of different resolution, the subindices also show different resolutions on the continuum between 0 and 1.0. For instance, the autonomy subindex is a 4-point scale from 0 to 1.0 (with 0.33 and 0.66 being the only other scores), whereas the choice subindex is a 28-point scale (with scores in 0.04 units between 0 and 1.0). One might suspect that this imbalance gives the subindices a different impact on the overall index, yet this is not the case. Quite the contrary, the four subindices of emancipative values have a fairly equal impact on the overall index of emancipative values. The same holds true for the four subindices of secular values. The details are documented in Appendix 2 (www.cambridge.org/welzel).

1.5 Index Dimensionality

Conceptually speaking, agnosticism, defiance, skepticism, and relativism all indicate a secular dissociation from sacred sources of authority. This suggests, but does not mean by necessity, that the four components reflect a single underlying dimension. Whether they do is an empirical question. The hierarchical factor analysis in Table 2.1 examines this question.[12] In the first stage of the analysis, I examine the dimensional structure of the twelve initial items across all respondents from all societies. The table shows that the twelve items group into the four dimensions of agnosticism, defiance, skepticism, and relativism; and they group together in the way in which the subindex calculations have summarized them. The respondents' scores on the four dimensions are extracted using an "oblique" rotation that allows the dimensions to be correlated. This is necessary in order to see if the four dimensions merge into a higher ordered dimension in the next stage of the analysis. As Table 2.1 shows, this is indeed the case: there is a single meta-dimension, secular values, unifying the four subdimensions.

One might suspect that the unidimensionality of the four subindices of secular values reflects a Western pattern that does not exist elsewhere. This is easily tested. Based on the culture zone scheme described in the Introduction (see Table I.2), I divide the WVS into Western and non-Western samples and test the dimensionality of the subindices separately for the two groups of samples. Before doing so, I reduce variation in the four subindices to individual-level differences within societies.[13] This step removes the between-societal correlation among the four subindices, which is so pronounced that it alone could be the source of their unidimensionality. Table 2.2 documents the results.

Table 2.2 shows each subindex's factor loading on the first and single underlying dimension. Because there is only one dimension, the four subindices are unidimensional. This is equally true for Western and non-Western samples. Even though the Western factor solution shows better test statistics, the difference is not dramatic. The concept of secular values can, therefore, not be disqualified as a specifically Western concept.

As we will see later, a more systematic response pattern in the West is a regularity. As we will also see, however, this does *not* reflect a Western bias, such that the WVS questions do not speak to non-Westerners. Instead, a more systematic response pattern is indicative of a higher level of cognitive mobilization among Western respondents – which in turn is the result of education and other aspects of technological advancement, not Westernness.

---

[12] Sample sizes vary between countries. This biases estimates when individual-level data are pooled, giving countries with the larger samples more weight. The bias is undesirable because differences in sample size exist for reasons that are of no theoretical interest. To eliminate the bias, samples must be weighted. There are two possibilities. One possibility is to weight each country sample for the proportion of the world population it represents. This approach is appropriate when the universe to which one infers is defined as the *world population*. The alternative is to weight national samples to equal size. This approach is appropriate when country-level conditions are analyzed as a source of variation of how people act and think. Then, population size is irrelevant. I follow this approach throughout this book. Hence, in all pooled individual-level analyses, I weight national samples to equal size.

[13] This is done by subtracting from each respondent's score the mean score of her society. Doing so eliminates all between-societal variation.

TABLE 2.3 *Measuring Emancipative Values with World Values Surveys/European Value Study Data.*

SINGLE ITEMS	L1 Loadings	Level-1 CONSTRUCTS	L2 Loadings	Level-2 CONSTRUCT
Toleration of Abortion	0.86			
Toleration of Divorce	0.85	Choice	0.77	
Toleration of Homosexuality	0.80			
Women's Equality: Politics	0.81			
Women's Equality: Education	0.77	Equality	0.73	
Women's Equality: Jobs	0.72			EMANCIPATIVE
Priority More Say: Local	0.77			VALUES
Priority More Say: National	0.77	Voice	0.68	
Freedom of Speech	0.60			
Independence a Desired Quality	0.73			
Obedience NOT a Desired Quality	0.71	Autonomy	0.60	
Imagination a Desired Quality	0.50			
Kaiser-Meyer-Olkin Measure	0.77		0.70	
Cronbach's α	0.68		0.65	
Explained Variance	60%		50%	
N			152,315 respondents from 95 societies	

Results are from hierarchical factor analysis with oblique rotation ("direct oblimin") at the first level (Δ: 0.20) and no rotation at level two. Factor analysis conducted with the country-pooled individual-level data of all ninety-five societies surveyed at least once by the WVS/EVS, using from each society the latest available survey (1995–2005). National surveys weighted to equal sample size. Number of extracted factors at both levels due to the Kaiser criterion. Pairwise exclusion of missing values.

The fact that autonomy, choice, equality, and voice belong together under the definition of emancipation suggests, but does not necessarily mean, that these four components reflect a single underlying dimension. To see if they do, Table 2.3

TABLE 2.4 *Dimensional Uniformity of Emancipative Values (within-societal variance).*

COMPONENTS	SAMPLES	
	Non-Western Samples	Western Samples
Choice Index	0.60	0.69
Equality Index	0.58	0.66
Voice Index	0.52	0.53
Autonomy Index	0.51	0.62
Kaiser-Meyer-Olkin Measure	0.56	0.64
Explained Variance	30%	39%
N	109,233	43,082

Entries are factor loadings on first-and-only dimension. Factor analysis conducted with the country-pooled individual-level data of all ninety-five societies surveyed at least once by the World Values Surveys/European Value Study (WVS/EVS), using from each society the latest available survey (1995–2005). National samples are weighted to equal size. Individual-level data are reduced to their within-societal variation by subtracting the country mean from each respondent's score on each variable. As Western, I categorize samples from societies grouped into one of the four Western culture zones in Table I.3 (p. 23) of the Introduction. Samples from all other societies are classified as non-Western.

shows the results of another hierarchical factor analysis, one similar to that performed for secular values in Table 2.1. The results are similar too. At the first stage of the analysis, the twelve initial items group into four dimensions – autonomy, choice, equality, and voice – exactly as the index calculation groups these items. At the second stage of the analysis, the four extracted dimensions merge into a single meta-dimension: emancipative values.

Table 2.4 demonstrates that the unidimensionality of the four subindices is not a uniquely Western pattern. Although the factor solution shows again somewhat better test statistics among Western samples, the pattern is basically the same across the Western/non-Western divide. As mentioned before, a more systematic pattern in Western responses does not indicate a cultural bias in the questions; instead it is indicative of higher levels of cognitive mobilization among Western societies. This leads to higher levels of conceptual organization among Western respondents, which manifests itself in more patterned responses. This is true for all sorts of questions, not only those that one might suspect appeal to Westerners in particular.[14]

[14] For instance, one can hardly claim that asking people for their confidence in institutions of order, such as the police and courts, has a particularly Western bias. Police forces and a court system exist in almost every society. Still, confidence ratings in these two institutions correlate more strongly in Western samples ($r = 0.69$; $N = 45,978$; $p < 0.001$) than in non-Western samples ($r = 0.35$; $N = 110,745$; $p < 0.001$). These figures are based on the latest available survey from each of the ninety-five societies surveyed once by the World Values Surveys (WVS), weighting national samples to equal size.

Based on the results of Tables 2.1 and 2.3, it would be justified to follow dimensional logic and extract the shared variation among the components of secular and emancipative values. Nevertheless, I prefer a compository index construction because it is a concept-driven logic that does not depend on specific assumptions about the empirical coherence among the index components. Moreover, the compository logic suggests that the very *combination* of components matters, which mandates that the unshared variance of each component is to be fully included in the index: in dimensional logic, by contrast, one discounts the unshared variance.

In compository logic, the empirical coherence among the index components becomes an object of explanation rather than a part of the measurement procedure itself. This opens important new insights, as we will see. Because this book centers on the theme of emancipation, the following discussion focuses on emancipative values rather than secular values.

2. QUALIFYING THE EMANCIPATIVE VALUES INDEX

2.1 Evolving Standards of Emancipation

One can easily think of better items to cover the themes of secularization and emancipation. But these were the best available items in the WVS and the only ones measured throughout consecutive waves.

It needs to be emphasized that the measures proposed here capture values at the standard of *our* era. For instance, if we had included the acceptance of homosexuality in a measure of emancipative values fifty years ago, no society would have scored high in emancipative values. Thus, different historical periods have different standards against which a person or society appears more or less emancipatory. These standards themselves evolve, pushing the front of emancipation farther ahead. Two hundred years ago, someone was strongly emancipatory if she supported the liberation of slaves and serfs. Hence, the recentness of some of the topics I use to measure emancipative values should not be taken to mean that emancipative values did not exist in earlier periods. They did. Still, the standards against which a position appeared emancipatory were lower.

If we eventually arrive at a situation in which the measure of emancipative values proposed here no longer shows much variation, the standard of emancipation will probably have moved farther ahead, and we will need to adjust the measurement accordingly. As will be seen, however, we are far from this point.

2.2 Normative Desirability

Scholars might argue that measuring and rank ordering societies on a scale of emancipative values is not a culturally neutral exercise but one that applies Western standards to societies in which these standards are alien. If this were so, the value measure could be dismissed as a case of intellectual imperialism. However, we cannot simply assume the alienness of emancipative values to non-Western cultures; it must be examined. It is an empirical question whether and to what extent emancipative values exist and develop in non-Western cultures. As will be seen throughout this book, emancipative values do exist and develop outside the West – provided technological advancement and other processes that widen people's action resources proceed. To demonstrate this claim, emancipative values must be measured across cultures under the same conceptual definition, despite the fact that these values first became prominent in the West.

A different issue is the question of whether emancipative values are a normatively desirable phenomenon. Chapters 5, 6, 9, and 12 demonstrate that they are. We will see that emancipative values come with an emphasis on civic norms that favor trusting, fair, and benign human interactions and enhance general well-being (Chapters 5 and 6). Also, emancipative values fuel democratizing mass pressures and environmental activism, thus helping to improve a society's democratic quality (Chapter 9) and ecological sustainability (Chapter 12). From a normative point of view, the civic-humanistic-democratic-ecological impetus of emancipative values is a quite desirable feature.

2.3 How Western Are Emancipative Values?

Emancipative values are, a priori, defined as the combination of orientations emphasizing freedom of choice and equality of opportunities. People's responses in the WVS are measured against this theoretical definition, no matter how closely the item responses reflect a coherent syndrome in people's minds.

Such a compository logic is preferable to a dimensional logic under two conditions: (1) the combination of given components has an a priori theoretical meaning, and (2) there are reasons to assume that this combination has important consequences, irrespective of whether the components always closely correlate.

These are precisely the conditions informing the concept of emancipative values. As the sequence thesis of emancipation theory suggests, the combined strength of the orientations that form emancipative values is consequential: this combined strength accounts for how effectively universal freedoms are guaranteed in a society. To test this assumption, we do not need to burden the concept of emancipative values with the demanding assumption that its components "reflect" in every population a coherent syndrome. In fact, we can treat the coherence of the components as a variable that is a target of explanation.

To examine the coherence of emancipative values, I estimate the consistency between the concept's four subsidiary orientations for each society separately and then see whether and to what extent the consistency varies between societies and whether it varies systematically in ways that can be understood as cognitive mobilization. One way to do this is to calculate the Cronbach's α (read: alpha) for the four subsidiary orientations.[15] Cronbach's α grows with a larger average correlation between the subsidiary orientations. Thus, a larger Cronbach's α indicates that the four orientations are more coherent. Since this coherence represents cognitive consistency in the respondents' minds, one can interpret stronger coherence as a measure of conceptual organization: people's conceptions are more organized when the four orientations merge into a more coherent syndrome in their minds. For a compository index, then, Cronbach's α is not a measure of index quality but a measure of the respondents' conceptual organization.[16] Calculating the α separately for each national population allows us to identify different degrees of conceptual organization between societies.

Taking this perspective, the left-hand diagram in Figure 2.1 plots the α of each society against the measure of technological advancement presented in the Introduction. Because this measure is based on indicators of education, information, and knowledge, it is straightforward to interpret it as a measure of cognitive mobilization. On the vertical axis, we see large cross-national variability in the α, ranging from a low α of almost 0, in Rwanda and Uganda, to a relatively high α of 0.65 in Austria and Denmark.

If the cross-national variability in the α indeed indicates different degrees of conceptual organization, we must conclude that people in African societies are conceptually the least organized. But this seems racist. African and other non-Western societies might appear less conceptually organized because they are asked Western questions and not because of lower levels of conceptual organization. If so, whether or not a society belongs to the West should explain a large proportion of the α's cross-national variability. By contrast, variation in cognitive mobilization should not make much of a difference when we take into account the Western/non-Western divide. If, however, cognitive mobilization continues to show a positive influence on the α, even as we take into account the Western/non-Western divide, it is safe to conclude that emancipative values grow more coherent as people's conceptual organization matures.

The regression models in Table 2.5 test these alternative possibilities. The dependent variable is the degree of emancipative values' coherence in a society, measured by the Cronbach's α. To examine Western influence, I use two variables. One is a dummy variable indicating whether or not a society belongs in one of the four Western culture zones shown in Table I.2 of the Introduction. Yet, since this is a very crude distinction, it might not account for much variance. For this reason, I also use a fine-grained variable to measure the strength of a Western tradition. One of the signature inventions of Western culture is liberal democracy

---

[15] Conducting the same analyses for the twelve constituent items yields similar results.

[16] I am not interested in the absolute values of the Cronbach's *α* but only in the cross-national *differences* in these values. I am especially not interested in whether the *α* value crosses some standard marker (e.g., a score of 0.70) considered as a threshold for a "sufficient" inter-item correlation. The compository logic defies the idea of a "sufficient" inter-item correlation because this logic does not base its measurement on the assumption of correlation.

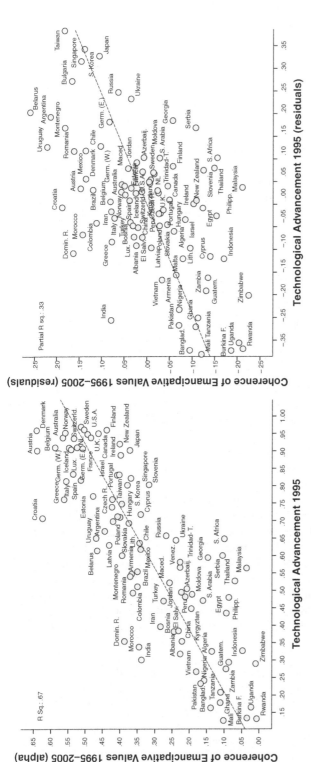

FIGURE 2.1 The Effect of Technological Advancement on the Coherence of Emancipative Values (before and after controlling for societies' belonging to the West and their democratic tradition).

Data Coverage: All societies for which data on technological advancement are available and which are surveyed at least once by the World Values Surveys/European Value Study (WVS/EVS), using the latest available survey (1995–2005). Number of covered societies is ninety-two, excluding Andorra, Hong Kong, and Iraq, for which the data on technological advancement are missing. Left-hand diagram shows the effect of technological advancement on the coherence of emancipative values without controls. The right-hand diagram shows the effect after controlling the societies' belonging to the West and their democratic tradition, illustrating the impact of technological advancement for constant Westernness and democratic traditions. For instance, the upper-right position of Bulgaria, Japan, Russia, Singapore, South Korea, and Taiwan in the right-hand diagram shows that, when a society's technological advancement is higher than lack of a Western-democratic tradition suggests, emancipative values are more coherent. Conversely, the lower-left position of Greece, Israel, Latvia, Luxemburg, and Poland in the same diagram shows that, when a society's technological advancement is lower than the presence of a Western-democratic tradition suggests, emancipative values are less coherent.

TABLE 2.5 *Explaining the Coherence of Emancipative Values.*

PREDICTORS	DEPENDENT VARIABLE: Emancipative Values' Coherence 1995–2005 (Cronbach's α over four subindices)		
	Model 1	Model 2	Model 3
Constant	0.19 (8.31)***	−0.02 (-0.66)[†]	0.04 (1.19)[†]
Western Society (dummy)	0.23(7.91)***		0.11(3.52)***
Democratic Tradition 1995	0.09(1.89)*		−0.01(0.24)[†]
Technological Advancement 1995		0.56(13.60)***	0.42(6.59)***
Adjusted R²	0.57	0.67	0.70
N (number of observations)	94	92	92

Entries are unstandardized regression coefficients (*b*'s) with T ratios in parentheses. Test statistics of heteroskedasticity (White test), mucollinearity (variance inflation factors), and influential cases (DFFITs) reveal no violation of ordinary least squares (OLS) assumptions. Significance levels: * $p < .100$; ** $p < .050$; *** $p < .005$;[†] not significant ($p > .100$). Data cover all ninety-five societies surveyed at least once by the World Values Surveys/European Value Study (WVS/EVS), aggregating emancipative values from the latest available survey, provided the measures of technological advancement and democratic tradition are available. Data on democratic tradition are missing for Hong Kong. Data on technological advancement are missing for Andorra, Iraq, and Hong Kong. For Zimbabwe, the 1995 score in technological advancement is estimated from the 2005 score, using OLS regression. As Western, I categorize societies grouped into one of the four Western culture zones in Table I.3 (p. 23) of the Introduction.

(Huntington 1996). Hence, the endurance of democracy in a society is a formidable indicator of how long this society has been under the influence of Western culture. And if liberal democracy is the institutional embodiment of emancipative values, the endurance of liberal democracy should shape these values and strengthen their coherence. To measure the endurance of liberal democracy, I use the *democracy stock index* by Gerring, Bond, Barndt, and Moreno (2005), as of 1995. This index measures a society's historically accumulated experience with democracy by adding over time the yearly democracy ratings provided by the Polity IV project (Marshall & Jaggers 2004). Among alternative measures of democracy, the authors qualify the democracy stock index as the one with the greatest impact on theoretically expected consequences of democracy. I standardize scores on this index into a scale from minimum 0 (no experiences with democracy) to 1.0 (richest experience). I label the index here and henceforth "democratic tradition." Among the societies of the WVS sample, a score of 0 is found in Saudi Arabia. The United States and Sweden have a score of 1.0, whereas a medium score of around 0.50 is found in Peru and the Philippines.

As Model 1 in Table 2.5 shows, when one estimates the coherence of emancipative values in each society based on whether the society belongs to the West and how long a democratic tradition the society has, we explain 57 percent of the cross-national coherence differences. As the coefficients show, a 1-unit increase in the democratic tradition comes with a 0.09-unit increase in the coherence of emancipative values – a very low translation rate. However, the simple fact that a society belongs to the West increases the coherence of emancipative values by 0.23 points on the α index. This testifies to a substantial impact of Western belongingness – which is actually not surprising given that Western societies are *defined* by an imprint from emancipatory movements in history. Because of this imprint, emancipative values should be more coherent in Western societies. In light of this result, measuring emancipative values seems to be a case of Western-centrism that judges non-Western societies against an alien standard.

This is one possible interpretation. The other is that the coherence of emancipative values is mostly a matter of conceptual organization, which grows with a society's cognitive mobilization. In this case, the stronger coherence of emancipative values in Western societies would not so much result from these societies' *historic* exposure to emancipatory movements but from their advanced cognitive mobilization *today*. In other words, the main reason why emancipative values are less coherent in non-Western societies is not that they are non-Western but that their cognitive mobilization is less advanced. This would imply that, as cognitive mobilization advances in non-Western societies, emancipative values become coherent in these societies.

This is precisely what the right-hand diagram of Figure 2.1 demonstrates: it shows the impact of cognitive mobilization on the coherence of emancipative values, controlling for a society's Westernness. Japan, Singapore, South Korea, and Taiwan are cases in point. Culturally speaking, these societies are definitely non-Western. Yet, these societies' cognitive mobilization is more advanced than their non-Westernness suggests, and this corresponds with a stronger coherence of emancipative values than their non-Westernness suggests. Conversely, Greece, Israel, Luxemburg, Malta, Poland, Latvia, and Lithuania's[17] cognitive mobilization is less advanced than these societies' belongingness to the West suggests – which corresponds to a weaker coherence of emancipative values than these societies' Westernness suggests.

More generally, we do not find non-Western societies to be a systematic exception from the logic that ties the coherence of emancipative values to a society's cognitive mobilization. Otherwise, the non-Western societies would cluster into a compact outlier position from the regression line in the two diagrams of Figure 2.1. But they are not in such an outlier position. Most (although not all) of them simply cluster at the lower end of the regression line, meaning that emancipative values in non-Western societies are less coherent because these societies' cognitive mobilization is less advanced. Hence, the low

---

[17] The Baltic states have a democratic tradition from the interwar period. Their cultural orientation is toward Scandinavia. Soviet communism has been imposed on them against their will, and so they were the first republics to break free from the Soviet empire, to adopt liberal democracy, and to join the Western alliance. Their cultural self-attribution is decidedly Western. For these reasons, I think that they are accurately grouped into the culture zone of the Returned West.

coherence of emancipative values in non-Western societies is a developmental phenomenon, not a manifestation of cultural immunity.

Confirming this interpretation, the third model in Table 2.5 shows that, once we take a society's cognitive mobilization into account, the effect of the democratic tradition on the coherence of emancipative values becomes *entirely* insignificant, whereas the effect of Western belongingness drops to less than half its size. By contrast, cognitive mobilization retains most of its positive impact on the coherence of emancipative values. Hence, the main reason for the coherence of emancipative values is cognitive mobilization today. Whether a society has an imprint from emancipatory movements in history also counts but is clearly less important. All this means that, even though non-Western societies start out at lower coherence levels of emancipative values than Western societies, they are as open as Western societies to the coherence-generating force of cognitive mobilization.

In conclusion, cross-national differences in the coherence of emancipative values are misinterpreted when they are understood as culture-biased differences in measurement quality. They reflect real differences in the advancement of cognitive mobilization – the intellectual component of the human empowerment process. Human empowerment is most advanced in Western societies, but other societies are catching up. So, if we are interested in the worldwide diffusion of this process, we have every reason to measure emancipative values around the globe.

2.4 Measurement Validity

For a compository index, internal coherence is not a quality criterion; it is a target of explanation. External validity, however, is certainly a quality criterion for a compository index. One way to look at external validity is to examine an index's associative strength with its theoretically expected correlates, including both antecedents and consequences.

Table 2.6 correlates the *emancipative values index* (EVI), as well as its four components with theoretically expected correlates at the individual and societal levels. At the individual level, two of the specified correlates – formal education and informational connectedness – are expected antecedents that give rise to emancipative values. Two other correlates – social movement activity and understanding democracy – are expected consequences that follow from emancipative values.[18]

---

[18] Formal education measures the highest school level a respondent attended, in ascending order on a 9-point scale. Informational connectedness measures the variety of sources a respondent uses to receive information, in ascending order on a 10-point scale. Social movement activity measures the variety of social movement activities a respondent has been or considers to be involved in, on a 7-point scale in ascending order. Understanding democracy measures how strongly a respondents' notion of democracy coincides with democracy's liberal definition, on a multipoint scale in ascending order. Measurement details of these and all other variables used in this chapter are documented in Appendix 2 (www.cambridge.org/welzel).

TABLE 2.6 *Correlation of Emancipative Values and Their Components with Assumed Antecedents and Consequences.*

	EV-INDEX	AUTONOMY	EQUALITY	CHOICE	VOICE	Self-ex. Values	N
Non-Western Surveys:							
Formal Education	0.28	0.17	0.17	0.16	0.13	0.17	113,310
Informational Connectedness	0.25	0.18	0.15	0.14	0.11	0.21	44,357
Social Movement Activity	0.18	0.09	0.08	0.14	0.12	NA[a]	100,891
Understanding Democracy	0.25	0.06	0.25	0.19	0.08	0.11	40,819
Western Surveys:							
Formal Education	0.31	0.24	0.18	0.24	0.15	0.29	51,212
Informational Connectedness	0.30	0.23	0.20	0.22	0.14	0.34	25,680
Social Movement Activity	0.38	0.23	0.24	0.30	0.24	NA[a]	52,326
Understanding Democracy	0.37	0.24	0.26	0.32	0.15	0.20	22,911
Societal Level:							
Technological Advancement	0.79	0.61	0.66	0.75	0.54	0.69	93
Democratic Achievement	0.80	0.48	0.67	0.65	0.60	0.72	86
Advancement & Achievement	0.84	0.58	0.72	0.76	0.59	0.73	86

Entries are Pearson correlation coefficients (r). Correlation analysis in the top two panels conducted with the country-pooled individual-level data of all societies surveyed at least once by the World Values Surveys/European Value Study (WVS/EVS), using the most recent survey from each society (ca. 1995–2005). Number of included societies in the top two panels is ninety-five for formal education and social movement activity and fifty for informational connectedness and understanding democracy (the latter two variables are only available from round five of the WVS). National samples in the top two panels are weighed to equal sample size.

In the lower panel, societal averages of the values measures are used from the latest available survey and correlated with technological advancement, democratic achievement, and the factor combination of the two (advancement & achievement), measured over the period 1995-2005. As Western I categorize samples from societies grouped into one of the four Western culture zones Table I.3 (p. 23). Samples from all other societies are classified as non-Western. All correlations significant at the .001-level (two-tailed). Gray-marked coefficients indicate strongest association with a given correlate of emancipative values.

[a] Not applicable: correlation would be semi-tautological because self-expression values include a component measure of social movement activity, namely signing petitions.

To make sure that the same validity conclusions hold over the Western/non-Western divide, the individual-level data are analyzed separately for Western and non-Western samples. At the societal level, technological advancement is an expected antecedent and democratic achievement an expected consequence of emancipative values. Together, they combine into "advancement and achievement," which measures a society's stage of human empowerment over the capability and guarantee domains. This is the third correlate at the societal level.[19]

To justify the summary of components into the EVI, we require the encompassing index to associate with the correlates at least as strongly as the strongest component does, in any instance. For most cases, the encompassing index should actually associate more closely with the respective correlates than does its strongest component.

Again, Table 2.6 shows a somewhat more pronounced correlation pattern for the Western than for the non-Western samples. Furthermore, correlations at the societal level are, as usual,[20] much stronger than at the individual level. Otherwise, the same conclusions apply to all three panels of the table.

All correlations in Table 2.6 are positive and statistically significant. If we had to rely on a single component of emancipative values, the "choice index" would be our best pick. Among the four components, this one usually shows the strongest association with the expected antecedents and consequences of emancipative values, followed by the "equality index." Nevertheless, in every instance but one, the encompassing EVI associates more strongly with its expected antecedents and consequences than does each of its components. In fact, there is not a single instance in which the encompassing EVI does not associate at least as strong as its strongest component.

In every instance, the EVI associates more closely with its expected antecedents and consequences than does the original version of Inglehart and Welzel's (2005) "self-expression values." This is obvious from a comparison of the correlations in the first with those in the last column in Table 2.6.

There are other value measures that scholars use to pinpoint the most salient cultural differences between societies. For instance, Hofstede (2001 [1980]), Suh

---

[19] Using the indicators of technological advancement and democratic achievement described in the Introduction, I take measures of them that are contemporaneous to emancipative values. "Advancement and achievement" is measured here as the average of technological advancement and democratic achievement, indicating the stage of human empowerment over the capability and guarantee domains. This is a reduced measure of human empowerment because it does not include the motivation domain, which is represented by emancipative values.

[20] The fact that aggregate-level attitudes show stronger correlations than their individual-level measures is not the result of "aggregation bias." On the contrary, aggregation eliminates random measurement error at the individual level and unmasks, for this reason, a correlation's true strength (on the widely misconceived problem of the "ecological fallacy," see Inglehart & Welzel 2005: 231–244).

et al. (1998) as well as Gelfand et al. (2004) use measures of "collectivism versus individualism" to describe cultural differences: collectivistic cultures place the authority of the group over the rights of the individual; individualistic cultures do the opposite. Another measure of collectivism versus individualism, labeled "embeddedness versus autonomy," is provided by S. Schwartz (1992, 2004, 2007): embeddedness describes a culture in which individuals emphasize their belongingness to closely knit in-groups; autonomy describes cultures in which they emphasize their independence from such groups. In addition, Gelfand et al. (2011) describe cultural differences in terms of "tightness versus looseness": tight cultures show low tolerance of deviant behavior; loose cultures do the opposite.

Conceptually speaking, one would expect that collectivism overlaps with embeddedness and tightness. By the same token, individualism should overlap with autonomy and looseness (Triandis 1995). Also, there is an obvious connection between these culture measures and societal development. As Table 2.7 shows, collectivism, embeddedness, and tightness associate consistently with low levels of development, as indicated by more than a dozen measures of a society's life quality, including – among other things – income, education, longevity, gender equality, rule of law, peace, security, and democracy. Conversely, individualism, autonomy, and looseness associate consistently with high levels of development.

Given that these alternative measures are so clearly linked with development, the obvious question is whether they provide a better indication of human empowerment's cultural domain than do emancipative values. Table 2.7 examines this possibility, correlating emancipative values with the same large set of indicators of societal development, including our two measures of human empowerment in the capability and guarantee domains: technological advancement and democratic achievement.

Not surprisingly, emancipative values correlate with technological advancement and democratic achievement, and with all other indicators of development, in the same way as the alternative measures of culture do. The correlations always point in the same direction and are of roughly comparable magnitude, except for "tightness versus looseness," whose associations are consistently weaker. The similarity of the correlation pattern between emancipative values, individualism and autonomy, is reassuring: it documents that emancipative values capture the same societal differences as other measures of culture. In fact, emancipative values capture these differences better in fourteen out of fifteen indicators of development: in all these instances, emancipative values correlate more strongly with development than do the alternative measures of culture. From that point of view, emancipative values are the preferable measure of the cultural domain of human empowerment.

This is true for a couple of additional reasons. First, emancipative values are available for ninety-five societies worldwide; the other measures exist for a considerably smaller number and variety of societies. Second, emancipative

TABLE 2.7 Correlations of Cultural with Noncultural Indicators of Development

Correlates (in 2000):	Emancipative Values (emancipation coded high)			Tightness/ Looseness (looseness coded high)	Collectivism/ Individualism (individualism coded high)	Embeddedness/ Autonomy (autonomy coded high)
	All Societies	Same Set of Societies as with Tightness/ Looseness	Same Set of Societies as with Collectivism/ Individualism			
Technological Advancement	.81***(89)	.87***(32)	.80***(50)	.36**(32)	.76***(50)	.30***(50)
Democratic Advancement	.79***(88)	.78***(32)	.84***(48)	.35*(32)	.76***(48)	.47***(46)
Gross Domestic Product (GDP)/ per capita	.80***(88)	.79***(26)	.82***(40)	.11†(26)	.80***(40)	.50***(46)
Urbanization	.58***(88)	.73***(31)	.52***(49)	.45*(31)	.50***(49)	.21†(49)
Schooling Years	.76***(63)	.73***(31)	.74***(44)	.30†(31)	.76***(44)	.46***(41)
Fertility	-.49***(85)	-.48***(29)	-.53***(44)	-.46**(29)	-.46***(44)	-.09†(44)
Infant Mortality	-.65***(87)	-.74***(31)	-.72***(47)	-.40**(29)	-.57***(47)	-.20†(45)
White Settler Mortality	-.31***(86)	-.32***(32)	-.32**(46)	.08†(32)	-.19*(46)	-.12†(46)
Human Development	.72***(88)	.86***(31)	.80***(48)	.36**(31)	.69***(48)	.49***(44)
Gender Empowerment	.89***(45)	.86***(22)	.90***(29)	.29†(22)	.82***(29)	.48***(44)
Rule of Law	.76***(92)	.83***(31)	.81***(49)	.06†(31)	.81***(49)	.45***(49)
Order and Stability	.72***(92)	.75***(31)	.77***(49)	.19†(31)	.73***(49)	.36***(49)
Continuous Peace	.66***(89)	.66***(31)	.70***(49)	.13†(31)	.63***(49)	.29***(48)
Consanguinity (logged)	-.71***(51)	-.64***(23)	-.66***(33)	-.57**(23)	-.58***(33)	-.33*(28)
Social Movement Activity	.71***(48)	.73***(19)	.82***(30)	.19†(19)	.82***(30)	.52***(46)

Entries are Pearson correlation coefficients (r) with number of societies in parentheses. Tightness/looseness is taken from Gelfand et al. (2011) and coded inversely. Component measures of collectivism/individualism are taken from Thornhill/Fincher et al. (2008) and combined as detailed in Appendix 2 (www.cambridge.org/welzel). The same appendix describes the sources of all other data in this table. Embeddedness/autonomy scores are calculated on the basis of the Schwartz items fielded in round five of the World Values Surveys (WVS). Significance levels (two-tailed): † $p \geq .100$; * $p < .100$; ** $p < .050$; *** $p < .005$. Coefficients in the second column from the left are marked in gray if, for the same set of societies, emancipative values show the stronger association with the respective correlate than tightness/looseness. Coefficients in the third column from the left are marked in gray if, for the same set of societies, emancipative values show the stronger association with the respective correlate than collectivism/ individualism. Correlates in bold letters represent the two components of human empowerment, in addition to emancipative values.

values are taken from random national samples that are representative of entire societies; the other cultural measures are taken from convenient samples of specific subpopulations, such as students. An exception is the embeddedness versus autonomy measure from the European Social Survey and the WVS. But, here, the number of measures is limited to fifty societies. Third, only emancipative values are available in considerable time series, so, among the existing cultural measures, only this one is suited to trace value change.[21]

For all these reasons, we can safely conclude that emancipative values are a valid and preferable measure of the cultural differences linked with human empowerment and other aspects of development.

2.5 How Real Are National Mean Scores?

Value preferences are a property of individuals. Accordingly, we measure values at the individual level in nationally representative mass surveys. But we often aggregate these individual-level measures to assess how prevalent certain values are in a given society. As we do this, the object of study changes from the individual to the society. With this change, what values mean in substantive terms changes as well. At the individual level, we deal with value *preferences* that characterize personalities. At the societal level, we deal with value *prevalences* that describe cultures.

From the viewpoint of culture, how prevalent certain values are in different societies is exactly what we want to know. In fact, the whole point of why surveys are conducted on the basis of nationally representative samples is to allow for an estimation of value prevalences among entire societies.

Some scholars might suspect that the prevalence of a value is a calculated artifact that doesn't represent a truly felt aspect of social reality. It might not be a Durkheimian "social fact." However, this suspicion is highly implausible, especially with respect to values. Values motivate actions in pursuit of these values. As a consequence, people exhibit and signal their values through communication and other forms of social interaction. Because of that, most people get a sense of which values are prevalent in their society. The prevalence of a value becomes an intuitively felt fact (Stimson 1999; Stimson, MacKuen, & Erikson 2002). As part of a society's psychological climate, the prevalence of a value has its very own – ecological – effects on people, no matter how strongly these people *themselves* prefer the prevalent value.

For this reason, it is important to examine emancipative values not only for their individual-level effects but also for their ecological effects. Doing so is to give the social prevalence of emancipative values its own consideration. This

---

[21] I searched the literature for other cross-national measures of culture that could show a stronger link than emancipative values with the capability and guarantee domains of human empowerment. I found indicators of the demographic prevalence of the so-called Big Five personality attributes, as well as the prevalence of "social dominance orientations." Apart from the fact that these indicators are only available for much smaller sets of societies, their link with human empowerment and societal development does not come close to emancipative values.

gives "culture" its due weight because culture is a collective property, manifest precisely in the prevalence of values.

However, the assumption that the prevalence of a value represents a cultural fact that is felt in similar ways by most members of a society hinges on distributional prerequisites. The assumption has more plausibility if the members of a society cluster in a bell-shaped, single-peaked curve around the average value-position of all respondents. Then, we have a real central tendency – a *cultural anchor point* around which the individual value positions of all members of a society gravitate.

The question is whether national mean scores of emancipative values meet this requirement. Consider the possibility that a society is polarized into two large groups, one showing a strong and the other a weak emphasis on emancipative values. In this case, we face a two-peaked distribution with the mean located somewhere in the middle, between two polar groups. In such a constellation, the mean does not represent a society's cultural anchor point, for there is no such anchor point in this case. The mean only represents a cultural anchor point if distributions are *single-peaked*, with sharply dropping frequencies as we move away from the mean. To what extent are these requirements met by emancipative values?

To examine how the populations of national societies distribute over emancipative values, I collapse the continuous 0–1.0 index of emancipative values into ten ascending categories of equal interval size, each covering a tenth (i.e., a range of 0.10 points) of the entire scale range. For instance, category "EV 01" summarizes people who score from 0 to 0.10 on emancipative values; "EV 02" summarizes people in the range from 0.11 to 0.20, and so forth, until category "EV 10" summarizes people scoring from 0.91 to 1.0.

Using this categorization, Figure 2.2 shows how nine selected populations distribute over emancipative values. Space restrictions do not allow me to display the distribution of each of the ninety-five societies, so I selected nine societies, arranging them in ascending order from left to right and from top to bottom. The arrangement starts with the Iraqi population as one of those with the weakest prevalence of emancipative values. The arrangement ends with the Swedish population as the one with the strongest prevalence of emancipative values. In the center, we find the Taiwanese population as one with a medium emphasis on emancipative values. Additional societies fill the ranges between these examples. As is evident, all nine societies show both single-peaked and mean-centered distributions over emancipative values. Among the ninety-five societies for which these graphics could be shown, there is *not a single exception* from this pattern. The population average in emancipative values adequately depicts a society's cultural anchor point in these values; it is a valid measure of the social prevalence of emancipative values.

In light of the previous results, I conclude that the index of emancipative values has sufficient quality in terms of theoretical foundation, construction logic, external validity, and distributional centeredness. So we can move on from here and look at real-world variation in emancipative values, within and between societies.

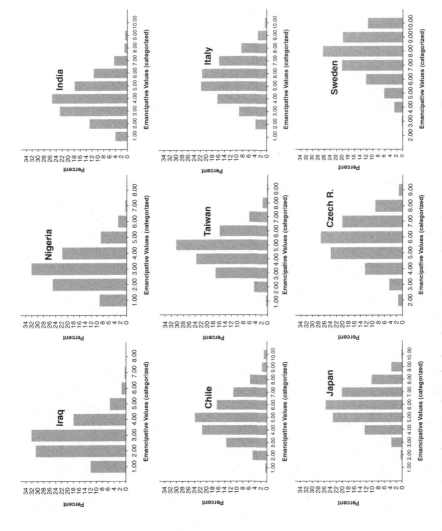

FIGURE 2.2 Emancipative Values' Single-Peaked and Mean-Centered Distributions.

3. VARIATION IN EMANCIPATIVE VALUES BETWEEN AND WITHIN SOCIETIES

3.1 Variation between Societies

Figure 2.3 maps each of our ninety-five societies' average position on secular values and emancipative values, using the most recent survey for each society. Given this book's focus on human emancipation, secular values are of interest here as a contrast medium to illuminate emancipative values.

FIGURE 2.3 The New Cultural Map of the World.
Data Coverage: Respondents from all ninety-five societies surveyed at least once by the World Values Surveys/European Value Study (WVS/EVS), using for each society the latest available survey. Total *N* (respondents) is 144,381. Societies in bold letters represent the largest population of their culture zone or its historic center. Here and throughout the remainder of this book, Germany is treated as two samples (West and East).

The two sets of values show a pronounced correspondence. The correlation coefficient is $r = 0.77$ ($p < 0.001$, two-tailed).[22] Accordingly, secular values and emancipative values share 60 percent variation. Despite this close association, there are good reasons to keep the two sets of values separate, as we will see.

There is a large cultural distance of almost 0.50 scale points between the least emancipative populations – Iraq, Jordan, and Pakistan – and the most emancipative ones: Sweden, Norway, and Switzerland. The same holds true for secular values, where an equally sizeable chasm separates the least secular populations – Jordan, Tanzania, and Bangladesh – from the most secular ones: Slovenia, the Czech Republic, and Belarus.

Of course, mean differences between societies hide divisions within them. Indeed, one can find respondents from every society on each corner of the cultural map in Figure 2.2. But the bulk of a society's respondents gravitate around the mean as their cultural anchor point. As the map shows, the average size of the orbit within which one finds two-thirds of a society's respondents covers about 10 percent of the map. Interestingly, the size of this orbit differs less than one might expect between small and big or between homogenous and heterogeneous societies: the gravitation orbit in India, a very large and very heterogeneous society, is hardly bigger than the gravitation orbit in Iceland, a very small and homogenous society.[23]

Variation in secular values and in emancipative values is present on roughly similar ranges of the two scales. Variation in secular values covers the range from about 0.15 to 0.65 scale points, whereas variation in emancipative values covers the range from about 0.20 to 0.75 scale points. In both cases, roughly half of the possible scale range is covered by real-world variation. Moreover, national populations gravitate equally densely around their anchor points in emancipative values and secular values: the societies' average standard deviation is 0.18 in emancipative values and 0.19 in secular values. Societal gravities absorb 30 percent of the individual-level variation in secular values and 37 percent in emancipative values.

Figure 2.4 shows the gravity centers and orbits of the ten culture zones. The gravitation of societies around the anchor points of culture zones accounts for, respectively, 62 and 72 percent of the cross-national variation in secular and emancipative values.[24] Even with the total variance among individuals, culture zones account for 19 percent of the variation in secular values and for 27 percent in emancipative values. Thus, there is a layered gravitation pattern:

---

[22] The individual-level correlation between the two sets of values is $r = 0.38$.

[23] Both samples show a standard deviation of 0.20 in emancipative values and of 0.19 in secular values, for the period 1995–2005.

[24] If we run a cluster analysis to create ten clusters of societies most similar in the two sets of values, we find more than 70 percent of the societies in the same cluster when they are in the same culture zone. Thus, the culture zone categorization comes close to a purely statistical cluster solution.

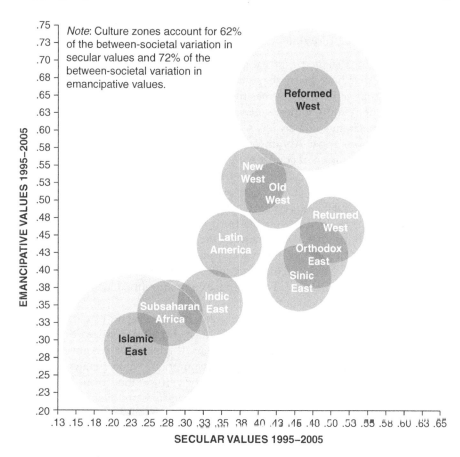

FIGURE 2.4 Culture Zones on the World Cultural Map.
Data Coverage: Respondents from all ninety-five societies surveyed at least once by the World Values Surveys/European Value Study (WVS/EVS), using the latest available survey for each society. Total *N* (respondents) is 144,381. Respondents per culture zone: Islamic East – 21,039; Indic East – 16,544; Sinic East – 8,952; Orthodox East – 20,727; Old West – 12,920; Reformed West – 8,150; New West – 8,560; Returned West – 12,796; Latin America – 19,184; sub-Saharan Africa – 17,203. Within each culture zone, national samples are weighted to equal size, treating all societies as equally important units of aggregation, regardless of population size. *Note*: Circles around the Islamic East and Reformed West show the orbit within which one finds two-thirds of the individuals surveyed in these culture zones. These orbits are of almost identical size for each culture zone.

1. The values of individuals gravitate around national anchor points, reflecting the fact that national societies develop as entities, with a common imprint left on all members. This partially homogenizes culture within societies.
2. The anchor points of national societies, in turn, gravitate around the anchor points of culture zones, reflecting the fact that societies of the

same culture zones are shaped by the same historic forces. Thus, societies of the same culture zones are on similar pathways of development.

These propositions suggest that values are *not* static; they co-evolve with the developments that have given shape to culture zones. Even though we do not have enough time series data to trace the process of value change over very long periods of time, cohort patterns leave important footprints. They chart the course of value change in a society's past (Inglehart 1977, 1990, 1997, 2008; Inglehart & Welzel 2005; Abramson 2013). This inference is safe because the alternative interpretation of cohort patterns as lifecycle effects has been conclusively disproven (Inglehart 2008; Welzel 2010; Abramson 2013).

Under these premises, Figure 2.5 traces values on the cultural map from the oldest to the youngest cohort, separately for each culture zone. The oldest cohort in each culture zone includes people born before 1920; the youngest cohort includes people born after 1980. Between these extremes, the traces follow the cohort succession in ten-year intervals, from people born between 1920 and 1930 to people born between 1970 and 1980. National samples are weighted to equal size in each culture zone. To maximize comparability, I include from each society only the most recent survey.

If it is true, as established theories suggest, that the values of older cohorts indicate a society's cultural position in the past, Figure 2.5 indeed depicts the global cultural change of the past eighty years (Inglehart & Abramson 1999; Flanagan & Lee 2003). If we accept this assumption, value change has been uniform: without fail, change moves in every culture zone from weaker to stronger secular and emancipative values. What differs are the starting points and distances covered: the starting points are lower and the distances covered are smaller in the Islamic East and sub-Saharan Africa, and so we still find these culture zones at the lower end of secular and emancipative values today. Relatively speaking, they are located even lower at the lower end than they used to. Yet, the secular-emancipative trend is evident even among societies of the Islamic East and sub-Saharan Africa.

The trend is stronger for some components of the two value indices than for others. With secular values, the progressive trend is strongest for the agnosticism and skepticism components. With emancipative values, the progressive trend is strongest for the choice and equality components. Yet, a progressive cohort trend exists for each component of the two sets of values. This is documented in Appendix 2 (www.cambridge.org/welzel).

A clustering of national societies on the two sets of values is also visible when we group societies into ascending stages of human empowerment. Remember that we distinguish between three stages of human empowerment with respect to democratic achievement: nondemocracies, hybrid regimes, democracies. Similarly, we distinguish between three stages of human empowerment in terms of technological advancement: traditional economies, industrial economies, knowledge economies. Figure 2.6 plots the centers of gravity for

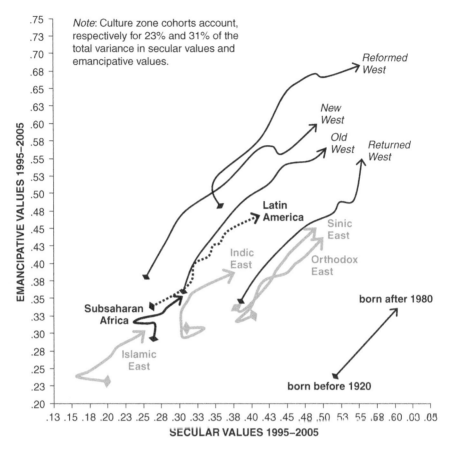

FIGURE 2.5 Cohort Traces on the World Cultural Map.
Data Coverage: Data are based on the latest available survey from each of the ninety-five societies surveyed at least once by the World Values Surveys/European Value Study (WVS/EVS). National samples weighted to equal size in each culture zone. Traces show value shifts from the earliest cohort (people born before 1920) to the latest cohort (people born after 1980) over a total of eight cohorts, separated by ten-year intervals: cohort 1 – people born before 1920, cohort 2 – people born between 1921 and 1930, cohort 3 – people born between 1931 and 1940, cohort 4 – people born between 1941 and 1950, cohort 5 – people born between 1951 and 1960, cohort 6 – people born between 1961 and 1970, cohort 7 – people born between 1971 and 1980, cohort 8 – people born after 1980. For number of respondents per culture zone, see Figure 2.4.

respondents living at these stages of human empowerment. The figure also displays the size of the orbits containing two-thirds of all respondents at each stage. The left-hand diagram shows this for stages of democratic achievement; the right-hand diagram for stages of technological advancement.

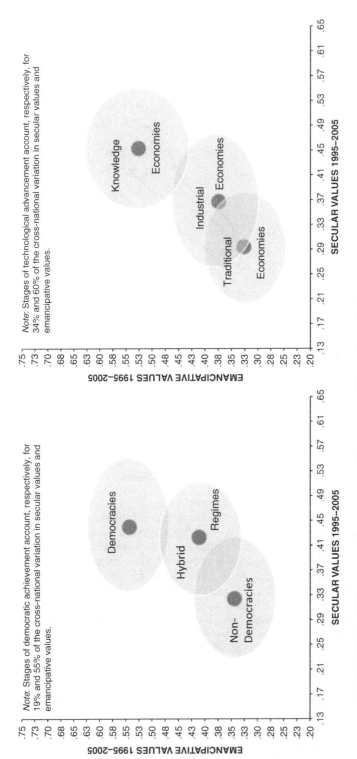

FIGURE 2.6 Global Value Differences by Democratic Achievement and Technological Advancement.

Data Coverage: Respondents from all ninety-five societies surveyed at least once by the World Values Surveys/European Value Study (WVS/EVS), using the latest available survey from each society. National samples are weighted to equal size (*N* = 1,000 per sample). Elliptic shadows demarcate orbits wherein we find two-thirds of the respondents of a given category. Left-hand diagram: number of respondents is 38,000 in the thirty-eight nondemocracies, 23,000 in the twenty-three hybrid regimes, and 33,000 in the thirty-three democracies. Right-hand diagram: number of respondents is 22,000 in the twenty-two traditional economies, 30,000 in the thirty industrial economies, and 42,000 in the forty-two knowledge economies. To inspect which societies are grouped into these categories, see Table I.1 in the Introduction.

As concerns stages of democratic achievement, respondents in democracies score highest on secular values (mean: 0.45; standard deviation [SD]: 0.08) and highest on emancipative values (mean: 0.55; SD: 0.09). Conversely, respondents in nondemocracies score lowest on secular values (mean: 0.32; SD: 0.11) and on emancipative values (mean: 0.35; SD: 0.06). Respondents in hybrid regimes score in between. Needless to say, these differences are statistically significant at the 0.001-level (two-tailed).

Considering stages of technological advancement, a similar pattern surfaces. Respondents in knowledge economies score highest on secular values (mean: 0.45: SD: 0.07) and on emancipative values (mean: 0.54; SD: 0.09). Respondents in traditional economies score lowest on secular values (mean: 0.29; SD: 0.07) and on emancipative values (mean: 0.33; SD: 0.05). Respondents in industrial economies score in between.

When one asks (a) whether emancipative values or secular values differ more over these two domains of human empowerment, and (b) whether democratic achievement or technological advancement vary the two sets of values more strongly, we get a clear answer to both questions. The three stages of democratic achievement account for 19 percent of the cross-national variance in secular values and 55 percent in emancipative values; the three stages of technological advancement account for 34 percent of the cross-national variance in secular values and 60 percent in emancipative values. These numbers point to two conclusions:

1. Technological advancement varies human values more strongly than democratic achievement does.
2. Emancipative values differ more strongly than secular values over both technological advancement and democratic achievement.

Emancipative values are more closely linked than secular values to the other two domains of human empowerment. Hence, emancipative values are the stronger manifestation of human empowerment in the domain of culture.

Figures 2.3 and 2.4 show that among the various culture zones, the New West – and within it especially the United States – is less secular than other Western societies. The United States is also somewhat less emancipative than most other Western societies. Thus, if one projects a regression line into Figure 2.3, it becomes clear that neither the New West in general nor the United States in particular are outliers from the positive association between secular values and emancipative values: these societies are inside the 95 percent confidence interval of the relationship between secular values and emancipative values. From this point of view, American exceptionalism is an ambivalent characterization. On one hand, American exceptionalism is an accurate characterization because the United States is less secular and emancipative than most other Western societies. On the other hand, it is an incorrect characterization because the United States lies within the general pattern of how secular and emancipative values relate to each other.

On closer examination, the relationship between secularization and emancipation is strongly heteroskedastic: there is much more variation in emancipative values on high levels than on low levels of secular values. Indeed, the relationship looks like one that exists when the variable on the horizontal axis operates as a necessary but insufficient condition of the one on the vertical axis: very high scores in emancipative values are only found if the scores in secular values are high; yet scores in emancipative values are not always high if scores in secular values are high. The latter condition is exemplified by societies from the Sinic East, the Orthodox East, and the Returned West. In Figures 2.3 and 2.4, these societies score high in secular values but not in emancipative values.

The idea that secular values are a necessary but insufficient condition of emancipative values resonates with Inglehart and Welzel's (2005) thesis of a sequential value change. The authors argue that the transition from traditional to industrial economies gives rise to secular values, but then this process slows down and the transition from industrial to knowledge economies gives rise to emancipative values. One pattern in Figure 2.6 (right-hand diagram) supports this thesis: traditional and industrial economies differ twice as much on secular values as on emancipative values (a difference of 0.08 compared to 0.04 scale points), whereas industrial and knowledge economies differ twice as much on emancipative values as on secular values (a difference of 0.16 compared to 0.08 scale points).

The idea that secular values are a necessary but insufficient condition of emancipative values makes indeed sense. Emancipation is the process by which people internalize authority over their own lives. For the internalization of authority to be possible, people must distance themselves from sources of authority that are external to them. This is what secular values are doing. Apparently, however, the preparatory work of secular values is not always completed: it does not always give rise to emancipative values. I suggest that this only happens when secular values result from expanding action resources among the people, which is not always the reason why these values are pronounced.

This is evident when we look at the types of societies in Figures 2.3 and 2.4 that score high on secular values but not on emancipative values. Without a single exception, these are societies from the Sinic and Orthodox East and the Returned West. The formative ideologies of these culture zones were Confucianism and communism – both inherently secular ideologies. Hence, the societies in the lower right part of Figure 2.3 have become secular for different reasons than growing action resources. This explains why strong secular values in these societies do not associate with strong emancipative values.

These findings confirm that secular values are not linked to human empowerment in the same unequivocal way as emancipative values. Since human empowerment is the guiding theme of this book, we will henceforth focus on emancipative values and leave secular values aside.

3.2 Variation within Societies

Different social experiences vary people's worldviews. Thus, I expect to find systematic differences in people's values according to group characteristics that vary people's social experience. Such characteristics include socially relevant biological characteristics, such as gender, age, and race. They also include characteristics of socioeconomic status, such as residential location, occupational position, household income, and educational achievement.

With respect to emancipative values, it follows from Chapter 1 that members of groups with larger action resources more strongly prefer emancipative values. Thus, one would expect people with higher occupational status, higher household incomes, and higher levels of education to place stronger emphasis on emancipative values. Since these groups are more frequent in urban than in rural areas, one would also expect urban respondents to emphasize emancipative values more than respondents from rural areas.

What about the members of distinct ethnic, linguistic, or religious minorities – should their values systematically differ from the majority? Emancipation theory suggests that whether distinct minorities place stronger or weaker emphasis on emancipative values than members of majority groups depends on the minority's socioeconomic status relative to the majority. There are minorities whose members are better off, as well as examples of minorities whose members are worse off than the majority. For instance, the Albanian and Turkish minorities in Southeastern Europe, the French-speaking groups in Canada and Switzerland, native Indians in Latin America, and African Americans in the United States are, on average, worse off than the majority in these societies. They command fewer action resources, so they should emphasize emancipative values less. On the other hand, members of the Flemish community in Belgium and residents of the Catalan region in Spain are on average better off than the majority in these nations. Commanding greater action resources, these minorities should place stronger emphasis on emancipative values than the respective majority. This pattern should not be a specialty of Western societies. Thus, the Chinese communities in Singapore and Malaysia should prefer emancipative values more than the Malay majorities in these societies because, on average, the Chinese are better off.

I expect one exception from this rule. If a better-off group owes its privileged status to a history of repression, the interest in justifying the privilege might make these groups reactionary. In this case, they emphasize emancipative values less – despite their greater action resources. In other words, if there is a group monopoly on certain resources to defend, valued freedoms are not generalized beyond the in-group: solidarity does not reach far in this case. This should weaken emancipative values because they aim at *universal* freedoms. A possible example is the white minority in South Africa. On average, its members possess greater action resources than members of the black majority, yet historically the whites acquired their privileged status through a history of exploitation, and this might weaken their emphasis on emancipative values. To generalize this point, I hypothesize that action resources make people prefer emancipative values only if these resources have not been gained through patterns of exploitation whose defense fosters a reactionary mindset.

As regards the effects of age and gender, one might have conflicting expectations. Because of sexual discrimination, women have, on average, fewer action resources in almost any society, which should weaken their emphasis on emancipative values. But as a tool to overcome their disadvantage, women should have a rational interest in emancipatory goals, especially when it comes to gender equality. This should strengthen their emphasis on emancipative values. Moreover, research shows that women have weaker social dominance orientations than men, and some argue that evolution has shaped this sexual bias in dominance orientations (Sidanius, Pratto, & Bobo 1994; Sidanius, Levin, Lin, & Pratto 2000). Since emancipative values contradict social dominance orientations, an evolution-shaped sexual bias should be visible in a female tendency toward stronger emancipative values.

With age, one might have conflicting expectations as well – depending on whether one sees age as a marker of lifecycle or cohort effects. If age is primarily a marker of lifecycle effects, younger people should emphasize emancipative values less than older people in most societies. The reason is that younger people usually control fewer action resources: they might not have finished their education yet and are at the beginning of their careers, in which case income, savings, and equipment are at a lower level. On the other hand, scholars point out that people's values take shape during their formative phase of socialization, which is, roughly speaking, the time in which people spend most of their teenage years (Inglehart 1977; Dalton 2006). If this is true, whether younger people emphasize emancipative values more than older people depends on whether action resources were more abundant during their adolescence than they were during the adolescence of the previous generation.[25] Now, we have seen that ordinary people's action resources have increased in most of the world in recent decades (see Figure I.1, p. 4). Taking this into account, the formative-socialization thesis suggests that younger people emphasize emancipative values more than older people.

Provided these expectations hold, the next question is whether gender, cohort, occupation, income, and education vary people's emancipative values *in the same way in every society*? If this is indeed the case, yet another question must be addressed: do similar group characteristics homogenize people's emancipative values across societies?

The set of graphs in Figures 2.7 and 2.8 provides answers to these questions. Each graph plots the scores in emancipative values found in two opposite groups

---

[25] I assume that what shapes adolescents' emancipative values, apart from parental transmission, is not so much the action resources that these people themselves control but the action resources they experience to be in the reach of the "typical" adult in their reference groups.

in each society: low versus high income, old versus young cohorts, rural versus metropolitan residents. Whenever these classifications are based on multipoint scales, I juxtapose the most distant groups. This should increase the chances of finding truly large within-societal value differences.

Each diagram shows an "isoline." This is the diagonal running from the lower left to the upper right corner. The isoline demarcates identical positions in emancipative values among two opposite groups. Thus, when two groups in a society – such as women and men – have identical emancipative values, this society's dot will be located on the isoline. A society dot's vertical distance from the isoline indicates by how many scale points the emancipative values of the group on the vertical axis exceeds or falls short of the emancipative values of the group on the horizontal axis. There are also a couple of projection lines in each diagram. The projection lines contrast the largest *within*-societal difference in emancipative values with the largest *between*-societal difference.

The graphs in Appendix 2 (www.cambridge.org/welzel) and Figures 2.7 and 2.8 show an astonishingly regular pattern. One of the graphs in Appendix 2 plots for each society the emancipative values of men against those of women. The dots fall almost perfectly on a straight line: the societies in which men place the strongest emphasis on emancipative values are also those in which women do so. In fact, the between-societal variation in emancipative values is 98 percent identical between women and men. We also observe that, in almost all of our ninety-five societies, women place more emphasis on emancipative values than do men. This is obvious from the fact that the society dots are, with less than a handful of exceptions, always located above the isoline.

That women place somewhat more emphasis on emancipative values than do men seems to be an anthropological universal.[26] However, the extent to which female emphasis exceeds male emphasis on emancipative values is very small and shows little variation; it is almost a constant. On average, women's emancipative values exceed those of men by just 0.02 scale points, which is within the margin of sampling error. Thus, the differentiation in emancipative values among men is almost perfectly reproduced among women (and the other way round), which means that gender by no means homogenizes emancipative values across societies. It is not surprising, then, that the biggest gender difference in emancipative values we find in our ninety-five societies (i.e., in Saudi Arabia), is eight times smaller than the largest between-societal difference in emancipative values among women alone. Saudi women emphasize emancipative values at an average of 0.32 scale points whereas Saudi men do so at an average of 0.25 scale points, which makes a significant within-societal difference of 0.07 scale points. By contrast, Swedish women emphasize emancipative values at an average of

---

[26] Women's higher score in emancipative values is solely due to the fact that gender equality is covered as a domain in emancipative values. In this domain, women score, on average, 0.10 scale points higher than men. Excluding this domain, gender differences in emancipative values are less uniform, smaller, and mostly insignificant.

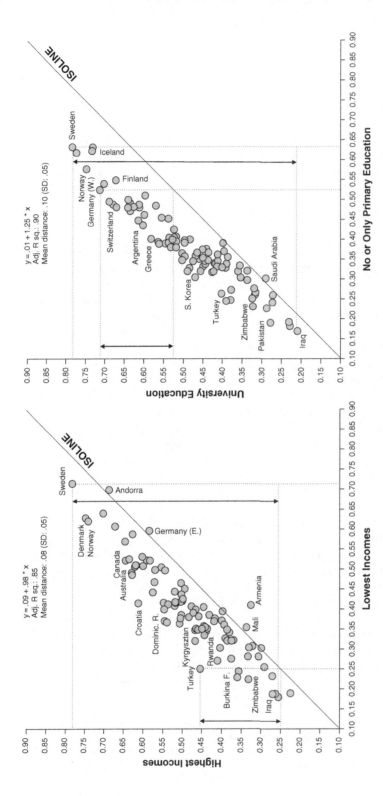

FIGURE 2.7 Group-Specific Emancipative Values by Society (income and education opposites).

Data Coverage: All respondents with valid data from all ninety-five societies surveyed at least once by the World Values Surveys/European Value Study (WVS/EVS), using the latest available survey (1995–2005). *Note*: The distances between projection lines indicated by double-headed arrows in both diagrams juxtapose (a) the largest *within*-societal difference between the two *opposite* groups and (b) the largest *between*-societal difference within the *same* group. This is to visualize how much the latter dwarfs the former.

0.76 scale points whereas Iraqi women do so at an average of 0.18 scale points, which makes a between-societal difference of 0.58 scale points.

Looking at differences in emancipative values by cohort, we find an even more pronounced uniformity: without the exception of a single society, people who were born after 1970 place stronger emphasis on emancipative values than do people born before 1950. This is evident from the fact that all society dots in the respective graph in Appendix 2 (www.cambridge.org/welzel) are placed above the isoline. Yet again, recentness in the cohort sequence does not homogenize emancipative values across societies. Instead, between-societal differences in emancipative values among older people are strongly echoed among younger people. The shared between-societal variation in emancipative values among these opposite cohorts amounts to fully 89 percent. The largest cohort difference in emancipative values within societies is found in Germany, where the difference amounts to 0.20 scale points: Germans born after 1970 emphasize emancipative values at an average of 0.70 scale points whereas Germans born before 1950 do so at an average of 0.50 scale points. But the largest between-societal difference in emancipative values among younger cohorts alone is 2.5 times larger, amounting to 0.50 scale points: young Swedes emphasize emancipative values at an average of 0.75 scale points whereas young Pakistani do so at an average of 0.25 scale points.

The pattern repeats itself for other group-related differences in emancipative values, including residential and occupational status, as well as income and education (again documented in Appendix 2; www.cambridge.org/welzel). With few, if any, exceptions, we find in our more than ninety societies that emancipative values are pronounced more among urban respondents than rural respondents, more among white-collar workers than blue-collar workers, more among high income earners than among low income earners, and more among people with university education than among people with little or no education. These are quasi-universal patterns. Once more, however, similar group characteristics by no means homogenize emancipative values across societies. On the contrary, between-societal differences in emancipative values in one group are mirrored to a large extent among people of the opposite group, yielding shared between-societal variations of 77, 96, 85, and 90 percent among opposite groups in residential status, occupational status, income, and education, respectively.

In any case, the largest within-societal difference found for any group characteristic, even focusing on the most distant groups in that characteristic, is always dwarfed by the largest between-societal difference among people *from the same* group. People's emancipative values vary far more between societies than over within-societal divisions.

This pattern holds when we examine ethnic, linguistic, and religious lines of division, juxtaposing for each society – in which such divisions carry some importance – the position of the most significant minority against the majority, as shown in Figure 2.8.

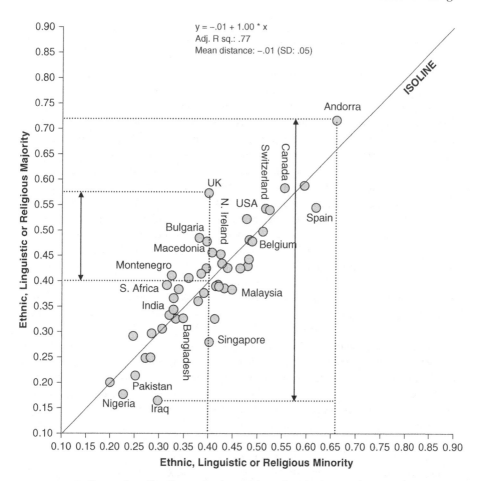

FIGURE 2.8 Group-Specific Emancipative Values by Society (ethnicity, language, religion).
Data Coverage: Respondents from a selection of the ninety-five societies surveyed at least once by the World Values Surveys (WVS), using the latest available survey from each society. Societies are selected for display when a significant proportion of the respondents report belongingness to a sizeable ethnic, linguistic, or religious minority of the respective society. *Note*: The distances between projection lines indicated by double-headed arrows juxtapose (a) the largest majority-minority difference *within* societies and (b) the largest difference among majorities *between* societies. As in the previous diagram, the difference between societies dwarfs that within societies.

Reflecting specific historical configurations, Figure 2.8 juxtaposes a different minority-majority division for each society. In some societies, these are ethnic divisions. In Malaysia and Singapore, for example, the most significant minority are ethnic Chinese. In South Africa, it is ethnic whites and in the United States, it is blacks. Some divisions are linguistic. This applies, for example, to the French-Flemish division in Belgium or the French-English division in Canada. Some of these divisions are linguistic and regional, like the Italian-French-German division in Switzerland. Some divisions are ethnic, linguistic, and regional, like the Kurdish-Turkish division in Turkey, the Kurdish-Iraqi division in Iraq, or the Turkish-Bulgarian division in Bulgaria. In other cases, the division is religious. In the Netherlands and Germany, it is a Protestant-Catholic division, in Nigeria a Christian-Muslim division, in India a Muslim-Hindu division, and in Iran a Shiite-Sunni division among Muslims.

The pattern of ethnic-linguistic-religious divisions is complex. Based on these divisions, we cannot generalize whether minority status is linked with a stronger or a weaker emphasis on emancipative values. But knowing whether the minority under consideration is better or worse off than the majority, we are able to make fairly accurate predictions about whether the members of this group emphasize emancipative values more or less than do members of the majority. If members of the minority are better off, they tend to emphasize emancipative values more than do members of the majority.

The dot for Iraq, for example, plots emancipative values among the Kurdish minority against those of Arab Iraqis. The Kurds are better off insofar as their oppression ended with the U.S. invasion and because they are not terrorized as seriously as the Arab Iraqis by suicide bombings. Accordingly, the Kurdish minority emphasizes emancipative values on average at 0.29 scale points, which is 0.13 scale points above the Arab majority (0.16).

We find minorities that place more emphasis on emancipative values than the majority group also in Malaysia and Singapore. Here, the minority position is taken by ethnic Chinese, who are economically better off than the Malayan majority groups in these societies. Thus, the Chinese minorities emphasize emancipative values at 0.40 scale points in Singapore and at 0.45 scale points in Malaysia, which compares to 0.26 and 0.38 scale points among the Malayan majorities in these two societies.

In Spain, the minority position is taken by the Catalans, who, on average, are economically better off than the Castilian majority. Accordingly, the Catalan minority emphasizes emancipative values, on average, at 0.62 scale points, in contrast to 0.55 scale points among the Castilian majority.

Members of the Albanian minority in Macedonia and Montenegro and of the Turkish minority in Bulgaria are economically much worse off than the respective majorities, and here we find minority status to be most clearly associated with a weaker emphasis on emancipative values: the Albanian minorities emphasize emancipative values at 0.39 scale points in Macedonia and at 0.32 scale points in Montenegro, which compares to 0.45 and 0.41 scale points, respectively, among the majorities in these societies.

This pattern is most pronounced in the United Kingdom, where the minority position is taken by immigrants from India, Pakistan, and Bangladesh. On average, they are economically worse off than the "white" majority of the

British, so members of these groups emphasize emancipative values less strongly: at 0.40 scale points compared to 0.58 scale points among the majority. This difference in values is not simply the result of imported cultural differences through migration. Migratory origin affects emphasis on emancipative values mostly insofar as it is an indicator of differences in action resources: before controlling for household income, formal education, and informational connectedness, migratory origin of one parent varies people's emancipative values by 0.05 scale points and migratory origin of two parents by 0.10 scale points – which is significant but modest. After these controls, migratory origin of one parent varies people's emancipative values by only 0.01 scale points and migratory origin of two parents does so by just 0.02 scale points. These proportions are far below the variation in emancipative values due to people's action resources.[27]

Another prominent case in which members of the smaller group are economically worse off than the larger group, and hence emphasize emancipative values significantly less, occurs with blacks in the United States: their emphasis on emancipative values averages at 0.46 scale points, which compares to 0.53 scale points among the white majority. The same applies to members of the French-speaking communities in Belgium, Canada, and Switzerland.

However, the idea that a better off minority emphasizes emancipative values more strongly than the majority holds, if – and only if – the minority did *not* acquire its superiority through a history of exploitation. Most obviously, members of the Afrikaans-speaking white minority in South Africa are, on average, better off than members of the black majority, yet their superior status is linked to a history of exploitation under the apartheid regime. Hence, members of this better-off minority do not emphasize emancipative values more strongly than the worse-off majority. In numbers, while Afrikaans-speaking white South Africans emphasize emancipative values on average at 0.31 scale points, black Africans emphasize these values at an average of 0.39 scale points.[28] This is a significant difference.

The Northern Irish case confirms this pattern. Members of the Protestant Free Church minority are economically better off than the Catholic majority, but this does not lead to a stronger emphasis on emancipative values among Northern Irish Protestants: the better-off minority owes its status to a history of repression. In numbers, the Protestant minority in Northern Ireland emphasizes emancipative values at 0.42 scale points, which compares to 0.45 scale points among the majority.

---

[27] Results are from a multilevel regression over some 50,000 respondents from fifty societies. The analysis is limited to WVS round five because the question on the parents' migratory origin has been fielded for the first time in this round.

[28] Note that this pattern does not include all white South Africans but only those interviewed in Afrikaans, which is not the majority of white African respondents. In light of the pattern we find here, speaking Afrikaans might indicate a continued identification with apartheid.

Despite these complex patterns, in general it holds true that the between-societal differences in emancipative values among significant ethnic, linguistic, and religious minorities are mirrored to a large extent among the majority groups. Indeed, between-societal differences among majorities reproduce themselves to 77 percent among minorities. Once more, the largest within-societal difference that we find in a minority-majority juxtaposition (0.17 scale points in the United Kingdom) is dwarfed by the largest between-societal difference in emancipative values, which is 0.50 scale points.

Emancipative values vary along social group characteristics within societies. But the variation is bounded within distinctive orbits around a society's gravity center in emancipative values. Thus, the nation varies people's values far more strongly than do even the most significant within-societal divisions. Comparing values on the level of national societies is a worthwhile thing to do.

KEY POINTS

We have seen that emancipative values can be measured at the individual level and at the societal level. These measures illustrate meaningful differences between societies from different culture zones. In addition, we have seen that differences in the coherence of emancipative values between societies are not caused by a Western cultural bias in the concept of emancipative values but rather reflect differences in the societies' cognitive mobilization – the intellectual strand of the human empowerment process. This finding underlines the validity of emancipative values as an indicator of the mentality that emerges with human empowerment. Furthermore, population averages in emancipative values validly measure a society's anchor point in these values.

The relationship of emancipative values to secular values is not uniformly linear. It appears more like a necessary but insufficient condition: emancipative values are strong only, but not always, if secular values are strong. If we interpret emancipation as a process by which people dissociate from external authority in order to internalize authority over their lives, the dissociation process that is manifest in secular values appears to be a necessary condition for the internalization process that advances with emancipative values. However, this does not seem to be a sufficient condition, especially if secularization has been achieved by historic forces that occurred in disconnect from the human empowerment process. Confucianism and communism are examples: these forces shifted societies' cultural position outside the otherwise close relationship between secular values and emancipative values. For this reason, emancipative values represent much better than secular values the cultural undercurrent of the human empowerment process. This justifies a focus on these values throughout the remainder of this book.

Compared to alternative measures of culture – including collectivism versus individualism, embeddedness versus autonomy, tightness versus looseness, the "Big Five" personality traits and social dominance orientations – emancipative values have better data quality because these values are taken from national representative samples. Moreover, emancipative values correlate more closely than any of the alternative culture measures with other indicators of human empowerment. Hence, emancipative values are the most valid indicator of the cultural domain of human empowerment.

Certain social characteristics, such as gender, cohort, income, education, and occupation, vary emancipative values in rather uniform ways: the group whose members control more action resources prefers emancipative values more strongly than the group with less control – provided the group with the greater control does not owe its advantage to a history of exploitation. However, group characteristics such as these by no means homogenize people's emancipative values across societies. On the contrary, between-societal differences by far outsize within-societal differences. This pattern demonstrates how strongly the human condition is shaped at the societal level.

Finally, population averages in emancipative values differ strongly across culture zones. On one hand, this underlines that population averages in emancipative values are meaningful indicators of cultural differences. On the other hand, there is a need for further investigation of what is behind the culture zone differences in emancipative values. This problem will be explored in the next chapter.

3

Multilevel Drivers

> There is no force so powerful as an idea whose time has come.
>
> – Everett Dirksen

Chapter 1 explained the theoretical relevance of emancipative values, whereas Chapter 2 showed how these values are measured and how they distribute over different social groups and across societies. In this chapter, we explore the social forces that shape emancipative values at different layers of reality: human individuals, national societies, and culture zones. The chapter is organized into three sections.

Section 1 pays closer attention to two universal determinants of emancipative values: birth cohort and formal education. I demonstrate that the emancipatory impulse of these two characteristics amplifies with the abundance of action resources in a society. Section 2 deepens this theme into multilevel models, showing that it is the part of action resources that most people in a society have in common, rather than what individuals have on top of others, which strengthens emancipative values. Among the three types of action resources, material ones strengthen emancipative values less than intellectual and connective resources do. Section 3 addresses the formative power of culture zones over emancipative values.

So far, scholars make little effort to sort out what exactly it is about culture zones that has such formative power. As we will see, culture zones *seem* to shape people's emancipative values because the culture zones differ in the action resources that *truly* shape these values. What is more, in testing the source thesis of emancipation theory I show that the culture zones' different propensities to proliferate action resources originate in different natural opportunity endowments.

1. SOCIAL DETERMINANTS OF VALUES

Chapter 2 showed that various group characteristics differentiate emancipative values. Among these characteristics, birth cohort and formal education stand out. These two characteristics are of particular interest because both are mirrors of social change: cohorts are in a continuous succession, and education has been continuously expanding in almost every society of the world in the past thirty years (see Figure I.1, p. 4). Thus, it seems worthwhile to study the impact of cohorts and education a bit more closely.

1.1 Birth Cohort

Values inspire the strategies that people pursue to master their lives (Kluckhohn 1951; Rokeach 1973; S. H. Schwartz 1992). They are long-term orientations that shape people's personal identity. Hence, people do not change their values easily. In fact, people change their values less easily as they get older because age increases the lifetime one has invested into one's identity and its defining values (Inglehart 1977, 1990; Flanagan 1987; Flanagan & Lee 2001, 2003). Conversely, values change more easily among younger than among older people. This has implications for the impact of action resources on emancipative values: when action resources grow to the same extent throughout all cohorts, emancipative values increase more among younger than among older cohorts. Hence, if growing action resources give rise to emancipative values, this process will leave its footprints in every cross-section of a population: at any point in time, younger cohorts emphasize emancipative values more than older cohorts. So, even if we do not have longitudinal data, the cohort pattern of a cross-section still hints at the course and pace of value change, revealing a society's value position in the past (Inglehart & Abramson 1999).

Figure 3.1 shows how birth cohorts differentiate people's emancipative values across societies in which ordinary people control different amounts of action resources. To distinguish societies with meager, modest, and abundant action resources, we classify them into traditional economies, industrial economies, and knowledge economies based on differences in technological advancement (see Table I.2). Using this classification, Figure 3.1 makes it evident that people throughout all cohorts place more emphasis on emancipative values when they live in technologically more advanced societies. In every birth cohort, people in knowledge economies emphasize emancipative values more than people in industrial economies, and people in industrial economies do it more than people in traditional economies.

Interestingly, the elevation of emancipative values by technological advancement is more than twice as large when societies ascend from industrial to knowledge economies than when they ascend from traditional to industrial economies. Thus, it seems that technological advancement favors emancipative values with *increasing* marginal returns.

Technological advancement elevates emancipative values regardless of the cohort into which people are born. Still, birth cohort matters. Independent of

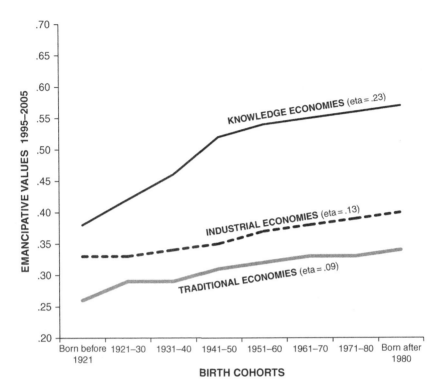

FIGURE 3.1 The Effect of Birth Cohort on Emancipative Values by Technological Advancement.

Data Coverage: Respondents with valid data from all ninety-five societies surveyed at least once by the World Values Surveys/ European Value Study (WVS/EVS), using the latest available survey from each society, with samples weighted to equal size (*N* = 1,000 per sample). Observations (*N*): 22,000 respondents in the twenty-two traditional economies; 30,000 respondents in the thirty industrial economies; 42,000 respondents in the forty-two knowledge economies.

technological advancement, younger cohorts emphasize emancipative values more than older cohorts – in all types of societies. This is an important finding in and of itself, hinting to a general trend toward emancipative values.

Technological advancement not only adds to the positive effect of birth cohort; it amplifies it. Cohort sequence strengthens emancipative values more in knowledge economies (η = 0.23) than in industrial economies (η = 0.13), and more in industrial economies than in traditional economies (η = 0.09).[1]

---

[1] *Eta* (Greek η) is a measure of association and can be interpreted like a correlation coefficient, with larger coefficients indicating a stronger association. Unlike the correlation coefficient *r*, the value of η is always positive, even if the association is negative.

It is noteworthy that the rise of emancipative values along the cohort sequence flattens out in knowledge economies: up to the cohort born between 1941 and 1950, the increase is steep; thereafter, the increase continues but is less steep. The shift in slope coincides with the first cohort whose members grew up after the two world wars. I interpret this pattern such that, in today's knowledge societies, there was a greater expansion of people's action resources from the prewar cohorts to the postwar cohorts than among the postwar cohorts. In simpler terms, a young adult in 1970 is more affluent, educated, and connected than a young adult in 1940. Likewise, a young adult in 2000 is more affluent, educated, and connected than a young adult in 1970. But the gain in affluence, education, and connectivity is considerably bigger from 1940 to 1970 than from 1970 to 2000.

1.2 Formal Education

Technological advancement increases ordinary people's control over action resources. One type of action resources is intellectual and depends on education. Education improves people's skills to digest information and to think for themselves. Also, education makes people more knowledgeable about options and possibilities. Thus, people with a higher level of education can usually take more advantage of freedoms. Furthermore, because education raises awareness, educated people get a sense of their advantage. Accordingly, education increases both the actual and perceived utility of freedoms. For this reason, education strengthens people's preference for emancipative values. As Figure 3.2 illustrates, this is true in a culturally universal way – despite large differences in the content and organization of education across different cultures.

But even though education makes people more emancipatory in every society, it does so only *relative* to a given society's gravity point in emancipative values. Relative to this gravity point, a university degree might shift a person's values 0.10 scale points toward a more emancipatory position. Still, if a society's gravity point on emancipative values is 0.25 in the case of Pakistan and 0.75 in the case of Sweden, the emancipative values of a typical Pakistani graduate score at 0.35 and those of a typical Swedish graduate at 0.85– fully 0.50 scale points apart.

However, the assumption that the emancipatory effect of education is of the same size in every society is too simplistic. In fact, there are good reasons to assume that, even though the effect is uniform in direction, it should vary in strength. Indeed, education's emancipatory effect should grow with the prevalence of education in a society.

The reason for this is *social cross-fertilization*. If an individual attribute has an inherent impulse – like the emancipatory impulse of education – this impulse becomes stronger, the more prevalent the attribute in question (e.g., education) is in a society. This is a matter of social cross-fertilization: through cross-overs, more prevalent education fertilizes education's inherent emancipatory impulse.

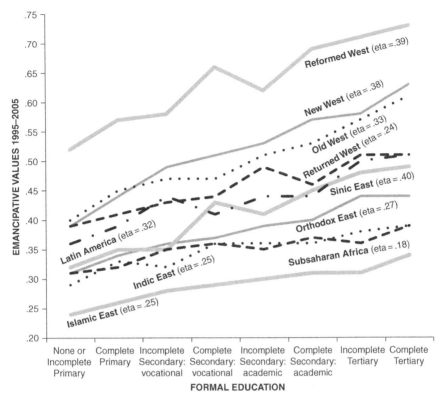

FIGURE 3.2 The Effect of Education on Emancipative Values by Culture Zone.
Data Coverage: Respondents with valid data from all ninety-five societies surveyed at least once by the World Values Surveys/European Value Study (WVS/EVS), using the latest available survey from each society, with samples weighted to equal size ($N = 1,000$ per sample). Number of respondents (N): 25,951 – Islamic East; 16,988 – Indic East; 8,887 – Sinic East; 20,269 – Orthodox East; 13,471 – Old West; 8,047 – Reformed West; 8,466 – New West; 11,585 – Returned West; 17,007 – sub-Saharan Africa; 19,155 – Latin America. The mean standard deviation for each educational category is 0.20 scale points on emancipative values.

Consequently, every person's emancipative values reach over and above what her or his own education alone suggests (see Box 3.1, below).

The logic of social cross-fertilization suggests two hypotheses about what happens when education becomes more prevalent: first, the level of emancipative values is higher for each individual than her or his own education suggests (the elevator effect); second, an increase in an individual's education brings a bigger increase in his or her emancipative values (the amplifier effect).

To test these hypotheses, Figure 3.4 uses the three-fold categorization of technological advancement as a proxy for the prevalence of education in a

---

Box 3.1 Social Cross-Fertilization and Reciprocal Goods

Social cross-fertilization is a regular but neglected phenomenon. Cross-fertilization is typical of *reciprocal goods* that grow through mutual recognition. The emphasis on universal freedoms that defines emancipative values is a case in point: respecting other people's freedoms is the easier the more people return the favor and reciprocate this respect.

We have seen that – in every society – individuals with higher education emphasize emancipative values more than do people with less education. Accordingly, there is an emancipatory tendency inherent in education. Cross-fertilization in this case means that the emancipatory tendency of an individual's education is fertilized through cross-overs deriving from the prevalence of education in the individual's society.

This happens through two mechanisms: social confirmation among people with higher education and social contagion of people with lower education. Both mechanisms operate on the condition that most people (a) signal their social tendencies and (b) receive the signals of others in ways that create a roughly accurate sense of what tendencies are prevalent in a society.

Thus, when education becomes more prevalent in a society, the emancipatory tendencies inherent in education are more frequently signaled and received. Especially people with higher education then feel confirmed in their emancipatory tendencies and follow them more freely. This is the *social confirmation mechanism*. Social confirmation "amplifies" the emancipatory tendency of higher education. In the hypothetical line diagram of Figure 3.3, the *amplifier effect* is visible in the trend lines' steepening angles from societies with less prevalent education to those with more prevalent education. Thus, in societies with more prevalent education, a difference in education between two individuals produces a bigger difference in their emancipative values. In multilevel models, amplifier effects show up as steepening "slopes": the angle (slope) at which the impact of education hits emancipative values steepens with the prevalence of education.

As education becomes more prevalent, everyone is more frequently exposed to education's emancipatory tendencies. This includes the shrinking segment of people whose lower level of education does not embody an emancipatory tendency. To keep pace with their surrounding society, even these people adopt some of the emancipatory tendencies. This is the *social contagion mechanism*. Social contagion "elevates" everyone's emancipative values above the level that their own education suggests. In the hypothetical line diagram of Figure 3.3, the *elevator effect* is visible in the trend lines' increasing levels from societies with less to those with more prevalent education. In multilevel models, elevator effects show up as rising "intercepts": the level (intercept) at which the impact of education hits emancipative values rises with the prevalence of education.

Box 3.1 (continued)

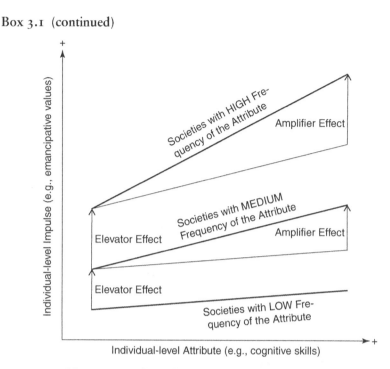

FIGURE 3.3 The Concept of Social Cross-Fertilization.

This conceptual graph illustrates a very regular but entirely undertheorized phenomenon: the cross-fertilization of an individual-level attribute's inherent impulse by the social prevalence of this very attribute. Cross-fertilization shows up in elevator and amplifier effects. An elevator effect is present when the social prevalence of an attribute increases the presence of its impulse among all individuals, whether they themselves carry the attribute or not. An amplifier effect is present when the social prevalence of an attribute multiplies its impulse among the carriers of the attribute. Amplifier effects reflect the mechanism of social confirmation; elevator effects reflect the mechanism of social contagion.

Both amplifier and elevator effects enhance an attribute's tendency *beyond* this attribute's presence among individuals. In that sense, we deal with truly contextual effects. Cultural phenomena should be analyzed via these contextual effects, for culture is essentially a contextual phenomenon: it denotes the prevalence patterns of social attributes and the psychological tendencies inherent to them.

society: education is least prevalent in traditional economies, more prevalent in industrial economies, and most prevalent in knowledge economies.

Given this distinction, Figure 3.4 reveals some striking regularities. Among people in each educational category, emphasis on emancipative values elevates

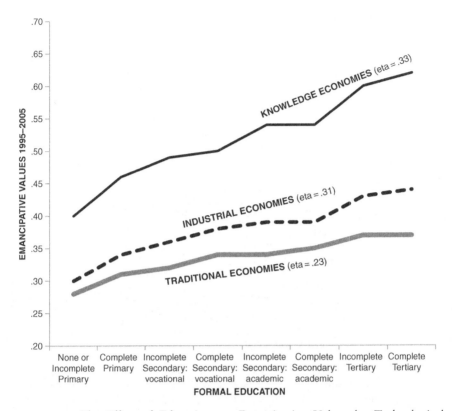

FIGURE 3.4 The Effect of Education on Emancipative Values by Technological Advancement.

Data Coverage: Respondents with valid data from all ninety-five societies surveyed at least once by the World Values Surveys/ European Value Study (WVS/EVS), using the latest available survey from each society, with samples weighted to equal size (*N* = 1,000 per sample). Number of respondents (*N*): 22,000 respondents in the twenty-two traditional economies; 30,000 respondents in the thirty industrial economies; 42,000 respondents in the forty-two knowledge economies.

with the prevalence of education, from traditional economies to industrial economies to knowledge economies. This pattern confirms the elevator hypothesis.

Moreover, the prevalence of education steepens the emancipatory impulse of education. For instance, in traditional economies, the difference in emancipative values between the least educated people (i.e., no or only elementary education) and the most educated people (i.e., a university degree) is only 0.09 scale points. This is much less than the standard deviation (0.20 scale points) in each educational category. In knowledge economies, by contrast, the difference in emancipative values between the least and the most educated people is 0.22 scale points:

more than double the difference in traditional economies. Industrial economies are between knowledge economies and traditional economies: the difference in emancipative values between the least and the most educated people is 0.15 scale points. This finding confirms the amplifier hypothesis.

2. MATERIAL, INTELLECTUAL, AND CONNECTIVE RESOURCES

Technological advancement increases people's action resources, including material means, intellectual skills, and connective opportunities. The sequence thesis of emancipation theory suggests that emancipative values emerge in response to people's growing control over action resources. Yet the thesis is silent about which type of action resources – material, intellectual, or connective – contributes more to rising emancipative values. This is an open question. To answer it, we must disentangle the three types of action resources. Because technological advancement is intimately linked to all three of them, we need to look for separate indicators of material, intellectual, and connective resources – at both the individual and societal levels.

To begin with the societal level, I follow the convention and use a society's per capita gross domestic product (GDP) in purchasing power parties as the indicator of material resources. To measure a society's intellectual resources, I use the number of schooling years obtained by the average person in a society. As an indicator of connective resources, I use internet access per 1,000 inhabitants. Each of these three indicators is taken from the year 2000; data sources are detailed in Appendix 3 (www.cambridge.org/welzel).

Even though the prevalences of these three action resources substantially overlap,[2] there is still a significant portion of separate variance.[3] Thus, it is possible that the three action resources differ in their explanatory power over emancipative values. This is indeed what we find in three separate regression analyses[4] using a society's emancipative values measured at or after 2000 as the dependent variable. Variation in emancipative values is explained to 57 percent by GDP/capita ($r = 0.76$, $N = 80$), 64 percent by schooling years ($r = 0.80$, $N = 60$), and 67 percent by internet access ($r = 0.82$, $N = 80$). Thus, the

---

[2] Technological advancement correlates with schooling years at $r = 0.93$ ($N = 93$), with internet access at $r = 0.81$ ($N = 139$), and with per capita GDP at $r = 0.84$ ($N = 136$). It is, hence, a formidable indicator of the prevalence of all three types of action resources. In a factor analysis, schooling years, internet access, and GDP/capita represent a single dimension: action resources. This dimension captures 90 percent of the variance in its three components. Technological advancement correlates with this dimension at $r = 0.95$ ($N = 88$).

[3] Depending on which pair of two among the three indicators we look at, the non-overlapping variance varies between 10 and 30 percent.

[4] A multivariate regression with all three resources as predictors produces inconclusive results because of too high collinearity (variance inflation factors are above 5.0).

explanatory power of GDP/capita is slightly but recognizably lower. Accordingly, material resources appear somewhat less important than intellectual and connective resources.

At the individual level, this conclusion is confirmed. At this level, I use the respondents' household income as an indicator of material resources, their formal education as an indicator of intellectual resources, and their informational connectedness as an indicator of connective resources. Because of random measurement error, individual-level data show much weaker correlation patterns than societal-level data, implying lower explanatory powers. This also means much lower collinearity, so we can test the impact of the three types of action resources on emancipative values simultaneously. But let's look at separate regressions for each type of resource first. In separate regressions of the respondents' emancipative values on each of the three types of resource, household income explains 4 percent of the variation ($r = 0.20$; $N = 300,156$), formal education explains 8 percent ($r = 0.29$; $N = 260,223$), and informational connectedness 17 percent ($r = 0.41$; $N = 69,381$).[5] In a multivariate regression that includes all three indicators simultaneously, we obtain similar results. It is again clear from these findings that material resources seem to matter less than intellectual and connective resources.

The problem of separate societal- and individual-level analyses is that they cannot tell us how action resources at these two levels interact in shaping emancipative values. To make such interactions visible, we must specify multi-level models in which individual- and societal-level effects are examined simultaneously.

Along these lines, Table 3.1 displays five multilevel models to examine the combined individual- and societal-level determination of emancipative values. As standard demographic controls, the models include biological sex and an indexed version of the respondents' birth year, with higher scores indicating later birth.[6] Under these premises, the following five models are specified:

1. A *material empowerment* model, using per capita GDP as a societal-level indicator of material resources and household income as an individual-level indicator.
2. An *intellectual empowerment* model, using average schooling years as a societal-level indicator of intellectual resources and formal education as an individual-level indicator.
3. A *connective empowerment* model, using the indexed number of internet hosts per 100,000 inhabitants as a societal-level indicator of connective resources and the measure of informational connectedness introduced in Chapter 1 as an individual-level indicator.

---

[5] The number of observations differs so much because the questions to measure informational connectedness were fielded in WVS round five for the first time.
[6] The index is at maximum 1.0 when the birth year is 1990 and at minimum 0 when the birth year is 1900.

TABLE 3.1 *Material, Intellectual, and Connective Empowerment as Explanations of Emancipative Values.*

	DEPENDENT VARIABLE: Emancipative Values					
PREDICTORS	Material Empowerment[a]	Intellectual Empowerment[a]	Connective Empowerment	Combined Empowerment	Combined Empowerment I[b]	Combined Empowerment II
• Constant	0.43***(55.9)	0.43***(47.1)	0.44***(47.4)	0.46***(47.5)	0.46***(47.5)	0.46***(46.3)
Societal-level Effects:						
• Per Capita GDP	0.51***(5.9)					
• Schooling Years		0.46***(9.7)				
• Internet Access			0.61***(9.2)			
• Technological Advancement[b]				0.52***(9.1)	0.52***(9.1)	0.41***(9.9)
Individual-level Effects:						
• Female Sex	0.02***(10.5)	0.02***(11.5)	0.03***(11.2)	0.03***(11.5)	0.03***(11.5)	0.03***(11.5)
Cross-level Interactions:						
• Birth Year (indexed)	0.14***(19.9)	0.11***(12.3)	0.09***(10.1)	0.07***(6.8)	0.07***(6.8)	0.07***(7.2)
* GDP/cap	0.28***(5.0)					
* Schooling Years		0.28***(6.6)				
* Internet Access			0.14***(2.6)			
* Technological Advancement[b]				0.28***(4.4)	0.28***(4.4)	0.17***(4.8)
• Household Income	0.09***(16.6)			0.02***(3.6)	0.02***(3.6)	0.02***(3.7)
* GDP/cap	N.S.					
* Schooling Years						

TABLE 3.1 (cont.)

	DEPENDENT VARIABLE: Emancipative Values				
PREDICTORS	Material Empowerment[a]	Intellectual Empowerment[a]	Connective Empowerment	Combined Empowerment I[b]	Combined Empowerment II
* Internet Access					
* Technological Advancement[b]				N.S.	N.S.
• Formal Education		0.12***(19.0)		0.10***(12.0)	0.10***(12.6)
* GDP/cap					
* Schooling Years		0.11***(4.2)			
* Internet Access					
* Technological Advancement[b]				0.21***(4.5)	0.12***(5.1)
• Informational Connectedness			0.08***(15.7)	0.04***(11.0)	0.04***(11.0)
* GDP/cap					
* Schooling Years			N.S.		
* Internet Access					
* Technological Advancement[b]				N.S.	N.S.
Reduction of Error (of total):					
Within-societal Variation of DV	08% (05%)	13% (09%)	08% (05%)	12% (08%)	12% (08%)
Between-societal Variation of DV	57% (20%)	60% (21%)	71% (25%)	79% (28%)	77% (27%)
Variation in Age Effect	36%	41%	13%	31%	40%

TABLE 3.1 (cont.)

		DEPENDENT VARIABLE: Emancipative Values			
PREDICTORS	Material Empowerment[a]	Intellectual Empowerment[a]	Connective Empowerment	Combined Empowerment I[b]	Combined Empowerment II
Variation in Income Effect	0	0	0	0	0
Variation in Education Effect	0	13%	0	28%	35%
Variation in Connectivity Effect	0	0	0	0	0
Total Variance Explained	25%	30%	30%	36%	35%
N (number of observations)	128,908 individuals in 81 societies	116,390 individuals in 62 societies	58,272 individuals in 45 societies	41,808 individuals in 33 societies	41,808 individuals in 33 societies

[a] The material and intellectual empowerment models cover data of all societies surveyed in the last two rounds of the World Values Survey (WVS), using the latest survey from each society (ca. 2000–2005) and weighting each national sample to equal size. The other models only cover data from WVS round five (ca. 2005) because the questions used to measure informational connectedness were only fielded then.

[b] In the first combined model, instead of technological advancement, I use the average of the gross domestic product (GDP) per capita, schooling years, and internet access to measure combined action resources at the societal level. In all models, societal-level variables are taken from the year of the survey.

Entries are unstandardized regression coefficients (*b*'s) with T ratios in parentheses. Societal-level variables are global-mean centered; individual-level variables (except female sex) are country-mean centered. Models calculated with HLM 6.01. Societal-level variables are global-mean centered; individual-level variables (except female sex) are country-mean centered. Reduction of error is calculated from change in random variance component relative to the empty model. Sixty-five percent of the total variance in emancipative values is within and 35 percent between societies. Significance levels:

* $p < .050$; ** $p < .010$; *** $p < .001$; N. S. not significant ($p > .050$).

4. A *first combined* model: this model summarizes the three societal-level indicators into an encompassing index of action resources and introduces each of the three individual-level indicators of action resources.[7]
5. A *second combined* model: this is the same as the first model but replaces the encompassing societal-level index of action resources with technological advancement; this is done to see if technological advancement is an acceptable surrogate for all three action resources.

The models do not assume that action resources affect people's emancipative values uniformly across societies. Instead, the models are built on the assumption that the effect varies in strength, depending on how prevalent control over a given resource is in a society. The assumption results from the idea of social cross-fertilization (see Box 3.3, p. 110). For instance, a highly educated person has more utility from freedoms than a less educated person, yet when there are many other people with high education, the highly educated person shares her utility with many others. Then, the emphasis on *equal* freedoms that inheres in emancipative values should be stronger than in a society in which our person has a unique utility from freedoms because her high level of education is rare.

To test this assumption, we separate individually unique resource possessions from socially prevalent ones. This is done by centering all individual-level variables on their societal-level means, measuring for each individual to what extent and in which direction her own command of action resources deviates from what is common in her society.[8]

To interpret the regression coefficients in Table 3.1, one has to recognize that *all* variables are normalized into a scale range from a theoretical minimum of 0 to a theoretical maximum of 1.0. With normalized scales, unstandardized regression coefficients of different independent variables are directly comparable concerning their contribution to emancipative values. Specifically, the coefficients tell us what fraction of its observed score an input variable adds to or subtracts from the constant to obtain a respondent's expected score in emancipative values. For instance, a coefficient of 0.30 for an input variable tells us that we add a fraction of 0.30 of this variable's observed score to the constant to obtain the respondent's expected score in emancipative values. We can also say that the coefficient tells us at what ratio differences in the input variable translate into differences in emancipative values.

Looking at the empowerment models in Table 3.1, the first thing to note is that female sex shows a significant and consistent effect on emancipative values.

---

[7] The societal-level indicators are summarized because too high collinearity makes it impossible to separate their simultaneous effects; by contrast, collinearity among the individual-level indicators is much lower, so they can be introduced as separate indicators simultaneously.

[8] There is another desirable property of using mean-centered individual-level variables. Doing so isolates the effect of each individual-level variable from *anything* that could possibly influence the societal mean in this variable. This is equivalent to a "country-fixed effects" model. A desirable property of these models is that they reduce omitted variable bias.

Admittedly, the effect is very small: all else kept equal, being a woman adds no more than 0.03 scale points to the approximately 0.45 scale points of the constant term in emancipative values. But the effect is robust against controls for other individual-level characteristics, including action resources.[9]

The next obvious result is that the societal-level manifestations of action resources have considerably larger coefficients than their individual-level manifestations. For instance, a 1-unit increase in the social prevalence of intellectual resources elevates people's emancipative values by a 0.46-unit, whereas a 1-unit increase in people's own intellectual resources only elevates their emancipative values by a 0.11-unit. Similar conclusions apply to material and connective resources. Thus, the level of action resources that is typical for most people in a society strengthens one's emancipative values much more than the level of action resources that one has on top of what most others have.

Confirming these results, the bottom of Table 3.1 shows that the societal-level inputs of our models explain two to five times more of the total variance in emancipative values than do the individual-level inputs. These findings confirm the emphasis that the theory of emancipation places on people's *joint* utilities from freedoms. Freedoms are a reciprocal good whose valuation is a cross-fertilization product of mutual recognition. The mutuality can grow only on the basis of joint utilities.

The societal prevalence of each of the three types of action resources raises people's emancipative values above the level that their own action resources suggest. This is another example of the elevator effect explained in Box 3.3.

In the case of intellectual resources, we also find an amplifier effect: an individual's own intellectual resources strengthen her emancipative values more when she lives in a society in which intellectual resources are more widespread. This is evident from the positive interaction between formal education at the individual level and schooling years at the societal level.

We have seen in Figure 3.1 that younger birth cohorts tend to prefer emancipative values more than older cohorts do. In Table 3.1, this finding is reflected in a uniformly positive effect of the birth year index on emancipative values. In the first model, for instance, we add to the constant a 0.14 fraction of a respondent's score on the birth year index to obtain a respondent's expected score in emancipative values: if a respondent is born in 1990, the score on the birth year index is at its maximum (1.0), and we add exactly 0.14 scale points to the constant. More generally, a 1-unit increase on the birth year index translates into a 0.14-unit increase in emancipative values. This means that we add about 0.05 scale points to emancipative values for every thirty years of later birth – the span of a generation. This may not seem like much, yet this is the pure effect of the birth year, holding everything else constant.

Even though the effect of birth year on emancipative values is uniformly positive, its strength varies significantly with the social prevalence of the type

---

[9] The female effect is solely due to the equality component of the emancipative values index.

of action resource under consideration. This is evident from birth year's positive interaction with the prevalence of each action resource: later birth generally strengthens emancipative values, yet it strengthens them more where more people are affluent, educated, and connected.

Back to our initial question: which action resource is more important for emancipative values? The first message is that all three resources contribute significantly to emancipative values. All of them do so at both the individual and societal levels, even though the typical disposition of action resources in a society strengthens people's emancipative values more than people's unique dispositions.

Still, there are recognizable differences in the relative importance of the three types of action resources. As we can see from the bottom of Table 3.1, the material empowerment model explains less within-societal variance in emancipative values than does the intellectual empowerment model (8 compared to 13 percent). The material empowerment model also explains less between-societal variance in emancipative values than do both the intellectual and connective empowerment models (57 compared to 60 and 71 percent). Of the three types of action resources, material resources are relatively less important than intellectual and connective resources.

Of course, the largest variance in emancipative values (79 percent at the societal level, 39 percent in total) is explained when all three types of resources are combined. This is obvious from the first combined model in Table 3.1. This model uses as a societal-level predictor of emancipative values the average of the three types of action resources and introduces each of them simultaneously at the individual level. The second combined model is identical to the first, except for the fact that the average of the three types of action resources at the societal level is replaced with technological advancement. Because the societal-level component of this model produces almost identical results to the previous one (the explained variance is just 1 percent lower), it is safe to conclude that technological advancement is a formidable indicator of the combination of all three types of action resources.

3. THE FORMATIVE POWER OF CULTURE ZONES

Emancipative values vary to a considerable extent across culture zones. Of the total variance in emancipative values among individuals, culture zones account for a significant 26.6 percent. Looking at national mean scores in emancipative values, culture zones account for 72.4 percent of the variation. This pattern reflects two regularities:

1. People internalize values through exposure to the cultural gravity of their reference society.
2. Similarities in trajectories of development among societies of the same culture zone cluster these societies' cultural gravities.

Among their belonging societies, culture zones capture *all* similarities that exist, even similarities we are not aware of.

Given this catch-all property, pointing out that culture zones explain a lot of variation in people's values is telling us little more than that history matters. The inherent unspecificity of this insight calls for a specification of the substantive characteristics through which culture zones cluster the values of the societies belonging to them.

3.1 How to Explain the Formative Power of Culture Zones

To estimate the formative power of culture zones, we must isolate the culture zones' purely *contextual* effect on the values of national societies. Otherwise, we identify a semi-tautological impact: because each national mean score in emancipative values contributes to the mean score of the respective culture zone, it is unavoidable that the culture zone mean scores explain some of the variation in the national mean scores. To avoid this tautology, we must ask the question "to what extent is a given society's mean score in emancipative values explained by the mean score of all *other* societies in the same culture zone?" This is the critical question because, if culture zones have genuine grouping power over emancipative values, then a society's emphasis on these values is determined merely by its membership in a particular culture zone. In other words, it is not a society's *own* characteristics but characteristics common among the *other* societies of its culture zone that shape this society's emphasis on emancipative values. If there is a genuine membership effect in this sense, this is an entirely contextual effect.

To isolate the merely contextual part of the culture zone's grouping power over emancipative values, I assign each society a contextual culture zone score in emancipative values: this is the average national mean score in emancipative values for all other societies of the same culture zone. Contextual culture zone scores (CCZS) are specific for each society, and even societies of the same culture zone do not share exactly the same score. In the next step, I examine to what extent these CCZS in emancipative values explain the national mean scores (NMS) in these values. This examination gives us an estimate of the truly contextual grouping power of culture zones. As Table 3.2 indicates, the CCZS explain 68.9 percent of the NMS of emancipative values.[10]

The next question is which specific characteristics of culture zones account for their grouping power. To answer this question, I calculate contextual culture zone scores in a number of specific characteristic over which culture zones differ and which might account for most of their clustering power over emancipative values. I use the CCZS in each of these specific characteristics to explain the emancipative values of our ninety-five societies and note the different explanatory powers in the left-hand column of Table 3.2. Then, I calculate to what

---

[10] To calculate culture zone means in emancipative values across the societies of a culture zone, each national sample is weighted to equal size. Weighting societies for their population size and calculating culture zone means on this basis produces similar results as those reported here.

TABLE 3.2 *Variance in National Mean Scores in Emancipative Values Explained by Clustering within Culture Zones (before and after "instrumentation").*

PREDICTORS	Explained Variance (%) in NMS of Emancipative Values	*Match Ratio* of Explained Variance (68.9 = 1)	N (Societies)
True CCZS in Emancipative Values[a]	68.9	1.0	95
Expected CCZS in Emancipative Values[b], by instrument:			
• Time since Neolithic Revolution	00.0	0.00	90
• 5-HTTLPR-Gene Frequency	00.0	0.00	49
• Demographic Big-Five Profile	00.0	0.00	51
• Cultural Looseness	03.0	0.04	33
• Bioclimate	11.3	0.16	91
• Female Fertility	22.0	0.32	85
• State Antiquity	23.0	0.33	85
• Mean Temperature	29.7	0.43	91
• Household Patrilocality	42.0	0.61	89
• Per capita GDP (logged)	43.3	0.63	94
• Disease Security	44.6	0.65	91
• Democratic Tradition	46.7	0.69	93
• Val$^{108/158}$Met-COMT Gene Frequency	48.9	0.71	50
• White Mortality	49.4	0.72	85
• Cool-Water Condition	49.4	0.72	93
• Cultural Individualism	50.1	0.73	77
• Consanguine Marriages	52.5	0.76	64
• Protestantism versus Islam	52.6	0.76	89
• Technological Advancement	62.1	0.90	91

CCZS, Contextual Cultural Zone Score; NMS, National Mean Score.

[a] All societies obtain the mean score in emancipative values of the *other* societies in the same culture zone: these are the societies' "true" CCZS in emancipative values. The predictive power of these with respect to the societies' *own* emancipative values indicates the degree of intrazone clustering in these values, which is 68.9 percent.

[b] I calculate "expected" CCZS in emancipative values by CCZS in the respective instrument variable (assigning all societies the mean in this instrument of the other societies in the same culture zone). Then I calculate the "expected" CCZS' predictive power with respect to the societies' own emancipative values and compare the predictive power with that of the "true" CCZS in emancipative values.

extent these explanatory powers match that obtained by the observed culture zone scores in emancipative values and note the match ratio in the middle column of Table 3.2. The largest match ratio identifies the culture zone characteristic with the biggest clustering power over emancipative values. Before discussing the results of Table 3.2, the next section introduces a variety of specific characteristics on which culture zones differ.

3.2 Specific Explanations of Culture Zone Effects

Culture zones differ in many characteristics that possibly influence their paths of development. We can order these characteristics according to how long they reach back in time. At the origin, then, there are natural endowments that did not change over the recent past. They represent more or less constant differences between culture zones. Such natural endowments might have worked as kickoff conditions that started long chains of path-dependent developments (McNeill 1990; Diamond 1997; Landes 1998; Nolan & Lenski 1999).

Among the natural endowments discussed in the development literature, climate receives increasing attention (Diamond 1997; Gallup & Sachs 2000; Dell, Jones, & Olken 2011). This is plausible when one acknowledges that climate sits at the beginning of a chain of developments from surplus agriculture to urban civilization to technological advancement. Technological advancement and other aspects of development need the presence of urban civilization as a starting platform. Civilization in turn requires the existence of surplus agriculture to feed urban populations. This is where climatic conditions matter: they influence (a) whether surplus agriculture is possible in the first place, (b) what type of surplus agriculture is suitable, and (c) how large a surplus is achievable on a given level of technology (Fernandez-Armesto 2002).

Extreme cold and heat, for instance, render desert and polar areas infertile. Absent vegetation in these areas makes any form of agriculture impossible. Without agriculture, urban civilization cannot emerge (Diamond 1997). Next to temperature, aridity limits agrarian potential. In the absence of continuous fresh water sources, producing agrarian surplus sufficient to sustain urban populations is impossible (Weischet & Cavides 1993). Historically, aridity has exempted large areas of sub-Saharan Africa and Central Asia from the rise of urban civilization (Midlarsky & Midlarsky 1999).

Even in the humid tropics, soil conditions are unsuited for most of the staple food crops needed to feed urban populations.[11] Rice is the exception but its cultivation requires so much labor coordination that a rigidly regulated type of

---

[11] This might seem a paradox in view of the thriving diversity of plant life in tropical rainforests. However, as lucidly pointed out by Weischet and Cavides (1993), as well as by Gallup and Sachs (2000), land cleared from tropical rainforest is quickly baked hard by intense sun exposure while seasonal heavy rains wash soil away. In addition, tropical temperatures accelerate plant life cycles and hence the depletion of soil nutrients.

agriculture is the result. This *regimented allotment cultivation* became prevalent in the subtropics, especially in alluvial regions, where central irrigation management yields large agrarian surpluses (Mann 1986). Indeed, alluvial regions in Mesopotamia, Egypt, India, and China became the cradle of urban civilization (McNeill 1990; Fernandez-Armesto 2002). But even though large-scale irrigation requires a certain level of technological advancement, its rigid regulation suffocates people's creativity, thus stalling further advancement (Wittfogel 1957; Jones 1987; Solomon 2011). The system of labor organization in this type of agriculture is accurately described by Powelson (1997) as *coercive feudalism*.

In stark contrast, the rare combination of moderately cold temperatures with continuous seasonal rainfall in Northwestern Europe gave rise to a categorically different type of surplus agriculture: *autonomous family farming*. According to Powelson (1997), this type of agriculture establishes *contractual feudalism* – a system of labor organization in which the lord–peasant relationship is less oppressive, family farms have more autonomy, and the peasantry writ large is in a better position to struggle for rights (Landes 1998). In fact, beginning in late medieval times, rights struggles became a signature feature of Western civilization and a defining element of its emerging emancipatory spirit (McNeill 1990; Finer 1999; Grayling 2007).

It appears inherently plausible to me that the emancipatory spirit of Western civilization originates in Northwestern Europe's contractual type of family farming, which in turn is favored by an ecological specialty: the combination of moderately cold temperatures with continuous rainfall and permanently navigable waterways (Chirot 1986). This "cool-water" condition' (CW condition) gives farming households more autonomy than they have in an irrigation-managed agrarian setting. The CW condition also enhances agrarian labor productivity: according to Gallup and Sachs (2000), agrarian return to labor in cold and rainy areas is four times higher than in the tropics and three times higher than in dry areas. As these authors demonstrate, the productivity advantage of the cold and rainy regions is not endogenous to these areas' greater technological and financial resources: controlling for differences in development, the productivity advantage of the CW zones remains – it is inherent to their *natural* endowment.

Offering existential autonomy and greater returns to labor, the CW condition provides an opportunity-rich environment. This opportunity endowment bestows greater initial utility on practicing and tolerating freedoms. I consider this natural opportunity endowment as the seed of Western civilization's affinity to emancipatory ideals. This proposition is part of my theory of emancipation. It is emancipation theory's *source thesis* (see Chapter 11 for a detailed elaboration of this thesis).

In my understanding, natural endowments are not deterministic. Rather, they open a possibility corridor within which human agency unfolds. The choices societies make cannot place them beyond the limits of the corridor, yet they decide whether a society moves along the corridor's floor or ceiling (Lal 1998).

Figure 3.5 illustrates this idea with respect to a relationship discussed in more detail in Chapter 11: the impact of the CW condition on a society's technological

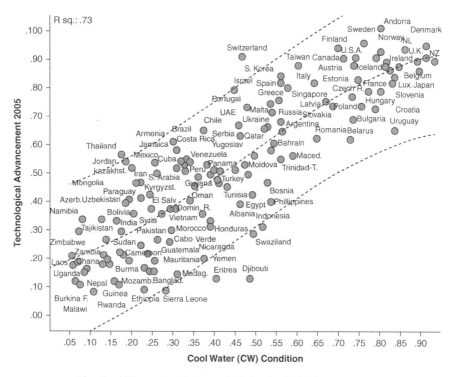

FIGURE 3.5 The Cool-Water Condition and Technological Advancement.
Data Coverage: All 142 societies for which data on both technological advancement and the cool-water condition are available. The cool-water index summarizes data on (a) the average annual temperature (inverted), (b) rainfall continuity across the seasons, and (c) the abundance of ice-free waterways on a society's territory. These data are taken from Gallup, Mellinger, and Sachs (2010) and summarized into a 0–1.0 index, as detailed in Appendix 11 (www.cambridge.org/welzel).

advancement – the most proximate determinant of emancipative values. The CW condition is naturally given, indicating the prevalence of relatively cold temperatures, continuous rainfall, and access to navigable waterways.[12] As the trendline

---

[12] I measure the CW condition by calculating the fraction of a society's arable territory in cold temperate and rainy zones in excess of the fraction in hot and dry zones. Then I factor in additional variation in (a) the exact amount of rainfall in the driest season on a country's territory and (b) the fraction of territory within a 100 km reach of ice-free waterways. The resulting index is at minimum 0 when all territory is in hot and dry zones, when there is no rain at all on the entire country's territory in the driest season and when no fraction of the territory is within a 100-km reach of ice-free waterways. The index is at maximum 1.0 when all territory is in cold temperate and rainy zones, when rainfall in the driest season is at the highest known level for national territory (ca. 200 mm, Solomon Islands), and when all territory is within a 100-km reach of ice-free waterways. Data are from the Harvard Geography project by Gallup, Mellinger, and Sachs (2010). Precise index construction is described in Chapter 11 and Appendix 11(www.cambridge.org/welzel).

in Figure 3.5 shows, the degree to which the CW condition is present favors a society's technological advancement. In fact, across the 145 societies for which both measures are available, the strength of the CW condition explains 73 percent of the variation in technological advancement. Nevertheless, societies distribute within a relatively broad corridor alongside the overall tendency. The width of that corridor is indicated by the upper and lower boundaries of the 95 percent confidence interval in Figure 3.5. Thus, each level of the CW condition allows societies to settle at varying levels of technological advancement, with some societies settling at the lower boundary and others at the upper boundary. Yet very few societies escape the boundaries of the corridor.

Exactly why the CW condition affects a society's technological advancement is discussed in Chapter 11. Yet, it is obvious from Figure 3.6 that culture zones differ significantly in the CW condition. These differences are, thus, a possible reason why culture zones differ in technological advancement and other aspects of development, including emancipative values. Indeed, most Western societies score at about 0.80 scale points in the CW condition (with the exception of Switzerland, which scores at 0.50). The *only* non-Western societies with such a strong CW condition are Japan and Uruguay. Most Eastern societies score considerably lower, in a range

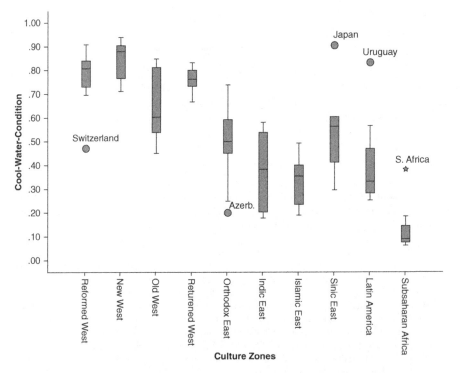

FIGURE 3.6 The Cool-Water Condition across Culture Zones.
Data Coverage: See Figure 3.5.

between 0.30 and 0.50 scale points. With a mean score of 0.10, sub-Saharan Africa shows by far the weakest CW condition. The exception is South Africa, which scores at 0.40. In light of these numbers, it appears plausible that emancipative values differ across culture zones because culture zones differ in the strength of the CW condition – a possible root cause of the developments leading to emancipative values.

There are plausible reasons to place climatic conditions at the beginning of historic path dependencies in the course of which certain cultures and their defining values take shape. Van de Vliert (2008; 2013) even goes so far to ascribe climate a direct influence on values. The author argues that societies whose average temperature is more remote from the human comfort zone (i.e., 22 degrees Celsius) must invest more resources into technology to cope with the thermal challenges of their environment. Thermal challenges program societies into a "promotion focus" to advance their technological capacity. All else equal, the promotion focus not only facilitates technological advancement; in interaction with advanced technology, it also accelerates the rise of emancipative values.[13] This reasoning suggests that emancipative values vary across culture zones because culture zones differ in their "bioclimates"; that is, in their thermal distance from the human comfort zone. To test this hypothesis, I use van de Vliert's bioclimate data.[14]

The *bioclimate theory* posits that distance from the thermal comfort zone in *both* directions – colder and hotter – is conducive to development. Accordingly, technological advancement and emancipative values rise in a U-shaped curve away from the thermal comfort zone. Other authors have different ideas about climatic influences on development. Instead of maintaining a *curvilinear* relationship between temperature and development, many scholars argue that development tends to advance *linearly* with decreasing temperature. Indeed, there is compelling evidence that both land productivity and labor productivity increase alongside falling annual mean temperatures (Deschenes & Greenstone 2007; Graff Zivin & Neidell 2010). This tendency goes even so far that seasonal frost enhances agrarian productivity (Masters & Wiebe 2000).[15] What is more, a longitudinal study by Dell, Jones, and Olken (2011) finds that the impact of temperature on agrarian productivity carries

---

[13] Van de Vliert tests this proposition with respect to "self-expression values" as defined by Inglehart and Welzel (2005). Because emancipative values constitute an improved measure of self-expression values, van de Vliert's reasoning should apply to emancipative values, too. Similarly, van de Vliert talks mostly about monetary resources; yet, I think that his logic applies even more directly to technological resources.

[14] I thank Evert van de Vliert for sharing his data with me.

[15] Colder temperatures decelerate nutrient depletion in soil and increase the return to labor. Of course, the tendency of colder temperatures to improve agrarian productivity does not go beyond *seasonal* frost: permafrost defies agriculture.

through all the way to economic prosperity writ large. And even small temperature fluctuations have an immediate effect on development. Thus, if colder climates are conducive to development, they should also be conducive to the cultural features linked with development – most notably emancipative values. In this case, emancipative values vary across culture zones because mean annual temperatures differ between culture zones. To test this hypothesis, I use data from Dell, Jones, and Olken (2011) on a society's mean annual temperature over the past fifty years.[16]

Still other authors see a more indirect influence of climate on culture. For instance, the *disease security theory* by Fincher, Thornhill, Murray and Schaller (2008) posits that lower annual temperatures diminish the threat of human livability from communicable diseases (see also Thornhill, Fincher & Aran 2008).[17] Higher disease security in turn lowers the need of in-group closure as a protective mechanism against infections – with far-reaching consequences for socializing patterns. Specifically, natural disease security shifts utility from avoiding out-group contact to pursuing it. This proposition formulates another variant of the source thesis: next to the CW condition, disease security represents another natural endowment that bestows utility on the practice and toleration of freedoms.[18] If this is correct, societies with greater natural security from diseases have been placed from the start on a path that is more favorable to freedom and emancipation. To test this hypothesis, I use data on a society's natural disease load from Murray and Schaller (2010).[19] The data measure to what extent a society's natural environment harbors various infectious diseases, not how large a proportion of the population actually falls ill. This is important because disease measures of the latter type are endogenous to technological advancement: technologically advanced societies have more elaborate medical and hygienic facilities that prevent infections even if there is a natural potential for them. Measuring *natural* disease load avoids this endogeneity.[20] Because I am interested in the role of disease security, I invert Murray and Schaller's measures, so that higher scores indicate a lower threat from diseases.

Thornhill and Fincher's disease security theory can be linked with Woodley and Bell's (2012) *consanguinity theory*. Consanguinity describes a marriage

---

[16] I thank Melissa Dell for sharing her data with me.

[17] The germs of nonzoonotic diseases thrive outside the body of a host. With the decrease of annual average temperatures, the livability of these diseases diminishes.

[18] The CW condition and disease security are mutually overlapping opportunity endowments: because the CW condition comes with lower annual temperatures, it causes higher disease security. In numbers, across the 165 societies for which both measures are available, the CW condition explains 51 percent of the variation in disease security.

[19] I thank Randy Thornhill for making me attentive to Murray and Schaller's article.

[20] That this is not a far-fetched possibility can be seen from the fact that, across the ninety-two societies for which measures of both disease security and emancipative values are available, the two correlate at $r = 0.65$ ($p < .001$).

pattern that seeks to keep the social circle of marriages narrow by preferring distant relatives over nonrelatives as marriage partners. Obviously, consanguinity is an aspect of the in-group closure emphasized by the *disease security theory*.[21] Not surprisingly, then, Woodley and Bell (2012) find that consanguinity concurs with some of the same correlates as low disease security, especially deficient democracy. This finding implies that consanguinity involves a weak emphasis on emancipative values because these values are strongly linked with democracy (as Chapter 8 will show).[22] Hence, emancipative values might vary across culture zones because consanguinity differs between culture zones. To test this possibility, I use Woodley and Bell's data on the presence of consanguinity in a society.

Another possible link is offered by what I would label *female integrity theory* (Hudson, Ballif-Spanvill, Caprioli, & Emmett 2012). Where natural disease threats favor consanguine marriages, in-group closure along kinship lines is more pronounced. This pattern goes often hand in hand with patrilocal household formation: married couples move into the household of the husband's parents. Patrilocality facilitates male bonding at the same time as it disrupts female alliances. The result is patriarchy – male control over female sexuality. Since patriarchy is antithetical to emancipative values, these values should be weak where patriarchy is strong. In light of these propositions, I treat patrilocal household formation as a proxy for patriarchy. To be precise, I calculate per country the percentage of married men living with their parents. Data are taken from the World Values Surveys (WVS).[23] Accordingly, I examine if emancipative values vary across culture zones because culture zones differ in patrilocal household formation.

Another measure of patriarchy is a high female fertility rate. Where fertility is high, women are largely reduced to their reproductive function, and their activity radius is pinned to the household. By implication of this, out-of-household life is monopolized by men. To estimate the influence of fertility, I use data from the World Development Indicators (World Bank 2010) on the female birth rate in 1980.[24] To avoid endogeneity problems, I chose on purpose

---

[21] Supporting this proposition, across the seventy-one societies for which measures of both disease security and consanguinity are available, the two correlate at $r = -0.50$ ($p < .001$).

[22] Indeed, across the fifty-one societies for which measures of both consanguinity and emancipative values are available, the two correlate at $r = -0.74$ ($p < .001$).

[23] There is the possibility that the spouses of married men live in a separate household. I assume, however, that this is a negligible percentage in most societies. Marriage in most instances implies living under the same roof.

[24] Female fertility correlates at $r = 0.63$ with consanguine marriages ($p < .004$; $N = 68$) and at $r = 0.32$ with patrilocal households ($p < .004$; $N = 80$) whereas the latter two correlate with each other at $r = 0.70$ ($p < .001$; $N = 46$). Thus, the three variables represent a single dimension, indicating a syndrome of patriarchal in-group closure. Factor loadings on the single dimension are 0.92 for consanguine marriages and 0.82 for both patrilocal household formation and female fertility ($N = 42$ societies). The overlapping variance among the three variables is 73 percent. Summarizing the three variables into an overall measure of patriarchal in-group closure, this measure correlates

a fertility measure from a time located considerably before emancipative values. Now, fertility is also interesting from a different point of view. *Unified growth theory* (Galor 2011) posits that development depends on a change in life strategy that redirects time investments from maximizing offspring to promoting skill. Part of this change in strategy is fertility control. Against this backdrop, it seems plausible that the opportunity endowments embedded in the CW condition encourage stronger fertility control, which in turn promotes development and its cultural consequences – emancipative values in particular. Hence, emancipative values might vary across culture zones partly because culture zones differ in fertility control. To test this possibility, I measure fertility control as the inverse of a society's fertility rate.

An increasing number of scholars suggest that genetic factors might play a role in societal development (Hatemi & McDermott 2012). Societal variation in the frequency of two genes calls particular attention: the Val$^{108/158}$Met polymorphism of the catechol-o-methyltransferase (COMT) gene and the long-allelic version of the 5-HTTLPR gene. Both genes affect the human reward system by influencing the emission level of stimulating hormones: dopamine in the case of the COMT gene; serotonin in the case of the HTTLPR gene. Data from the *allele frequency database* (ALFRED) at Yale University seem to suggest that both genes exist in different frequencies in different populations (cf., alfred. med.yale.edu). What is more, both genes seem to be linked with traits that supposedly make people more receptive to emancipative values. In the case of the COMT gene, there is a positive link with two of the "Big Five" personality traits that should increase people's affinity to emancipative values: openness and extraversion. Likewise, the demographic prevalence of the COMT gene shows a negative link with the personality trait that should diminish people's affinity to emancipative values: neuroticism (Stein, Fallin, Schork, & Gelernter 2005; Wichers et al. 2008).[25] In the case of the HTTLPR gene, there is a positive link of its long-allelic version with cultural individualism – a trait that also should enhance people's affinity to emancipative values (Chiao & Blizinski 2010).

Why exactly genetic predispositions to certain traits seem to prevail in some societies but not in others might be explained by the source thesis of emancipation theory. When natural opportunity endowments, such as the CW condition, bestow utility on freedoms, traits that prompt people to claim, assert, and use freedoms are beneficial. Openness, extraversion, and individualism are such traits: because they predispose people to follow intrinsic motivations, these traits involve the use of freedoms. People with these traits have a competitive advantage then and are more likely to prosper. Prospering people are more likely to be

---

at $r = -0.65$ with disease security and at $r = -0.82$ with the CW condition ($p < .001$; $N = 42$). Since disease security and the CW condition reach further back in time than patriarchal in-group closure, the evident conclusion is that lack of the opportunities endowed by the CW condition and disease security induce patriarchal in-group closure.

[25] The other two traits are "agreebleness" and "conscientiousness." For the definition and measurement of the Big Five personality traits, see Matthews, Deary, and Whiteman (2003).

seen as role models. They become preferred partners and reproduce in larger proportions for this reason. Hence, genes that predispose people to traits linked with greater affinity to emancipative values might have become more prevalent among populations whose natural endowment gives freedoms greater utility. If so, emancipative values should differ across culture zones partly because culture zones differ in the frequency of particular genes such as COMT and HTTLPR. To test this possibility, I use data from Chiao and Blizinski (2010) who have gathered information on the demographic frequency of the HTTLPR gene. Equivalent data on the COMT gene are taken from Inglehart, Ponarin, and Welzel (forthcoming). Demographic frequencies of these genes are available for some fifty societies.[26]

If these reflections have a grain of truth, the demographic frequency of openness, extraversion, neuroticism, and individualism are more proximate causes of a population's affinity to emancipative values than are gene distributions. To test this possibility, I use data on the per country prevalence of openness, extraversion, and the inverse of neuroticism from Schmitt et al. (2012) and data on the prevalence of cultural individualism from Hofstede (2001 [1980]) and Suh et al. (1998).

Another trait that is supposedly favored by opportunity-rich environments is "cultural looseness." Cultural looseness, the opposite of tightness, measures how large a diversity of behaviors and lifestyles a society tolerates. Since emancipative values incorporate this type of tolerance, it is straightforward to assume that culturally loose societies are more strongly predisposed to embrace emancipative values. If so, emancipative values vary across culture zones partly because culture zones differ in "looseness." To test this possibility, I use data on the demographic prevalence of cultural looseness for some thirty societies from Gelfand et al. (2011).

Natural endowments and the traits that are supposedly favored by them are purely exogenous conditions; they are beyond a society's control.[27] Moreover, these factors reach so far back in time that they are placed at the origin of the causal funnel toward emancipative values. Thus, there must be more proximate causes of these values. Still reaching far back in time, although not as far as a society's natural endowment, are historic breakthroughs that elevate societies to a whole new stage of development. Among the early breakthroughs, two call recent attention: the adoption of agriculture and state formation. For instance, Putterman (2008) argues that societies in which agriculture has been adopted earlier in historic time tend to be more advanced until this day. Bockstette,

[26] I interpret these data with a strong note of caution for two reasons. First, it is not exactly clear if the gene frequencies are estimated from equivalent samples of the respective populations. Second, so far, we cannot pinpoint the exact selection mechanism that explains how different gene frequencies across populations come about. Nevertheless, I consider it legitimate to document the evidence for the existence of a gene-culture link and to speculate about its underlying reason.

[27] In the future, this might change through the expansion of our technological capacities to control climate change and genetic engineering. But, for now, this is not yet in sight.

Chanda, and Putterman (2002) claim the same for "state antiquity," a measure of the historic endurance of functioning state orders. Thus, the longer the adoption of surplus agriculture and the formation of states date back in a society's history, the more developed it tends to be. If one understands development as the accumulation of knowledge, these propositions are plausible because an early start is an advantage in a cumulative process. Since emancipative values are a consequence of development, the beginning of agriculture and state order should also affect these values. In other words, it is possible that emancipative values vary across culture zones because culture zones differ in the timing of agriculture and state order. To test this possibility, I use data on the timing of these two factors from Putterman (2008) and Bockstette, Chanda, and Putterman (2002).

Institutional legacies from the colonial era are much closer to the present than the Neolithic Revolution and "state antiquity." Among these legacies, Acemoglu, Johnson, and Robinson (2001) emphasize the role of *"inclusive institutions"* – inclusion referring to market access and political representation. The authors argue that the extent to which societies adopted inclusive institutions in the colonial era explains their level of development until this day. Inclusive institutions evolved in late medieval times under Western Europe's contractual type of feudalism (Powelson 1997) or what North, Wallis, and Weingast (2009) call "open access orders." From their European origin, inclusive institutions were transplanted to those colonial areas where Europeans could settle in large numbers because the mortality was low. Thus, Acemoglu, Johnson, and Robinson use historic data on "white settler mortality" as an instrument for inclusive institutions and show that societies are still more developed today where this mortality has historically been low. Again, since emancipative values are intimately linked with development, white settler mortality should also affect the societies' propensity to adopt emancipative values. In other words, it is possible that emancipative values vary across culture zones because culture zones differ in white settler mortality. To test this possibility, I use the mortality data published by Acemoglu, Johnson, and Robinson (2001).

A key manifestation of inclusive institutions is democracy. Indeed, some authors claim that emancipative values are endogenous to democracy (Vanhanen 2003; Hadenius & Teorell 2005). This claim is informed by the idea of "institutional learning": as part of their socialization, people embrace the values that their societies' institutions embody (Rustow 1970; Jackman & Miller 1998). If this is correct, it is clear that institutions need time to exert a socialization effect. Accordingly, democracy should shape values through its long-term endurance, not its momentary presence. Indeed, as Gerring et al. (2005) show, democracy impacts on other social phenomena much more by its endurance than by its momentary presence. Accordingly, emancipative values vary across culture zones because culture zones differ in their democratic traditions. To test this possibility, I use the democratic tradition index introduced in Chapter 2.

Next to institutional legacies, the literature emphasizes ideological legacies (Lal 1998). Inspired by Weber (1958 [1904]), various authors suggest that the emancipatory signature of Western civilization originates in the individualistic-egalitarian legacy of Protestantism (Dumont 1986; Lal 1998). By contrast, Islam's alleged tradition of patriarchy, hierarchy, and authority is often described as antithetical to the emancipatory tradition of Protestantism (Huntington 1996; Kuran 2004). Thus, it is conceivable that emancipative values vary across culture zones because culture zones differ in the imprint from Protestantism and Islam. To test this possibility, I use data on the percentages of Protestants and Muslims during the 1980s from the Quality of Governance Database (Quality of Governance Institute 2012). Following Inglehart and Welzel (2005), I construct a Protestantism versus Islam index by subtracting the fraction of Muslims from that of Protestants in a society. Scores on this index grow positive as Protestants outnumber Muslims and negative in the opposite case.[28]

Finally, the sequence thesis of the theory of emancipation suggests that the most proximate cause of emancipative values is control over resources of action. If this is correct, emancipative values vary across culture zones because culture zones differ in the action resources of the average person. To measure the action resources typical for most people in a society, I use the technological advancement index and per capita GDP. Whereas technological advancement indicates all three types of action resources equally, per capita GDP is mostly a measure of material resources in particular. Since emancipative values are supposed to originate in all three types of action resources, I hypothesize that technological advancement captures a larger portion of the culture zone variation in emancipative values than per capita GDP does.

The various conditions proposed here are by no means mutually exclusive. Instead, we can think of them as being located at different stages in the causal funnel toward emancipative values. At which stage they are located depends on how far back they reach in time: root causes reach farthest back in time; proximate causes are most recent; intermediate causes lie in between. At the origin, then, there are natural opportunity endowments – including the CW condition and disease security. These endowments permanently bestow greater utility on freedoms. Slowly but steadily, this opportunity endowment favors the selection of emancipatory traits such as individualism. Emancipatory traits predispose people to claim, assert, and use freedoms. Where these traits became prevalent, ideological and institutional traditions with an emancipatory spirit took root more easily. Most notably, this is true for the Protestant religion and representative institutions. Opportunity-rich settings are safer and more permissive; they shift utility from breeding many children to building individual skills,

---

[28] Using instead a set of dummy variables to indicate a society's historic imprint from either Protestantism, Islam, Catholicism, Orthodox Christianity, Buddhism, or Confucianism showed weaker results.

and from population growth to technological advancement. As a result of technological advancement, people gain control over the action resources that predispose them to the emancipative values as we know them today.

In the next step, we estimate for each of these conditions how much of the culture zone's clustering power over emancipative values it explains. Specifically, I calculate how well the average presence of a condition in a given society's culture zone explains this society's overall emphasis on emancipative values. These estimates are shown in the left-hand column of Table 3.2. The critical question is how close this explanatory power matches the one obtained from the societies' contextual culture zone score in emancipative values. The matching score is given in the middle column of Table 3.2.

In light of how far each condition reaches back in time, its explanatory power provides a benchmark to assess its "truth" status as a cause of the culture zones' clustering power over emancipative values. For instance, when a very remote condition, like the CW condition, shows a higher explanatory power than a more proximate condition, this speaks strongly against the truth status of the proximate condition. More generally, when a proximate condition has less explanatory power than a remote one, this *undermines* the truth status of the proximate condition while it *underlines* that of the remote condition.

3.3 Test Results

If we examine Table 3.2, the first thing to recognize is that the CW condition belongs to the most remote factors. Nevertheless, culture zone differences in the CW condition explain 49 percent of the cross-national variation in emancipative values. This proportion captures 72 percent of the culture zones' clustering power over emancipative values. This is more than many of the more proximate conditions capture, including genetic population profiles, demographic personality profiles, cultural looseness, the time since the adoption of agriculture and state formation, democratic traditions, and even per capita GDP. This undermines the truth status of these conditions as causes of the culture zones' clustering power over emancipative values. What is more, none of the conditions reaching as far back in time as the CW condition surpasses the CW condition's explanatory power. In fact, the bioclimate, mean annual temperatures, and disease security have weaker explanatory powers. Only the white mortality reaches as far back in time as the CW condition and shows an equally strong explanatory power. In line with this finding, the white mortality and the CW condition correlate at $r = -0.71$ ($p < 0.001$; $N = 93$). This makes sense. Historically, white mortality was higher where the CW condition was weaker because white people evolved under Europe's CW features and showed higher mortality in climates lacking these features. Thus, it is certain that in this environment-mortality relationship the environment is the cause. Hence, the evidence in Table 3.2 underlines the truth status of the CW condition as the root cause behind the culture zones' clustering power over emancipative values.

If this is so, we can accept as proximate causes only those conditions that are temporally closer to emancipative values than the CW condition and, at the same time, surpass this condition's explanatory power. There are only four conditions that meet this requirement. These include, in the order of their explanatory power: cultural individualism, consanguine marriages, Protestantism versus Islam, and technological advancement. Of these four conditions, Protestantism versus Islam and, especially, technological advancement show the strongest explanatory power. In the case of these two conditions, the explanatory power weighs more because they cover two dozen more societies than consanguine marriages and a dozen more societies than cultural individualism.

Focusing on these two conditions, the two-stage least squares regression in Table 3.3 demonstrates that Protestantism versus Islam and technological advancement *completely* absorb the clustering power of culture zones over emancipative values. In the first stage of the regression, I use contextual culture zone score in both Protestantism versus Islam and technological advancement to predict the observed culture zone scores in emancipative values. Together, the culture zone clustering in

TABLE 3.3 *Explaining Culture Zone's Clustering Power over Emancipative Values (two-stage least-squares regression).*

	DEPENDENT VARIABLES	
PREDICTORS	Stage 1: True CCZS in Emancipative Values	Stage 2: True NMS in Emancipative Values
Constant	0.29 (34.66)***	0.00 (0.11)[†]
True CCZS in Protestantism versus Islam	0.10 (16.89)***	
True CCZS in Technological Advancement	0.26 (20.08)***	
Expected CCZS in Emancipative Values		0.97 (15.19)***
Residual CCZS in Emancipative Values		0.49 (1.63)[†]
Adjusted R^2	0.96	0.73
N (societies)	87	87

Entries are unstandardized regression coefficients (*b*'s) with T-ratios in parentheses. Significance levels: * $p < .100$; ** $p < .050$; *** $p < .005$; [†] not significant ($p > .100$). Data cover all societies that have valid data on all variables of this analysis and are surveyed at least once by the World Values Surveys/European Value Study (WVS/EVS), aggregating emancipative values from the latest available survey.
CCZS, Contextual Culture Zone Scores; NMS, National Mean Scores
In the first regression stage, true CCZS in technological advancement and Protestantism versus Islam are used to calculate expected and residual CCZS in emancipative values. In the second stage, these expected and residual CCZS are used to explain true NMS in emancipative values

Protestantism versus Islam and technological advancement predicts fully 96 percent of the culture zone clustering in emancipative values, with technological advancement contributing the larger share to this prediction. Figure 3.7 illustrates the 96 percent overlap between the observed and predicted cultural zone scores in emancipative values. What this tells us is that culture zones cluster emancipative values because culture zones differ in Protestantism versus Islam and in technological advancement. Thus, when we use in the second stage of the regression the predicted culture zone scores in emancipative values to explain the national mean scores in these values, we explain 73 percent of the variation. This percentage even surpasses the clustering power of culture zones over emancipative values, which we estimated as 68.9 percent.

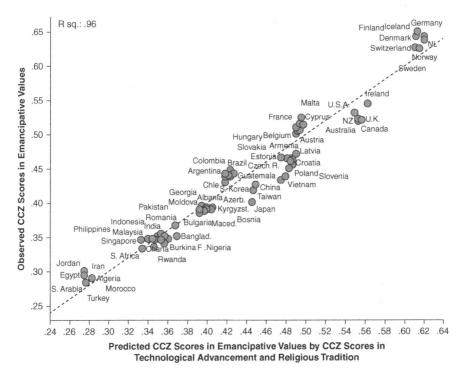

FIGURE 3.7 Observed and Predicted Culture Zone Scores in Emancipative Values. Contextual culture zone scores (CCZS) assign each society the mean score of a given variable of all other societies of the same culture zone. Thus, the vertical axis shows for each society the mean culture zone score in emancipative values of all other societies in the same culture zone. The horizontal axis shows predictions of these CCZS for each society, based on a society's CCZS in technological advancement and in Protestantism versus Islam. Simply put, the plot shows how well a society's culture zone environment in emancipative value is predicted by its culture zone environment in technological advancement and religious tradition.

These results suggest that two forces shape a society's gravity point in emancipative values. To a minor part, the gravity point depends on religious legacies that once infused the seed of an emancipatory spirit into a society's culture. This part is visible in the effect of Protestantism versus Islam. To a major part, the gravity point in emancipative values depends on the action resources that technological advancement today puts into ordinary people's hands.

The clustering power of culture zones over emancipative values is *completely* explained by culture zone differences in Protestantism versus Islam and technological advancement. Hence, we do not need to invoke the totality of all existing differences between culture zones to account for their explanatory power over values. We can be more specific. Of course, our gain in specificity does not tell us why culture zones differ in Protestantism versus Islam and technological advancement. But the source thesis of emancipation theory offers a plausible answer. Where the CW condition is strong, it endows farm households with existential autonomy and offers a larger return to labor on land. The CW condition also enhances disease security. In combination, the CW condition and disease security provide an opportunity-rich environment that bestows greater utility on freedoms. When freedoms have greater utility, it becomes more rewarding to invest time in one's skills and creativity. Investing time instead into raising many children then incurs higher opportunity costs. Accordingly, investments redirect from maximizing fertility to promoting innovation. The result should be technological advancement. Historically, areas with a strong CW condition, high disease security, and stronger fertility control should have been predisposed to ideologies with an emancipatory appeal, such as Protestantism, and resistant to ideologies with a patriarchal appeal, such as Islam. Together, Protestantism versus Islam and technological advancement eventually feed emancipative values.

I will discuss these propositions in light of the historical record in Chapter 11, but let me emphasize already here that the evidence strongly supports each of these propositions. This is obvious from the path diagram in Figure 3.8. What we see is the result of separate, temporally ordered regressions, each of which uses the full set of societies with available measures.[29] The main flow of impact runs from the timeless CW condition to fertility control in 1980 to technological advancement in 1995 to emancipative values in 2000–2005, with explained variances of 67 percent (fertility control), 81 percent (technological advancement), and 77 percent (emancipative values). Chapter 11 puts the sequence shown in Figure 3.8 into historical context, discussing when the impact of the CW condition began to unfold and why. For now, we shall leave it with a key

[29] To obtain a goodness of fit for the entire path diagram in Figure 3.8, one needs to reduce the sample to the set of societies with measures on all involved variables. This reduces the number of societies to eighty-three. Specifying the same paths as those in Figure 3.8 for these eighty-three societies and examining them as an integrated path model produces similar results. Goodness-of-fit statistics for the entire model are above the acceptance threshold of 0.90.

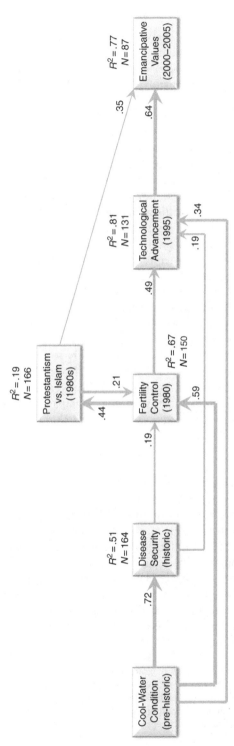

FIGURE 3.8 Temporally Ordered Path Model of the Source Thesis of the Emancipation Theory.

Entries are standardized regression coefficients (β weights) obtained from a sequence of temporally ordered, stepwise regressions. Each regression uses all variables to the left of the dependent variable as independent variables while dropping all insignificant effects from each model. All effects are significant at the 0.05 level. Diagnostic statistics for heteroskedasticity (White test), multicollinearity (VIFs), and influential cases (DFFITs) reveal no violation of ordinary least squares (OLS) assumptions in any of these regressions. Using listwise deletion to reduce the sample to societies with measures on all variables shrinks the sample to eighty-three cases. Running a path analysis in AMOS with this reduced sample while specifying all paths displayed here yields similar path coefficients, with the goodness-of-fit statistics (GFI, CFI, IFI) surpassing the 0.90 acceptance threshold.

conclusion: the source thesis of emancipation theory offers a plausible and evidence-supported explanation of culture zone differences linked with the human empowerment process.

Note that the path model in Figure 3.8 is probabilistic, not deterministic: it explains much but not all variation in societies' development. Opportunity endowments provide possibility corridors that societies cannot escape. But the institutional and ideological choices that societies make at some point in their history decide if they place themselves at the floor or the ceiling of their corridor. And this can make a big difference.

KEY POINTS

Emancipative values are shaped at different levels of social reality, including in ascending order of aggregation: human individuals, national societies, and culture zones. Greater action resources and, in particular, greater intellectual resources strengthen emancipative values at each of these levels. But the emancipatory impulse of action resources operates most strongly at the societal level. It is people's *shared* level of action resources, rather than what they have on top of others, that strengthens emancipative values. This confirms the emphasis that the theory of emancipation places on *joint* utilities.

Action resources also account for the strong formative power that culture zones seem to exert on their societies' emancipative values. Societies' emancipative values cluster in culture zones. And the clustering accounts for two-thirds of the cross-national variation in emancipative values. This is not surprising because culture zones are a catch-all category that captures every historically emerged commonality among their societies. However, when we try to identify which specific characteristic accounts for most of the culture zone's formative power, it turns out that this is technological advancement – a combined measure of all three types of action resources. Hence, culture zones shape their societies' emancipative values mostly because these zones differ in technological advancement.

Of course, this does not answer the question of why culture zones differ in technological advancement. But preliminary evidence suggests that natural opportunity endowments that bestow greater utility on freedoms provide the initial seed. When in history and why this seed fertilized is discussed in Chapter 11.

4

Tracing Change

> Changing values are transforming virtually every important aspect of society, from economic motivations, to the role of religion, to political institutions.
>
> – Ronald Inglehart

We have looked at differences in emancipative values from a cross-sectional point of view. It is now time to change perspective and examine emancipative values in the longitudinal dimension. We analyze change in values over time, tracing the rise of emancipatory orientations over recent decades and generations.

Scholars have put much more effort into analyzing cultural *differences* than cultural *change* (Triandis 1995; Hofstede 2001 [1980]; Schwartz 2006). An exception is the work of Inglehart and a few other authors whose work indeed focuses on cultural change (Inglehart & Abramson 1999; Flanagan & Lee 2003; Inglehart & Welzel 2005; Inglehart 2008; Abramson 2013). The findings of this group improve our understanding of how lifecycle effects, period effects, and cohort effects play together in shaping value change. One key finding is that age-related differences in values do not reflect lifecycle dynamics, such that people always start out with more emancipatory orientations in young age and turn more conservative as they get older. Instead, the pattern that shows young people to hold emancipatory orientations more strongly than older people emerges when people from subsequent generations grow up under steadily improving living conditions. In short, cohort effects dominate over lifecycle effects.

Another major finding is that people make periodic adjustments in their values in tandem with economic cycles. But these adjustments are made around relatively stable anchor points that continue to distinguish the generations in each economic cycle (Inglehart & Welzel 2005: 101; Welzel 2007b; Inglehart 2008). What is more, both the cohort differences and the periodic adjustments follow a single principle – the utility ladder of freedoms: when existential conditions become more pressing, freedoms lose utility and values shift to a less emancipatory position; conversely, when existential conditions become more permissive, freedoms gain utility and values move to a more emancipatory position. Hence, the cohort differences in emancipative values reflect a generational ascension on the utility ladder of freedoms; the periodic adjustments in these values reflect cyclical fluctuations up and down that same ladder (Welzel 2007b; Inglehart 2008).

So far, this pattern is well documented for the "voice" component of emancipative values, more widely known as *postmaterialism*. But voice is only one of the four components of emancipative values, next to choice, equality, and autonomy. Thus, this chapter is concerned with changes in the entire set of emancipative values. Moreover, the issue of causality is not as rigorously addressed in previous analyses as it could be. For this reason, this chapter documents and explains change in emancipative values with a strong focus on the causality issue.

This is done in two ways. Building on the documentation of change in emancipative values in the first section, section 2 presents a dynamic shift model to explain the increase in emancipative values over the more recent period. Section 3 then estimates from current cohort patterns the level of emancipative values for periods reaching much further back in time than survey data are available. On the basis of these estimates, I simulate a temporal order test, examining the dominant directions of impact among the three elements of human empowerment: action resources, emancipative values, and civic entitlements. The findings confirm the sequence thesis of emancipation theory: human empowerment advances in a sequence from action resources to emancipative values to civic entitlements.

Before we enter the analysis, a methodological remark is due. The World Values Surveys/European Value Study (WVS/EVS) is not a panel study that interviews the same people repeatedly. Hence, value change cannot be studied at the individual level. We can only look at societal-level evidence, investigating how a society's average value position changes over time. However, if we are interested in cultural change, this a qualification rather than a restriction. Culture is not a property of individuals; it is a property of societies. As a collective property, culture is manifest in the value position around which most people in a society gravitate. As Chapters 2 and 3 have shown, a society's average score on emancipative values is a valid representative of its cultural gravity point: the average score measures the most common value position in a given population. The cultural gravity of national societies is forceful, as we have seen. The reason lies in the fact that people's values are shaped by conditions that are most common in their society. These commonalities are exactly what aggregate numbers, such as societal averages, tap. Hence, there is no ecological fallacy, aggregation bias, or some other methodological pitfall involved when we analyze value change and its determinants at the societal level.

I. THE RISE OF EMANCIPATIVE VALUES

The following documentation focuses on statistically significant changes in emancipative values. In national samples of a size of about 1,000 respondents, changes from one time point to another are significant when they surpass 0.05 scale points.

From 1981 to 2008, the WVS has conducted some 250 surveys around the globe. In 140 instances, we can measure change in emancipative values from one round of surveys to the next. These changes cover mostly a five-year period. Of the statistically significant changes among these, eight are negative whereas forty-four are positive. Thus, on a five-year horizon, increases in emancipative values outnumber decreases by a factor of five. A documentation of these and the following numbers can be found in Appendix 4 (www.cambridge.org/welzel).

In seventy-five instances, we can measure change in emancipative values over three WVS rounds. These changes typically cover a ten-year period. Of the significant changes over this time horizon, four are negative whereas forty-one are positive. Thus, on a ten-year horizon, increases in emancipative values outnumber decreases by a factor of ten.

In yet another fifty instances, we can measure change in emancipative values over four rounds, involving a change of fifteen years or more. Of the significant changes among these, three are negative whereas thirty are positive. Again, increases outnumber decreases by a factor of ten.

Finally, in fourteen instances, we can measure change in emancipative values over five rounds, covering fully twenty-five years. Of these fourteen changes, all are significant and positive. If anything is clear from these numbers, it is that emancipative values are on the rise. By and large, the change figures confirm the rising trend of emancipative values, as suggested by the cohort pattern in Figure 2.5.

The human empowerment framework addresses developmental processes that advance at a glacial pace. Such processes become visible only in the long run. For this reason, we concentrate the following consideration on societies with a sizeable time coverage. We focus first on the fourteen societies with the WVS's full-time coverage of twenty-five years and then on the fifty societies with a temporal coverage of at least ten years. By focusing on longer time distances, we run a lower risk of confusing the trend with a cycle.[1]

The rise of emancipative values is most pronounced in postindustrial knowledge economies. So let's concentrate for a moment on these societies, where the

---

[1] Assume a variable increases with cyclical ups and downs on a long-term upward slope. Assume further that you measure change over a given time interval and you coincidentally take the first measure in an upward cycle and the second in a downward cycle. Now, the longer the time interval is over which you take these two measures, the less likely it is that you miss the trend: over a longer time, enough increase accrues that you see it even if the first measure is taken in an upward cycle and the second in a downward cycle.

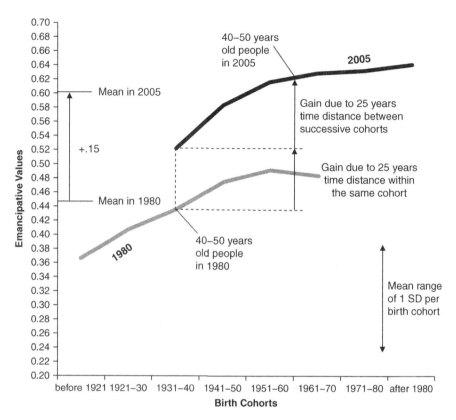

FIGURE 4.1 The Rise of Emancipative Values between and within Cohorts (knowledge economies, ca. 1980–2005).
Data Coverage: Earliest and latest World Values Surveys (WVS) from Australia, Canada, France, West Germany, Italy, Japan, the Netherlands, Norway, Sweden, the United States, and the United Kingdom. Each national sample weighted to equal size.

pattern is clearest. Figure 4.1 narrows down the analysis to the eleven societies that are knowledge economies and for which data for the full time span from 1980 to 2005[2] exist. Across these societies and the twenty-five-year time span, there is an increase in emancipative values of 0.15 scale points.[3] This increase covers almost a third of the entire range of cross-national variability in emancipative values.

The increase in emancipative values can be broken down into two components:

---

[2] The correct dates would be 1981–83 and 2005–08. For reasons of brevity, I round these dates.
[3] Societies are weighted to equal sample size. If we weight them for their population size, the amount of increase in emancipative values is the same.

1. the *intercohort* component: emancipative values rise through the time distance between successive cohorts;
2. the *intracohort* component: emancipative values rise through the passage of time within the same cohorts.

The inter cohort increase is visible in the upward slope of both lines in Figure 4.1: in 1980 as well as 2005, emancipative values increase from older to younger cohorts. As the flattening trend lines show, the tendency that a younger cohort emphasizes emancipative values more than the previous one seems to level off, especially after the cohort born between 1950 and 1960.

Despite the apparent fading of the intercohort increase, emancipative values grow pronouncedly between 1980 and 2005. The increase happens in *each* cohort: the line for 2005 hovers above the one for 1980 in every cohort. The vertical distance between the two lines for 1980 and 2005 represents the intracohort increase.

Comparing the inter- and intracohort increase reveals that they are even. The oldest cohort covered at both the beginning and the end of the observation period was born between 1930 and 1940. Between 1980 and 2005, this cohort's emancipative values increase from 0.44 to 0.53 scale points: a rise of 0.09 scale points within twenty-five years. In 1980, members of this cohort are forty to fifty years of age. Twenty-five years later, in 2005, people of that age score at 0.62 scale points in emancipative values: another 0.09 scale points above the position at which the forty- to fifty-year-olds from 1980 are in 2005. Hence, there is a gain in emancipative values of 0.09 scale points over a twenty-five-year time distance within the same cohort. In addition, there is a gain in emancipative values of another 0.09 scale points over a twenty-five-year time distance between cohorts. The gains between and within cohorts are equal.

Appendix 4 (www.cambridge.org/welzel) shows changes in the four subsidiary components from which emancipative values are calculated. We find inter- and intracohort increases in the same direction and in a comparable range in each of the components as those found in the overall index of emancipative values. The change pattern documented here is not driven by a specific component of emancipative values.

Moreover, the value changes from 1980 to 2005 depicted in Figure 4.1 are not the result of a short-term fluctuation, from a temporary low in 1980 to a temporary high in 2005. Instead, the temporal difference reflects a continuous move over time toward stronger emancipative values. This becomes evident when we plot emancipative values over all five rounds of the WVS from 1980 to 2005. This is also shown in Appendix 4.

The rise of emancipative values is most pronounced in knowledge economies. But even when we look outside of knowledge economies, significant increases in emancipative values outnumber decreases. Furthermore, Figure 2.5 has shown that the cohort pattern in societies from all ten culture zones of the globe points to an increase in emancipative values. Still, despite the overall progressive trend, the increases vary in amount. There are even cases of stagnation and a few cases of significant decline. These variations raise the question: can we explain the direction and the amount of change in emancipative values?

2. A DYNAMIC SHIFT MODEL

2.1 Establishing Dynamic Association

If the sequence thesis of emancipation theory is correct, then the direction and amount of change in the prevalence of emancipative values is a reaction to the direction and amount of change in most people's action resources.

As we have seen in Chapter 3, technological advancement is our best indicator of the combination of all three types of action resources, including intellectual skills, material means, and connective opportunities. Unfortunately, the measure of technological advancement is not available in sufficient time series to establish a dynamic association with emancipative values.[4] Alternative indicators of action resources at the societal level include the spread of internet access, the number of schooling years of the average person, and the per capita gross domestic product (GDP). Internet access is not suited for longitudinal analyses because the spread of the internet is a recent phenomenon that did not exist before 1990. Schooling years are patchy in terms of country coverage: we lose more than a dozen societies if we base the longitudinal analysis on schooling years. Thus, we are left with per capita GDP as the only measure of action resources with a sufficiently rich coverage of space and time.

As we have seen in Chapter 3, of our three types of action resources, per capita GDP is the one with the weakest influence on emancipative values. But this is a relative statement. Even as the weakest of the three types of resources, per capita GDP nevertheless shows a strong impact on emancipative values. Also, per capita GDP strongly correlates with the other types of action resources.[5] Hence, when better indicators are not available, it is defensible to examine the impact of action resources on emancipative values using per capita GDP.[6]

Per capita GDP and emancipative values are strongly associated, as we have seen. However, this association is purely cross-sectional. It does not evidence a dynamic association between the two variables. This presents a limitation because the association between any two variables can be causal only if these variables *coevolve*. For this to be true, changes, not only levels, in the two variables must be associated (Harrison 1987; Alexander & Welzel 2010).

---

[4] The earliest measure is from 1995. Since then, measures are available for only one more point in time at the time of this writing.

[5] Measured in the year 2000, per capita GDP correlates with schooling years at $r = 0.86$ ($N = 95$) and with internet access at $r = 0.89$ ($N = 170$).

[6] This is all the more true in a sample that does not include rent-seeking oil economies, which are rich but do not increase ordinary people's intellectual and connective resources in the same proportion as their material benefits. These economies are absent from my sample.

Dynamic association is no final proof of causation; yet it is a precondition.[7] Hence, we examine if there exists a dynamic association between per capita GDP and emancipative values. To do so, we test whether change in emancipative values associates with change in per capita GDP in the expected direction and at a corresponding rate.[8]

According to the sequence thesis of emancipation theory, people change their values in reaction to changes in their control over action resources. This thesis assumes that significant changes in action resources directly affect people's living conditions and are felt instantaneously for this reason. Consequently, perceptible changes in action resources trigger responses in people's values toward more or less emphasis on emancipation as soon as these changes are felt (even though younger cohorts' values might respond more pronouncedly than those of older cohorts). Hence, the model does not assume a measurable time lag in the response of values to changes in action resources. From this point of view, the reason why values usually change slowly is not that values never could change more quickly. Instead, values usually change slowly because people's action resources usually change slowly too – as does any development of glacial pace. For this reason, I choose change measures in emancipative values and in per capita GDP such that they temporally coincide for each society.[9] For instance, when change in emancipative values is measured from 1980 to 2005, change in per capita GDP is measured over the same period.[10]

Figure 4.2 illustrates how changes in emancipative values over a period of at least ten years associate with changes in per capita GDP over the same period.[11] The analysis is limited to fifty societies for which longitudinal evidence of this

---

[7] Note that for a causal relationship between two changes to exist, one change does *not* need to be completed before the other. It is perfectly possible that between two contemporaneous changes one is driving the other. Sunset and temperature drop occur contemporaneously but sunset is driving the drop in temperature. In the political world, Stimson (1999) shows this for the relationship between public opinion change and policy change: they are contemporaneous, but opinion change is driving policy change more than the other way round.

[8] Since Cronbach and Furby (1970), the analyses of change scores has been discredited. But recently, a growing literature rehabilitated the analyses of change scores as reliable, valid, and essential to the understanding of dynamic relations (Liker, Augustyniak, & Duncan 1985; Allison 1990; Miller & Kane 2001).

[9] I also estimated the regression models of the following analyses using a change measure in per capita GDP that dates for each society ten years before the change measure in emancipative values. These models showed a weaker and less significant effect of change in GDP on change in emancipative values. This supports my argument that emancipative values respond instantaneously to changes in action resources.

[10] The GDP measures used to calculate change over time must be comparable over time. Thus, all GDP measures must be based on the same reference year. I chose the year 2000 as the base year.

[11] In a univariate comparison of changes in emancipative values across societies, one had to standardize changes for the different temporal distances over which they are observed. However, when we relate change in emancipative values to concomitant change in other variables whose amount of change is measured over exactly the same period as that in emancipative values, differences in temporal distance are controlled.

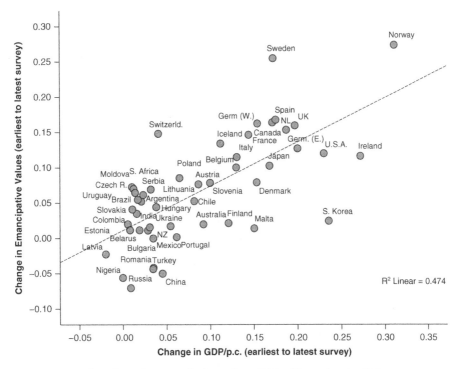

FIGURE 4.2 The Effect of Economic Growth on Rising Emancipative Values.
Data Coverage: All societies surveyed at least twice by the World Values Surveys/
European Value Study (WVS/EVS) over a temporal distance of at least ten years.
Change in the per capita gross domestic product (GDP) calculated as the difference in
real per capita GDP at constant US$ (base year 2000) from the time of the earliest to that
of the latest survey. GDP figures are indexed with 1.0 being equivalent to US$70,000.
Growth in China looks smaller than one would think because it is the growth in its
absolute per capita GDP value, not the percentage of growth. For most societies, change
covers the periods from ca. 1990 to 2000, 1995 to 2005, or 1990 to 2005. For the eleven
knowledge societies analyzed in Figure 4.1 (plus Argentina and Hungary), the temporal
coverage is ca. 1980 to 2005. Note that, unlike in a univariate analysis, differences in
temporal coverage do not need to be controlled in a bivariate analysis as long as the two
variables always cover the same temporal range for a given society.

length is available.[12] We see a clearly positive relationship between change in per
capita GDP and change in emancipative values: knowing the direction and
amount of change in per capita GDP, we can explain almost 50 percent of the
direction and amount of change in emancipative values. On average, an increase

[12] The mean length of the observation period from the earliest to the latest point in time is fifteen
years, and, for most societies, it covers the period from about 1990 to about 2005.

in per capita GDP of about 0.15 scale points over fifteen years yields an increase of 0.10 scale points in emancipative values over the same period. A 0.15 points increase in the per capita GDP index corresponds to an increase of US$ 10,000 over the entire period or US$ 670 per year.

There are two outliers: South Korea shows a smaller increase and Sweden a bigger increase in emancipative values relative to what the per capita GDP growth in these societies suggests. On the other hand, Norway shows such an extreme increase in its per capita GDP that it provides a critical case for the assumption that sizeable increases in material wealth trigger corresponding increases in emancipative values.[13] And Norway confirms this assumption, showing an increase of 0.27 scale points in emancipative values – the largest increase among all surveyed societies. By contrast, decreases in emancipative values are modest, and they are found only in a small number of societies. In each of these the growth in material wealth remains below 0.05 scale points or is negative. The latter is typical of some post-Soviet societies, including Russia, for which our observation period coincides with the transition shock. Thus, even though the relationship between growth in material wealth and rising emancipative values is by no means deterministic, it is clearly recognizable.

Apparently, there is a dynamic association between material wealth and emancipative values. Yet, before attributing causality to this association, three issues must be addressed. The first issue relates to omitted variable bias, the second to endogeneity, and the third to reciprocity.

2.2 Treating Omitted Variable Bias, Endogeneity, and Reciprocity

To begin with the first issue, we must make sure that the dynamic association is not caused by change in an omitted "third" variable that is responsible for both the change in material wealth and emancipative values. A possible candidate for such a third variable is democratization. Hadenius and Teorell (2005), for instance, suspect that emancipative values emerge in the process of democratization. These authors' arguments imply that the link between democratic institutions and emancipative values exists because institutional change drives the change in values. If this is an accurate assumption, the massive extensions of civic entitlements that accompanied the global wave of democratization account for the rise of emancipative values. Hence, the dynamic association between material wealth and emancipative values would be driven by expanding civic entitlements and vanish once we control for that. To examine this possibility, we regress change in emancipative values simultaneously on change in material wealth and on change in civic entitlements. To measure civic entitlements,

---

[13] Between 1980 and 2005, Norway's per capita GDP increased by about 0.30 scale points, corresponding to international US$21,000 at constant prices of 2000. This means an average annual increase of US$840 over this period.

I use the citizen rights index presented in the Introduction and detailed in Chapter 8.

The second issue relates to endogeneity. To interpret the dynamic association between material wealth and emancipative values as change in wealth driving concurrent change in values, we must make sure that change in wealth is not endogenous to values at the beginning of the change. In case such endogeneity is in place, change in material wealth is triggered by emancipative values present before that change. Causality would then operate in the opposite direction. To foreclose this possibility, we must include the level of emancipative values at the beginning of the change period among our predictors. In this way, we remove the endogenous variation in wealth change and isolate its exogenous part (King, Keohane, & Verba 1994; Pascarella & Wolniak 2004).[14] The same happens with change in civic entitlements: controlling for emancipative values before the change, we isolate that part in the change of civic entitlements which is exogenous to emancipative values.

When one regresses emancipative values at the end of the change period on a set of predictors, among them emancipative values at the beginning of that period, one actually explains change in emancipative values. Indeed, by including the start level of the dependent variable among the predictors of its outcome level, all other predictors estimate the outcome level of the dependent variable *insofar as it shifted away from* the start level (Pike 2004).[15] Hence, our model shows to what extent and into which direction change in material wealth and change in civic entitlements shift the resulting level of emancipative values away from the start level.

Furthermore, the lagged dependent variable carries with it any prior influence on emancipative values, including influences we are not even aware of. Because of that, including the lagged dependent variable further reduces the problem of omitted variable bias.

The third problem to be considered is reciprocity. Simultaneous change in a pair of variables does not tell us which change is driving which. This information gap is a possible source of error: we might define as the driving change what is in fact the driven one. To avoid this possible error, we must

[14] Against recent criticism by Achen (2001), Keele and Kelly (2006) defend the use of lagged dependent variables in autoregressive models as appropriate for most cases of application.

[15] Regressing the *change* in emancipative values on a set of predictors, including the start-level of emancipative values (change score model), is equivalent to regressing the *level* of emancipative at the end of the change on these predictors, again including the start-level of emancipative values (autoregressive model). This is true for the sizes, directions, and significances of the effects of all predictors, except the start-level of emancipative values: the latter has a negative effect in the change score model, reflecting an inverse stock-to-flow relation, but a positive effect in the autoregressive model, reflecting the values' temporal self-perpetuation. In both cases, coefficients of the other predictors are to be interpreted as the *shift* they yield in emancipative values from the start to the end of the observation period.

switch what we think is the driving and the driven change and estimate the model in the opposite direction as well. The goal of this estimation is to make sure that the impact flow isn't stronger in the direction opposite to our assumption.

However, this method leads to a conclusive result only if we dissolve the symmetry between the two simultaneous changes. Symmetry means that the relationship between a pair of variables looks the same in both directions of impact – unless we include additional sources of determination that possibly dissolve the symmetry. Two such sources of determination indeed dissolve the symmetry, provided the paired variables receive a different impact from these sources. These sources are *autonomous and heteronomous determination*. By autonomous determination, I mean how strongly each of the paired variables is determined by earlier manifestations of *itself*. Heteronomous determination means how strongly each of them is determined by a *third* variable. Autonomous and heteronomous determination complement the *reciprocal determination* of two paired variables. In fact, the reciprocal determination of two paired variables shrinks with increasing autonomous and heteronomous determination. The interesting point now is that the shrinkage in the reciprocal determination is more pronounced for that one of the two paired variables which is under a stronger autonomous and heteronomous influence. The reason is simple: greater autonomous and heteronomous determination of one paired variable makes this particular variable less susceptible to the reciprocal impact of the other. Hence, a system of two regressions that switches the direction of impact among a pair of variables, but includes in both directions the dependent variable's autonomous and heteronomous determination, will turn the reciprocity of the pair *asymmetric*: the variable of the pair with the stronger autonomous and heteronomous determination will show a stronger impact on its counterpart than the counterpart shows on this variable. For a given pair of reciprocal variables, this method identifies the one with the stronger impact on the other. In this way, we can distinguish the driving change from the driven one between two concurrent changes.

This is inherently logical. If, in a pair of concurrent changes, one is more determined by its own dynamic or by the dynamic of a third variable, this one drives the concurrent change with its counterpart. To model this logic, we estimate a bidirectional and dynamic system of equations that specifies each of two reciprocal variables at a later time, T_2, as a function of (a) *itself* at an earlier time T_1 to capture the *autonomous* determination; (b) *change* in a third variable from the earlier time T_1 to the later time T_2 to capture the *heteronomous* determination; and (c) *change* in the paired variable from the earlier time T_1 to the later time T_2 to capture the *reciprocal* determination.

Now, if we treat emancipative values and material wealth as the paired variables and civic entitlements as the third variable, and if we denote values as V, wealth as W, entitlements as E, the regression coefficient as b, and the error term as 3, we can write a dynamic system of reciprocal equations, as follows:

	Autonomous Determination	Heteronomous Determination	Reciprocal Determination
Eq. (1) $V(T_2) = c + b_1{}^*V(T_1) +$		$b_2{}^*\Delta E(T_2-T_1) +$	$b_3{}^*\Delta W(T_2-T_1) + 3$
Eq. (2) $W(T_2) = c + b_1{}^*W(T_1) +$		$b_2{}^*\Delta E(T_2-T_1) +$	$b_3{}^*\Delta V(T_2-T_1) + 3$

Assume that wealth is more strongly determined by its earlier presence than values are determined by their earlier presence. This would mean that $W(T_2)$ in equation (2) is more strongly determined by $W(T_1)$ than $V(T_2)$ in equation (1) is determined by $V(T_1)$. Assume further that wealth is more strongly determined by preceding change in entitlements than values are determined by preceding change in entitlements. This would mean that $W(T_2)$ in equation (2) is more strongly determined by $\Delta E(T_2-T_1)$ than $V(T_2)$ in equation (1) is determined by $\Delta E(T_2-T_1)$. From this, it would follow suit that $\Delta W(T_2-T_1)$ in equation (1) has a stronger effect on $V(T_2)$ than $\Delta V(T_2-T_1)$ in equation (2) has on $W(T_2)$. In other words, the concurrent changes in material wealth and emancipative values are *a*symmetrically reciprocal: change in material wealth drives change in emancipative values more than change in emancipative values drives change in material wealth. Such asymmetry in the reciprocal dynamic between these two variables would be seen in such a way that the b_3 coefficient in equation (1) is more significant and has more determining power than the b_3 coefficient in equation (2).[16]

2.3 Results

Table 4.1 shows what we find when we test our model empirically.[17] As is obvious, neither material wealth nor emancipative values are significantly determined by preceding change in civic entitlements. And, even though both material wealth and emancipative values are significantly determined by their prior presence, this is more strongly the case for wealth than for values: prior values explain 56 percent of their later presence whereas prior wealth explains 74 percent of its later presence. This means that wealth is more self-determined than values, which in turn implies that wealth is less susceptible to preceding change in values than values are to preceding change in wealth. Accordingly, change in values explains 28 percent of the variation in subsequent wealth, whereas change in wealth explains 48 percent of the variation in subsequent values. It looks indeed as if, in the coevolution of wealth and values, change in wealth drives values more than change in values drives wealth.

[16] The determining power is visible in the partial r^2, which is the reason why Table 4.1 displays each predictor's partial r^2 in parentheses. The partial r^2 is the squared partial correlation coefficient.

[17] Since I test a reciprocal *system* of equations rather than two separate equations, I use the procedure of seemingly unrelated regression in STATA. The logic of this method is described by Greene (2003: 378–425).

TABLE 4.1 *A Reciprocal System of Shifts in Material Wealth and Emancipative Values (seemingly unrelated regression [SUR]).*

| | DEPENDENT VARIABLE | |
PREDICTORS	Emancipative Values at T_2^a	Per capita GDP at T_2^a
Constant	0.02†	0.03†
Dependent Variable at T_1^b	0.97 (0.56)***	1.12 (0.74)***
Δ Citizen Rights, T_1 to T_2	–0.00 (0.00)†	–0.04 (0.04)†
Δ Per capita GDP, T_1 to T_2	0.65 (0.48)***	
Δ Emancipative Values, T_1 to T_2		0.60 (0.28)***
Adjusted R^2	0.72	0.89
N	49	49

Entries are unstandardized regression coefficients with partial r-squares in parentheses. Δ-variables measure change from the time of the earliest survey to the time of the latest survey, for all societies for which the temporal distance between these surveys is at least ten years. For most societies, this covers the periods from ca. 1990 to 2000, 1995 to 2005, or 1990 to 2005. For the eleven knowledge societies analyzed in Figure 4.1 (plus Argentina and Hungary), the temporal coverage is ca. 1980 to 2005. Note that, unlike in a univariate analysis, differences in temporal coverage do not need to be controlled in a multivariate analysis as long as the involved variables always cover the same temporal range *for a given society*.

The model includes each society once, so there can be no serial correlation.

Regression diagnostics for heteroskedasticity (White test), multicollinearity (variance inflation factors), and influential cases (DFFITs) reveal no violation of ordinary least squares (OLS) assumptions.

Significance levels: † $p \geq .100$, * $p < .100$, ** $p < .050$, *** $p < .005$.
[a] T_2: Time point at latest available survey
[b] T_1: Time point at earliest available survey

The second important result of Table 4.1 is that preceding change in civic entitlements does not at all affect subsequent values. This finding is at odds with the claim that emancipative values are endogenous to democratic institutions. The two partial regression plots in Figure 4.3 contrast the difference in impact that change in material wealth and change in civic entitlements have on subsequent values.

The cases illustrating the differential impact of wealth and entitlements are those in which changes in these two variables do not match. These cases are critical in testing whether emancipative values result (a) from preceding growth in wealth even when no extension of entitlements occurred, or (b) from extensions of entitlements even when no growth in wealth occurred.

All knowledge economies in our sample belong to category (a): being stable democracies, they experienced no significant extension in entitlements, but wealth did increase considerably during the observation period. Typical representatives of this group are Iceland, Germany, Japan, and the United States. Now, if emancipative values result from extensions of civic entitlements but not from growth in material wealth, there should be no increase in emancipative

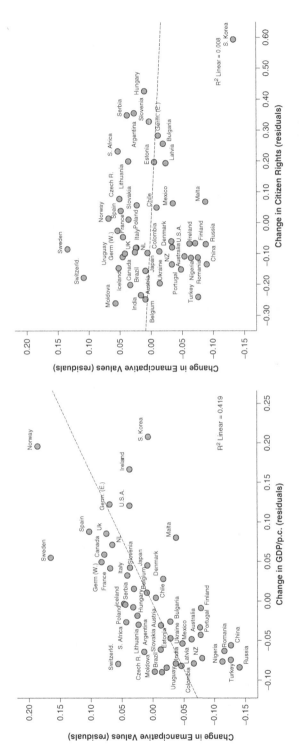

FIGURE 4.3 The Effects of Economic Growth and Rights Extensions on Rising Emancipative Values (mutually controlled).

Data Coverage: All societies surveyed at least twice by the World Values Surveys/European Value Study (WVS/EVS) over a temporal distance of at least ten years. Change period covered for most societies is ca. 1990 to 2000, 1995 to 2000, or 1990 to 2005. Note that China's negative score on the GDP change axis in the left-hand diagram does not indicate a negative growth rate in China. Instead, it indicates that China's absolute per capita GDP grew less relative to what the change in its citizen rights score suggests. This makes sense when one recognizes that China's citizen rights hardly changed (they remained stable on a very low level): most other societies with similar stability in citizen rights showed higher growth in their absolute per capita GDP than China. Thus, China's absolute per capita GDP grew somewhat less than the stability in its citizen rights suggests. This explains the slightly negative residual and confirms that, if per capita GDP grows less than what change in citizen rights suggests, then emancipative values also grow less than change in citizen rights suggests.

values in these societies. However, these societies experienced sizeable increases in emancipative values.

Conversely, there are a number of societies in which the global wave of democratization led to a profound extension of civic entitlements while material wealth did not significantly increase in our observation period. This is category (b), which is most clearly represented by post-Soviet societies, including the Baltic states, and Ukraine, and societies in sub-Saharan Africa, such as Nigeria. If emancipative values result from extensions of civic entitlements but not from growth in material wealth, there should be pronounced increases in emancipative values in these societies. Again, however, emancipative values change in unison with material wealth but not with civic entitlements: they stagnate instead of increasing in this group of societies.[18]

Could these results be artifacts of a selection bias among the fifty societies included in the analyses? Looking at the sample of societies, this seems rather implausible. The sample includes societies from all world regions, and they represent a large variety in start levels, as well as in patterns of change among our variables of interest. In addition, in each world region and culture zone, the societies with the largest populations and the biggest economies are included: France and Italy in the Old West, Germany and the United Kingdom in the Reformed West, the United States and Australia in the New West, Poland and Hungary in the Returned West, Russia and Ukraine in the Orthodox East, Turkey in the Islamic East, India in the Indic East, China and Japan in the Sinic East, Brazil and Argentina in Latin America, and Nigeria and South Africa in sub-Saharan Africa. Sampling bias is, thus, an unlikely source of these results.[19]

Admittedly, it is possible that the results are specific to the particular period under consideration here, which is mostly the 1990s and early 2000s. Thus, to establish that the patterns found here are temporally generalizable, we must extend the time perspective.

3. A LONG-TERM TEMPORAL ORDER MODEL

The previous analysis gets us closer to a causal interpretation because it shows that there is a dynamic relationship between emancipative values and its determinants – a necessary condition for a causal mechanism to be at work. However, even though the dynamic shift model focuses on the longest period under observation, this is still a relatively short and recent time span. Hence, the pattern

---

[18] The stagnation of emancipative values in post-Soviet societies might be a reason for their reversion to authoritarianism.

[19] No question, some regions (e.g., sub-Saharan Africa, Middle East) are underrepresented whereas others (e.g., Europe) are overrepresented as concerns their share among the global number of national societies. Assuming that the included societies are typical of their region, this bias can be rectified by a weighting scheme. Doing so, and using the scheme in a weighted-least squares regression, does not produce substantially different results.

we find with this model allows us little temporal generalization. This raises the question of how one could establish causality on a wider temporal basis. Here, the crucial questions are temporal order and direction of impact.

We have three elements of human empowerment – action resources, emancipative values, and civic entitlements – and they all are very closely related to each other. Whatever measures of the three elements we use, they always correlate with each other above $r = 0.75$. But correlation is not causation. To examine causality, one needs longitudinal data to see what was there before and what came thereafter. Also, our three main elements are intertwined in a reciprocal system of human empowerment. For this reason, effects can operate simultaneously in different directions. In the dynamic shift model, we focused on explaining emancipative values. Yet, in a temporal order test, we might generalize the perspective not only temporally but also in the sense that we analyze the entire system of human empowerment, looking at each of the three elements as a function of the other two. Doing so reveals if the system of human empowerment is symmetrically reciprocal (i.e., operating equally strong in each direction) or whether there are dominant directions of impact.

3.1 A Generalized Temporal Order Model

If we had sufficient longitudinal data, what we would ideally do is analyze each of the three elements of human empowerment, measured at a reference time, T_o, as a function of the other two elements, measured at an earlier time, T_{-1}. In this way, we test if a predictor element at T_{-1} has an effect on the outcome element at T_o. Yet, to see if a predictor element's effect is truly exogenous, we control it for dependence on prior measures of the outcome element. This is done by including measures of the outcome element from an even earlier time, T_{-2}, among the predictor elements. Doing so "parses out" the predictor elements' endogeneity to the outcome element (King, Keohane & Verba 1995: 251). Moreover, the inclusion of a lagged measure of the outcome element reduces the problem of omitted variable bias because the lagged measure carries with it every prior influence on the outcome element, including influences we don't know.

In other words, we test if the earlier appearance of an element *A* has an effect on the later appearance of an element *B* – independent of *A*'s determination by an even earlier appearance of *B*. Then we do the same in the opposite direction, examining if earlier *B* has an effect on later *A*, independent of *B*'s determination by even earlier *A*. If only one of these two effects is significant, we have a one-directional system of causation. If both effects are significant, we have a reciprocal system of causation. But even if the system is reciprocal, it can be asymmetrically reciprocal, with the impact flowing more strongly in one direction than in the other.

We extend this logic from two elements to the three elements of human empowerment, modeling each element as an outcome of earlier measures of the other two – taking into account the earlier elements' dependence on even earlier measures of the outcome element. So letting R, V, and E denote resources, values, and entitlements, we test the following three models:

1. $R(T_0) = c + b_1 * V(T_{-1}) + b_2 * E(T_{-1}) + b_3 * R(T_{-2}) + \varepsilon$
2. $V(T_0) = c + b_1 * R(T_{-1}) + b_2 * E(T_{-1}) + b_3 * V(T_{-2}) + \varepsilon$
3. $E(T_0) = c + b_1 * V(T_{-1}) + b_2 * R(T_{-1}) + b_3 * E(T_{-2}) + \varepsilon$

where c is a constant, b_1 to b_3 are regression coefficients, and ε is an error term.

The gray-shaded parts of the equations mark the direction of impact postulated by the sequence thesis of emancipation theory. Accordingly, resources should have a positive effect on values, and then the two together should have a positive effect on entitlements – with values having the stronger effect. Conversely, the effect of entitlements on values should be much weaker than the opposite effect – once we control for resources. In other words, in disjunction from resources, entitlements should affect values much less than the latter affect entitlements.

3.2 Proxy Measures for a Time-Pooled Cross-Sectional Database

Can we create a database to test this model on a wider temporal scope? Our preferred measure of action resources is technological advancement, yet the measure is not available before 1995. For this reason, we used per capita GDP as a surrogate, and this is good enough for the dynamic shift models just estimated – as long as we focus on more recent periods. But for times earlier than the mid-1960s, no GDP data are available on a broad country basis: the World Bank's development indicators series does not go back that far.

However, Vanhanen (2003) provides resource measures and democracy measures for all independent countries for times reaching back to 1850–60. The temporal intervals of these data are decades, from 1850–60 to 1990–2000. These are relatively large time intervals but when we deal with human empowerment, we face a glacial process that advances slowly. Thus, significant progress becomes visible only after considerable time, which justifies the use of wide time intervals. From Vanhanen's measures, we can create proxy measures for action resources and civic entitlements.

To begin with action resources, I use Vanhanen's estimates of a given society's literacy and urbanization rates. In today's world, literacy rates no longer differentiate between societies very strongly but decades ago they did. My assumption is that societies with higher literacy rates have more action resources in terms of intellectual skills. Higher rates of urbanization, for their part, indicate a denser and more differentiated population; this means greater action resources in terms of connective opportunities. To combine the two measures, I weight a society's urbanization rate by its literacy rate using multiplication. Thus, if the urbanization rate is 0.60 (60 percent) and the literacy rate is 0.50 (50 percent), the final score for the proxy of action resources is 0.50 * 0.60 = 0.30. Like Vanhanen, I use a multiplicative instead of an additive combination because I assume that intellectual and connective resources amplify rather than supplement each other. That this measure is a reasonable proxy for action resources is evident from the fact that the proxy measure for 2000 correlates with technological advancement in 2000 at $r = 0.91$ ($N = 180$; $p < .001$, two-tailed). The correlation of an additive combination of literacy and urbanization with technological advancement is more than 0.10 points lower.

As a proxy for civic entitlements, I use Vanhanen's index of democratization, standardized into a 0–1.0 scale (0 indicating no democracy, 1.0 indicating maximum democracy). The index is based on Dahl's (1973) two-dimensional definition of "polyarchy" as the interaction of (a) political inclusion/participation and (b) political competition/pluralism. Political inclusion/participation is measured as the turnout in national parliamentary elections (calculated for the adult residential population); political competition/pluralism is the seat share not captured by the largest party in parliament. After standardization, these two indices are multiplied to yield the overall index of democratization. Note that this index has the intended property that, when the participation rate is 100 percent because all voters vote whereas pluralism is zero because all votes go to one party (a situation closely approximated by societies of the former Soviet bloc), the index of democratization yields a score of 0. The multiplicative combination treats the components of participation and pluralism as necessary but insufficient conditions of democracy, as intended by Dahl's original definition.

Arguably, a high degree of both participation and pluralism requires a strong institutionalization of civic entitlements. Hence, the index of democratization is a reasonable proxy for civic entitlements at times for which a direct measure of the latter is not available. Empirically, this is obvious from the fact that the measure of civic entitlements used in the previous section correlates with Vanhanen's index of democratization in 2000 at $r = 0.88$ ($N = 170$; $p < 0.001$, two-tailed).[20]

Data for emancipative values are unavailable for any society before 1981, and even then they exist for only two dozen societies. However, the previous analyses suggest that the cohort differences in emancipative values show the footprints of value change in a society's past. Stunning in its simplicity, the basic pattern is that younger cohorts emphasize emancipative values more than do older cohorts. As Figure 2.5 has shown, this regularity is cross-culturally universal. What differs is merely how pronounced the pattern is. Because we have seen that the younger cohorts' stronger emancipative values are definitely not a lifecycle

---

[20] Another indicator of democracy with a wide temporal scope is the *democracy-autocracy index* from the Polity Project. Using this index instead of that by Vanhanen in the analyses of Table 4.2 produces the same pattern with weaker results: civic entitlements are still determined by emancipative values and action resources, and they continue to have no effect of their own on either emancipative values or action resources. The weaker pattern found with the Polity proxy echoes the validity test by Alexander and Welzel (2011). A similar result is shown at the end of Chapter 8.

phenomenon, it is certain that the cohort differences reflect generational value change. If this is true, the cohort differences provide a valid basis to estimate how much weaker a society's emancipative values have been in the past. Hence, we can estimate how much weaker a society's emancipative values have been a decade ago by calculating how much weaker these values are among the cohort born a decade before the youngest cohort. Likewise, we can estimate how much weaker the emancipative values of this society have been two, three, four, and even five decades ago by calculating how much weaker these values are among cohorts born this number of decades before the youngest cohort. Doing so, we obtain backward estimates for each society whose recent emphasis on emancipative values is known and for which the cohort differences in these values are also known. Restricting ourselves to cohorts that include at least fifty respondents per society, we can do this six decades back in time, covering the decennial sequence from 1940–1950 to 1990–2000.

Unfortunately, the world is complicated, and there are two more things to be considered. To begin with, backward estimates derived solely from cohort differences of a recent cross-section ignore that emancipative values do not only rise through the cohort succession. As Figure 4.1 has shown, emancipative values also rise through the time trend within each cohort. Neglecting the trend factor, we certainly overestimate each society's past emancipative values. In fact, we overestimate them the more, the further back in time our estimates reach because – with each decade in the past – we miss a bigger chunk of the trend. To correct this error, we must subtract from the backward estimates the average decennial increase in emancipative values, multiplied by the number of decades that the retrospection reaches back. By a rough estimate, the recent decennial increase in emancipative values within cohorts has been 0.05 scale points, on average.[21] This suggests to subtract from each retrospective estimate another 0.05 points for every decade it reaches back into the past.[22]

---

[21] Among a constant set of ten advanced postindustrial democracies, emancipative values rose by 0.05 scale points, from an average of 0.51 to an average of 0.56 in the period between 1990 and 2000. For this calculation, the ten societies are weighted to equal sample size and include Canada, France, Germany (West), Italy, Japan, the Netherlands, Norway, Sweden, the United States and the United Kingdom.

[22] There are good reasons to assume that the time trend is a more recent phenomenon, linked with the rise of knowledge economies in the postindustrial era. This suggests that the emancipatory trend picked up speed, starting from a base of zero during World War II. To model this assumption, I employ a backward deceleration factor, so that the trend decreases for each decade further back in time. If the trend started from a zero-base and then continuously approached the 0.05-point decennial increase of the recent decade, the backward deceleration factor amounts to 0.01 points for every decade back in the past. Thus, I assume a decennial increase in emancipative values of 0.05 scale points from 1990 to 2000, 0.04 points from 1980 to 1990, 0.03 points from 1970 to 1980, 0.02 points from 1960 to 1970, 0.01 points from 1950 to 1960, and 0 from 1940 to 1950. The regression results in Table 4.2 are based on estimates using this deflator. Not using the deflator produces weaker results, but the conclusions as concerns the determination pattern among the three elements of human empowerment remain the same.

The second complication is that the time trend has certainly not been uniform across all societies. Instead, societies on a higher level of emancipative values today obviously climbed to this level by a more pronounced emancipatory trend than did societies on a lower level of these values today. Hence, the recently reached level of emancipative values indicates how strong the emancipatory trend has been in this society. This allows us to calculate *specific* decennial subtraction scores for each society, rather than subtracting the same scores across the board. We calculate country-specific subtraction scores by weighting the 0.05-point subtraction score for each society's recent level of emancipative values.[23] As a result, decennial subtraction scores are larger for societies with higher levels of emancipative values today. An immediate consequence of this adjustment is that societies whose levels of emancipative values are far apart today were closer to each other in the past. This implication is intuitively plausible. Postmaterialist orientations, for instance, did not become a mass phenomenon before the late 1960s, and even this only in the most advanced postindustrial societies. Likewise, societies whose gender norms and sexual liberties appear advanced today were probably not quite as traditional as the most traditional societies of today, but they were certainly closer to them.

Figure 4.4 compares different retrospective estimates of emancipative values across culture zones. The left-hand diagram shows estimates derived solely from the cohort differences of today. The right-hand diagram shows the estimates after country-specific decennial subtractions. It is clear that, whereas the emancipative values of Western societies remain equally different from non-Western societies throughout the entire period in the left-hand diagram, they are closer to non-Western societies at the beginning of the estimation period in the right-hand diagram.[24] In addition, the right-hand diagram displays a considerably steeper increase in emancipative values in all culture zones than does an estimation based solely on the cohort pattern. For the reasons outlined earlier, I assume that the right-hand diagram reflects past cultural changes more accurately.

In summary, we derive retrospective estimates of emancipative values for a given decade by three pieces of information:

1. *Cohort differences*: we subtract from a society's recent emancipative values the difference in these values between the youngest cohort and the cohort that is born as many decades before the youngest as the number of decades the retrospective estimate reaches back.

---

[23] Western societies in which the emancipatory trend has been most pronounced have an average score in emancipative values of 0.60 scale points. I equate 0.60 with 1.0 and standardize all other scores for this value. Then I use these standardized scores as weights with which I multiply the 0.05-point decennial subtraction score.

[24] In the left-hand diagram, the least emancipative culture zone, the Islamic East, and the most emancipative culture zone, the Reformed West, are 0.35 scale points apart at the beginning of the estimation period. In the right-hand diagram, they are 0.23 scale points apart. In both diagrams, they are 0.40 scale points apart at the end of the estimation period.

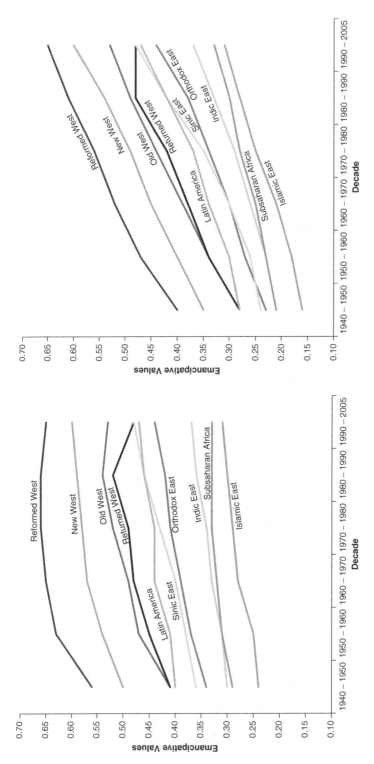

FIGURE 4.4 Culture Zone Differences in Backward Estimates of Emancipative Values (with and without trend adjustment).
Left-hand diagram displays backward estimations of emancipative values without country-specific trend adjustments; the right-hand diagram shows estimates with country-specific trend adjustments. A description of the logic of the backward estimation procedure is found in Section 3.2. A detailed documentation is provided in Appendix 4 (www.cambridge.org/welzel). The analysis includes all societies surveyed once by the World Values Surveys/European Value Study (WVS/EVS) ($N = 95$). Which society belongs to which culture zone can be seen from Table I.3 (p. 23) of the Introduction. To obtain culture zone estimates, each society is weighted to equal sample size.

2. *Decennial trend*: for further subtraction, we assume a constant score of 0.05 points for each additional decade in the past.

3. *Outcome level*: we use a given society's outcome level in emancipative levels to adjust the 0.05-point decennial subtraction score, assuming steeper trends with higher outcome levels.

Substantively speaking, this estimation procedure recognizes that emancipative values have been rising (1) by the succession of cohorts and (2) by an emancipatory trend throughout all cohorts, the steepness of which differs (3) with the outcome level of emancipative values. Appendix 4 (www.worldvaluessurvey.org/publications/) documents the technical details of this estimation procedure, together with those of alternative procedures.

Under these premises, we probe into simulation and estimate emancipative values for eighty-four countries over six decades (of all ninety-five countries surveyed once we lack cohort data for ten). This provides a data matrix of 504 country-per-decade observations. For seventy-four of the eighty-four countries, we also have the proxy measures of action resources and civic entitlements, as reported in Appendix 4 (www.cambridge.org/welzel). Theoretically, this sums up to 444 country-per-decade observations in a time-pooled cross-sectional dataset. Yet, when we introduce double-time lagged variables, we lose two decades with seventy-four countries each, leaving us with 296 country-per-decade observations. Still, not all seventy-four countries were independent in every decade from 1940 to 2000. Hence, the proxy measures of action resources and civic entitlements are not available in every decade either. In the worst situation, this leaves us with 230 country-per-decade observations. As the replication data in Appendix 4 document, the seventy-four societies included in this dataset show no sampling bias: they are from all world regions, include the largest population of each region, and cover the whole range of variation in all three variables of interest.

3.3 Findings

Using this newly created dataset, Figure 4.5 plots for each of our ten culture zones how action resources, emancipative values, and civic entitlements increase from the first decade of observation, 1940–50, to the last decade of observation, 1990–2000. It is evident that the elements of human empowerment coevolve and that progress clearly prevails in each of them: there is a long-term global trend toward human empowerment.

Figure 4.5 divides the picture according to the two mechanisms posited by the human empowerment model in Figure 1.1. The left-hand diagram shows the "utility-valuation" mechanism due to which expanding action resources give rise to emancipative values. The right-hand diagram shows the "value codification" mechanism according to which rising emancipative values lead to wider civic entitlements. In both diagrams, increases over the two dimensions are

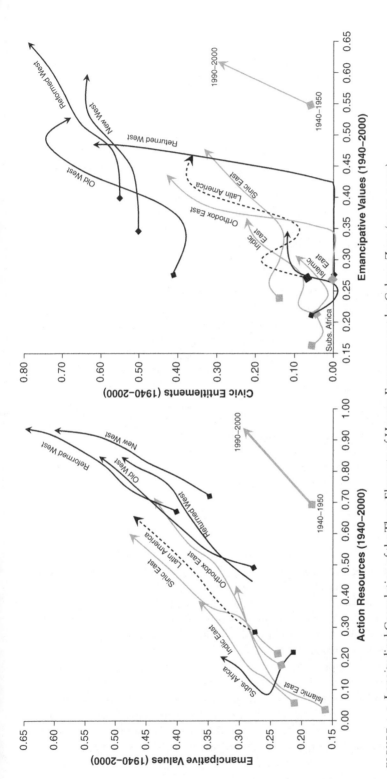

FIGURE 4.5 Longitudinal Coevolution of the Three Elements of Human Empowerment by Culture Zone (1940–2000).

Arrow tail is a culture zone's position in the decade 1940–50; arrow head is its position in the decade 1990–2000. Trace from tail to head covers decades between 1940–50 and 1990–2000 in ascending temporal order. Each culture zone's score on the three variables is the average in a given decade over the societies belonging to the respective culture zone, with each society weighted equally. Calculating culture zone averages by weighting societies for their population size produces similar results because the population-richest societies are the trend setters in their culture zone. Emancipative values for previous decades are estimated from the cohort differences in these values in the most recent survey, using society-specific trend adjustments (as detailed in Appendix 4 [www.cambridge.org/welzel]).

concomitant. In the relationship between emancipative values and civic entitlements, however, a growth in values usually precedes that in entitlements. This is evident from a pattern in which the trend lines move to the right first before a steep move upward follows. This is particularly obvious for the societies in the two ex-communist zones: the Orthodox East and the Returned West. For the latter especially, we see a build-up of emancipative values for quite some time, until the downfall of Soviet imperialism opens the gate for democratization. Once this happened, these societies' civic entitlements jumped rapidly to where rising emancipative values should have pulled them already, were it not for the overriding veto of the Red Army. What we see here is the deeper reason for the downfall of Soviet-type communism: its growing contradiction with people's values.

The right-hand diagram of Figure 4.5 discloses another historical pattern. The link between emancipative values and civic entitlements is similar in the sense that, over the short or long term, rising emancipative values bring wider civic entitlements among both Western and non-Western societies. But although the rise of emancipative values in non-Western societies is more recent and linked with steeper gains in civic entitlements, the flatter gains among Western societies unfold on a higher plateau from the start. Most likely, the West's higher plateau of civic entitlements reflects its historic imprint from emancipatory movements, especially the Enlightenment, and the early rights struggles inspired by these movements. However, at the time when Western societies began to be shaped by emancipatory gains, they used their power to deny such gains to the societies they colonized.[25] Even after the colonial period, Western societies propped up authoritarian regimes in Latin America, Africa, and Asia for a prolonged period. Hence, because of blockades erected by colonialism and neocolonialism, emancipative values in non-Western societies had to surpass a higher threshold to yield the same gains in civic entitlements as those observed in Western societies.

Incorporating this historic pattern, the three panel regressions in Table 4.2 examine the causal relationship between the three elements of human empowerment, as formalized by the model in Section 3.1. What we have at hand is a time-pooled cross-sectional dataset consisting of seventy-four societies with up to six repeated observations for each society. The repeated observations are organized decadewise, ordered from 1940–50 to 1990–2000. To handle the problem of serially correlated observations, estimations are based on panel-corrected standard errors (Beck & Katz 1995; Beck 2001).

Table 4.2 indicates that action resources at time T_0 obtain no effect from either emancipative values or civic entitlements at T_{-1}, controlling for these elements' dependence on action resources at T_{-2}. Emancipative values, however,

---

[25] The exception are the "white" settler colonies. White settlers benefitted from the same emancipatory gains, including property rights and political representation, as their sending countries' populations.

TABLE 4.2 *Long-Term Temporal Order Test among the Three Components of Human Empowerment (using proxies).*

Lagged Predictors	Dependent Variables at time T_o:		
	Action Resources[a]	Emancipative Values[b]	Civic Entitlements[c]
Action Resources at time T_{-1}		0.07 (4.17)***	0.26 (1.76)*
Emancipative Values at time T_{-1}	0.08(0.70)[†]		0.93(4.80)***
Civic Entitlements at time T_{-1}	−0.00(0.09)[†]	0.01(0.90)[†]	
Dependent Variable at time T_{-2}	0.93(29.20)***	0.89(15.60)***	0.33(1.50)[†]
Constant	0.14(3.72)***	0.08(5.90)***	−0.21(−3.40)***
Adj. R^2	0.93	0.91	0.70
N (observations)	232	260	253
N (societies)	68	74	74
N (decades)	max. 4, mean 3.4	max.4, mean 3.5	max.4, mean 3.4

Time-pooled cross-sectional regressions with panel-corrected standard errors calculated in STATA 11.2. Entries are unstandardized regression coefficients with their panel-corrected T values in parentheses.

T_{-1} is the decade preceding any given decade (T_o); T_{-2} is any decade preceding T_{-1}.

Tests for heteroskedasticity (White test), influential cases (DFFITs), and multicollinearity (variance inflation factors) reveal no violation of ordinary least squares (OLS) assumptions.

Significance levels (two-tailed): [†] $p \geq .100$, * $p < .100$, ** $p < .050$, *** $p < .005$.

Included are all societies with available measures on each of the involved variables.

[a] Analysis in this column represents equation (1) from Section 3.1. Proxy for action resources is a combined and indexed measure of a society's literacy and urbanization rates in given decade from Vanhanen (2003).

[b] Analysis in this column represents equation (2) from Section 3.1. Emancipative values in a given decade are estimated from the contemporary cohort pattern in these values with society-specific trend adjustments, as detailed in Appendix 4 (www.cambridge.org/welzel).

[c] Analysis in this column represents equation (3) from Section 3.1. Proxy measure for a society's civic entitlements in a decade is Vanhanen's index of democratization for that decade. See Vanhanen (2003).

Measurement procedures and data are documented in Appendix 4.

do obtain an independent and positive effect from action resources, although none from civic entitlements. Civic entitlements, for their part, obtain an effect from both action resources and emancipative values, but the one from emancipative values is considerably stronger.

The two partial regression plots in Figure 4.6 illustrate the differential impact of action resources and civic entitlements on emancipative values. Even though the regression coefficient for action resources on emancipative values is not particularly large, it has a very small standard error and hence explains a considerable proportion of the subsequent variation in emancipative values, namely, 45 percent. By contrast, civic entitlements account for only 7 percent

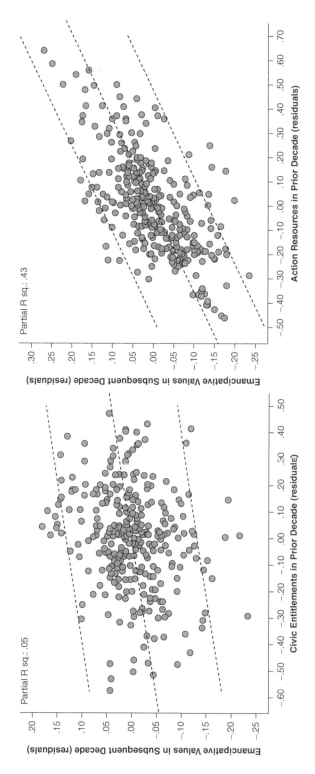

FIGURE 4.6 Partial Effects of Prior Action Resources and Civic Entitlements on Subsequent Emancipative Values (time-pooled cross-sectional regression with panel-corrected standard errors).

Data are from a time-pooled cross-sectional matrix covering seventy-four societies over six decades from 1940–1950 to 1990–2000, as described in Section 3.2 and documented for replication in Appendix 4 (www.cambridge.org/welzel). Partial plots are from a regression of emancipative values estimated for a given decade on action resources and civic entitlements of the *preceding* decade.

of the subsequent variation in emancipative values. Controlling for the temporal self-perpetuation of emancipative values, the latter effect vanishes completely.

It is noteworthy that these findings generalize the temporal pattern over the six decades under consideration: the sequence T_{-2}-T_{-1}-T_0 does not refer to any particular three-decade sequence; it extends to any three-decade sequence between 1940–50 and 1990–2000, covering more than a half century.[26] Also, it cannot be emphasized enough that, based on this simulation, the link between emancipative values and civic entitlements is one-directional, running from values to entitlements but not the other way round. The two partial regression plots in Figure 4.7 visualize this result. In the left-hand diagram, we see that earlier civic entitlements explain only an insignificant 4 percent of the variance in later emancipative values; in the opposite direction, however, earlier emancipative values explain 38 percent of the variance in later civic entitlements. Interestingly, as the quadratic fit curve indicates, emancipative values favor civic entitlements with increasing marginal returns. The liberating impulse of emancipative values becomes increasingly powerful as these values grow strong. This pattern is at odds with an influential literature that considers values as endogenous to institutions.

To demonstrate the robustness of these findings, Figure 4.8 shows what happens when we respecify the three-equation system of Table 4.2 in various ways, using "seemingly unrelated regressions" and "multiple imputations." The figure focuses on a comparison between the effects of entitlements on values in equation (2) with the effect of values on entitlements in equation (3). The technical details of these model variations are documented in Appendix 4 (www.cambridge.org/welzel) and need not concern us here. The bottom line is clear: the link between emancipative values and civic entitlements is always much stronger when we specify it as an effect of earlier values on later entitlements than when we specify it in the opposite direction.

KEY POINTS

This chapter documented the rise of emancipative values. In line with the human empowerment model, the rise is most pronounced in knowledge economies. Yet, in almost all societies with a time series of at least ten years, there is an increase in emancipative values. Moreover, the cohort pattern in all ten culture zones of the world indicates a glacial trend toward stronger emancipative values.

To test the sequence thesis of emancipation theory, we used a *dynamic shift model* for the more recent period and a *temporal order model* for more than a half-century time span to explain the rise of emancipative values. The dynamic shift model shows that the amount of increase in emancipative values is well explained by the amount of increase in a society's per capita income (an indicator of material

---

[26] There are four such three-decade sequences: (1) 1940–50, 1950–60, 1960–70; (2) 1950–60, 1960–70, 1970–80; (3) 1960–70, 1970–80, 1980–90; and (4) 1970–80, 1980–90, 1990–2000.

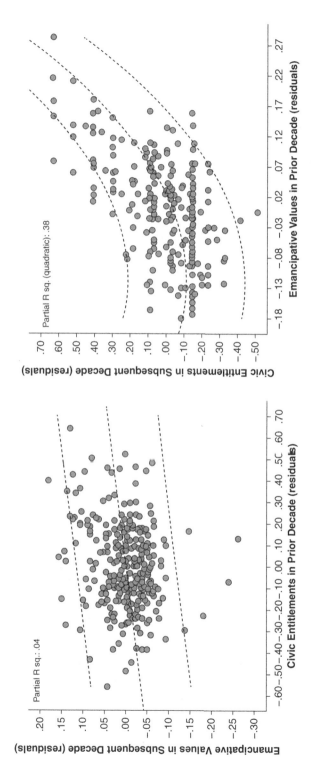

FIGURE 4.7 Asymmetry between the Reciprocal Effects of Prior Civic Entitlements on Subsequent Emancipative Values and Prior Emancipative Values on Subsequent Civic Entitlements (time-pooled cross-sectional regression with panel-corrected standard errors).

Data are from a time-pooled cross-sectional matrix covering seventy-four societies over six decades from 1940–1950 to 1990–2000, as described in Section 3.2 and documented for replication in Appendix 4 (www.cambridge.org/welzel). Partial plots are from a system of regressions in two opposite directions, one from prior entitlements to subsequent values (left-hand diagram), the other from prior values to subsequent entitlements (right-hand diagram). Both regressions control the effect of the prior input variable for its dependence on even prior variation of the outcome variable. The inclusion of this double-lagged control explains the smaller N here compared to Figure 4.6. The straight line of dots in the right-hand diagram all are ex-communist observations dating back to times when the threat of Soviet intervention shielded regimes from mass pressures that would otherwise emanate from emancipative values.

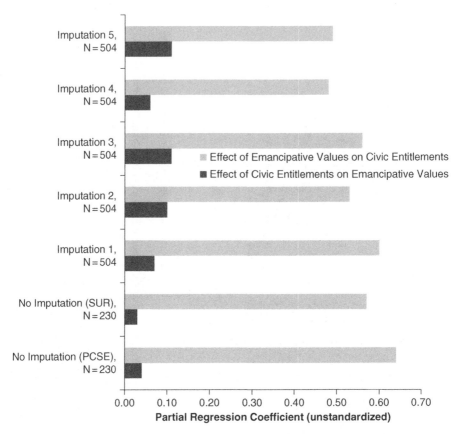

FIGURE 4.8 Comparing the Reciprocal Effects of Emancipative Values and Civic Entitlements from Alternative Specifications of the Three-Equation System in Table 4.2. Each pair of bars is from another specification of the three-equation system in Table 4.2. Basis is the time-pooled cross-sectional dataset described in Section 3.2, using proxy measures for action resources and civic entitlements, as well as backward estimates of emancipative values from eighty-four societies over six decades. The bars compare the partial effect of earlier emancipative values on later civic entitlements in equation (3) of Table 4.2 with the partial effect of earlier civic entitlements on later emancipative values in equation (2) of this table. The upper five pairs of bars are from a multiple imputation of the missing values in the original data matrix. The second lowest pair of bars is from a seemingly unrelated regression (SUR) of the three-equation system, using the original data matrix. The lowest pair of bars is from a regression analysis of the same data using panel corrected standard errors (PCSE). For technical documentation, see Appendix 4 (www.cambridge.org/welzel).

action resources and a proxy for other types of action resources). By contrast, extensions of civic entitlements contribute nothing to explaining the increase in emancipative values. This finding disconfirms the idea, repeatedly stated in the literature, that emancipative values are endogenous to democracy.

The long-term temporal order model should be interpreted with caution. It is more of a thought experiment based on informed estimates of emancipative values for past decades, not on data truly observed in these decades. However, if one considers the assumptions that inform these estimates as defensible, the conclusions are far-reaching. To begin with, there is a uniform and long-term global trend toward human empowerment in each of its three components, including emancipative values. Furthermore, when one looks at what came first and what thereafter, a clear causal pattern surfaces: action resources cause emancipative values; then action resources and emancipative values together cause civic entitlements; civic entitlements, in turn, have no effect of their own on either action resources or emancipative values.

These findings suggest that objective utilities, manifest in resources, shape subjective values, and that subjective values together with objective utilities shape legal guarantees, visible in entitlements. This is exactly the order of appearance suggested by the sequence thesis of emancipation theory, one of the three core hypotheses informing the human empowerment framework.

According to these findings, institutions that guarantee universal freedoms complete the human empowerment process but do not initiate it. This is important to note because this insight contradicts an increasingly prominent view that considers "inclusive institutions" as the cause of all development (Acemoglu & Robinson 2012).

Following these results, there is no endogenous explanation of action resources from within the system of human empowerment. Thus, to explain action resources, we need to invoke exogenous factors outside the human empowerment process itself. This part of the human empowerment story is addressed by the second key hypothesis: the source thesis. Chapter 11 deals in detail with this part of our theory,

PART B

EMANCIPATIVE VALUES AS A CIVIC FORCE

5

Intrinsic Qualities

Happiness is not something ready made. It comes from your own actions.

– Dalai Lama

The sequence thesis of emancipation theory starts from a utility assumption: freedoms have utility for humans because our intellectual powers enable us to choose a course of action for a valued purpose. However, our potential to choose an action of our liking is not always readily usable: we need to control action resources to be able to do what we would like to. Control over action resources corresponds directly with existential conditions. Pressing conditions mean that action resources are largely beyond our control; permissive conditions mean the opposite.

Freedoms always embody *potential* utility: at any time, people could take advantage of freedoms if they only had the resources needed to do what they desire. Yet, the *actual* utility of freedoms varies because people's control over action resources also varies. The persistence of freedoms' potential utility is the seed of the human quest for freedoms; variation in their actual utility is the reason why the quest adapts.

The quest for freedoms adapts through the sequence of coping mechanisms depicted in Figure 1.2 (p. 53). Since humans evolved as a cooperative species, people do not move in isolation through this sequence. Instead, the passing of the sequence is a socially embedded process in which people adjust their *shared* values to their *joint* utilities and, based on that, reach a common sense of well-being.[1] The collective passage through the adjustment sequence can stabilize societies in two opposite equlibria, as Figure 1.2 has shown. One equilibrium perpetuates

---

[1] The "common" sense of well-being is not a metaphor. Quite the contrary, when we look at distributions of life satisfaction data from the WVS, these distributions show an astounding clustering around national mean scores. The clustering indicates that each national population has indeed a common sense of well-being.

human oppression; the other one advances human empowerment. Both equlibria shape a society's entire fabric.

This chapter examines the adjustment sequence, focusing on the type of motivations and levels of well-being that become most common as entire societies pass through the sequence. We proceed in four steps. Section 1 summarizes the adjustment sequence. Section 2 translates the sequence into testable hypotheses, whereas Section 3 describes the variables and measurements used in the analyses. Section 4 reports the findings. As always, the chapter concludes with a summary of key points.

1. THE WELL-BEING–UTILITY LINK

As outlined in Chapter 1, the human mind is the product of a long process of brain evolution. Evolution shaped the mind as a utility-pursuing device. Evolution managed to do this by linking people's subjective well-being to their objective utility. Insofar as people recognize their utilities as shared, a common sense of well-being emerges. Hence, it is not just individuals but entire societies that pass through the adjustment sequence. In other words, the utility logic underlying this sequence does not only shape individual mindsets; it also shapes collective mentalities.

Linking our subjective well-being to our objective utilities keeps our lives in touch with reality. Sometimes, this link can become lost: individuals and even entire societies can get trapped in doing things that harm them. Yet time punishes the continuation of malicious practices with failure and decay, as much as it rewards beneficial practices with success and florescence (Diamond 2005). By sorting out failure and success, time drives selection. Selection operates in favor of practices that yield individual and mutual benefit (Wilson 2009). But when the two contradict each other, mutual benefit trumps individual benefit: if most individuals seek for benefit at the expense of their group, this particular group is put at a disadvantage in competition with others. Consequently, it will be subordinated or dissolve. Over the long run, then, group selection gives cooperative behavior primacy over selfish behavior (Bowles & Gintis 2011). The prevalence of cooperation over selfishness in given groups has focused human evolution on realizing *joint* rather than *unique* utilities. Accordingly, the human motivational system has been shaped in this way: our sense of well-being is tied to the pursuit of joint utilities (Kaplan, Gurven, & Lancaster 2007). The functioning of this well-being–utility link is vital to the flourishing of societies and their people. To sustain the link, individuals and groups must process the sequence of adjustment functions shown in Figure 1.2 (p. 53). Let us briefly recapitulate the stages of the sequence.

First, the human mind must recognize the utilities embodied in given circumstances, and it must value these utilities accordingly (valuation mechanism). Second, the mind must encourage action toward the realization of valued utilities (activation mechanism). Third, the mind has to obtain satisfaction from successfully realized utilities (satisficing mechanism). Fourth, this satisfaction feeds back to the start of the sequence in stabilizing the value placed on the recognized utilities (feedback mechanism). Fifth, the solidarity mechanism makes sure that the adjustment sequence does not operate in such a way that isolated individuals pursue their unique utilities so as to increase only their own well-being. Instead, we deal with group-embedded individuals who pursue jointly valued utilities in mutual cooperation, from which they obtain a common sense of well-being. Again, not only individual mindsets but whole collective mentalities take shape by passing through the adjustment sequence.

The sequence of coping mechanisms makes the human quest for freedoms adaptive to existential pressures beyond our momentary control. Depending on the presence or absence of these pressures, the adaptation can go in two opposite directions, as shown by the two ideal-typical equilibria in Figure 1.2: an equilibrium in which the pursuit of freedoms is dormant and another one in which it is vibrant.

The dormant equilibrium stabilizes human oppression; the vibrant equilibrium advances human empowerment. The source of both equlibria is control over action resources. If most people do not control basic resources of action, the median person sees little utility in freedoms. Accordingly, people place little value on freedoms and take no action to pursue them. This is evident in the weakness of emancipative values. With weak emancipative values, people's life strategy focuses on material well-being and the ascertainment of goods and income. This is an extrinsic strategy because it is driven by external necessities. In this condition, little satisfaction is obtained from pursuing freedoms, and this feeds back to people's values, reinforcing the weak emphasis on emancipative values.

If, by contrast, most people control significant action resources, they see a high utility in freedoms. Accordingly, they place more value on freedoms: emancipative values emerge. Driven by emancipative values, people refuse to be remote-controlled and instead wish to commit themselves to self-chosen goals. Self-direction encourages an intrinsic life strategy that aims at feelings of fulfillment. The priority shifts from material to emotional well-being and from life's external circumstances to its inner qualities. To follow self-chosen commitments, by necessity, implies to exercise freedoms. Hence, exercising freedoms becomes a source of satisfaction. The obtained satisfaction feeds back to people's values: it reinforces the emphasis on freedoms inherent in emancipative values. Again, people pass through this sequence not as atomized individuals but within the stream of their society in close interaction with others. Thus, people recognize *joint* utilities from *equal* freedoms, *share* the valuation of these freedoms, take *solidary* action to assert their jointly valued freedoms and obtain a *common* sense of well-being when their actions are successful.

Both extrinsic and intrinsic strategies are a source of satisfaction, if they achieve their pursued goals. Yet, the type of strategy harbors different satisfying potential. As Headey, Muffels, and Wagner (2012) point out, different strategies engage people in different types of "games," and the nature of the game offers different possibilities to satisfy its participants. Extrinsic strategies focus people's energies on material well-being. The game they play is competition for material things: it is an *acquisition game*. Because material things are "rival goods," acquisition is a zero-sum game in which what one party gains the other loses. In acquisition games, the satisfaction of one group is counterbalanced by the dissatisfaction of another group. Thus, acquisition games make collective well-being gains unlikely, if not impossible. Even for those who win, their gains may not give them a feeling of inner fulfillment. Material acquisitions can saturate our consumption needs and the need for status recognition, but they cannot generate the feeling of fulfillment – the deepest source of satisfaction for a self-aware species. Fulfillment is only achievable upon bringing our inner talents to fruition. Fulfillment is an inherently emotional reward; it is something deeply felt (Maslow 1988 [1954]).

Prioritizing fulfillment focuses people's energies on a different type of game, one that aims to bring inner talent to fruition: it is a *thriving game*. In contrast to acquisition games, thriving games are often synergetic rather than competitive. Talents complement each other and even where the same talents come together, as in an orchestra, they often cross-fertilize in achieving a common experience from which everyone benefits. True feelings of fulfillment derive from achieving something bigger than oneself, from serving a higher purpose that adds value to the lives of others. Thus, intrinsic strategies do not only yield more fulfillment for the individual but are also beneficial for the society. Part of this benefit is a stronger common sense of well-being: the benevolence involved when more people commit themselves to self-transcendent goals creates a gentler climate that elevates everyone's sense of well-being, over and above what everyone's personal situation suggests. Social cross-fertilization should be a pronounced phenomenon in this context. Intrinsic strategies need mutual recognition to come to fruition: thriving games are goodwill games, and that is a quickly exhausted moral resource if others do not return the goodwill. Behaving like an altruist in an environment of egoists quickly shows its limits (Axelrod 1986).

People are not entirely free to prioritize intrinsic over extrinsic strategies, even if they correctly calculated that the former have higher satisfying potential. To be sustainable, intrinsic strategies need a supportive social environment. Moreover, extrinsic strategies are more useful to cope with scarcity. If daily life is a struggle to get the things one needs, prioritizing the material basis of life is absolutely functional. Still, the fact remains that a higher satisfying potential resides in the emotional qualities of life. Because of this, strategies change from extrinsic to intrinsic well-being – once scarcity fades persistently.[2] In a nutshell, *extrinsic priorities prevail in a population only as long as necessary, whereas intrinsic*

---

[2] Individuals might get stuck in a once-habitualized strategy, so strategy change is easier from one generation to the next than within the life course. To test this hypothesis, we needed panel data, which are unavailable for multinational settings.

priorities begin to dominate as soon as possible. In other words, extrinsic priorities are evolutionary "programmed" as a means toward intrinsic priorities as their end. As a part of this evolutionary programming, the highly satisfying reward for intrinsic priorities anchors the quest for freedoms in the human motivational system.

2. HYPOTHESES

These considerations can be condensed into three hypotheses concerning the evolution of value priorities, life strategies, and sense of well-being:

1. *Valuation Hypothesis*: More widespread action resources give rise to more widely shared emancipative values.
2. *Activation Hypothesis*: As emancipative values become more widely shared, the dominant life strategies in a population shift from an extrinsic focus on material circumstances to an intrinsic focus on emotional qualities.
3. *Satisfaction Hypothesis*: As intrinsic life strategies become more prevalent, a strong sense of general well-being becomes more common.

Of these three sequential hypotheses, Chapter 3 already confirmed the first one. Hence, this chapter focuses on the two subsequent hypotheses. As was the case for the first hypothesis, I propose that two qualifications apply to hypothesis 2 and 3 as well. First, people pass through the hypothesized processes with the stream of their society, not as atomized individuals. Because of that, we see stronger connections among the resources, values, and strategies that people have in common than among the resources, values, and strategies that set them apart from what is most typical of their society. Second, the hypothesized sequence is not specific to Western cultures; instead, its logic is evolutionary rooted and, thus, operates culture-invariant.

3. DATA AND MEASUREMENTS

The thesis that these mechanisms operate invariantly across cultures plainly contradicts the position of cultural relativism. Advocates of this position would argue that what I suggest reflects a Western logic. Hence, this logic should be inapplicable to non-Western cultures. Indeed, two prominent theses – the *Asian values thesis* (Yew 1994) and the *clash of civilization thesis* (Huntington 1996) – imply that the emphasis on equal freedoms inherent in emancipative values is a culture-specific feature of societies with strong Western traditions. So, which point of view is true, developmental universalism or cultural relativism? To answer this question conclusively, the proposed linkages have to be tested against the strength of Western traditions. If the linkages hold against this control, they are not Western-specific but universal. If they do not hold up, they are Western-specific rather than universal.

As I argue in Chapter 2, the strength of a Western tradition is visible in the historic persistence of democracy. To measure the persistence of democracy, I use the already introduced *democracy stock index* as of 1995 (Gerring et al. 2005). The richness of a society's democratic tradition measured by this index is considered by its authors as that one aspect of democracy with the strongest impact on other social phenomena. As in previous chapters, I label the democracy stock index "democratic tradition" and interpret it as an indication of the strength of Western traditions in a society.[3]

Alternatively, I use a dummy variable indicating a society's belongingness (coded 1) or non-belongingness (coded 0) to one of the four Western culture zones described in the Introduction (see Table I.3, p. 23).

To conclude that cultural relativism is accurate, either the democratic tradition or belongingness to the West must disrupt the hypothesized effects. Specifically, the effect of emancipative values on intrinsic well-being strategies and the effect of intrinsic well-being strategies on the general sense of well-being should operate only within the confinements of a Western tradition but not beyond it, if cultural relativism is correct. In this case, the hypothesized effects must vanish or greatly diminish as we control for the democratic tradition or Western belongingness.

To measure people's sense of general well-being, I use a question on overall life satisfaction asked in World Values Surveys (WVS) variable V22.[4] The wording of this question is:

All things considered, how satisfied are you with your life as a whole these days? Using this card on which 1 means you are "completely dissatisfied" and 10 means you are "completely satisfied," where would you put your satisfaction with your life as a whole?

I normalize responses into a range from 0 for the least satisfied position to 1.0 for the most satisfied one. Anything between 1 and 10 on the original scale becomes a fraction of 1.0 after rescaling.

A huge literature suggests that general well-being is the result of various domain-specific well-beings (for overviews see Veenhoven 2000; Lykken 2000; Diener, Lucas, & Scollon 2006; Fischer & Boer 2011). Among the domain-specific well-beings, material well-being is a key domain. To measure material well-being, I use a question on financial satisfaction, asked in WVS variable V68:

How satisfied are you with the financial situation of your household? Please use this card again to help with your answer.

[3] I experimented with Dreher, Gaston, and Marten's (2008) cultural globalization index, which measures the per capita density of IKEA stores and McDonalds restaurants in a society. But this index produces weaker results than the democratic tradition index.

[4] Variable numbers mentioned here and throughout this book refer to the master questionnaire of WVS round five.

The show card displays a 1–10 scale, which I again normalize into a range from 0 for the weakest sense of material well-being to 1.0 for the strongest sense.

A different domain of general well-being is emotional well-being, that is, a sense of feeling happy. To measure emotional well-being, I use a question on happiness, asked in WVS variable V10:

Taking all things together, would you say you feel: very happy, rather happy, not very happy or not at all happy.

I rescale the answers into 0 for "not at all happy," 0.33 for "not very happy," 0.66 for "rather happy," and 1.0 for "very happy."

Life satisfaction and feeling happy are sometimes combined into an overall index of subjective well-being (Inglehart, Foa, Peterson, & Welzel 2008). But doing so blurs the distinction between the emotional subdomain of well-being (feeling happy) and the overall sense of well-being (life satisfaction). In the context of this chapter, it is important to sustain this distinction because I am interested in the different contributions that emotional and material well-being make to general well-being, under varying circumstances. The idea that these contributions vary by circumstances is supported by the fact that the correlation between happiness feelings and life satisfaction is by no means uniform across societies. On the contrary, correlations vary from a low of $r = 0.14$ in Zambia to a high of $r = 0.60$ in Greece (statistically significant in every national sample). Given that these differences might indicate culture-specific meanings of happiness, it is all the more important to examine the hypothesized effects with controls for possible Western bias.

Material well-being relates to external living conditions that are not inherent to a person. For this reason, I label material well-being as *extrinsic* well-being. Emotional well-being, by contrast, describes an inner state of mind, inherent to a person. Thus, I label emotional well-being as *intrinsic* well-being.

Examining how well people sense they are doing, both extrinsically and intrinsically, does not tell us how much these domains of well-being contribute to people's general well-being. Nor does it tell us how much emphasis people place on these different domains of well-being. Also, the WVS does not ask people directly how much their extrinsic and intrinsic well-being contribute to their general well-being.

Nevertheless, we can measure to what extent extrinsic and intrinsic well-being affect people's general well-being by estimating the proximity of these domain-specific well-beings to general well-being. In so doing, we infer the relative importance of domain-specific well-beings from their proximity to general well-being. This actually has an advantage: because respondents have not conscientiously constructed the proximity patterns in their responses, these patterns are certainly not an artifact of social desirability. This is a safe conclusion because the respective questions are scattered all over the WVS questionnaire; they are not located next to each other. Thus, we have an "implicit" psychological measure, which is known to avoid social desirability bias.

To estimate how much people's general well-being depends on their extrinsic and intrinsic well-beings, we calculate for each individual how close the extrinsic and intrinsic well-being scores are to the general well-being score. The premise is that general well-being takes shape on the basis of specific well-beings. For this reason, it is a fair assumption that the proximity of a person's general well-being to a given type of specific well-being indicates the importance of this type of specific well-being for that person's general well-being. Accordingly, one can further assume that a person prioritizes a given type of specific well-being to the extent of its importance. Thus, the proximity of a person's extrinsic and intrinsic well-beings to his or her general well-being indicates how strongly the person prioritizes these specific well-beings.[5] Having a measure of the individuals' well-being priorities, we also calculate an average societal score for each priority, estimating the prevalence of these priorities in a given society. At both the individual and societal levels, priority scores are bound between a theoretical minimum of 0 (no priority for a given strategy)[6] and a theoretical maximum of 1.0 (maximum priority for a given strategy).[7]

Based on the data and variables just described, I test the above listed hypotheses by examining global cross-cultural variation in values, strategies, and well-being at the societal and individual levels.

4. FINDINGS

4.1 The Activation Hypothesis

Table 5.1 shows two multilevel models in which the respondents' priority for intrinsic well-being is the outcome variable. I hypothesize that emancipative values strengthen the priority for intrinsic well-being in two ways: (a) within the same societies, individuals with stronger emancipative values have a stronger priority for intrinsic well-being; (b) the social prevalence of emancipative values elevates people's priority for intrinsic well-being above the level that their own emancipative values suggest.

---

[5] Extrinsic and intrinsic well-being are more specific than general well-being. Thus, it is reasonable to assume that the two specific well-beings generate the general well-being. From this, it follows that the general well-being's proximity to the specific well-beings indicates how strongly the general well-being is tied to each of them. It is equally reasonable to assume, then, that the specific well-being to which the general well-being is more closely tied is the one that people prioritize to obtain general well-being.

[6] Example: If extrinsic well-being is at its minimum 0 and general well-being at its maximum 1.0, the person's general well-being is entirely untied from her extrinsic well-being. In this case, the absolute value of the difference between the two is 1.0. But the inverse is 1 − 1 = 0, which is the priority score for the extrinsic strategy in this case, indicating no priority.

[7] Example: If extrinsic well-being is at its minimum 0 and general well-being, too, at its minimum 0, the person's general well-being is entirely tied to her extrinsic well-being. In this case, the absolute value of the difference between the two scores is 0. But the inverse is 1 − 0 = 1, which is the priority score for the extrinsic strategy in this case, indicating highest priority.

TABLE 5.1 *Multilevel Model Explaining Well-Being Priorities.*

| | DEPENDENT VARIABLE: Priority for Intrinsic Well-being | | | |
| | Model 1 | | Model 2 | |
PREDICTORS	b	S. E.	b	S. E.
• Constant	0.80***	0.00	0.80***	0.00
Societal-level Effects:				
• Western Society (dummy)	0.03*	0.01		
• Democratic Tradition			0.03†	0.02
• SV Prevalence[a]	0.09*	0.05	0.11*	0.05
• EV Prevalence[b]	0.16***	0.06	0.18**	0.06
Individual-level Effects:				
• Birth Year (indexed)	-0.00†	0.01	0.00†	0.00
• Female Sex	0.01*	0.00	0.01*	0.00
• Formal Education	0.01***	0.00	0.02***	0.00
• SV Preference[a]	0.03***	0.01	0.03***	0.01
Cross-level Interactions:				
• EV Preference[b]	0.02**	0.01	0.02**	0.01
* Western Society	0.01†	0.01		
* Democratic Tradition			0.02†	0.02
Error Reduction (%):				
– Within-societal Variance of DV	16.5		16.5	
– Between-societal Variance of DV	57.1		55.7	
N	114,274 individuals in 73 societies			

Multilevel models calculated with HLM 6.02. Entries are unstandardized regression coefficients (b) and their robust standard errors. Individual-level variables are country-mean centered. Societal-level variables are global-mean centered. Error reduction calculated as percent reduction of random variance relative to empty model.

Data cover each of the ninety-five societies with valid data surveyed at least once by the World Values Surveys/European Value Study (WVS/EVS), using the latest available survey from each society. Time coverage is ca. 1995 to 2005. National samples weighted to equal size without changing the overall N. Significance levels: $^\dagger p \geq .100$; $^* p < .100$; $^{**} p < .050$; $^{***} p < .005$.
[a]SV, Secular Values; [b]EV, Emancipative Values

Both hypotheses hold true. Among individuals within the same societies, a 1-unit increase in emancipative values comes with a 0.02-unit increase in intrinsic priorities. Even though this is indeed a very tiny contribution, it is significant and robust against controls for sex, birth year, education, and secular values. What is more, the positive contribution of emancipative values to intrinsic priorities is not moderated by either a society's democratic tradition or its belongingness to the West. This is evident from the insignificance of these two variables' interaction with an individual's emancipative values. In other words, even in societies with little democratic tradition and even in societies outside the West, stronger emancipative values involve a slight tendency toward stronger intrinsic priorities.

The impact of an individual's own emphasis on emancipative values is robust but very small. By contrast, the impact of the social prevalence of emancipative values is much larger: a 1-unit increase in the prevalence of emancipative values comes with a 0.16- or 0.18-unit increase in intrinsic priorities for all individuals within the same societies. Thus, emancipative values affect well-being strategies much more by their social prevalence than by their individual preference. In other words, for a person to prioritize intrinsic well-being, it is more important that she shares an emphasis on emancipative values with many others than that her own emphasis on these values exceeds that of most others.[8] Accordingly, the intrinsic impulse of emancipative values is a cross-fertilization product of the mutual sharing of these values. This is inherently plausible. It is difficult to freely follow the intrinsic impulse of emancipative values when one emphasizes these values in isolation. The reason is that intrinsic strategies tend to create more individuality, and individuality encounters lower tolerance when emancipative values are not widely shared. Hence, the intrinsic impulse of emancipative values needs to be widely shared to come to fruition. This finding is robust against controls for secular values, Western culture, and democratic traditions. It explains almost 60 percent of the between-societal variation in intrinsic strategies.

Figure 5.1 groups respondents from all societies surveyed by the WVS into the ten ascending categories of emancipative values introduced earlier. The vertical axis in Figure 5.1 shows the simultaneous impact of people's extrinsic and intrinsic well-beings on their general well-being, as indicated by the regression coefficients for the two types of well-being. These impacts are shown separately for people in each of the ten ascending categories of emancipative values.

Figure 5.1 reveals an extremely pronounced pattern. At a strength of emancipative values from 0 to 0.50 scale points, the impact of intrinsic well-being fluctuates around a factor of 0.30, whereas the impact of extrinsic well-being declines slightly from a factor of 0.55 to 0.50. However, at a strength of emancipative values from 0.50 to 1.0 scale points, the impact of extrinsic well-being drops sharply from a factor of 0.50 to 0.15. At the same time, the impact of intrinsic well-being increases almost as sharply, from a factor of 0.30 to 0.48. At a strength of emancipative values from 0.60 to 0.70 scale points, the effects of extrinsic and intrinsic well-being break even. In the highest of the ten categories of emancipative values, we find a complete reversal in the impact of extrinsic and intrinsic well-being compared to what we find in the lowest category. Hence,

---

[8] This conclusion is safe because individual-level variables are centered on the mean of their respective society. This eliminates all between-societal variation and reduces individual-level variables to their within-societal variation. Moreover, mean-centering is equivalent to a country-fixed effects model. These models are known to diminish omitted variable bias as concerns country-level characteristics.

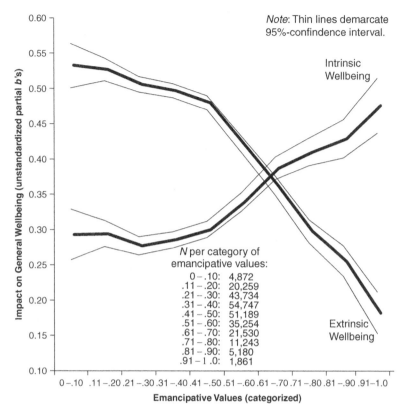

FIGURE 5.1 The Effect of Emancipative Values on Well-Being Priorities.
Data Coverage: Respondents with valid data from all societies surveyed at least once by the World Values Surveys/European Value Study (WVS/EVS), using the most recent survey. National samples are weighted to equal sample size without changing the overall *N*.

emancipative values change people's well-being strategies by strengthening their priorities for intrinsic well-being and weakening those for extrinsic well-being.[9]

4.2 The Satisfaction Hypothesis

The satisfaction hypothesis suggests that the prioritized well-being strategy affects the level of people's general well-being: supposedly, an intrinsic priority

[9] The strong evidence in Figure 5.1 does not contradict the weak individual-level effect in the multilevel models. The reason is that most people in different categories of emancipative values in Figure 5.1 are people from different societies, whereas the weak individual-level effect in the multilevel models refers to people in the same societies.

contributes more to general well-being than does an extrinsic one. The interesting question is whether the prioritized strategy affects in and of itself the general well-being level – *independent* of the strategy's success in achieving a sense of well-being in its prioritized domain. This is an important consideration because, if a strategy affects general well-being only via its success, all we need to look at is the sense of well-being achieved in a given domain. In this case, we do not need to know how strongly this domain is prioritized. To figure out whether the *priority* placed on a domain has an effect independent from the *sense* of well-being achieved in this domain, we must distinguish the two. Then we can see if the priority placed on a domain contributes to general well-being – in addition to what the achieved sense of well-being in this domain contributes. Only if such an additional contribution exists is it safe to conclude that it matters what we prioritize and not merely that we *achieve* what we prioritize. To put it simply, the question is whether indeed "the journey is the reward."

To answer this question, let's consider certain facts. To begin with, most people's sense of extrinsic well-being is relatively low, whereas their sense of intrinsic well-being is relatively high. Indeed, the global mean score in extrinsic well-being is 0.49 scale points (standard deviation [SD]: 0.29; $N = 206,516$) whereas that for intrinsic well-being is 0.67 scale points (SD: 0.25). Thus, two-thirds of all respondents from around the world have a weaker sense of extrinsic than intrinsic well-being. Also, for two-thirds of the respondents, their general well-being is closer to their extrinsic than to their intrinsic well-being. The closer proximity to extrinsic well-being indicates a greater importance of this domain for people's general well-being and, hence, a stronger priority for the extrinsic domain of well-being. Yet, since extrinsic well-being is usually low, prioritizing it ties people's general well-being to their low extrinsic well-being. Hence, prioritizing extrinsic well-being lowers people's general sense of well-being – simply because extrinsic well-being tends to be notoriously low.

Conversely, when people prioritize intrinsic well-being, this elevates their general well-being to the usually high level of intrinsic well-being. Consequently, the intrinsic priority positively affects people's general well-being: it ties general well-being to the domain in which satisfaction is apparently more readily achieved. But that tie itself is not easily made; it depends on values.

The two multilevel models in Table 5.2 demonstrate that this reasoning is right on target. The models explain people's general sense of well-being by various societal- and individual-level predictors. As societal-level predictors, I use the societies' mean sense of well-being in both the extrinsic and intrinsic domains as well as the societies' mean priorities placed on these two domains. At the individual-level, I measure in what direction and to what extent the respondents' own sense of extrinsic and intrinsic well-being deviates from their societies' mean sense of well-being in these two domains. Likewise, I measure in what direction and to what extent the respondents' own priorities for the two domains deviates from their society's mean priorities. In this way, I separate the individual- and societal-level effects of the same variable. Doing so reveals to what

TABLE 5.2 *Multilevel Model Explaining General Well-Being*

PREDICTORS	DEPENDENT VARIABLE: General Well-being Level			
	Model 1		Model 2	
	b	S. E.	*b*	S. E.
• Constant	0.62***	0.00	0.63***	0.00
Societal-level Effects:				
• Western Society (dummy)	−0.01†	0.01		
• Democratic Tradition			−0.03*	0.01
• Sense of *Extrinsic* Well-being	0.88***	0.03	0.88***	0.03
• Sense of *Intrinsic* Well-being	0.17***	0.03	0.17***	0.02
• Priority for *Extrinsic* Well-being	−0.70***	0.04	−0.69***	0.04
• Priority for *Intrinsic* Well-being	0.24***	0.04	0.22***	0.40
Individual-level Effects:				
• Birth Year (indexed)	0.00†	0.00	0.00†	0.00
• Female Sex	0.00†	0.00	0.00†	0.00
• Formal Education	0.01*	0.00	0.01*	0.00
• Sense of *Extrinsic* Well-being	0.47***	0.02	0.47***	0.02
• Sense of *Intrinsic* Well-being	0.29***	0.02	0.29***	0.02
Cross-level Interactions:				
• Priority for *Extrinsic* Well-being	−0.39***	0.02	−0.39***	0.02
* Western Society	0.08*	0.04		
* Democratic Tradition			0.14†	0.07
• Priority for *Intrinsic* Well-being	0.35***	0.02	0.35***	0.02
* Western Society	−0.02†	0.04		
* Democratic Tradition			0.08‖	0.06
Error Reduction (%):				
– Within-societal Variance of DV	56.8		54.3	
– Between-societal Variance of DV	93.8		93.8	
N	114,274 individuals in 73 societies			

Multilevel models calculated with HLM 6.02. Entries are unstandardized regression coefficients (*b*) with their robust standard error (S.E.). Individual-level variables are country-mean centered. Societal-level variables are global-mean centered. Explained variance calculated as percent reduction of random variance relative to empty model. Data cover each of the ninety-five societies with valid data surveyed at least once by the World Values Surveys/European Value Study (WVS/EVS), using the latest available survey from each society. Time coverage is ca. 1995 to 2005. National samples weighted to equal size without changing the overall *N*.
Significance levels: †$p \geq .100$; *$p < .100$; **$p < .050$; ***$p < .005$

extent a variable affects people's general well-being when a high score in the variable is socially shared, compared to when a high score is individually unique.

Inspecting the coefficients in Table 5.2, we find that if a society's average extrinsic well-being increases by 1 unit, a given person's general well-being increases by 0.88 units. The contribution of intrinsic well-being is much smaller: a 1-unit increase in the average intrinsic well-being of a society increases a given person's general well-being by 0.17 units. What is more, a 1-unit increase in a person's own extrinsic well-being translates into a 0.47-unit increase in her or his general well-being. The contribution of intrinsic well-being is again smaller: a 1-unit increase in a person's own intrinsic well-being generates a 0.29-unit increase in her or his general well-being. In combination, a 1-unit increase in extrinsic well-being for both one's society and for oneself yields 1.35 units of an increase in one's general well-being. For intrinsic well-being, the corresponding increase is 0.46 units. From this perspective, it seems as if extrinsic well-being is far more important than intrinsic well-being.

However, this calculation does not take into consideration the impact of the priority placed on these two domains of well-being. If we do take this into consideration, we receive an entirely different result. A 1-unit increase in one's society's average priority for extrinsic well-being comes with a *decrease* (!) in one's general well-being by 0.70 units, and a 1-unit increase in one's own priority for extrinsic well-being corresponds to another 0.39-unit decrease in one's general well-being. Hence, the *priority* placed on extrinsic well-being almost cancels the gain obtained from extrinsic well-being itself. In numbers, the gain of 1.35 units obtained from extrinsic well-being itself is counteracted by a 1.09-unit loss from prioritizing extrinsic well-being. This means a net gain of only 0.26 units in one's general well-being for a 1-unit gain in both sensing and prioritizing extrinsic well-being by one's society as well as by oneself. In a nutshell, people's extrinsic well-being is notoriously so low that emphasizing this domain of well-being drags down one's general wellbeing to that low level.

By contrast, a 1-unit increase in one's society's average priority for intrinsic well-being comes with a 0.24-unit increase in one's general well-being. Furthermore, a 1-unit increase in one's own priority for intrinsic well-being translates into a 0.35-unit increase in one's general well-being. Hence, the priority placed on intrinsic well-being adds to the gain obtained from the sense of intrinsic well-being. In numbers, the gain of 0.46 units from the sense of intrinsic well-being is augmented by an additional 0.59-unit gain from prioritizing this domain of well-being. This means a net gain of 1.05 units in one's general well-being for a 1-unit gain in both sensing and prioritizing intrinsic well-being by one's society as well as by oneself. In summary, the gains from intrinsic well-being outmatch those from extrinsic well-being by 1.05 to 0.26, or a factor of 4.

These estimations control for a society's democratic tradition and its belongingness to the West. Since there is no disturbance of the reported pattern by these culture-specific factors, the pattern is universal. In fact, both Western belongingness and the democratic tradition show a negligibly small effect on people's general well-being. And neither Western belongingness nor the democratic tradition moderate in any significant way the effect of people's intrinsic priorities on their general well-being. The latter is evident from the insignificant interactions of these two variables with intrinsic priorities at the individual level.

Omitted variable bias is not a problem here because Western belongingness and the democratic tradition tap a host of other fundamental differences between societies, from cultural to institutional to developmental differences: Western societies and societies with a long democratic tradition are culturally more individualistic, economically more developed and institutionally more impartial than non-Western societies and more so than societies with a shorter or no democratic tradition.[10]

Figure 5.2 visualizes the societal-level findings from the two multilevel analyses. The left-hand diagram shows the impact of emancipative values on priorities for intrinsic well-being; the right-hand diagram shows the impact of intrinsic priorities on a society's general well-being. In both diagrams, we see partial effects: these effects are obtained after we control for the overall sense of intrinsic well-being in each society. In this way, we isolate the priority for intrinsic well-being from the achieved sense of intrinsic well-being. Thus, we see that emancipative values increase the priorities for intrinsic well-being – independent of what the sense of intrinsic well-being contributes to these priorities (left-hand diagram). Likewise, we see that priorities for intrinsic well-being increase the sense of general well-being – independent of what the sense of intrinsic well-being contributes (right-hand diagram). There are a few outliers from the general pattern in both relationships. For instance, among societies with a similar sense of intrinsic well-being as the Zambians and Zimbabweans, the latter two should have much higher priorities for intrinsic well-being or much weaker emancipative values, in order to fit the pattern. Zambia is also a striking outlier from the relationship between intrinsic priorities and general well-being, together with Pakistan, Guatemala, and Malta. But these outliers are a just a few insulated cases with no obvious commonality. Hence, it is futile to speculate about the reasons for their strange locations: one reason could be cultural specificities in the understanding of the term 'happiness' but we have no solid evidence to support this conclusion. In any case, the basic point is that, by far, most societies fit the general pattern pretty well.

Our findings hold across a culturally diverse sample of societies around the world. They describe a cross-cultural pattern rather than a culture-specific one. This conclusion is safe because the multilevel models demonstrate that neither the democratic tradition nor Western belongingness alter the effect of emancipative values on well-being priorities or that of the well-being priorities on the general sense of well-being.[11] But such an alteration should exist if cultural

---

[10] The democratic tradition correlates with cultural individualism at $r = 0.56$ ($N = 50$; $p < 0.001$), with the per capita gross domestic product at $r = 0.67$ ($N = 188$; $p < 0.001$) and with rule of law at $r = 0.65$ ($N = 179$; $p < 0.001$). Western belongingness correlates with the same features, respectively, at $r = 0.45, 0.67$ and 0.66 (all significant at the 0.001-level). Data are from 1995 or 2000 and taken from the same sources as in Table 11.1 (p. 345).

[11] This is evident from the insignificant cross-level interactions in the multilevel models. Their insignificance proves that democratic tradition and Western belongingness neither moderate the effect of people's emancipative values on their intrinsic well-being priority nor that of their intrinsic well-being priority on their general sense of well-being.

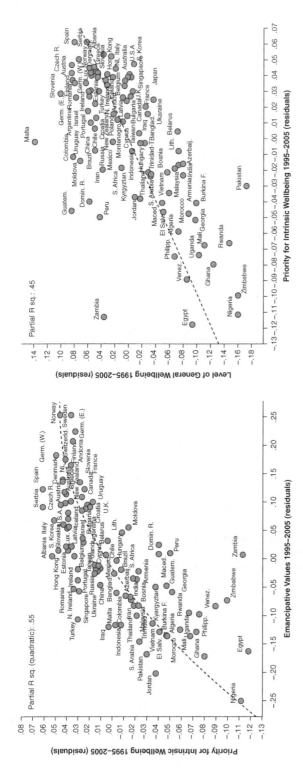

FIGURE 5.2 The Determination and Impact of Intrinsic Well-Being Priorities (controlling for levels of well-being).

Left-hand Diagram: Holding the different populations' level of intrinsic well-being constant, their average priority focuses more on intrinsic well-being when emancipative values are more prevalent. This tendency accounts for 55 percent of the cross-national variance.

Right-hand Diagram: Holding the different populations' level of intrinsic well-being constant, their average level of general well-being is higher when their average priority for intrinsic well-being is stronger. This tendency accounts for 45 percent of the cross-national variance.

Data Coverage: All ninety-five societies surveyed once by the World Values Surveys/European Value Study (WVS/EVS), using the most recent survey: data coverage period is ca. 1995 to 2005.

relativism is accurate. In fact, these effects should be systematically strengthened by Western features, even to the extent that they vanish in the absence of these features. However, this is obviously not the case. Hence, the utility ladder of freedoms indeed constitutes an evolutionary root principle that shapes human motivations in culture-invariant ways. This is an important insight because it lends credibility to the human empowerment framework's claim for universality.

KEY POINTS

This chapter tested if the utility ladder of freedoms is a root principle that shapes human motivations in the way the theory of emancipation suggests. How exactly the utility ladder of freedoms is supposed to shape human motivations has been outlined by the adjustment sequence depicted in Figure 1.2 (p. 53). Because the initial mechanism of this sequence, the valuation mechanism, has already been positively tested, this chapter focused on the two subsequent mechanisms. Of these, the activation mechanism posits that emancipative values favor intrinsic well-being priorities over extrinsic ones, shifting the focus of life from material conditions to emotional qualities. Next, the satisfaction mechanism states that intrinsic priorities yield a stronger sense of general well-being than do extrinsic priorities. Moreover, I assumed social cross-fertilization to play a strong role in this context because emancipative values and intrinsic priorities are reciprocal goods that need mutual recognition to come to fruition. Hence, I expected that emancipative values and intrinsic priorities show the hypothesized effects primarily insofar as these values and priorities are *socially shared*, and much less in as far as they are *individually unique*.

Cross-cultural, multilevel evidence from representative population samples around the world strongly confirms all of these propositions. Controls for a society's belongingness to the West and its democratic tradition provide no indication that these mechanisms are specific to Western cultures.

These findings are important because they testify to the universal behavioral relevance of emancipative values: these values change people's life priorities and, hence, most likely their life strategies as well. And emancipative values do this in the same way wherever they become widely shared. As these values spread, they encourage people to follow their own intrinsic impulses. This enhances a public's civic agency and makes it less easily remote-controlled. The intrinsic impetus of emancipative values has all kinds of consequences. Most importantly, when people begin to focus on their own impulses and encourage others to do the same, command systems in every social domain – from economics to politics to religion – lose control over people. As the following chapters will illustrate, the intrinsic impetus of emancipative values overcomes collective action dilemmas because the impetus strengthens people's motivation to voice shared concerns, to initiate and join social movement activities, and to confront power holders (see Chapter 7). By the same token, the intrinsic impetus of emancipative values questions dictatorship and authoritarian policy styles and generates legitimacy beliefs that value democracy inherently for the freedoms that define it (see Chapters 8 and 10). Last, but not least, the intrinsic impetus of emancipative values provides both a motivational driver and a moral resource for the global "rights revolution" that has empowered people in general as well as specifically disadvantaged groups, such as women and homosexuals (see Chapter 9).

6

Benign Individualism*

I believe that every human mind feels pleasure in doing good to another.

– Thomas Jefferson

Chapter 4 showed that emancipative values are on the rise throughout the postindustrial world and beyond. Furthermore, Chapter 5 illustrated that the rise of emancipative values involves profound changes in people's entire life strategy. In light of these findings, emancipative values constitute a significant phenomenon. Hence, it is important to understand the further implications of these values. Unless we do so, we miss the gist of global cultural change.

There is a heated controversy over the implications of emancipative values. The debate centers on the accurate interpretation of modernization and one of its signature features: individualization. The dispute echoes a fundamental dissent among social observers on whether individualization is in harmony or in conflict with human nature, whether individualization diminishes or advances human well-being, and whether it is a curse or a blessing for society. With their emphasis on freedom of choice and equality of opportunities, emancipative values embody the spirit of individualization: as we have seen in Chapter 2, emancipative values correlate closely with societal-level measures of individualism. Accordingly, the debate over the good and evil of individualization touches directly on emancipative values.

This chapter reviews the controversy and conducts an empirical test to resolve it using a number of new items fielded for the first time in a global cross-cultural setting in the fifth round of the World Values Surveys (WVS). The items fall into three domains, each of which allows one to separate socially *benign* orientations

* Some insights of this chapter are foreshadowed in less elaborate form in a journal article by Welzel (2010).

191

from socially *harmful* orientations. Socially benign orientations yield positive externalities because they involve a concern for the well-being of the world beyond oneself and one's in-group. Socially harmful orientations yield negative externalities because they lack such concern. I consider the former synonymous to *pro-civic* orientations and the latter to *anti-civic* orientations.

The first group of items addresses the pro-civic/anti-civic distinction by asking people how important it is to take care of other people and the environment, separating *unselfish* from *selfish* orientations. The second group of items addresses the pro-civic/anti-civic distinction by asking people how much they trust remote others, separating *trustful* from *distrustful* orientations. The third group of items addresses the pro-civic/anti-civic distinction by asking people how strongly they welcome diversity between people, separating *humanistic* from *xenophobic* orientations.

I hypothesize that emancipative values represent a benign version of individualism and that they associate for this reason with pro-civic orientations in each of these three domains.

When pro-civic individualism dominates, the nature of social capital transforms. Indeed, I argue that pro-civic individualism brings a sea change from a dominance of imposed affiliations that chain us to prefixed groups toward chosen affiliations in which we are free to connect and disconnect as we like. Hence, individualization does not erode social capital; it transforms the nature of social capital, changing it from a *captivating* into a *liberating* property (a separate treatment of this important point follows in the Conclusion, see especially Figure C.2, p. 394). This transformation is inherent to the logic of human empowerment and closely linked with the emergence of emancipative values.

To demonstrate these points, the chapter is organized into four sections. Section 1 reviews the opposing claims about individualism. Section 2 describes how we can subject the opposing claims to an empirical test. In the third section, I introduce the data and variables used to conduct the examination. Section 4 presents the findings. I conclude with a summary of key points.

1. CIVICNESS AND INDIVIDUALISM: A CONTRADICTION?

Going back to Tocqueville (1994 [1837]), one may define "civicness" as a benign mentality characterized by a concern for the well-being of the outer world beyond one's ego and in-group. Civicness in this sense includes:

1. an *unselfish* orientation toward others and the environment,
2. a *trustful* orientation that bridges group boundaries,
3. a *humanistic* orientation that welcomes people's diversity.

These mental attributes are foreshadowed in Lasswell's (1951) "democratic character" and Rokeach's (1968) "open-mind." Ever since, pro-civic orientations are considered the key psychological attribute of a thriving civil society that harbors and cultivates social capital (Almond & Verba 1963; Dahl 1973;

Putnam 1993; Verba, Schlozman, & Brady 1995; Uslaner 2002, 2004). To learn pro-civic orientations, people must overcome the protective instinct of insider-favoritism and outsider-discrimination (Popper 1971 [1962]). The dispute is whether rising emancipative values make it more or less difficult to overcome the protective instinct.

Flanagan and Lee (2003) consider it more difficult. These authors interpret emancipative values[1] as anti-civic because they equate the inherent individualism of these values with selfishness. In their eyes, emancipative values make people increasingly self-centered and diminish their concern for others. The authors claim that emancipative people "seem to be, at base, more self-serving" (263) and that emancipative values not only erode people's loyalty to the community "but also their willingness to make sacrifices for other individuals" (267). Flanagan and Lee conclude that the rise of emancipative values nurtures a "trend toward a growing politics of narrow self-interests." Echoing Putnam's (2000) thesis of declining civic engagement, the authors claim that the selfish tendency of emancipative values leads to the dissolution of social affiliations, social capital, and civil society.

Inglehart and Welzel (2005: 141–144, 293–295) interpret emancipative values in the opposite way. They, too, see emancipative values as individualistic but do not view individualism as a corrosive force. They define individualism as an orientation that sees *every* human being, first and foremost, as an autonomous person in his or her own right rather than a group member (Dumont 1986). Because this view places all humans on equal footing, it defies unbridgeable group distinctions. For this reason, individualism allows for a universal form of humanism that cuts through group boundaries and makes people more open to concern for remote and dissimilar others. Concern for others in one's immediate in-group constitutes the primordial form of collectivism. Collectivism in its primordial form has little to do with humanism: it is simply group-egoism. In contrast to collectivism, humanism involves respect and concern for others with whom there is no immediate relation. Humanism in this sense actually requires a sense of individualism. From this point of view, emancipative values are pro-civic, not despite but *because* they embody individualism.

The debate over the nature of individualism goes back to the classics of sociology (Durkheim 1988 [1893]; Toennies 1955 [1887]). To use Wellman's (1979) terms, social researchers disagreed from the beginning in their views of individualism as "community lost" (Freud 2005 [1930]; Riesman 2001 [1961]; Putnam 2000) or "community liberated" (Simmel 1984 [1908]; Florida 2002; Turner & Maryanski 2008). Flanagan and Lee's portrayal of emancipative values as anti-civic exemplifies the community-lost belief. It assumes that human beings do not use the freedoms that individualization grants them in sociable ways. The community-lost view implies a particular notion of human

---

[1] "Libertarian values" in their terminology.

nature: ordinary people are seen as lacking the capacity to regulate themselves, so they need the disciplinary force of group bonds to be kept from all kinds of unsocial behavior.

Inglehart and Welzel's depiction of emancipative values as pro-civic echoes the community-liberated argument. From this point of view, individualization emancipates: it occurs when receding existential constraints liberate people from their dependence on narrow, uniform, and closed support groups that they have not chosen. Thereby, individualization frees people to affiliate with communities as wide, diverse, and open as they like them. Individualism in this understanding bestows civic agency: the capacity to shape one's social environment in voluntary cooperation with others. Hence, individualization does not undermine society but transforms it, shifting the mode of affiliation from imposed to chosen loyalties. Toennies (1955 [1887]) described this process as a transition from community (*Gemeinschaft*) to association (*Gesellschaft*).

The debate about the true character of individualism is ongoing in psychology as well. Triandis (1995) includes self-interest in his definition of individualism, following Hofstede (2001 [1980]) who declares selfishness to be an inherent facet of individualism. Kagitcibasi (1997, 2005) and S. Schwartz (2004), by contrast, delimit the notion of individualism to autonomy and criticize the merging of autonomy and selfishness into individualism. Both authors argue that individual autonomy can be manifest in either unselfish or selfish versions and should not be reduced by definition to just one of its two possible variants. Which version prevails under what circumstances should be a matter of empirical investigation, not of axiomatic definitions.

From the viewpoint of emancipation theory, individualization is altogether an empowering process. Individualization diminishes people's dependence on support groups they have not chosen at the same time as it increases their chances to join and form groups which they prefer. Thus, individualization does not bring the end of people's tendency to connect. Instead, it brings the freedom to connect and disconnect as people choose. As a consequence, social relations, group loyalties, and collective affiliations become more of people's liking. As this happens, society gains in intrinsic value.

So far, this debate proceeds on purely theoretical ground. There is no systematic evidence as to whether emancipative values actually represent a pro-civic form of individualism that associates with unselfish, trusting, and humanistic orientations. Empirically, the "true" nature of emancipative values is an unresolved question that deserves closer examination, especially since these values are on the rise. The analyses of this chapter test how emancipative values relate to pro-civic orientations, including unselfishness, trust, and humanism. If emancipative values are anti-civic, they associate with selfishness instead of unselfishness, with distrust instead of trust, and with xenophobia instead of humanism. If emancipative values are pro-civic, they associate with these orientations in the opposite way.

2. ANALYTICAL STRATEGY

To resolve the debate about the pro-civic versus anti-civic nature of emancipative values, we examine how emancipative values associate with three manifestations of civicness: unselfishness, trust, and humanism. To achieve generalizable results, we examine these associations in a broadly cross-cultural setting with evidence taken from all over the world, using data from the fifth and most recent round of the WVS, conducted in 2005–8. I limit the analyses to this round of the WVS because this is the only one in which the WVS fields questions suited to measure unselfish orientations, generalized trust, and humanistic orientations. This leaves us with some 60,000 individuals from roughly fifty societies around the globe, as documented in Appendix 6 (www.cambridge.org/welzel). Because these fifty societies include the largest national populations from each global region and culture zone, we represent almost 80 percent of the world population. Hence, there is little reason for concern that the findings are contaminated by a bias in country selection.

We investigate the association of emancipative values with the three indications of civicness by spatial and statistical analyses, using multilevel models. The models estimate the association between emancipative values and the three indications of civicness simultaneously at the individual and societal levels and under control of additional variables. In light of the results from previous chapters, I expect the phenomenon of social cross-fertilization to apply (see Box 3.1, p. 110): the pro-civic or anti-civic impulse of an individual's emancipative values is amplified by the prevalence of these values in a given society.

3. CONCEPTS AND MEASUREMENT

3.1 Pro-Civic Orientations

3.1.1 Unselfishness

A suitable tool to measure unselfishness is a condensed, ten-item version of the *personal value instrument* by Schwartz (1992, 2004, 2007). The instrument addresses ten personal values, including *power, achievement, hedonism, stimulation, self-direction, universalism, benevolence, tradition, conformity,* and *security.*

Several studies find that these values are organized by two overarching polarities (Schwartz & Boehnke 2004; Fontaine, Poortinga, Delbeke, & Schwartz 2008). One polarity aligns the values of power and achievement against benevolence and universalism. Schwartz characterizes this polarity as a conflict between "self-enhancement" (power, achievement) and "self-transcendence" (benevolence, universalism). This characterization is plausible because power and achievement are goals that aim at improving one's own standing, whereas the goals of benevolence and universalism indicate wider concerns that transcend oneself. Accordingly, it is not far-fetched to describe this polarity as one between *selfishness* (self-enhancement) and *unselfishness* (self-transcendence). Since this is a simpler terminology, I use it here.

The second polarity aligns deference and security against self-direction and stimulation. Schwartz describes this polarity as reflecting the conflict between "embeddedness" (conformity, security) and "autonomy" (self-direction, stimulation). This is an adequate description, but one can understand this polarity also in terms of *collectivism* versus *individualism*: the goals of self-direction and stimulation emphasize the actualization of the potentials of the individual, whereas conformity and security imply deference to the norms and authority of the community. Since individualism versus collectivism is a widely known concept, I prefer this terminology.

The ten-item version of the personal value instrument is worded as follows:

"Now I will briefly describe some people. Using this card, would you please indicate for each description whether that person is very much like you, like you, somewhat like you, not like you, or not at all like you?" The response options are coded 1 to 5 from "very much like me" to "not at all like me." The items read as follows (labels in brackets are not read out):

V80 [Self-Direction]   It is important to this person to think up new ideas and be creative; to do things one's own way.

V81. [Power]   It is important to this person to be rich; to have a lot of money and expensive things.

V82. [Security]   Living in secure surroundings is important to this person; to avoid anything that might be dangerous.

V83. [Hedonism]   It is important to this person to have a good time; to "spoil" oneself.

V84. [Benevolence]   It is important to this person to help the people nearby; to care for their well-being.

V85. [Achievement]   Being very successful is important to this person; to have people recognize one's achievements.

V86. [Stimulation]   Adventure and taking risks are important to this person; to have an exciting life.

V87. [Conformity]   It is important to this person to always behave properly; to avoid doing anything people would say is wrong.

V88. [Universalism]   Looking after the environment is important to this person; to care for nature.

V89. [Tradition]   Tradition is important to this person; to follow the customs handed down by one's religion or family.

It is common to center the respondents' ratings of each of these items on the particular respondent's average rating. The resulting ratings are mean-deviation scores.[2] These scores yield larger positive numbers the higher a respondent rates a single item relative to her average rating. Analogously, scores obtain larger negative numbers the lower the respondent rates a single item relative to her

---

[2] Technically, one subtracts from each value rating the respondent's average rating over all values.

average rating. Thereby, one isolates the respondents' *value priorities*. This is important because the association-opposition structure of values refers to people's *relative* value priorities rather than to their *absolute* support and rejection levels.

In contrast to emancipative values, the personal values instrument is not based on compository logic but on dimensional logic (see Box 2.1, p. 60). This means that value combinations are not measured in the way in which a theoretical concept defines them; instead, value combinations are measured in the way in which they associate in people's mindsets. Because the personal value instrument is commonly used in this way, I continue the established practice and extract the value combinations from a dimensional analysis.[3]

The left-hand diagram in Figure 6.1 shows how the personal values group themselves when one applies a varimax-rotated two-factor solution to the mean-centered items, using the country-pooled individual-level data of WVS round five. As expected, the values group themselves in a way that reflects the two polarities between individualism versus collectivism and unselfishness versus selfishness.[4] I save scores on the individualism versus collectivism factor and the unselfishness versus selfishness factor as two separate variables for each respondent. The factor scores have a mean of 0 and standard deviation (SD) of 1.0. As with all other variables, I recode these scores into a scale range from minimum 0 for the most collectivistic and selfish position to 1.0 for the most individualistic and unselfish position. On both dimensions, a score of 0.5 describes the neutral position between the end poles.

It is possible that the dimensional pattern in the left-hand diagram of Figure 6.1 describes how personal values associate and polarize among people from different societies. It might not describe how these values associate and polarize among people from the same societies. Such an inconsistency between the dimensional patterns across and within societies would contradict the idea of estimating people's values from a single pattern. To find out whether this concern is justified, we isolate the pure within-societal variation in the personal value items and run the same factor analysis again. The result of this analysis is shown in the right-hand diagram of Figure 6.1. As this diagram illustrates, the personal values align in essentially the same way as before. There is no inconsistency between the dimensional patterns across and within societies. Hence, we can estimate people's values from a single pattern.

---

[3] Applying compository logic, I have also calculated the value combinations of individualism versus collectivism and unselfishness versus selfishness in the way the conceptual definition stipulates them. I have reestimated the following analyses with these compository indices instead of the dimensional extractions. Results are substantially the same.

[4] Tradition and hedonism do not load as strongly and not as unequivocally on the individualism versus collectivism dimension and are not included in the extraction of factor scores for this reason.

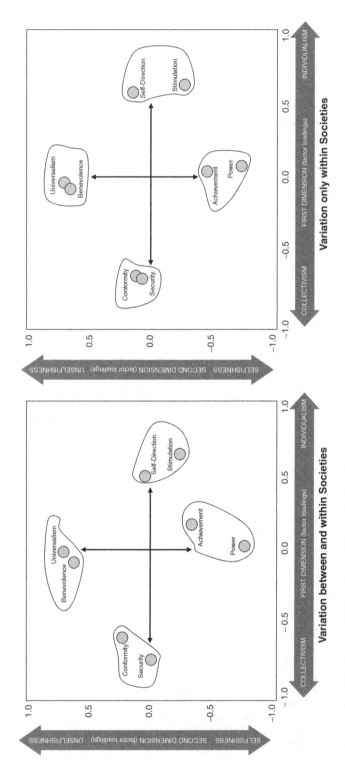

FIGURE 6.1 The Personal Value Space (dimensional analyses).

Data Coverage: 66,029 respondents from all fifty-two societies surveyed in World Values Surveys (WVS) round five (ca. 2005) with valid data on the personal value items. National samples are weighted to equal sample size without changing the overall *N*. Scores on the eight value items are centered for each respondent on his or her mean rating over all items.

3.1.2 *Trust*

Apart from unselfishness, another manifestation of civicness is trust. Trust in others is a core component of social capital – the key resource needed to overcome collective action blockades (Fukuyama 2000; Hardin 2002; Uslaner 2002). Indeed, scholars consider trust in others a psychological facilitator of the peaceful and voluntary activities that feed civil societies. Civil society, in turn, is seen in the literature as the main source of pressures to keep governments accountable and responsive (Putnam 1993; Anheier, Glasius, & Kaldor 2001; Fung 2003; Warren 2001; Bernhard & Karakoc 2007). Especially when it comes to collective actions that cut across group boundaries, scholars agree that what societies need is *generalized* trust. Generalized trust derives from trust in close others and then extends to unspecified others to eventually include even remote others (Fukuyama 1995b, 2000; Hardin 2002; Uslaner 2002). Following these rationales, generalized trust adds up over trust in close, unspecific, and remote others—but with increasing weights along this sequence, reflecting these trust objects' expanding contribution to the generality of trust.

The fifth round of the WVS includes three questions asking for trust in close people: "your family" (V125), "your neighbors" (V126), and "people you know personally" (V127). From the same battery, I take another three items to measure remote trust. The items do indeed address trust in remote people: "people you meet for the first time" (V128), "people of another religion" (V129), and "people of another nationality" (V130). For all six items, I recode the trust levels "not at all," "not very much," "somewhat," and "completely" as 0, 0.33, 0.66, and 1.0, respectively.

Located between trust in close and remote others is trust in unspecified others. Two additional questions ask for trust in people with no further specification of these people. Question V23 simply asks if "most people can be trusted" or if "one can't be too careful enough," whereas question V47 asks on a 10-point scale whether "most people would try to take advantage of you" (1) or "whether people would try to be fair" (10). I recode the first variable into a dummy with 0 for the nontrusting and 1.0 for the trusting response. The second variable is rescaled from minimum 0 for the nontrusting to maximum 1.0 for the trusting response. These two measures indicate unspecific trust.

Now that we have measures of close, unspecific, and remote trust we can add them up to measure generalized trust, using increasing weights to account for these domains' expanding contribution to the generality of trust. Thus, close trust flows into the overall measure with a weight of 1, unspecific trust with a weight of 2, and remote trust with a weight of 3. The sum of the scores is then divided by the sum of weights, which keeps the generalized trust score in a range from minimum 0 to maximum 1.0. The generalized trust variable is very fine-grained and has a mean of 0.46, an SD of 0.18, and shows an almost perfect normal distribution. Appendix 6 (www.cambridge.org/welzel) documents the details of this measurement procedure.

Note that the generalized trust measure is not a latent variable in the sense that all of its components are interchangeable parts of a single dimension. It is by no means assumed that a respondent who has close trust also has unspecific trust or that a respondent who has unspecific trust also has remote trust. In fact, I assume that these trust components are often decoupled. But this possibility is precisely the reason why generalized trust should be measured as the average over all trust domains: only respondents with high trust scores across the board should be considered as people with high generalized trust. If generalized trust is defined as the overall trust across multiple trust domains, we have to measure it that way, no matter how much the domains overlap empirically. Thus, I follow once more a compository logic of index construction (see Box 2.1).

3.1.3 Humanism

In addition to unselfish orientations and generalized trust, a third indication of civicness is a humanistic orientation. I define humanism as an orientation that resists judging people by their origin and instead welcomes human diversity (Appiah 2006). Screening the WVS questionnaire, I identify five questions that fit this definition. They measure whether and to what extent people (1) reject a similarity-centered ideal of citizenship, (2) appreciate ethnic diversity, (3) dissociate from divisive identities, (4) support helping the poor in the world, and (5) refuse to kill other people in war. As before, I construct compository indices for people's support of these themes, measuring orientations against a theoretically predefined standard, regardless of exactly how these orientations are dimensionally organized in the respondents' minds.

The question used to measure the denial of a similarity-centered ideal of citizenship is phrased as follows:

"In your opinion, how important should the following be as requirements for somebody seeking citizenship of your country? Specify for each requirement if you consider it as very important, rather important, or not important."

Respondents are confronted with four requirements. I consider the requirements "having ancestors from my own country" (V217) and "being born on my country's soil" (V218) as an indication of a similarity-centered ideal of citizenship: it requires fellow citizens to be similar by origin or culture. To measure the rejection of such an ideal, I code both items in ascending order of *rejection*, assigning scores of 0 for "very important," 0.33 for "rather important," and 1.0 for "not important" on each item.[5] Then I calculate the average score over the two items for each respondent. This procedure yields a 5-point index from minimum 0 to maximum 1.0, indicating refusal of a similarity-centered ideal of citizenship.

---

[5] The coding scheme assumes that "rather important" is closer to "very important" than to "not important."

The question used to measure the appreciation of ethnic diversity reads:

"Turning to the question of ethnic diversity, with which of the following views do you agree? Please use this scale to indicate your position: 1 "ethnic diversity erodes a country's unity," 10 "ethnic diversity enriches life."

I rescale the responses to this question into a 10-point index from 0 for the least supportive and 1.0 for the most supportive attitude toward ethnic diversity.

Another question asks respondents about their identity. Two of the statements for which respondents rate their support on a 4-point scale address identities that defy group divisions: "I see myself as a world citizen" (V210) and "I see myself as an autonomous individual." Indeed, cosmopolitanism and individualism deny rather than reify group boundaries: these are universal identities. Two other statements refer to the identification with the local community (V211) and the national community (V212). These identifications reinforce group boundaries. They are divisive for this reason. On this basis, I calculate for each respondent how strong her or his universal identities are relative to the divisive ones by subtracting the latter from the former. I standardize the difference into a scale from minimum 0 (the divisive identities completely outweigh the universal ones) to maximum 1.0 (the opposite case).

To measure how strongly people support helping the poor in the world, round five of the WVS includes the following question (V178):

"Thinking of your own country's problems, should your country's leaders give top priority to reducing poverty in the world or should they give top priority to solving your own country's problems? Use this scale where 1 means 'top priority to reducing poverty in the world' and 10 means 'top priority to solving my own country's problems.'"

I rescale the responses into a range from minimum 0, for prioritizing "solving my own country's problems," to maximum 1.0, for prioritizing "helping the poor in the world." Fractions of 1.0 indicate intermediate priorities.

Finally, the WVS asks people if they are willing fight in war for their country (V75). I code the pacifist response "no" as 1.0 and "yes" as 0.

Examining the relationship among the five measures representing (1) the rejection of similarity-centered citizenship ideals, (2) the appreciation of ethnic diversity, (3) a universal identity, (4) solidarity with the poor in the world, and (5) unwillingness to go to war, it turns out that all five measures correlate positively with each other and that each has a positive loading on a common underlying dimension.[6] Based on these findings, it would be justified to extract the overlapping variance of the five indices in a dimensional factor scale that weights each component differently for its share in the overlapping variance. However, with respect to the definition of a humanistic orientation, each of the five components is equally important, irrespective of how much variance it

[6] Analysis based on the country-pooled individual-level data: $N = 42,507$ respondents in forty societies.

shares with the other components. Hence, if we want to measure humanism in the way it is theoretically defined, compository logic is preferable. Thus, I average the five components, giving equal weight to each one (see Box 2.1, p. 60). The overall mean on this very fine-grained humanism index is 0.41 (SD = 0.16), and the index shows an almost perfect normal distribution. National mean scores on the humanism index can be any fraction of 1.0, as shown in Appendix 6 (www.cambridge.org/welzel).

3.2 Control Variables

Sociodemographic controls for birth year, biological sex, and formal education are routinely included in multivariate models. In the context of this analysis, these controls are not by themselves of much interest. They only serve as a robustness check.

Because the analyses in this chapter focus on civic orientations, it is reasonable to assume that civic entitlements favor these orientations. At least, this is plausible from an institutional learning perspective: since civic entitlements embody civic norms, they instill these norms into people who are socialized under these entitlements (Rustow 1970; Jackman & Miller 1998). Hence, civic orientations should flourish when civic entitlements are well institutionalized. Possibly, the institutional civicness effect is so powerful that not much of a civic impact is left to emancipative values. To test this possibility, I include civic entitlements in all models as a societal-level control variable. To measure civic entitlements, I use the citizen rights index used in previous chapters and described in detail in Chapter 8. I take measures averaged over the five years preceding the survey.[7]

Another variable looming prominently in any civicness study is membership in voluntary associations. The standard assumption is that membership in associations breeds civic orientations and does so at both the individual and societal levels (van Deth 2006; Paxton 2007; van der Meer, Grotenhuis, & Scheepers 2009). Again, the civicness effect might be so powerful that no civic impact is left to emancipative values, at either the individual or societal level.

At the individual level, I measure membership in associations as the sum of a respondent's memberships in organizations that operate for the benefit of the wider community, with an emphasis on active rather than passive membership. These associations are introduced with the question:

"Now I am going to read off a list of voluntary organizations. For each one, could you tell me whether you are an active member, an inactive member, or not a member of that type of organization?"

Among the listed associations, four contribute to public goods that reach beyond the well-being of just the members: "sport or recreational organizations" (V25),

---

[7] I reexamined all models using the measure of democratic traditions instead of citizen rights, but this measure generally produced weaker results as concerns the impact of institutions.

"art, music, or educational organizations" (V26), "environmental organizations" (V29), and "humanitarian or charitable organizations" (V31). For each association, I code nonmembership o, inactive membership 0.50, and active membership 1.0. I average the scores across the four types of associations. This yields a multipoint index with minimum o for no involvement in any of the four associations to 1.0 for active involvement in all four. This index construction follows a large literature that emphasizes (a) the importance of active in contrast to passive involvement and (b) the importance of associations enriching local community life and seeking public goods (van Deth 2006; Morales & Geurts 2007; Mackerle-Bixa, Meyer, & Strunk 2009).[8]

Association membership is used as a control variable at both the individual and societal levels. At the societal level, association membership measures the prevalence of associational activity in a society. As the prevalence measure, I use the national mean of the individual-level membership index.[9]

4. RESULTS

4.1 Emancipative Values Related to Individualism and Unselfishness

Figure 6.2 plots the sequence from weaker to stronger emancipative values in a space with individualism versus collectivism as the horizontal dimension and unselfishness versus selfishness as the vertical dimension.[10] Respondents in each of the ten categories of emancipative values are plotted with their mean scores in individualism versus collectivism and unselfishness versus selfishness.

As is evident, the sequence from weaker to stronger emancipative values associates with a sequence from collectivism to individualism, as expected. However, the association is much weaker in the lower categories of emancipative values, from EV01 to EV05, than in the upper categories, from EV06 to EV10. In other words, variation in the deficiency of emancipative values makes less of a difference than variation in their prevalence. As regards unselfishness versus selfishness, there is less differentiation across the different categories of emancipative values than there is in individualism versus collectivism. And again, from EV01 to EV05, the differentiation is much weaker than from EV06 to EV10. Hence, the individualistic-unselfish impulse of emancipative values surfaces more strongly when people cross the midpoint into the upper half of the scale: this is the threshold dividing deficient from prevalent emancipative values.

---

[8] I used various alternative summaries of association membership. None of these showed stronger civicness effects than the one chosen here.

[9] Using percentages of respondents per society being active or a just a member in one, two, three, or all four of the covered associations shows in none of the models stronger civicness effects than using national mean scores.

[10] The 1 standard deviation circle in Figure 6.2 depicts the average size of the area within which one finds two-thirds of the respondents of a given category of emancipative values.

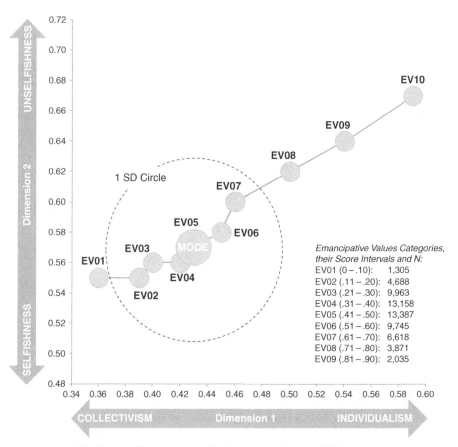

FIGURE 6.2 The Trace of Emancipative Values in the Personal Value Space.
Data Coverage: Respondents with valid data from all fifty-two societies surveyed in World Values Surveys (WVS) round five (ca. 2005). National samples are weighted to equal sample size.

This pattern already contradicts the anti-civic interpretation of emancipative values. Advocates of this interpretation claim that too strong an emphasis on emancipative values favors selfishness: this suggests that emancipative values associate with selfishness *particularly* at high levels of these values. The evidence, however, shows the exact opposite.

With respect to unselfish orientations, Figure 6.3 illustrates the combined effects of individual preferences for emancipative values and these values' social prevalence. To make the combined effects visible, we look at the individual-level effect of emancipative values separately for societies with a different prevalence of these values. To simplify things, I collapse prevalences of emancipative values

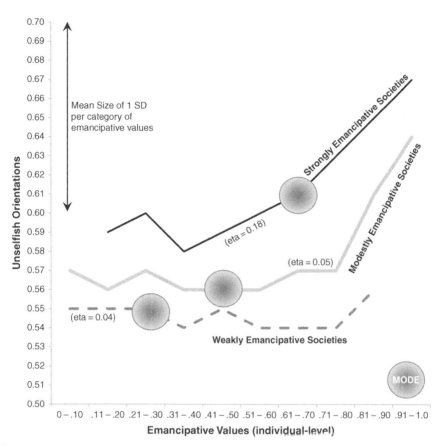

FIGURE 6.3 Multilevel Effects of Emancipative Values on Unselfish Orientations.
Data Coverage: Respondents with valid data from all fifty-two societies surveyed in World Values Surveys (WVS) round five (ca. 2005). National samples are weighted to equal sample size (N = 1,000 per society). Number of observations: weakly emancipative societies (EVI score below 0.37) – 17,000 respondents from seventeen societies (Burkina Faso, China, Egypt, Ghana, India, Indonesia, Iran, Iraq, Jordan, Mali, Morocco, Russia, Rwanda, Thailand, Turkey, Ukraine, Vietnam); moderately emancipative societies (EVI score between 0.37 and 0.48) – 15,000 respondents from fifteen societies (Brazil, Bulgaria, Chile, Colombia, Cyprus, Malaysia, Mexico, Moldova, Poland, Romania, South Africa, South Korea, Thailand, Trinidad-Tobago, Zambia); strongly emancipative societies (EVI score above 0.48) – 20,000 respondents from twenty societies (Andorra, Argentina, Australia, Canada, Finland, France, Germany (East), Germany (West), Italy, Japan, Netherlands, Norway, Serbia, Slovenia, Spain, Sweden, Switzerland, United Kingdom, United States, Uruguay).

into three broad categories, as shown in Appendix 6 (www.cambridge.org/welzel). The first category, labeled "*weakly* emancipative societies," covers societies in which the prevalence of emancipative values is in a range from 0.23 to 0.37 scale points. The second category, "*moderately* emancipative societies," includes societies with a prevalence of emancipative values from 0.38 to 0.47 scale points. Strongly emancipative societies are those with a prevalence of emancipative values from 0.48 to 0.73 scale points. These cut-off points are chosen empirically so that each category covers about an equal number of individuals and societies.

Using this classification, Figure 6.3 depicts separately for weakly, moderately, and strongly emancipative societies how the emancipative values of individuals relate to unselfish orientations. In weakly emancipative societies, the sequence from weak to strong emancipative values is a flat line on the unselfishness dimension. In other words, there is no relationship between emancipative values and unselfishness in weakly emancipative societies. Already, this finding is in contradiction with the anti-civic interpretation of emancipative values, which suggests a *negative* relationship of these values with unselfishness. In moderately emancipative societies, there is no relationship between emancipative values and unselfishness from categories EV02 to EV06, but from EV07 to EV10 the relationship turns sharply positive, leading to a recognizable net gain in unselfishness in EV10. In strongly emancipative societies, the relationship between emancipative values and unselfishness is strongly positive over most of the scale range of emancipative values. Hence, the social prevalence of emancipative values unleashes and amplifies the unselfish impulse of an individual's preference for these values.

Moreover, the prevalence of emancipative values elevates people's unselfishness above the level that their own preference for these values suggests. This is evident from the fact that, among respondents who place the same emphasis on emancipative values, the level of unselfishness is higher when emancipative values are more prevalent in the surrounding society. Thus, when emancipative values are more widespread, every person is more unselfish, irrespective of his or her own preference for emancipative values.

Table 6.1 employs multilevel analyses to test the statistical robustness of the spatial analysis. The left-hand model in Table 6.1 examines the effect of emancipative values on individualism, the right-hand model examines their effect on unselfishness, using various controls.[11] Under societal-level effects, we see whether and in what direction the social prevalence of emancipative values affects a society's mean levels of individualism and unselfishness. As is obvious from both models, and in line with what we have seen from the spatial analyses, more prevalent emancipative values raise a society's mean levels of individualism

---

[11] To stay consistent with the use of 0–1.0 indices, the factor score variables for individualism versus collectivism and unselfishness versus selfishness are standardized into this scale range, with the maximum of 1.0 representing the individualism and unselfishness poles.

TABLE 6.1 *Effects of Emancipative Values on Individualism and Unselfishness (multilevel models).*

PREDICTORS	DEPENDENT VARIABLES	
	Individualism (multipoint scale from 0 to 1.0)	Unselfishness (multipoint scale from 0 to 1.0)
• Constant	0.46***	0.56***
Societal-level Effects:		
• EV-Prevalence[a]	0.22 (5.40)***	0.12 (3.58)***
• Association Membership	0.13 (3.61)***	N. S.
• Civic Entitlements	−0.03 (−2.23)*	0.04 (1.85)*
Individual-level Effects:		
• Female Sex	−0.03 (−13.68)***	0.02 (12.44)***
• Birth Year (indexed)	0.11 (12.32)***	−0.14 (−17.50)***
• Formal Education	0.02 (6.46)***	0.01 (2.23)*
•Association Membership	0.05 (6.34)***	0.02 (4.45)***
Cross-level Interactions:		
•EV-Preference[a]	0.13 (13.87)***	0.03 (3.56)***
* EV-Prevalence[a]	0.47 (4.98)***	0.61 (2.36)**
* Association Membership (society level)	N. S.	N. S.
* Civic Entitlements	N. S.	0.10 (3.19)**
Reduction of Error:		
Within-societal Variation of DV	10.5%	06.0%
Between-societal Variation of DV	56.3%	48.6%
Variation in Effect of EV[a]	48.7%	50.6%
N (number of observations)	61,429 individuals in 49 societies	

Entries are unstandardized regression coefficients (*b*'s) with T ratios in parentheses based on robust standard errors. Individual-level variables are country-mean centered. Societal-level variables are global-mean centered. Hierarchical linear models calculated with HLM 6.01. Eighty-two percent of the total variance in unselfishness versus selfishness is within-societal variation, 18 percent is between-societal variation. Reduction of error calculated from change in random variance component relative to empty model.

Data cover all respondents with valid data from all fifty-two societies surveyed in the World Values Surveys (WVS) round five (ca. 2005). National samples are weighted to equal size without changing the overall N.

Significance levels: *p < .100; **p < .050; ***p < .005; N.S. not significant (p > .100).
[a]EV, Emancipative Values

and unselfishness. The effects are about equally strong: a 1-unit increase in the prevalence of emancipative values elevates individualism and unselfishness by about 0.22 units each.

Some societal-level characteristics might absorb the individualistic and unselfish effects of prevalent emancipative values. These characteristics include a society's overall membership in associations and its civic entitlements. Yet the effects of prevalent emancipative values hold up when we control for a society's association membership and its civic entitlements. More than that, emancipative values trump the effects of association membership and civic entitlements. The latter are hardly significant after controlling for emancipative values.

Under individual-level effects, we find that a respondent's preference for emancipative values also affects his or her individualism and unselfishness, and it does so in the same direction as does the social prevalence of emancipative values. In other words, respondents who prefer emancipative values more strongly tend to be more individualistic and unselfish. In numbers, a 1-unit increase in a respondent's emancipative values elevates her individualism by a 0.13-unit and her unselfishness by a 0.03-unit. These contributions, and the latter one in particular, are tiny, and they are at any rate much smaller than what the prevalence of emancipative values contributes to people's individualism and unselfishness. What is more, for both individualism and unselfishness, the effect of a respondent's preference for emancipative values is amplified by the prevalence of these values in the respective society. This is obvious from the positive interactions between individual preferences for emancipative values and their social prevalence.

In explaining individualism, other variables add to the effect of emancipative values. This is true for association membership at both the societal and individual levels. At both levels, association membership brings a significant shift toward individualism, not collectivism. This might be surprising when one thinks of association membership as a collective experience. From this point of view, one would expect association membership to favor collectivism rather than individualism. However, we know from a large body of research that participation both requires and fosters a sense of agency, self-efficacy, and personality strength (Sniderman 1975; Verba, Nye, & Kim 1978; Verba, Schlozman, & Brady 1995). Since these states of mind are elements of individualism, it is not so surprising to find that association membership strengthens individualism rather than collectivism. Moreover, if we interpret collectivism as group egoism, this finding tells us that membership in public goods-seeking associations operates against group egoism. At any rate, individualism is not as antisocial, as often suggested.

Formal education also strengthens individualism, whereas older people and women tend on average to be less individualistic than younger people and men. The sex difference is negligible, however, with women being 0.03 scale points less individualistic than men. The sex difference probably reflects the fact that women are, in every society, more insecure than men and, for this reason, depend more on in-group protection.

Later birth, by contrast, results in a stronger individualistic orientation. Since birth year is standardized into a 0–1.0 scale, with birth in 1900 set at minimum 0 and birth in 1990 at maximum 1.0, the coefficient of 0.11 for birth year means that a person born in 1990 is 0.11 scale points more individualistic than someone born in 1900, holding everything else equal. Chapter 4 showed a similar age pattern for emancipative values. And we have seen that the age pattern reflects a cohort effect rather than a lifecycle effect: younger people are not more emancipatory because people get less emancipatory as they age; instead, younger people are more emancipatory because of an intergenerational rise of emancipative values. Against this backdrop, the strong link of individualism with emancipative values suggests that, in the case of individualism, too, the age pattern reflects a cohort effect rather than a lifecycle effect. Supposedly, there is an intergenerational rise of individualism.

In relation to unselfishness, emancipative values are the only variable with a highly significant effect at the societal level. At the individual level, female sex continues to show a negligible effect and birth year a moderate effect, but both switch signs. Holding other things equal, female sex contributes slightly to unselfishness: women are, on average, 0.02 scale points more unselfish than men. This might reflect the fact that women are in literally every society socialized into care-taking roles, which should leave an unselfish imprint on women (Chafetz 1988; Hakim 2003). Alternatively, the stronger unselfish orientation of women might be the result of a naturally evolved "femininity" principle that makes women more solidarity-oriented (Sidanius, Pratto, & Bobo 1994; Sidanius, Levin, Lin, & Pratto 2000).

Later birth shows a modest *negative* effect on unselfishness: holding everything else equal, a person born in 1990 is 0.14 scale points more selfish than someone born in 1900. Contrary to the pattern found for individualism, this is probably not a cohort effect. A cohort effect here would mean that there is an intergenerational decline of unselfishness. But this possibility is incompatible with the intergenerational rise of emancipative values and the fact that these values favor unselfishness. Hence, the age pattern in the case of unselfishness is more likely the result of a lifecycle effect: people become more unselfish as they age. This is indeed plausible. Older people have usually found themselves and their place in society; hence, they tend to be less obsessed with the effort of personal profiling. However, until we have a longer time-series with the personal value instrument, we cannot prove this interpretation. For now, it remains a matter of theoretical plausibility.

In any case, these findings suggest that, when emancipative values rise, people tend to become more rather than less unselfish. This result confirms the pro-civic interpretation of emancipative values on the first testing ground. So let's move to the next one.

4.2 Emancipative Values Related to Trust and Humanism

Figures 6.4 and 6.5 illuminate the combined individual- and societal-level effects of emancipative values on generalized trust (Figure 6.4) and on humanistic orientations (Figure 6.5). The individual-level effects can be seen from the slopes of the trend lines, which are increasing from respondents with weaker to those with stronger emancipative values – except for people in weakly emancipative societies when it comes to generalized trust. The societal-level effects can be seen in the different levels of the trend lines: the levels elevate as emancipative values are more prevalent. At least this is always true as we move to strongly emancipative societies. Interactions between the societal- and individual-level effects of emancipative values can be seen in the different slopes of the trend lines: they become steeper as emancipative values become more prevalent – again, especially as we move to strongly emancipative societies. This shows that the trusting and humanistic impulses of people's own emancipative values amplify as these values become more prevalent in the societies surrounding people. These elevator and amplifier effects evidence once more the phenomenon of social cross-fertilization: the impulses residing in an individual preference for emancipative values are fertilized and brought to fruition by the social prevalence of these values (see Box 3.1, p. 110).

The multilevel models in Table 6.2 confirm the findings of the spatial analyses. We find that both individual preferences for emancipative values and these values' social prevalence increase trust as well as humanism. For both trust and humanism, the individual preference for emancipative values has a weaker effect than the social prevalence of these values. For instance, a 1-unit increase in the social prevalence of emancipative values brings a 0.35-unit increase in trust, whereas a 1-unit increase in the individual preference for emancipative values brings only a 0.13-unit increase in trust. Likewise, a 1-unit increase in the social prevalence of emancipative values comes with a 0.58-unit increase in humanism, whereas a 1-unit increase in the individual preference for emancipative values only yields a 0.15-unit increase in humanism. Emancipative values affect trust and humanism more by their social prevalence than by individual preferences. In addition, the social prevalence of emancipative values amplifies the trust and humanism effects of an individual preference for these values: a 1-unit increase in the product of the social prevalence and individual preference yields an extra 0.48-unit increase in trust and an extra 0.75-unit increase in humanism.

These findings underscore the cross-fertilizing role of emancipative values. It is the *socially shared* emphasis more than the *individually unique* emphasis on these values that unleashes their civic impulses.[12] Again, this pattern confirms the social dimension of emancipation theory, with its emphasis on joint utilities and shared values.

---

[12] This is a safe conclusion because, at the individual level, scores on the emancipative values index are societal-mean centered, measuring each individual's deviation from his or her society's mean score. In this way, we separate the individually unique from the socially shared emphasis on emancipative values.

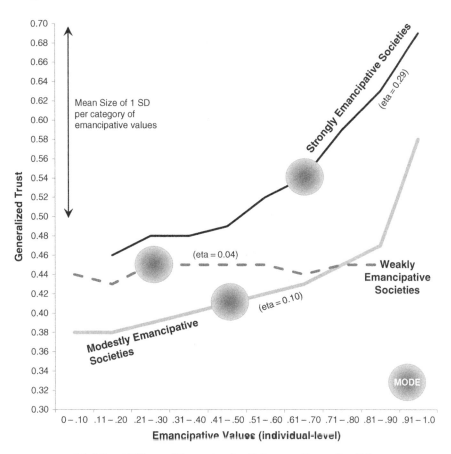

FIGURE 6.4 Multilevel Effects of Emancipative Values on Generalized Trust.
Data Coverage: Same as Figure 6.3.

Looking at the control variables in Table 6.2, female sex, birth year, formal education, association membership, and civic entitlements also affect either trust or humanism or both, yet none of these variables exceeds the civicness effects of emancipative values. In the case of association membership and civic entitlements, this is especially noteworthy because much of the literature declares them the strongest sources of civicness. Yet, the civic benefits of emancipative values are more impressive.[13]

---

[13] As a sidenote, the societal-level effects of emancipative values on unselfishness, trust, and humanism are not rendered insignificant or absorbed by technological advancement or some other indicator of economic development. This is shown in the supplementary analyses of Appendix 6 (www.cambridge.org/welzel).

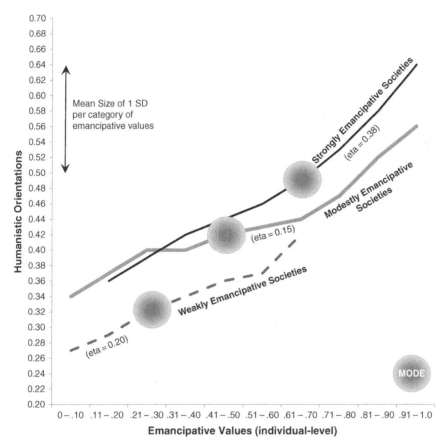

FIGURE 6.5 Multilevel Effects of Emancipative Values on Humanistic Orientations. *Data Coverage*: Same as Figure 6.3.

KEY POINTS

The evidence presented in this chapter confirms the pro-civic nature of emancipative values. Emancipative values unambiguously favor generalized trust and humanistic orientations. With respect to unselfishness, the pattern is more complicated but, even here, it is evident that emancipative values increase rather than decrease unselfishness. The latter is true in a double sense: first, the societal-level relation between emancipative values and unselfishness is strongly positive; second, the individual-level relation between the two turns from a nonexisting one into a pronouncedly positive relation as emancipative values become more prevalent in a society.

TABLE 6.2 *Effects of Emancipative Values on Trust and Humanism (multilevel models).*

PREDICTORS	DEPENDENT VARIABLES	
	Generalized Trust (12-point scale)	Humanistic Orientations (multipoint scale)
•Constant	0.47 (48.55)***	0.41 (67.60)***
Societal-level Effects:		
• EV-Prevalence[a]	0.35 (2.02)**	0.58 (6.28)***
• Association Membership	0.21 (1.83)*	N. S.
• Civic Entitlements	N. S.	N. S.
Individual-level Effects:		
• Female Sex	−0.01 (−1.97)*	0.02 (7.26)***
• Birth Year (indexed)	−0.10 (−9.79)***	N. S.
• Formal Education	0.05 (5.84)***	0.04 (5.63)***
• Association Membership	0.05 (6.08)***	N. S.
Cross-level Interactions:		
• EV-Preference[a]	0.13 (10.23)***	0.15 (11.73)***
* EV-Prevalence[a]	0.48 (2.74)***	0.75 (4.78)**
* Association Membership (societal level)	−0.41 (−2.27)**	N. S.
* Civic Entitlements	.11 (2.13)**	N. S.
N (number of observations)	56,471 individuals in 49 societies	40,476 individuals in 41 societies
Reduction of Error:		
Within-societal Variation of DV	05.0%	07.0%
Between-societal Variation of DV	33.9%	73.3%
Variation in Effect of EV[a]	47.0%	53.2%

Entries are unstandardized regression coefficients (b's) with T ratios in parentheses based on robust standard errors. Individual-level variables (except sex) are country-mean centered. Societal-level variables are global-mean centered. Hierarchical linear models calculated with HLM 6.01. Reduction of error calculated from change in random variance component relative to empty model.

Data cover all respondents with valid data from all fifty-two societies surveyed in the World Values Surveys (WVS) round five (ca. 2005). National samples are weighted to equal size without changing the overall N.

Significance levels: *p < .100; **p < .050; ***p < .005; N. S. not significant (p > .100).
[a] EV, Emancipative Values

The relationship of emancipative values with pro-civic orientations follows, once again, the logic of social cross-fertilization. At the individual level, we see that significant civic impulses reside in emancipative values. But these impulses remain weak if they receive no social confirmation because emancipative values are not widely shared. The civic impulses residing in emancipative values are a reciprocal good: to be unlocked, they need mutual recognition through a widely shared inspiration from emancipatory ideals.

Emancipative values are closely linked with individualism, yet they tie individualism to pro-social orientations. These values proliferate a benign form of individualism. Egocentric forms of individualism may also exist, but this is not what emancipative values measure. Quite the contrary, the civic productivity of emancipative values qualifies them as a powerful source of social capital. Indeed, the evidence suggests that emancipative values constitute a moral resource that infuses a civic force into modern society. On the basis of this, one would expect that emancipative values vitalize civil society in that they generate more collective action and social movement activity. The next chapter explores these expectations in detail.

7

Collective Action[*]

If you have right on your side, you have no fear.

– Nonviolent female protestor in Egypt

Throughout most of history, ordinary people did not play an active role in politics. They lacked the resources as well as the values that one needs to voice claims. Apart from short-lived revolts here and there, politics was entirely an elite game. The idea that institutions would be tailored to the demands of the people and that people would take action to enforce their own claims was implausible for most of the time. The onset of modernity, however, brought a game change. Rising levels of prosperity, literacy, and connectivity among wider population segments reshape mass publics, making their members both capable and willing to voice claims and to take action on their behalf. Where this happens, societies are infused with civic agency.

The first signs of this sea change surfaced with the liberal revolutions of the seventeenth and eighteenth centuries (Markoff 1996; Grayling 2007; Tilly & Wood 2009). Ever since, we see that, in place after place, social movements rise to campaign for the rights of the people (Clark 2009; Carter 2012). In mature democracies, social movements have become a constant source of influence on government, keeping elected officials under permanent pressure (Tarrow 1998; McAdam, Tarrow, & Tilly 2003; Meyer 2004; Kriesi 2009; Keane 2009). In new democracies, social movements have frequently mobilized people against the predemocratic regime, often so powerfully that the pressure was decisive in triggering transitions to democracy (Foweraker & Landman 1997; Karatnicky & Ackerman 2005; Schock 2005; Ulfelder 2005; Welzel 2007a; Teorell 2010). Furthermore, social movement activities around the world turned

---

[*] Some insights of this chapter are foreshadowed in a less elaborate way and with much less emphasis on their theoretical relevance in a journal article by Welzel and Deutsch (2011).

increasingly less violent over recent decades and became more successful this way in achieving emancipatory goals (Chenoweth & Cunningham 2013). This observation resonates with the key finding of this chapter: rising emancipative values indeed motivate nonviolent social movement activities.

Since the beginning of cross-national survey programs in the 1970s, scholars note an expansion of social movement activities (SMAs) that confront power holders with claims from their citizenry (Barnes & Kaase et al. 1979; Norris 2002; Dalton 2004; Inglehart & Welzel 2005). SMAs are mostly and increasingly unarmed and include such events as strikes, boycotts, demonstrations, blockades, sit-ins, petitions, and other joint acts of voicing claims (Tarrow 1998; Schock 2005; Carter 2012; Chenoweth & Cunningham 2013).

Where nonviolent SMAs are widespread and frequent, we find vital civil societies in which people exert civic agency in shaping their societies' agendas. Hence, SMAs are a major manifestation of human empowerment; they are of inherent interest precisely because of that. This chapter argues that the connection of SMAs to human empowerment is evident in these activities' strongest inspirational force: emancipative values. Indeed, I hypothesize that both individual preferences for emancipative values and the social prevalence of these values encourage SMAs.

When joint acts of voicing claims are frequent, this is testimony to a public whose members find raising their voice valuable. To value the voicing of claims is in and of itself an emancipative value. Thus, a connection of SMAs to emancipative values seems self-evident. This chapter theorizes and analyzes this connection.

Usually, people make claims because they want to overcome grievances. Thus, the deprivation literature considers the occurrence of SMAs an indication of grievance (Gurr 1970; Muller 1979; Opp 1990, 1994). In the explanation of collective violence, this approach has a point indeed. However, the SMAs I refer to differ in kind from violent collective action because they are peaceful. To focus on nonviolent SMAs is adequate for three reasons. First, SMAs have turned more nonviolent around the globe in recent decades (Schock 2013). Second, nonviolent SMAs have proven to be more successful in achieving emancipatory goals, from democratic institutions to gender equality to same sex marriage (Chenoweth & Cunningham 2013). Third, precisely these achievements place nonviolent SMAs right into the center of interest of the theory of emancipation.

Interestingly, SMAs are most typical of flourishing societies. In fact, there is a strong positive correlation between literally every quality-of-life indicator, be it material prosperity, life expectancy, years of schooling, measures of "good governance," or subjective well-being, and the incidence of nonviolent SMAs (Welzel, Inglehart, & Deutsch 2005). One might conclude that people raise their voice the most where they have the least to criticize.

The same conclusion seems to apply within societies as well. If we examine who participates in SMAs, it is usually not the most deprived groups. No doubt, some members of disadvantaged groups, such as ghetto-dwelling immigrants, have joined urban riots and other spontaneous outbreaks of collective violence from time to time (Snow, Vliegenhart, & Corrigall-Brown 2007). But they are not the main recruitment pool for peaceful acts of voicing claims. These acts belong to the repertoire of the educated, the informed, the connected, and the relatively well-off (Inglehart 1990; Norris 2002). Again, it seems as if those people raise their voice the most who have the least to criticize.

When one sees the voicing of claims as the outcome of deprivation, this pattern is paradoxical. But when one views the voicing of claims as a sign of empowering conditions that enable and motivate people to raise their voice, there is no paradox in the positive relationship between SMAs and thriving societies. This chapter examines this relationship, focusing on a particular element that has been largely overlooked: the impact of emancipative values on SMAs.

Section 1 discusses the relationship between emancipative values and SMAs in theory and outlines the study design to examine this relationship empirically. Section 2 describes the database and measurements used to execute the study design. Section 3 reports the findings, demonstrating in what direction and to what extent emancipative values shape SMAs at individual and societal levels. Special emphasis is placed on the dynamic relationship that takes into account change in values and actions over time. I conclude with a summary of key points.

1. THEORY: VALUES AND ACTION

1.1 Values, Norms, and Interests

People's actions are partly intentional, and values constitute a central element in people's intentions. Values are consequential in that they guide people's actions toward valued goals (Triandis 1995; S. Schwartz 2004). When we focus on *collective* actions, the guiding power resides in *shared* values that are held by wider segments of society.

Shared values are not the only guide of collective action. Social norms and group interests also drive collective action. Yet, compared to norms and interests, values are a particularly powerful motivator of action. Let me elaborate.

Social norms guide action via external sanctions. In the absence of external sanctions, norms lose their power to guide actions. The exception is when people have internalized the norm. But then the norm has become a value and is no longer merely a norm. To perpetuate a norm's guiding power in the absence of sanctions, the norm needs to become a value (Lal 1998).

In contrast to norms, values are internalized ideals that define people's intrinsic preference structure. For this reason, values do not need external sanctions to guide actions. Values are the basis of people's capacity for self-regulation. Thereby, values are a moral resource from which societies can profit.

Legal regulations, for instance, involve lower monitoring costs when people's values commit them voluntarily to a legal norm (Axelrod 1986; Coleman 1990).

In addition to social norms and shared values, group interests also guide collective action. Still, in comparison to interests as well, values carry a motivational advantage. The advantage carries as long as interests remain primarily instrumental. Group interests always originate in an instrumental purpose: the specific group's standing relative to rival groups. The problem lies precisely in the instrumental origin of group interests: instrumentality ties acts to voice the group interest to cost-benefit calculations about an act's likely success in serving the interest. The bigger the group, the more members calculate that their contribution to the group's success is insignificant (Olsen 1987 [1965]). Hence, most members of a group abstain from action to voice the group's interest. If the group in question does not have a powerful organization, its interest will not be taken care of in this case. Hence, collective actions that depend on cost-benefit calculations among large numbers of individuals are regularly blocked (Coleman 1990; Ostrom 1990).

It is illuminating to think about the circumstances under which group interests overcome this motivational block. For this to happen, the interest's instrumentality must fade. The interest must eventually become an inherent part of people's social identity, in which case voicing the interest obtains *intrinsic* value. In other words, embedding interests in identities bestows intrinsic value on their expression, which unties collective actions from cost-benefit calculations. Hence, we are back to the original point: to overcome the motivational blocks of norms and interests, one needs to anchor them as values in people's intrinsic preference system.

Values are constitutive elements of our personal identities. For this reason, the expression of our valued goals in our actions becomes an end in itself – irrespective of the action's success in achieving the valued goal. Exhibiting one's values through one's actions fulfills an identity-building purpose that gives value-guided action an expressive utility. Because of their expressive utility, values are less vulnerable to collective action blockades.

Based on these considerations, I conclude that the intentional drive of SMAs is rooted more strongly in intrinsic values than in extrinsic norms or in instrumental interests. Among the values that potentially drive SMAs, I consider emancipative values of paramount importance. This is true for two reasons. First, SMAs have throughout history been most powerful when they voiced emancipatory claims, especially claims for the entitlement of disadvantaged groups (Markoff 1996; Foweraker & Landman 1997; Tarrow 1998; Clark 2009; Carter 2012). This suggests that emancipative values are the chief motivational source of the most vigorous SMAs. Second, independent of the specific claim that is voiced, the mere fact that people take things into their own hands and voice a joint claim is already in and by itself an act of emancipation. By its very nature, such an act should be more appealing to people who have already internalized emancipative values.

1.2 The Value-Action Link

If the link between emancipative values and SMAs exists in the way I suppose, it is a lethal link that dictators must avoid at all costs. Because emancipative values aim at entitlements that dictators deny, these values delegitimize dictatorship when they emerge in a dictatorial system. When SMAs claim emancipatory goals under dictatorial rule, this already signals that the regime has lost control over the society. Indeed, SMAs with emancipatory goals have frequently terminated dictatorship and triggered successful transitions to democracy (Schock 2005; Ulfelder 2005; Thompson 2004; Welzel 2007a). Examples range from Portugal in 1974 to Argentina in 1983 to South Korea in 1987 to Czechoslovakia in 1989 to Tunisia in 2011.

Dictators can apply two strategies to disrupt the link between emancipative values and SMAs: ideological propaganda and increasing levels of repression. Yet, either strategy works only as long as the engine of the human empowerment process – the expansion of people's action resources – does not ignite. It goes without question that dictatorships put considerable effort into propaganda. The purpose of these efforts is to prevent the emergence of desires that long for the entitlements that the regime denies. Therefore, every dictatorial regime will try to discourage emancipative values. But propaganda has its limits. As far as I can see, dictators have not been able to eradicate the utility ladder of freedoms: they have not been able to prevent people from longing for emancipatory gains when an increase in action resources enhances the utility of such gains. This is obvious from the analysis in Chapter 4. As this analysis shows, deficiencies in civic entitlements do not suppress emancipative values, if people's action resources have been growing. The denial of entitlements and the propaganda justifying this denial do not prevent people from valuing emancipation, once increased action resources bestow utility on emancipatory goals.

The second strategy of dictators to disrupt the value-action link is to increase the risk of engaging in SMAs. This is done by sustaining a credible threat of repression. I hypothesize, however, that – once emancipative values are widely shared – repression does not discourage people's participation in SMAs. Peripheral preferences with little intrinsic value are easily discouraged from action. But this is different for values because they are intrinsic. Intrinsic values inspire people with a sense of what is morally just, and a sense of justice bestows utility on expression. For emancipative values, the expressive utility is even higher because expressing one's values through action is itself an emancipatory act. Emancipatory goals thus embody an expressive utility of exceptional strength. And when these utilities are widely shared, the solidarity effect often overcomes the fear of repression. Hence, I suggest that increasing repressive threats does not discourage SMAs once emancipative values are widely shared. As we will see, the true reason why repression seems to discourage SMAs is that whenever SMAs are rare, emancipative values are weak.

One could make a case that SMAs in democratic and nondemocratic societies are two different species because, in nondemocratic societies, these actions involve a much higher risk of punishment and are often directed against the incumbent regime. In democracies, by contrast, SMAs are protected by law, and regime change is almost never their claim. From this point of view, one might conclude that SMAs should be studied separately in democratic and nondemocratic societies. I, however, argue that it is better to examine SMAs simultaneously across societies at different levels of democracy while taking into account these differences as a potential determinant of SMAs. This is preferable under the assumption that emancipative values motivate SMAs in both democratic and nondemocratic systems. If they emerge in nondemocracies, emancipative values motivate SMAs with a claim for civic entitlements that the regime denies. If they grow strong in democracies, emancipative values motivate SMAs with claims for better practice, further extension, and stronger substantiation of civic entitlements. Thus, emancipative values motivate SMAs with a focus on entitlements in *any* type of system in which these values become prevalent. These suggestions involve the further assumption that the value-action link between emancipative values and SMAs is *not* disrupted by deficiencies in democracy. To test this assumption, the link must be examined across societies at all levels of democracy while including the level of democracy among the predictor variables.

Translating emancipative values into SMAs requires many things. One is a network of activists with the skills and resources to initiate mass campaigns. Yet, activists have it easier in a public in which emancipative values are relatively widespread. For one, appeals to raise the people's voice resonate strongly with emancipative values. Moreover, since we know that emancipative values grow strong among people with significant action resources, people with these values are not only eager but also capable of taking action. In addition, activists themselves are more numerous in a public with stronger motivation and ability. Quite plausibly, a society of capable and motivated people provides a fertile breeding ground for SMAs.

For all these reasons, I assume that emancipative values are the chief inspirational source of SMAs. I hypothesize that individuals with emancipative values have a stronger tendency to initiate and join SMAs, yet this tendency is more pronounced in societies in which more people share emancipative values: the expressive impulse inherent in people's own emancipative values is reinforced when these values are more prevalent – a case of social cross-fertilization (see Box 3.1, p. 110).

Before we move on to review recent findings in the study of SMAs, a qualification is due. It is well understood that each single SMA is a unique phenomenon, specific to the circumstances of a particular place and time. This unquestionable fact might suggest to study SMAs from an event-history perspective. The typical question in this perspective is to ask why a particular SMA occurred at a certain place and time. But this approach has its blind side. Instead of asking why people participate in a particular SMA at a particular place and time, an equally relevant question asks why people in some societies *generally* participate more in SMAs, regardless of space and time. From an event-history perspective, the first question is more interesting, but this book is written from an evolutionary perspective. From this point of view, the second question is more interesting: why do some people generally participate more in SMAs, irrespective of occasion, place, and time? And why do some societies have more of these people so that their *chronic* level of SMAs is higher? To answer this type of question, we must search for systematic factors that transcend the specificities of each single SMA. The following review focuses only on studies that are inspired by this type of question.

1.3 The Standard Model of SMAs

Few studies of SMAs test rival theories on a broad basis of cross-national evidence.[1] Even fewer studies do so using a multilevel approach to examine how individual-level traits and societal-level conditions simultaneously shape people's actions. Among the exceptions is a study by Dalton, van Sickle, and Weldon in 2010 (henceforth: DVW). Thus far, the DVW study provides the broadest analyses of SMAs, using survey data from round four of the World Values Surveys (WVS) with a coverage of some fifty societies worldwide.

DVW specify a human empowerment model of SMAs. The model shows how individual- and societal-level manifestations of empowerment strengthen SMAs. However, from the perspective of human empowerment, the DVW model is incomplete in a central aspect.

Out of the three components of human empowerment – resources, values, entitlements – the DVW model specifies only two at the societal level, ignoring the value component at this level. In light of what we have seen so far, this is a drawback. The previous chapters provide ample evidence that emancipative values are not only important as an attribute of individuals. What matters more is *how prevalent* these values are throughout a population. The phenomenon of social cross-fertilization that we encountered repeatedly in previous chapters supports this point powerfully. Thus, ignoring how the prevalence of emancipative values motivates SMAs necessarily overestimates the effects of other components of human empowerment, namely resources and entitlements.

For these reasons, I reexamine the DVW model of SMAs. After presenting the data and measurements, I proceed in four steps. First, I extend the DVW model to new data from the fifth and most recent round of the WVS. This shows whether their results are replicable with a different sample of societies from a later point in time. The replication indeed confirms the results of the DVW model. Second, I modify the DVW model by including the prevalence of emancipative values as an additional predictor of SMAs at the societal level. Doing so

---

[1] The exceptions include Roller and Wessels (1996), Welzel (1999), Norris (2002: chapter 10), Inglehart and Catterberg (2003), Inglehart and Welzel (2005: chapter 9).

not only produces stronger results but also alters the findings in an important point: among the three components of human empowerment, values are most important in fueling SMAs. Third, I test the robustness of the value-action link against the entire set of societies covered by the WVS, examining whether inflicting higher risks of repression weakens the link. As we will see, this is not the case: if emancipative values are widespread, they translate into SMAs even under high risks of repression. Fourth, I enter new ground in modeling change in SMAs as a function of change in emancipative values, looking at dynamic effects that allow for a causal interpretation. As will become obvious, there is a truly dynamic relationship between values and actions, such that a rise in emancipative values motivates a corresponding increase in SMAs, holding other things constant.

2. DATA AND MEASUREMENTS

2.1 Data

Replicating what has been found for a particular set of societies over a specific period of time with new data is important to strengthen confidence in previous results. DVW test their model using round four of the WVS, which was conducted in about fifty societies between 1999 and 2001. Round five of the WVS was fielded between 2005 and 2008 in about fifty societies as well, but twenty of these were not included in round four, providing a considerably different country sample.[2] After replication of the DVW model with WVS round five data, I modify the model and test it against the entire set of societies covered by the WVS, using the most recent survey from each society. The approximately ninety societies included in this analysis represent almost 90 percent of the world population. In the final step, I change the perspective from cross-sectional to longitudinal evidence, looking at patterns of concurrent change in emancipative values and SMAs. This part of the study limits the evidence base to about fifty societies for which a sufficient time span of at least ten years is covered. But even this smaller sample covers societies from all ten culture zones in the world, including the population-richest society from each world region. Furthermore, the societies represent the full range of variation in all variables of interest. Thus, it is unlikely that the findings of this chapter are due to selection bias.

2.2 The Dependent Variable: Peaceful SMAs

The analysis of SMAs on the basis of survey data does not aim at explaining why people join a specific SMA with a specific goal at a particular time and place.

---

[2] Societies covered in round five but not round four of the WVS include Andorra, Australia, Brazil, Burkina Faso, Colombia, Cyprus, Ghana, Guatemala, Iraq, Malaysia, Mali, New Zealand, Norway, Rwanda, Switzerland, Taiwan, Thailand, Trinidad and Tobago, and Zambia.

Survey-based research of SMAs is not interested in the particularities of single SMAs. Instead, the aim is to explain patterns that transcend the specificities of each SMA. The main questions of interest are why certain types of SMAs become part of people's *action repertoires* and why the repertoires of entire populations expand. From the human empowerment perspective, the interesting feature of action repertoires is their permanent availability: repertoires can be activated for various goals at various times. Thus, action repertoires transcend the particularities of location and time; they are an empowering feature for precisely this reason.

DVW examine a 6-point index that measures in how many out of five SMAs a respondent says that he or she has participated. These activities include: "signing petitions," "joining in boycotts," "attending peaceful demonstrations," "joining unofficial strikes," and "occupying buildings or factories."[3] DVW (p. 62) report positive, fairly strong and highly significant correlations between country-level measures of these self-reported SMAs and observational data on actual SMAs.

The WVS neither asks for the specific goal behind the SMA in question, nor for a particular time when such an activity has been undertaken. For the measurement of action repertoires, this is an advantage. How recently a respondent undertook an action and for what purpose does not matter when the issue is whether or not the action is part of a respondent's repertoire. For the repertoire, it only matters whether people have once acted in the way in question or at least intended such action. When this is the case, the action in question is part of a given person's repertoire. In the case of a reported intention to act, the action is at least part of people's *imagined* repertoire – an important precondition for the action to become part of the *practiced* repertoire. When the action is in the repertoire, people can choose it at will for varying purposes at various times.

Slightly deviating from DVW, I use the SMA index introduced by Welzel (2010). The deviation is unavoidable because round five of the WVS cancelled the two most unpopular actions, "joining unofficial strikes" and "occupying buildings or factories," from the questionnaire. This leaves us with three SMAs: "signing petitions," "joining in boycotts," and "attending peaceful demonstrations."[4]

---

[3] These items are introduced in the WVS by asking "Now I'd like you to look at this card. I'm going to read out some forms of political action that people can take, and I'd like you to tell me, for each one, whether you have done any of these things, whether you might do it, or would never under any circumstances do it."

[4] In round five of the WVS, two half-split versions of the questionnaire have been fielded. In Ballot A, the wording has been changed from "lawful" into "peaceful" demonstrations. In Ballot B, the original wording (lawful) has been kept. No systematic differences have been discovered depending on the use of the adjective. Yet, in upcoming rounds, the wording will be permanently changed from lawful to peaceful. The latter is more appropriate to cover nonviolent but forbidden SMAs in nondemocracies.

The reasons to drop the other two activities are threefold. First, unofficial strikes and occupying buildings stand out by far as the least popular forms of SMAs. In fact, unofficial strikes and occupying buildings are used in most samples by such minor proportions of the respondents (usually below 5 percent) that responses are within the margin of sampling error. Considering these activities clearly cannot reveal systematic variation. Second, these activities (in particular "occupying buildings") are closer to the violence threshold, so including them blurs the focus on peaceful action. Third, because of this conceptual difference, unofficial strikes and occupying buildings show consistently the weakest loadings on the underlying SMA dimension.[5] For these reasons, one does not lose much by dropping unofficial strikes and occupying buildings from the measurement of SMAs. It is actually a gain in conceptual clarity because the three remaining activities are less ambiguous with respect to violence.

Using petitions, boycotts, and demonstrations, I create the SMA index in two versions. The first version codes "have done" for each activity 1.0 and everything else 0 and averages the codes over the three activities, yielding a 4-point index from 0 for no activity, 0.33 for one activity, 0.66 for two, and 1.0 for all three.[6] The second version takes advantage of the fact that we also have information on whether or not a respondent "might do" the respective activity, indicating readiness to act. Taking this additional information into account makes sense for a number of reasons.

Under the notion of repertoires, reported readiness to act should not be ignored because readiness already indicates something meaningful: the respective action is anticipated and thus psychologically part of the repertoire, even if it has not yet been practiced. Thus, reported action, reported readiness, and reported refusal represent different positions on a single continuum, ranging from an absent SMA repertoire in the case of refusal to act, to an anticipated but not yet practiced repertoire in the case of readiness to act to, to a practiced repertoire in the case of actual action. In a repertoire measure, readiness is therefore to be treated differently from refusal and should not be lumped together with the latter in the 0 category. Readiness should accordingly at least obtain some weight in the SMA repertoire index. But it is also clear that readiness should have less weight, and perhaps much less weight, than action, if the difference between anticipated and practiced repertoires is to be emphasized.

---

[5] Calculated over the country-pooled individual-level data, factor loadings on the single underlying dimension are 0.79 (petitions), 0.77 (boycotts), 0.75 (demonstrations), 0.71 (unofficial strikes), 0.61 (occupying buildings) in WVS I (1981–83). In subsequent waves, loadings deviate insignificantly from these numbers.

[6] It is sometimes argued that petitions should be studied separately because they are an easy activity. This is true for participating in a petition. But petitions must be organized by people, and this is not an easy activity. Thus, when many people participate in petitions, there are also many people organizing them. Hence, the argument that petitions are different because they are easy does not apply when we look at social prevalence measures of this activity.

For these reasons, I weight readiness greater than 0 but place it closer to refusal than to action. Concretely, refusal is coded 0, readiness 0.33, and action 1.0 for each of the three SMAs. Then I average scores over all three actions. This procedure yields a more fine-grained 0–1.0 index than the first index version, indicating a person's SMA repertoire, including both the anticipated and practiced repertoires, but with a premium placed on the practiced one.

All of the following results have been obtained in practically identical form with both versions of the SMA index. This is not surprising because, at the individual level, the two indices correlate at $r = 0.93$ in the country-pooled data using the most recent survey of each society covered by the WVS ($N = 231,068$). Nevertheless, I display the results from the second version of the SMA index because it takes into account more information and has better scale quality: a reliability test[7] yields a Cronbach's α of 0.69 for the three activities when readiness to act is taken into account, compared to an α of only 0.58 when it is not.[8]

As mentioned, the three SMAs are one-dimensional. But dimensionality shall not concern us. Even if the three types of SMAs were not uniformly one-dimensional across and within all societies, with a compository definition of action repertoires it is nevertheless appropriate to summarize these activities in a single index: repertoires are defined by the variety of included activities – no matter how strongly these activities correlate and no matter whether they correlate in the same way in all places. The compository logic is appropriate whenever the measured concept has an a priori theoretical definition (see Box 2.1, p. 60). Because this is the case here, I measure people's responses against the theoretically predefined standard, and not how the response patterns are dimensionally organized.

2.3 Explanatory Variables

As potential explanations of SMAs, the DVW model covers two domains of human empowerment at the societal level: resources and entitlements. Specifically, DVW operationalize people's action resources by a society's per capita gross domestic product (GDP) for the year of the survey. This resonates with the *resource mobilization approach* in social movement theory: SMAs are more prevalent in societies whose affluence diffuses greater action resources into wider segments of the population (McCarthy & Zald 1977). DVW operationalize people's entitlements to action by the rule of law index from the World Bank "good governance" database for the year of the survey. This measure

---

[7] Results are based on the pooled individual-level data of WVS rounds three to five, covering some 240,000 individuals in about ninety societies.

[8] WVS round five fields a follow-up question asking for each SMA whether or not it "has been done in the past five years." The version of the SMA index that recognizes intention explains as much variation as the one that does not (i.e., 56 percent) as concerns the SMAs a respondent has taken in the past five years. Thus, the version that recognizes intention is as valid an indicator of executed repertoires as the one that doesn't. The result is based on the country-pooled individual-level data.

represents the *opportunity structures approach* in social movement research: SMAs are more prevalent in societies in which more credible entitlements widen the opportunities of action (Meyer 2004).

Participation in SMAs not only depends on societal-level circumstances; it is also shaped by individual-level characteristics. Thus, the DVW model specifies education as a personal resource of participation. This resonates with a large literature showing education to be one of the strongest individual-level determinants of participation (Barnes & Kaase 1979; Verba, Schlozman, & Brady 1995; Inglehart & Catterberg 2003). Moreover, DVW operationalize membership in associations as a personal opportunity of participation, following another widely shared assumption in the literature: people who are more involved are better networked and thus encounter more opportunities for joint action (Putnam 2000; Norris 2002).

Taking into account psychological factors, DVW introduce two additional variables at the individual level: a leftist orientation and postmaterialist values. In accordance with the literature, DVW expect that both postmaterialist values and leftist orientations increase participation in SMAs (Opp 1990; Bernhagen & Marsh 2007).

Finally, the DVW model covers *grievance theory*. Advocates of this theory argue that a major motivation to participate in SMAs is dissatisfaction with some social deficiency or system failure (Walker, Wong, & Kretzschmar 2002). The DVW model specifies grievance with measures of a respondent's personal and political dissatisfaction. More precisely, life satisfaction is used as an inverse measure of personal dissatisfaction and trust in parliament as an inverse indicator of political dissatisfaction.

I replicate the DVW model with the fifth and most recent round of the WVS, using the slightly modified SMA index just described. After replicating the DVW model on the basis of new data, I extend the theoretical scope of the model in the next step. This is done by including a prevalence measure of values among the societal-level variables. As a measure of values, I am not using the short version postmaterialism index. As we have seen, with its emphasis on people's voice, postmaterialism covers only two of the twelve items that constitute the wider construct of emancipative values. Hence, the wider construct of emancipative values is a more powerful predictor of SMAs than its narrower constituent (evidence is available in Table 2.6, p. 80).

Moreover, I respecify two individual-level variables and two societal-level variables in ways that make more sense. To begin with the societal-level variables, I replace the rule of law index with the citizen rights index presented in the Introduction and analyzed in detail in Chapter 8. Rule of law is a less valid measure of civic entitlements than citizen rights. Favorable rule of law scores, as used by the World Bank, simply mean strength in law enforcement. Law enforcement can be strong even in nondemocratic states, such as Singapore, in which case it is not an indication of guaranteed but, to the contrary, of denied entitlements to action. By contrast, the citizen rights index is a direct measure of civic entitlements, and one that has more validity than alternative measures. The latter point is demonstrated in Chapter 8.

I replace per capita GDP with the index of technological advancement presented in the Introduction. Per capita GDP is high in some oil exporting countries. In these cases, per capita GDP indicates patrimonial state structures that repress rather than enhance people's chances to voice their claims (Ross 2001; Conrad & DeMeritt 2013). In addition to material resources, intellectual and connective resources are relevant as well. As shown in Chapter 3, the technological advancement index is a decent measure of all three types of resources – material, intellectual, and connective. Per capita GDP, by contrast, is a direct measure of material resources only.

As concerns the individual-level variables, instead of using distrust in parliament, I use distrust in government as the indicator of political dissatisfaction. This respecification is informed by the idea that governments are usually more in the focus of attention and, for this reason, are more likely to be the target of people's dissatisfaction than are parliaments (Catterberg 2003). Next, I find leftist orientations a problematic measure, especially in a cross-cultural dataset that includes societies in which left and right have different meanings or are not such salient ideological categories as in a typically Western context (Bernhagen & Marsh 2007). For this reason, I replace leftist orientations with political interest. The latter has been found in scores of studies to be an important psychological determinant of political activity, including SMAs (Heitzman et al. 2009).

In a separate step, I test the robustness of the value-action link. For this purpose, I extend the cross-sectional analyses to include all societies with valid data ever surveyed by the WVS. Doing so widens the country base from roughly fifty to almost ninety societies. The key issue is the robustness of the value-action link against the risks of repression. To examine this topic, I replace the citizen rights index with a direct indicator of the risk of repression, using Gibney, Wood, and Cornett's (2008) political terror scale (for a discussion see Davenport & Armstrong 2004; Conrad & DeMeritt 2013).

The final analysis is longitudinal and looks at concurrent changes in emancipative values and SMAs. Since the WVS is not a panel study, change can only be analyzed at the societal level. Thus, I employ Δ-variables that measure change in emancipative values, civic entitlements, action resources, and SMAs, from the earliest to the latest available survey, provided these are at least ten years apart. This minimum time span is chosen to obtain change measures that more likely reflect the long-term trend than short-term cycles.[9] Change in the resource

---

[9] If a variable shows cyclical fluctuations on an increasing trend line, one is more likely to capture the increase the more temporally distant any pair of two measures is taken. If the two measures are distant, one more likely captures an increase, even if the later measure is taken in a downward cycle and the earlier measure in an upward cycle. Of course, the more accurate method to isolate the trend from cycles is to calculate moving averages. But we do not have enough points in time for this.

component of human empowerment is measured by per capita GDP, instead of technological advancement, because the latter measure is not available in sufficient time series. As always, I standardize every variable into a scale range from minimum 0 to maximum 1.0, with fractions of 1.0 indicating intermediate positions.[10]

3. FINDINGS

3.1 Replicating the DVW Model with WVS Round Five

The multilevel models in Appendix 7 (www.cambridge.org/welzel) replicate the DVW study with data from WVS round five. Despite differences in the exact operationalization of the dependent variable, as well as in the sample and in the time of the surveys, the models in Appendix 7 confirm the results of DVW on four points. First, in societies with wider entitlements and more abundant resources, more individuals participate more extensively in SMAs. Second, people's leftist orientations and postmaterialist values have modestly positive effects on SMAs, yet these effects grow in strength when entitlements are wider and resources more abundant. Third, people's formal education and association membership have strongly positive effects on SMAs and these are invariant across societies with different entitlements and resources. Fourth, indications of grievance, like personal and political dissatisfaction, show either a very small or no effect at all on SMAs.

In summary, the conclusions of the DVW model hold for a different sample of societies from another period of time. The incorporation of SMAs into people's repertoire is basically a matter of two key components of human empowerment: action resources and civic entitlements.

3.2 Extending the DVW Model

There is room to improve the DVW model in two ways. First, and most important, the theoretical reach can be extended by including the value component of human empowerment not only at the individual level but also at the societal level. DVW operationalize postmaterialist values as the value component of human empowerment but specify this component only at the individual level, not the societal level. This overlooks that value orientations not only

---

[10] The only other difference to the DVW model is that I replace their group membership index with the association membership index introduced in Chapter 6. DVW sum up membership in all associations asked for. In light of the literature that shows that associations differ in their effects by type, I find this procedure unconvincing (van der Meer, Grotenhuis, & Scheepers 2009). From a social capital perspective, one would like to focus on membership in associations that are horizontally organized and are engaged in the provision of public goods. Also, one would rate active membership higher than passive membership.

matter as an individual-level trait of persons. The *prevalence of values through-out a society* is an important contextual attribute of a society's psychological climate. This has become evident in our repeated observation of social cross-fertilization (see Box 3.1, p. 110): an impulse that is inherent in an individual orientation unfolds more freely when that orientation is more prevalent in a society. Thus, if postmaterialist orientations predispose people to voicing joint claims, this impulse will unfold more freely if postmaterialism is more prevalent in a society. Accordingly, we extend the DVW model by includ-ing an aggregate measure of the prevalent orientation.

Second, postmaterialism is a component of the broader concept of emanci-pative values, and I hypothesize that the activating impulse is more powerful with the broader concept. Hence, I replace postmaterialism with emancipative values at both levels of analyses.

After these modifications, Table 7.1 specifies three alternative models:

1. an *entitlements model* using the citizen rights index instead of the rule of law index;
2. a *resources model* using the alternative indicator of action resources, that is, the technological advancement index instead of per capita GDP;
3. a *values model* using the social prevalence of emancipative values.

The respecification of the individual-level variables yields a 5 percentage points higher explained variance: the explained within-societal variation in SMAs increases from 13 to 18 percent. It turns out that political interest has more than twice as strong an activation effect than leftist orientations ($b = 0.22$ compared to 0.09), whereas individual preferences for emancipative values have an almost three times stronger activation effect than preferences for postmateri-alist values ($b = 0.22$ compared to 0.08). Also, whereas distrust in parliament does not have a significant activation effect, distrust in government does have such an effect, although it remains small ($b = 0.04$).

Comparing the societal-level components of the three models, it is obvious that entitlements, resources, and values each operate in the same direction. Recognizing that these are three distinct but interrelated elements of human empowerment, this is not surprising. Thus, entitlements, resources, and values each enhance SMAs in a population, and each of them amplifies the activation effects of both political interest and emancipative preferences at the individual level: political interest and emancipative preferences enhance SMAs more when citizen rights are more extensive, when technological advancement is further ahead, and when emancipative values are more prevalent. But when we compare these effects' relative strengths, it is obvious that the prevalence of emancipative values explains considerably more cross-national variation in SMAs (i.e., 62 percent) than do either citizen rights (49 percent) or technological advancement (25 percent). The prevalence of emancipative values is also the strongest ampli-fier of these values' activating impulse at the individual level—as the idea of social cross-fertilization suggests.

TABLE 7.1 *Reanalyzing the Standard Model of Social Movement Activities with World Values Surveys Round Five Data (nonrival models).*

PREDICTORS	DEPENDENT VARIABLE: Social Movement Activity (SMA-Index)		
	Model 1 (Entitlements)	Model 2 (Resources)	Model 3 (Values)
• Constant	0.29 (20.9)***	0.30 (17.2)***	0.29 (24.1)***
Societal-level Effects:			
• Entitlements: Citizen Rights	0.47 (6.4)***		
• Resources: Technological Advancement		0.27 (3.5)***	
• Values: EV-Prevalence[a]			0.91 (9.6)***
Individual-level Effects:			
• Dissatisfaction with Life	0.03 (3.9)***	0.03 (3.9)***	0.03 (3.9)***
Cross-level Interactions:			
• Distrust in Government	0.04 (4.7)***	0.04 (4.7)***	0.04 (4.6)***
* Entitlements: Citizen Rights	N. S.		
* Resources: Technological Advancement		N. S.	
* Values: EV-Prevalence[a]			N. S.
• Association Membership	0.16 (12.3)***	0.16 (12.5)***	0.16 (12.3)***
* Entitlements: Citizen Rights	N. S.		
* Resources: Technological Advancement		N. S.	
* Values: EV-Prevalence[a]			N. S.
• Formal Education	0.12 (12.2)***	0.12 (11.8)***	0.12 (11.8)***
* Entitlements: Citizen Rights	0.09 (1.9)*		
* Resources: Technological Advancement		N. S.	
* Values: EV-Prevalence[a]			N. S.
• Political Interest	0.22 (18.6)***	0.22 (18.1)***	0.22 (18.2)***
* Entitlements: Citizen Rights	0.17 (3.1)**		
* Resources: Technological Advancement		0.12 (2.3)*	
* Values: EV-Prevalence[a]			0.25 (2.6)**
• EV-Preference[a]	0.22 (12.2)***	0.22 (13.0)***	0.22 (14.2)***
* Entitlements: Citizen Rights	0.52 (6.4)***		
* Resources: Technological Advancement		0.46 (7.1)***	
* Values: EV-Prevalence[a]			0.90 (7.3)***

TABLE 7.1 (cont.)

PREDICTORS	DEPENDENT VARIABLE: Social Movement Activity (SMA-Index)		
	Model 1 (Entitlements)	Model 2 (Resources)	Model 3 (Values)
Reduction of Error:			
Within-societal Variation of DV	18%	18%	18%
Between-societal Variation of DV	49%	25%	61%
Variation in Effect of Political Interest	15%	10%	10%
Variation in Effect of Emancipative Values	46%	53%	62%
N (number of observations)	54,664 respondents in 46 societies		

Entries are unstandardized regression coefficients with T values in parentheses, based on robust standard errors. Significance levels: N. S. $p \geq .100$ (not significant), $^* p < .100$, $^{**} p < .050$, $^{***} p < .005$. Individual-level variables are country-mean centered, societal-level variables are global-mean centered. Percent error reduction calculated from change in random variance component related to empty model. Models calculated with HLM 6.01. Data cover all societies and respondents from WVS round five (ca. 2005) with valid data, with national samples weighted to equal size.
^{a} EV, Emancipative Values

It is noteworthy that citizen rights are indeed a stronger indicator of entitlements than the rule of law index: citizen rights in Table 7.1 explain more cross-national variation in SMAs (namely, 49 percent) than does rule of law in Appendix 7 (44 percent [www.cambridge.org/welzel]). Technological advancement, for its part, is about as strong an indicator of capabilities as per capita GDP: technological advancement in Table 7.1 explains about the same amount of cross-national variation in SMAs as does per capita GDP in Appendix 7. Hence, we could use either indicator, yet I find technological advancement preferable for the known theoretical reasons.

The considerable differences in explained variance obtained by the three societal-level indicators of human empowerment suggest that these indicators are not so highly correlated that it is impossible to separate their effects. Indeed, collinearity diagnostics show that variance inflation factors remain within tolerable limits (below 5.0) for any pair of the three indicators. Thus, I rerun the regression models by including pairs of two of the three indicators. The results of these rival models are shown in Table 7.2.

As the three models in Table 7.2 illustrate, paired with the prevalence of emancipative values, neither entitlements nor resources increase a society's SMAs. This finding corrects the DVW model in an important point: civic entitlements and action resources *seemingly* increase SMAs because they exist largely in conjunction with prevalent emancipative values. In disjunction from them, both resources and entitlements show much weaker and even insignificant effects on SMAs.

TABLE 7.2 *Reanalyzing the Standard Model of Social Movement Activity with World Values Surveys Round Five Data (rival models).*

PREDICTORS	DEPENDENT VARIABLE: Social Movement Activity		
	Model 1 (Entitlements vs. Resources)	Model 2 (Resources vs. Values)	Model 3 (Values vs. Entitlements)
• Constant	0.30 (21.0)***	0.30 (24.2)***	0.30 (24.7)***
Societal-level Effects:			
• Entitlements: Citizen Rights	0.53 (5.4)***		N. S.
• Resources: Technological Advancement	N. S.	N. S.	
• Values: EV-Prevalence^a		0.99 (9.1)***	0.70 (4.6)***
Individual-level Effects:			
• Dissatisfaction with Life	0.03 (3.8)***	0.03 (3.8)***	0.03 (3.9)***
• Distrust in Government	0.04 (4.9)***	0.04 (4.9)***	0.04 (4.6)***
• Association Membership	0.15 (11.9)***	0.15 (11.9)***	0.16 (12.3)***
• Formal Education	0.11 (11.5)***	0.11 (11.5)***	0.12 (12.2)***
Cross-level Interactions:			
• Political Interest	0.22 (19.1)***	0.22 (18.8)***	0.22 (18.6)***
* Entitlements: Citizen Rights	N. S.		N. S.
* Resources: Technological Advancement	N. S.	N. S.	
* Values: EV-Prevalence^a		N. S.	N. S.
• EV-Preference^a	0.23 (13.1)***	0.23 (14.9)***	0.22 (14.2)***
* Entitlements: Citizen Rights	0.37 (2.5)**		N. S.
* Resources: Technological Advancement	N. S.	N. S.	
* Values: EV-Prevalence^a		0.88 (4.3)***	0.85 (3.4)***
Reduction of Error:			
Within-societal Variation of DV	17%	17%	17%
Between-societal Variation of DV	48%	61%	62%
Variation in Effect of Political Interest	15%	11%	13%
Variation in Effect of Emancipative Values	45%	59%	60%
N (number of observations)	54,664 respondents in 46 societies		

Entries are unstandardized regression coefficients with T values in parentheses, based on robust standard errors. Significance levels: N. S. $p \geq .100$ (not significant), * $p < .100$, ** $p < .050$, *** $p < .005$. Individual-level variables are country-mean centered, societal-level variables are global-mean centered. Percent error reduction calculated from change in random variance component related to empty model. Models calculated with HLM 6.01. Data cover all societies and respondents from WVS round five (ca. 2005) with valid data. National samples are weighted to equal size without changing the overall N.
^{a}EV, Emancipative Values

One might suspect that these results are an artifact of the peculiar sample of round five of the WVS. But they are not. Looking at the full-blown evidence of the WVS, including all 240 surveys from rounds one to five, we still find that emancipative values increase SMAs. This is evident from Figure 7.1. To simplify things, the diagram uses the categorization of societies as weakly, moderately, and strongly emancipative introduced in Chapter 6. Based on this categorization, the diagram illustrates the combined individual- and societal-level effects of emancipative values on SMAs, evidencing three regularities.

First, regardless of the prevalence of emancipative values, we see a genuine individual-level effect: whether a society is weakly, moderately, or strongly emancipative, individuals in these societies have a wider SMA repertoire when their preference for emancipative values is stronger. Second, regardless of the individuals' own preference for emancipative values, we see a genuine societal-level effect: individuals with the same preference for emancipative values have a wider SMA repertoire when they live in a strongly emancipative society.[11] Third, the social prevalence of emancipative values amplifies the activating impulse of an individual preference for these values: moving from individuals with weak to those with strong emancipative values comes with a stronger increase in SMAs when these values are more prevalent.

The impact of the prevalence of emancipative values is more obvious when we contrast strongly and moderately emancipative societies than when we contrast moderately and weakly emancipative societies. This pattern is familiar from some of the analyses in previous chapters: differences in the lower half of the emancipative values index are less consequential than differences in the upper half. The power of emancipative values grows stronger as they pass the threshold from deficiency to prevalence.

Figure 7.1 demonstrates that the combined individual- and societal-level effects of emancipative values on SMAs is not an artifact of recent WVS rounds but exists across the full-blown evidence of the WVS. Again, these effects remain robust against controls for entitlements and resources. This is evident from an additional set of multilevel models in Appendix 7 (www.cambridge.org/welzel).

3.3 Repression and Mobilization

The extent to which civic entitlements are present or absent does not matter for SMAs, once we control for the prevalence of emancipative values. This might be surprising because, quite plausibly, the absence of civic entitlements should

---

[11] To further validate this finding I examined whether the prevalence of emancipative values per society correlates with the average size of 'nonviolent campaigns' between 1990 and 2005, using the campaign measures from the NAVCO2 dataset (Chenoweth & Lewis 2013). It turns out that the prevalence of emancipative values indeed correlates positively and significantly with non-violent campaign size at $r = 0.62$ ($N = 44$; $p < .001$). The evidence is presented in Appendix 7 (www.cambridge.org/welzel).

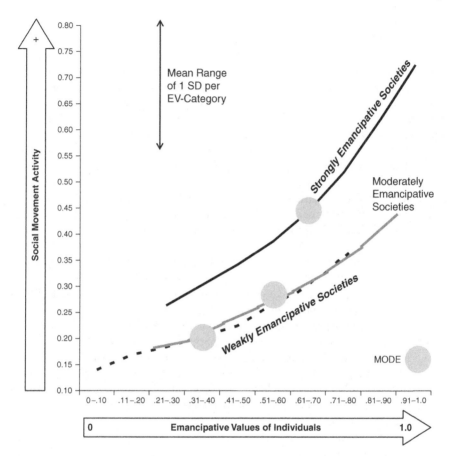

FIGURE 7.1 Multilevel Effects of Emancipative Values on Social Movement Activity. *Data Coverage*: Respondents with valid data from a total of 232 surveys conducted from the World Values Surveys (WVS) rounds one to five between ca. 1980 and 2005. All national surveys at a time weighted to equal size (N = 1,000 per survey). Number of observations: weakly emancipative societies – 63,000 respondents from sixty-three surveys (with 4, 5, 20, 16 and 18 surveys in rounds one, two, three, four, and five, respectively); moderately emancipative societies – 91,000 respondents from ninety-one surveys (with 13, 20, 16, 26, and 16 surveys in rounds one, two, three, four, and five, respectively); strongly emancipative societies – 78,000 respondents from seventy-eight surveys (with 2, 17, 16, 21, and 22 in rounds one, two, three, four, and five, respectively).

discourage SMAs. The reason is simple: with absent entitlements, SMAs are not legally protected, if not outrightly forbidden, so pursuing them risks repressive measures of unpredictable scale. Indeed, the literature on political opportunity structures attributes a strongly discouraging effect to the risks induced by the denial of civic entitlements (Opp 1994; Francisco 1995, 2005; Davenport 2005,

2007; Tilly 2007). In line with this literature, Model 1 in Table 7.1 confirms that SMAs diminish under narrower civic entitlements: this conclusion follows directly from the positive effect of citizen rights on SMAs. However, this finding is not robust: once we control for the prevalence of emancipative values, the effect of citizen rights on SMAs turns insignificant.

The latter result suggests that the discouraging effect of repressive threats is conditional: repressive threats discourage SMAs *only in conjunction* with a low prevalence of emancipative values. Conversely, the expressive impulse of emancipative values encourages action even with a high risk of repression – especially as the solidarity experience from widely shared emancipative values grows strong.

However, this is an informed guess so far. To test this suggestion directly, I replace the citizen rights index with a direct indicator of repressive threats, using Gibney, Wood, and Cornett's (2008) political terror scale. Based on reports by Amnesty International and other sources, the scale measures the violation of citizen rights through repression and terrorism (for a discussion of the political terror scale, see Davenport & Armstrong 2004; Conrad & DeMeritt 2013). Measurement details are documented and data displayed in Appendix 7 (www.cambridge.org/welzel).

Now, we extend the evidence by including all societies ever surveyed by the WVS, using the most recently available survey from each society. Accordingly, we use a society's score on the political terror scale over the five years before the respective survey has been conducted. Among the least repressive societies (scoring at 0), we find countries like Sweden or the United Kingdom; among the most repressive societies (scoring at 1.0), we find countries like Belarus or Iran.

As the first model in Table 7.3 shows, when we examine the effect of repressive threats merely by itself, expectations from the literature are confirmed. The risk of repression diminishes the prevalence of SMAs in a society. In numbers, a 1-unit increase in risk comes with a 0.27-unit decrease in SMAs. Needless to say, this is a highly significant effect. Moreover, even though repressive threat does not offset the effect of emancipative preferences on SMAs, it does weaken this effect: emancipative preferences encourage SMAs less in riskier societies. This is obvious from the negative interaction between repressive threat and individual preferences for emancipative values. In numbers, a 1-unit increase in an individual's preference for emancipative values increases SMAs by a 0.22-unit, but from this we must subtract a 0.39-unit for a 1-unit increase in the product between this individual's emancipative values and the risk of repression in the respective society. What does that mean? Assume an individual scores 0.60 on emancipative values, and the society's repressive threat score is 0.60 (about the level of Russia). In this case, the individual's emancipative values increase her SMAs by (0.22 * 0.60 =) 0.13 scale points, yet in turn the negative interaction with repressive threat diminishes SMAs by (0.39 * 0.60 * 0.60 =) 0.14 scale points. Thus, the negative interaction with the risk of repression can easily eat up the otherwise positive effect of an individual's emancipative values on SMAs.

TABLE 7.3 *The Role of Repressive Threats (multilevel models).*

PREDICTORS	DEPENDENT VARIABLE: Social Movement Activity (SMA-Index)		
	Model 1 (Risk)	Model 2 (Values)	Model 3 (Risk vs. Values)
• Constant	0.29 (20.9)***	0.29 (24.1)***	0.29 (39.8)***
Societal-level Effects:			
• Risk of Repression	−0.27 (−6.0)***		N. S.
• EV-Prevalence[a]		0.91 (9.6)***	1.09 (10.1)***
Individual-level Effects:			
• Dissatisfaction with Life	0.03 (3.9)***	0.03 (3.9)***	0.03 (3.9)***
• Distrust in Government	0.04 (4.7)***	0.04 (4.6)***	0.04 (4.6)***
• Association Membership	0.16 (12.3)***	0.16 (12.3)***	0.16 (12.3)***
• Formal Education	0.12 (12.2)***	0.12 (11.8)***	0.12 (11.8)***
Cross-level Interactions:			
• Political Interest	0.22 (18.6)***	0.22 (18.2)***	0.21 (33.3)***
* Risk of Repression	−0.17 (−3.1)**		−0.17 (−3.7)***
* EV-Prevalence[a]		0.25 (2.6)**	N. S.
• EV-Preference[a]	0.22 (12.2)***	0.22 (14.2)***	0.28 (19.7)***
* Risk of Repression	−0.39 (−5.3)***		N. S.
* EV-Prevalence[a]		0.90 (7.3)***	0.99 (5.0)***
Reduction of Error:			
Within-societal Variation of DV	18%	18%	18%
Between-societal Variation of DV	29%	61%	61%
Variation in Effect of Political Interest	15%	10%	10%
Variation in Effect of Emancipative Values	47%	62%	62%
N (number of observations)	194,414 respondents in 88 societies		

Entries are unstandardized regression coefficients with T values in parentheses, based on robust standard errors. Significance levels: N. S. *p* ≥.100 (not significant), * *p* < .100, ** *p* < .050, *** *p* < .005. Individual-level variables are country-mean centered, societal-level variables are global-mean centered. Percent error reduction calculated from change in random variance component related to empty model. Models calculated with HLM 6.01.

Data cover all of the ninety-five societies with valid data surveyed at least once by the World Values Surveys/European Value Study (WVS/EVS), using the latest available survey from each society (ca. 1995–2005). Risk of violence measured for each society over the five years before and at the time of the survey. National samples are weighted to equal size without changing the overall N.

[a] EV, Emancipative Values

Again, however, these results are not robust. As Model 3 of Table 7.3 shows, controlling for the social prevalence of emancipative values, repressive threat is no longer relevant for SMAs. This is true in a double sense. For one, repressive threat does not in and of itself lower SMAs; it only does insofar as it exists in conjunction with a low prevalence of emancipative values. This is obvious from the fact that the negative societal-level effect of repressive threat on SMAs in Model 1 turns insignificant after we control for the prevalence of emancipative values in Model 3. Next, repressive threat does not in and of itself weaken the activating impulse of individual-level emancipative values. Again, repressive threat does this only insofar as it exists in conjunction with a low prevalence of emancipative values. This is obvious from the fact that the negative interaction of repressive threat with individual-level emancipative values in Model 1 turns insignificant after we control for these values' interaction with their social prevalence in Model 3. Now, we see a strengthening of the activating impulse of the individuals' emancipative values by the social prevalence of these values. In other words, a person's emancipative values translate more easily into actions when many other people also prefer emancipative values – once more a case of social cross-fertilization (see Box 3.1, p. 110). This tendency is entirely undisturbed by repressive threat. In other words, a higher risk of repression does not disrupt the value-action link when widely shared emancipative values create solidarities that seek expression in collective action.

The partial regression plots in Figure 7.2 visualize these findings. The left-hand diagram shows that, when we control for the prevalence of emancipative values, repressive threat no longer decreases SMAs. By contrast, the right-hand diagram shows that prevalent emancipative values increase SMAs pronouncedly, even controlling for the risk of repression. Of course, repressive threat and emancipative values tend to match: where emancipative values are prevalent, the risk of repression tends to be low and vice versa.[12] However, this relationship is far from being perfect, and a number of critical cases show where the two fall apart.

Consider, for instance, the positions of Brazil and Singapore. Singapore's leftward position in the left-hand diagram means that Singapore has lower repressive threats than other societies at its level of emancipative values. Now, if lower risks encourage SMAs *independent from* emancipative values, then Singapore should have more SMAs than societies at its level of emancipative values. However, the country's downward position on the vertical axis shows that this is not the case.

Conversely, Brazil's rightward position indicates that repressive threats in Brazil are higher than in other societies at Brazil's level of emancipative values. Again, if higher risks discourage SMAs *independent from* emancipative values, then Brazil should have less SMAs than societies at its level of emancipative

---

[12] To be precise, emancipative values and repressive threats correlate at $r = -0.66$ ($N = 89$; $p < 0.001$), indicating a shared variance of 44 percent.

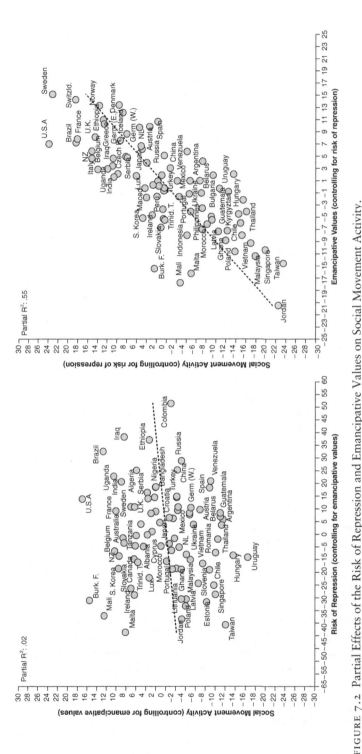

FIGURE 7.2 Partial Effects of the Risk of Repression and Emancipative Values on Social Movement Activity.

Left-hand Diagram: The plot shows whether societies that have higher (lower) repressive threats than societies at their level of emancipative values, also have less (more) social movement activities than societies at their level of emancipative values. The widely scattered distribution of societies around the flat regression line shows that this is not the case. Hence, repressive threats do not affect social movement activities independent from emancipative values.
Right-hand Diagram: The plot shows whether societies that have stronger (weaker) emancipative values than societies at their level of repressive threats, also have more (less) social movement activities than societies at their level of repressive threats. The narrow distribution of societies around the steep regression line shows that this is indeed the case. Hence, emancipative values do affect social movement activities independent from repressive threats.
Data Coverage: All of the ninety-five societies with valid data surveyed at least once by the World Values Surveys (WVS), using the most recent survey from each society (N = 88).

values. However, the country's upward position on the vertical axis shows that this is not the case. Hence, these societies' repressive threats show no influence on SMAs in isolation from emancipative values. This is a generally valid statement, as is obvious from the widely scattered distribution of societies around the regression line in the left-hand diagram of Figure 7.2.

Now, Singapore's leftward position in the right-hand diagram of Figure 7.2 means that Singapore has weaker emancipative values than other societies at *its* level of repression. If weak emancipative values discourage SMAs independent from repressive threats, Singapore should have less SMAs than societies at its level of repression. Indeed, the country's downward position on the vertical axis confirms that this is the case.

By contrast, Brazil's rightward position indicates stronger emancipative values than in other societies at Brazil's level of repression. If stronger emancipative values encourage SMAs independent from repressive threats, Brazil's SMAs should be higher than in societies at its level of repression. Brazil's upward position on the vertical axis confirms this expectation. As the narrow distribution of societies around the regression line shows, it is generally true that when a society has stronger emancipative values than societies at its level of repression, then it also has more SMAs than these societies.

In summary, the two partial plots illustrate two things with impressive clarity: (1) on similar levels of emancipative values, higher repressive threats do not decrease SMAs and lower repressive threats do not increase SMAs (left-hand diagram); (2) on similar levels of repressive threats, more prevalent emancipative values increase SMAs and less prevalent ones decrease SMAs. This effect is pronounced in both directions.

Repression and emancipation are negatively related, as one would expect. But this does not mean that emancipative values rise in response to shrinking repression. Instead, emancipative values emerge when action resources expand – even when the risk of repression is high. As this happens, emancipative values encourage SMAs that claim civic entitlements; once these entitlements are guaranteed, the risk of repression diminishes as a consequence (Conrad & DeMeritt 2013). This mechanism creates the negative cross-sectional relationship between repressive threat and emancipative values. Chapter 9 provides evidence for this mechanism: many regimes whose repressive character inflicted high risks on citizens for a long time – like South Korea, Chile, and former Czechoslovakia – adopted civic entitlements as a reaction to swelling SMAs that were fueled by rising emancipative values. Repressive threat then decreased as a byproduct of the civic entitlements that were guaranteed in the process of democratization.

3.4 A Dynamic Perspective

Thus far, no one has used the longitudinal evidence of WVS data to test whether given hypotheses about the causes of SMAs hold in a dynamic perspective. This is a serious shortcoming because, in the absence of dynamic relations, causality cannot be established. So what does the longitudinal evidence look like?

Examining societies for which SMAs can be measured over the entire time span from WVS rounds one to five (roughly from 1980 to 2005), we are left with the dozen postindustrial knowledge societies shown in Figure 4.1 (p. 143). If we weight these societies' samples to equal size and then look at how SMAs developed across this pool of societies from about 1980 to 2005, we obtain the picture in Figure 7.3. As in Figure 4.1, we subdivide respondents into birth cohorts, using ten-year intervals, from older cohorts on the left to younger cohorts on the right.

Updating previous findings by Welzel, Inglehart, and Deutsch (2005), Figure 7.3 shows the same cohort pattern, in the shape of an inverted U. Apparently, people in the middle-age cohorts are more active than people in younger and older cohorts. This can be interpreted as a lifecycle effect: usually, people are at the climax of their family and career responsibilities in

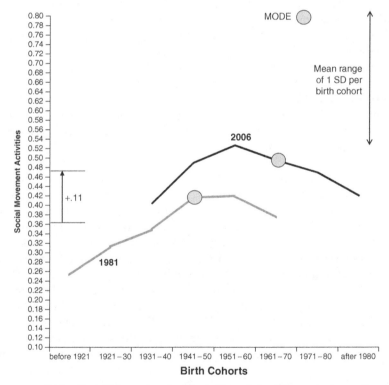

FIGURE 7.3 Rising Social Movement Activity in Knowledge Economies (ca. 1980–2005). *Data Coverage*: World Values Surveys (WVS) rounds one and five from Australia, Canada, France, West Germany, Italy, Japan, the Netherlands, Norway, Sweden, the United Kingdom, and the United States. Each sample weighted to equal size without changing the overall *N*.

middle age, and this more intense involvement in collective duties creates a stronger urge to voice one's claims with like-minded others. However, there is no lifecycle effect in the sense that people's action repertoire narrows as they progress in the lifecycle. This is obvious from the fact that all cohorts, including the older ones, increase their action repertoire as they age from about 1980 to 2005. On average, SMA repertoires grow by 0.11 scale points over this twenty-five-year time span. This increase is statistically significant. It is also truly glacial because it went through all birth cohorts without affecting the cohort differences: the curve in 1980 is simply elevated to a higher action level in 2005. In this respect, the increase in SMAs resembles the increase in emancipative values shown for the same societies and time span in Figure 4.1 (p. 143). The resemblance suggests that the rise of emancipative values is the motivational force driving the increase in SMAs.

Before examining this possibility, let me add a few qualifications to the change pattern evidenced in Figure 7.3. As Appendix 7 (www.cambridge.org/welzel) shows, the same pattern applies separately for each of the three types of activity – petitions, demonstrations, boycotts – covered by the SMA index. Even though the three activities take place on considerably different levels, with petitions being a more widespread activity than demonstrations and boycotts, the patterns are the same in each of the three activities. All three of them show an inverted U-shaped cohort pattern, and all three of them show a glacial increase throughout all cohorts over the past twenty-five years, from about 1980 to 2005. Furthermore, these increases are not a cyclical artifact. It is quite possible that most postindustrial societies are surveyed during a downturn in their mobilization cycles in 1980 and an upturn in 2005. In this case, the increase in SMAs would not reflect a glacial trend. But this is not the case. Instead, as Appendix 7 shows, SMAs increase continuously throughout the five successive rounds of the WVS. This does not mean that cyclical patterns are entirely absent but, in as far as they are recognizable, they appear to be fluctuations along a glacial upward trend.

Can one establish for a broader selection of societies that change in emancipative values is the motivating force behind change in SMAs? One can. For this purpose, we look at all societies from WVS rounds one to five for which at least two different surveys in time exist. As an additional restriction, we limit ourselves to societies with at least ten years between the earliest and latest survey. This leaves us with the almost fifty societies introduced in Chapter 4 (see Figure 4.2, p. 147). I restrict the analysis to societies with reasonable temporal evidence because I am not interested in short-term mobilization cycles. Instead, I am interested in glacial changes in people's action repertoire.

Given these premises, Figure 7.4 shows how change in SMAs is related to change in emancipative values. It is evident that a large majority of societies experience increases rather than decreases in the level of emancipative values from the earliest to the latest available survey. The exceptions are Estonia, Latvia, Mexico, Nigeria, Romania, Russia, and Turkey. As we saw in

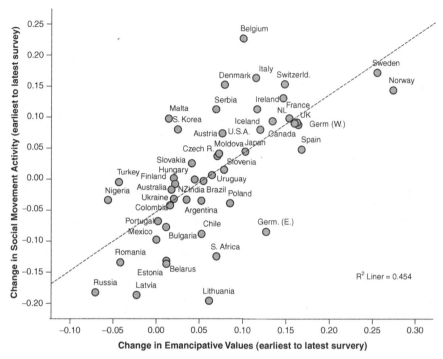

FIGURE 7.4 The Effect of Change in Emancipative Values on Change in Social Movement Activities.

Data Coverage: All of the fifty societies with valid data surveyed at least twice over a temporal distance of at least ten years by the World Values Surveys (WVS) ($N = 49$, no social movement activity for China at time of the earliest survey). Temporal coverage for most societies is from ca. 1990 to 2000, 1995 to 2005, or 1990 to 2005. For the eleven knowledge societies analyzed in Figure 7.3 (plus Argentina and Hungary), the temporal coverage is ca. 1980 to 2005. Note that, unlike in a univariate analysis, differences in temporal coverage do not need to be controlled for in a bivariate analysis as long as the two variables always cover the same temporal range for a given society.

Figure 4.2 (p. 147), each of these societies experiences over this period of time little, if any, increase in its absolute per capita GDP level.[13] Moreover, none of these societies is categorized as a knowledge economy in Table I.1 (p. 4) of the Introduction.

Most of the societies in Figure 7.4 that experience an increase in emancipative values from the earliest to the latest survey also experience an increase in SMAs

---

[13] In Figure 4.2, this is also true for China (which shows exceptional GDP growth rates in percentages of its GDP but, since it is still a low-income society, not yet in its *absolute* per capita GDP). China is not included in the analysis of Figure 7.4, however, because questions on SMAs were not asked in the Chinese WVS prior to round five.

over the same period. The exceptions are East Germany, Poland, Lithuania, Chile, Argentina, and South Africa. These societies show a slight or considerable decrease in SMAs despite a significant increase in emancipative values. In all these societies, the earliest survey took place during a transition to democracy, which in each of these societies was accompanied by an extraordinary upward cycle in mass mobilization. Levels of SMAs were, accordingly, exceptionally high and dropped back to normal after the transition. This is reflected in these instances by a decrease in SMAs and has been noted by Inglehart and Catterberg (2003) as the "post-honeymoon decline."

The transition factor does not offset but it certainly disturbs the otherwise strong and positive relationship between change in emancipative values and change in SMAs. Hence, we should examine the effect of changes in emancipative values on changing SMAs while holding changes in civic entitlements constant. Furthermore, since we have seen in Chapter 4 that changes in emancipative values depend on changes in per capita GDP, we should examine the effect of changing emancipative values on changing SMAs holding changes in per capita GDP constant. In other words, the dynamic effect of emancipative values on SMAs should be examined under control of changes in civic entitlements and changes in per capita GDP.[14] In so doing, we examine in which of its three domains – resources, entitlements, values – progress in human empowerment is more conducive to SMAs.

With these premises in mind, I follow the logic outlined in Chapter 4 and specify a dynamic shift model in which the level of the dependent variable at the time of the latest survey (i.e., time T_2) is modeled as a function of (1) the dependent variable's own level at the time of the earliest survey (i.e., time T_1) and (2) the change from time T_1 to time T_2 in the independent variables of interest.

More precisely, I model SMAs at time T_2 as a function of:

1. the *level* of SMAs at time T_1; and
2. the *changes* in emancipative values, in per capita GDP, and in civic entitlements from time T_1 to time T_2.

In contrast to the previous analyses, this model is dynamic for two reasons. First, to explain SMAs at time T_2, we include the lagged dependent variable, that is, SMAs at time T_1, among the predictors. Including the lagged dependent variable means that we explain SMAs at time T_2 insofar as they are unexplained by SMAs at time T_1. This procedure makes the model dynamic because we actually explain change in SMAs, that is, the extent to which SMAs at time T_2 are above or below their level at time T_1. The effect of the lagged dependent variable shows how strongly SMAs are self-perpetuating from time T_1 to time

---

[14] Technological advancement is the better indicator of action resources but cannot be used here because there are no longitudinal data.

T_2.[15] The second feature that makes the model dynamic is the introduction of the independent variables as change measures. This reveals to what extent change in these variables from time T_1 to time T_2 shifts SMAs at time T_2 above or below their level at time T_1.

Including the lagged dependent variable has two more advantages. For one, we remove endogeneity from the model: the effects of the other independent variables on SMAs at time T_2 are shown under the condition of these variables' *independence from* SMAs at time T_1. Next, the lagged dependent variable carries with it every influence on prior SMAs that we do not address by a specific independent variable. Thus, we diminish the problem of omitted variable bias.

Since all three independent variables – emancipative values, per capita GDP, and civic entitlements – are normalized into a 0–1.0 range, the change measures of each of them is in a theoretical range from –1.0 to +1.0, with negative scores indicating decrease and positive scores indicating increase in the respective variable from time T_1 to time T_2.

The analysis in Table 7.4 puts the previous findings into a dynamic perspective. What do we find? As the intercept indicates, on average across the forty-eight societies, SMAs increase slightly and do so just significantly by 0.08 scale points. Thus, extending the evidence from the dozen postindustrial societies examined in Figure 7.3 to a much more diverse array of societies, the increase in SMAs is less pronounced.

That the increase is not larger is partly due to a demobilization effect: in a considerable number of societies, civic entitlements increased substantially as the result of SMA-driven regime transitions (Ulfelder 2005; Welzel 2007a). Examples include Argentina, the Baltic states, Chile, the Czech Republic, South Korea, Ukraine, and others. After a completed transition, SMA levels dropped to normal. Accordingly, we see that expanding civic entitlements affect SMAs negatively: SMAs drop by a 0.10 fraction of the change score in citizen rights. Therefore, if citizen rights increase by their maximum, that is, by +1.0 scale points (as they almost did in the Czech and Slovak republics), SMAs drop by 0.10 scale points.

Change in per capita GDP affects SMAs in the opposite way, showing a positive sign: when per capita GDP increases from the earliest to the latest survey, the level of SMAs in the latest survey rises a 0.32 fraction of the GDP change score above the level in the earliest survey. However, the positive effect of GDP growth is less significant than the negative effect of expanding citizen rights.

---

[15] The pronounced self-perpetuation of the societies' SMA levels (visible in the strong effect of an earlier SMA level on its later level) shows that the SMA index measures long-term differences in *chronic action repertoires* rather than short-term fluctuations in *cyclical action events*. The exception to this generalization is that societies surveyed during democratic transitions are usually on a singular peak in SMAs. An example are the SMA data from the Baltic countries in the 1990 round of the WVS.

TABLE 7.4 *Dynamic Model of Rising Social Movement Activity.*

PREDICTORS	DEPENDENT VARIABLE: Social Movement Activity at time T_2^b
• Constant	0.08 (1.92)*
• Dependent Variable at time T_1^a	0.61 (5.35)***
• Δ Citizen Rights from time T_1 to T_2	−0.10 (−2.17)**
• Δ GDP/p.c. from time T_1 to T_2	0.32 (1.99)*
• Δ EV-Prevalence^c from time T_1 to T_2	0.72 (3.96)***
N (number of observations)	48
Adjusted R^2	0.73

Entries are unstandardized regression coefficients with T ratios in parentheses. Significance levels: * $p < .100$; ** $p < .050$; *** $p < .005$. Test statistics for heteroskedasticity (White test), mulitcollinearity (variance inflation factors), and influential cases (DFFITs) indicate no violation of ordinary least squares (OLS) assumptions.

Data cover all societies surveyed at least twice by the World Values Surveys/European Value Study (WVS/EVS), provided the earliest available survey (T_1) and the latest available survey (T_2) are at least ten years apart. For most societies, the temporal distance from T_1 to T_2 covers the periods from ca. 1990 to 2000, 1995 to 2005, or 1990 to 2005. For the eleven knowledge societies analyzed in Figure 4.1 (plus Argentina and Hungary), the temporal coverage is roughly 1980 to 2005. Note that, unlike in a univariate analysis, differences in temporal coverage do not need to be controlled for in a multivariate analysis as long as all involved variables always cover the same temporal range for a given society.

The model includes each society once, so there can be no serial correlation.

^{a} T_1, time point of earliest available survey
^{b} T_2, time point of latest available survey
^{c} EV, Emancipative Values

By contrast, change in emancipative values shows a stronger and more significant effect on SMAs than change in citizen rights. As is the case with change in per capita GDP, the effect is positive – in fact, strongly positive. In numbers, growth in emancipative values elevates SMAs in the latest survey by a 0.72 fraction of the value change score. Rising emancipative values show an even stronger effect on SMAs than in the bivariate analysis of Figure 7.4, in which the *b*-coefficient for changing emancipative values is 0.60. The key difference between the two analyses in Figure 7.4 and Table 7.4 is that, in the latter, the effect of changing emancipative values is controlled for changes in civic entitlements. Controlling for changes in civic entitlements holds constant the effect of post-transitional demobilization. This makes the dynamic effect of emancipative values comparable across societies with different regime dynamics. Apparently, this brings the effect more strongly to the surface.

The dynamic regression of Table 7.4 confirms with more causal validity what the previous cross-sectional models suggests: among the three components of human empowerment, emancipative values turn out to be most important in shaping SMAs. In activating people, the value component of human empowerment is the most central one.

KEY POINTS

Replicating the standard model of SMAs with a different WVS sample from another period of time largely confirms an important conclusion: SMAs are more strongly shaped by human empowerment than by grievance. In another key point, however, the findings here go beyond the standard model: looking at which component of human empowerment is the most important one in enhancing SMAs, it is the value component rather than the resource and entitlement components. Thus, values matter for SMAs in four ways:

1. The preference for emancipative values encourages people to voice their claims with like-minded others.
2. This encouragement is strengthened by social solidarity when more people share emancipative values.
3. Hence, societies with more prevalent emancipative values encourage more widespread and frequent SMAs.
4. Imposing higher risks of repression does not weaken the value-action link. Quite the contrary, repression vanishes under the imprint of this link.

These conclusions hold against various controls and in a longitudinal perspective that looks at the dynamic concurrence of rising emancipative values and emerging SMAs.

The results support what we found in Chapters 5 and 6. Emancipative values represent an inherently activating and, at the same time, civic orientation. Because emancipative values motivate people to initiate and participate in joint activities and because their expressive utility helps to overcome collective action blockades, these values infuse societies with civic agency and create new social capital. For this reason, emancipative values provide a major force of democratization. The following chapters illuminate this point from various angles.

PART C

DEMOCRATIC IMPULSES OF EMANCIPATIVE VALUES

8

Entitling People[*]

The defenders of every kind of regime claim that it is a democracy, and fear that they might have to stop using the word if it were tied down to any one meaning.

        – George Orwell

Emancipation theory considers democracy as the institutional manifestation of people power. Thereby, it links democracy to two preinstitutional manifestations of people power: action resources and emancipative values. The theory interprets these preinstitutional manifestations as the social fundament in which democracy is grounded. Thus, measures of democracy with a stronger link to action resources and emancipative values tap the social grounding of democracy better than measures with a weaker link. These measures are better representatives of democracy's origin in preinstitutional manifestations of people power; from the viewpoint of human empowerment they are more valid indicators of democracy.

How appropriate is it to evaluate measures of democracy first and foremost through the lens of human empowerment? Section 1 of this chapter answers this question, proposing five different points of view from which an evaluation of democracy under the criterion of human empowerment appears appropriate. Then I portray the new index of "citizen rights" used earlier in this book as a measure of institutionalized people power. Here I detail how this index is built and why. The purpose is to create an index that captures the empowering nature of democracy better than other measures do. In Section 2, I test whether the index meets this purpose, and the result is that it does. Section 3 discusses the causal connection between democracy and the preinstitutional manifestations of people power. We will see that these are indeed antecedents rather than consequences of democracy. Section 4 demonstrates why democracy's embedding in

---

[*] This chapter greatly profits from my work with Amy Alexander and Ronald Inglehart on "effective democracy" (cf. Alexander & Welzel 2011; Alexander, Inglehart, & Welzel 2012).

preinstitutional empowerments is easily overlooked – a pitfall that the human empowerment framework avoids. Specifically, I show that scholars' preoccupation with mass preferences for democracy has obscured the fact that these preferences affect systemic democracy if – and only if – they are grounded in emancipative values. Ungrounded preferences, by contrast, are irrelevant for systemic democracy. I conclude with a summary of key points.

I. MEASURING DEMOCRACY

I.I People Power as the Core Meaning of Democracy

In its literal meaning, "government by the people," the ideal that ultimately inspires democracy is *empowering ordinary people to govern their lives* (Macpherson 1977; Holden 1992; Philpott 1995; Sen 1999; Canovan 2006). Democracy's specific contribution to this purpose is of an *institutional* nature. Consequently, democracy's functionality is limited to what can be achieved by crafting legal norms. These legal norms include, first and foremost, the entitlements that establish "democratic citizenship" (Kymlicka 1995). I call them civic entitlements. They base a society on the rights of its constituents (Saward 2006). Rights are guarantees. They empower people in that they permit them to practice freedoms in their private and public lives (Dahl 2000: 45; Held 2006: 265).

There are various meanings of democracy, and many of these are contested (Held 2006: 2). Yet, I claim that "people power" is the root meaning from which most other meanings take their justification. This claim can be substantiated from four points of view:

1. *popular views* of democracy held by ordinary people around the world;
2. *social activists' views* of democracy evident in the goals for which democracy movements of the past and present struggle;
3. *constitutional views* of democracy manifest in the priority of stipulations in model constitutions of democracy;
4. *scholarly views of democracy* championed by leading theorists.

To begin with the views of democracy held by people around the world, there is broad evidence from the Global Barometers Surveys and the World Values Surveys (WVS) that what first comes to people's mind when they think about democracy is the rights that entitle people to self-govern their private lives and to cogovern public life (Dalton, Shin, & Jou 2007; Diamond 2008). It is by no means true, as some scholars postulate, that ordinary people consider democracy primarily as a means of redistribution (Boix 2003; Acemoglu & Robinson 2006). Redistribution is, in fact, the least popular notion of democracy (see Chapter 10 for detailed evidence). The survey evidence unequivocally shows that, when one confronts people with the word "democracy" – be it in Africa, Asia, Latin America, the Middle East, or Europe – they emphasize, before anything else, the civic entitlements that empower them. Throughout the world, people power is the prime meaning of democracy for most people.[1]

Looking at the goals for which democracy movements of the past and present struggle points to the same conclusion. Modern democracy originates in the liberal revolutions of the eighteenth century (Grayling 2007: 6). These were popular upheavals against tyranny, and they became engraved in our memory through rights-setting acts of historic significance. This is most obvious for the U.S. *Declaration of Independence* in 1776 and the French *Declaration des Droits de L'Homme et des Citoyens* in 1789 (Finer 1999; O'Donnell 2004; Donnelly 2006). These declarations entitled considerable shares of the population to govern their private lives and to exert control over public government. This achievement established *partial* democracy in which the majority of the adult population, including the working class and women, still remained excluded from suffrage. Nevertheless, establishing partial democracy was a crucial precursor to the achievement of *full* democracy: entitling part of the public encouraged further claims, until universal suffrage extended democracy to the entire adult citizenry late in the nineteenth century (Markoff 1996; McAdam, Tarrow & Tilly 2003).[2]

Since then, people's struggles for democracy continues and expands. Within established democracies, civil rights and equal opportunity movements continue to fight for the advancement of democracy's empowering qualities (Tarrow 1998). Beyond established democracies, people power movements continue to pressure for the introduction of democratic procedures (Huntington 1991; Schock 2005; Thompson 2004). From the American Revolution to the Color Revolutions of today, people's struggles for democracy aim at the rights that entitle people to govern their lives (Ackerman 1991, 1998; Markoff 1996; Foweraker & Landman 1997; Karatnycky & Ackerman 2005; Canovan 2006).

Looking at the order in which constitutions are organized, model constitutions of democracy – including those of the United States, France, or Germany – start with the rights of the people (Ackerman 1991; Canovan 2006; Donnelly 2006). This order of priority signals that the basis of democracy is civic entitlements. In terms of constitutional priorities, the core meaning of democracy is people power.

In political theory, conceptions of democracy vary widely, ranging from Schumpeter's (2003 [1943]) minimalist understanding of "electoral democracy" to Barber's (1984) maximalist understanding of "strong democracy." Yet, each of these understandings includes at least some civic entitlement as its central element. Even in the most minimalist understanding – electoral democracy – the basis of democracy is a civic entitlement, in this case, every person's equal right

---

[1] I qualify this conclusion in Chapter 10. For the moment, it is enough to say that democracy's empowering features constitute the prime understanding of democracy in all parts of the world, whether democratic or nondemocratic.

[2] The exact date is the introduction of universal (male and female) suffrage in 1893 in New Zealand.

to a free vote in regular and competitive elections. As much as the various understandings of democracy differ in scope, they all have one thing in common: in the democratic condition, people are more entitled than in the nondemocratic condition (Held 2006: 263). Thus, one can say that different conceptions of democracy operate with different notions of how far people power ought to reach; yet they all operate with a notion of people power as the core meaning of democracy.

In addition to democracy's literal meaning, four perspectives support the same conclusion: (1) the dominant popular understanding of democracy, (2) the claims of past and present democracy movements, (3) the priorities of order in model constitutions, and (4) the notions of democracy in political theory, all imply that people power is the root idea of democracy. Since people power is institutionalized by entitling a society's constituents to perform freedoms, citizen rights that specify these freedoms by law constitute democracy's institutional core. *People power through citizen rights* is hence the most condensed definition of democracy.

Democracy is the institutional element of human empowerment. This is a qualification and limitation at the same time. As a strictly institutional phenomenon, democracy operates on the basis of preinstitutional empowerments. Visionary concepts of democracy, such as Habermas's (1996) "deliberative democracy" and Held's (1993) "cosmopolitan democracy," discuss various preinstitutional empowerments as conditions to be in place before democratic institutions can realize their empowering purpose. Rawls's (1971) *Theory of Justice*, Dahl's (1989) *Democracy and Its Critiques*, and the whole liberal tradition of thought point in the same direction. Thus, democratic theory champions a "socially embedded" notion of democracy (Merkel 2004) that understands the role of democracy in the context of preinstitutional empowerments. These preinstitutional empowerments are of both a material and a mental nature. Materially, they include such things as participatory resources; mentally, they include such things as participatory values (Verba, Schlozman, & Brady 1995; Dahl 2000: 69). The human empowerment framework addresses these as action resources and emancipative values. This framework unifies democracy and its social prerequisites in a single scheme without denying these elements' distinctive roles in empowering the people.

1.2 Citizen Rights as First-Order Tools of Democracy

From the viewpoint of human empowerment, two conceptions of democracy are misconceptions: *electoral reductionism* and *unordered eclecticism*. Electoral reductionism is present when scholars limit the meaning of democracy to regular, competitive, and fair elections. From the viewpoint of people power, this is reductionist because elections are only one among many institutional tools to empower people; elections are anchored in a variety of citizen rights that include voting rights, among many others. The viewpoint of people power suggests an operationalization of democracy that covers all institutional tools that empower people, not simply elections. The growing literature on "electoral authoritarianism" supports this point of view (Levitsky & Way 2002, 2010; Bunce & Wolchik 2010).

Unordered eclecticism is present when scholars fail to define the essence of democracy and instead provide a catalogue of observed features without ordering them by their instrumental value to democracy's guiding idea. Eclectic catalogues of this type might include such features as competitive elections, multiparty systems, associational pluralism, press freedom, separation of powers, rule of law, and a set of citizen rights. The problem with this enumerative approach is that, if citizen rights are mentioned at all, they are listed as just one bullet point among others. The enumerative approach overlooks that citizen rights are of higher instrumental value to democracy's core idea – people power – than is any other institutional feature of democracy. Citizen rights are first-order tools of democracy because they are directly instrumental to the empowerment of people. Other institutional features of democracy, such as an independent judiciary, exist to protect the rights of the people or to make these rights operate properly. Existing for this purpose, such features are indirectly instrumental to people power. They are second-order tools of democracy (Brettschneider 2007). The viewpoint of people power suggests a more focused operationalization of democracy that concentrates on first-order tools instead of listing tools of different order in an eclectic catalogue of observables. Understanding democracy as "people power through citizen rights" solves this problem. Understanding democracy in this way is broader than electoral reductionism but more focused than unordered eclecticism.

The institutional feature most directly instrumental to the idea of people power is citizen rights. It is the inherent purpose of rights to empower their beneficiaries by entitling them to practice some form of freedom. To be empowered, people who live in state-organized societies need two forms of freedom: freedoms to follow their personal preferences in their private lives and freedoms to make their political preferences count in public life (Beetham 1999; O'Donnell 2004; Saward 2006; Williams 2006). Under the idea of self-governance, both forms of freedom are equally important (Brettschneider 2007). The first form of freedom is private and granted by autonomy rights; the second form is public and granted by participation rights. This distinction resembles Berlin's (2006 [1957]) differentiation between "negative" and "positive" freedom. To institutionalize people power completely, both freedoms must be granted together and in equal proportion.

One might argue that democracy is, above all, a political concept, in which case it is sufficiently established by participation rights alone, with no need for autonomy rights. However, the democratic idea of having people participate in politics only makes sense when one thinks of people as autonomous actors who are in the position to recognize and express a preference. Hence, personal autonomy is essential even under a minimalist understanding of democracy and needs protection by its own set of rights (Dahl 1989: 104–105). Accordingly, democracy requires the enactment of autonomy rights as much as that of participation rights. As Brettschneider (2007: 8, fn. 4) correctly notes, "democracy and rights are not in tension but part of a coherent, unified theory of self-government."

From the viewpoint of people empowerment, citizen rights – both personal and political – constitute the core definitional tool of democracy.[3] Focusing on citizen rights is thus an appropriate account of democracy's root meaning (Beetham 1999; Sen 1999; O'Donnell 2004; Williams 2006).

1.3 Democracy's Gradual Nature

Assume that the full list of known citizen rights would include five autonomy rights and five participation rights, each of which is of equal importance. The five autonomy rights could include the freedoms to choose (1) how to earn and spend one's money; (2) what to learn and which sources of information to access; (3) which religion and belief, if any, to practice; (4) where to live; and (5) with whom to live and how. The five participation rights could include the freedoms (1) to express one's political preferences in public; (2) to campaign for one's preferences, mobilize support for them, and organize supporters; (3) to litigate political authorities for violations of one's rights; (4) to run for public office; and (5) to have a free vote, equal in weight to that of all others, in elections, initiatives, and referenda.

More rights could be added to this list, or the list could be extended by subdividing some general rights into several more specific ones. But no matter how we approach this theme, the key point is that as long as one can list a decent number of essential rights, democracy is not a binary all-or-nothing phenomenon. Instead, democracy varies by degree. It varies by degree between the entire absence of institutionalized people power when not a single right is guaranteed and the full presence of institutionalized people power when each known right is guaranteed. These are absolute endpoints on a continuum that can be scaled in fractions of the known maximum of citizen rights. This fractional scale has a natural minimum at 0, when no citizen right is granted, and a natural maximum at 1.0, when all are granted. The numerical values of these endpoints are directly interpretable, and there are a number of natural cut-off points, as depicted in Figure 8.1.

---

[3] I include social rights in my concept of civic entitlements but on a lower status. The reason is that, from an empowerment perspective, social rights are not ends in themselves. Instead, the function of social rights is strictly *compensatory* with respect to autonomy rights and participation rights (which are ends in themselves from an empowerment perspective). In other words, the purpose of social rights to enable those to exercise their participation and autonomy rights who otherwise lack the means to do so.

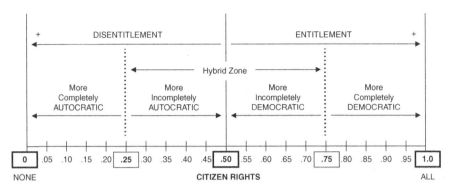

FIGURE 8.1 Institutionalized People Power as the Scope of Citizen Rights.

On a scale of citizen rights with minimum 0 and maximum 1.0, the 0.50 mark is an intuitively meaningful cut-off point. Below this point, regimes deny more rights than they guarantee, so they disentitle people more than they entitle them. Entitlements being more absent than present classifies all regimes below the 0.50 mark as more "autocratic" than "democratic." To simplify things, we might call them "autocracies," even though we must keep in mind that these regimes still vary in how completely autocratic they are. By contrast, all regimes above the 0.50 mark guarantee more rights than they deny, so they entitle people more than they disentitle them. This classifies regimes above the 0.50 mark as more "democratic" than "autocratic." Again, for simplicity, we might call these regimes "democracies" but, once more, we have to keep in mind that they still vary in how completely democratic they are.

The 0.25 and 0.75 marks provide equally meaningful cut off points. The 0.75 mark divides democracies into those closer to the democratic maximum (democracies above 0.75 scale points) and those closer to the neutral point (democracies below 0.75 scale points). This classifies the former as more "completely" democratic and the latter as more "incompletely" democratic. To simplify things, we might call them "incomplete" and "complete" democracies, respectively, even though they vary in exactly how incompletely or completely democratic they are. Among regimes that are more autocratic than democratic, the 0.25 mark operates in similar fashion, separating more "completely" autocratic regimes (autocracies below 0.25) from more "incompletely" autocratic regimes (autocracies above 0.25). Again, for reasons of brevity, we might call them incomplete and complete autocracies, although they still vary in how incompletely and completely autocratic they are.

Summing this up, the continuum of institutionalized citizen rights can be collapsed into four scale zones:

1. *Complete Autocracies*: citizen rights score between 0 and 0.25 scale points.
2. *Incomplete Autocracies*: citizen rights score between 0.25 and 0.50 scale points.

3. *Incomplete Democracies*: citizen rights score between 0.50 and 0.75 scale points.
4. *Complete Democracies*: citizen rights score between 0.75 and 1.0 scale points.

People power differentiates between autocracy and democracy as much as it differentiates within these categories, accounting for how completely autocratic and democratic societies are. Democracies are more completely democratic the closer they come to the maximum of civic entitlements. Autocracies are more completely autocratic the closer they come to the minimum of civic entitlements. Thus, the differences that separate autocracies from democracies and the differences that separate complete from incomplete versions of these two categories are differences on the same continuum: the scope of civic entitlements. A categorization of societies is possible after one has identified their position on this continuum. Contrary to Sartori's (1984) dictum, categorization follows grading rather than the other way round.

Autocracies, in a categorical sense, are defined by the fact that they deny more civic entitlements than they guarantee. But even autocracies differ in the degree to which they deny civic entitlements. It might appear as a semantic paradox to think of autocracies as differing in the degree to which they lack democracy. But this way of thinking is inherently logical when the categorization of a society as autocratic is derived from its score on a democracy index. In fact, when autocracies are defined by their lack of democracy, differentiating them by how much they lack democracy makes perfect sense.

1.4 A Conditional Measure of Citizen Rights

Under the notion of people empowerment, personal autonomy rights and political participation rights together form citizen rights (Brettschneider 2007). In combination, personal autonomy rights and political participation rights constitute not just electoral democracy but liberal democracy in a more substantive sense (Ottaway 2003).

Based on this premise it is evident that, in order to measure how democratic a society is, we must measure the extent to which both personal autonomy rights and political participation rights are guaranteed. The burgeoning literature on "illiberal democracies" and "electoral authoritarianism" reminds us that when any of these two basic sets of rights is insufficiently institutionalized, we deal with some version of a hybrid regime that is neither completely democratic nor completely autocratic (Collier & Levitsky 1997; Diamond 2002; Levitsky & Way 2002; Ottaway 2003; Merkel 2004).

If one considers autonomy rights as indicative of personal liberty and participation rights as indicative of political inclusion, then democracy in any substantive sense of the word can only mean that *both* autonomy rights and participation rights are sufficiently guaranteed, combining high degrees of personal liberty and political inclusion.[4] Deficiencies in either of these two characteristics suffice as a failure to create democracy, providing some diminished form of autocracy instead, namely, "inclusive autocracy" when participation rights are sufficiently guaranteed but autonomy rights are not, and "liberal autocracy" when autonomy rights are sufficiently guaranteed but participation rights are not. When none of these rights is sufficiently guaranteed, we face an undiminished form of autocracy that needs no further adjective. Thus, we obtain another four-fold typology, as depicted in Figure 8.2:

1. (Pure) *Autocracies* are autocracies in an undiminished sense because they deny most autonomy rights as well as most participation rights, scoring below 0.50 scale points on both.
2. *Liberal Autocracies* grant most autonomy rights but deny most participation rights, scoring above 0.50 scale points on the former but below 0.50 on the latter.
3. *Inclusive Autocracies* deny most autonomy rights but grant most participation rights, scoring below 0.50 scale points on the former but above 0.50 scale points on the latter.
4. (Minimal) *Democracies* grant most autonomy rights, as well as most participation rights, scoring above 0.50 scale points on both. Since the crossing of just the midpoint on both rights is a modest requirement, it is fair to speak about democracies in a minimal sense here.

Apart from classifying regimes, it is of inherent interest where on the citizen rights continuum in Figure 8.1 a regime is located. For that, we need a precise score of a regime's citizen rights, which must somehow be calculated from the scores on autonomy rights and participation rights. Assuming that fine-graded scores of both autonomy and participation rights exist in a 0–1.0 range, there are two possibilities to calculate from these an overall citizen rights score: the average and the product of autonomy and participation rights. The two possibilities can create dramatically different scores. Consider a society that scores 0.80 in participation rights and 0.40 in autonomy rights. Averaging the two, we obtain a citizen rights score of 0.60 scale points. This score classifies a society as an incomplete democracy on the citizen rights continuum in Figure 8.1. But if we multiply the constituent scores, we obtain 0.32 scale points on the citizen rights index (CRI), which classifies a society as an incomplete autocracy. Since the type of combination creates differences of such categorical scope, it is an essential question which combination is more appropriate.

---

[4] Of course, what "sufficient" means is not self-evident. For reasons of simplicity, let's assume "sufficient" means that citizen rights are guaranteed to *more than half* of their known scope in both rights domains. This implies that we cross the threshold from deficiency to sufficiency on both domains as we cross the midpoint of the theoretical scale range. If both rights domains are measured on a scale from 0 to 1.0, then a score of 0.51 or higher is the threshold of sufficiency.

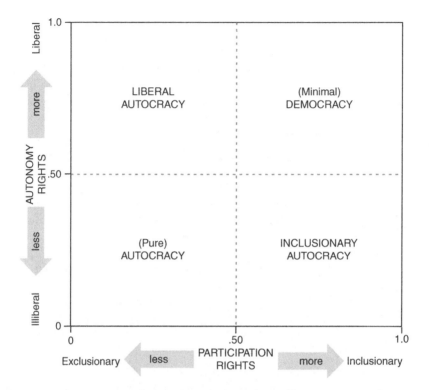

FIGURE 8.2 A Regime Typology by Autonomy Rights and Participation Rights.
It is assumed that the theoretical scale midpoint on both rights domains divides the
deficiency zone (below the midpoint) from the sufficiency zone (above the midpoint).
Thus, deficiency in both domains establishes pure autocracy, deficiency in one domain
establishes a diminished form of autocracy, and sufficiency in both establishes democracy
in a minimal sense.

Averaging the two rights scores would make sense if we have reason to
consider autonomy rights and participation rights as *complementary* with
respect to their unifying construct – democracy. In this case, one component's
contribution to democracy is undiminished by deficiency in the other.
Multiplication, by contrast, makes sense if we have reason to assume that the
two sets of rights represent conceptually distinct domains that do not simply
complement each other but instead condition each other, such that participation
rights contribute more to democracy the more autonomy rights are in place, and
vice versa. With this assumption, we do not want deficiencies in one domain to
be compensated by sufficiency in the other. This is exactly what multiplication
prevents from happening: it weighs down each component's contribution for
deficiency in the other. Hence, multiplication models necessary yet insufficient
conditionality among components (Goertz 2006).

Box 8.1   Conditional and Complementary Indicator Combinations

In the logic of compository index construction (see Box 2.1, p. 60), measures of two or more attributes are combined into an overall index, if they form an empirically consequential combination of attributes. An important question refers to the combinatory logic according to which the attributes work together. There are two possibilities: *additive* combination through mutually *complementary* contributions, or *multiplicative* combination through mutually *conditioning* contributions.

For instance, if we think that the contributions of autonomy rights (AR) and participation rights (PR) to democracy are complementary, this implies that each component's contribution is independent of the other: more AR contribute the same to democracy on each level of PR; and more PR contribute the same to democracy on each level of AR. This assumption calls for an additive combination by averaging AR and PR.

However, if we think that one component's contribution depends on the other, so that AR contribute more to democracy when there are more PR and vice versa, then these are conditional contributions that amplify each other. This assumption calls for a multiplicative combination of AR and PR because multiplication is the mathematical expression of mutual conditionality. When using 0–1.0 scales, multiplication is equivalent to weighting: one weighs down one component for deficiency in the other.

I find the conditionality assumption more convincing in this case. Autonomy rights do not simply add to participation rights. Instead, autonomy rights make participation rights more effective, and vice versa: being accustomed to exercising rights in one domain of life enhances one's efficacy in exercising rights in another domain of life. Thus, the private and public domains of rights condition each other's efficacy of use. Hence, I apply a conditional logic that weighs down the contribution of participation rights to citizen rights for deficiencies in autonomy rights, and vice versa. This is done by multiplying the two rights scores.

The appropriateness of the conditional logic is plausible from yet another angle. Let's assume once more a regime with a 0.80 score in participation rights and a 0.40 score in autonomy rights. According to the classification in Figure 8.2, this is a diminished version of autocracy, namely, inclusive autocracy. Now, averaging the two scores yields a citizen rights score of 0.60, which is in the zone of incomplete democracy in Figure 8.1. That is inherently inconsistent: autocracy and democracy are incompatible categories. Calculating the product of the two rights scores avoids this inconsistency. With the product of participation rights and autonomy rights, only democracies in Figure 8.2 achieve a score that places them in the zone of democracies in Figure 8.1 (although not necessarily so, as we will see).

1.5 Indicators and Their Combination

In searching for indicators of citizen rights, the freedom ratings by Freedom House (FH) are an obvious choice. These ratings include two components. FH's *civil liberties* cover freedoms that are roughly equivalent to autonomy rights. The organization's *political rights* cover freedoms corresponding, by and large, with participation rights. Thus, to measure citizen rights, one could follow the convention and simply average FH's civil liberties and political rights ratings.[5] However, in view of the last section, this procedure is inappropriate because it treats different domains of rights as complementary when, in fact, they are mutually conditional. Thus, a multiplicative combination of the civil liberties and political rights scores is preferable (see Welzel 2006: 882 for a validation of this point).

Before proceeding with an interactive combination of autonomy rights and participation rights, the quality of the FH ratings can be improved by incorporating information from another data source: the Cingranelli and Richards (CIRI) human rights data project (Cingranelli & Richards 1999, 2010). For every society since 1981, this project provides an 8-point index of personal *integrity rights* and a 10-point index of political *empowerment rights*. The distinction between these two sets of rights overlaps roughly with FH's distinction, such that CIRI's integrity rights correspond with FH's civil liberties and CIRI's empowerment rights with FH's political rights.[6]

An important difference between the FH and CIRI indices is how they are obtained. As documented in its annual reports, FH does not use other officially documented information to rate societies but instead relies on the judgment of regional experts (Freedom House 2012). This procedure goes with all the advantages and disadvantages of the experts' subjectivity, as shown by Bollen and Paxton (2000). CIRI, by contrast, relies on documented rights violations, as reported by the U.S. State Department and Amnesty International, and it uses a standard coding scheme to transform the information included in these documents into index scores that measure how strongly certain types of rights are respected in a society. If both methods have their own bias, the difference in method is actually an advantage because, in combination, each method's bias weighs less. Accordingly, I combine the two methods by averaging the FH civil liberties and the CIRI integrity rights indices into a *combined index of autonomy rights* for each year and society for which both indices are available. Likewise, I average the FH political rights and the CIRI empowerment rights indices into a

---

[5] This is done after having reverted their polarity (so that higher scores measure more rights) and after standardizing the scales into a range from minimum 0 to maximum 1.0.

[6] For the years 2000 to 2005, for instance, CIRI's integrity rights correlate more closely with FH's civil liberties ($r = 0.68$, $p < 0.001$, $N = 187$) and CIRI's empowerment rights more closely with FH's political rights ($r = 0.84$, $p < 0.001$, $N = 188$) than CIRI's integrity rights and empowerments rights correlate with each other ($r = 0.53$, $p < 0.001$, $N = 187$).

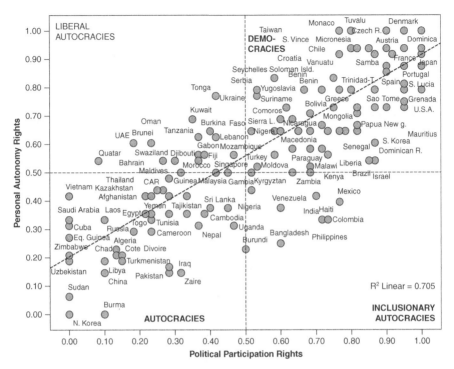

FIGURE 8.3 Distribution of Regimes over the Two Domains of Rights (in 2000). *Data Coverage*: All societies in the world with valid data (*N* = 154).

combined index of participation rights for each year and society for which both indices are available.[7] Appendix 8 (www.cambridge.org/welzel) documents these data.

Figure 8.3 exemplifies, for the year 2000, how participation rights and autonomy rights relate to each other.[8] The figure shows all societies in the world for which both measures are available. As one would expect, the two sets of rights are strongly positively correlated. In fact, the two sets of rights share 70 percent overlapping variance. The correspondence between the two sets of rights can also be seen in the fact that most societies are located in the lower left and upper right quadrants, reflecting a predominance of regimes that *consistently disentitle* their constituents (being both illiberal and exclusive), or *consistently entitle* them (being both liberal and inclusive). By contrast, liberal autocracies that entitle people in the domain of autonomy rights but keep

---

[7] For both combinations, this is done after standardizing all indices into a scale range from minimum 0 and maximum 1.0.

[8] The scattergram looks similar for any other year between 2000 and 2010, the latest year with available data at the time of this writing.

them disentitled in the domain of participation rights are rare, showing a certain concentration among the oil-exporting monarchies of the Middle East.[9] Inclusive autocracies that entitle people in the domain of participation rights while keeping them disentitled in the domain of autonomy rights are also rare, showing a concentration in South Asia and Latin America.

Yet, the correspondence between the two sets of rights is far from perfect. Almost a third of the variation in autonomy rights is not absorbed by the variation in participation rights (and vice versa). Thus, we find, at each level of participation rights in Figure 8.3, that autonomy rights vary in a range of about 0.40 scale points. In the middle zone of participation rights, from 0.30 to 0.70 scale points, autonomy rights vary even in a range of 0.60 scale points.

It follows from this distribution that weighting a society's participation rights for the presence of autonomy rights, or vice versa, yields an index of citizen rights with far more variation than there is in either of its two components or in their simple average. To be precise, in 2000 the variance coefficient over all societies is 0.41 for autonomy rights, 0.51 for participation rights, 0.44 for the average of the two, but 0.72 for their product.[10] Weighting the two sets of rights by each other actually means to weight them down for deficiencies in the other. Necessarily, this produces a lower citizen rights score for almost any combination of participation rights and autonomy rights than the average of the two provides. Indeed, while the global mean of the averaged autonomy and participation rights scores is 0.63, the mean of the weighted scores is 0.46. The discounting effect is especially pronounced for (a) societies in the middle zone of the two sets of rights and (b) societies with discrepant scores on the two sets. These discounts are fully intended by the conditional combination logic.

Figure 8.4 summarizes how I combine FH and CIRI information on different sets of rights into the citizen rights index. At the first level of generalization, I combine rescaled versions of the CIRI empowerment rights index and the FH political rights index additively by calculating their average. The resulting index measures the scope of legally granted and practically respected participation rights. I also combine rescaled versions of the CIRI integrity rights index and the FH civil liberties index additively by calculating their average. The resulting index measures the scope of legally granted and practically respected autonomy rights. At this level of generalization, I choose additive combinations because the indices that are combined measure the same domain of rights, although with different methods. Additive combinations average out each method's unique bias.

---

[9] I suppose that, if we included a specific measure of women's rights into the autonomy rights measure, the oil-exporting monarchies would no longer show up as liberal. At the time of this writing, there was not enough time to probe into this refinement, however. The task is left for future work. For a separate analysis of women's rights, consider Chapter 9.

[10] The variance coefficient is the ratio of a variable's standard deviation to its mean. The coefficient takes into account that standard deviations can only be compared across equal means.

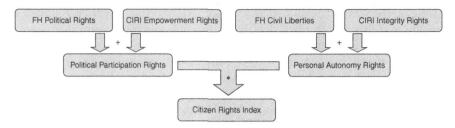

FIGURE 8.4 The Citizen Rights Index.
An additive combination is used to average out measurement bias among indicators supposedly measuring the same rights domain. A multiplicative combination is used to qualify distinctive rights domains for deficiencies in the other.

At the second level, I combine political participation rights and personal autonomy rights multiplicatively because here we combine separate domains of rights that condition each other. Mutual conditionality among components is mathematically expressed by multiplication.

Alexander and Welzel (2011) apply the same conditional logic: they qualify citizen rights by rule of law so as to measure what they call "effective democracy." Their index of effective democracy correlates with my citizen rights index at $r = 0.90$ ($p < 0.001$, $N = 185$) in 2000[11] and shows a similar distributional pattern. If given a choice, I would prefer the index of effective democracy because it provides an even more rigorous measure of democracy than the citizen rights index (for a validation, see Alexander, Inglehart, & Welzel 2012). Nevertheless, I use the citizen rights index for the analyses in this book because this index covers a wider time period, going back to 1981. This time coverage is needed for the longitudinal analyses in subsequent chapters.[12]

2. MEASUREMENT PERFORMANCE

2.1 Distributional Patterns

To assess the citizen tights index (CRI), we examine whether the societies' empirical distribution over the index conforms to the index's theoretical intention. The CRI is designed to favor the completion of civic entitlements. Given the emphasis on *complete* entitlements, incomplete entitlements constitute a deficiency almost as grave as absent entitlements. Thus, the CRI should place incomplete entitlements closer to absent entitlements than to complete entitlements. From this, it follows that the scoring of democracies on the CRI should

---

[11] The correlation is similar for other years.
[12] One of the components of Alexander and Welzel's (2011) effective democracy index, the World Bank rule of law index, is only available since 1996, which limits the possibility of longitudinal analyses.

stand out: they should be more distant from the other regime types in Figure 8.2 than these are from each other. Put differently, the step from diminished autocracy to democracy should be bigger than that from undiminished to diminished autocracy, if the completion of civic entitlements is emphasized. This is an inescapable implication of the CRI's conditional logic.

Figure 8.5 uses the regime typology of Figure 8.2 and shows the mean score, standard deviation, and score range of each of the four regime types on the CRI. The figure also displays the location of these scores in the scale zones of Figure 8.1. By and large, the empirical distribution over the CRI meets the index's intention. Undiminished autocracies and the two types of diminished autocracies differ only weakly on the CRI: on average, autocracies score at 0.08 scale points – which is, of course, in the completely autocratic zone of Figure 8.1. Liberal autocracies score, on average, at 0.19, still in the completely autocratic zone of Figure 8.1. Inclusive autocracies score only somewhat higher, at 0.27 scale points – again in the autocratic zone of Figure 8.1, albeit in the incompletely autocratic section. The societies in these three regime categories cluster very densely around their category's mean CRI score. Democracies stand out.

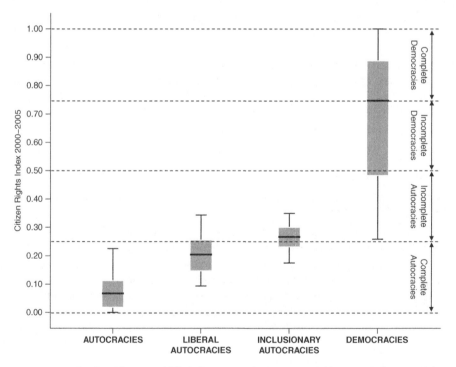

FIGURE 8.5 Regime Types and Their Scores on the Democratic/Autocratic Zones of the Citizen Rights Index (year 2000).
Data Coverage: All societies in the world with valid data (N = 180).

Their mean score is 0.75 scale points – far above all the nondemocratic regime categories. Indeed, democracies, in the definition of Figure 8.2, are the only regime category whose mean score is located in the democratic zone of Figure 8.1, right on the border between the incompletely and completely democratic sections. Yet, democracies, by the definition of Figure 8.2, are minimal democracies only: the minimal requirement is that they score just above 0.50 on both sets of rights. This still allows for great variation on the CRI among these minimally democratic regimes: they vary from 0.26 to 1.0 scale points.[13] For a democracy in this minimal sense to be placed in the democratic zone of Figure 8.1, it must achieve a score higher than 0.70 on *both* sets of rights.

The distributional pattern in Figure 8.5 meets the intended measurement properties of the CRI: the difference between absent and incomplete entitlements is much smaller than that between incomplete and complete entitlements. As implied by the conditional logic, scores on the CRI place a premium on complete civic entitlements.

2.2 Reassessing the Global Democratization Trend

Measuring citizen rights in a conditional way discounts participation rights to the extent that autonomy rights are lacking, and vice versa. As a result, the CRI sets a high standard for measuring a society's degree of democratization. Measured against a higher standard, the global democratization wave of recent decades does not look as impressive as it appears with less demanding measures of democracy. To demonstrate this point, the two line charts in Figure 8.6 plot the global percentage of societies that (a) represent the four regime types from our four-fold typology (left-hand diagram) and (b) the four scale zones on the CRI (right hand diagram), for each year from 1981 to 2010.[14]

Looking at the left-hand diagram, it is evident that the two diminished versions of autocracy do not show much movement. From 1981 to 2010, the proportion of societies in these two categories remains consistently below 20 percent. The decisive change happens among pure autocracies and minimal democracies. Until 1988, pure autocracies fluctuate around the 50 percent line and democracies around the 30 percent line. But then, within three years (!) they switch positions: autocracies plummeting to a 30 percent representation and democracies jump to a 50 percent representation in the global state system. Since then, autocracies approach the 25 percent line while democracies approach the 60 percent line. This pattern looks familiar, resembling very much what Doorenspleet (2000) characterizes as the "global explosion of democracy."

---

[13] A score of 0.26 on the CRI is the minimum possible score for democracies in the definition of Figure 8.2: the requirement to have a score of at least 0.51 in both autonomy rights and participation rights yields a score of 0.51 * 0.51 = 0.26.

[14] Newer data were unavailable at the time when this analysis was completed.

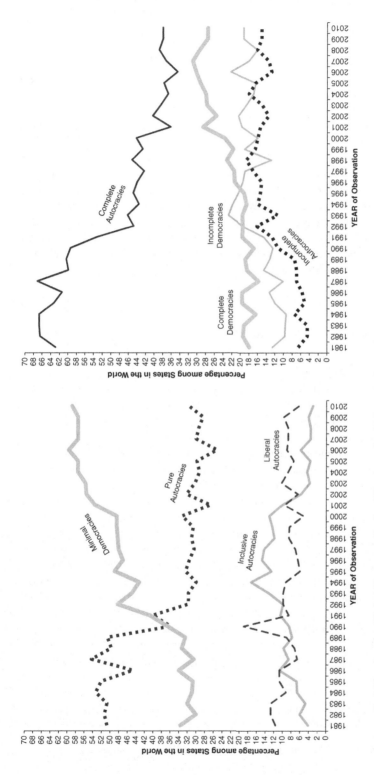

FIGURE 8.6 Tracing the Global Democratization Wave on the Citizen Rights Index (1981–2010).
Left-hand Diagram: Regime Typology from Figure 8.2. *Right-hand Diagram*: Scale Zone from Figure 8.1.
Data Coverage: All societies in the world with valid data N varies over the years from 141 to 188 countries.

However, democracies in the left-hand diagram of Figure 8.6 are democracies in a minimal sense. Thus, when we evaluate them under the completion criterion, many of them show incomplete civic entitlements on the CRI. In that sense, they are deficient democracies. Consequently, the democratic trend looks more modest if we trace it along the four scale zones in Figure 8.1. This is obvious from the right-hand diagram in Figure 8.6. As this diagram documents, there is a pronounced shrinkage of complete autocracies, with a particularly deep drop in the early 1990s, when Soviet-type communism collapsed. Overall, the percentage of complete autocracies falls by almost 30 percentage points, from some 65 percent in 1981 to 38 percent in 2010. But this loss is not compensated by a corresponding increase of complete democracies. In fact, complete democracies increase only from 18 percent in 1981 to 28 percent in 2010. This result contrasts starkly with the left-hand diagram, where democracies in a minimal sense became the clear majority of societies in the world. In contrast, complete democracies, by the definition of Figure 8.1, are far from a majority position. They are still outnumbered by complete autocracies. Moreover, there are other winners of the shrinkage of complete autocracies, namely, hybrid regimes: incomplete autocracies grow by 9 percentage points, from 7 percent in 1981 to 16 percent in 2010; incomplete democracies grow by 6 percentage points, from 13 to 19 percent over the same period. At any rate, from the viewpoint of civic entitlements, complete democracies are fewer today than standard accounts of the global democratization trend suggest.

Overall, the distributional patterns of the CRI are in accordance with the conditional logic that informs its construction. As implied by the conditional logic, whether a regime does not entitle citizens at all or only does so partially makes less of a difference than whether or not a regime entitles citizens completely. It is the completion of entitlements that matters.

2.3 Empowerment Linkages

A chief criterion of measurement performance is *nomological validity*, that is, how strongly a measure is linked with other phenomena – phenomena that are not themselves part of the measure but represent theoretically expected correlates, consequences, or antecedents of it (Adcock & Collier 2001; Denton 2008).

The CRI is essentially a democracy measure, so the nomological validity of the CRI must be assessed against criteria relevant to democracy. Democracy is about people power, so human empowerment is democracy's key conceptual link to other aspects of reality. In the logic of nomological validity, then, a democracy index is a more valid measure of people power the more closely it associates with other – preinstitutional – aspects of human empowerment. Accordingly, we can assess the external validity of various democracy indices by examining how strongly they associate with preinstitutional aspects of human empowerment. The more strongly an index associates, the better it taps democracy's supposed link to empowering qualities in its social context.

The human empowerment framework continues a tradition in political theory. This tradition sees democracy as a socially embedded regime that is conditioned by features of its social context (Lipset 1959, 1960; Dahl 1973; Putnam 1993). In this tradition, modernization theory emphasizes various *socioeconomic* features as embedding conditions of democracy (Bollen & Jackman 1985; Vanhanen 1997, 2003; Boix 2003; Boix & Stokes 2003; Acemoglu & Robinson 2006). The civic culture approach, by contrast, emphasizes certain *sociocultural* features as embedding conditions of democracy (Lasswell 1951; Almond & Verba 1963; Putnam 1993; Verba et al. 1995; Inglehart 1997).

As shown in Figure 1.1 (p. 44), the human empowerment framework integrates socioeconomic and sociocultural conditions into a single scheme in which each condition constitutes a distinct empowering quality in the social context of democracy. Figure 8.7 rearranges the causal sequence of Figure 1.1 into a model of embedding shells. At the core of the model, I situate civic entitlements. As a manifestation of an empowering political regime, civic entitlements are embedded in an empowering sociocultural context. The clearest manifestation of such a context is the prevalence of emancipative values because these values give people an empowering motivation, encouraging them to take their lives into their own hands. In turn, emancipative values are embedded in an empowering socioeconomic context based on widespread action resources, including intellectual skills, material equipment, and connective opportunities. The best indicator of all three types of resources is the index of technological advancement described in the Introduction. In summary, as an empowering institutional setup, democracy should reflect the empowering qualities in its preinstitutional context.

FIGURE 8.7 The Shell Model of Human Empowerment.

This scheme situates the two sets of embedding conditions and their core, democracy, in a single framework that highlights human empowerment as the integrating theme, without diluting each component's distinct contribution.

In the human empowerment perspective, the CRI can be considered a nomologically valid measure of democracy if this index is closely associated with technological advancement and emancipative values. But, to conclude that the CRI is the *most* valid measure of democracy, it must associate more closely than any of its four components with technological advancement and emancipative values.

To establish association, it is irrelevant whether the association exists because citizen rights are associated as an *antecedent* or as a *consequence* with technological advancement and emancipative values. In either case, association is indicative of the extent to which the CRI represents empowering qualities in the social context of democracy, be it as an antecedent or consequence of these qualities.

However, the sequence thesis of emancipation theory suggests that empowering contexts condition democracy rather than democracy conditioning these contexts. The reasons for this causal proposition are clear. Since democracy entitles people to exercise freedoms, democracy can become a useful tool in the hands of the people, if – and only if – these people are both capable and eager to exercise freedoms. This is a demanding precondition: it requires empowering socioeconomic and sociocultural conditions to be in place. Empowering socioeconomic conditions, manifest in technological advancement, make people capable to exercise freedoms. Empowering sociocultural conditions, manifest in emancipative values, make people eager to exercise freedoms. Democracy then completes people's empowerment by entitling them to exercise freedoms. To achieve this purpose, democratic institutions need a preinstitutional context that already embodies empowering qualities.

The sequence thesis suggests that democracy is conditioned by empowering features of its social context but does not produce this context. Evidence supporting this proposition has been presented in Chapter 4 (see Table 4.2, p. 164). Viewing democracy as conditioned by empowering qualities in its social context implies that democracy associates with prior rather than subsequent context measures. To mirror this assumption, temporal order is important. Hence, I relate the various measures of democracy to measures of technological advancement and emancipative values that predate the democracy measures by ten years. I choose this rather large time distance to leave no ambiguity about the temporal order. If we can establish association between democracy and its supposed antecedents in this temporal order, we examine the causal quality of this association in the next step. The crucial issue here is endogeneity: do technological advancement and emancipative values exert an effect on later democracy independent of their imprint from earlier democracy? To answer this question, we isolate the variation in technological advancement and emancipative values that is independent from prior democracy and see if this independent variation continues to affect subsequent democracy, in which case we have evidence of a truly exogenous impact.

TABLE 8.1 *Correlations of Empowering Social Conditions in 1995 with Civic Entitlements in 2005*

2005 CIVIC ENTITLEMENTS	1995 EMPOWERING SOCIAL CONDITIONS	
	Technological Advancement	Emancipative Values
FH Civil Rights	0.64*** (136)	0.70*** (80)
FH Political Rights	0.61*** (136)	0.68*** (80)
CIRI Integrity Rights	0.56*** (136)	0.59*** (80)
CIRI Empowerment Rights	0.52*** (136)	0.70*** (80)
FH Civil + Political Rights^a	0.63*** (136)	0.69*** (80)
CIRI Integrity + Empowerment Rights^b	0.61*** (136)	0.71*** (80)
Personal Autonomy Rights^c	0.66*** (136)	0.70*** (80)
Political Participation Rights^d	0.59*** (136)	0.71*** (79)
Average Citizen Rights^e	0.64*** (136)	0.73*** (79)
Citizen Rights Index^f	**0.69*** (136)**	**0.75*** (79)**

Entries are Pearson correlations (r) with the number of societies with valid data in parentheses. Strongest correlations are marked in gray. Overlapping N between civic entitlements and emancipative values is less than 95 because I only include the values measures from the World Values Surveys rounds three and four (1990–95). This is done to keep the values measure temporally prior to the civic entitlements measures.
FH, Freedom House; CIRI, Cingranelli and Richards
^{a} Average of FH Civil and Political Rights
^{b} Average of CIRI Integrity and Empowerment Rights
^{c} Average of FH Civil Rights and CIRI Integrity Rights
^{d} Average of FH Political Rights and CIRI Empowerment Rights
^{e} Average of c and d
^{f} Product of c and d

Table 8.1 shows zero-order correlations between measures of technological advancement and emancipative values,[15] from 1995 on one hand, and various measures of citizen rights from 2005, on the other hand. The result is straightforward: even though all component measures of citizen rights associate significantly and positively with both technological advancement and emancipative values, the CRI associates more closely with both technological advancement ($r = 0.69$, $N = 136$) and emancipative values ($r = 0.83$, $N = 79$) than any of its four components, and more closely than any of their additive combinations. Hence, among the various possibilities to combine components of citizen

[15] In fact, the emancipative values measures are taken from WVS rounds two to four and thus cover the time period from 1990 to 2000. The mean measurement point in time, however, is 1995. Wherever only the round two measure from 1990 or only the round four measure from 2000 was available, I calculated the expected value for 1995 based on the respective regression formula and substituted the 1995 expected value for the 1990 and 2000 measure.

rights into an overall index, the multiplicative combination of the CRI is the most valid one.

The next question is how well the CRI performs in comparison with alternative measures of democracy. Does the CRI tap democracy's link with empowering social conditions as well as do the alternative measures? Indeed it does. Using the year 2005 as a common base, the CRI outperforms the Polity Project's *autocracy-democracy index* (Marshall & Jaggers 2004). While the CRI correlates at $r = 0.69$ with technological advancement and at $r = 0.83$ with emancipative values, the autocracy-democracy index correlates at 0.53 and 0.65 with these empowering qualities.[16] The CRI also outperforms the democratic tradition measure by Gerring et al. (2005). The latter correlates at 0.57 and 0.70 with the two empowering qualities. The CRI performs about equally well as Vanhanen's (2003) *index of democratization*, whose latest measure in 2000 correlates at 0.77 with both of the empowering qualities. The same holds true for the World Bank's *voice and accountability index* (Kaufman, Kraay, & Mastruzzi 2008). The 2005 measure of this index correlates at 0.77 and 0.78 with the empowering qualities. In the same ballpark, the 2005 *democracy index* by *The Economist* (2007) correlates at 0.71 and 0.80 with the empowering qualities.

However, the latter two indices are unequal contenders because they incorporate cultural indicators.[17] In this way, they extend the definition of democracy beyond the institutional domain. This is undesirable for three reasons. First, democracy is defined as an institutional concept; hence, its measurement should be strictly limited to institutional characteristics. Second, incorporating features of democracy's cultural context into the measure of democracy itself deprives us of the possibility to examine the link between the two. For the same reason, the correlation between democracy and its cultural context is semi-tautological when aspects of the cultural context are incorporated into the measure of democracy.

Among the democracy measures with a clear institutional focus, only one really outperforms the CRI in tapping democracy's link with empowering societal conditions. This is Alexander and Welzel's (2010) *effective democracy index*: the 2005 measure of this index correlates at 0.81 with technological advancement and at 0.85 with emancipative values. But measures of this index are available only since 1996 because one of its components, the World Bank's rule of law measure, is not available before that year. Hence, the index of effective democracy is of limited use for longitudinal analyses. For this reason, I stick to the CRI for the following analyses.

---

[16] Correlations of democracy with technological advancement reported in this paragraph are based on 128 to 133 societies; correlations with emancipative values on 78 to 81 societies. Needless to say, all reported correlations are statistically significant at the 0.001-level.

[17] Both *The Economist*'s democracy index and the World Bank's voice and accountability index use data from the WVS that partly overlap with emancipative values.

3. VALIDATING DEMOCRACY'S SOCIAL EMBEDDEDNESS

3.1 Removing Endogeneity

We have seen in Chapter 4 that the strong association between emancipative values and citizen rights does not exist because emancipative values are somehow "endogenous" to citizen rights, as some scholars claim (Hadenius & Teorell 2005). With the measures used in this chapter, we can subject the endogeneity assumption another, rather rigid test. So far, we related measures of technological advancement and emancipative values from 1995 to measures of citizen rights taken ten years later, namely in 2005, assuming a causal direction from technological advancement and emancipative values toward citizen rights. But we can also relate the measures of technological advancement and emancipative values from 1995 to measures of citizen rights taken ten years before, that is, in 1985. Then we can look at whether technological advancement and emancipative values associate more closely with prior or subsequent measures of citizen rights. A stronger association with prior citizen rights would suggest that technological advancement and emancipative values associate with citizen rights primarily as their consequence. A stronger association with subsequent citizen rights would suggest that technological advancement and emancipative values associate with citizen rights primarily as their condition.

We can do even more. Perhaps there is at least partial endogeneity, such that technological advancement and emancipative values depend in part on prior citizen rights. In as far as endogeneity exists, we can remove it and isolate the nonendogenous parts of technological advancement and emancipative values (King, Keohane, & Verba 1994). Then we can see if these nonendogenous parts still show a significant and positive effect on subsequent citizen rights, controlling for these rights' temporal self-perpetuation. This is done by regressing citizen rights from 2005 on measures of technological advancement and emancipative values from 1995 while controlling for citizen rights in 1985. Including citizen rights from 1985 into the regression takes care of three things:

1. We control the temporal self-perpetuation of citizen rights, analyzing only that part of citizen rights that is unrelated to its prior level.
2. We isolate the nonendogenous parts of technological advancement and emancipative values, examining the effects of these variables only insofar as they are unaffected by prior citizen rights.
3. Controlling for prior citizen rights includes *every* prior influence on citizen rights that is not specifically addressed; because of that, omitted variable bias is not an issue.

The whole procedure is a conservative test of endogeneity because it assumes that citizen rights in 1985 are themselves perfectly exogenous: we pretend that these rights carry no influence whatsoever from even earlier technological advancement and emancipative values. This procedure assumes maximum

TABLE 8.2 *Effects of Empowering Social Conditions on Subsequent Civic Entitlements (before and after eliminating endogeneity)*

PREDICTORS	DEPENDENT VARIABLES	
	2005 Citizen Rights *before* Eliminating Endogeneity[a]	2005 Citizen Rights *after* Eliminating Endogeneity[b]
1995 Technological Advancement	0.70*** (128)	0.49*** (128)
1990–95 Emancipative Values	0.81*** (79)	0.63*** (79)

Entries are bivariate correlation coefficients (r) in the middle column and multivariate, partial correlation coefficients (partial r) in the right column, with number of observations in parentheses.

[a] 2005 citizen rights are regressed separately on 1995 technological advancement and 1990–1995 emancipative values.

[b] 2005 citizen rights are regressed separately on 1995 technological advancement and 1990–1995 emancipative values, yet, in both regressions, 1985 citizen rights are included as an additional predictor. Thus, we examine the effects of technological advancement and emancipative values on citizen rights ten years later, controlling for these two variables' dependencies on citizen rights ten years before. In so doing, we isolate these variables' exogenous effect.

possible endogeneity for technological advancement and emancipative values, setting the bar high for detecting a nonendogenous effect on citizen rights. If, despite this high bar, we still detect a nonendogenous effect, the conclusion that this effect is indeed exogenous is safe.

Table 8.2 displays the results of this analysis. They are straightforward. The zero-order effects of technological advancement (b = 0.70) and of emancipative values (b = 0.81) on subsequent citizen rights are stronger than these two conditions' dependence on prior citizen rights (b = 0.65 in the case of technological advancement, b = 0.71 in the case of emancipative values). Furthermore, even after removing technological advancement's and emancipative values' partial dependence on prior citizen rights, these two conditions retain a highly significant and strongly positive effect on subsequent citizen rights (b = 0.49 in the case of technological advancement, b = 0.63 in the case of emancipative values). From another angle, these results assure that we can interpret technological advancement and emancipative values as qualities of the social context of democracy that indeed condition democracy rather than being produced by it.

3.2 Disclosing Cultural Embeddedness

Recent evidence seems to indicate that mass preferences do not really matter for democracy. For instance, Inglehart (2003: 54) shows that democratic mass preferences explain only a minor proportion of the cross-national variation in democratic institutions. In line with this finding, Fails and Pierce (2008) show that, after proper controls, mass preferences for democracy show no impact whatsoever on subsequent democracy.

However, against this dismissive interpretation of mass preferences Inglehart (2003) and Welzel (2006, 2007a) emphasize three things. First, people's overt regime preferences don't indicate an *intrinsic* preference for democracy, which is a preference for democracy's own sake based on an appreciation of the freedoms that define democracy. Second, an *intrinsic* preference for democracy depends on emancipative values because these values emphasize democracy's defining freedoms. Third, with regard to emancipative values, mass preferences show a very strong and robust impact on subsequent democracy, controlling for dozens of additional variables.

To further illustrate these points, I create an index of democratic preferences that assigns respondents a minimum score of 0 under two conditions: the respondent strongly endorses the army rule and strong leaders and at the same time rejects the idea of democracy. The index has a maximum of 1.0 with the opposite configuration and a neutral point at 0.50, indicating equal endorsement or rejection of democracy and the army rule/strong leaders.[18] Hence, this index balances preferences for democracy against conflicting preferences for the authoritarian alternatives of democracy, as is standard practice (Klingemann 1999; Shin & Tusalem 2007).

However, the theory of emancipation suggests that democratic preferences are relevant for a society's civic entitlements, if – and only if – these preferences are grounded in emancipative values. Democratic preferences that are ungrounded in emancipative values are irrelevant to a society's civic entitlements. By splitting people's democratic preferences into the part that is matched by their emancipative values and the part that overshoots these values, we separate grounded and ungrounded democratic preferences: the part of the democratic preferences matched by emancipative values is grounded in these values[19]; the part that overshoots them is ungrounded.[20] For each respondent, grounded and ungrounded democratic preferences are calculated in such a way that they vary from minimum 0 to maximum 1.0. On this basis, I calculate for

---

[18] Item wording and other details of this measure are documented in Appendix 8 (www.cambridge.org/welzel). In different nuances, this democratic preference index is in wide use.

[19] Since democratic preferences and emancipative values are measured on the same 0–1.0 scale, the part of democratic preferences matched by emancipative values is the given score in emancipative values when democratic preferences overshoot emancipative values (which is true for 88.9 percent of all 240,000 respondents for which both variables exist). When democratic preferences fall short of emancipative values, the score in democratic preferences itself is the matching part.

[20] The part of democratic preferences overshooting emancipative values is the difference obtained by subtracting the score in emancipative values from the score in democratic preferences. For the 11.1 percent of all respondents whose democratic preferences do not overshoot their emancipative values, the ungrounded preference score has been set at 0, indicating an absent overshoot.

each society a national mean score in grounded and ungrounded democratic preferences.[21]

Using these definitions, Figure 8.8 shows two partial plots from a regression that explains citizen rights by both ungrounded and grounded preferences for democracy. The left-hand diagram shows the partial association of citizen rights with people's ungrounded preferences for democracy; the right-hand diagram shows the partial association with grounded preferences. As is immediately obvious, the citizen rights of a society depend in no way on ungrounded democratic preferences: the regression line in the left-hand diagram is almost flat, and societies distribute widely and unsystematically around it. Even the slight upward slope would vanish if we excluded Malta and Ghana from the sample. The extreme position of these societies turns them into "leverage" cases that angle the regression line toward their location. In any case, it is clear that when ungrounded preferences for democracy are stronger, this does not do any good to a society's citizen rights. In societies where ungrounded preferences for democracy are very strong, as in Bangladesh, Iraq, Morocco, or Tanzania, citizen rights profit not at all. The right-hand diagram, by contrast, shows a pronounced positive impact of grounded democratic preferences on citizen rights, albeit with decreasing marginal returns. Overall, the strength of grounded mass preferences for democracy explains 60 percent of the cross-national variation in citizen rights measured later. Some outliers exist, like Belarus, Mali, and Malta. Yet they share no obvious commonality and, apart from these isolated cases, all other societies fit fairly well into the overall pattern.

The evidence for an absent link between democratic mass preferences and systemic democracy in the left-hand diagram of Figure 8.8 resonates with similar findings by Hadenius and Teorell (2005) and by Fails and Pierce (2008). These authors raise skepticism against any explanation of democracy that invokes mass preferences. Following their advice, researchers should abandon the assumption of a close link between political regimes and mass preferences (O'Donnell & Schmitter 1986; Higley & Burton 2006). However, this advice is mistaken because it ignores the distinction between grounded and ungrounded preferences for democracy. As the recent literature on "democrats with adjectives" suggests, standard measures of democratic preferences are inconsequential: they measure motivationally irrelevant preferences that do not guide mass actions toward democratic goals. The reason is that these preferences lack a solid grounding in emancipative values (Schedler & Sarsfield 2006; see also Bratton & Mattes 2001; Rose & Shin 2001; Mattes & Bratton 2007; Shin & Tusalem 2007). Unless we use emancipative values to qualify people's preferences for

---

[21] The two newly created variables are normally distributed at both the individual level and the societal level, and at both levels they correlate negatively at $r = -0.44$ and $r = -0.54$, respectively. Almost identical results are obtained when one separates the matching and nonmatching parts of democratic preferences by regressing them on emancipative values and saving the predicted and residual scores as two variables.

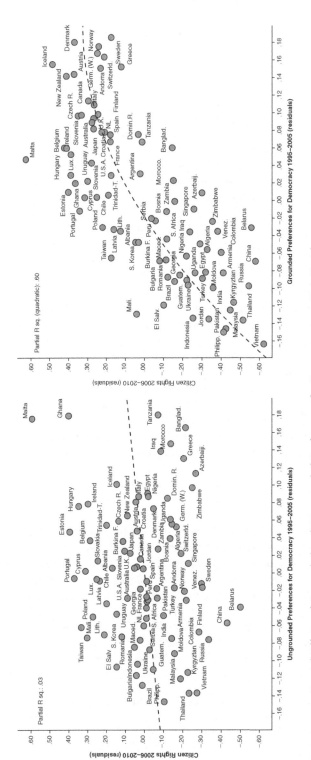

FIGURE 8.8 Partial Effects of Grounded and Ungrounded Preferences for Democracy on Civic Entitlements.

Left-hand Diagram: The plot shows whether, on the same level of "grounded" democratic preferences, more "ungrounded" democratic preferences correlate with wider citizen rights. As the wide distribution of societies around the flat regression line shows, this is not the case. Thus, holding grounded democratic preferences constant, ungrounded democratic preferences do not improve citizen rights.

Right-hand Diagram: The plot shows whether, on the same level of ungrounded democratic preferences, more grounded democratic preferences correlate with wider citizen rights. As the relatively narrow distribution of societies around the upward regression line shows, this is obviously the case. Thus, holding ungrounded democratic preferences constant, grounded democratic preferences help improving citizen rights.

Data Coverage: All societies with valid data surveyed at least once by the World Values Surveys (WVS), using the most recent survey ($N = 87$). *Grounded preferences for democracy* is that part of democratic preferences matched by emancipative values; *ungrounded preferences for democracy* is the part that overshoots emancipative values.

democracy, these preferences can mean anything, including lip service to a fashionable term whose defining freedoms are not really valued. In this case, it is not surprising that people's democratic preferences do not prompt them to act in pursuit of citizen rights. As a consequence, civic entitlements are disconnected from these preferences.

At this point in history, democracy is almost ubiquitously preferred, so what matters today is not whether democracy is preferred but whether it is preferred for the proper reason. The proper reason, from the emancipatory perspective, is that people prefer democracy because they value the freedoms through which democracy emancipates them. This is why emancipative values matter.

KEY POINTS

From the viewpoint of human empowerment, the purpose of democracy is to institutionalize people power. This purpose is realized first and foremost through civic entitlements. Civic entitlements are equally important in two mutually conditioning domains: political participation rights and personal autonomy rights. To operationalize the mutual conditionality of these two domains of rights, I created a citizen rights index that combines scores on these two domains multiplicatively, not additively. The citizen rights index has been tested for its measurement performance, with positive results. We have seen that, when we measure democracy as citizen rights, democracy is a socially grounded regime that closely reflects empowering qualities in democracy's social context, including action resources and emancipative values. We have also seen that democracy represents empowering qualities in its social context less as an antecedent than as a consequence of these qualities.

It also became obvious that mass preferences were prematurely declared irrelevant for democracy because scholars mistakenly interpret explicit mass preferences for democracy as a population's intrinsic valuation of democracy. At a time in which it has become common to prefer democracy to its authoritarian alternatives, the question is no longer whether people prefer democracy. The question is whether they prefer it for the proper reason: an intrinsic valuation of democracy's defining freedoms. The latter depends on how strongly people have internalized emancipative values.

Because democracy's inherent purpose is to empower people, one needs the human empowerment framework to fully understand democracy. Designed to institutionalize people power, democracy is a socially grounded regime that depends on empowering qualities on the preinstitutional basis of democracy. Human empowerment is an integrated phenomenon: it denotes empowering regime qualities within empowering social contexts that enable and encourage people to exercise freedoms. To further evidence these points, the next chapter examines in more general terms the dynamic relationship between emancipative values and citizen rights in both directions of impact.

9

The Rights Revolution[*]

> The efforts to stigmatize, and in many cases to criminalize, temptations to violence have been advanced in a cascade of campaigns for "rights" – civil rights, women's rights, children's rights, gay rights, and animal rights. These movements are tightly bunched in the second half of the 20th century, and I will refer to them as the rights revolutions.
>
> – Steven Pinker 2011

Human empowerment is the emancipation of people from external domination. Emancipation requires equal freedoms, and such freedoms are granted through citizen rights. Ironically, as large as the theme of citizen rights looms in our time, it has literally been absent throughout most of history. But since the onset of preindustrial capitalism, starting with the abolition of slavery and feudal privileges, history takes a new turn: the granting of rights to common people, the steady differentiation of these rights, and their continuous extension to new groups and territories become a major trend of development – indeed a signature theme of modernity itself (Marshall 1950; Moyn 2010). This tendency is visible in a chain of milestone documents from the *Habeas Corpus Act* in 1640 to the *Virginia Bill of Rights* in 1776, and the *Universal Declaration of Human Rights* in 1948 to the *Convention on the Rights of Persons with Disabilities* in 2006 (Donnelly 2003; Ishay 2008).

In what some call a *rights revolution* (Epp 1998; Franck 2001; Ignatieff 2000; Pinker 2011), the tendency to expand the rights of common people has intensified over recent decades. The rights revolution is evident in the growing prominence of rights discourses in the international arena (Moravcsik 2000; Landman 2005, 2006; Simmons 2009; Pegram 2010), the granting of rights in democratizing societies (Foweraker & Landman 1997; Beetham 1999; Donnelly

[*] I am grateful to Amy Alexander and Ronald Inglehart for their extensive input to an earlier draft of this chapter. I am also indebted to Roberto Foa for his insightful comments.

2003; Brettschneider 2007), and the attribution of rights to underprivileged groups, women being by far the largest (UNIFEM 2000; Walter 2001; Strom 2003; Coleman 2004). More recently, new rights are attributed to the increasingly visible group of lesbians, gays, bisexuals, and transsexuals (LGBTs) (Ungar 2000; Mertus 2007; Smith 2008; Wilson 2009).

The rights revolution represents the trend toward human empowerment in the domain of institutions. Another manifestation of this trend is apparent in the domain of culture. Here, we have seen that mass values are becoming more emancipatory, shifting toward greater emphasis on freedom of choice and equality of opportunities.

The concurrence of expanding citizen rights and rising emancipative values is no coincidence. Both trends are linked to the growing prominence of social movements whose supporters claim citizen rights and appeal to emancipative values to justify these claims (Markoff 1996; Foweraker & Landman 1997; Risse, Ropp, & Sikkink 2011). Citizen rights and emancipative values are mutually intertwined through their common focus on empowerment. Citizen rights empower people because they generalize entitlements against exclusive group privileges. Emancipative values empower people because they mobilize their desire for generalized entitlements.

The link between emancipative values and citizen rights is a key manifestation of the nexus between culture and institutions. As social theorists from Weber (1958 [1904]) to Parsons (1964) to Coleman (1990) have recognized, the culture-institution nexus is a society's configurative force. Understanding this nexus is to understand a society.

Institutions are the formal rules that prescribe a society's operations. A key component of these rules is the rights that a society's constituents do or do not possess. Culture is the representation of institutions in people's mindsets. Part of this representation includes the values that people attribute to the rights granted or denied to them. Thus, by studying the connection between values and rights, one studies a core arena of the culture-institution nexus.

Various theories assume that societies sustain given institutions only as long as the culture supports them; that is, as long as social actors believe in the value of these institutions (Almond & Verba 1963; Parsons 1964; Easton 1965; Eckstein 1966, 1998). In that sense, *institutions are value-dependent*. But the value-dependence of institutions varies: it is larger the more the proper functioning of institutions needs people's voluntary commitment (Coleman 1990). And the need for people's voluntary commitment tends to increase (Elias 1984 [1939]). The reason is one of modernity's major transformations: individualization (Bell 1973; Beck 2002). Individualization releases people's intrinsic motivations, makes them self-driven, unchains them from group bonds they haven't chosen, and diminishes their susceptibility to conformity pressures (Wellman 1979; Florida 2002). Control of people's behavior shifts from external sources of authority into people themselves, to their own values – which is altogether an emancipatory process (Flanagan & Lee 2003). As the emancipatory trend continues, governing bodies find it increasingly difficult to invoke their authority to guide people's behavior. Increasingly, governing bodies are forced to persuade and convince. Policies, including those that define rights, increasingly need people's voluntary commitment to achieve their purpose. Hence, people's values gain greater impact on the making of rights. This tendency is at the heart of the human empowerment trend.

These reflections suggest that citizen rights depend on emancipative values. Thus, citizen rights and emancipative values concur because values drive rights, more than rights drive values. This is an important suggestion because it contradicts the increasingly prominent idea that institutions are the source of all development (North, Wallis, & Weingast 2009; Acemoglu & Robinson 2012).

Until now, we did not examine how change in emancipative values relates to change in citizen rights in both directions of impact. What is missing is an analysis of the dynamic relationship between values and rights in a truly reciprocal perspective, focusing on how changes in the two variables over both shorter and longer periods of time relate to each other. Focusing on change is necessary for a causal interpretation of the values-rights linkage because causality is a dynamic concept: change in a supposed outcome variable is driven by change in a supposed input variable. So, what we test is whether the concurrence of changing rights and changing values is driven by the move in values or by the move in rights. We conduct this test while considering a third possibility: the concurrence of change in rights and values is of no inherent causal quality because both are driven by change in external factors.

The enormous rights literature is infused with assumptions about the reciprocity between rights and values (Donnelly 2003; Freeman 2003; Beitz 2009). Thus, claims for every possible reciprocity pattern exist. However, there are no studies that test alternative reciprocity patterns across a wide array of societies. In fact, there is not a single cross-national analysis of the relationship between rights and values (a) in both directions; (b) in a dynamic way, with a focus on concurrent changes; (c) for different rights domains; and (d) with controls for plausible third causes.

This chapter presents such an analysis in five sections. Section 1 discusses in theory what kind of reciprocity pattern is most likely to be expected for values and rights. Section 2 outlines the methods to test the expectation and briefly describes the country sample based on longitudinal data from the World Values Surveys (WVS). Section 3 introduces the variables, and section 4 reports the findings. I conclude with a discussion of their implications.

1. THEORY: THE VALUES-RIGHTS NEXUS

1.1 The Direction of Impact

The history of rights is the history of social movements fighting for these rights (Markoff 1996; Foweraker & Landman 1997; Schock 2005; Tilly 2007). This is not surprising. Establishing rights expands entitlements, and this always means abandoning privileges in which the privileged have a vested interest. This is why the underprivileged – whether defined by sex, race or class – almost always have to fight for their rights. Yet, for the underprivileged to be ready to fight, values must change.

For the most part, history is a story of societies that are stable despite appalling inequalities (Nolan & Lenski 1999). The reason is that the under-privileged learn through socialization to accept their discrimination. To break this pattern, a value change is necessary: discrimination must appear illegitimate, first among the underprivileged themselves but then also within the wider society. Otherwise, rights claimants will not appear, or they will not mobilize support (Tarrow 1998; McAdam, Tarrow, & Tilly 2003). The emergence and support of rights claims is contingent on concurrent value changes.

There is abundant evidence showing that underprivileged groups continue to accept their discrimination even long after their equality before the law has been established. For instance, scholars point to various instances in which gender inequality persists because women continue to believe in their inferiority, despite the fact that formal equality is legally guaranteed (Rowlands 1995; Kabeer 1999; Sen 1999; Nussbaum 2000). Hence, rights are often ineffective because they lack the concurrent change in values that is needed to upset people about rights violations. Given the rich evidence of this pattern, the opposite idea – that rights improvements are the main reason why values change in support of rights – is less plausible.

The sequence thesis of the human empowerment framework makes the same proposition. Underprivileged people begin to believe in their rights not because these rights are guaranteed. On the contrary, a belief in rights usually emerges under the *very denial* of these rights. Yet, the sequence thesis suggests that this process is highly contingent: it happens only if people have acquired the action resources that one needs to take advantage of rights. Only then do people see utility in rights and begin to value them. With action resources, people also acquire bargaining power: they are now capable of challenging the privileges that bloc their rights. Hence, the main reason why values change in support of rights is that growth in action resources – including skills, equipment, and connectivity – increase people's utility from rights, whether they already possess them or not. Subjective values change in response to changing objective utilities. This keeps human values in touch with reality, which is vital for our functioning. The effectiveness of rights depends on this utility-value link.

Change in values can drive change in rights when mechanisms exist through which mass values pave their way to institutions. I can think of at least two such mechanisms: people's voting behavior in societies with fairly free elections and people's activity in social movements, whether there are free elections or not.

1.2 Causal Mechanisms

To demonstrate across many societies and over a considerable period of time the mechanisms through which changing values pave their way to institutions would require an elaborate and costly research design that goes beyond the capacities of this study. So, we have to leave the mechanism question as a black box and test hypotheses merely about the observable outcomes of the supposed mechanism. Nevertheless, I shall try to put together at least some arguments about mechanisms that appear inherently plausible and for which there is supportive evidence.

In societies with free elections, newly emerging values transpire through opinion polls, media coverage, and elections. When the new values can no longer be ignored, candidates will run campaigns that appeal to the new values. In cases in which these values are emancipatory, rights are likely to enter the agenda of candidates. If the new values become the cultural mainstream, these candidates win majorities and the propagated rights are implemented in laws. Research on the congruence between the policy preferences of voters and representatives in democracies suggests that this mechanism indeed works (Schmitt & Wessels 2003; Dalton 2006; Lax & Philipps 2012). As at least the evidence from the United States indicates, the mechanism works in such a way that change in public opinion drives change in policies, rather than the other way round (Page & Shapiro 1992; Stimson 1999; Stimson, MacKuen, & Erikson 2002). This is particularly well documented for policies around abortion and same-sex marriage, which touch on two of the more specific rights domains considered in this chapter: women's rights and LGBT rights.

In semi-authoritarian regimes where competitive elections are heavily manipulated, rising emancipative values might not as easily translate into rights improvements. The reason is the very purpose of authoritarian structures: shielding those in power from mass desires. This seems to be even more true in outright authoritarian regimes that do not hold competitive elections at all. However, Zavadskaya and Welzel (2013) show that power holders in semi-authoritarian regimes are not quite as shielded from mass influences as one might think. In fact, mass protests against electoral fraud, as well as an electoral defeat of the incumbent, are significantly more likely where emancipative values have grown stronger. Even in outright authoritarian regimes, mass protests have frequently led to regime change toward democracy (Thompson 2004; Karatnycki & Ackerman 2005; Schock 2005; Ulfelder 2005). By definition, such regime transitions come with rights improvements.[1] What is more, mass protests against authoritarian regimes are more powerful and more likely to be successful when they are driven by emancipative values (Welzel 2007a). This complements the findings in Chapter 7, where we saw that emancipative values strongly encourage peaceful mass protest, regardless of whether there is a threat of repression.

Unless propped up by outside forces, authoritarian regimes are not as shielded from mass desires as one might think. Often, these regimes stay in power not because they suppress mass desires for rights; instead, they are most of the time

---

[1] This is true by definition because my operationalization of democracy actually centers on rights (see Chapter 8).

not confronted with such desires. One reason is that the cultural breeding ground of these desires – emancipative values – has not yet matured. Supporting this point, WVS data show that in a couple of authoritarian societies – among others China, Pakistan, Saudi Arabia, and Vietnam – people evaluate their rights situation very favorably.[2] There is a striking regularity behind this pattern: where people express satisfaction with a deficient rights situation, emancipative values are weak. This is obvious from Figure 9.1: across the eighty-four societies for which these data are available, the weakness of emancipative values is responsible for 58 percent of people's satisfaction with deficient rights.[3] Hence, people's judgment of their rights situation tells us more about their subjective values than about their objective rights situation.[4]

[2] One might assume that, out of fear, respondents in authoritarian systems rate the rights situation favorably even though they are dissatisfied with it. On the other hand, people in these societies are not often asked about their opinion and might be particularly eager to express it when given the chance. If both impulses conflict with each other, the easiest way out would be nonresponse. In this case, one would expect a particularly high nonresponse rate in the most authoritarian societies covered by the WVS. However, the nonresponse rate is 3.2 percent in the societies classified as nondemocratic in Table I.2 (p. 21) of the Introduction. This negligible proportion makes it implausible that many respondents rate the rights situation favorably when, in fact, they are unhappy about it. In other words, I believe that many people are indeed as satisfied with the rights situation as the say. This interpretation is more easily reconcilable with the fact that, most of the time, repressive regimes are not confronted with mass pressures for rights. A plausible reason for such satisfaction is weak emancipative values: when these values are weak, people have no strong expectation about their rights, in which case they are easily satisfied. By contrast, when emancipative values grow, people have higher expectations about their rights and are eager to express their dissatisfaction, in case these expectations are not met. Consequently, social movement activity grows even in the face of repressive threats, as Chapter 7 has shown. In conclusion, most authoritarian regimes do not survive because they repress rising emancipatory aspirations; they survive because such aspirations do not rise in the first place.

[3] The vertical axis in Figure 9.1 uses a WVS question (V164) asking people what they think the respect level is for human rights in their country, from no respect at all to full respect. I recode the 4-point response format into a scale from 0 (no respect) to 1.0 (full respect) and subtract from each respondent's judgement her country's citizen rights score of the same year (which is in the same 0–1.0 scale range). This yields a difference index in which larger positive numbers indicate how much people's rights evaluation overrates the actual situation, whereas larger negative numbers indicate how much their evaluation underrates the actual situation. Finally I calculate for each country her respondents' average evaluation.

[4] An alternative interpretation is that people's evaluation of the rights situation shows what they know about rights, in which case informational connectedness and formal education should be strong correlates of people's misjudgment of the rights situation. Indeed, using the country-pooled individual data of WVS round five, including some 53,000 respondents from fifty societies, formal education correlates at $r = -.08$ and informational connectedness at $r = -0.18$ with rights misjudgments. Emancipative values, by contrast, correlate at $r = -0.34$ with rights misjudgments and also trump the other two predictors in a multivariate regression. I could find no stronger correlate of rights misjudgments than emancipative values. Hence, I think the conclusion is safe that these misjudgments indicate satisfaction with a deficient rights situation among people with weak emancipative values. This is inherently plausible: for someone who does not embrace emancipative values, rights are less important. Hence, such a person is more likely to be satisfied with a deficient rights situation.

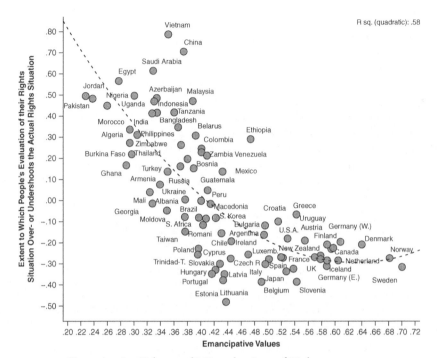

FIGURE 9.1 Emancipative Values and Misevaluations of Rights.
Analysis includes all eighty-four societies with available data surveyed once by the World
Values Surveys (WVS), using the latest available survey from each society. Time coverage
thus varies from about 1995 to 2005. Vertical axis is the difference between people's
rating of their society's human rights situation and the society's actual citizen rights score
at the year of the survey. The difference index has a theoretical minimum of –1.0 in cases
in which all people of a society would rate its rights situation the worst when actually it is
the best. The theoretical maximum is +1.0 in cases in which all people of a society rate
their rights situation the best possible when it is actually the worst. It is worthwhile to note
how close indeed Vietnam, China, and Saudi Arabia are to this situation. As a comparison
of this diagram with Figure 10.6 in Chapter 10 reveals, people's assessment of rights and
democracy tells us more about expectation standards than about objective situations.

These findings suggest that semi-authoritarian and authoritarian structures
do not shield power holders from mass desires for rights. These structures persist
not because they suppress mass desires for rights but because, most of the time,
they are not confronted with such desires. But when emancipative values give
rise to such desires, the authoritarian shields begin to erode under swelling social
movement activity. Hence, in authoritarian settings, it might take longer than in
democratic settings for the link between value change and rights improvements
to emerge. Yet, it should emerge in authoritarian regimes, too. When it does, we
face the very demise of authoritarianism. By the same token, authoritarian
systems that remain stable and make no rights improvements most likely

experience no growth in emancipative values – the reason why it is easy for them to avoid improving on rights.

Now, if all this is flawed, and changes in values and rights only concur in democratic societies, we will see no general concurrence in a sample that covers all types of regimes, including semi-authoritarian and authoritarian ones. Hence, to test whether rising emancipative values and rights improvements concur across different regimes, our sample must include different regimes, not just democracies.

2. METHODS

To study the concurrence of changing values and rights, we need longitudinal data to measure change. But how is it possible to decide which among two concurrent changes is the driving one? To answer this question, we employ the same approach as for the dynamic shift models in Chapter 4.[5]

The basic idea is to estimate a system of *reciprocal* regressions, one from changing values on changing rights and another in the opposite direction, and then compare the regression coefficients. However, this method leads to conclusive results only if we can dissolve the symmetry in the reciprocal relationship between the two paired variables. To do so, we need to "disturb" the reciprocal determination between the paired variables. This can be done by bringing in additional sources of determination – sources that potentially affect the paired variables differently. If one of the paired variables is indeed more affected by these other sources of determination, this particular variable's reciprocal determination will become smaller – smaller especially than the reciprocal determination of its paired counterpart. This will turn the reciprocity asymmetric: among the paired variables, the stronger effect will now run from the one with the smaller to the one with the larger reciprocal determination. Thus, by uncovering the asymmetry in a reciprocal relationship, we can identify which of two concurrent changes is the driving one and which is the driven one.

To uncover the asymmetry in the reciprocal determination between changes in values and rights, we introduce two additional sources of determination: *autonomous determination* and *heteronomous determination*.

Autonomous determination means how strongly each of two concurrent changes is driven by its own inertia, as indicated by temporal autocorrelation. Heteronomous determination means how strongly each of two concurrent changes is driven by third changes outside the reciprocal system. Now, if

---

[5] Note that, for a causal relationship between two changes to exist, one change does not need to be completed before the other. It is perfectly possible that, between two contemporaneous changes, one is the driver and the other the driven. Sunset and temperature drop occur contemporaneously but sunset is driving the drop in temperature. In the political world, Stimson (1999) shows this for the relationship between public opinion change and policy change: they are contemporaneous, but opinion change drives policy change more than the other way round.

among two concurrent changes, one shows more autonomous and heteronomous determination, this one's reciprocal determination will become smaller than the reciprocal determination of its paired counterpart. The reciprocity turns now asymmetric and this will show up by one of the two changes having a stronger effect on the other in a system of regressions specified in the two opposite directions of impact.

Thus, we estimate a system of reciprocal regressions by taking both change variables' autonomous and heteronomous determination into account. In the first step, we look at how change in values and change in rights affect each other, controlling for both variables' autonomous determination. Formally speaking, we model rights at time T_2 as a function of (1) rights at time T_1 and (2) change in values from time T_1 to time T_2. Conversely, we model values at time T_2 as function of (1) values at time T_1 and (2) change in rights from time T_1 to time T_2. Letting V denote values, R denote rights, c a constant, and ε an error term, we write:

$$R(T_2) = c + b_1{}^* R(T_1) + b_2{}^* \Delta V(T_2 - T_1) + \varepsilon \qquad \text{(Eq. 1a)}$$

$$V(T_2) = c + b_1{}^* V(T_1) + b_2{}^* \Delta R(T_2 - T_1) + \varepsilon \qquad \text{(Eq. 1b)}$$

In both models, we explain the outcome variable under control of its prior level, which is equivalent to explaining change in the outcome variable: we explain its later level insofar as it has shifted away from its prior level.[6] Accordingly, the b_2-coefficient of the first equation tells us to what extent change in values shifts subsequent rights away from their initial level.[7] Similarly, the b_2-coefficient of the second equation tells us to what extent change in rights shifts subsequent values away from their initial level.[8] If one of the two change variables shows more autonomous determination over time, this one is less susceptible to the other's influence, which implies that it is driving the reciprocal relationship.

In the second step, we include external changes that plausibly influence either or both of the changes within the reciprocal system. Letting E denote a vector of the changes in the external variables, we extend the models as follows:

$$R(T_2) = c + b_1{}^* R(T_1) + b_2{}^* \Delta V(T_2 - T_1) + b_3{}^* \Delta E(T_2 - T_1) + \varepsilon$$
$$\text{(Eq. 2a)}$$

---

[6] Against criticism by Achen (2001), Keele and Kelly (2005) defend the use of lagged dependent variables in autoregressive models as appropriate for most cases of application.

[7] Against criticism by Cronbach and Furby (1970), the recent literature rehabilitates the analyses of change scores as essential to the understanding of dynamic relations (Liker, Augustyniak, & Duncan 1985; Allison 1990; Miller & Kane 2001).

[8] Using the Δs as the dependent variable produces the same coefficients for all independent variables in such models, except the lagged dependent variable.

$$V(T_2) = c + b_1{}^*V(T_1) + b_2{}^*\Delta R(T_2 - T_1) + b_3{}^*\Delta E(T_2 - T_1) + \varepsilon$$

$$(Eq.2b)$$

If change in values drives the reciprocal system more strongly than change in rights, the b_2-coefficient in equation (2a) will be larger[9] and more significant than that in equation (2b).

The equations are not independent of each other. They represent a reciprocal system. This produces biased estimates if the error terms of the two equations are correlated. To correct this possible bias, I use Zellner's (1962) algorithm, called "seemingly unrelated regression" (Srivastava & Gilles 1987; Greene 2003).

Note that these models take care of endogeneity. If values are an endogenous feature of rights, so that prior rights trigger subsequent value changes, equation (2a) takes this into account by controlling the effect of value change for rights at T_1. So what we get is the effect of value change insofar as it is free from an influence of rights. The same holds true in the opposite direction: what we get in equation (2b) is the effect of changes in rights insofar as it is free from the influence of values.[10]

Another advantageous property of this system of equations is that it eliminates omitted variable bias. This is true because the inclusion of the lagged dependent variable takes into account every prior influence on the dependent variable, including influences not specifically addressed by a separate independent variable.

I run models in two versions: a short-term model and a long-term model. In the short-term model, we include all societies that the WVS has covered at least twice. For these societies, we look at every change between two adjacent rounds of the WVS. This gives us some 130 society-by-wave units in which societies appear in repeated observations. By contrast, in the long-term model, we examine change from the earliest to the latest available survey, provided these surveys are at least ten years apart. This limits the analyses to fifty societies.

The short- and long-term models have complementary advantages. The short-term model covers more observations but shorter time spans; for the long-term model, the opposite is true. If the same pattern appears in both models, we can be more confident about the validity of the findings.

After presenting the regression models, I subject the results to a plausibility check, testing expectations that must be met if change in values drives change in

---

[9] This assumes that the magnitudes of the unstandardized regression coefficients are directly comparable, which is the case when the variables are measured in equivalent units, relating to each variable's maximum scale range. This measurement standardization is done in this chapter as it is done throughout this book (see Box 2.2 , p. 64).

[10] Nevertheless, I conduct a Durbin-Wu-Hausman test, examining whether value change in equation (2a) and change in rights in equation (2b) are endogenous (Davidson & MacKinnon 1993). As documented in Appendix 9 (www.cambridge.org/welzel), the results are negative: there is no endogeneity. Hence, there is no need to use instrumental variables for either value change or change in rights: a two-stage least squares regression is not the appropriate method here.

rights more than the other way round. For this purpose, I extend the analyses in two directions. First, I extend the temporal perspective back in time, estimating values for the year 1975 – a point in time before the major rights expansions of the global democratization trend. Second, I test if one finds a similar reciprocity pattern between values and rights in a newly emerging rights domain: LGBT rights.

In the long-term models, we look at value change from the earliest to the latest survey, provided there is at least ten years distance between these surveys. Doing so reduces the ninety-five societies covered by the WVS to fifty – the same sample we used for the dynamic shift models in Chapter 4. As the replication data in Appendix 9 (www.cambridge.org/welzel) show, there is no selection bias in this reduced sample. The fifty societies are distributed over all regions of the world, cover each culture zone, and represent the global diversity in levels of development and type of regime. The sample includes from each region of the world the largest societies by both population size and size of the economy.

In the short-term model, we treat change between any two adjacent rounds of the WVS as an observation. A dozen more societies are added to the short-term model because more societies are observed over two successive rounds of the WVS. The replication data in Appendix 9 (www.cambridge.org/welzel) list the societies of both samples.

3. DATA AND VARIABLES

3.1 General and Group-Specific Citizen Rights

Citizen rights encompass any set of rights that entitle people. This definition includes both general citizen rights granted equally to all citizens and group-specific citizen rights granted specifically to members of underprivileged groups, such as women and LGBTs. The latter rights do not contradict but further specify general citizen rights for groups whose particular disadvantage justifies such additional specifications. Both general and group-specific citizen rights are inspired by the same idea: human empowerment.

Throughout the subsequent analyses, I use the term "citizen rights" in the sense of general citizen rights with no group-specific attribution. From this, I distinguish group-specific citizen rights and examine those of women and LGBTs. There are more group-specific citizen rights, such as those of disabled persons or children. However, there are no data suitable for a longitudinal analysis across a wide range of societies.

3.1.1 *General Citizen Rights*

To measure citizen rights, I use the citizen rights index (CRI) portrayed and validated in Chapter 8. In our sample, the low end in citizen rights is represented by China (0), Vietnam (0.01), Belarus (0.05), Nigeria (0.06), and Egypt (0.07). At the high end, we find Iceland (1.0), the Netherlands (0.99), Norway (0.97), and Sweden (0.95). The mean citizen rights score is 0.64, the level of South Africa.

Change in rights from the earliest to the latest survey covers the period from 1990 to 2005 for most societies in our sample. Over this observation period, positive shifts outnumber negative shifts by thirty to nineteen. The mean shift is +0.26, which we find in Bulgaria and Uruguay. The largest negative shift is –0.17 in Turkey. Compared to 1990, the first observation for Turkey, the change reflects a more restrictive rights practice due to rising Islamism. The largest positive shift is +0.74 in Hungary. As the only ex-communist society, Hungary was already surveyed in 1981, so this big improvement reflects the transition from authoritarian rule under communism to democracy, as present in 2005. It is important to note that these changes in citizen rights reflect shifts in the actual practice of rights, not just the formal guarantee.

3.1.2 Group-Specific Citizen Rights

3.1.2.1 WOMEN. The Cingranelli-Richards Human Rights Data Project analyzes human rights reports by the U.S. State Department and Amnesty International (Cingranelli & Richards 1999, 2010). The project provides various indices for different sets of rights. Each index measures on a multipoint ordinal scale how much the rights in question are respected in a society's daily practice. There are separate indices for women's political, economic, and social rights. A list of the rights included in each of these domains is provided in Appendix 9 (www.cambridge.org/welzel).

I average and standardize all three indices into a fine-grained overall index of women's rights from minimum 0 to maximum 1.0. The lowest women's rights score is 0.19 (Nigeria); the highest is 1.0 (Norway). The mean score is 0.62, the level of Spain or Italy. Over the observation period, positive shifts outnumber negative ones by eighteen to eleven. The mean shift is +0.14, a score to which New Zealand is closest. The largest negative shift is –0.22 in Poland: as in other ex-communist societies, the rights situation of women deteriorated with the breakdown of communism's fairly equal gender treatment. The largest positive shift is +0.33 in the United States.

3.1.2.2 LESBIAN, GAY, BISEXUAL AND TRANSGENDER. A newly emerging domain of rights relates to LGBTs. Because this area is new, there are no longitudinal data. By contrast, we know from Chapter 4 that emancipative values are on the rise since at least three decades. Thus, it seems safe to conclude that emancipative values have been on the rise before LGBT rights gained prominence. Accordingly, I interpret any link between emancipative values and LGBT rights as an effect of values on rights. Should we find such an effect, we have additional plausibility that emancipative values are indeed a source of the rights expansions linked to human empowerment.

I use data from the International Gay and Lesbian Human Rights Commission (2010) on the absence (coded 0) or presence (coded 1) of the legal recognition of same-sex relationships, legalization of same-sex marriage, the right of LGBTs for child adoption, access of LGBTs to the military, antidiscrimination laws, and legal protection for expressing one's sexual identity. This provides a 7-point index that I normalize into a range from 0 to 1.0.

The lowest LGBT score in our sample (0) is found in Algeria and Vietnam. The highest score (1.0) is found in Belgium, Sweden, and the Netherlands. The mean LGBT score is 0.52, a level found in the Czech Republic, Japan, and Peru. Because older data do not exist, no change scores can be calculated.

3.2 Control Variables

As controls, I include variables that loom large in the democratization literature. The reason is obvious: rights improvements are a main achievement and purpose of democratization. The three factors with the strongest evidence for an impact on democratization include economic development (Boix 2003; Teorell 2010), global linkages (Rudra 2005; Levitsky & Way 2010), and exogenous contagion (Starr 1991; Weijnert 2005; Gleditsch & Ward 2006).

3.2.1 *Economic Development*

From the viewpoint of human empowerment, economic development is important because it enhances people's action resources. Usually, I prefer the index of technological advancement presented in the Introduction as a measure of action resources. However, this indicator is unavailable in a time series, so it cannot be used in longitudinal analyses. Hence, I rely on the most prominent indicator of economic development: per capita gross domestic product (GDP) (Barro 1997). As a measure of *human* development in a broader sense, the United Nations Development Program (2011) propagates the human development index (HDI), a composite measure of prosperity, education, and longevity. To measure human development insofar as it benefits women, the UNDP provides the gender development index (GDI), which is the women's HDI relative to men.

The analyses use all three indicators alternately, but only the strongest results are reported, which are obtained by per capita GDP. Results with the HDI and GDI are literally identical to using a logged measure of per capita GDP; these results are reported in Appendix 9 (www.cambridge.org/welzel). They show no alteration of the reciprocity pattern between values and rights found with per capita GDP.

I use indexed per capita GDP scores in purchasing power parities measured in U.S. dollars at constant prices of the year 2000. Data are taken from the World Development Indicators (World Bank 2008). The maximum GDP level (US $70,000 in Norway) is set at 1.0. The lowest index score in per capita GDP is 0.02 (Nigeria). The mean GDP level is 0.21, which is about the level of Poland. Over the observation period, positive shifts outnumber negative ones by forty-eight to two. The largest negative shift is −0.02 (Latvia), the largest positive one is +0.31 (Norway). The mean shift is +0.09 (a gain of about US$6,000 over an approximately twenty-year period).

3.2.2 Global Linkages

To measure a society's linkages to networks of global exchange, I use Dreher, Gaston, and Martens's (2008) globalization index. The index summarizes information on a society's integration into social, economic, and political networks of global exchange, as detailed in Appendix 9 (www.cambridge.org/welzel). The lowest score is 0.38 in Belarus, an isolated resort of autocracy in Europe. The highest score is 0.93 in Belgium, which hosts key international institutions. The mean linkages score is 0.70, the level of Argentina.

There is not a single negative shift in linkages over the observation period. The largest positive shift is +0.35 in Slovenia, the first post-Yugoslav society to integrate into the European Union. The mean shift is +0.17, a level found in Chile, the Czech Republic, and Japan.

3.2.3 Exogenous Contagion

Shifts in either rights or values might be triggered by similar shifts in neighboring societies. The reason is obvious. No society exists in a vacuum but is influenced by things happening in its neighborhood. However, societies are embedded in the culture zones described in the Introduction. These zones constitute clusters of societies with shared historical legacies, which suggests that societies pick up trends mostly among societies of the same culture zone.

To come to terms with this consideration, I create variables that assign each society the mean change in values and rights of all other societies in its own culture zone. Alternatively, I assign each society an *adjusted* mean change in values and rights; that is, mean changes weighted for the population size of the respective societies. This is done under the assumption that trends in larger populations obtain more attention and are, hence, more likely to be trend-setting for other societies within the same culture zone. However, results with the population size-adjusted means are weaker than those with the simple means. For this reason, the tables in the findings section report results with the simple means.

4. FINDINGS

4.1 Visual Evidence

Let's start with a look at the bivariate relationship between values and rights. Figure 9.2 shows this relationship for citizen rights; Figure 9.3 shows it for women's rights. Both figures compare the relationship between the earliest observation in the left-hand diagram with the latest observation in the right-hand diagram. These observations are ten or more years apart; for most societies, the earliest observation is in 1990 and the latest in 2005.

For citizen rights, the model fit improves: the overlapping variance between values and rights is 22 percent at the earliest observation but 57 percent at the

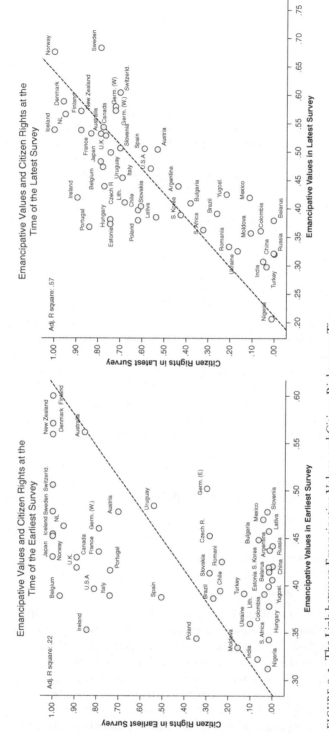

FIGURE 9.2 The Link between Emancipative Values and Citizen Rights over Time.

Data Coverage: All fifty societies with valid data that are surveyed at least twice by the World Values Surveys/European Value Study (WVS/EVS) over a temporal distance of at least ten years.

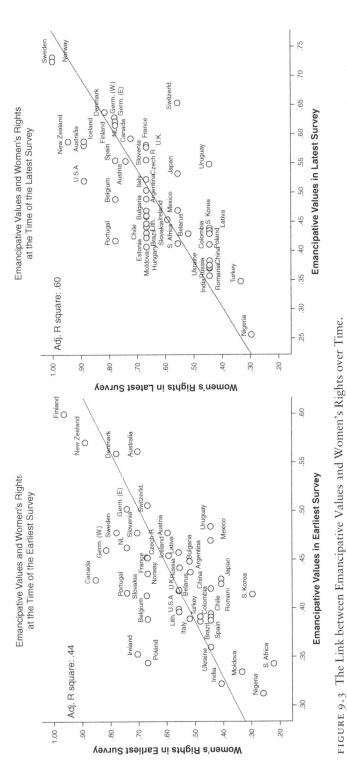

FIGURE 9.3 The Link between Emancipative Values and Women's Rights over Time.
Data Coverage: All of the fifty societies with valid data that are surveyed at least twice by the World Values Surveys/European Value Study (WVS/EVS) over a temporal distance of at least ten years.

latest.[11] Logically, the fit between two variables can improve over time, only if both variables move closer to each other or if one moves closer to the other. Now, emancipative values improved on average by 0.07 scale points while citizen rights improved on average by 0.26 scale points. By necessity, the massive fit improvement must result primarily from shifts in the variable that made the larger move: rights. In other words, rights moved more toward congruence with values than values moved toward congruence with rights.

Indeed, a group of young democracies – including Argentina, Hungary, South Korea, Mexico, Slovenia, and Bulgaria – represents a lower-right outlier in the left-hand diagram of Figure 9.2. The outlying position of these societies indicates that, at the time of the earliest observation, citizen rights were largely deficient relative to these societies' emancipative values. For Slovenia and Bulgaria, whose first observation is in 1990, this situation is measured at the beginning of the transition to democracy. For Argentina, Hungary, and South Korea, whose first observation is in 1981, this situation is measured before the transition to democracy. This is also true for Mexico, whose earliest observation is in 1990. At the time of the latest observation, in about 2005, democratic transitions were completed, and citizen rights improved greatly in each of these societies. As a result, citizen rights moved into a closer fit with people's emancipative values, which themselves did not change as much within this limited period: values are more solidly anchored and change glacially for this reason.

Figure 9.3 illustrates a fit improvement nearly as impressive in the relationship between values and women's rights, from 44 to 60 percent.[12] But although emancipative values improved on average by 0.07 scale points, women's rights improved by 0.15 scale points – more than twice as large a shift. This indicates that most of the fit improvement results from the move in rights. Again, rights adjust more to values than values to rights. Does this conclusion hold, testing the reciprocal system of regressions proposed earlier? Tables 9.1 to 9.4 display regression results for this system.

4.2 Regression Results

The three models in the left-hand panel of Table 9.1 explain citizen rights at time T_2 by themselves at time T_1 and change in values from time T_1 to time T_2. The right-hand panel reverses the causal arrow, explaining values at time T_2 by themselves at time T_1 and change in rights from time T_1 to time T_2. The gray-shaded regression coefficients in the left-hand panel tell us to what extent change in values contributes to elevating rights above their initial level. The gray-shaded coefficients in the right-hand panel tell us to what extent change in rights contributes to elevating values above their initial level.

---

[11] Less pronounced, we find the same pattern with the 130 observations of the short-term shift sample: the overlapping variance increases from 46 to 61 percent.

[12] In the short-term sample of 130, the improvement is from 60 to 65 percent.

TABLE 9.1 A Reciprocal System of Dynamic Relationships (long-term shift model with citizen rights).

| | DEPENDENT VARIABLES | | | | | |
| | Citizen Rights at time T_2 | | | Emancipative Values at time T_2 | | |
PREDICTORS	Model 1–1	Model 1–2	Model 1–3	Model 2–1	Model 2–2	Model 2–3
Constant	0.40 (8.1)***	0.25 (2.4)**	0.10 (0.9)†	0.06 (0.4)†	0.00 (0.1)†	0.14 (1.8)*
Dependent Variable (DV) at time T_1	0.41 (4.2)***	0.47 (4.0)***	0.64 (5.8)***	0.99 (6.3)***	0.94 (7.3)***	0.71 (3.9)***
$\Delta(T_2 - T_1)$ Emancipative Values	0.82 (1.7)*	1.10 (2.0)**	0.91 (2.1)**			
$\Delta(T_2 - T_1)$ Citizen Rights				−0.08 (−2.1)**	0.01 (0.3)	−0.02 (−0.4)
$\Delta(T_2 - T_1)$ Economic Development		−0.08 (−0.2)†	0.59 (1.8)*		0.65 (6.7)***	−0.03 (−0.2)†
$\Delta(T_2 - T_1)$ Global Linkages		0.57 (1.6)†	0.48 (3.7)***		−0.10 (−0.9)†	0.84 (3.8)***
Exogenous Change in DV						
Adjusted R^2	0.54	0.57	0.66	0.49	0.74	0.62
N	49	48	48	49	48	48

Entries are unstandardized regression coefficients with T values in parentheses. Estimates are calculated with the "sureg" procedure in STATA, conducting a seemingly unrelated regression for each of the three two-equation systems (Models 1–1 and 2–1, 1–2 and 2–2, 1–3 and 2–3). Δ variables measure change from the earliest survey at time T_1 to the latest survey at time T_2. For each society, time T_1 is measured at least ten years before time T_2. Since each society appears only once in this dataset, no test for serial correlations is necessary.

In each model, regression diagnostics for heteroskedasticity (White test), multicollinearity (variance inflation factors), and influential cases (DFFITs) reveal no violation of ordinary least squares (OLS) assumptions.

T_1: Year of earliest available survey (mostly 1990 or 1995)
T_2: Year of latest available survey (mostly 2000 or 2005)
Significance levels: † $p \geq .100$, * $p < .100$, ** $p < .050$, *** $p < .005$

We compare the coefficients in the two panels that belong to the same pair of equations. Thus, we compare the gray-shaded coefficients (a) in models 1–1 and 2–1, (b) models 1–2 and 2–2, and (c) models 1–3 and 2–3.

Models 1–1 and 2–1 show the reciprocal system without external controls. In this configuration, change in values shows a strongly positive effect, adding a 0.82 fraction of the change score in values to the elevation of rights. The effect is significant at the 0.08 level. Conversely, change in rights shows a significant but very weak and negative effect: one subtracts a 0.08 fraction of the change score in rights from emancipative values. With no other control than both variables' autonomous determination, the dynamic in the relationship between values and rights operates positively in only one direction: from values to rights.

Does this conclusion hold when controlling for plausible third causes? To answer this question, we introduce two of the three controls at a time.[13] In so doing, the effect of change in values becomes more significant and more strongly positive. This happens because change in values covaries with change in the controls, yet some of these changes in the controls are of no direct relevance for the shift in rights. Thus, changing values carry some of the irrelevant changes, which diminishes their effect on shifting rights. Now, by including in the model the changes in the controls, we decouple changing values from other irrelevant changes, bringing their effect more clearly to the surface. In other words, the effect of changing values on shifting rights surfaces more clearly under otherwise equal conditions – a premise realized with external controls.

By contrast, the effect of change in rights turns positive but becomes insignificant with external controls.[14] The reason for the switch in sign and loss of significance is more complicated. On further inspection, it turns out that great improvements in citizen rights often come with a temporary deterioration in economic development: one reason is that, before completion, regime transitions create an insecure investment climate. Since economic development is a driver of value change (as Chapter 4 has shown), the slightly negative effect of rights improvements on economic development is echoed in a slightly negative effect on value change. But, once we control for economic development, this negative effect vanishes: it is a spurious effect that only shows up because of the way in which rights improvements affect economic development.

Replicating this analysis with the short-term sample, we cover smaller shifts but include more than twice as many observations. Table 9.2 shows the results. As before, change in values has a strongly positive and highly significant effect in all models. The effect of change in rights is this time always positive and becomes

---

[13] Including all three controls at once exhausts the degrees of freedom in the small sample of the short-term shift model.

[14] These two results hold true, too, for the third possible combination of two external controls: economic development and exogenous contagion. The results also hold true when we include as an additional predictor the temporal length of the Δ variables. To save space, these models are shown in Appendix 9 (www.cambridge.org/welzel).

TABLE 9.2 *A Reciprocal System of Dynamic Relationships (short-term shift model with citizen rights).*

DEPENDENT VARIABLES

PREDICTORS	Citizen Rights at time T_2			Emancipative Values at time T_2		
	Model 1–1	Model 1–2	Model 1–3	Model 2–1	Model 2–2	Model 2–3
Constant	0.16 (6.4)***	0.11 (3.8)***	0.09 (3.2)***	0.01 (0.3)†	0.04 (1.7)*	0.05 (2.4)**
Dependent Variable at time T_1	0.76 (19.7)***	0.84 (21.0)***	0.80 (22.0)***	1.04 (23.2)***	0.96 (21.5)***	0.88 (16.5)***
$\Delta(T_2-T_1)$ Emancipative Values	1.06 (3.6)***	0.99 (3.8)***	1.30 (4.7)***			
$\Delta(T_2-T_1)$ Citizen Rights				0.03 (1.4)†	0.08 (2.8)**	0.06 (2.5)**
$\Delta(T_2-T_1)$ Economic Development		−0.46 (−1.3)†			0.52 (4.7)***	
$\Delta(T_2-T_1)$ Global Linkages		0.15 (0.8)†	0.06 (0.3)†		−0.15 (−2.4)**	
Exogenous Change in DV			0.73 (5.5)***			1.30 (4.9)***
Adjusted R^2	0.79	0.85	0.83	0.80	0.83	0.83
Durbin Watson	1.70	1.80	2.00	1.70	1.80	2.00
N	133	126	131	133	126	131

Entries are unstandardized regression coefficients with T values in parentheses. Estimates are calculated with the "sureg" procedure in STATA, conducting a seemingly unrelated regression for each of the three two-equation systems (Models 1–1 and 2–1, 1–2 and 2–2, 1–3 and 2–3). Δ variables measure change from an earlier survey at time T_1 to a later survey at time T_2. Observations are included in a time-series cross-sectional dataset in which each society appears in repeated observations.

In each model, regression diagnostics for heteroskedasticity (White test), multicollinearity (variance inflation factors), and influential cases (DFFITs) reveal no violation of ordinary least squares (OLS) assumptions.

T_1: Year of previous survey
T_2: Year of subsequent survey
Significance levels: † $p \geq .100$, * $p < .100$, ** $p < .050$, *** $p < .005$

significant with external controls. Accordingly, rights improvements affect value change more significantly under otherwise equal conditions – a premise realized by introducing external controls. But, even when significant, change in rights shows a very weak effect. At the most, we add a 0.09 fraction of the change score in rights to the elevation of values.

The basic conclusion remains the same: an always significant and strongly positive effect operates from values to rights; in the opposite direction, from rights to values, the effect is always weak and not always significant and positive.

Let's turn to the relationship between values and women's rights. Table 9.3 examines this relationship in the long-term perspective, mirroring the analysis in Table 9.1. In all three model pairs, change in values affects rights much more strongly than change in rights affects values. As the size of the regression coefficients indicates, change in values contributes more than five times as much to the shift in rights as change in rights contributes to the shift in values. This holds true both with and without external controls.

Table 9.4 confirms the reciprocity pattern found in Table 9.3 in the short-term perspective. Again, the reciprocity pattern is profoundly asymmetric: it operates more strongly from values to rights than in the opposite direction. Once more, this holds true with and without external controls.

What about the external control variables' own effects? Economic development shows significant and positive effects only on values but never on rights. This finding provides an even stronger confirmation of the human empowerment model than the temporal order test in Chapter 4. According to the sequence thesis of emancipation theory, economic development gives rise to emancipative values because it expands people's action resources; in so doing, economic development increases the utility of the freedoms that emancipative values emphasize. Moreover, because popular pressures for the guarantee of freedoms require the emergence of values that emphasize these freedoms, the effect of economic development on rights improvements operates through its effect on emancipative values. Hence, economic development has no effect on rights improvements once we control for rising emancipative values.

Looking at the other external controls, contagion always shows significant and positive effects on values but not always on rights. Controlling for development or contagion, globalization usually shows no significant effect on rights, and, if its effect on values is significant, it is always weak (and sometimes negative). In any case, values are more strongly determined by these external forces than are rights. This explains why values are less susceptible to change in rights than rights are to change in values. Consequently, values show up as the driver in the reciprocal relationship with rights.

As documented in Appendix 9 (www.cambridge.org/welzel), these results hold for a series of alternative model specifications. The results of Appendix Table 9.5 are of particular interest from a social movement perspective. They show that an increase in social movement activities affects rights improvements less strongly than an increase in emancipative values. This might be surprising if

TABLE 9.3 *A Reciprocal System of Dynamic Relationships (long-term shift model with women's rights).*

| | DEPENDENT VARIABLES | | | | | |
| | Women's Rights at time T_2 | | | Emancipative Values at time T_2 | | |
PREDICTORS	Model 1–1	Model 1–2	Model 1–3	Model 2–1	Model 2–2	Model 2–3
Constant	0.24 (4.3)***	0.28 (3.8)***	0.27 (3.2)***	−0.08 (−1.2)†	−0.01 (−0.1)†	0.03 (0.4)†
Dependent Variable (DV) at time T_1	0.52 (5.1)***	0.48 (4.5)***	0.48 (4.5)***	1.30 (8.3)***	1.06 (8.3)***	0.93 (5.9)***
$\Delta(T_2\_T_1)$ Emancipative Values	1.50 (6.9)***	1.30 (4.3)***	1.50 (6.8)***			
$\Delta(T_2\_T_1)$ Women's Rights				0.33 (4.7)***	0.16 (2.9)***	0.30 (5.2)***
$\Delta(T_2\_T_1)$ Economic Development		0.02 (0.1)†			0.56 (5.7)***	
$\Delta(T_2\_T_1)$ Global Linkages		−0.01 (−0.1)†	−0.01 (−0.1)†		−0.08 (−0.9)†	−0.01 (−0.1)†
Exogenous Change in DV			−0.07 (−0.4)†			0.77 (4.0)***
Adjusted R^2	0.57	0.60	0.58	0.51	0.75	0.65
N	46	46	46	46	46	46

Entries are unstandardized regression coefficients with T value in parentheses. Estimates are calculated with the "sureg" procedure in STATA, conducting a seemingly unrelated regression for each of the three two-equation systems (Models 1–1 and 2–1, 1–2 and 2–2, 1–3 and 2–3). Δ variables measure change from the earliest survey at time T_1 to the latest survey at time T_2. For each society, time T_1 is measured at least ten years before time T_2. Since each society appears only once in this dataset, no test for serial correlations is necessary.

In each model, regression diagnostics for heteroskedasticity (White test), multicollinearity (variance inflation factors), and influential cases (DFFITs) reveal no violation of ordinary least squares (OLS) assumptions.

T_1: Year of earliest available survey
T_2: Year of latest available survey
Significance levels: † $p \geq .100$, * $p < .100$, ** $p < .050$, *** $p < .005$

TABLE 9.4 *A Reciprocal System of Dynamic Relationships (short-term shift model with women's rights).*

PREDICTORS	DEPENDENT VARIABLES					
	Women's Rights at time T_2			Emancipative Values at time T_2		
	Model 1–1	Model 1–2	Model 1–3	Model 2–1	Model 2–2	Model 2–3
Constant	0.10 (3.8)***	0.10 (3.4)***	0.10 (3.3)**	0.00 (0.4)†	0.03 (1.5)†	0.04 (2.0)**
Dependent Variable (DV) at T_1	0.83 (18.3)***	0.81 (17.8)***	0.82 (18.1)***	1.06 (23.9)***	0.97 (21.6)***	0.90 (17.2)***
$\Delta(T_2\_T_1)$ Emancipative Values	0.97 (5.8)***	0.73 (4.2)***	0.98 (5.8)***			
$\Delta(T_2\_T_1)$ Women's Rights				0.20 (4.8)***	0.14 (3.4)***	0.19 (4.9)***
$\Delta(T_2\_T_1)$ Economic Development		0.40 (1.8)*	0.09 (0.6)†		0.40 (3.6)***	
$\Delta(T_2\_T_1)$ Global Linkages		−0.13 (−1.3)†	−0.11 (−0.5)†		−0.16 (−2.4)***	−0.11 (−1.8)*
Exogenous Change in DV						1.09 (4.3)***
Adjusted R^2	0.75	0.78	0.75	0.80	0.84	0.83
Durbin Watson	2.10	2.00	2.10	2.10	2.00	2.10
N	126	122	126	126	122	126

Entries are unstandardized regression coefficients with T values in parentheses. Estimates are calculated with the "sureg" procedure in STATA, conducting a seemingly unrelated regression for each of the three two-equation systems (Models 1–1 and 2–1, 1–2 and 2–2, 1–3 and 2–3). Δ variables measure change from an earlier survey at time T_1 to a later survey at time T_2. Observations are included in a time-series cross-sectional dataset in which each society appears in repeated observations.

In each model, regression diagnostics for heteroskedasticity (White test), multicollinearity (variance inflation factors), and influential cases (DFFIT's) reveal no violation of ordinary least squares (OLS) assumptions.

T_1: Year of previous survey
T_2: Year of subsequent survey
Significance levels: † $p \geq .100$, * $p < .100$, ** $p < .050$, *** $p < .005$

one assumes that rights improvements need the mass pressures that derive from social movement activities. Under this assumption, one would think that the effect of increasing emancipative values is conditional: it depends on the translation of these values into social movement activities. But Chapter 7 has demonstrated that this condition is a given: rising emancipative values usually do translate into increasing social movement activity, even under repressive threats. Conversely, not all social movement activities are motivated by emancipative values. Hence, what matters for rights improvements is not whether there is an increase in social movement activities but whether there is an increase in social movement activities that are motivated by emancipative values. The regression model in Appendix Table 9.5 demonstrates this point: if we partition the increase in social movement activities into the component that is predicted by the increase in emancipative values and the component that is not, it is only the predicted component that improves rights. Only those social movement activities which are inspired by emancipative values matter.

4.3 Model Extensions

4.3.1 *Extending the Temporal Scope*

We have seen that changes in values and rights tend to concur. But there might be periods in which the two dissociate, and a more or less pronounced misfit between values and rights builds up. If we can go back in time and find a point where the misfit was sizeable, what should we expect to happen in the subsequent period when values indeed drive the move in rights? The expectation is clear: the initial misfit between values and rights drives the subsequent change in rights toward closing their distance to values. By contrast, values are not driven by this logic because they change for other reasons, such as economic development.

In a sense, Figure 9.2 already confirms this expectation. The left-hand diagram shows that, at the beginning or before major regime transitions, citizen rights are greatly deficient relative to people's values in the Baltic societies, East Germany, Hungary, Bulgaria, South Korea, Argentina, Slovenia, and Mexico. But, as the right-hand diagram shows, after the completion of the regime transitions, citizen rights had greatly improved in all these societies – to a level at which they fit people's values much more closely.

If we think of a time when the misfit between emancipative values and citizen rights could have been particularly large, the time at the onset of the global democratization trend is a good candidate. That would be around the year 1975 (Huntington 1991). A misfit between values and rights at this time is likely because, during the Cold War, right- and left-wing dictatorships were propped up by the two superpowers. By outside forces, authoritarian regimes were artificially shielded from inside pressures. This protective shield allowed these regimes to ignore the rise of emancipative values and the swelling desires for rights that these values feed. Intuitively, Huntington (1984: 214) felt this when noting that, based on their own economic and cultural make-up, several societies in Eastern Europe, most notably

"Czechoslovakia would certainly be a democracy today (and probably Hungary and Poland also) if it were not for the overriding veto of the Soviet presence" [parentheses in the original]. Applied to our framework, this thesis suggests that, at the beginning of the global democratization trend in about 1975, there was a pronounced misfit between emancipative values and citizen rights, especially in the then-authoritarian regimes. Indeed, this misfit might be the deeper reason why the democratization trend set in once the superpowers gave up shielding the authoritarian regimes from domestic pressures.

Unfortunately, we have no measures of emancipative values for the time around 1975. However, we know pretty much for certain how strongly emancipative values are autocorrelated over time and how much the cohort difference affects their pace of change. Hence, we can use the temporal distance from each society's first real measure of emancipative values to 1975 to estimate emancipative values in 1975. Appendix 9 (www.cambridge.org/welzel) describes this estimation in detail. We also have a proxy of each society's citizen rights in 1975 using the combined Freedom House civil and political rights ratings. As detailed in Appendix 9, scores have been adjusted downward to establish equivalence with the more conservative citizen rights scores.

Using these estimates as a thought experiment, Figure 9.4 plots citizen rights in 1975 against the societies' estimated emancipative values in 1975. As we can see, rights were indeed greatly deficient relative to people's values wherever regime transitions were still to come. This is most obvious for the then-communist societies, as well as for South Korea, Uruguay, and Chile. But, in 1975, this group is joined by Spain. At this point in time, Spain had still to make its democratic transition.[15] Yet, it had completed the transition by the time of our first *real* observation in 1981: in this year, Spain's citizen rights are sufficient relative to people's values (see Figure 9.2, left-hand diagram). These critical cases suggest that major rights expansions are driven by the tendency to bring rights in line with people's values.

Let us test directly the suggestion that a given misfit between values and rights drives the subsequent move in rights but not in values, toward reducing the misfit. We measure the misfit by the residuals of rights in 1975 that are unexplained by the estimated values in that year. The two diagrams in Figure 9.5 display this misfit on the horizontal axis. Misfit scores are larger the more the rights are deficient relative to people's values. Note that the misfit is measured *before* the global democratization wave. On the vertical axis, the left-hand diagram displays each society's change in values *after* 1975, all the way to 2005. Likewise, the vertical axis in the right-hand diagram shows each society's change in rights *after* 1975, all the way to 2005. So what we see is a temporally ordered relationship, showing how the values-rights misfit in 1975 drives the changes in these two variables long after 1975.

The result is straightforward: the more the rights in 1975 fall short of what the values of this year call for, the more the rights grow after 1975. In other words,

[15] The initial event, General Franco's death, happened on November 22, 1975.

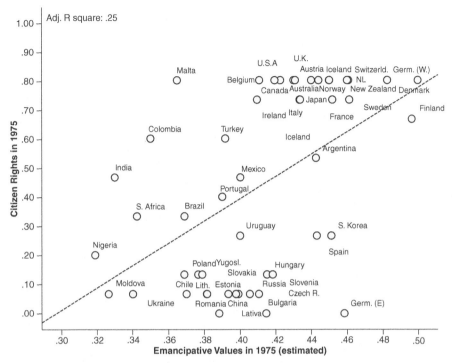

FIGURE 9.4 Estimated Link between Emancipative Values and Citizen Rights in 1975. *Data Coverage*: All of the fifty societies with valid data that are surveyed at least twice by the World Values Surveys/European Value Study (WVS/EVS) over a temporal distance of at least ten years.

rights move toward reducing their misfit to values. This tendency explains 52 percent of the rights extensions from 1975 to 2005. By contrast, values do not move as a function of the values-rights misfit: the value changes after 1975 are unexplained by the values-rights misfit in 1975. Indeed, had emancipative values moved toward reducing the initial misfit with citizen rights, these values should have declined over the three decades in Figure 9.5. As Chapter 4 has shown with ample evidence, the contrary was the case. At any rate, the results of this thought experiment identify values as the driving variable and rights as the driven one.

4.3.2 *Extending the Domain of Rights*

In the long run, values and rights should tend to move into correspondence with each other on any rights domain that reflects the human empowerment trend. One such domain is LGBT rights. LGBT rights are a recent domain of legislation, so contemporary LGBT rights are subsequent to the rise of emancipative values. But are they systematically related to these values?

Figure 9.6 shows that contemporary LGBT rights are strongly positively influenced by the growth of emancipative values since the first observation.

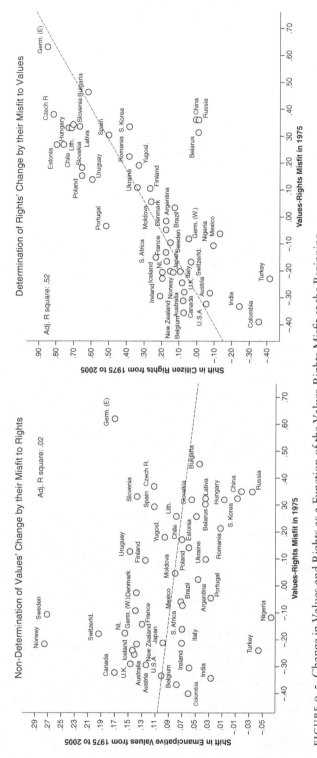

FIGURE 9.5 Change in Values and Rights as a Function of the Values-Rights Misfit at the Beginning.

Data Coverage: All of the fifty societies with valid data that are surveyed at least twice by the World Values Surveys/European Value Study (WVS/EVS) over a temporal distance of at least ten years.

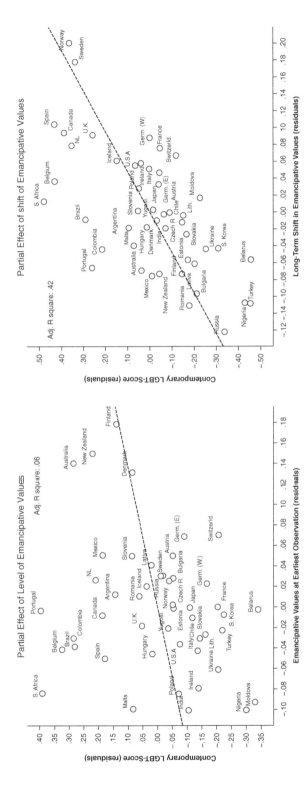

FIGURE 9.6 Emancipative Values and Lesbian, Gay, Bisexual, Transgender (LGBT) Rights (stock and flow effects).

Data Coverage: All of the fifty societies with valid data that are surveyed at least twice by the World Values Surveys/European Value Study (WVS/EVS) over a temporal distance of at least ten years.

This finding is robust controlling for both development and globalization (see Appendix 9 for further robustness checks). After all, emancipative values relate as closely to LGBT rights as they relate to women's rights and citizen rights. The temporal order of this relationship leaves little doubt about its direction. LGBT rights emerged very recently, in fact long after the generational rise of emancipative values gained momentum. Hence, the close relationship evidences an effect of values on rights rather than the other way around.

KEY POINTS

Four insights need to be emphasized. First, the close reciprocity between values and rights is genuine because it does not break down when we control for external influences. Second, the reciprocity is profoundly asymmetric, operating more strongly from values to rights than in the opposite direction. Third, even though values are quite strongly shaped by development and contagion, they have an independent effect on rights that largely absorbs the effects of these external influences. Fourth, the reciprocal effect of rights on values is weak but still positive and significant, especially as concerns women's rights. This is good news for rights advocates: by framing values and claiming rights, one contributes to the cycle of human empowerment.

A strong impact of values is expected from the viewpoint of human empowerment. Rights do not tell us what people want; they are exogenous to people's desires. Values, by contrast, directly represent people's desires. Human empowerment implies that people's values obtain more weight in how societies develop. Thus, in domains affected by the human empowerment trend, people's values should have a great impact, especially on rights.

For most of human history, it did not matter what most people wanted because ordinary people had neither the means nor the skills to reflect, shape, and express their values in ways that could challenge those in power. Human empowerment changes this, making common people more capable and willing to act as agents of their own values. This puts people and their values into the driver seat of history, as Elias claimed long ago.

The Paradox of Democracy*

> Democracy is the theory that the common people know what they want, and deserve to get it good and hard.
>
> – H. L. Mencken

The global democratization trend of recent decades has opened wide areas of the world to comparative survey research. Researchers embrace this opportunity and analyze questions that ask people around the world how strongly they desire democracy. Apparently, great majorities of almost every society express a strong desire for democracy, even where authoritarian practices persist (Klingemann 1999; Inglehart 2003).

However, the very universality of democratic desires presents a paradox. Despite these desires' prevalence, the majority of political regimes around the world are deficient democracies, hybrid regimes, and renewed or continued versions of autocracy. Chapter 8 demonstrated this point (see also Rose 2009; Alexander & Welzel 2011; Levitsky & Way 2010). As it seems, widespread popular desires for democracy coexist easily with deficient and even absent democracy. Indeed, we have seen in Chapter 8 that knowing what percentage of a population expresses a strong desire for democracy predicts less than 30 percent of a society's actual level of democracy.

This paradox raises doubts that democratic desires are the best yardstick for assessing a population's affinity to democracy. Quite likely, the universality of democratic desires hides profound differences in people's understanding of democracy (Schedler & Sarsfield 2006). Similar differences might exist with respect to how ready people are to step up for their democratic desire and take action to enforce it (Welzel 2007b). Thus, scholars in the meanwhile recognize

---

* I am indebted to Alejandro Moreno who co-authored a previous, still unpublished version of this chapter.

the need to qualify people's democratic desires for the kind of understanding and the type of values that drive these desires.

One such qualification has been provided in Chapter 8, with strong results. When one couples people's desires for democracy with emancipative values, one enhances the predictive power with respect to a society's actual level of democracy from 30 to 70 percent. Qi and Shin (2011) report similar findings: the predictive power of people's democratic desires is greatly enhanced when these desires go together with critical evaluations of a society's institutions. This finding resonates well with results of this chapter, although we will see that emancipative values are the reason *why* people evaluate institutions critically.

The reason why the grounding of democratic desires in emancipative values enhances these desires' democratic impact so dramatically lies in the very nature of emancipative values. Emancipative values emphasize freedom of choice and equality of opportunities – precisely the ideals that are democracy's inspirational source (Dahl 2000; Held 2006). In addition, emancipative values generate an intrinsic drive to take action in pursuit of their emphasis on freedoms. This has been shown in Chapter 7. Thus, whenever democratic desires are decoupled from emancipative values, people want democracy for reasons other than the equal freedoms that define democracy. Accordingly, people are not ready to stand up for these freedoms. In these cases, power holders can satisfy people's democratic desires by achievements that are propagated as democratic when, in fact, they are not.

This proposition suggests two hypotheses about the impact of emancipative values on desires for democracy.[1] On the one hand, emancipative values hardly affect the *strength* of people's democratic desires because these desires are almost uniformly strong. On the other hand, emancipative values change the *nature* of democratic desires in targeting these desires at an unequivocally liberal version of democracy, not just anything propagated as democracy. Plausible as these hypotheses are, they have never been tested because conclusive evidence was not available until recently. The most recent round of the World Values Surveys (WVS) has changed this situation. For the fifth round of the WVS I devised a question asking people how they define "democracy."

Based on this and other new democracy questions, this chapter demonstrates that emancipative values do indeed shape people's democratic desires and that they do so in a twofold way. First, stronger emancipative values prompt people to define democracy more unequivocally in liberal terms; that is, in terms of the equal freedoms through which democracy empowers the people. Second, people

---

[1] Emancipative values evolve around issues, such as gender roles, that are relevant early in the life course. In comparison, democracy is an abstract and remote concept that requires a certain amount of cognitive maturation to establish itself in people's mindset. In other words, views of democracy take shape later in the life course than emancipative values. For this reason, it is fair to assume that emancipative values influence views of democracy more than these influence emancipative values. This chapter, accordingly, assumes the causal arrow to run from values to views of democracy rather than the other around.

with strong emancipative values internalize demanding evaluation standards that make them critical in assessing their society's democratic quality. In combination, emancipative values generate a *critical-liberal* desire for democracy. Importantly, the critical-liberal impulse of emancipative values is independent of two other sources of influence: people's cognitive mobilization and their socialization under democracy. Finally, the critical-liberal impulse of emancipative values explains why widespread democratic desires can coexist with deficient or absent democracy: where this is the case, democratic desires lack the critical-liberal grounding that emancipative values create.

To demonstrate these points, this chapter is organized into four sections. Section 1 presents my guiding theoretical perspective: democratic mobilization. This perspective assumes that, in order to have an impact on a society's regime, people's views of democracy must be shaped in ways that make it easy to mobilize people into democratic reform movements. The second section describes new measures of three distinct aspects of people's views of democracy: the notion of what democracy means, the assessment of one's society's democratic quality, and the strength of the desire for democracy. Section 3 formulates the hypotheses of how I think emancipative values affect these views. The fourth section presents the results. The chapter closes with a summary of key points.

1. THEORY: DEMOCRATIC MOBILIZATION

Power holders have a vested interest in preserving their power. Vested interests in power create a natural tendency among elites to resist democratic reforms because such reforms shift power from the elites to the people. Thus, democratic reforms often need to be enforced against elite resistance by mobilizing mass pressure (Foweraker & Landman 1997; McAdam, Tarrow, & Tilly 2003; Schock 2005; Ulfelder 2005). The pro-democratic impulses of mass pressures have been demonstrated for both the introduction of democratic rights in undemocratic regimes and the persistence of these rights in democratic regimes (Welzel 2007a).

Mass publics can be mobilized for various reforms, democratic or nondemocratic, depending on what beliefs prevail in a population. With respect to the chances of democratic mobilization, mass beliefs matter in three aspects.

First, there must be a widespread desire for democracy; otherwise people cannot be mobilized for goals advocated in the name of democracy. Second, people must have a proper notion of democracy; otherwise their democratic desires can be mobilized for any goal propagated in the name of democracy, including nondemocratic goals. Third, people must assess the democratic quality of their society as deficient; otherwise, they see their democratic desire satisfied and will not join democracy movements.

To examine these three aspects of people's views of democracy, round five of the WVS fields a new series of questions designed to address (1) the liberalness of people's notion of democracy, (2) the criticalness of their assessment of democracy, and (3) the strength of their desire for democracy. These questions allow us to qualify people's democratic desires and to estimate on this basis the potential for democratic mobilization.

2. MEASURING PEOPLE'S VIEWS OF DEMOCRACY

2.1 Liberalness of the Notion of Democracy

Knowing how strongly people desire democracy is meaningless unless we also know how people understand democracy. Only if people understand democracy in the way prescribed by its liberal definition can we be sure that democratic desires are not mobilized for nondemocratic goals in the name of democracy. Hence, we must measure people's notion of democracy.

Round five of the WVS asks respondents to indicate their agreement with ten meanings of democracy. Each meaning is phrased as a short statement and is rated on a scale from 1 for no agreement at all to 10 for complete agreement. The wording of this and all other questions used in this chapter are documented in Appendix 10 (www.cambridge.org/welzel). The ten statements represent four different notions of democracy:

1. a *liberal* notion: equal freedoms of the people are the meaning of democracy;
2. a *social* notion: redistributive justice is the meaning of democracy;
3. a *populist* notion: the delivery of "bread and butter" and "law and order" are the meaning of democracy; and
4. an *authoritarian* notion: extra powers for military and religious leaders are the meaning of democracy.

Of these four notions, only the liberal and social notions are compatible with democratic theory. The liberal notion in particular garners the most consensus in political theory and is championed by prominent theorists such as Rawls (1971), Dahl (1973), Sartori (1984), Huntington (1991), and Sen (1999). In the real world, liberal democracy is the dominant form of democracy (Diamond 2008).

The social notion of democracy is more contested, depending on whether one prefers a market-liberal or a social-liberal version of democracy (Held 2006). As an ideal type, the market-liberal version grants individuals only personal and political rights but no social rights. This ideal of democracy is based on the belief that individuals are themselves responsible for their well-being. The social-liberal version, by contrast, assumes that people's well-being depends on circumstances beyond their control, which mandates a social right to compensation for unjust disadvantage (Marshall 1950). Despite these differences over social rights, both the market-liberal and the social-liberal versions of democracy embrace personal and political rights. These rights signify the minimal consensus among theoreticians of democracy.

Of course, the ubiquitous use of the term "democracy" in public discourse does not always accord with democratic theory. In fact, many people are unfamiliar with democratic theory. Hence, people might adopt whatever notion of democracy dominates their society's discourse. Especially in societies where authoritarian rulers abuse the term "democracy" for their own interests and control the media, people might be left with a twisted notion. What is more, precisely because the term "democracy" is used in different contexts with different meanings, people might feel free to fill it with whatever they value as a desirable outcome of politics. At least, this seems to be a reasonable possibility that deserves investigation.

To test this possibility, I devised items for WVS round five asking for notions of democracy that definitely conflict with democratic theory but which nevertheless might find people's support, even if mistakenly so. These items address features of politics that many people value highly and that they might define as features of democracy for this reason. These items also address features of politics that authoritarian and populist rulers might propagate as characteristics of democracy. This is the rationale behind the items proposing populist and authoritarian features as definitions of democracy.

As Figure 10.1 shows, the liberal notion is addressed by four items referring to free elections, referenda votes, civil liberties, and equal rights. The social notion is addressed by two items relating to state benefits and income redistribution. The populist notion is covered by another two items relating to economic growth as a bread-and-butter issue and fighting crime as a law-and-order issue. The authoritarian notion is covered by two items favoring military intervention and religious authority as definitions of democracy.

The factor analysis in Table 10.1 reproduces these distinct notions of democracy.[2] The liberal notion is manifest on the positive pole of the first dimension; the authoritarian notion appears on the negative pole of this dimension; the populist and social notions both represent dimensions of their own. The social notion constitutes the weakest dimension that covers the least variation in people's understanding of democracy. Also, the social notion of democracy determines people's preferences for democracy the least: if we regress the strength of people's expressed preference for democracy[3] on the four distinct notions of democracy, the social and populist notion together explain *less than 1 percent* of the variance in people's democratic preference. By contrast, the liberal versus authoritarian notion explains 18 percent.[4] These results plainly contradict a prominent model of democracy. According to this model, popular

---

[2] Note that each respondent's ratings are centered on this respondent's mean rating over all items. This procedure isolates item *priorities*, which is important to uncover the association-opposition structure among the items.

[3] For this analysis, I use the democratic preference index introduced in Chapter 8.

[4] Regression results are for 54,024 respondents from fifty societies from each of the world's ten culture zones.

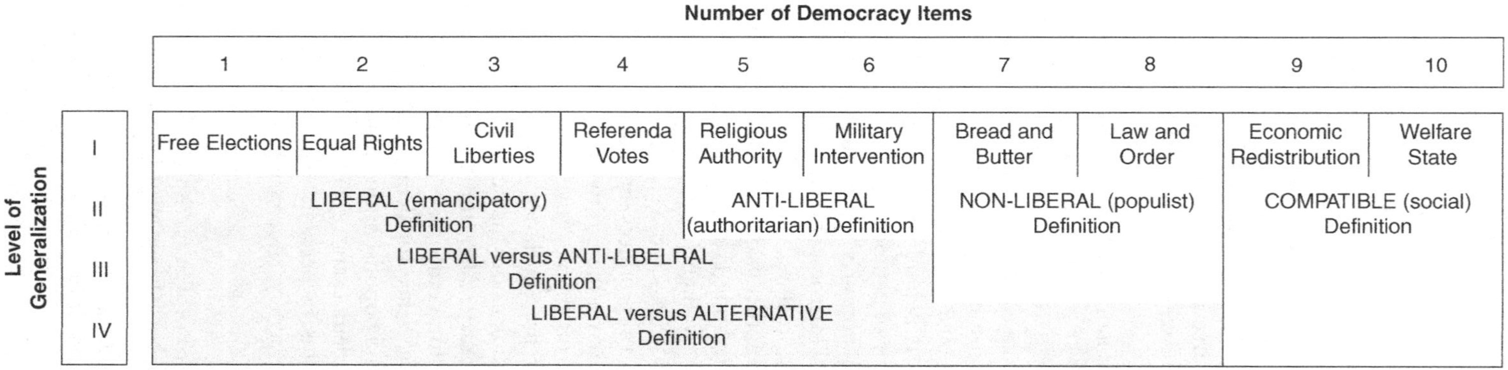

Number of Democracy Items

Level of Generalization	1	2	3	4	5	6	7	8	9	10
I	Free Elections	Equal Rights	Civil Liberties	Referenda Votes	Religious Authority	Military Intervention	Bread and Butter	Law and Order	Economic Redistribution	Welfare State
II	LIBERAL (emancipatory) Definition				ANTI-LIBERAL (authoritarian) Definition		NON-LIBERAL (populist) Definition		COMPATIBLE (social) Definition	
III	LIBERAL versus ANTI-LIBELRAL Definition									
IV	LIBERAL versus ALTERNATIVE Definition									

FIGURE 10.1 Summarizing Definitions of Democracy.

The qualification of understandings of democracy based on bread-and-butter and law-and-order as "non-liberal" does not mean that these goods are incompatible with liberal democracy. Yet they are no distinctive definitional features of liberal democracy: bread-and-butter and law-and-order may be or may not be delivered by any type of regime, whether democratic or not. By contrast, the redistributive understanding of democracy is included in the social-liberal definition of democracy but is excluded from the market-liberal definition. Hence, if one wants to avoid narrowing down the meaning of liberal democracy to any of its two variants, we cannot count the redistributive understanding either in favor or against the liberal definition of democracy. It must be left open to the democratic process itself where, between the market-liberal and the social-liberal ideals, a society places itself.

TABLE 10.1 *Empirical Dimensions in Popular Definitions of Democracy.*

	Dimensions		
Items	Dimension 1: Liberal vs. Authoritarian Definition	Dimension 2: Populist Definition	Dimension 3: Social Definition
Free Elections	0.63		
Equal Rights	0.60		
Civil Liberties	0.53		
Referenda Votes	0.50		
Military Intervention	−0.70		
Religious Authority	−0.73		
Bread-and-Butter		0.76	
Law-and-Order		0.73	
Economic Redistribution			0.68
Welfare State			0.62
Explained Variance	24%	14%	12%
N	58,524 respondents from 50 societies		

Entries are factor loadings. Items are standardized for each respondent's mean rating over all items. Factor analysis specified with varimax rotation under the Kaiser criterion. Data source is the country-pooled individual-level dataset of the World Values Surveys (WVS) round five (ca. 2005). National samples are weighted to equal size without changing the overall N.

preferences for democracy are motivated by the median voter's interest in redistribution (Boix 2003; Acemoglu & Robinson 2006). If this were true, the social notion of democracy would dominate people's democratic preferences. But this is not the case in any one society surveyed by the WVS, including highly unequal societies like Brazil and poor societies like Burkina Faso.

One way to group people's notions of democracy into a smaller number of summary measures is to rely on the dimensional analysis. On this basis, one can assign each respondent a factor score on each extracted dimension, indicating this respondent's position on the respective continuum. If we do so, we follow the dimensional logic and measure people's notions of democracy as they are organized in people's mind – regardless of theoretical definitions of democracy.

However, I am not interested in measuring how notions of democracy are organized in people's mind without reference to a theoretical norm. This approach is inappropriate for a concept as inherently normative as democracy. For this reason, I abstain from dimensional logic and follow instead the logic of compositiory index construction, as outlined in Box 2.1 (p. 60). That is, I measure people's notions of democracy against a theoretically predefined norm. If some people's notions differ from what the norm prescribes, these people's notions will score low when measured against the norm. If other people's notions are in accordance with the norm, their notions will score high when measured against the norm. Should the world be like this, then this is exactly what I want to measure.

I use the liberal meaning of democracy as the norm for two reasons: first, the liberal meaning embodies the emancipatory idea of human empowerment, which is the inspirational core of democracy; second, the liberal meaning is most firmly grounded in democratic theory (Sen 1999; Dahl 2000; Held 2006; Brettschneider 2007).

Against the standard of liberal democracy, the authoritarian notion of democracy is *anti*-liberal: it reverses the meaning of democracy when one defines the political authority of the military or religious leaders as democracy. Democracy means, on the contrary, the unequivocal subjection of the military and religion to civil and secular authority. The populist notion of democracy is *a*-liberal: economic growth and fighting crime could be considered as prerequisites or outcomes of democracy, yet they do not *define* democracy. Neither economic growth nor fighting crime are exclusive properties of democracy. Both democracies and nondemocracies might or might not have economic growth, and they both might or might not put effort into crime prevention; but whether or not they do has no bearing on whether they are democracies or nondemocracies. Thus, the authoritarian as well as the populist notion rival the liberal notion; these are alternative meanings and should hence be treated that way. From this, it follows that one can qualify a person's notion of democracy as unequivocally liberal only if the person emphasizes the liberal meanings of democracy and at the same time rejects the authoritarian and populist meanings.

The social notion of democracy is not necessarily part of the liberal notion, but it is fully compatible with the liberal notion. If one endorses both civic freedoms and redistributive justice as meanings of democracy, one favors a social-liberal notion of democracy (Held 2006). If one endorses civic freedoms but rejects redistributive justice as meanings of democracy, one favors a market-liberal notion of democracy. Yet, both are liberal conceptions of democracy. Consequently, one cannot narrow down the liberal notion to either of these two. This leads to a clear conclusion: if one wants to measure the dominance of the liberal over rival definitions, but not over compatible definitions of democracy, the social notion of democracy must neither be counted against nor counted in favor of the liberal notion. In practical terms, this means that we measure liberal notions of democracy without building in a preference for either the market-liberal or the social-liberal model of democracy.

A person's notion of democracy is truly liberal to the extent that she both supports the liberal notion of democracy and rejects the nonliberal notions. Thus, I calculate each person's average support of the four liberal meanings of democracy and then subtract from this her average support of the four non-liberal meanings. The calculation of this and all other variables is detailed in Appendix 10 (www.cambridge.org/welzel). I standardize the resulting difference index into a range from 0 to 1.0. The minimum 0 indicates complete dominance of the nonliberal over the liberal notion of democracy; the maximum 1.0 indicates the exact opposite. A score of 0.50 indicates that the two notions are even.

2.2 Criticalness of the Assessment of Democracy

Unless people perceive the democratic quality of their society as deficient, even a decidedly liberal notion of democracy cannot be mobilized for democratic reforms. Thus, round five of the WVS asks people to assess the democratic quality of their society on a 10-point scale from 1 ("not at all democratic") to 10 ("fully democratic"). Again, I transform this question into a 0–1.0 scale.

However, one cannot judge how critical people's assessment is without reference to a society's actual democratic quality. I take information about the actual democratic quality from the citizen rights index introduced in Chapter 8. I use a society's score on the citizen rights over the five years preceding the survey as the yardstick to measure how critically a respondent assesses his or her society's democratic quality. People's democracy assessment is less critical the higher they rate their society's democratic quality relative to its actual quality. By the same token, someone's democracy assessment is more critical the lower it is relative to a society's actual democratic quality. Critical assessments in this sense indicate the strength of people's *democratic expectations*. At least this is true when there is a desire for democracy, which we know is usually the case.

Following these reflections, I calculate how much people's assessment of their society's democratic quality exceeds or falls short of the actual quality by subtracting the former from the latter. This is straightforward because both measures exist in the same scale range. As detailed in Appendix 10 (www. cambridge.org/welzel), I rescale the resulting index into a range from 0 to 1.0. On the final index, the minimum 0 indicates the most uncritical assessment: someone rates his or her society's democracy best when in fact it is worst. The maximum 1.0 indicates the most critical assessment: someone rates his or her democracy worst when in fact it is best. The midpoint at 0.50 indicates that respondents assess their society's democratic quality equal to its actual quality.

2.3 Qualifying Desires for Democracy

A third aspect of people's views of democracy is how strongly they wish to live in a democracy. The WVS addresses this aspect by another 10-point scale from 1 ("not at all important" to live in a democracy) to 10 ("absolutely important"). As before, I transform this scale into a range from 0 to 1.0.

Democratic desires are important for democratic mobilization because, in the absence of democratic desires, one cannot mobilize people for goals advocated in the name of democracy. But the democratic desire needs further qualification. It needs to be qualified for the liberalness of people's notion of democracy, so we know the desire can only be mobilized for liberal goals. And it needs to be qualified for the criticalness of people's assessment of democracy, so that we know the desire can be mobilized at all because people see democracy as deficient.

Following this logic, I qualify people's democratic desires in two steps. In the first step, I weight the strength of people's democratic desire for the liberalness of people's notion of democracy. The resulting index measures democratic desires conditionally, showing how strongly people desire democracy *on the condition* that they understand democracy in liberal terms. The index is at minimum 0 if someone either does not wish to live in a democracy or has a completely non-liberal notion of democracy. The index is at maximum 1.0 if someone both strongly wishes to live in a democracy and has an unequivocally liberal notion of democracy. Intermediate positions on either component yield fractions of 1.0.

In the second step, I condition liberal democratic desires by how critically people assess democracy, speaking about the desire for democracy in an even more conditional way: the strength of the desire for democracy on the double condition that people (a) define democracy in liberal terms and (b) assess the democratic quality of their society as deficient. This is the critical-liberal desire for democracy.

The critical-liberal desire for democracy is at minimum 0 if a respondent does not wish at all to live in a democracy, or understands democracy in completely nonliberal terms, or is entirely uncritical of the society's democratic quality. The index is at its maximum 1.0 if a respondent strongly wishes to live in a democracy, and understands democracy unequivocally in liberal terms, and is most critical of the society's democratic quality. Intermediate positions on either of these components yield fractions of 1.0.

I do by no means assume that people's desire for democracy, their notion of democracy, and their assessment of it reflect interchangeable facets of a single underlying dimension. Hence, the critical-liberal desire is not to be mistaken as a latent variable. Instead, it is a multidimensional construct that weighs democratic desires for inherently relevant qualities – precisely because these qualities do not come automatically with the desire itself. With this approach, I once again follow a conditional logic of index construction as outlined in Box 8.1 (p. 259).

3. HYPOTHESES

I expect to confirm four hypotheses that describe what I think are inherent impulses of emancipative values. The basic assumption is that the notion of democracy as equal freedoms for everyone becomes intrinsically appealing under emancipative values, for these values emphasize universal freedoms. This assumption suggests four hypotheses:

   1. Emancipative values anchor people's desire for democracy in an unequiv-
      ocally liberal notion of democracy.[5]

---

[5] A colleague once disqualified this hypothesis as tautological. I agree that there is an obvious plausibility in this hypothesis. Yet, this does not make it tautological but simply logical. There remains a conceptual boundary between what people value in life and how they idealize democracy. For the two to be connected, people have to cross this boundary. As plausible as this cross-over might be, it is not self-evident that it happens. Hence, demonstrating it is worthwhile.

2. Emancipative values tie people's desire for democracy to a critical assessment of a society's democratic quality.

3. Emancipative values show these effects at both the individual and societal levels, but the mechanism of social cross-fertilization applies: the critical-liberal impulse of an individual's emancipative values is amplified by the social prevalence of these values.

4. The impact of emancipative values on democratic orientations is independent of people's cognitive mobilization, as well as of their socialization under democracy.

The most important control variable at the societal level is democratic traditions. To assume a strong effect of democratic traditions on people's views of democracy is plausible from the viewpoint of "democratic learning." From this point of view, adopting the "proper" views of democracy is a matter of being socialized into a long collective experience with democratic institutions (Rustow 1970; Jackman & Miller 1998; Rohrschneider & Peffley 2003). To test this proposition, I use the democratic traditions index introduced in Chapter 2. The index measures each society's historically accumulated experience with democracy. As outlined in Chapter 2, the democratic tradition index is also a formidable measure of Western legacies. Thus, when using this index, we do not need an additional measure to depict cultural differences along a Western/non-Western fault line: on the democratic traditions index, this fault line is fully manifest, with Western societies having on average much longer democratic traditions than non-Western societies. Indeed, cross-national differences in the democratic tradition covary to 81 percent with our ten global culture zones and to 57 percent with the dichotomous Western/non-Western division. Thus, by taking democratic traditions into account, I test whether the supposed effects of emancipative values are culture-bound or operate beyond Western contexts.

At the individual level, some researchers give people's views of democracy primarily a cognitive reading: people's views reflect what people *know* about democracy (Shin & Tusalem 2007; Norris 2011). Thus, at the individual level, we test the effect of emancipative values on views of democracy against cognitive variables, including people's level of education, their political interest, and their informational connectivity. Looking at informational connectivity also provides a test of whether people adopt liberal notions of democracy because of their exposure to democratic norm diffusion through global communications. Gender and age are included as routine demographic controls.

I present the findings in three steps. First, I demonstrate that the qualified measures of people's desires for democracy bring differences to the surface that are invisible otherwise. This is shown in bar diagrams that exhibit how strongly the different desires are held by populations of different culture zones around the world. The purpose of this analysis is to demonstrate that people's desires for democracy are indeed very different, which underlines the need for explanation. The second step probes into explanation, using line graphs to examine the combined individual- and societal-level effects of emancipative values on people's desires for democracy. The third step extends this analysis into multilevel regression models in which the individual-level effect of emancipative values is controlled for the impact of cognitive mobilization while the societal-level effect is controlled for democratic traditions.

4. FINDINGS

4.1 Culture Zone Differences

The left-hand diagram of Figure 10.2 plots for each culture zone how strongly people understand democracy in liberal terms, *before* qualification (dark gray bars) and *after* qualification (light gray bars). Before qualifying people's understanding for how unequivocally liberal it is, it seems as if there is little difference, which confirms previous research (Dalton, Shin, & Jou 2007). Indeed, the extent to which people understand democracy in liberal terms is above 0.70 scale points in each culture zone. People's notions of democracy vary to only 4 percent between culture zones.

The picture changes drastically when we qualify people's notion of democracy for how unequivocally liberal it is. Ratings plummet considerably. Moreover, they plummet to different degrees, making culture zone differences strikingly evident. To be precise, the extent to which people emphasize the liberal against nonliberal notions of democracy varies from a high of 0.74 scale points in the Reformed West to a low of 0.55 scale points in the Islamic East. If one takes into account how unequivocally people understand democracy in liberal terms, about 20 percent of the individual-level variance is explained by culture zones. People in the Islamic East, the Indic East, and sub-Saharan Africa understand democracy the least unequivocally in liberal terms. In this regard, a big rift separates these cultures from the West.

With desires for democracy, we make a similar observation. Figure 10.3 depicts for each culture zone the average strength of people's desire for democracy, *before* qualification (dark gray bars) and *after* qualification (light gray bars). Before qualification, it seems that the desire for democracy is similarly strong across the globe. In all culture zones, the desire for democracy scores at 0.77 scale points or higher. Again, people's desire for democracy varies to only 4 percent between culture zones. After qualifying the desires for how strongly they are grounded in an unequivocally liberal notion of democracy, the picture changes drastically. Desire levels are generally much lower, and they vary considerably between culture zones. As before, people of the Reformed West show the strongest liberally grounded desire, scoring at about 0.67 scale points. And once more, people in the Islamic East are found at the bottom, at 0.44 scale points. Again, the individual-level

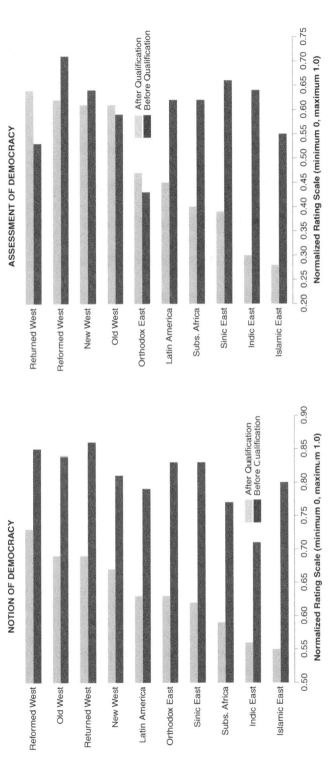

NOTION OF DEMOCRACY

Reformed West
Old West
Returned West
New West
Latin America
Orthodox East
Sinic East
Subs. Africa
Indic East
Islamic East

After Qualification
Before Qualification

0.50 0.55 0.60 0.65 0.70 0.75 0.80 0.85 0.90

Normalized Rating Scale (minimum 0, maximum 1.0)

ASSESSMENT OF DEMOCRACY

Returned West
Reformed West
New West
Old West
Orthodox East
Latin America
Subs. Africa
Sinic East
Indic East
Islamic East

After Qualification
Before Qualification

0.20 0.25 0.30 0.35 0.40 0.45 0.50 0.55 0.60 0.65 0.70 0.75

Normalized Rating Scale (minimum 0, maximum 1.0)

FIGURE 10.2 Notions and Assessments of Democracy by Culture Zone (before and after qualification).

Data Coverage: Respondents with valid data from all fifty societies surveyed in the World Values Surveys (WVS) round five (ca. 2005). National samples are weighted to equal size (N = 1,000 per society). Societies per culture zone: Islamic East – Egypt, Iran, Iraq, Jordan, Morocco, Turkey; Indic East – India, Indonesia, Malaysia, Thailand; Orthodox East – Bulgaria, Moldova, Romania, Russia, Serbia, Ukraine; Sinic East – China, Japan, South Korea, Taiwan; Old West – Andorra, Cyprus, France, Italy, Spain; Reformed West – Finland, West Germany, Netherlands, Norway, Sweden, Switzerland; New West – Australia, Canada, New Zealand, United States; Returned West – East Germany, Poland, Slovenia; Sub-Saharan Africa – Burkina Faso, Ghana, Mali, Rwanda, South Africa, Zambia; Latin America – Argentina, Brazil, Chile, Mexico, Peru, Trinidad-Tobago, Uruguay.

Left-hand diagram measures how liberal people's notion of democracy is. "Before qualification" indicates how strongly people support just the four liberal notions of democracy. "After qualification" means how strongly they support the four liberal notions and at the same time reject the four nonliberal notions. Right-hand diagram measures how democratic people assess their society. "Before qualification" is just their assessment. "After qualification" is their assessment relative to the society's "true" level of democracy, with higher scores indicating a more critical rating.

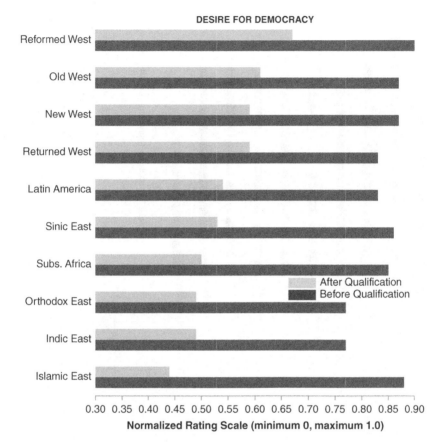

FIGURE 10.3 Desires for Democracy by Culture Zone (before and after qualification). *Data Coverage*: Same as for Figure 10.2. "Before qualification" measures just the desire for democracy. "After qualification" measures the desire on the condition that is linked with an unequivocally liberal notion of democracy.

variation in people's views of democracy that is due to culture zone differences jumps from 4 to 20 percent after proper qualification.

The right-hand diagram of Figure 10.2 plots for each culture zone at what level people rate their society's democratic quality, again *before* qualification (light gray bars) and *after* qualification (dark gray bars). The pattern is familiar. Before qualification, ratings vary in a more limited range than after qualification, and, in all culture zones, except the Orthodox East, democracy ratings are above 0.50 scale points. Accordingly, people around the world rate their societies as rather more than less democratic. This includes people in the Islamic East, which is odd when one recognizes that, at the time of these surveys, there hardly was a democracy in the Islamic East – with the exception of Turkey. Apparently, then, many people overrate their societies' democratic quality. They rate democracy uncritically.[6] Hence, qualifying people's ratings for how critically they assess democracy, relative to the actual democratic quality, uncovers a wide chasm between the most critical rating in the Returned West (0.64) and the least critical rating in the Islamic East (0.27).

There is indeed a deep cultural rift between Islamic and Western societies over democratic orientations. At times, this rift has been disputed (Inglehart & Norris 2003), but it is fully visible after we qualify otherwise superficial measures of people's views of democracy. The assertion that the democratic deficits of the Islamic world have little to do with deficiencies in people's democratic attitudes needs to be reconsidered.

4.2 The Effect of Emancipative Values without Controls

It is not culture zones themselves that vary people's views of democracy but their difference in emancipative values. Indeed, culture zones differ just as much in emancipative values as they differ in people's views of democracy, showing the same Western/non-Western chasm. Thus, if we replace the culture zones with their mean scores on emancipative values, these mean scores explain all the variance in people's views of democracy that seems to be explained by culture zones.[7] According to this finding, it is worthwhile to have a closer look at how emancipative values shape people's views of democracy.

Emancipative values can affect people's desires for democracy in two ways. First, a person's own preference for emancipative values can shape his or her desire for democracy, irrespective of how prevalent these values are in the person's society. Second, the prevalence of emancipative values in a person's

---

[6] This resonates with the evidence from Chapter 9, where we found that many people in authoritarian societies with a miserable human rights record nevertheless judge their society's rights situation very favorably (see Figure 9.1, p. 284). The correlation between uncritical rights judgments and uncritical democracy ratings in the country-pooled individual-level data is $r = .62$ across some 45,000 respondents from forty-three societies. The societal-level correlation is $r = .85$ ($N = 43$). Both uncritical rights judgments and uncritical democracy ratings correlate strongly negatively with emancipative values, suggesting that *weak* emancipative values keep people uncritical. At the individual level, emancipative values correlate at $r = -.34$ and $r = -.40$ with uncritical rights judgments and uncritical democracy ratings, respectively. At the societal level, the correlations are $r = -.68$ with uncritical rights judgments ($N = 80$) and $r = -.82$ with uncritical democracy ratings ($N = 50$). The fact that uncritical judgments are strongly predicted by weakness in emancipative values has to be seen in connection with another fact: the very low nonresponse rate to these evaluation questions even in authoritarian societies (see Chapter 9). Together, these two pieces of evidence disconfirm the interpretation that many people in authoritarian societies are critical but do not dare to express their criticism out of fear from sanctions.

[7] If we regress the liberalness of people's notion of democracy on a set of dummies representing the ten culture zones (using the New West as the reference category), we explain 20 percent of the variation among 63,914 respondents from fifty societies. Replacing the culture zone dummies with a variable that assigns each respondent the mean score of his or her culture zone in emancipative values, we explain precisely the same proportion of variance in the liberalness in people's notion of democracy. Thus, culture zones vary people's notion of democracy because the prevalence of emancipative values varies across culture zones. Similar results are obtained for the criticalness of people's assessment of democracy.

society can shape his or her desires for democracy, irrespective of how strongly the person him- or herself prefers these values. In other words, emancipative values can shape desires for democracy through both their individual preference and their social prevalence.

To visualize the individual-level impact of emancipative values, we group the individual respondents into ten ascending categories on the emancipative values index, ordered from weaker to stronger emphasis on these values. To visualize the societal-level impact of emancipative values, we categorize societies according to how prevalent emancipative values are, distinguishing "weakly," "moderately," and "strongly emancipative" societies. This distinction was introduced in Chapter 6.

Based on these categorizations, the left-hand diagram of Figure 10.5 plots the strength of the respondents' desire for democracy on the vertical axis against the strength of their emancipative values on the horizontal axis, separately for weakly, moderately, and strongly emancipative societies.

The strength of the desires for democracy is consistently above 0.80 scale points. Whether a society is weakly, moderately, or strongly emancipative does not vary the desire level. As the slopes show, stronger preferences for emancipative values among individuals strengthen the desire for democracy slightly at best. And this is only the case when these values have surpassed a certain prevalence level: in weakly emancipative societies, there is no linear relationship between people's emancipative values and their democratic desires – the slope is U-shaped.

Looking at notions of democracy, a different pattern surfaces. The left-hand diagram of Figure 10.4 shows how people's preference for emancipative values varies the liberalness of their notion of democracy. Again, this is shown separately for weakly, moderately, and strongly emancipative societies. In each of the three types of society, there is a recognizable upward slope indicating that individuals with stronger emancipative preferences define democracy more unequivocally liberal, and they do so irrespective of how prevalent emancipative values are in their society. Still, the prevalence of emancipative values matters in two ways. First, irrespective of how strongly the individuals themselves prefer emancipative values, their liberal notion of democracy is stronger when emancipative values are more prevalent in their society. This is evident from the fact that the data line of weakly emancipative societies is below that of moderately emancipative societies, which in turn is below that of strongly emancipative societies. Second, when emancipative values are more prevalent in a society, the individuals' own preferences for emancipative values strengthen their liberal notion of democracy more pronouncedly. This is evident from the fact that the slopes of the three data lines become steeper from weakly to moderately to strongly emancipative societies. The joint individual-level and societal-level impact of emancipative values varies people's liberal notion of democracy by about 0.28 scale points.

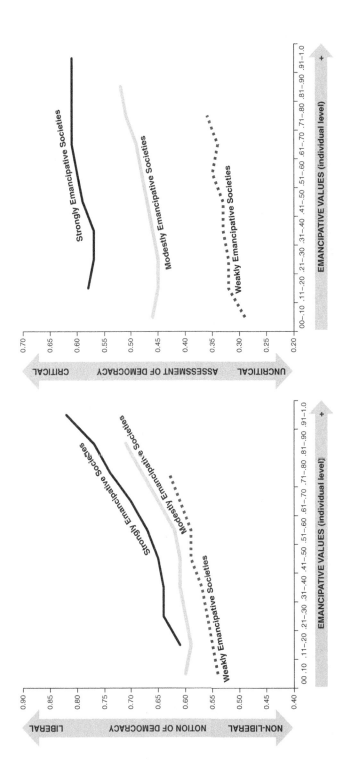

FIGURE 10.4 Multilevel Effects of Emancipative Values on Liberalness in Notions and on Criticalness in Assessments of Democracy.

Data Coverage: All respondents with valid data from all fifty societies surveyed in World Values Surveys (WVS) round five (2005). Samples are weighted to equal size (N = 1,000 per society). Weakly emancipative societies (emancipative values index [EVI] below 0.37) include Burkina Faso, China, Egypt, Ghana, India, Indonesia, Iran, Iraq, Jordan, Mali, Morocco, Russia, Rwanda, Thailand, Turkey, Ukraine, Vietnam; moderately emancipative societies (EVI score between 0.37 and 0.48) include Brazil, Bulgaria, Chile, Colombia, Cyprus, Malaysia, Mexico, Moldova, Poland, Romania, South Africa, South Korea, Trinidad-Tobago, Zambia; strongly emancipative societies (EVI score above 0.48) include Andorra, Argentina, Australia, Canada, Finland, France, Germany (East), Germany (West), Italy, Japan, Netherlands, Norway, Serbia, Slovenia, Spain, Sweden, Switzerland, United Kingdom, United States, Uruguay.

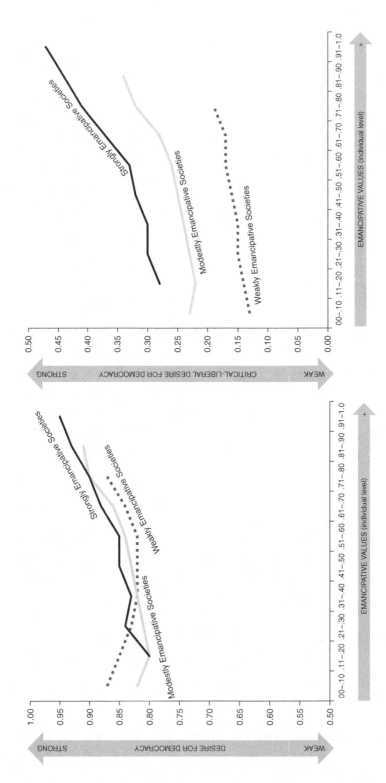

FIGURE 10.5 Multilevel Effects of Emancipative Values on Unqualified and on Critical-Liberal Desires for Democracy.
Data Coverage: Same as in Figure 10.4.

The right-hand diagram of Figure 10.4 illustrates how emancipative values vary the criticalness of people's rating of democracy. Again, strong effects are evident. The combined individual-level and societal-level impact of emancipative values varies the criticalness of people's rating of democracy to about the same extent as it varies the liberalness of their notion of democracy, namely, by 0.32 scale points. But, in contrast to liberal notions, critical assessments vary much more with the social prevalence of emancipative values than with individual preferences for them. The large co-variation of critical assessments with the social prevalence of emancipative values is evident from the large distances between the data lines for weakly, moderately, and strongly emancipative societies. The small co-variation of critical assessments with individual preferences for emancipative values is evident from the fact that the slopes of the three data lines point only slightly upward. The reason for this pattern is that critical assessments are measured against the societies' actual levels of democracy, which are constant within societies. Thus, bigger differences surface between than within societies.

The liberalness of people's notion of democracy and the criticalness of their assessment of democracy are key qualifications of people's desire for democracy. Because emancipative values vary these qualifications quite strongly, they must also vary the qualified desire for democracy, that is, the critical-liberal desire for democracy. The right-hand diagram of Figure 10.5 demonstrates that this is indeed the case. The combined individual- and societal-level impact of emancipative values varies the critical-liberal desire for democracy by 0.32 scale points. Note that the critical-liberal desire combines features of the liberal notion and the critical assessment. Hence, the strong individual-level variation in liberal notions and the strong societal-level variation in critical assessments now both show up. The data lines are fairly steep (the feature of liberal notions), as well as quite distant (the feature of critical assessments).

The next question is whether these findings are robust and hold when we control for other plausible influences on people's desires for democracy, namely, the length of a society's democratic tradition and the individuals' cognitive mobilization.

4.3 The Effect of Emancipative Values after Controls

The multilevel models in Table 10.2 confirm the previous findings when we include these controls. In the following, we focus on the last model because it explains the most qualified view of democracy: the critical-liberal desire for democracy. On average, people's critical-liberal desire for democracy scores at 0.27, which is at about a fourth of the possible maximum.

Among individuals within the same societies, a 1-unit increase in emancipative values comes with a 0.11-unit increase in the critical-liberal desire. This is by far the strongest individual-level contribution to a critical-liberal desire, stronger than the effects of informational connectedness, political interest, and formal

TABLE 10.2 *Effects of Emancipative Values on Popular Views of Democracy (multilevel models).*

Predictors	Dependent Variables				
	Strength of Desire for Democracy	Liberalness in Notion of Democracy	Criticalness in Rating of Democracy	Liberal Desire for Democracy	Critical-Liberal Desire for Democracy
• Constant	0.58(81.7)***	0.67(119.6)***	0.45(40.8)***	0.58(81.7)***	0.27(37.4)***
Societal-level Effects:					
• Democratic Tradition	N.S.	N.S.	0.12(2.4)**	N.S.	0.07(2.1)*
• EV-Prevalence	0.58(5.4)***	0.55(6.6)***	0.70(5.9)***	0.58(5.4)***	0.68(8.3)***
Individual-level Effects:					
• Female Sex	−0.01(−3.3)***	−0.01(−4.6)***	−0.01(−2.4)**	−0.01(−3.3)**	−0.01(−5.5)***
• Birth Year (indexed)	0.10(6.0)***	0.05(6.9)***	N.S.	0.10(6.0)***	0.05(6.3)***
Cross-level Interactions:					
• Formal Education	0.07(9.7)***	0.05(9.3)***	N.S.	0.07(9.7)***	0.03(8.0)***
* Democratic Tradition	N.S.	N.S.	N.S.	N.S.	N.S.
* EV-Prevalence	N.S.	N.S.	N.S.	N.S.	N.S.
• Political Interest	0.06(7.2)***	0.01(2.3)**	−0.04(−7.6)***	0.06(7.2)***	0.01(2.3)**
* Democratic Tradition	N.S.	N.S.	N.S.	N.S.	N.S.
* EV-Prevalence	N.S.	N.S.	N.S.	N.S.	N.S.
• Informational Connectedness	0.06(6.6)***	0.02(3.6)***	N.S.	0.06(6.6)***	0.02(4.2)***
* Democratic Tradition	N.S.	N.S.	N.S.	N.S.	N.S.
* EV-Prevalence	N.S.	N.S.	N.S.	N.S.	N.S.
• EV-Preference	0.15(9.5)***	0.12(10.4)***	0.04(4.0)***	0.15(9.5)***	0.11(11.5)***
* Democratic Tradition	N.S.	0.10(1.8)*	0.11(2.1)*	N.S.	0.08(1.9)*
* EV-Prevalence	0.77(3.7)***	0.32(2.1)**	−0.31(−2.2)*	0.77(3.7)***	0.30(2.6)**

Reduction of Error:					
Within-societal variation of DV	05.3%	09.2%	03.2%	10.1%	09.1%
Between-societal variation of DV	08.9%	70.5%	69.3%	66.6%	80.9%
Variation in effect of values	27.9%	45.9%	07.7%	45.1%	48.5%
N (number of observations)	44,201 respondents in 45 societies				

Models estimated with HLM 6.01. Entries are unstandardized regression coefficients with T ratios in parentheses based on robust standard errors. Individual-level variables are country-mean centered, societal-level variables are global-mean centered.

EV, Emancipative Values.

Data cover all societies from World Values Surveys (WVS, round five (ca. 2005) with valid data. National samples are weighted to equal size.

education. This is remarkable because the latter three are important indicators of (a) cognitive mobilization and (b) exposure to democratic norm diffusion through global communications. One would assume that these variables create greater awareness of democracy's defining features and – because of this greater awareness – shape people's views toward a more liberal and critical orientation. As the positive coefficients of all three variables show, this is the case. Yet, emancipative values clearly trump the effects of the cognitive variables. Even combined, informational connectedness, political interest, and formal education contribute less to a critical-liberal desire than do emancipative values alone. Thus, orientations toward democracy are more an *evaluative* matter than a *cognitive* matter: people's responses to democracy questions indicate less what people *know* about democracy than what they *wish* democracy to be.

The social prevalence of emancipative values influences things in the same direction as individual preferences for these values. Specifically, a 1-unit increase in the social prevalence of emancipative values comes with a 0.68-unit increase in people's critical-liberal desires. This is a far stronger and more significant contribution than that of a society's democratic tradition. A 1-unit increase in the latter only comes with a 0.07-unit increase in critical-liberal desires. Hence, critical-liberal desires for democracy are not simply a function of being socialized into a lasting democratic tradition.

Moreover, the social prevalence of emancipative values amplifies the critical-liberal impulse of an individual preference for these values: a 1-unit increase in the product of individual- and societal-level emancipative values comes with an additional 0.30-unit increase in people's critical-liberal desires. This is obvious from the coefficient for the interaction term between the social prevalence of emancipative values and individual preferences for them. The existence of this interaction illustrates the mechanism of social cross-fertilization (see Box 3.1, p. 110): when an individual-level attribute has an inherent tendency, the tendency unfolds more freely when the attribute in question is more prevalent in a society. Thus, the critical-liberal tendency of emancipative values develops more freely when these values are more prevalent in a society.

As in previous chapters, emancipative values affect other social phenomena more through their social prevalence than through the individual preference for them: the shared emphasis on emancipative values matters more than the individually unique emphasis. This pattern confirms the emphasis that the human empowerment framework places on collectively shared features of empowerment.

As the models in Table 10.2 show, similar findings apply to the constituents of the critical-liberal desire: the liberal notion of democracy and the critical assessment of democracy. Only the unqualified desire for democracy (see the first model in Table 10.2) stands out, showing a much weaker determination pattern. Bare of the critical-liberal fundament, the strength of the desire for democracy is a quite meaningless phenomenon. In the analysis of Table 10.2, this is evident in a weak determination pattern.

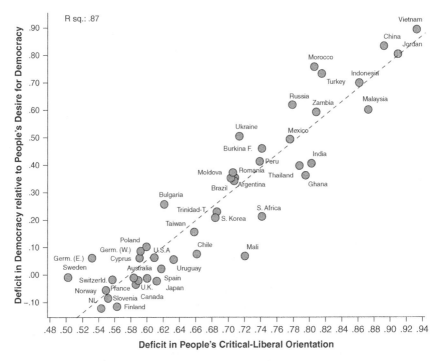

FIGURE 10.6 Democratic Deficits and Deficits in Critical-Liberal Mindedness.
Data Coverage: All of the fifty societies with valid data surveyed in World Values Surveys (WVS) round five (ca. 2005). Horizontal axis is the inverse of the combination of critical assessments of democracy with liberal notions of what democracy means: scores are higher the more this combination is absent. Vertical axis is the level difference between people's desire for democracy and the given society's actual degree of democracy (as indicated by the citizen rights index in the year of the survey): scores are higher the more the level of democracy falls short of what people seem to desire. In simple terms, the diagram shows that, when a society's level of democracy falls far short of people's desire for democracy, the critical-liberal orientation is largely absent in this society. In fact, elites can afford to undersupply democracy relative to what people seem to want the more these people lack the critical-liberal orientation. China, Indonesia, Jordan, Malaysia, Turkey, and Vietnam are the examples of this pattern.

Figure 10.6 demonstrates this point in fullest clarity: the extent to which a society's actual level of democracy falls short of people's desire for democracy is explained to 87 percent by the absence of a critical-liberal fundament. There are many societies whose actual "democraticness" – seemingly – falls far short of people's desire for democracy. China, Jordan, and Vietnam are on top of the list: this is where we have no democracy, in apparent contradiction to widespread desires for it. Yet, these democratic deficits are only seemingly in contradiction to people's democratic desires: wherever the seeming contradiction occurs, people's democratic desires lack the critical-liberal grounding. In the absence of a critical-liberal orientation, people mistakenly consider their society as democratic and see their democratic desire satisfied when in fact democracy is largely absent. Consequently, mass desires for democracy that lack the critical-liberal grounding provide no source of pressure for democratic reform. In all these cases, the democratic deficits can persist without provoking mass opposition.

This insight might change our view of authoritarian survival. Where authoritarian regimes manage to persist, the reason might not be that they are able to repress opposing mass preferences. More likely, opposing mass preferences are actually not in place because the processes that feed emancipative values and their subsequent critical-liberal impulses have not yet set in.

KEY POINTS

With unqualified measures of democratic desires, we are confronted with the coexistence paradox: strong desires for democracy coexist easily with the lack of democracy. With qualified measures, the paradox dissolves: wherever democracy is absent or deficient, people's desire for democracy lacks the critical-liberal grounding that emancipative values provide.

These results resonate with recent findings. Qi and Shin (2011) show that the predictive power of democratic desires with respect to a society's actual democraticness increases considerably if these desires go together with a critical assessment of institutions. However, these authors do not place this result into a wider context because they make no effort to highlight the sources of the citizens' criticality. To the contrary, they pitch the impact of critical assessments against that of emancipative values, ignoring the fact that these values do not operate against critical assessments but actually encourage them – as we have seen. Critical citizens are the product of emancipative values.

Another related finding is provided by Norris (2011) who shows that Inglehart and Welzel's (2005) "self-expression values" do not strengthen people's desire for democracy. We have seen that the same holds true for emancipative values, which is not surprising because these values are an improved measure of self-expression values. Norris reads her finding as a disapproval of Inglehart and Welzel's theory, which she thinks posits that stronger emancipative values make people's desire for democracy stronger.

However, Inglehart and Welzel (2005: 178–185) have themselves demonstrated a weak effect of emancipative values on the desire for democracy. As they point out, the role of emancipative values is not to strengthen the democratic desire *but to reshape the nature* of this desire by grounding it in a strong aspiration for freedoms coupled with an urge to take action. Without the fundament of emancipative values, a strong desire for democracy is inconsequential.

This insight makes particular sense in the human empowerment framework. This framework suggests that emancipative values empower people motivation-wise because these values make people eager to take their lives in their own hands. As abundant evidence has shown, emancipative values grow stronger in response to more widespread action resources based on higher education, easier connectivity, and better equipment. As the evidence also shows, when people dispose of significant action resources and when they are strongly inspired by emancipative values, they are much more likely to join forces and to voice shared claims. Ignoring the voices of people who have the means and will to coordinate themselves is a costly and eventually unsustainable option for those in power. For this reason, we find that governments are more responsive, accountable, and democratic where emancipative values are widely shared (Welzel & Dalton 2013).

The findings of this chapter fit into the sequence from action resources to emancipative values to civic entitlements. In fact, they provide additional clarity on how emancipative values improve the conditions for democratic mobilization. Consider the evidence that emancipative values focus people's desire for democracy ever more sharply on democracy's liberal qualities: because of this, people's desire for democracy can only be mobilized for the sake of liberal democracy. Or, consider the evidence that emancipative values couple people's desire for democracy with a more critical rating of their society's actual democratic quality: because of this, it is easier to mobilize this desire into pressures to improve the democratic quality of one's society. In conclusion, emancipative values shape the conditions of democratic mobilization: where emancipative values grow strong, these conditions become favorable.

PART D

EMANCIPATIVE VALUES IN HUMAN CIVILIZATION

11

The Redirection of Civilization[*]

> Cultures do not exist as simply static "differences" to be celebrated but compete
> with one another as better and worse ways of getting things done.
>
> – T. Sowell 1996: 378

The theory of emancipation derives its description of human empowerment
from a single evolutionary principle: the utility ladder of freedoms.
Accordingly, human empowerment is a development that elevates societies on
the utility ladder of freedoms. Two theses of the theory address separate aspects
of causality in this ascension. The sequence thesis [italic letters] addresses the
endogenous causation of human empowerment, that is, the dominant flow of
impact among its three elements: action resources, emancipative values and civic
entitlements. Specifically, the sequence thesis suggests that, as expanding action
resources increase the objective utility of freedoms, growth in freedoms' subjective valuation and in their legal guarantees follow subsequently, giving rise to
emancipative value and to civic entitlements. Chapters 4, 8 and 9 provided
conclusive evidence in support of this sequence.

In contrast to the sequence thesis, the source thesis [italic letters] addresses the
exogenous causes of human empowerment. Exogenous causality refers to the
original source of human empowerment, which cannot itself be an element of the
process. Since we have not yet dealt thoroughly with the exogenous causes of
human empowerment, this chapter examines the source thesis. The source thesis
posits that human empowerment originates in a particular environmental condition. This condition harbors two natural forms of existential security and

* A preliminary draft of this chapter has been co-authored as a conference paper by myself, Amy
Alexander, Jan Delhey, Roberto Foa, Ronald F. Inglehart, Ronald C. Inglehart, Jan Mueller, and
Serban Tanasa. The preliminary version was presented at the Western Regional Science annual
meeting 2012 on Kauai but has not been published to avoid conflict with this chapter. I thank my
co-authors as well as Ronald Fischer, Michele Gelfand, Jacob Gerner Hariri, Patrick Nolan, Jeffrey
Sachs, and Randy Thornhill for their invaluable input.

existential autonomy, both of which bestow on freedoms an initial utility that is otherwise lacking. I identify this environmental condition in what I call the *cool-water condition* (CW condition).

The CW condition is a combination of (1) moderately cold climates, (2) continuous rainfall over all seasons, and (3) permanently navigable waterways. Why is this condition significant? First, colder temperatures with mild seasonal frost kill microbes and, thus, diminish infectious diseases (Jones 1987; Landes 1998). Colder temperatures also decelerate soil depletion, which improves land productivity (Masters & Wiebe 2000; Easterly & Levine 2003). Second, continuity of rainfall over the seasons further improves land productivity and, combined with colder temperatures, keeps water sources healthier (Dell, Jones & Olken 2011). Moreover, colder temperatures greatly diminish physical exhaustion from work, which is conducive to labor productivity (Deschenes & Greenstone 2007; Graff Zivin & Neidell 2010). Third, availability of permanently navigable waterways is a lubricant of economic exchange and democratizes market access (Gallup & Sachs 2000).

In combination, colder temperatures, continuous rainfall, and navigable waterways generate the CW condition. Under this condition, soil is arable without irrigation and small farming households in the possession of an iron plow and an ox can work large sections of land on their own. There is not much need of community support and no need of extended families with many children to provide armies of land laborers. No central power can monopolize access to water as a means to control people under the CW condition (Jones 1987; Landes 1998; Solomon 2011).

As concerns the situation of ordinary people, the CW condition embodies an original form of existential security, "disease security," as well as an original form of existential autonomy, "water autonomy." Building on recent breakthroughs in sociobiological theory by Fincher, Thornhill, Murray and Schaller (2008), I define disease security as a low natural incidence of communicable diseases (see also Thornhill, Fincher & Aran 2008). The idea of "water autonomy," by contrast, is foreshadowed in the work of Wittfogel (1957) and has been rediscovered by Midlarsky and Midlarsky (1999), yet little attention has been paid to it since then. Water autonomy simply means equal, easy, and permanent access to safe and clean water for all people on a given territory.

Using geographic data from Gallup, Mellinger, and Sachs (2010) and historic estimates of development from Maddison (2007) and Vanhanen (2003), I demonstrate that the CW regions of our planet score exceptionally high on disease security and, by definition, have a high degree of water autonomy. Next, I demonstrate that the base process of human empowerment – mass scale technological advancement[1] – began to accelerate to its industrial pace first in the CW regions and remains until today closely linked with an area's

---

[1] The qualification "mass scale" is intended to indicate the development of technologies that are used by wide population segments, not just the elites.

original disease security and water autonomy. Applying *unified growth theory* (Galor 2011), I identify the mechanism that mediates the impact of a society's original disease security and water autonomy on its technological advancement today: the upgrading of the workforce's value. With higher existential security and autonomy, it is rewarding to reallocate time from maximizing fertility to improving skills. As a result, the size of the workforce is kept small while its quality improves. For employers, this means that the factor costs for labor are high. Once rising urban markets increase labor demand, costly labor establishes an incentive to search for technologies that save labor (Landes 1998). I analyze these mechanisms in a path model that demonstrates a flow of impact along the following sequence: geographical conditions dating back to prehistoric times → disease security and water autonomy dating back to historic times → fertility control in recent time → technological advancement today.

As Chapter 4 has shown, technological advancement on a mass scale is the base process of human empowerment from which emancipative values and civic entitlements follow. Hence, by identifying the environmental root cause of technological advancement, we provide an exogenous explanation of the complete human empowerment process.

However, I also demonstrate that the advantages of high disease security and water autonomy did not begin to surface before 1450–1500 CE. The reason for the delay is that these advantages need vibrant urban markets to come to fruition, and no mature urban civilization emerged in CW regions before this time. The causes of the late maturation of CW regions are two-fold. First, given their large migratory distance from the human origin in East Africa, CW regions were populated later than the original, semiarid areas of civilization in the Middle East, India, China, and Southeast Europe. The larger migratory distance also means a larger diffusion distance from the original centers of agriculture and urbanity in the Middle East. Second, CW regions embody a delay factor that postpones the abandonment of the foraging lifestyle. Ironically, the delay factor originates precisely in the higher initial utility that the CW regions bestow on freedoms: this utility discourages an early abolition of the free foraging lifestyle. As a consequence, the full-scale adoption of surplus agriculture is delayed. So is the flourishing of urban civilization because it needs surplus agriculture to feed urban populations. But once this initial postponement is overcome, the CW condition turns into an accelerator of technological advancement for the same reason: the higher utility of freedoms under this condition. Once urban markets begin to flourish, water autonomy creates derivative autonomies, such as autonomy in marketing one's ideas, skills, and produce – the engine of technological advancement. The latter two points are demonstrated by evidence from the Standard Cross-Cultural Sample, an anthropological dataset of the lifestyles of historic populations around the world (Divale 2004).

Finally, I present evidence for what I call the *contagion thesis*. Human empowerment is breaking free from its confinement to the CW condition, and globalization is the reason for its detachment from this particular environmental condition. There are still more than enough places in the world where people continue to live in poverty and oppression. Yet global communications are tearing down the veil of ignorance that used to shield rulers from mass expectations for a better life. As these expectations diffuse, human empowerment begins to globalize. The following sections flesh out these arguments and present the evidence. The chapter closes with a summary of key points.

1. THE COOL-WATER CONDITION AS AN EXOGENOUS CAUSE

We have seen broad evidence showing that human empowerment starts from action resources and that emancipative values as well as civic entitlements follow subsequently. Hence, if we can explain expanding action resources, we explain the entire human empowerment process.

Throughout this book, it became clear that all three types of action resources – material means, intellectual skills, and connective opportunities – expand through mass scale technological advancement. Hence, the question of the exogenous causes of action resources boils down to the causes of mass scale technological advancement.

If the causes we are searching for are to be truly exogenous, they must not be human achievements. Otherwise, we continue to explain human achievement in one domain with human achievement in another domain. In this case, we remain entrapped in endogeneity and fail to explain human achievement in the first place. Clearly, the requirement for exogeneity eliminates institutions and ideologies from the list of possible root causes.

Now, if one thinks of the causes that are most indisputably exogenous to any type of human achievement, environmental conditions are an obvious candidate (Diamond 1997; Landes 1998; Nolan & Lenski 1999; Olsson & Hibbs 2005). But are there any links between environmental conditions and indicators of development? Indeed, there are such links. For instance, Gallup and Sachs (2000) document strong correlations across the globe between a society's per capita gross domestic product (GDP) and its territory's navigable waterways. Likewise, productivity and prosperity of societies around the world increase alongside falling annual mean temperatures and continuous rainfall over all seasons (Masters & Wiebe 2000; Deschenes & Greenstone 2007; Graff Zivin & Neidell 2010). A recent longitudinal study by Dell, Jones, and Olken (2011) shows that even small fluctuations in temperature and rainfall over time have an immediate impact on growth and prosperity, controlling for potentially confounding factors.

Apparently, the advantageous environmental condition consists in the combination of cool temperatures with continuous seasonal rain and permanently navigable waterways – the CW condition. This combination is prevalent in certain geographic zones. Using the Koeppen-Geiger climate classification, these features are prevalent in zones categorized as "temperate: no dry season" and "cold: no dry season" (Peel, Finlayson, & McMahon 2007).[2] Gallup, Mellinger, and Sachs (2010) provide data indicating the fraction of every society's inhabitable territory located in the various climate zones of the Koeppen-Geiger classification. Calculating on this basis the fraction of each society's CW territory,[3] this fraction correlates at $r = 0.70$ with societies' technological advancement in 2005 ($p < 0.001$; $N = 134$). Worldwide, the fraction of a society's CW territory explains roughly 50 percent of the cross-national variation in technological advancement. Indeed, the technologically most advanced populations are highly concentrated in our planet's CW territories: Western Europe, the coastal areas of North America, Japan and South Korea, Southeast Australia, New Zealand, Uruguay, and the cape region of South Africa.

Despite climatic fluctuations, the *big pattern* with regard to which territories on the globe are hotter and which colder and which are dryer and which rainier can be considered as more or less constant over the last couple of centuries (Peel, Finlayson & McMahon 2007; Kuhle 2011). Hence, the CW-environment describes a condition that is temporally very remote; it is definitely older than the explosive development that humanity experiences since just a couple of centuries (Landes 1998). The CW condition is, thus, *perfectly exogenous* to the technological achievements of today, of past decades and even of recent centuries. The very exogeneity of the CW condition eliminates all ambiguity concerning the possible causal direction in the strong connection between the CW condition and technological advancement. The possibility that the connection exists because technological advancement has produced the CW condition can be excluded with certainty. The causal arrow can only run from the CW condition to technological advancement. This still leaves us with uncertainty about the intervening mechanism that explains the strong connection, but there is no ambiguity about its direction.

Civilization matured considerably earlier outside the world's CW territories. Indeed, millennia before urban civilization emerged in CW territories, it existed in the Oriental band from the Middle East to China (Jones 1987; McNeill 1990; Levine 2001; Modelski 2003; Goldstone 2009). But despite millennia of urban culture, none of the Oriental civilizations pioneered the scientific technology explosion that set the stage for the Industrial Revolution (Hall 1989). Instead, this happened where urbanity matured latest: Western Europe and Japan – the only two urban civilizations in CW territories in preindustrial times (Jones 1987; McNeill 1990; Powelson 1997). These observations raise two questions:

---

[2] These are coded as zones "cf" and "df" in the Koeppen-Geiger scheme.

[3] To be precise, I calculate for each society the fraction of its habitable territory in cold or temperate and wet zones that it has in excess of the fraction in hot and dry zones, based on the Koeppen-Geiger classification as detailed in Appendix 11 (www.cambridge.org/welzel). Data are taken from Gallup, Mellinger, and Sachs (2010).

1. What makes societies in CW areas prone to technological advancement once they have reached urban maturity?
2. Why did societies in CW areas reach urban maturity late?

Paradoxically, the answer to both questions lies in the same factor: the initial utility of freedoms under CW conditions. Technological advancement requires time investments in innovation and the marketing of ideas. More such time is available when people are existentially secure because then they need to spend less time for making things safe. Likewise, people have more time for innovation and marketing when they are existentially autonomous because then they are less preoccupied with executing the orders of authorities. If these assumptions are correct, the link between technological advancement and the CW condition exists because this condition harbors some original form of existential security and autonomy.

Indeed, CW territories embody two original forms of security and autonomy: disease security and water autonomy. Because of that, freedoms have higher initial utility in CW areas and people in these areas are more prone to freedoms. This explains both the delayed advancement and its subsequent acceleration in CW areas. Since foraging is a freer lifestyle than agriculture, and because people in CW areas are more prone to freedoms, these people stick to foraging as long as possible. This decelerates the emergence of surplus agriculture and urban markets. But once the delay is overcome and urban markets begin to flourish, the initial utility of freedoms turns into an accelerator: autonomies deriving from the CW condition under emerging urbanity, now set free more time for innovation and marketing. The following sections evidence these propositions.

2. EVIDENCING THE COOL-WATER EFFECT

First, let's look at the two original forms of existential security and autonomy: disease security and water autonomy. Disease security means a low natural incidence of communicable diseases. Using historic disease data from Murray and Schaller (2010), disease security correlates across the globe at $r = 0.73$ ($N = 165$; $p < .001$) with the fraction of a society's CW territory. This relationship is not explained by the fact that CW societies are richer and have better health provision for this reason: although CW societies are richer, the CW condition favors disease security independently from prosperity.[4]

Disease security correlates with the CW condition because the lower temperature of CW zones hampers parasites. But disease security does not reflect

---

[4] After controlling for per capita GDP in 1995 (or some other year), the association between the fraction of the area in cold-temperate and rainy zones and disease security drops from $r = 0.74$ to a partial r of 0.60 but remains positive and highly significant ($p < 0.001$; $N = 156$). The partial r for per capita GDP is 0.22. This shows that the historic data on disease security primarily indicate an area's *natural* disease load, much more than disease security achieved through prosperity in recent times. The disease measure is *not* endogenous to prosperity.

another signature feature of CW zones: continuous rainfall. Is there something about this feature that accounts for the CW zones' propensity to accelerated technological advancement? I suggest the responsible factor is *water autonomy*: equal, easy, and permanent access to safe and clean water for all individuals on a territory.

Autonomous access to water cancels a historic route to despotism: control over people through irrigation management (Wittfogel 1957; Mann 1986; Jones 1987; McNeill 1990; Midlarsky & Midlarsky 1999; Solomon 2011; Bentzen, Kaarsen, & Wingender 2012).[5] Giving rulers less control over their subjects, water autonomy is the source of subsequent autonomies once commercial urban centers emerge – including autonomy in market access, in skill allocation, and in profit acquisition (Powelson 1997; Landes 1998). With these autonomies, people can reap the benefits of their creativity, which is a stimulus for innovation – the source of technological advancement.

To create a precise measure of the CW condition, I calculate the fraction of a society's inhabitable area in CW zones that exists in excess of the fraction in dry and hot zones, according to the Koeppen-Geiger classification (data from Gallup et al. 2010). If all area is in the CW zone and none in the dry and hot zones, the score is 1.0. If none of the area is in the CW zone and all is in dry and hot zones, the score is 0. If all area is in neither zone or in both zones to equal parts, the score is 0.50. However, these area proportions still show considerable variation in (a) the amount of continuous rainfall as well as (b) in the abundance of permanently navigable waterways. Hence, I use a weighting procedure to factor in this uncovered variation. In this way, I obtain a very fine-grained version of the ultimate *cool-water index* (CWI). It varies between 0 for the complete absence of the CW features to 1.0 for their maximal presence. The CWI is, at the same time, a measure of water autonomy. The exact steps of the index construction are detailed in Appendix 11 (www.cambridge.org/welzel).

Figure 11.1 illustrates the astonishingly strong effect of the CWI on technological advancement in 2005. If we refer to both disease security and the CWI, these two natural endowments explain fully 90 percent of the cross-regional variance and 74 percent of the cross-national variance in contemporary technological advancement around the world ($N = 139$). But, even though the two are intertwined, the impact of the CWI is considerably stronger than that of disease security. Under mutual control, the CWI accounts for 72 percent of the global cross-regional variance and 45 percent of the cross-national variance in technological advancement, compared to 18 and 14 percent accounted for by disease security. This justifies a focus on the outstanding impact of the CWI. The obvious questions are how far this impact reaches back in time and what mechanism explains it.

---

[5] Even though Wittfogel's (1957) thesis that irrigation predated bureaucracy is contested, it is beyond doubt that large-scale irrigation facilitates power concentration (Mann 1986). Conclusive evidence presented by Bentzen, Kaarsen, and Wingender (2012) confirms this point.

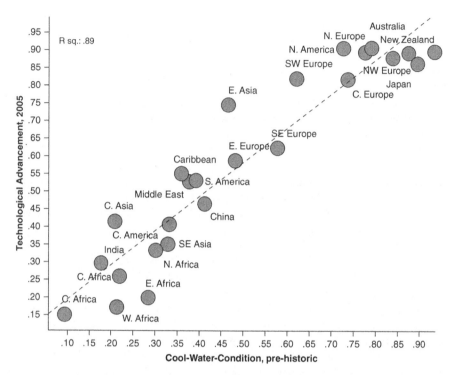

FIGURE 11.1 The Impact of the Cool-Water Condition on Technological Advancement. Data are available for 142 societies. For better readability, they are summarized into twenty-five global regions. Note that the global cross-regional variation accounts for 75 percent of the cross-national variance in water autonomy and 81 percent of the cross-national variance in technological advancement. Across all 142 societies, water autonomy accounts for 73 percent of the variation in technological advancement (see Figure 3.5, p. 125). For more descriptive details and data documentation, see Appendix 11 (www.cambridge.org/welzel).

The direct indicator of technological advancement used for contemporary times is not available for historic times. Hence, to explore the impact of water autonomy on technological advancement over historic periods, we must use reasonable proxies for technological advancement. Figure 11.2 uses as an indicator of technological advancement the proxy from Vanhanen (2003) introduced in Chapter 4. This proxy combines data on a society's literacy and urbanization rates. The proxy is available decennially going back to the decade 1850–60. In each decade, measures are available for all independent states at the time. For periods before 1850, I use as an alternative proxy Maddison's (2007) per capita income estimates for thirty-one exemplary territories from around the world. Missing data for intermediate time points are interpolated as detailed in Appendix 11 (www.cambridge.org/welzel). For every decade from 1500 to 2010, I correlate these proxies for technological advancement with

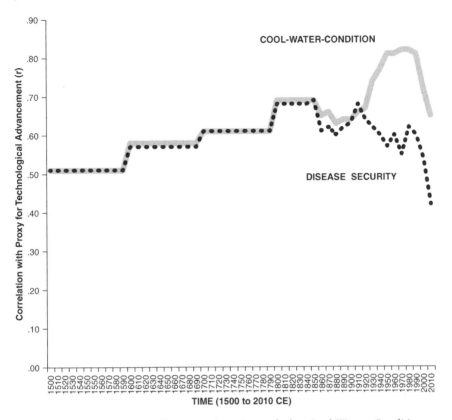

FIGURE 11.2 The Impact of Disease Security and the Cool-Water Condition on Technological Advancement over Time and across the World (from the beginning of the modern era until today).

For the decades from 1850 to 2000, the diagram uses the proxy of technological advancement introduced in Chapter 4, based on data from Vanhanen (2003) on urbanization and literacy rates. For the decades from 1500 until 1850, Maddison's (2007) estimates of per capita incomes for 31 exemplary territories from around the world are used instead of Vanhanen's urbanization and literacy estimates. For 2010, per capita gross domestic product (GDP) in purchasing power parities from the World Bank's (2010) World Development Indicators Series is used. Number of societies covered by data varies over time. For more descriptive details and data documentation, see Appendix 11 (www.cambridge.org/welzel).

the CWI (and disease security). Since the CWI indicates features of the natural environment that exist prior to the technological advancement of recent decades and centuries, I interpret these correlations as reflecting the impact of the CWI on technological advancement. Figure 11.2 traces the impact of the CWI to the origin of the modern era: the rise of urban capitalism in the age of European Humanism around 1500 CE.

Despite some fluctuation, Figure 11.2 shows that the impact of the CWI on the technological advancement of the world's major territories is consistently high all the way from 1500 to 2010 – albeit with a recent dip that I address at the end of this chapter.

The CW condition is a natural endowment for which no prior human cause exists, and its impact on technological advancement is evident since the beginning of the modern era. This suggests that this condition is indeed a root cause of technological advancement.

3. EXPLANATIONS OF THE COOL-WATER EFFECT

There must be causes that are more proximate to technological advancement – causes that explain the impact of the CW condition. To sort out which causes these might be, Table 11.1 correlates contemporary technological advancement with a variety of potential causes looming prominently in the development literature. Table 11.2 uses multivariate regressions to examine which of these potential causes absorbs the technological impact of the CW condition. Arguably, the potential cause that absorbs most of the technological impact of the CW condition explains why that impact exists.

Since recently, an increasing number of scholars suggest genetic factors as a source of differences in development (Hatemi & McDermott 2012). Societal variation in the frequency of two genes calls particular attention: the $Val^{108/158}Met$ polymorphism of the catechol-o-methyltransferase (COMT) gene, and the long-allelic version of the 5-HTTLPR gene. Both genes affect the human reward system by influencing the emission of stimulating hormones: dopamine in the case of the COMT gene; serotonin in the case of the HTTLPR gene. Data from the *allele frequency database* (ALFRED) at Yale University seem to suggest that both genes exist in different frequencies in different populations (cf., alfred.med.yale.edu). What is more, both genes are linked with traits that supposedly stimulate innovation and experimentation – the driving activities of technological advancement. In the case of the COMT gene, there is a positive link with two of the Big Five personality traits that supposedly encourage innovation and experimentation: "openness" and "extraversion." Likewise, the demographic prevalence of the COMT gene shows a negative link with the personality trait that supposedly discourages innovation and experimentation: "neuroticism" (Stein, Fallin, Schork, & Gelernter 2005; Wichers et al. 2008).[6] In the case of the HTTLPR gene, there is a positive link of its long-allelic version with cultural individualism – a trait that supposedly stimulates innovation and experimentation (Chiao & Blizinski 2010).

Since the CW condition bestows initial utility on freedoms, innovation and experimentation are rewarding activities under this condition. Possibly, then, the

---

[6] The other two traits are "agreebleness" and "conscientiousness." For the definition and measurement of the Big Five personality traits, see Matthews, Deary, and Whiteman (2003).

TABLE 11.1 *Testing the Predictive Power of the Cool-Water Condition on Technological Advancement against Alternative Predictors (bivariate correlations).*

PREDICTORS of Technological Advancement	CORRELATION with Technological Advancement 2005	N (societies)
• Fertility Control, 1980	0.87***	141
• Cool Water, historic	0.84***	142
• State Integrity, 2000	0.78***	143
• Civic Entitlements, 2000	0.73***	130
• Disease Security, historic	0.72***	143
• Order and Stability, 2000	0.71***	143
• Cultural Individualism, 1990s	0.70***	84
• Consanguinity (logged)	−0.70***	66
• Val$^{108/158}$Met COMT Gene	0.52***	50
• Democratic Tradition, until 2000	0.51***	151
• White Settler Mortality, historic	−0.44***	108
• Cultural Looseness, 1990s	0.40**	33
• Continuous Peace, post WWII	0.36***	142
• State Antiquity Index	0.36***	121
• % Muslims, 1990s	−0.33***	142
• % Protestants, 1990s	0.31***	140
• Time since Neolithic Revolution	0.28***	138
• Long-allele 5-HTTLPR Gene	0.27*	46
• % Catholics, 1990s	0.19**	142
• Neuroticism (Big 5), 1990s	0.18†	44
• Extraversion (Big 5), 1990s	0.16†	44
• Openness (Big 5), 1990s	−0.02†	44

Entries are correlation coefficients (r). Included are all societies with available data on the respective variables.
Significance levels (two-tailed): † $p \geq .100$, * $p < .100$, ** $p < .050$, *** $p < .005$
For documentation of data and variables, see Appendix 11 (www.cambridge.org/welzel).

CW condition establishes a selective advantage for genes favoring the traits that encourage innovation and experimentation. If so, the technological impact of the CW condition should be largely absorbed either by the demographic prevalence of the respective genes or by the prevalence of their supposedly favored traits. To see if this is the case, I control in separate regressions the effect of the CW condition on technological advancement for the demographic prevalence of the Val$^{108/158}$Met COMT gene, the long-allelic HTTLPR gene, and these genes' presumably favored traits: openness, extraversion, and neuroticism, as well as individualism. Data for demographic variation in the COMT gene are from Inglehart et al. (forthcoming), data for the HTTLPR gene from Chiao and Blizinski (2010). Data for demographic variation in personality types are from Schmitt et al. (2012) and data for cultural individualism from Hofstede (2001 [1980]) and from Suh, Diener, Oishi, and

TABLE 11.2 *Testing the Predictive Power of the Cool-Water Condition on Technological Advancement against Alternative Predictors (multivariate regressions).*

Alternate PREDICTORS	Simultaneous EFFECTS on Technological Advancement 2005			
	Cool Water Controlling for Disease Security and Alternate Predictor	Disease Security Controlling for Cool Water and Alternate Predictor	Alternate Predictor Controlling for Cool Water and Disease Security	N
• Fertility Control	0.41***	0.28***	0.61***	131
• State Integrity	0.52***	0.33***	0.47***	138
• Civic Entitlements	0.63***	0.29***	0.36***	127
• Long-allele 5-HTTLPR Gene	0.68***	0.37**	0.57***	48
• Order and Stability	0.59***	0.29***	0.38***	138
• Cultural Individualism	0.66***	0.17†	0.34***	81
• State Antiquity Index	0.69***	0.35***	0.34***	123
• Cultural Looseness	0.79***	0.19†	0.32*	31
• Democratic Tradition	0.62***	0.39***	0.30***	137
• Consanguinity (logged)	0.66***	0.32**	−0.25*	67
• Neuroticism (Big 5)			0.25†	
• Openness (Big 5)	0.51***	0.36**	0.03†	48
• Extraversion (Big 5)			0.00†	
• White Settler Mortality	0.70***	0.32***	−0.21**	105
• Time since Neolithic Revolution	0.70***	0.35***	0.22**	132
• % Muslims			−0.12†	
• % Protestants	0.67***	0.36***	0.02†	136
• % Catholics			0.05†	
• Continuous Peace	0.67***	0.36***	0.09†	137
• Val[108/158]Met COMT Gene	0.72***	0.17†	0.17†	49

Entries are partial correlation coefficients to indicate each predictor's partial explanatory power over technological advancement. Each line represents a separate regression of technological advancement simultaneously on the cool-water (CW) condition, disease security, and one of the alternate predictors shown in the left-hand column. Example: in the first line, the coefficient 0.41 indicates the partial effect of the CW condition, 0.28 that of disease security, and 0.61 the one of fertility control.

Tests for heteroskedasticity (White test), influential cases (DFFITs), and multicollinearity (variance inflation factors) reveal no violation of ordinary least squares (OLS) assumptions in any regression series. Significance levels (two-tailed): †$p \geq .100$, *$p < .100$, **$p < .050$, ***$p < .005$

Gray-shaded coefficients show the strongest effect for each regression. For detailed description of variables and data sources, see Appendix 11 (www.cambridge.org/welzel).

Triandis (1998). Appendix 11 (www.cambridge.org/welzel) provides more detailed descriptions and replication data.

Additional cultural traits that supposedly affect technological advancement include "cultural looseness," and consanguinity, as well as Protestantism and Islam. Cultural looseness measures how much a society tolerates deviating behavior. Following Gelfand et al. (2011), from whom I take data on the demographic prevalence of cultural looseness, this trait should stimulate innovation and experimentation; hence, it should be conducive to technological advancement. Consanguinity relates to a marriage pattern that keeps the marriage circle narrow in preferring (distant) relatives over nonrelatives. According to Woodley and Bell (2012), from whom I take estimates of the demographic prevalence of consanguinity, the effect on technological advancement is expected to be negative. In line with the literature, Protestantism is expected to have a positive effect on technological advancement (Lal 1998), whereas Islam's effect should be negative (Kuran 2004). I take data on the proportion of Protestants and Muslims per society from the Quality of Governance Database (Quality of Governance Institute 2012). If the expectations about the effects of these cultural traits on technological advancement are correct, any one of them should largely absorb the technological impact of the CW condition.

Another set of factors discussed in the development literature relates to long-lasting institutional path dependencies. These include the timing of the Neolithic Revolution (Putterman 2008) and "state antiquity," a measure of the historic endurance of functioning state orders (Bockstette, Chanda, & Putterman 2002). The proponents of these measures argue that the longer the Neolithic Revolution and a functioning state date back in a society's history, the more time this society had to expand its stock of knowledge, which should be visible in technological progress today. Thus, it is quite possible that the technological effect of the CW condition is absorbed by these factors.

A colonial pattern with a lasting influence on development has been identified by Acemoglu, Johnson, and Robinson (2001). These authors claim that where the "white settler mortality" was high, development was hampered, whereas it was boosted where the white settler mortality was low. Acemoglu, Johnson, and Robinson justify this thesis with an institutional argument: development depends on "inclusive institutions." These institutions evolved in Western Europe and were transplanted only to those colonial areas where a low "white" mortality allowed Europeans to settle in large numbers: temperate or cold areas outside the tropics. Conversely, in tropical areas where a high 'white' mortality hindered large-scale European settlement, smaller numbers of European colonizers came to extract natural resources. Finding physical work insufferable, European rent-seekers forced indigenous people and slaves imported from Africa to work on plantations and in mines. Tropical areas were, thus, left with a legacy of "labor-repressive" institutions – a manifest hindrance to human capital formation (Engerman & Sokoloff 1997).

The thesis that development favors democracy is one of the most researched topics in political science, mostly with confirmatory results (Teorell 2010). The opposite thesis, however, that democracy also favors development has produced conflicting evidence (Krieckhaus 2004). Yet, as Gerring et al. (2005) show, most results are misleading because they test an immediate effect of democracy on development, ignoring that the impact of democracy lies in its *long-term* endurance. Thus, they claim that the democratic tradition shows a pronounced effect on development. Possibly, then, the democratic tradition absorbs the effect of the CW condition on technological advancement.

Other institutional factors that might mediate the technological effect of the CW condition include contemporary qualities of the state. Thus, I measure "state integrity"' by a low incidence of corruption among the office holders in a society, using the *control of corruption* index from the World Bank's quality of governance project (Kaufman, Kraay, & Mastruzzi 2008). From the same data source, I use the *political stability and absence of violence index* to measure order and stability in more recent times. Then I measure "continuous peace," using Gleditsch et al.'s (2002) *armed conflict dataset*. The variable indicates for each society the number of armed conflicts in which it has been involved since the end of World War II. The most strongly emphasized factor among institutional economists refers to civic entitlements that guarantee universal freedoms. These entitlements provide what North et al. (2009) call "open access orders" or what Acemoglu and Robinson (2012) label "inclusive institutions." To examine if civic entitlements absorb the technological impact of the CW condition I use the citizen rights index described in Chapter 8.

Finally, I introduce a variable labeled "fertility control," which is simply the inverse of a society's fertility rate. The variable is informed by *unified growth theory* (Galor 2011). From the viewpoint of this theory, low fertility indicates that people sacrifice their demographic productivity for their economic productivity. The evidence strongly supports this interpretation: low levels of fertility associate strongly with high levels of education, which is an investment in one's economic productivity.[7] Theoretically, the pronounced polarity between low fertility/high education, on the one hand, versus high fertility/low education on the other, reflects opposite strategies of life time investment: a *quality-building* strategy versus a *quantity-breeding* strategy (Becker & Barro 1988; Guinnane 2008). The breeding strategy is a time investment in demographic productivity; the building strategy is a time investment in economic productivity. And while a breeding strategy supplies cheap mass labor, a building strategy generates

---

[7] The correlations between a society's fertility rate and the average person's mean years of schooling in this society are: $r = -0.80$ ($p < 0.001$; $N = 91$) in 1960; $r = -0.86$ ($p < 0.001$; $N = 93$) in 1970; $r = -0.85$ ($p < 0.001$; $N = 97$) in 1980; $r = -0.82$ ($p < 0.001$; $N = 98$) in 1990; $r = -0.78$ ($p < 0.001$; $N = 94$) in 2000. Controlling the fertility-education nexus for per capita GDP, the partial correlation between fertility and education drops to -0.58 in 1970, -0.56 in 1980, -0.62 in 1990, and -0.61 in 2000 but remains highly significant ($N = 76, 80, 82, 82$; $p < 0.001$ at all time points, respectively).

a workforce of limited size but high quality. Clearly, keeping fertility under control is the basis of the building strategy. According to unified growth theory, the transition from quantity-breeding to quality-building is necessary to enter an era of mass scale technological advancement (Boserup 2011 [1970]; Blumberg 2004; Galor 2011). The reason is obvious: once the rise of urban markets increases labor demand while cheap mass labor is in short supply, labor is costly. High labor costs combined with an increasing demand for labor encourages technological advancement to save labor costs (Jones 1987; Landes 1998).

There is indeed evidence that the two pre-industrial CW civilizations – Western Europe and Japan – had later marriages and lower fertility than other urban civilizations *already in preindustrial times*. For Western Europe, the evidence is documented in Hajnal (1983), Laslett (1989) and Hartman (2004), for Japan in Kiyoshi (1999) and Bentley, Ziegler, and Streets-Salter (2010). In both CW civilizations, women did not marry before their early to mid-twenties, practiced fertility control before marriage, and marriage was tied to establishing one's own household–a pattern known as "neolocal" household formation. The neolocal pattern required a premarital period of accumulating savings, equipment, and skills.[8]

Table 11.1 shows *uncontrolled* effects on technological advancement for each of the variables that potentially absorb the technological impact of the CW condition. Table 11.2 shows these variables' *partial* effects on technological

---

[8] A late average age of women's first marriage is a strong indicator of low fertility: the percentage of women in a society married below the age of twenty correlates at $r = 0.71$ ($N = 158$; $p < 0.001$) with the fertility rate (data taken from Gapminder at www.gapminder.org). Hence, evidence showing that the two civilizations in CW areas – Western Europe and Japan – had later marriages before preindustrial times is important. It lends credibility to my argument that water autonomy establishes an incentive for lower fertility once urban markets flourish. The evidence indeed exists. Based on an examination of forty-five studies, Flinn cited in Hajnal (1982) calculates a mean age of first marriage for women in Northwestern Europe over the preindustrial era of twenty-five years, with a standard deviation of six years. This corresponds with Hajnal's (1982) estimate of a female average marriage age of twenty-three for the preindustrial period in Northwestern Europe. For other preindustrial urban civilizations, from Eastern and Southern Europe to the Middle East, India, and China, Hajnal estimates much lower marriage ages, usually in the late teens. His estimate for China, for instance, is 17.5 years. Japan lies in between the Western and non-Western pattern. Kiyoshi (1999: 132) reports a female marriage age of 20.2 years at the beginning of the Tokugawa period in around 1600, followed by a continuous rise throughout the Tokugawa period – a period that brought an increasing economic florescence of urban centers. Figures for the year 1800 confirm the pattern of late marriages in the West, early marriages in the East, and Japan in between: the figures are seventeen years for India, eighteen years for Egypt, nineteen years for Russia and China, twenty-one years for Japan, and twenty-three years for the United States and the United Kingdom (data taken from Gapminder at www.gapminder.org). Historic fertility estimates support the argument that water autonomy favored fertility control already in preindustrial times. For the year 1800 (a time before industrialization picked up speed in most societies), estimates for the number of born children per women are as follows: 4.0 Denmark; 4.1 Japan; 4.4 France; 5.5 China and Italy; 6.0 India; 6.7 Bangladesh, Pakistan, and Russia; 6.8 Mexico; 6.8 Zimbabwe; 7.2 Ethiopia; and 7.3 Iran. Hence, at beginning of the industrial age, fertility in urban civilizations is only low in the West and Japan.

advancement, controlling for the CW condition and disease security. These can be compared with the partial effects of the CW condition and disease security further to the left. Comparing the partial effects, we see how much of the technological impact of the CW condition and disease security is absorbed and how much is untouched by each of the other variables.

In Table 11.1, all variables – except the COMT gene and the Big Five personality traits – show a significant effect on technological advancement in the expected direction. Among the variables measured for more than a hundred societies, the largest uncontrolled effect on technological advancement derives from fertility control ($r = 0.87$), followed by the CW condition ($r = 0.84$), state integrity ($r = 0.78$), civic entitlements ($r = 0.73$), disease security ($r = 0.72$), order and stability ($r = 0.71$), the democratic tradition ($r = 0.51$), white settler mortality ($r = -0.44$), state antiquity ($r = 0.36$), and continuous peace ($r = 0.36$). Thus, only fertility control trumps the uncontrolled impact of the CW condition on technological advancement.

Controlling each of these variables' effects for the impact of the CW condition and disease security, the effect sizes drop considerably in the case of most variables. For instance, the effect of state integrity drops from $r = 0.78$ to $r_{partial} = 0.47$ and that of the democratic tradition from $r = 0.51$ to $r_{partial} = 0.30$. For all variables, except fertility control, the partial effect on technology is *much weaker* than that of the CW condition, which withstands the control of every other variable. The partial effect of disease security withstands all controls except two: controlling for cultural individualism or cultural looseness, disease security no longer shows a significant effect on technological advancement. Accordingly, the technological impact of disease security is entirely mediated by its effect on these two cultural traits.[9] And even though the technological impact of disease security is recognizable, it is always considerably below that of the CW condition.

Two of the most prominent variables in the development literature show a largely diminished or completely insignificant effect once we control for the CW condition: Protestantism and the white settler mortality. In fact, these variables' technological effects are largely explained by the CW condition. Protestantism and the institutions of white settlers evolved *exclusively* in societies where the CW condition is pronounced, and this is the reason why these factors seem to have a strong effect on technological advancement. Once we control for the CW condition, the apparent effect largely diminishes or vanishes.

Another variable of recent prominence is the timing of the Neolithic Revolution. As Putterman (2008) and Easterly, Comin, and Gong (2010) argue, an early adoption of agriculture means a developmental head start. Since development is path-dependent and self-perpetuating, the advantage that societies obtain from this head start should be visible until today in technological advancement. The

---

[9] This finding evidences an important side strand of causality: disease security favors looser cultures that allow for more diversity. More diversity in turn generates an intellectual climate conducive to experimentation and innovation – the engines of technological advancement.

uncontrolled regression of technological advancement on the timing of the Neolithic Revolution supports this view. But after controlling for the CW condition, an earlier transition to agriculture shows only a weak effect on technological advancement today. Hence, the effect of an early transition to agriculture is largely conditional: it depends on its connection with the CW condition.

The only variable that seriously diminishes and clearly exceeds the technological impact of the CW condition is fertility control: under mutual controls, the technological impact of the CW condition amounts to an $r_{partial}$ of 0.41, whereas that of fertility control amounts to an $r_{partial}$ of 0.61. This suggests that the CW condition favors technological advancement mainly because it enhances fertility control.

This conclusion rests on the assumption that fertility control is not itself endogenous to technological advancement. Some scholars might question this assumption. The reason is that technological advancement produces prosperity (Romer 1990), and it has been argued that fertility declines because of rising prosperity (Becker 1981; Becker & Barro 1988). If this is correct, fertility control is a consequence of technological advancement and not a cause of it. In this case, fertility control could not explain the impact of the CW condition on technological advancement.

The two-stage least-squares regressions in Table 11.3 test this possibility, using per capita GDP to measure prosperity based on the same year as fertility control. In the first stage, we instrument fertility control with the CW condition, disease security, and per capita GDP. The results of this regression show that fertility control is more strongly determined by the CW condition than by per capita GDP. The three instruments explain 69 percent of the cross-national variance in fertility control. Of these 69 percent, only 5 percent are accounted for by per capita GDP.[10] Because disease security is insignificant, the CW condition accounts for most of the remaining 64 percent of explained variance in fertility control. In version B of this first-stage regression, we instrument fertility control only with the CW condition and disease control, leaving out per capita GDP. We explain almost the same amount of variance: 63 percent. In the second stage, we use the two instrumented versions of fertility control – each one at a time – to predict technological advancement in 2005. The version in which fertility control is instrumented without per capita GDP explains just 5 percentage points less variance in technological advancement than does the version in which fertility control is instrumented under the inclusion of GDP. In short, there is very little endogeneity of fertility control to prosperity. Nevertheless, in the subsequent analyses, we will use a measure of fertility control from which we eliminate the small influence of prosperity.

As far as one can tell, the cross-national fertility differences found in 1980 are not only representative for this particular time. Instead, they partly reflect differences reaching back to preindustrial times. Indeed, the numbers in footnote 8 document similarity in the fertility pattern between 1800 and later times in at least one critical point: Japan and the West are at the forefront of low fertilities.

---

[10] The partial correlation coefficient of GDP/p.c. is 0.23, so the partial r squared is 0.05.

TABLE 11.3 *Examining the Developmental Endogeneity of Fertility Control (two-stage least-squares regressions).*

PREDICTORS	STAGE 1(Fertility Control 1980 is DV)		STAGE 2 (Technological Advancement 2005 is DV)	
	Version A	Version B	Version A	Version B
• Constant	0.21(5.70)***	0.15(5.19)***	−0.12(−3.28)***	−0.11(−2.55)***
• Cool Water, historic	0.62(6.08)***	0.68(9.13)***		
• Disease Security, historic	0.12(1.06)†	0.28(3.29)***		
• GDP/p.c. (indexed), 1980	0.22(2.21)**			
• Expected Fertility Control			1.11(18.65)***	1.10(16.19)***
Adjusted R^2	0.69	0.63	0.81	0.76
N (societies)	96	96	84	84

Entries are unstandardized regression coefficients with their T values in parentheses.

Tests for heteroskedasticity (White test), influential cases (DFFITs), and multicollinearity (variance inflation factors) reveal no violation of ordinary least squares (OLS) assumptions.

In the first stage, cool water and disease security dating back to historic times as well as gross domestic product (GDP)/p.c. in 1980 (version B without the latter) are used as instruments to calculate expected scores of fertility control in 1980. In the second stage, these expected scores are used to predict technological advancement in 2005.

Significance levels (two-tailed): $^{†} p \geq .100$, $^{*}p < .100$, $^{**}p < .050$, $^{***}p < .005$

In fact, in 1800 these are the only areas with low fertilities, reflecting the exceptionally strong presence of the CW condition.

All this suggests that the CW condition encourages the transition from breeding strategies to building strategies. From the viewpoint of the utility ladder of freedoms, this is indeed highly plausible.

The CW condition grants water autonomy: equal, easy, and permanent access to safe and clean water. As an original form of existential autonomy, water autonomy is the source of derivative autonomies, including autonomy in market access – once commercial urban centers emerge (Jones 1987; Landes 1998; Midlarsky & Midlarsky 1999; Solomon 2011). With existential autonomies, building skills is a time investment into one's market value. For this reason, marrying early to breed many children is a time investment with high opportunity costs. Once urban markets flourish, the subsequent autonomies deriving from water autonomy strongly encourage fertility control and skill formation. And people had fairly effective means to control fertility even in preindustrial times, provided this was the prevalent preference (Lipsey, Carlaw, & Bekar 2005).

The historic pattern seems to confirm this proposition. Late medieval Western Europe and Japan were the only two civilizations with high water autonomy to reach urban maturity in preindustrial times (see Figure 11.1). All other Eurasian civilizations, from Eastern and Southern Europe to the Middle East to India and China, as well as the urban Amerindian civilizations, show a much weaker presence of the CW condition than do Japan or Western Europe. Accordingly, Powelson (1997) finds that Western Europe and Japan are the only two preindustrial civilizations that did not develop *coercive feudalism*. Instead, they established *contractual feudalism* – a form of feudalism that acknowledges the autonomies of farmers, village communities, and corporations. In both Western Europe and Japan, this pattern was linked with late marriages, fertility limitation by means of monogamy and taboos on out-of-wedlock sex, an emphasis on skill formation over the prolonged premarital period and "neolocal" instead of "patrilocal" household formation after marriage (Hartman 2004; Bentley et al. 2010).

4. THE GREAT REDIRECTION OF CIVILIZATION

The explosive acceleration of technological advancement in modern time started with the scientific revolution in the fifteenth century (Braudel 1993; Landes 1998; Goldstone 2009). Before this turning point, we find a strikingly different pattern. This is evident from Figure 11.3. The diagram examines Maddison's (2007) historic per capita income estimates for thirty-one exemplary territories around the world: the assumption is that territories with higher per capita incomes are richer because they have developed more productive technologies. Under this premise, Figure 11.3 is a powerful illustration that global history takes a sharp turn around 1500 CE: the strong positive correlation between the CW condition and development literally leaps out, reversing a negative correlation that goes all the way back to the year 1 (Appendix 11 [www.cambridge.org/welzel] gives a detailed documentation of the correlation pattern). The switch in the signs of the correlations in 1500 coincides with the late achievement of urban maturity in the two CW civilizations: Western Europe and Japan.[11] Since then, the CW civilizations' technological advancement accelerated exponentially, and European settlement transplanted technological advancement to other, unurbanized CW areas outside Eurasia – hence the increase in the magnitude of the correlations until 1900.

The dotted line in Figure 11.4 plots over time the correlation between a country's per capita income and its migratory proximity to the human origin in East Africa (see Appendix 11 [www.cambridge.org/welzel]). The migratory proximity is a rough indicator of how early modern humans arrived on a given territory: the more proximate the territory, the earlier the arrival of humans. Interestingly, the correlation of income with the earliness of human arrival is the exact mirror image of its correlation with the CW condition: it is moderately

---

[11] To be more precise, Japan's urban florescence started some hundred years later than that of Western Europe, around 1600, when the Tokugava period began.

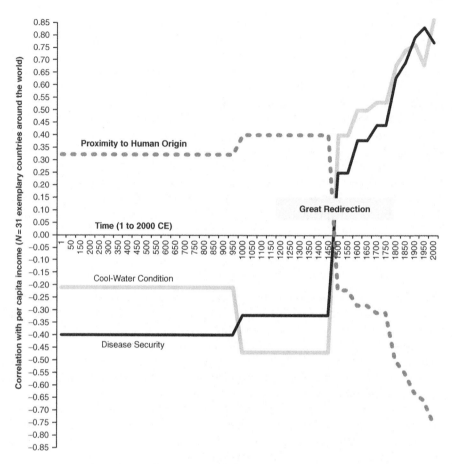

FIGURE 11.3 The Impact of Disease Security and the Cool-Water Condition on Per Capita Incomes over Time and across the World (before and after the Great Redirection). Diagram uses Maddison's (2007) historic estimates of per capita incomes for 31 exemplary countries from around the world. The diagram shows the trend after interpolating missing data for periods with no estimates. For more descriptive details and data documentation, see Appendix 11 (www.cambridge.org/welzel).

positive from the year 1 to the year 1500 when it reverses itself dramatically into a strongly negative correlation that persists until today.

Does our theory explain this turn in history? It does if one keeps in mind that the link between the CW condition and development is conditional: it depends on flourishing urban capitalism – a condition not prevalent before the fifteenth century in Western Europe and not before 1600 in Japan, the only urban CW civilizations of preindustrial times (Jones 1987; McNeill 1990; Powelson 1997; Bentley et al. 2010). Other CW areas – including the coastal zones of North America, the South of South America, the

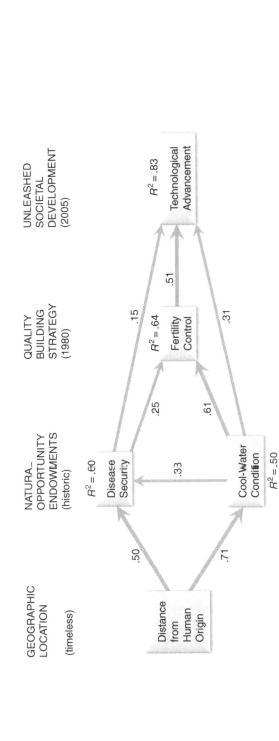

FIGURE 11.4 Causal Flow from Prehistoric Environmental Conditions to Current Technological Advancement (source thesis). Entries are partial correlation coefficients, calculated with AMOS 19.01. Units of observation are national societies: *N* is 127, including all societies with available data on each variable. Fertility Control in this model is *exogenous* to prosperity: it is the residuals in fertility control not predicted by per capita gross domestic product (GDP) in the same year. Goodness-of-fit measures: GFI .94, NFI .97, IFI .97, CFI .97. All effects are significant at the .001-level. To inspect the data matrix for the 127 societies included in this analysis, see Appendix 11 (www.cambridge.org/welzel).

Southeast of Australia and New Zealand – did not reach the mature urban stage of civilization until Europeans colonized these areas. What explains the belatedness of urban civilization in Eurasian CW areas and its absence in outer-Eurasian CW areas before European settlement?

The explanation probably lies in the migratory distance of the CW areas from the origin of modern humans in East Africa, in combination with a delay factor linked to water autonomy that slows down the transition from foraging to agriculture in CW areas. As a matter of fact, a society's score on the CWI correlates at $r = 0.71$ ($p = .000$; $N = 158$) with its migratory distance from the human origin in East Africa, indicating that inhabited areas with the most prominent CW condition are most distant from the origin of humanity. For this reason, modern humans arrived much later in these areas than in others. Hence, the clock of technological advancement started much later there than in areas with low water autonomy. The CW areas' greater migratory distance also meant greater diffusion distance from the early centers of agriculture and urbanization in the Middle East. As a consequence, the diffusion of surplus agriculture and urban life reached the CW areas late.

Besides migratory distance, there are reasons to believe that the CW condition itself embodies a delay factor as concerns the transition from foraging to agriculture. If so, the CW condition lowers technological advancement until the agrarian transition and the emergence of markets, but greatly accelerates it thereafter. We return to this point later. In combination, the evidence points to three conclusions:

1. The breakthrough into the era of accelerated technological advancement happened in CW areas because the breakthrough needed a level of existential security/autonomy that these areas naturally harbor.
2. The breakthrough was recent because the CW areas' migratory distance and an inherent delay factor led to late urban maturation in these areas.
3. Both the delay factor and the accelerated development after its overcoming originate in the same CW feature: the high utility that these areas' conditions bestow on freedoms.

5. PINPOINTING THE ORIGIN: THE SOURCE THESIS

These reflections and insights integrate into a theory that is complete in the sense that it traces human empowerment over various stages from its origin to its outcome. To begin with, areas harboring original forms of existential security and autonomy are placed in large migratory distance from the human origin in East Africa and in large diffusion distance from the earliest centers of agriculture and urbanity in the Middle East. Partly for this reason and because of an inherent delay factor, urban civilization occurred late in the CW areas. Once that happened, however, the original form of existential autonomy became the source of derivative forms of existential autonomy, including autonomy in marketing one's skills. Existential autonomies in an emerging market economy further increase the utility of freedoms. Consequently, people have an incentive to focus their life on quality building rather than on quantity breeding. In other words, ordinary people limit fertility and invest time in their own and their children's skills. Another reason for limited fertility is the high disease security in areas with high water autonomy: higher disease security lowers infant mortality, which reduces the birth rate needed to sustain the workforce.[12] The quality building strategy is further encouraged by the fact that rain-fed grain farming demands fewer laborers per unit of cultivated land than does irrigation-managed agriculture, especially rice cultivation. As a consequence of the quality-building strategy, there is no abundance of cheap labor. Once, however, the flourishing of urban markets increases labor demands, a scarcity of cheap labor stimulates investment in technologies that save costly labor. The result is larger investments in technological knowledge – the modern progress engine.

This reasoning suggests three testable propositions:

1. Since prehistory, areas with water autonomy and disease security prevail in large migratory distance from the human origin in Africa.
2. Coming to fruition late in history, disease security and water autonomy encourage quality-building strategies that persist since premodern times and are visible in fertility control at early points in contemporary time.
3. Fertility control at earlier points in contemporary time shows a positive impact on technological advancement in recent time.

The time-sequenced path analysis across 130 nations in Figure 11.4 strongly confirms each of these propositions – with respect to *contemporary* technological advancement. However, the evidence is not limited to technological advancement as it stands nowadays. Instead, Figure 11.2 showed that the technological impact of the CW condition goes back all the way to the origin of the Great Redirection: it is a persistent feature since this turn in human history, although there are recent signs of a slow fading of the CW condition's technological impact. I address this point in the last section of this chapter.

6. FROM EXPLOITATION TO EMANCIPATION

Before the modern technology era, development differed sharply on two accounts. First, technological advancement was much slower (Nolan & Lenski 1999; Morris 2010). Second, technological advancement did not empower common people; on the contrary, it increased state capacities to exploit people

---

[12] Indeed, disease security explains at least 40 percent of the cross-national variation in infant mortality, in every year from 1985 to 2005 across 175 societies. Controlling for a society's per capita GDP of the same year, disease security still explains some 12 percent of the cross-national differences in infant mortality. The effect is highly significant and, of course, negative: higher disease security comes with lower infant mortality. The partial effect of per capita GDP accounts for 11 percent of the cross-national variation in infant mortality.

(Mann 1986). Indeed, while states continuously increased their control over people, quality of life on a mass scale showed no real improvement until the modern technology era. As Maddison's (2007) estimates suggest, fifteen centuries of agrarian civilization brought little recognizable improvement in the life expectancies and per capita incomes of ordinary people. Galor (2011) characterizes the premodern agrarian centuries as the long Malthusian epoch in which material improvements were mostly eaten up by population growth.

Both features of the premodern era – the slowness of development and its exploitative nature – were a consequence of low water autonomy in early civilizations. As Wittfogel (1957) acknowledged, early Eurasian civilizations from the Middle East to India and China evolved as "hydraulic societies": their agrarian systems were based on large-scale irrigation infrastructure involving canals, dams, dikes, locks, pumps, pipes, bridges, and other complex architectural features – all of which require central coordination of cheap mass labor (Landes 1998; Solomon 2011). Within such a setting, people's access to water resources is elite-controlled: they have low water autonomy. Confirming this suggestion, the left-hand diagram of Figure 11.1 shows that the score on the CWI is 0.41 for China, 0.36 for the Middle East, and 0.17 for India. The African predicament is fully visible here, with a CWI score of 0.09 for Central Africa. This compares to 0.88 for both Japan and Western Europe (and the emphasis is indeed on *Western* Europe: the CWI scores for Southern and Eastern Europe are 0.57 and 0.48, respectively). With low water autonomy, the agrarian surplus depends on collective irrigation management. The control over mass labor needed to sustain large-scale irrigation favors despotism (Wittfogel 1957; Jones 1987; Midlarsky & Midlarsky 1999; Solomon 2011). A new study using global quantitative evidence across nations and over time strongly confirms this point (Bentzen, Kaarsen, & Wingender 2012).

At times, despotic regimes encourage technological advancement, yet only as long as it does not threaten despotism (Goldstone 2009). Until the Great Redirection, technological advancement in the Middle Eastern, Indian, and Chinese empires was ahead of Europe and Japan: these empires were farther advanced in mathematics, medicine, and astronomy; they invented porcelain, gun powder, silk, paper, printing, and the compass. What is more, the Chinese empire initiated large-scale naval operations almost a hundred years before the Europeans did. However, as Goldstone (2009) notes, at some point, each of these empires reverted to dogmatism, thus suffocating the innovative thrust. To sustain despotism, the empires did not allow research and inquiry to break free from dogmatic control. For instance, it has been argued that after 1433 CE, the Chinese empire took seafaring under strict control to prevent the merchant class from growing too independent (Jones 1987; Hall 1989; Solomon 2011).

As Western Europe and Japan reached the mature urban stage, civilization took hold where natural conditions gave rulers less control over people. Rulers had to acknowledge personal autonomies, autonomous social entities, and autonomous social sectors and territories (Powelson 1997). Under these conditions, the key activity driving development – intellectual inquiry – was freed from political control (Jones 1987; McNeill 1990). This happened earlier in Western Europe than in Japan because Western Europe reached the stage of flourishing urban capitalism more than a hundred years before Japan (Modelski 2003). Japan also lacked the innovative impulses that Western Europe obtained from its system of competing states (Jones 1987; Hall 1989; Landes 1998; Goldstone 2009). Nevertheless, Japan was the first non-European civilization to emulate the Western technology explosion. Among the non-European urban civilizations, Japan was best situated in terms of people's water autonomy and the derivative autonomies that follow once urbanization sets in.

7. THE INITIAL DELAY OF COOL-WATER AREAS

The CW areas in Eurasia and even more so those outside Eurasia are located in large migratory distance from the early centers of surplus agriculture and urban life, which spread along the ancient civilization belt from the Middle East to China. From a diffusionist point of view, migratory distance is a plausible reason for the delayed maturation of urban civilization in the Eurasian CW areas, as well as its absence in the non-Eurasian CW areas before European settlement. In addition to the migratory distance, I suggest that the belated urban maturation of the CW areas is also linked to a delay factor inherent to the CW condition itself. Ironically, that delay factor turned into an acceleration factor once the initial delay was overcome. Let me explain.

Some societies in history did not abandon the foraging lifestyle because agriculture is impossible under certain conditions. This is true of polar and subpolar regions, as well as steppes and deserts. In some other habitats, the transition is possible but not urgent (unless enforced from outside) because the richness of the flora, fauna, and water resources are benign to the foraging lifestyle. Notably, this is true of tropical rainforests and the initially forested CW areas (Fernandez-Armesto 2002.

The weaker urge to adopt agriculture is important when one considers what anthropology reveals about humans' preferred choice between foraging and agriculture. Agriculture did not improve the quality of the human diet; actually, there is evidence for a slightly negative effect on life expectancy (Blumberg 2004). In addition, agriculture meant a transition to a rigid work schedule and the sacrifice of individual freedoms for collective discipline under the authority of overlords (Nolan & Lenski 1999). For a self-aware being with a desire for freedom, this is indeed a sacrifice (Deci & Ryan 2000; Maryanski & Turner 1992; Turner & Maryanski 2008). As Veenhoven (2010) speculates, human life satisfaction probably deteriorated in the transition from foraging to agriculture. Consequently, humans would make the transition only if overpopulation, climatic change, or other exogenous events *forced* them to do so. Hence, in environments where the transition could be delayed, it indeed was.

If these assumptions are correct, we should see that – among societies of about the same age – the foraging lifestyle is preserved longer under the CW condition than otherwise. But we should also see that, among societies with an equal persistence of foraging, the CW condition is conducive to market exchange, which is an engine of development. All else being equal, the CW condition should encourage market exchange because the existential autonomies that the CW condition embodies turn markets into a greater opportunity than in settings with lesser autonomies.

If we had data on human societies throughout recorded history, from different places at different times and on different levels of subsistence, we could test these assumptions. Fortunately, a suitable data source exists: the Standard Cross-Cultural Sample founded by Murdock and White (1969) and enriched since then with ethnographic descriptions by hundreds of anthropologists (Ember & Ember 1998; Divale 2004). The units of observation are 186 local populations across the world, each of which "reproduces a specific way of life" (Divale 2004). Local populations are drawn from all inhabited continents and all levels of subsistence, from foraging to industrialization. The time range is from 1750 BCE for the Babylonians, 110 CE for the Romans, 1530 CE for the Incas, to 1930 for the Irish, and 1950 for the Japanese. Most of the studied populations are historic and therefore at the preindustrial level of subsistence. Many of these populations no longer exist, and a large proportion of them practiced a foraging lifestyle, including the !Kung Bushmen, the Tuareg, Lapps, Mongols, Inuit, Hurons, Maoris, and Yanomamo. Hence, the Standard Cross-Cultural Sample covers conditions typical of most of human history, rather than our very recent industrial and postindustrial past. The data are, thus, suited to test some of the effects of water autonomy for their temporal and spatial universality.

The Standard Cross-Cultural Sample measures basic lifestyle variables, from marriage patterns to child-rearing habits to subsistence technology and political organization. Most of these variables are ordinal 4- or 5-point scales, measured in a coding scheme in which 1 indicates the absence and 4 or 5 the complete presence of the property of interest.[13] The codings are based on expert judgments of ethnographic records or archeological evidence. The subjective element certainly involves considerable measurement error, but the Standard Cross-Cultural Sample provides a detailed documentation of coding standards and is widely acknowledged in anthropology as the most important source of systematic data on societal differences across space and time.

The Standard Cross-Cultural Sample also includes climatic information that allows us to measure the CW condition by combining the prevalence of mild and cooler temperatures with the continuity of precipitation. Besides the CW condition, other variables of interest include the age of a society, disease security, the extent of reliance on foraging, the urbanization rate (proxied by population density), the

---

[13] As always, I have transformed every variable into a range from minimum 0 to maximum 1.0, with intermediate positions as fractions.

level of state formation, and the extent of market exchange, as well as the sexes' reproductive autonomy and an emphasis on individual self-reliance and excellence as personal qualities. Appendix 11 (www.cambridge.org/welzel) provides a documentation of the data I take from the Standard Cross-Cultural Sample.

As before, a population's score on the CWI correlates positively with its disease security ($r = 0.45$; $p < 0.001$; $N = 180$) and negatively with its migratory distance from the origin of humanity ($r = -0.58$; $p < 0.001$; $N = 179$) as well as its age ($r = -0.31$; $p < 0.001$; $N = 179$). Thus, areas with high water autonomy are more benign for two reasons: by definition, they provide easy and equal access to water resources, but they also harbor fewer sources of disease. On the other hand, these areas are more distant from the origin of humanity and constitute younger habitats for this reason.

In every human habitat, populations initially followed a foraging lifestyle. As time passed, pressures to abandon foraging and adopt agriculture accrued, yet these pressures accrued to different degrees, depending on a habitat's ecological conditions. With high water autonomy, the pressures were lower because the richness of the fauna, flora, and water resources is less easily depleted. Still, time should diminish a population's reliance on foraging.[14] Hence, controlling for the CW condition, the time since modern humans live in a habitat should show a negative partial effect on foraging. The path model in Figure 11.5 confirms this expectation: the effect of human habitat age on a population's reliance on foraging amounts to $r_{partial} = -0.30$ ($p < 0.005$; $N = 63$).

At the same time, populations in equally old habitats should show a stronger continuation of foraging if the CW condition is more strongly pronounced. Accordingly, controlling for human habitat age, the CW condition should show a positive partial effect on foraging. This expectation, too, is confirmed by the path model in Figure 11.5: the effect of a population's CW condition on its reliance on foraging amounts to $r_{partial} = 0.36$ ($p < 0.005$; $N = 63$).

In other words, CW populations quit foraging later because (a) these populations occupied their habitats more recently and because (b) their higher water autonomy delayed the transition. Since subsequent stages of development – including urbanization and state formation – follow from the abandonment of foraging, CW populations became late developers.

But once CW societies abandon foraging and begin to settle around urban markets, one of their key tendencies turns out to be advantageous: from water autonomy follow derivative autonomies, including autonomy in marketing one's skills and products, which is conducive to market exchange as soon as markets emerge. Confirming this assumption, the path model in Figure 11.5 shows that, at similar levels of urbanization, the CW condition is conducive to market exchange, showing a partial effect of $r_{partial} = 0.27$ ($p < 0.005$; $N = 63$).

---

[14] One reason is the continuous diffusion of agriculture after its invention. This made it more likely that, with the passage of time, extant foraging populations were exposed to agrarian societies in their neighborhood and forced into competition with them.

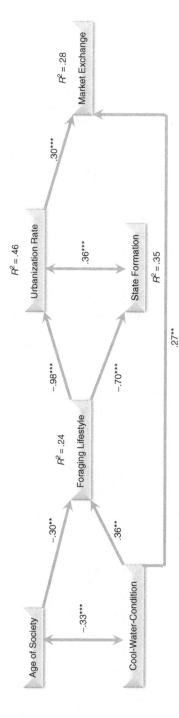

FIGURE 11.5 The Initial Delay and Subsequent Acceleration of Development by the Cool-Water Condition (the anthropological record). Entries are standardized path coefficients, calculated with AMOS 19.01. Number of observations (N) is sixty-three populations from the Standard Cross-Cultural Sample (including all societies for which every variable is available). Model is recursive. Goodness-of-fit measures: GFI .95; IFI .96; CFI .96; NFI .91. Urbanization Rate is proxied by Population Density. Exactly which variables from the Standard Cross-Cultural Sample are used here is documented in Appendix 11 (www.cambridge.org/welzel). Included Societies spread all over the world and existed from 1700 BCE to 1930 CE, covering some 3,500 years of history.

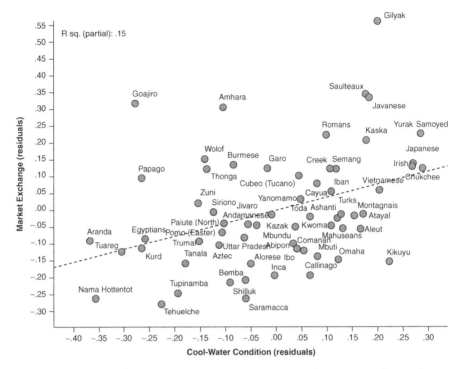

FIGURE 11.6 The Historic Impact of the Cool-Water Condition on Market Exchange (controlling for age of society).
Data Coverage: All societies from the Standard Cross-Cultural Sample with valid data on the respective variables.

Figure 11.6 visualizes the partial effect of the CW condition on market exchange. Even though the effect is only moderately strong, its significance is all the more noteworthy because it surfaces across populations of a truly remarkable diversity in both space and time, ranging from the Aztecs in 1500 CE to the Japanese in 1950. Consider, for instance, two societies at the upper right end of the regression line: a typical Japanese community in 1950 and a typical Irish community in 1930. These two populations are of different cultural background in two different places at different times. Yet, controlling for their age and other factors, their CW condition is equally strong – and so is their degree of market exchange. Or consider two societies at the lower left end of the regression line: the Nama Hottentot in sub-Saharan Africa, as they lived in 1860, and the Aranda in Central Australia, as they lived in 1900. Again, the two populations are of different cultural background in two different places at different times. Yet, controlling for their age and other factors, their CW condition is equally weak – and so is their degree of market exchange. Of course, across space and time, the CW condition explains only a portion of the differences in market exchange. Yet, it is a significant proportion.

Could these findings be a result of selection bias? This is indeed a possibility because the inclusion of populations for which measures on all variables of interest exist reduces the Standard Cross-Cultural Sample from initially 186 to 63 populations. For this reason, the results of this analysis must to be taken with a serious note of caution. Still, it remains true that the available evidence from the anthropological record confirms what the theory suggests. Moreover, we can exclude selection bias on the values of our main independent and dependent variable as a source of error. Comparing the means, medians and standard deviations in the CW condition and market exchange between the populations included in the path model and the excluded ones, no significant differences exist.

Given that market exchange is a chief engine of technological advancement, the anthropological record confirms my explanation of the historical paradox of the CW areas' belated but explosive development: water autonomy delays the aban-donment of a foraging lifestyle and hence delays the emergence of cities and markets, but once they emerge, water autonomy accelerates technological advancement.

The proposition that further autonomies follow from water autonomy can be subjected to additional tests. To do so, I look at the impact of the CW condition on the sexes' reproductive autonomy and the emphasis on self-reliance and individual excellence as personal qualities, under control of population density or state formation (depending on whichever has the stronger effect). The idea that water autonomy nurtures derivative autonomies implies that, throughout history, in populations with a stronger CW condition the sexes had more reproductive autonomy and emphasized self-reliance and individual excellence more. Reproductive autonomy measures to what extent women's and men's agreement is needed for marriage and to what extent household formation is oriented toward the monogamous, neolocal nuclear family. An emphasis on self-reliance and individual excellence as personal qualities is measured by the emphases on these qualities in the education of children.

Figure 11.7 illustrates the partial effects of water autonomy on these two variables: as expected, the effects are significantly positive and moderately strong (in the case of self-reliance and individual excellence) or strong (in the case of reproductive autonomy). However, even a relatively weak partial effect is remarkable, if it is significant, because what we see here are effects that seem to *persist* throughout our history. Operating over a longer period of time, even a relatively weak effect accumulates to large differences in outcomes.

8. EXPLOITATIVE AND EMANCIPATORY CIVILIZATIONS

With the breakthrough into the age of science, development not only acceler-ated; its logic diverted from perfecting human exploitation into advancing human empowerment. This diversion gave rise to an entirely new configuration of civilization. Compared to this new configuration, all previous configurations were *exploitative* in character: their main purpose was to sustain the well-being of a small, hereditary elite (Diamond 1997).

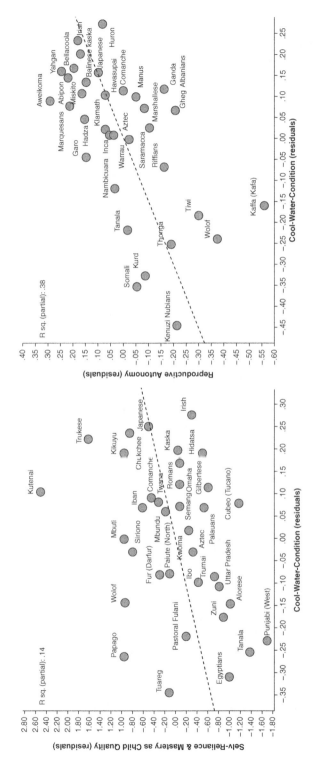

FIGURE 11.7 The Historic Impact of the Cool-Water Condition on Family Formation Patterns (controlling for state formation and urbanization). Left-hand Diagram: Partial relationship is statistically significant at the .001 level and controlled for state formation. Right-hand Diagram: Partial relationship is statistically significant at the .001-level and controlled for population density. *Data Coverage*: All societies from the standard Cross-Cultural Sample with valid data on the respective variables.

North, Wallis, and Weingast (2009) describe the new configuration in institutional terms, characterizing it as an "open access order." Acemoglu and Robinson (2012) likewise describe the new configuration in institutional terms, focusing on its "inclusive institutions." Fukuyama (2012) has similar things in mind when pinpointing "adaptive institutions" as the key characteristic of the new configuration. These characterizations are without doubt insightful. Yet, couching the new configuration in institutional terms focuses on the symptoms. In my eyes, the best characterization of the new configuration lies in its spirit, which is inherently emancipatory: it is the idea of liberating people from external domination over their lives, giving them equal opportunities to pursue happiness and focusing the purpose of government on the well-being of the people.

The emancipatory sprit originates in a natural environment, manifest in the CW condition, that bestows existential autonomies on people. These autonomies enabled and encouraged people to mobilize resistance against oppression. From this resistance emerged a *contractual order* with *consensual institutions*, which range from (1) voluntary marriage to (2) market organization to (3) political representation. The key principle of consensual institutions is agreement. The agreement principle derives from the bargaining power with which existential autonomies endow people. The existential autonomies harbored by the CW condition made universal freedoms useful and desired and this happened before the contractual order framed these freedoms legally. Consensual institutions (or open, inclusive, and adaptive institutions—whatever terms we use) evolve as consequences, not causes, of existential autonomies at the grassroots of society. The purpose of these institutions is to certify utilities and values that are in place *before* their certification. Where institutional guarantees of freedoms are effective, the reason is not the quality of these guarantees themselves. The true reason why guarantees work is that the utility of these guarantees is already widely valued.

By contrast, where the absence of the CW condition makes peasants dependent on centrally organized water supply, *coercive institutions* emerged and gave rise to *patriarchal orders*, the opposite of contractual orders. Coercive institutions include (1) pre-arranged marriages with patrilocal household formation instead of voluntary marriages with neolocal household formation, (2) rent seeking economies with repressive labor relations instead of market economies with contractual labor relations, and (3) patronage and confiscation instead of representation in return for taxation in the political realm. Such patriarchal orders characterize the exploitative configuration of civilization.

The emancipatory configuration of civilization began to take shape after 1500 CE and differs on every account from the exploitative configuration that prevailed until then. To simplify things, this contrast is captured by the schematized juxtaposition in Figure 11.8.

Let's briefly summarize Figure 11.8. If intensive agriculture is adopted in CW areas, a *rain-watered type* of agrarian system evolves. This type of agriculture favors a distinct organization of economic activities. The key point about rain-

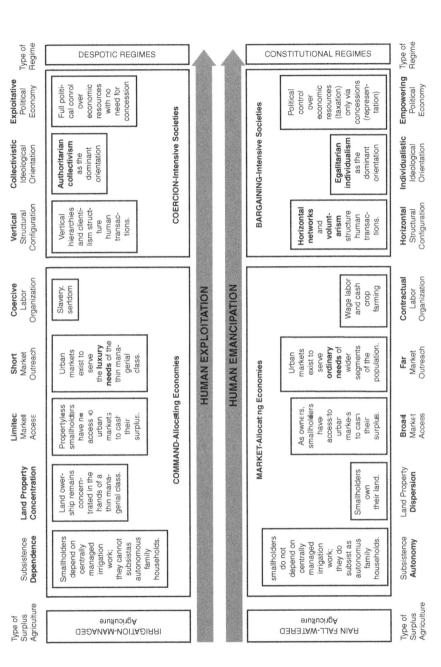

FIGURE 11.8 Juxtaposing the Emancipatory and Exploitative Configurations of Civilization.

watered agriculture is that smallholders are *existentially autonomous* because they can cultivate land on their own. Existential autonomy orients people toward entitlements and motivates them to fight for these entitlements. Eventually, this emancipatory spirit contributes to a wider dispersion of property titles on land. Landowning smallholders have economic agency because they can access urban markets to sell their surplus. Milder forms of contractual feudalism leave more surplus in the hands of the smallholders (Powelson 1997).

In this setting, a greater proportion of surplus is market allocated. Markets are more widely accessed and have greater outreach, serving the needs of common people. Market allocation increases the incentive to produce surplus and to invest in productivity-increasing technology. Consequently, the surplus eventually grows larger. Thus, richer and more sizeable urban populations emerge.

The commercial exchange networks of far-reaching urban markets provide the infrastructure for a civil society with autonomous actors who have the resources, skills, and motivation to coordinate their actions for jointly valued goals. This generates civic agency. Civic agency bestows bargaining power on social actors against political authorities. If authorities try to access economic resources via taxation, they have to make concessions in the form of political representation. As rulers grant representation in return for taxation (a deal often enforced in liberal revolutions), a social contract is forged, documented in statutes and constitutions.

Thus, *market-allocating economies* create *bargaining-intensive societies*, which result in *constitutional regimes* with political authority consented and controlled by wider segments of the population. These features establish the contractual order with its consensual institutions.

Under a contractual order, human transactions are structured by *horizontal networks* and social bonds are forged on the basis of *voluntarism*. The dominant orientation in society is a *meritocratic* form of individualism that values each person equally by his or her merits. The emancipatory spark inspiring the contractual order operates in harmony with productive human motivations. Hence, it unleashes people's creative energies, which makes possible the explosion of ideas needed to trigger an Industrial Revolution.

The success of the emancipatory type of civilization resides in its *double regulatory strength*. The double regulatory strength consists in strong organizing capacities on the part of the state and strong mobilizing capacities on the part of the society. The symbiosis of the two is forged by a social contract that tailors the state's powers toward the well-being of its constituents.

On the time scale of history, it took long until the civilization process gave rise to the emancipatory configuration on the territorial scope of entire countries, and not just of city states.[15] To understand why time was a crucial factor one has to see that the emancipatory configuration evolved under the CW condition. This

---

[15] On the territorial scale of city states, elements of emancipatory civilization, such as citizen rights, occurred in nascent form earlier in history. Classic Athens, the Roman Republic, and the historic

condition bestows autonomies on people and these autonomies motivate effective resistance against power concentrations. Thus, the formation of state capacities is blocked under the CW condition until state formation is pursued under the explicit recognition of people's autonomies. But this required the evolution of an encompassing mechanism of preference negotiation – a mechanism encompassing enough to aggregate the preferences of an entire country's population. The mechanism in question emerged from the principle "no taxation without representation." Taxation in return for representation allowed regulatory capacities to develop on two parallel paths: the organizing capacities of the state and the mobilizing capacities of society. Once this regulatory co-evolution was in motion, the emancipatory type of civilization proved enormously successful. Its regulatory capacities quickly outperformed those known from exploitative forms of civilization on every account. This is particularly true of technological advancement – the ultimate source of a society's powers.

The explosion of technology that emerged from the emancipatory configuration of society allowed the West to rise to global dominance: Figure 11.9 provides a stylized depiction of this course of history. In the eras of colonialism and imperialism, the West itself became an exploiter of previously exploitative civilizations. But the West could not monopolize the spirit of emancipation. Instead, the spirit was turned against the West in the era of decolonization: the colonized societies claimed and asserted their right for liberation from Western domination. Since then, the spirit of emancipation is globalizing: as we saw in Chapter 2 (Figure 2.5), emancipative values are on the rise in every culture zone across the globe.

The rising spirit of emancipation does not equate to Westernization because the desire to live free from external domination is universally human. Ironically, the diffusion of the emancipatory spirit actually evidences a *de*-Westernization of the world. Because emancipative values evolve in response to better living conditions, their growth indicates that other societies are catching up. As this happens, the West's global dominance fades.

9. FADING NATURAL ADVANTAGES: THE CONTAGION THESIS

There is conclusive evidence that environmental conditions exert a powerful impact on the base process of human empowerment: technological advancement. Through their impact on technological advancement, environmental conditions indirectly affect the two consecutive elements of human empowerment:

republics in Northern India might be counted as examples. Yet, as long as this configuration did not emerge on the territorial scale of an entire nation, it could not compete with large empires. And as long as this was the case, it seemed as if the exploitative organization of society was superior to the emancipatory organization. For the longer period of civilized history, despotism seemed superior to freedom. The deceptive nature of this impression became obvious once emancipatory societies eventually emerged on the territorial scale of entire nations.

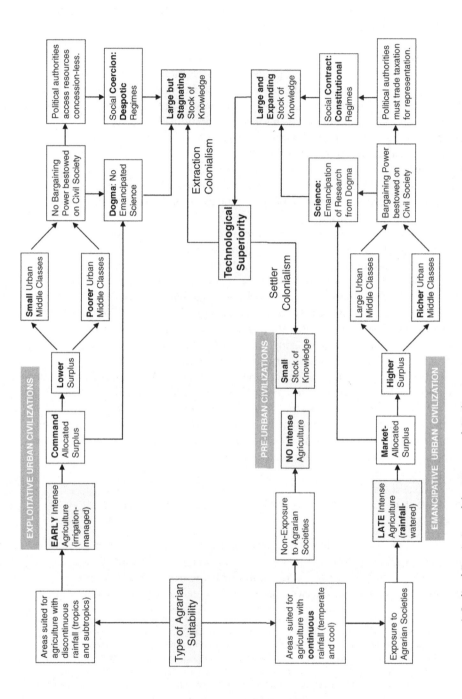

FIGURE 11.9 A Stylized Depiction of the History of Civilization.

emancipative values and civic entitlements. Hence, environmental conditions have been important for the entire human empowerment process. The industrial take-offs of Western Europe and Japan, together with European settlement in North America, Australia, and New Zealand, advanced human empowerment in all of the world's CW zones.

Now, many readers will ask "How great is a theory that leaves us with such a bleak, deterministic outlook?" Against this possible criticism, I want to point out that my theory is not deterministic but probabilistic. Certain natural endowments are givens, and they place societies within a possibility corridor from which they cannot escape. But this corridor can be broad, as Figure 3.5 (p. 125) has shown. The choices that societies make, some of them perhaps accidental, decide whether they move along the floor or the ceiling of their possibility corridors. What is more, and that could be another turn in history, there is accruing evidence that the determining power of natural endowments is shrinking, thus widening the possibility corridor for all societies. And I believe that global communications and the internet are responsible. Humans have always been programmed for social learning, but this potential was limited in social and geographic space. The internet is about to completely unlock this potential, which widens the choices that societies can make. Today, even people in backward areas can easily get a rough sense of how things are done in other places and how they are done better. And they can more easily connect with like-minded others to mobilize pressure for change. No question, there are still more than enough tyrants and corrupt power holders in this world, and their final days are not counted yet. But their lives become more difficult under rising popular pressures.

A symptom of this historic sea change is that life improvements decouple from advantageous natural endowments. Technological advancement in particular is becoming untied from its original limitation to CW areas. The emergence of India, a largely tropical society, to the forefront of information technology is a striking example. If this trend continues, we will observe an increasing dissociation of the human empowerment process from its previous confinements.

A sign that this decoupling is just about to happen is the weakening explanatory power of the CW condition. Since the 1980s, the CW condition shows a weakening impact on technological advancement: across the world, the explanatory power of the CW condition decreased from 67 percent in 1980 to 42 percent in 2010. Appendix 11 (www.cambridge.org/welzel) documents the evidence for this statement.

The regression analyses in Table 11.4 demonstrate why societies' progress in technological advancement is being decoupled from the CW condition. The covered period is 1980 to 2010. Since our direct measure for technological advancement is unavailable for the twenty-year time span covered in Table 11.4, I use the proxy for technological advancement from Vanhanen (2003) introduced earlier, combining a society's literacy and urbanization rate. From 1980 to 2010, all societies increase their score on this proxy. Yet, they progress to different degrees. The models explain this difference.

TABLE 11.4 *The Diminishing Impact of Natural Conditions and the Rising Impact of Globalization on Technological Advancement.*

PREDICTORS	DEPENDENT VARIABLE: Δ Technological Advancement[a] 1980–2010						
	Model 1	Model 2	Model 3	Model 4	Model 5	Model 6	Model 7
• Constant	0.20	0.09	0.16	0.15	0.20	0.11	0.17
	$(7.45)^{***}$	$(3.09)^{***}$	$(4.25)^{***}$	$(4.28)^{***}$	$(6.94)^{***}$	$(1.31)^{n.s.}$	$(2.59)^{**}$
• Cool-Water Condition	−0.11	−0.17	−0.10	−0.07	−0.12	−0.39	−0.44
	$(-2.21)^{**}$	$(-3.64)^{***}$	$(-1.93)^{*}$	$(-1.26)^{n.s.}$	$(-2.33)^{**}$	$(-3.95)^{***}$	$(-5.87)^{***}$
• Δ Social Globalization[b]		0.69				0.59	0.47
		$(5.02)^{***}$				$(2.25)^{**}$	$(2.11)^{**}$
• Δ Economic Globalization[b]			0.15			0.09	0.22
			$(1.02)^{n.s.}$			$(0.46)^{n.s.}$	$(1.18)^{n.s.}$
• Δ Political Globalization[b]				0.24		0.23 $(1.27)^{n.s.}$	
				$(2.25)^{**}$			
• Δ Civic Entitlements					0.05		0.03
					$(0.99)^{n.s.}$		$(0.43)^{n.s.}$
Adjusted R^2	0.06	0.32	0.03	0.11	0.06	0.35	0.42
N (societies)	65	62	61	63	61	62	57

Regression diagnostics for heteroskedasticity (White test), multicollinearity (variance inflation factors), and influential cases (DFFITs) reveal no violation of ordinary least squares (OLS) assumptions.

Significance levels: $^{n.s.}$ $p \geq .100$, * $p .100$, ** $p .050$, *** $p .005$

[a] Proxy measure: urbanization rate times literacy rate in 1980 and 2000, subtracting the former product from the latter.

[b] Dreher et al.'s (2008) globalization indices in 1980 and 2000, standardized into a range from minimum 0 to maximum 1.0 and subtracting the 1980 from the 2000 index.

As is evident, the CW condition has a negative effect on progress in technological advancement: societies with a stronger CW condition exhibit higher levels of technological advancement since a long time, yet they make less additional progress since 1980. In other words, naturally disadvantaged societies are catching up: they are overcoming their disadvantage. Progressing global integration favors this process: societies that engage more in exchange with other societies make more progress in their technological advancement than do societies that engage less. This is obvious from the positive effects of the indicators for social, economic, and political globalization that I take from Dreher, Gaston, and Martens (2008).

Interestingly, the positive effect of globalization is stronger for social than for economic and political globalization. Social globalization measures cross-border exchange between people and global communications, including such things as tourism, phone conversations, letter correspondence and internet usage. By contrast, economic globalization is about the exchange of goods while political globalization measures commitment to international treaties. The stronger impact of social globalization on progressing technological advancement makes sense from a social learning point of view: learning to progress happens primarily through communications between people. Figure 11.10 visualizes the findings of Table 11.2 (Model 2), depicting the partial effects of the CW condition and rising social globalization under mutual control.

In line with these findings, a recent analysis demonstrates across some 180 nations that the impact of the CW condition on decennial growth rates in per capita GDP shrank monotonically from $b = 0.78$ for the decade 1960–70 to $b = 0.55$ for the decade 2000–10. Moreover, 56 percent of the shrinking impact of the CW condition is explained by a parallel rise in the world's mean globalization score (Welzel 2013).

KEY POINTS

As this chapter has shown, the source thesis of emancipation theory explains some striking patterns of human history. The thesis posits that the CW areas' naturally higher disease security and water autonomy bestow on freedoms more initial utility than elsewhere. CW areas are naturally located a few steps above on the utility ladder of freedoms. This leads to two paradoxical effects.

First, since foraging is a freer lifestyle than agriculture, the transition to agriculture was delayed in CW areas. Hence, societies in these areas were late developers: urban markets emerged later than in the old Oriental civilizations, and technological advancement lagged behind for a long time.

Second, once urban markets emerged they became more vibrant in CW areas because water autonomy creates derivative autonomies once markets are in place. These derivative autonomies continue to bestow further utility on freedoms in CW areas, which now turns out to be an accelerator of technological advancement. With autonomy in market access, ordinary people have an incentive to

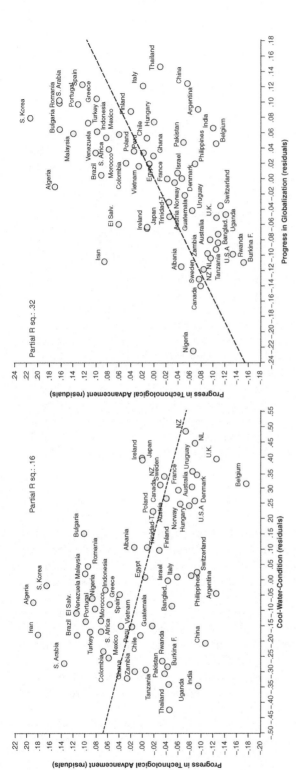

FIGURE 11.10 Diminishing Impact of Natural Conditions and the Rising Impact of Globalization on Technological Advancement.

Left-hand Diagram: Positive (negative) residuals on the horizontal indicate to what extent a society's cool-water (CW) condition is stronger (weaker) than one would expect knowing its progress in globalization. Positive (negative) residuals on the vertical axis indicate to what extent progress in a society's technological advancement is higher (lower) than one would expect knowing the society's progress in globalization. The relationship indicates that, if a society's CW condition is stronger than expected, its progress in technological advancement is lower than expected. Thus, controlling for progress in globalization, the CW condition negatively affects progress in technological advancement.

Right-hand Diagram: Positive (negative) residuals on the horizontal indicate to what extent a society's progress in globalization is higher (lower) than one would expect knowing its CW condition. Positive (negative) residuals on the vertical axis indicate to what extent progress in a society's technological advancement is higher (lower) than one would expect knowing the society's CW condition. The relationship indicates that, if a society's progress in globalization is higher than expected, its progress in technological advancement is higher than expected too. Thus, controlling for the CW condition, progress in globalization positively affects progress in technological advancement.

The two diagrams are partial regression plots from the same multivariate regression: the dependent variable is progress in technological advancement from 1980 to 2010, using the combined literacy and urbanization rates as a proxy. The independent variables are the CW index (which is without a specific time) and progress in a society's degree of globalization from 1980 to 2000, using Dreher, Gaston, and Martens' (2008) index of social globalization. All variables are standardized from minimum 0 to maximum 1.0. Progress is the difference in the technological advancement and globalization levels between 1980 and 2000, subtracting the former from the latter.

avoid a quantity-breeding strategy and instead pursue a quality-building strategy in their reproductive behavior: they sacrifice demographic for economic productivity. This creates a less numerous but more valuable workforce. Rising labor demands in urban centers must, therefore, be met by technologies that save costly labor. The result is accelerated technological advancement.

As a consequence, action resources make their way into the hands of wider segments of the population. More widespread action resources further increase the utility of freedoms. In recognition of this, people adopt emancipative values. Inspired by emancipative values, people claim civic entitlements and take action on their behalf if rulers refuse to provide effective guarantees. Overwhelmed by popular solidarity, rulers eventually give in: civic entitlements are guaranteed and respected in practice. As this happens, a first full cycle of human empowerment is completed. Then the next cycle might start, creating more action resources, stronger emancipative values, and wider civic entitlements. Of course, exogenous shocks can stop human empowerment or even revert it at any point in time. But there is no preset inner limitation beyond which human empowerment could never advance. The reason for the absence of a preset limitation lies in the simple fact that, no matter how much we improve, the world will always be imperfect.

The human empowerment process started in the CW areas of Western Europe, it was emulated by the CW area of Japan, and it was transplanted by European settlement to the CW areas of Northern America and Australia as well as New Zealand. Hence, human empowerment is far advanced in all of the world's CW areas. However, in the era of globalization the human empowerment process begins to dissociate from the advantageous CW condition and to diffuse elsewhere. Human empowerment begins to globalize. This process de-Westernizes the world as the West's monopoly over human empowerment erodes. The next chapter deals with the sustainability challenge that the global diffusion of human empowerment poses. I will argue that human empowerment holds in itself the key to master the sustainability challenge.

12

The Sustainability Challenge

I think . . . that an honest appraisal of the facts leads to the conclusion that by far the most likely outcome of the next nine decades is that both Africa gets rich and that no catastrophic climate change happens.

– Matt Ridley 2011

Once in motion, the human empowerment process has proven enormously successful in a double sense. For one, human empowerment gives room to people's quest for emancipation, which creates more happiness among people-powered societies. Thus, the process creates its own basis of legitimacy. Next, societies that progress in human empowerment mobilize intellectual creativity at an unprecedented level. For this reason, people-powered societies move to higher levels of technological advancement than do societies that delimit people power. As a consequence, people-powered societies dominate the global order.

But there is a paradox. The very success of human empowerment threatens to destroy its own basis. Continuing human empowerment incurs a degree of ecological destruction that challenges the sustainability of this process. As we will see, human empowerment is indeed strongly associated with a larger ecological footprint: people-powered societies put a heavy burden on the environment.

Ironically, though, at the same time as human empowerment threatens its own sustainability, it holds the key to mastering that challenge. As I will demonstrate, people-powered societies pressure their governments for environmental protection and achieve higher environmental quality for this reason. The net effect of human empowerment on a society's ecological sustainability is therefore neutral, not negative. There is actually reason to believe that the net effect will turn positive in the near future. The reason lies in the motivational element of human empowerment: emancipative values. As these values grow stronger, ordinary people's environmental concerns translate more easily into environmental activism that puts governments under popular pressures.

To flesh out these findings, the chapter proceeds in three sections. Section 1 gives a brief overview of the contested terrain in the sustainability debate. Section 2 derives some hypotheses from this debate and describes the measurements used to test them. Section 3 reports the results. As always, the chapter ends with a summary of key points.

1. THE SUSTAINABILITY DEBATE

A heated debate is going on about the sustainability challenge and its relationship to human progress. Going back to the Club of Rome report (Meadows et al. 1972), advocates of the sustainability challenge point out that the most advanced societies are destroying life on this planet as they continue to progress. The conclusion of this camp is that humanity must leave its destructive progress path. The clear implication is to discontinue the human empowerment process (Homer-Dixon 2000; Meadows et al. 1972; Meadows, Randers, & Meadows 2004; Wright 2004; Diamond 2005; Tainter 2007; Moran et al. 2008).

The rational optimists (Ridley 2010), by contrast, maintain that only the human empowerment process itself holds the key to solving the sustainability challenge (Simon 1996, 1998; Goklany 2007; Ponting 2007; McAnany & Yoffee 2010). These people admit that technological advancement has enhanced human impact on the environment to a level that indeed threatens the sustainability of human civilization. But meeting the challenge is only possible by further increasing our technological know-how, so we produce, consume, and live with "greener" technologies that keep our environmental impact within our societies' biological carrying capacity.

A related debate addresses the impact of values on environmentalism. Inglehart (1995) argues that a key component of emancipative values – postmaterialism – is conducive to green orientations because postmaterialists are no longer narrowly concerned with their material living standard. They are more broadly concerned with the quality of life, which includes an intact natural environment. Accordingly, in societies where postmaterialism is stronger, environmentalism should be more prevalent (Milbrath 1984; Rohrschneider 1990; Dalton 1994). Since emancipative values derive from the same source and have the same impulses as their postmaterial component, the same conclusion should apply to emancipative values: where emancipative values are stronger, environmentalism should be more prevalent.

Other scholars, however, point out that environmental concerns are widespread. They are by no means only found in societies in which postmaterialism (or emancipative values for that matter) are strong. Even in developing societies where these values are still weak, one finds large proportions of people voicing environmental concerns. In light of this evidence, researchers argue that, rather than subjective values, objective problems fuel environmentalism: obviously, people in poorer societies are more directly exposed to environmental damage and voice environmental concerns for this reason (Dunlap & Mertig 1997;

Dunlap 2008; Freymeyer 2010). Yet, both can be true: environmentalism is nourished by environmental problems in developing societies and by value change in developed societies. If so, the critical question is whether the consequences of environmental concern differ, depending on the two types of motivations driving them.

Rohrschneider, Miles, and Peffley (2013) argue exactly that: these authors hypothesize that value-induced environmental concerns are more likely to translate into environmental activism. I build on this idea but extend it to the broader concept of emancipative values, which I include as both an individual- and a societal-level predictor of environmental activism.

2. MEASUREMENTS

To examine how a society's progress in human empowerment affects its environmental outlook, I use three indicators. To begin with, I use the ecological footprint in the year 2010, measured in global hectares per person in a society (Global Footprint Network 2012). The measure is available in annual time series since the early 2000s. It indicates the area of biologically productive land and sea needed to produce the resources that a society consumes (Wackernagel & Rees 1998; Lenzen & Murray 2003). The deepest ecological footprints are found among rich oil-exporting societies, like the United Arab Emirates (10.68 hectares per capita) and Qatar (10.51), followed by advanced knowledge societies, with Denmark (8.26), Belgium (8.00), and the United States (8.00) on top of the list. The lightest ecological footprint is found in poor societies, with East Timor (0.44), Bangladesh (0.62), and Afghanistan (0.62) at the bottom of the ranking. From the viewpoint of the ecological footprint, people-powered societies are to be blamed: they all leave a deep footprint.

Things look very different from the perspective of another ecological indicator: the *environmental performance index*. Published by the Yale Center for Environmental Law and Policy (2012), the index uses a dimensional weighting scheme to summarize twenty-five indicators on a 0–100 index, measuring the state of "environmental health" and "ecosystem vitality" in a society. The indicator is available since the mid-2000s in an annual time series. While the ecological footprint measures a society's environmental impact, the environmental performance index measures a society's environmental quality. And while people-powered societies have a heavy environmental impact, they nevertheless have high environmental quality (Roller 2005). Thus, we find people-powered societies at the top of the rankings in environmental quality, with Switzerland, Latvia, and Norway leading the list. At the bottom we find disempowering societies: Uzbekistan, Turkmenistan, and Iraq.

The seeming paradox that empowering societies have a heavy environmental impact at the same as their environmental quality is formidable suggests that human empowerment does not necessarily deteriorate ecological sustainability. To measure ecological sustainability, I calculate the ratio of a society's biocapacity (measured in global hectares per capita) to the ecological footprint. The ratio operationalizes the assumption that a society's footprint is more sustainable the more the biocapacity exceeds it and less sustainable the more the biocapacity falls short of it. To eliminate skewness in the distribution of the biocapacity-to-footprint ratio, I take logs of the ratio. As I do with all variables, scores are standardized into a scale ranging from minimum 0 to maximum 1.0. On this scale, a score of 0.50 indicates the sustainability threshold: the biocapacity equals the footprint. Scores above 0.50 indicate how much the biocapacity overshoots the footprint; scores below 0.50 indicate how much the biocapacity falls short of the footprint.

To assume that better environmental quality produces human empowerment is nonsensical. It is far more plausible that the relationship exists because something in the human empowerment process makes societies take action for better environmental quality. Most likely, this "something" is emancipative values. These values bring an emphasis on life quality issues, including environmental quality. However, because environmental concern is supposedly not only high where emancipative values are pronounced but also where these values are not yet strong, the role of values must go beyond just environmental concerns. Building on the work of Rohrschneider, Miles, and Peffley (2013), I hypothesize that the impact of emancipative values lies in the *political mobilization* of environmental concerns, that is, the translation of these concerns into environmental action. Given the activating impulse of emancipative values evidenced in Chapters 6 and 7, this is indeed a plausible hypothesis.

To test the hypothesis, I use three questions from the fifth round of the World Values Surveys (WVS) asking people how serious a problem they think "global warming," the "loss of biodiversity," and "pollution" are. Each problem's seriousness is rated on a 4-point scale from "very serious" to "not at all serious." I code the response options 0, 0.33, 0.66, and 1.0 from not at all to very serious and calculate the average perceived seriousness across the three problems for each respondent, yielding a 9-point index from 0 to 1.0.[1]

Distinct from environmental concern is the priority that people assign to environmental protection. Policy priorities become virulent when we deal with conflicting goals, and among various conflicting goals the creation of jobs is usually a very popular one. Hence, the WVS asks respondents to indicate if they think that environmental protection should take priority over creating jobs or if they think it should be the other way round. Using this question, I code an economic priority 0, an environmental priority 1.0, and an undecided position 0.50.

Plausibly, environmental priorities gain in political importance to the extent that they are mobilized into social movement activity (SMA). Hence, I measure

---

[1] The index is justified as a compository index by the definition of environmental concern: it is the overall concern across the domains addressed in the questionnaire. It is not assumed that the three concerns are interchangeable. From the definitional point of view, interchangeability is, strictly speaking, irrelevant. For the logic of compository measurements, see Box 2.1 (p. 60).

environmental priorities *conditionally*, that is, only insofar as they translate into SMA. This is done by weighting environmental priorities for the SMAs introduced in Chapter 7. This yields an *index of environmental activism* with minimum 0 when a respondent either prioritizes jobs over the environment or abstains from participation in SMAs, to 1.0 when a respondent both prioritizes the environment over jobs and participates in SMAs. The index measures environmental priorities on the condition that they combine with SMAs, or SMAs on the condition that they combine with environmental priorities.

Environmental activism in this sense is not a latent variable: its components are not combined because they reflect a single underlying dimension (see Box 8.1, p. 259). Quite the contrary, the components are distinct, and this is exactly the reason why they are combined: their very combination generates something genuinely new – environmental activism. This is neither social activism nor environmental priorities alone but the very combination of the two. At any rate, I hypothesize that emancipative values ease the translation of environmental concerns into environmental activism.

The following section examines, first, how the three components of human empowerment affect a society's environmental impact, its environmental quality, and its overall ecological sustainability. These analyses are performed at the societal level. Then, I use multilevel models to isolate the microlevel mechanism underlying the macrolevel findings. Specifically, I analyze how emancipative values affect environmental activism and, in particular, the translation of environmental concern into environmental activism. Appendix 12 (www.cambridge.org/welzel) documents the data of the subsequent analyses.

3. FINDINGS

3.1 Ecological Sustainability

Table 12.1 shows the results of a series of multivariate regressions in which environmental indicators are the dependent variables and the three components of human empowerment are the independent variables. The purpose is to find out which component of human empowerment affects which environmental aspect the most. The analyses are limited to societies covered by WVS round five, so the three human empowerment measures can be kept contemporaneous, indicating conditions around the year 2005. This reduces the country sample to fifty societies. Yet, this is not an odd sample. Especially with respect to global ecological sustainability, the sample is highly indicative because it includes from each world region those societies with the largest economies and biggest populations: China and Japan in East Asia; India and Indonesia in South Asia; Turkey and Iran in the Middle East; Russia and Poland in Eastern Europe; Germany, France, Italy and the United Kingdom in Western Europe; the United States in North America; Mexico in Central America; Brazil and Argentina in South America; and South Africa in sub-Saharan Africa, as well as Australia and New Zealand.

TABLE 12.1 *The Impact of the Components of Human Empowerment on Different Aspects of Ecological Sustainability.*

PREDICTORS (2005)	DEPENDENT VARIABLES (2010)								
	Environmental Impact[a]			Environmental Quality[b]			Ecological Sustainability[c]		
Technological Advancement	0.37 (6.22)***		0.39 (3.30)***	0.21 (3.10)***		0.34 (5.83)***	−0.46 (−2.87)**		−0.23 (−1.66)†
Emancipative Values		0.18 (1.46)†	0.61 (3.95)***		0.31 (2.20)**	0.83 (5.94)***		1.00 (2.99)***	0.33 (0.94)†
Civic Entitlements		0.09 (1.49)†	0.07 (2.07)*		0.07 (1.37)†	0.01 (0.31)†		−0.04 (−0.79)†	0.17 (1.60)†
Constant	−0.08 (−2.21)**	−0.09 (1.83)*	−0.04 (−1.98)*	0.36 (9.40)***	0.29 (6.61)***	0.43 (15.3)***	0.25 (2.80)**	0.29 (2.69)**	0.48 (7.16)***
Adjusted R^2	0.80		0.64	0.62	0.58	0.55	0.14	0.00	0.02
N	48		48	52	51	50	48	48	47

Evidence limited to World Values Surveys (WVS) round five. Test statistics of heteroskedasticity (White test), multicollinearity (variance inflation factors), and influential cases (DFFITs) reveal no violation of ordinary least squares (OLS) assumptions. Significance levels:

$p < .050$; $^{**}p < .010$; $^{***}p < .001$; † not significant ($p > 1.0$)

[a] Ecological Footprint in global hectares per capita, standardized into a theoretical range from 0 to 1.0 (Global Footprint Network 2012).

[b] Environmental Performance Index, standardized into a theoretical range from 0 to 1.0 (Yale Center for Environmental Law and Policy 2012).

[c] Ratio of Biocapacity/per capita to Ecological Footprint/per capita (in global hectares per capita), logged and standardized into a theoretical range from 0 to 1.0.

For the environmental indicators, I use the latest available measures, which are from 2010. Hence, the environmental indicators are measured after human empowerment, following the assumption that the association between environmental indicators and human empowerment reflects the impact of human empowerment on the environment. Since environmental data are not available in sufficient time series, no longitudinal models can be estimated.

Given these limitations, Table 12.1 reveals some interesting results. Let us consider first the determination of the societies' environmental impact. Among the three components of human empowerment, one would expect that the one with the most direct material implications has the most powerful environmental impact. The reason is that the human impact on the environment originates in the exploitation, consumption, and processing of materials. Among the three components of human empowerment, technological advancement most directly affects the material basis of human existence because technologies involve extensive processing of materials. Indeed, Table 12.1 shows that technological advancement enhances a society's environmental impact more than the other two components of human empowerment. In fact, neither of the other two components is significant under control of technological advancement. In total, human empowerment explains 80 percent of the cross-national variation in a society's environmental impact and the technology component of human empowerment alone is responsible for this impact.

Figure 12.1 illustrates the environmental impact of technological advancement. It is obvious that the impact is not constant over all levels of technological advancement but increases with the level of technological advancement. Hence, a quadratic function provides a better fit to the data, explaining fully 85 percent of the cross-national variation in the societies' environmental impact. From this evidence, it seems clear that technological advancement proceeds with steeply increasing ecological damage.

In light of these findings, it is tempting to conclude that human empowerment has negative consequences for global ecological sustainability and that the origin of the problem lies indeed in the source component of human empowerment: technological advancement. Isn't then the best contribution to global ecological sustainability to stop our investment in better technologies?

The answer would seem to be affirmative – until we take an alternative perspective and consider how human empowerment affects a society's environmental quality. This is shown in the middle panel of Table 12.1. As we can see from the signs of the coefficients, human empowerment affects a society's environmental quality in a positive way: environmental quality improves with progress in human empowerment. Looking at the components of human empowerment, technological advancement now shows a positive effect on a society's environmental quality. Most likely, this reflects that, at higher levels of technological advancement, more effort is invested in "smart" technologies that reduce emissions, waste, and other damaging consequences. But this assumes a motivational force that redirects investments into "greener"

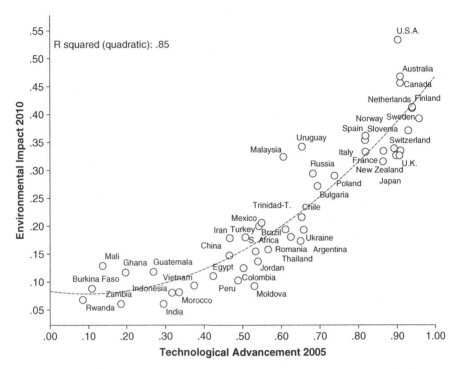

FIGURE 12.1 The Effect of Technological Advancement on a Society's Environmental Impact.
Data Coverage: All of the fifty societies with valid data surveyed in round five of the World Values Surveys (WVS).

technologies. And the results of Table 12.1 indeed point to such a motivational force: emancipative values. We achieve the best model fit by including emancipative values, and they associate with the steepest increase in environmental quality among the three components of human empowerment: controlling for civic entitlements, a 1-unit increase in emancipative values comes with a 0.83-unit increase in a society's environmental quality; controlling for technological advancement, a 1-unit increase in emancipative values associates with a 0.31-unit increase in environmental quality (compared to a 0.21-unit increase for a 1-unit increase in technological advancement).

Figure 12.2 illustrates the effect of emancipative values on a society's environmental quality: merely by themselves, emancipative values explain 58 percent of the cross-national differences in environmental quality.

Paradoxical as it may seem, different aspects of human empowerment affect ecological sustainability in opposite ways. Indeed, at the same time as technological advancement deepens a society's ecological footprint, emancipative values improve its environmental quality.

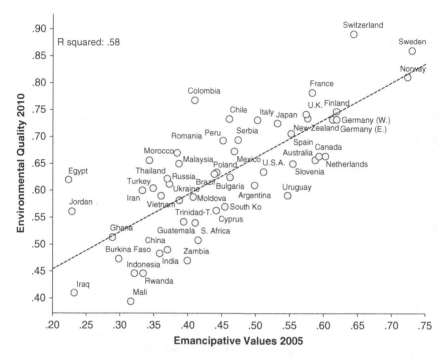

FIGURE 12.2 The Effect of Emancipative Values on a Society's Environmental Quality. *Data Coverage*: All of the fifty societies with valid data surveyed in round five of the World Values Surveys (WVS).

Together, these findings suggest that the overall effect of human empowerment on global ecological sustainability is neutral: the negative effect of technological advancement is counterbalanced by a positive effect of emancipative values (civic entitlements have no effect in either direction). By and large, the right-hand panel in Table 12.1 confirms this expectation. The explained variance in ecological sustainability is zero in two of the models. Hence, we cannot conclude that human empowerment deteriorates global ecological sustainability. The first model in the right-hand panel actually points slightly in the opposite direction. This is the only model explaining at least some variation in global ecological sustainability, and it demonstrates the simultaneity of the negative effect of technological advancement and the positive effect of emancipative values: when both technological advancement and emancipative values are included as predictors of ecological sustainability, technological advancement shows a significantly negative effect whereas emancipative values show a significantly positive effect. Importantly, however, the positive effect of emancipative values slightly outweighs the negative effect of technological advancement. As a consequence, the net effect on ecological sustainability is slightly positive.

It is worthwhile to look more closely at the numbers in the first model that explains ecological sustainability in Table 12.1. An important property is the fact that a score of 0.50 in the ecological sustainability marks the threshold separating unsustainability (below 0.50) from sustainability (above 0.50). Hence, the world must aim at a score of 0.50 or above. Now, the constant in ecological sustainability is 0.25. From this, we subtract approximately a 0.45 fraction of the score in technological advancement. Both the median and the mean in technological advancement are at about 0.60 scale points, so for the most common case we subtract 0.45 * 0.60 = 0.27 scale points from the constant of 0.25. Rounding up, this gets us to a score of zero in ecological sustainability. Yet, to this we add a 1.0 fraction of the observed score in emancipative values, which is identical to the observed score itself. Thus, we need a level of emancipative values of at least 0.50 scale points to compensate for the negative effect of technological advancement on ecological sustainability. At a level of technological advancement of 0.60 scale points, societies with a score of 0.50 or more in emancipative values indeed exist. Argentina and Uruguay are two examples. This suggests that the continuation of the human empowerment process becomes ecologically sustainable precisely through the rise of emancipative values.

Figure 12.3 visualizes the neutral overall effect of the human empowerment process on global ecological sustainability. To do so, we summarize the three components of human empowerment into an overall index by calculating the average of the three components.[2] The regression line is perfectly flat. As human empowerment progresses, we find as many societies above the regression line as we find below; thus, progress in human empowerment leaves us with no reliable prediction of a society's ecological sustainability. The fact, however, that the regression line runs 0.07 scale points below the sustainability threshold tells us that the world is currently in an unsustainable condition. This conclusion is reinforced if we weight the societies in Figure 12.3 for the size of their populations: the regression line then drops further below the sustainability threshold because most societies with large populations (China, India, the United States, Japan, Germany, etc.) are below the sustainability threshold.

A clear division between "ecological debtor" societies (those below the sustainability threshold) and "ecological creditor" societies (those above the sustainability threshold) lies in the fact that creditors have higher biocapacity. This is because of vast areas of thinly populated territory. Canada, Brazil, Russia, and Australia are examples. Debtors, by contrast, are societies whose entire territory is densely populated. Japan and the Netherlands are the prime examples. The fact that we find both creditors and debtors at advanced levels of human empowerment illustrates that the idea of trading ecological credits is reasonable.

At any rate, the regression line in Figure 12.3 is at least not dauntingly below the sustainability threshold (even when factoring in population size). This suggests

---

[2] A factor analysis gives no indication that differential weights would be justified: all three components have a factor loading of 0.91 on the single underlying factor.

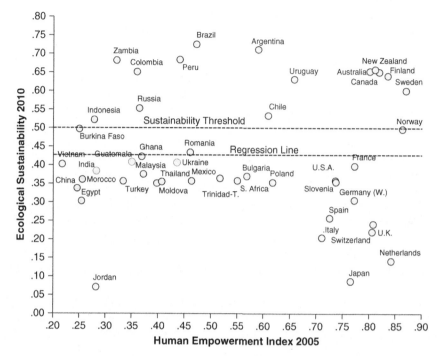

FIGURE 12.3 The Effect of Human Empowerment on a Society's Ecological Sustainability.
Data Coverage: All of the fifty societies with valid data surveyed in round five of the World Values Surveys (WVS).

that sustainability is an achievable goal. In order to achieve it, it makes sense to focus on the most positive ecological force in the human empowerment process: emancipative values.

3.2 Environmental Activism

We have to make sure that the positive ecological effect of emancipative values is not a methodological artifact of using aggregated data. Hence, we shall identify the micromechanism by which emancipative values become ecologically relevant. I hypothesize that emancipative values do indeed become ecologically relevant, but not because they increase people's environmental concern. Instead, emancipative values become ecologically relevant because they ease the *translation* of environmental concern into environmental activism. If this is true, it underlines from another angle that emancipative values procreate social capital.

To test this hypothesis, I build on the model of environmental activism introduced by Rohrschneider, Miles, and Peffley (2013), using similar variables. What differs is that I use the index of emancipative values instead of the narrower concept of postmaterialism. In addition, I introduce emancipative values at the societal level, not only at the individual level. There are good reasons to assume that values affect other social characteristics, not only by their individual preference but also by their societal prevalence. As we have seen throughout this book, there is ample evidence for this assumption. In fact, the general pattern is such that emancipative values affect other phenomena more by the socially shared emphasis than by the individually unique emphases on emancipatory goals. I assume that this is also the case for environmental activism. To isolate the individually unique emphases on emancipative values from the socially shared emphasis, individual-level variation in emancipative values is country-mean centered, measuring each respondent's deviation from the mean emphasis on these values within his or her society.[3]

Table 12.2 shows the results of the multilevel model. The societal-level components of the analysis illustrate that, among the three components of human empowerment, only the prevalence of emancipative values affects environmental activism. The effect is highly significant and positive: a 1-unit increase in the prevalence of emancipative values associates with a 0.36-unit increase in environmental activism. Note that this effect exists fully independent of the individuals' own preference for emancipative values: the prevalence of emancipative values elevates a person's environmental activism above the level that *his or her own* preference for these values suggests. Controlling for emancipative values, neither the prevalence of environmental concerns in a society nor the environmental quality affect environmental activism. The first model in Table 12.2 explains 53 percent of the between-societal variance in environmental activism, and the prevalence of emancipative values alone is responsible for this explanation.

At the individual level, people's formal education, their environmental concerns, and their preference for emancipative values show the expected positive effects on environmental activism, with emancipative values showing the strongest effect: a 1-unit increase in a person's preference for emancipative values enhances this person's environmental activism by a 0.25 unit. This compares to a 0.13-unit increase and a 0.18-unit increase for a 1-unit increase in a person's formal education and environmental concerns. Since the 0.25-unit contribution by individual preferences for emancipative values is less than the 0.39-unit contribution by these values' social prevalence, it is safe to conclude that environmental activism is more strongly encouraged by the socially shared emphasis than by the individually unique emphases on emancipatory goals. Yet, the effect is positive for both the socially shared and the individually unique emphases and even mutually reinforcing. The latter is obvious from the positive interaction between individual preferences for emancipative values and their social prevalence.

Interestingly, individual preferences for emancipative values not only interact with their social prevalence; they also interact with the environmental quality.

---

[3] Centering individual-level variables on country means is equivalent to a country-fixed effects model. These models reduce the problem of omitted variable bias.

TABLE 12.2 *The Effects of Emancipative Values on Environmental Activism (multilevel models).*

	DEPENDENT VARIABLE: Environmental Activism		
PREDICTORS	**Values-Model**	**Technology-Model**	**Institutions-Model**
• Constant	0.20 (17.44)***	0.20 (14.38)***	0.20 (15.03)***
Societal-level Effects:			
• EV^a-Prevalence	0.39 (3.54)***		
• Technological Advancement		0.03 (0.33)†	
• Civic Entitlements			0.04 (0.86)†
• Average "Green" Concern	0.08 (0.88)†	0.08 (0.68)†	0.06 (0.57)†
• Environmental Quality	0.08 (0.61)†	0.20(1.13)†	0.22(1.86)*
Individual-level Effects:			
• Female Sex	-0.02 (-5.68)***	-0.02 (-5.68)***	-0.02 (-5.70)***
• Birth Year (indexed)	0.05 (3.20)***	0.05 (3.25)***	0.05 (3.21)***
• Formal Education	0.13 (11.74)***	0.14 (11.80)***	0.14 (11.76)***
• Economic Egalitarianism	0.01 (1.06)†	0.01 (1.10)†	0.01 (1.08)†
Cross-level Interactions:			
• Personal "Green" Concern	0.18 (10.61)***	0.18 (10.30)***	0.18 (9.84)***
* EV^a-Prevalence	0.69 (3.32)***		
* Technological Advancement		0.37 (2.50)**	
* Civic Entitlements			0.12 (1.55)†
* Average "Green" Concern	0.03 (0.16)†	0.07 (0.46)†	0.03 (1.50)†
* Environmental Quality	0.15 (0.70)†	-0.15 (-0.51)†	0.35 (2.12)**
• EV^a-Preference	0.25 (13.51)***	0.25 (13.31)***	0.25 (13.58)***
* EV^a-Prevalence	0.58 (2.49)**		
* Technological Advancement		0.28 (1.78)*	
* Civic Entitlements			0.15 (1.63)†
* Average "Green" Concern	0.52 (2.76)**	0.56 (2.52)**	0.45 (1.77)*
* Environmental Quality	0.79 (3.54)***	0.57 (1.86)*	0.91 (4.71)***

Percent Error Reduction:

Within-societal Variation in DV	14.2%	14.2%	14.2%
Between-societal Variation in DV	52.9%	28.6%	34.7%
Variation in Awareness Effect	66.4%	65.4%	65.5%
Variation in Value Effect	46.9%	44.8%	34.3%
N (number of observations)	42,505 respondents in 40 societies		

Entries are unstandardized regression coefficients with T ratios in parentheses based on robust standard errors. Calculations with HLM 6.08. Respondents weighted to obtain equal sample size for each society (without changing the overall N). Individual-level variables are country-mean centered; societal-level variables are global-mean centered. All individual-level effects specified as random. Percent error reduction calculated relative to empty model. Significance levels:

$^{†} p \geq .100, \ ^{*} p < .100, \ ^{**} p < .050, \ ^{***} p < .005.$

Replacing the emancipative values index with the voice index at both levels of analysis, the error reduction in the between-societal variation of the DV is 20.8 percent, that in the within-societal variation 12.6 percent, 41.8 percent in the awareness effect, and 46.1 percent in the values effect.

Source: World Values Surveys (WVS), round five (ca. 2005).

^{a} EV – Emancipative Values

This interaction is positive as well: individual preferences for emancipative values encourage more environmental activism when the environmental quality increases. Of course, this effect makes sense only if we interpret its underlying causality inversely: environmental quality improves as a consequence of the environmental activism that emancipative preferences induce.

One of the most interesting findings in Table 12.2 is the strong positive interaction between people's environmental concerns and the social prevalence of emancipative values. This interaction evidences that people's environmental concerns translate more easily into environmental activism if emancipative values are more prevalent. How pronounced this interaction really is can be seen from Figure 12.4.

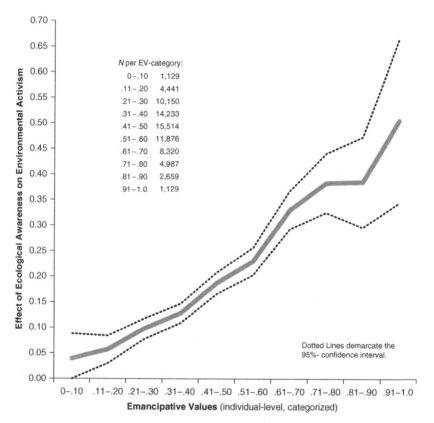

FIGURE 12.4 Emancipative Values as an Amplifier of the Impact of Ecological Awareness on Environmental Activism.
Vertical axis shows the magnitude of the unstandardized regression coefficient of ecological awareness on environmental activism. *Data Coverage*: Respondents with valid data from all of the fifty societies surveyed in World Values Surveys (WVS) round five. National samples are weighted to equal size ($N = 1,000$ per sample).

The horizontal axis in Figure 12.4 divides the individual respondents of WVS round five into the ten ascending categories of emancipative values introduced in Chapter 2. The vertical axis shows how strongly people's environmental concerns affect their environmental activism, displaying the sign and magnitude of the unstandardized regression coefficient. As is obvious, the magnitude of the coefficient increases monotonically and steeply from an insignificant $b = 0.05$ among people in the lowest category of emancipative values, to a highly significant $b = 0.50$ among people in the highest category of emancipative values.

KEY POINTS

On the time scale of history, societies entered the path of accelerating human empowerment late. Ever since, the human empowerment process is a success model. Not only do people-powered societies generate more well-being; they also outcompete other societies in terms of their system capacity. They dominate the global order for these reasons.

But the very success of human empowerment seems to erode its own sustainability through environmental damage. And, indeed, the source component of human empowerment – technological advancement – shows a negative environmental impact, as indicated by the ecological footprint.

Ironically, though, human empowerment holds in itself the key to mastering the sustainability challenge. Inspired by rising emancipative values, people-powered societies shift priorities to life quality issues, and these issues include living in an intact natural environment. Hence, the prevalence of emancipative values in a society is a strong and reliable predictor of its environmental quality: when these values are more prevalent, the quality of the environment tends to be better.

Looking at the micromechanism that explains the positive effect of emancipative values on a society's environmental quality, I find that environmental concern is *not* the mechanism. People who prefer emancipative values more strongly do not necessarily have stronger environmental concerns. The reason is that people often express environmental concern because of their direct exposure to environmental degradation, irrespective of whether they prefer emancipative values or not. Yet, emancipative values ease the translation of environmental concerns into environmental action: the more prevalent emancipative values are in a society, the easier are the individuals' environmental concerns mobilized into environmental action. These findings underscore the mobilizing and activating impulse of emancipative values, underlining their relevance as a social capital-building, civic force – with one additional qualification: it is a green force.

The good news is that the positive effect of emancipative values outweighs the negative effect of technological advancement. This leads to an interesting paradox: despite the fact that emancipative values feed themselves from an ecologically damaging process, these values' positive ecological effect outweighs their source's negative effect. As emancipative values continue to increase, a sustainable future becomes more likely.

Conclusion

> Every human has four endowments – self awareness, conscience, independent will and creative imagination. These give us the ultimate human freedom. . . . The power to choose, to respond, to change.
>
> – Stephen Covey

The first section of this Conclusion summarizes the major insights of this book. Figure C.1 provides a synopsis. In the second section, I outline how these insights account for seven of the most fundamental facts about democracy. Section 3 discusses the links of the human empowerment framework to some related concepts of major importance, including existential security, the human need hierarchy, and social capital. Section 4 asks whether the key set of orientations that emerges with human empowerment – emancipative values – improves the moral stature of our species. The final section provides a condensed restatement of the theory of emancipation.

1. KEY INSIGHTS

We have seen massive evidence for a multitude of trends toward human empowerment. Every bit and piece of this evidence makes sense within a single theory: the evolutionary theory of emancipation. This theory locates the source of the empowerment trend in the human desire for emancipation, that is, a life free from external domination. The theory explains the origin of this desire and outlines when it grows strong and when not.

The root premise of the theory of emancipation is evolutionary: all existence is under a permanent reality check. Nothing that lives – including societies and their culture – escapes selection for better reality-coping qualities. About 150,000 years ago, selection resulted in human intelligence. Intelligence has been selected because of its reality-coping qualities. These reside in the power of imagination. Imagination is an inherently emancipatory feature because it

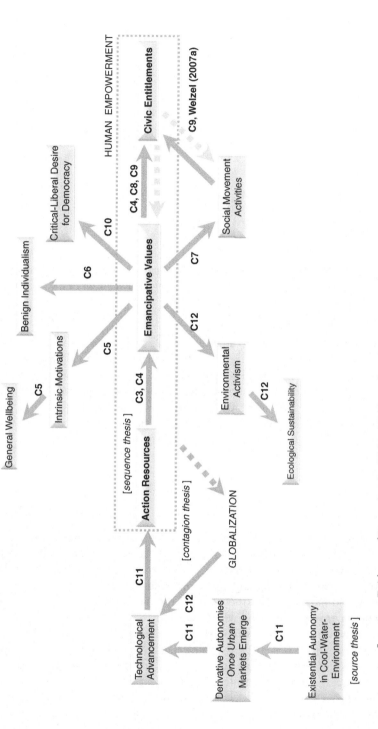

FIGURE C.1 Summary Evidence of Emancipative Values' Role in the Human Empowerment Process.
The letter 'C' and its respective number indicate in which chapter of this book the evidence for the effect depicted by an arrow is provided. The *evolutionary theory of emancipation* consists of the *source thesis*, the *sequence thesis*, and the *contagion thesis*, each of which derives from a single root principle: the *utility ladder of freedoms*.

bestows agency on humans: it allows them to reflect on constraints on their existence and to plan strategies to overcome them. With agency comes an inner drive to free human existence from external constraints. But to sustain its reality-coping quality, the quest for freedom adapts flexibly to the severity of the constraints themselves.

To keep the quest for freedom adaptive, the human mind processes four coping mechanisms. Three of the four mechanisms are ordered sequentially. The fourth operates on each of the first three, transforming the selfish pursuit of one's own utilities into the cooperative pursuit of joint utilities. This makes the adjustment sequence a collective one through which people pass together, in unison with members of their reference groups. Reference groups in turn are not isolated but embedded in larger populations. Hence, people move with the stream of entire societies through the sequence.

The first mechanism, valuation, means that people value the freedoms that they are capable of exercising based on the action resources available to them. The second mechanism, activation, means that people take action for the freedoms they value. The third mechanism, satisfaction, means that people obtain satisfaction from taking action in pursuit of their valued freedoms. Satisfaction feeds back to the first mechanism, reinforcing the valuation of freedoms from which the sequence starts. The fourth mechanism, solidarity, operates on each of the other three: it generalizes the freedoms that people value for themselves to all others whom they perceive as equals. How far solidarity reaches depends on how widely similar action resources disperse. Solidarity's reach is short if there are narrow group monopolies on action resources. Solidarity's reach is far when there are no impermeable group boundaries in the disposition of action resources.

The adjustment sequence stabilizes societies in two contradictory cycles, each of which is self sustaining until mutual confrontation. I call these cycles the *vicious cycle* and the *virtuous cycle*.

The vicious cycle is rooted in a situation in which most people lack the capability to exercise freedoms because their action resources are chronically deficient. The clearest case of this is when most people are poor, illiterate, and isolated in local groups – the default case throughout most of our history. In this situation, hardly anyone sees value in universal freedoms because hardly anyone is able to make much use of such freedoms – even if they were guaranteed by law. Accordingly, emancipative values remain dormant, and people abstain from taking action in pursuit of freedoms. In other words, power holders are under no pressure to guarantee freedoms, so, indeed, it does not cross their mind to grant them. As a result, ordinary people suffer from the absence of all three elements of human empowerment: they lack the resources that would enable them to exercise freedoms, they lack the values that would inspire them to exercise freedoms, and they lack the entitlements that would allow them to exercise freedoms. People in such a society are entrapped in disempowerment.

The same logic operates in the opposite direction in situations in which many people control significant action resources, including material means, intellectual skills, and connective opportunities. Technologically advanced societies represent this condition most clearly. Most people in these societies have a high living standard, are well educated, and can easily connect to like-minded others, irrespective of locality. In these situations, and in the many societies approaching these conditions, people recognize the use of universal freedoms and value them accordingly: emancipative values emerge. Inspired by emancipative values, people take action on behalf of freedoms. This is evident in all kinds of social movement activity, the most vigorous of which voice emancipatory goals: people-power movements, equal opportunity movements, civil rights movements, women's rights movements, gay rights movements, children's rights movements, and so forth. Confronted with people who are capable and motivated to stand up together for their freedoms, the denial and betrayal of freedoms become unsustainable options for rulers. At some point, they guarantee freedoms and begin to adhere to these guarantees in practice. As a consequence, ordinary people benefit from the presence of all three elements of human empowerment: action resources, emancipative values, and civic entitlements. This is a virtuous cycle that describes thriving societies.

The sequence thesis suggests that, if freedoms grow, they do so along a sequence from objective utilities to subjective valuations to legal guarantees. Accordingly, action resources constitute the founding element, emancipative values the linking element, and civic entitlements the completing element of human empowerment. Institutions that guarantee universal freedoms are the product, not the cause, of this process. This must be emphasized against the mantra in development economics that propagates institutions as the cause of everything.[1] Applying a dynamic shift model and a temporal order model, Chapters 4 and 9 have confirmed this sequential ordering in the growth of freedoms.

Because the vicious cycle of human disempowerment is self-sustaining, societies in this cycle can be very stable. This explains why oppression could prevail throughout most of "civilized" history and why ordinary people rarely stood up to throw off the yoke of tyranny. But, on confrontation with societies in the virtuous cycle, disempowering societies become unstable. Until recently, this was not obvious. It took a long time for civilization to mature in habitats whose natural conditions favor the initiation of the human empowerment cycle (see Chapter 11). This did not happen before the maturation of urban civilization in what I call *cool-water areas* (CW areas) in the early modern era. Since then, empowering societies dominate over disempowering societies and destabilize them. Empowering societies mobilize people's intellectual creativity on a much larger scale than do disempowering societies. Intellectual mobilization nurtures

---

[1] A case in point is the chapter in Acemoglu and Robinson's (2012) recent book titled *Institutions, Institutions, Institutions*. As a side note, their definition of institutions includes informal institutions, which makes the notion so broad that it incorporates culture. Accordingly, the claim that institutions but not culture explain development is self-defeating.

the empowering societies' technological advancement – the basis of their superior system capacities and, hence, global dominance. On confrontation with empowering societies, people in disempowering societies become aware of their dismal condition and begin to question its inescapability and justification. Hence, disempowering societies become unstable. They are on retreat, as the worldwide expansion of democracy and the global rights revolution indicate (see Chapters 8 and 9).

The reason why the human empowerment process started in CW areas resides in the fact that these areas harbor two natural forms of existential security and existential autonomy: disease security and water autonomy (Chapter 11). Higher disease security means a lower incidence of communicable diseases. Higher water autonomy means easy, equal, and permanent access to water resources. The source thesis suggests that higher disease security and water autonomy in the CW areas bestow a higher initial utility on freedoms in these areas. This has led to two paradoxical effects.

First, since foraging is a freer lifestyle than agriculture, the transition to agriculture was delayed in CW areas. Another reason for the delay is the peripheral location of the CW areas to the early centers of agriculture and urbanization in the Middle East and India: because of this, the diffusion of civilization reached the CW areas later (Chapter 11). At any rate, societies in the CW areas were late developers: urban markets emerged much later than in the Oriental civilizations, and technological advancement lagged behind. In fact, it lagged behind for millennia, throughout the entire Malthusian era preceding the rise of preindustrial capitalism and the Industrial Revolution.

Second, once urban markets emerged, they became more vibrant in CW areas because water autonomy creates derivative autonomies as soon as markets are in place. These derivative autonomies bestow further utility on freedoms, which now becomes an accelerator of technological advancement. With autonomy in market access, ordinary people have an incentive to avoid a quantity-breeding strategy and instead follow a quality-building strategy: people sacrifice demographic productivity for economic productivity. This creates a limited but valuable workforce. Rising labor demands in urban centers have, thus, to be met by technologies that save costly labor. The result is accelerated technological advancement on a mass scale.

As a result of technological advancement, action resources become available for wider segments of the population. More widespread action resources further increase the utility of freedoms. In recognition of this, people adopt emancipative values. Inspired by emancipative values, people make claims for civic entitlements and take action on their behalf if rulers deny guarantees. At some point, civic entitlements are guaranteed, completing an initial cycle of human empowerment. Unless disrupted by exogenous shocks, the cycle can continue to spiral upward, creating more action resources, stronger emancipative values, and wider civic entitlements. There is no preset limit to human empowerment because, no matter how much we improve, the world will always be imperfect.

The linkages in the human empowerment cycle operate more strongly over its socially shared components than the individually unique components. This cannot be emphasized enough. Looking at a person's action resources, it is the part she has in common with most other people in her society, rather than what she has on top of others, that strengthens her emancipative values (Chapter 3). Likewise, it is the part of her emancipative values she shares with most people that encourages her to join forces with others and take action for emancipatory goals (Chapter 7). Hence, the human empowerment cycle feeds itself from socially shared utilities far more strongly than from individually unique utilities. It is altogether a cooperative process whose benefits are reciprocal.

The human empowerment cycle started first in the CW areas of Western Europe, it was emulated by the CW area of Japan, and it was transplanted by European settlement to the CW areas outside Eurasia: North America, Australia, and New Zealand. Hence, human empowerment is far advanced in all of the world's CW areas.

However, in the era of globalization, the human empowerment process begins to dissociate from the advantageous CW condition. It diffuses elsewhere and begins to globalize. The worldwide flow of communication contributes to this diffusion because it allows for cross-border learning on an unprecedented scale (Chapter 11).

Human empowerment poses a sustainability challenge because its founding element – action resources – derive from an ecologically damaging process: technological advancement. Paradoxically as it may seem, however, the human empowerment process incorporates the solution to its own problems. In giving rise to emancipative values, human empowerment nurtures environmental activism and hence redirects societies toward sustainable "green" technologies. Above a certain threshold, the positive ecological effect of emancipative values outweighs the negative ecological effect of their source: the sustainability challenge is manageable (Chapter 12).

Human empowerment is driven by the emancipatory quest for universal freedoms. At each new level, yet another hindrance to the shared practice of freedoms can become the target of this quest – the true source of most of the social movement activity of today and in the past. Thus, there is no inherent limit at which the emancipatory drive must stop. With each achieved goal, the quest for further emancipation can be extended to another injustice. And injustice will continue to exist.

2. DEMOCRACY REVISITED

Evolution has instilled in the human mind an adaptive quest for freedom – a quest that hibernates under existential pressures but awakens with widening existential opportunities. The adaptivity of the human quest for freedom explains, within a single framework, some of the most significant features of democracy and its history, including:

1. why people desire democracy and why this desire is not a constant but varies;
2. why mass preferences for democracy often coexist with deficient and absent democracy;
3. why democracy emerged late in history but has been remarkably successful ever since;
4. why mass upheavals in history and even today often have no democratic impetus;
5. why mass upheavals with a democratic impetus are difficult to start but difficult to resist once they begin;
6. why rulers are sometimes still able to deny democracy or to deprive it of its substance; and
7. why the desire for democracy emerges in the absence of democracy but continues to flourish under its presence.

Let me outline these points in more detail.

1. Why people desire democracy and why this desire is not a constant but varies. An influential school of thought argues that the desire for democracy is rooted in an interest in redistribution among the low-income segments of a population (Boix 2003; Acemoglu & Robinson 2006). But, even though an entire theory building rests on this assumption, not a single piece of evidence supports it. On the contrary, as Chapter 10 has shown, in no society of the world do people understand democracy primarily as a means of redistribution. Instead, most people around the globe understand democracy in terms of its universal freedoms. What is more, freedoms are in every society more highly valued by economically prosperous people who command action resources, especially if these population segments are sizeable and connected through wide inroads with the general population. The economically deprived, by contrast, often value authoritarianism over freedoms. This evidence conforms to the sequence thesis of emancipation theory: people value freedoms more when widespread action resources increase their joint utility from freedoms. And because the dispersion of action resources varies greatly between societies, how strongly the people value freedoms also varies greatly. Differences in emancipative values are indicative of this variation.

2. Why mass preferences for democracy often coexist with deficient or absent democracy. Mass preferences for democracy are widespread across the globe. But these preferences account for very little variation in the societies' degree of democratization. Indeed, mass preferences for democracy often coexist with deficient or absent democracy. Yet, wherever this is the case these preferences lack grounding in emancipative values. Preferences for democracy that are detached from emancipative values are largely irrelevant for systemic democracy because ungrounded preferences do not motivate people to take action for the freedoms that define democracy. What matters is not the preference for democracy but the values that motivate that preference.

3. *Why democracy emerged late in history but has been successful ever since.* Throughout most of history, ordinary people lived in miserable conditions. Before the modern era, common people were everywhere poor, illiterate, and isolated in small communities. Deprived of action resources, ordinary people lack the capability and motivation to challenge powerholders. Since this was the prevailing condition over most of history, freedoms were mostly absent.

Although late, modernity changed this condition profoundly. Starting with preindustrial capitalism in the fifteenth century, history begins to turn from a story of unchallenged despotism into story of freedom movements: ever since, group after group and society after society struggles for the guarantee of freedoms. Where the struggles succeed, a twofold success follows. For one, free societies mobilize their people's intellectual creativity to the fullest extent; hence, they outperform unfree societies in technological advancement and other achievements that elevate a society's system capacities. Next, free societies allow their people to pursue their well-being in their own and mutually agreed ways; this contributes to enhanced general well-being. Arguably, societies that generate more well-being among their people are more widely supported. Competing for legitimacy with unfree societies, this is a crucial advantage.

4. *Why mass upheavals in history and even today often have no democratic impetus.* The history of states is pierced with examples in which the unentitled rebel against tyranny. But only a small proportion of these upheavals focused their claims on freedoms. More often, rebellions were food riots or other outbreaks of collective frustration without an emancipatory program. More often than not, they ended in suppression or disorder. The most frequent result of these types of unrest is the reinstallation of tyranny, whether old or new. Modern examples of this type of rebellion include the communist revolutions in Russia, China, Cuba, and Vietnam and the Islamic Revolution in Iran. It remains to be seen if the Arab Spring belongs to this class of desperation outbreaks.

A commonality of outbreaks without democratic inspiration is that their basis of mass support consists of impoverished segments of the population. I know of no counterfactual to this regularity. Members of these groups lack significant action resources. Since freedoms have little utility for people with deficient action resources, guarantees of freedoms have little appeal. Consequently, a systemic change to a democratic system that guarantees freedoms is an unlikely outcome of desperation outbreaks.

Regardless of whether mass upheavals do or do not have a democratic impulse, the leadership is usually recruited from the "intelligentsia": the highly educated stratum of the population. The reason is obvious. Members of the intelligentsia concentrate the skills needed to phrase credible blames and plausible solutions and to organize a campaign. But the condition of the intelligentsia differs markedly between upheavals with a democratic impulse and those without it. If a society's intelligentsia does not represent a sizeable population segment with broad inroads from the wider society but instead constitutes a small isolated circle, its members are likely to establish themselves as a new dictatorial class – like Lenin's "professional revolutionaries." This is a utility distribution question: if intellectual resources are highly concentrated among a small group, the utility of this group is to establish a *monopoly* on freedoms. This results in a new form of dictatorial rule, not democracy.

If, by contrast, the intellectual leaders of a mass protest represent a large social segment with wide inroads from the population, intellectual skill as an action resource loses its social distinctiveness and the joint utility of freedoms extends into the population. It thus becomes pointless to establish a group monopoly on freedoms. Instead, universal entitlements to freedoms are claimed. In this case, the mass upheaval obtains a democratic inspiration.

5. Why mass upheavals with a democratic impetus are difficult to start but difficult to stop once they begin. Mass upheavals with a democratic impulse are rare in history. They are almost nonexistent before the onset of preindustrial capitalism. I am aware of only two examples of upheavals with a democratic impulse during the long pre-industrial period. In both cases, the rebels were freeholders who had bargaining power because they served in the army and could boycott military campaigns: the *hoplites* in ancient Athens and the *plebeians* in ancient Rome (Finer 1999).[2] For both groups, the boycotts were successful and resulted in their enfranchisement: they obtained the freedom to vote.

Beginning with preindustrial capitalism, upheavals with a democratic impulse become more frequent. The initial events were the liberal revolutions of the seventeenth, eighteenth, and nineteenth centuries in the Netherlands, England, North America, and France. Even though these events extended suffrage and other freedoms only to certain qualified groups, these entitlements encouraged the extant excluded groups, such as women and the working class, to fight for the same freedoms. Since then, mass pressures have become an increasingly frequent factor of democratization. As a consequence, liberal democracy has evolved through several waves of rights extensions, and it has been diffusing in waves throughout the global state system.

The beginning of mass-pressured democratization coincides with a profound transformation of populations. Beginning with preindustrial capitalism, continuing with industrialization, and accelerating with the rise of postindustrial knowledge societies, modernization has transformed impoverished, illiterate, and secluded subjects into equipped, skilled, and connected actors with both the capability and the motivation to pursue shared values, including freedoms.

Initiating a mass upheaval with a claim for freedoms is difficult because it needs many people with abundant action resources who are united by a strong emancipatory inspiration: only then are many people capable and motivated to join a freedom campaign. This is a rather demanding condition. Yet, whenever the masses join a freedom campaign, it is likely to be successful precisely because these conditions are met. Then, the popular claim for freedoms carries the

---

[2] In Rome, this happened between 494 and 287 BCE and in Athens around 410 BCE.

power of solidarity and is difficult to resist. Even repressive regimes with rulers determined to stay in power had to get out of the way once confronted with swelling nationwide protests.

6. *Why rulers are sometimes still able to deny democracy or to deprive it of its substance.* In societies in which most people lack action resources and are uninspired by emancipative values, mass pressures for universal freedoms won't emerge and persist. In this case, elites are shielded from domestic pressures to democratize. Then, democratizing pressures can only come from outside. Yet, for outside pressures to be effective, a society's elites must depend on foreign aid or must be susceptible to international influences. But, even then, the absence of domestic pressures allows elites to get their way. They might concede a constitution that guarantees freedoms, but, in the absence of domestic pressures, it is easy for elites to disrespect these guarantees in practice, which leads to corrupted democracy.

To prevent elites from corrupting democracy, preinstitutional sources of power must be widespread among the people. Preinstitutional sources of people power involve, again, action resources and emancipative values. They are sources of people power because they enable and motivate people to take action in pursuit of jointly valued freedoms. These sources of power are preinstitutional because resources and values reside in preinstitutional domains of social reality: existential conditions in the case of resources and psychological orientations in the case of values. Only if these preinstitutional sources of power are in place is there a constant source of social pressures to keep the elites' self-interest in check. In today's mature democracies, this is largely the case. As a result, social movements, nongovernmental organizations, and critical media continue to advocate for people's freedoms, including those of specifically disadvantaged groups, such as women, homosexuals, and ethnic minorities.

Freedoms are a cross-fertilization product: their benefits come to fruition through mutual recognition and toleration. Hence, freedoms are not subject to decreasing marginal utility such that their benefits diminish with each additional gain. Quite the contrary, freedoms have increasing marginal returns, and this is the reason why free societies continue to be driven by freedom campaigns.

7. *Why the desire for democracy emerges in the absence of democracy but continues to flourish under its presence.* The sequence thesis suggests that people's valuation of freedoms increases when widespread action resources enhance joint utilities from freedoms. This means that the subjective value of freedoms can rise even in the absence of a guarantee for freedoms. Indeed, as the history of democracy shows, claims for freedoms emerged under the very denial of freedoms. Guarantees of freedoms were not the source of these claims but the response to them. Once freedoms are guaranteed, the subjective value of freedoms persists as long as their objective utility does not erode. This explains why, in mature democracies, advocacy for people's freedoms does not wane but continues and extends to new groups and domains.

3. THE UTILITY LADDER OF FREEDOMS

The theory of emancipation informs a broad and yet coherent framework, centered on the idea of human empowerment. This framework is broad because it addresses each of the three major domains of social reality, looking at (1) existential conditions in the economic domain, (2) psychological orientations in the cultural domain, and (3) institutional regulations in the legal domain. Yet the framework is coherent because it addresses each domain under the same theme: what it contributes to enhance people's power to exercise freedoms. Against this background, an important question to ask is how the human empowerment framework relates to other concepts that have been proven useful. Here, I address three of these: the need hierarchy, existential security, and social capital.

In previous work, Inglehart and Welzel (2005) characterize the emergence of emancipative values as an ascension from the survival level to the thriving level in the *hierarchy of human needs* (Maslow 1988 [1954]). By contrast, this book explains the rise of emancipative values as ascension on the *utility ladder of freedoms*: the more people's lives change from a source of pressures to a source of opportunities, the more instrumental is it to exercise and tolerate freedoms, so as to take advantage of what a more promising life has to offer. Interestingly, ascending in the hierarchy of needs is the same as climbing the utility ladder of freedoms. At the survival level of the needs hierarchy, existential pressures keep the utility of freedoms low: freedoms are not helpful in executing what pressures force one to do. Conversely, at the thriving level of the needs hierarchy, existential opportunities enhance the utility of freedoms: freedoms are crucial to take advantage of what opportunities offer one to choose. However, the utility ladder does not simply rephrase the needs hierarchy. It actually explains why the evolutionary direction in the needs hierarchy is oriented from pressure to opportunity or from survival to thriving, instead of the other way round. The reason is that both natural and cultural selection favor features that enhance control over reality. This point is central because freedoms gain utility precisely with higher levels of reality control. Consequently, the tendency of selection to favor reality-controlling features works *upward* on the utility ladder of freedoms.

This is why natural selection produced intelligence and why cultural selection produced democracy – the two success formulae in biology and society. On different levels, both intelligence and democracy bestow powers. In both instances, these powers reside in the capacity to exercise freedoms.

If we understand intelligence as the capacity to think independently and democracy as the power the cast an independent vote, it is evident that freedom is the link between both. John Dewey (1980 [1860]) and Karl Raimund Popper (1971 [1962]) described the intellect-democracy link most lucidly, pointing out that political freedom requires intellectual freedom and that the freedom to think for oneself cannot be tolerated without the freedom to make people's preferences heard and count in politics. The intellect-democracy link is manifest in the fact that societies with more advanced knowledge are more democratic and that educated people in every society tend to be more democratic in their orientations. Georg Buechner (1958) once condensed this connection saying that "the power of reason and the power of the people are the same." Steven Pinker's (2012) "escalator of reason" expresses a similar idea: as societies become governed less by coercion and more by reason, they become inherently more democratic. Hence, the "escalator of reason" is integrated into the utility ladder of freedoms.

In previous work, Inglehart, myself, and our co-authors emphasized existential security and material resources as the basis from which emancipative values emerge. This is fully compatible with the human empowerment framework, yet this framework goes beyond existential security and material resources. Beyond existential security, it emphasizes existential opportunities; and beyond material resources, it emphasizes action resources. Action resources include material resources, yet they also include intellectual and connective resources. This is an important extension because we have seen that the latter two types of resources have an even larger impact. Similarly, existential opportunities include existential security, yet they also include existential autonomy: to be capable of acting for a valued purpose you need resources; however, these resources need not only to be safe, you also must be autonomous in deciding how to use them. We looked at two primal manifestations of existential security and existential autonomy: disease security and water autonomy. We have seen that both are important in widening existential opportunities. But autonomy has proven even more important than security.

The concept with probably the most astonishing career in the social sciences in recent decades is *social capital*, commonly understood as the trust, norms, and networks that facilitate collective action (Coleman 1990; Putnam 1993, 2000). Now, the perspective of human empowerment allows us to see social capital in a new light. We can distinguish between two versions of social capital: versions that *disempower* people because they chain them to specific groups from which there is no escape, and versions that *empower* people because they make it easy for them to disconnect from unchosen groups and reconnect with the type of people they like. We might call the first version *captivating social capital* and the second version *liberating social capital*.

This distinction allows us to reconsider what has generally been described as the erosion of social capital. Through the lens of human empowerment, we do not see such a general erosion. What we see instead is a *transformation* of captivating into liberating social capital. In fact, this transformation is another way of describing the very essence of the human empowerment process. Because of that, the transformation of social capital is closely linked with rising emancipative values. Strong evidence for this point is shown in Figure C.2.

Social capital is manifest in how people trust and interact. Figure C.2 depicts the transformative force of emancipative values in replacing captivating forms of trust and interaction with liberating ones. The left-hand diagram shows this for trust, the right-hand one for interaction. The erosion of captivating social capital is illustrated for vertical trust and social conformism. Vertical trust is a

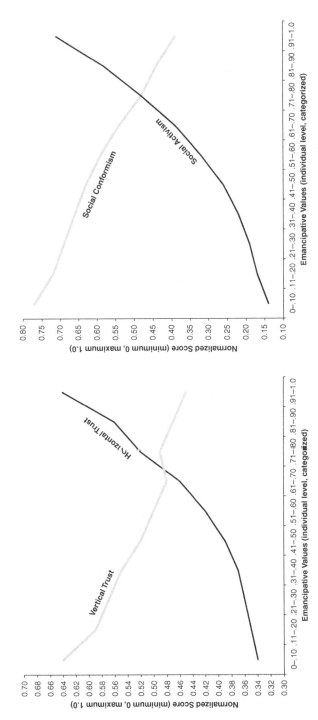

FIGURE C.2 The Transformative Force of Emancipative Values: Replacing Captivating with Liberating Social Capital.
Vertical trust measures the average confidence in three vertical institutions (army, police, courts), which is the inverse of the skepticism index described in Chapter 2. Horizontal trust is the average confidence in three out-groups (people one meets for the first time, people of a different nationality, people of a different religion), described by Delhey, Newton and Welzel (2012) as 'out-group trust.' Social conformism is the support for two statements on one's goals in life: "making one's parents proud" and "doing a lot of what my friends expect." Social activism is the social movement activity index described in Chapter 7.

captivating form of trust because it ties people to command hierarchies; social conformism is a captivating form of interaction because it ties people's doings to others' expectations. The emergence of liberating social capital is shown for horizontal trust and social movement activities. Horizontal trust is a liberating form of trust because it opens people to associate with equals; activity in social movements is a liberating form of interaction because it gives people opportunities to voice their claims. As Figure C.2 shows with striking clarity, captivating social capital indeed erodes as dramatically as liberating social capital emerges when emancipative values grow strong. These values are a transformative civic force in procreating forms of social capital that empower the people. In light of these insights, the concept of human empowerment adds value to the concept of social capital: it distinguishes different types of social capital and suggests which transitions between these types happen as human empowerment proceeds.

4. MORAL PROGRESS

Early on, social theorists expressed the fear that human nature is unchangeable and that our species' moral development cannot keep pace with technological progress for this reason (Spengler 1926 [1918]). Yet, there are better and worse sides to our nature, and cultural change can bring the better sides to dominate. As Karl Popper emphasized (1971 [1962]), one side of human nature – the "spirit of the horde" – is the tribal instinct of insider-favoritism and outsider-discrimination. Yet, the capacity for empathy, solidarity, and justice is also part of our nature. The question, thus, is not if human nature is good or bad but whether development brings the better or the worse side to dominance. Recent work in philosophy, psychology, and economics – including Kwame Appiah's *The Honor Code* (2012), Steven Pinker's *Our Better Angels* (2011), and Richard Florida's *The Creative Class* (2002) – recognizes the power of cultural change and how this change favors our better moral qualities.

Indeed, we have seen plenty of evidence that cultural change is happening, and the rise of emancipative values is its most forceful manifestation. As emancipative values give societies a more humanitarian, civic, democratic, and ecological outlook, the better side of our nature begins to dominate. Rising emancipative values are a grass-roots process that creates bottom-up receptivity to the trickling-down of humanitarian norms from global discourses.

Emancipative values enhance people's self-regulatory capacity. This includes the capacity to control selfish impulses. In a way, these values bring more, not less, self-restraint. There is no reason to fear the loss of social controls that disciplined people in traditional society. These controls, and the captivating forms of social capital in which they are embodied, are not needed where emancipative values grow strong. They actually become dysfunctional.

Interestingly, emancipative values harbor a property that is inherent in what Kohlberg (1971, 1981) considers the "highest stage of moral judgment" – moral autonomy: in judging things, people think for themselves and derive conclusions from their own convictions; they rely less on external sources of institutionalized authority (Kohlberg, Levine, & Hewer 1983). This has wide-ranging consequences.

For one, people commit themselves to projects and missions that represent their own inner values. This changes the nature of society profoundly. Society itself gains in intrinsic quality because the ways in which people interact become more authentic expressions of their inner values.

Next, people become less prone to turning a blind eye to social injustice. Instead, people are more easily upset about incidents of injustice. This does not eliminate immoral behavior but it raises moral pressures. A clear indication is the increasing proliferation of watchdog institutions and the vibrancy of critical media that Keane (2009) describes as "monitory democracy." Under monitory democracy, the twin pattern of insider favoritism/outsider discrimination continues to exist, but there is greater effort to bring such malicious behavior to light. Where these efforts are successful, the disclosure effect is often irresistible, forcing office holders in politics, business, and elsewhere to step down and take the consequences. In short, where emancipative values emerge, this indicates the rise of a thriving society inspired by the spark of the Enlightenment.

5. A COMPLETE THEORY OF EMANCIPATION

Let me finish the journey of this book with a condensed restatement of the theory. The theory of emancipation provides a threefold *human empowerment framework*, focusing on ordinary people's action resources, emancipative values, and civic entitlements. The theory derives its description of human empowerment from three central theses: the *sequence thesis*, the *source thesis*, and the *contagion thesis*. All three theses are integrated by a single evolutionary principle, metaphorically labeled the *utility ladder of freedoms*. Accordingly, human empowerment advances as societies ascend the utility ladder of freedoms. This process brings a game change in the nature of life: life transforms from a source of threats into a source of opportunities for most people in a given society. As this happens, practicing and tolerating universal freedoms becomes increasingly instrumental in taking advantage of the opportunities that a more promising life has on offer.

The sequence thesis and the source thesis address two distinct dimensions of causality in this process. The sequence thesis addresses the *endogenous* causation of human empowerment. It suggests that, as growing action resources increase the objective utility of freedoms, growth in freedoms' subjective valuation and in their legal guarantees follow subsequently, giving rise to emancipative values and civic entitlements. Once a utility-value-guarantee cycle is completed, another cycle can start from a higher plateau, and human empowerment proceeds.

Of course, there is no iron law preventing human empowerment from stagnation or recession. Yet evolution has shaped humans as a species gifted with an intellect to pursue utilities, as much as existential conditions allow. Herein resides the seed of the human desire for emancipation; that is, an existence free from external domination. This desire does not guarantee that human empowerment always progresses; yet it makes sure that the human effort is directed toward more instead of less empowerment. Humans are programmed to ascend rather than descend the utility ladder of freedoms: they stop their ascension as long as necessary to continue it as soon as possible.

Compared to the sequence thesis, the source thesis addresses *exogenous* causality. It posits that the human empowerment process originates in two primordial forms of existential security and autonomy, both of which bestow on freedoms an initial utility that is otherwise lacking. These two features are embodied in a natural endowment that I call the *cool-water condition* (CW condition). The CW condition is a combination of moderately cold climates with continuous rainfall over all seasons and permanently navigable waterways. This condition indeed harbors a primordial form of existential security (i.e., disease security), as well as a primordial form of existential autonomy (i.e., water autonomy). These endowments explain why the human empowerment process started in some CW areas, diffused into all other CW areas, and remained limited to these areas before the process started to globalize.

This is where the contagion thesis comes in. It suggests that human empowerment is about to break free from its initial CW condition. In the era of global communications, the florescence of people-powered societies in terms of human prosperity and liberty has reached ubiquitous visibility. If the desire for emancipation was not a natural human aspiration, the heightened visibility of emancipatory achievements wouldn't garner much attention in other parts of the world. Yet, it strikes a chord with people around the world who still live in poverty and oppression but no longer in ignorance. Global communications enables these people to question their condition and join forces to mobilize for change. As this happens, human empowerment begins to detach from its original source. This does not mean the Westernization of the world but, on the contrary, its de-Westernization. For the West's monopoly over human empowerment is about to fade.

References

Abramson, P. (2013). "The Rise of Postmaterialism Reconsidered." In Dalton, R. J. & C. Welzel (eds.), *The Civic Culture Transformed: From Allegiant to Assertive Citizens*. New York: Cambridge University Press, forthcoming.

Acemoglu, D., S. Johnson, & J. A. Robinson (2001). "The Colonial Origins of Comparative Development." *American Economic Review* 91: 1369–401.

Acemoglu, D., S. Johnson, & J. A. Robinson (2002). "Reversal of Fortune: Geography and Institutions in the Making of the Modern World Income Distribution." *Quarterly Journal of Economics* 117: 1231–94.

Acemoglu, D. & J. A. Robinson (2006). *Economic Origins of Democracy and Dictatorship*. New York: Cambridge University Press.

Acemoglu, D. & J. A. Robinson (2012). *Why Nations Fail*. London: Crown Publishing Group.

Achen, C. (2001). "Why Lagged Dependent Variables Can Suppress the Effects of Other Independent Variables." *Conference Paper* (Midwestern Political Science Association Annual Meeting, Chicago).

Ackerman, B. (1991). *We the People I: Foundations*. Cambridge: Harvard University Press.

Ackerman, B. (1998). *We the People II: Transformations*. Cambridge: Harvard University Press.

Adcock, R. & D. Collier (2001). "Measurement Validity: A Shared Standard for Qualitative and Quantitative Research." *American Political Science Review* 95: 529–45.

Africa Progress Panel (2012). *Africa Progress Report 2012*. Geneva: Africa Progress Panel (online at www.Africaprogresspanel.org).

Alexander, R. D. (1987). *The Biology of Moral Systems*. New York: de Gruyter.

Alexander, A. & C. Welzel (2010). "Empowering Women: The Role of Emancipative Values." *European Sociological Review* 27: 364–384.

Alexander, A. & C. Welzel (2011). "Measuring Effective Democracy: The Human Empowerment Approach." *Comparative Politics* 43: 271–289.

Alexander, A., R. Inglehart & C. Welzel (2012). "Measuring Effective Democracy: A Defense." *International Political Science Review* 33: 41–62.

Allison, P. D. (1990). "Change Scores as Dependent Variables in Regression Analyses." *Sociological Methodology* 20: 93–114.

Almond, G. A. & S. Verba (1963). *The Civic Culture: Political Attitudes in Five Western Democracies*. Princeton: Princeton University Press.

Anand, S. & A. Sen (2000). "Human Development and Economic Sustainability." *World Development* 28: 2029–49.

Anheier, H. K., M. Glasius, & M. Kaldor (2001). *Global Civil Society 2001*. Oxford: Oxford University Press.

Ansell, C. & J. Gingrich (2003). "Reforming the Administrative State." In B. Cain, R. J. Dalton, & S. E. Scarrow (eds.), *Democracy Transformed?* New York: Oxford University Press, pp. 164–91.

Appiah, K. A. (2006). *Cosmopolitanism: Ethics in a World of Strangers*. New York: W.W. Norton.

Appiah, K.A. (2012). *The Honor Code: How Moral Revolutions Happen*. New York: W. W. Norton.

Aung San Suu Kyi (1995). *Freedom from Fear and Other Writings*. New York: Penguin.

Avery, J. (2003). *Information Theory and Evolution*. Danvers: World Scientific.

Axelrod, R. (1986). "An Evolutionary Approach to Norms." *American Political Science Review* 80: 1095–111.

Bagozzi, R. P. (1982). "The Role of Measurement Theory Construction and Hypothesis Testing." In C. Fornell (ed.), *A Second Generation of Multivariate Analysis* (vol. 1). New York: Praeger, pp. 5–23.

Bagudu, N. (2003). *Minority Rights: A Definitive Manual*. Jos: League for Human Rights.

Bainbridge, D. (2000). *Data Protection*. Welwyn Garden City: CLT Professional Publishers.

Bairoch, P. (1995). *Economics and World History*. Chicago: University of Chicago Press.

Bakan, D. (1966). *The Duality of Human Existence*. Boston: Beacon Press.

Baker, R. J. (2007). *Mind Over Matter*. Hoboken: John Wiley.

Barber, B. (1984). *Strong Democracy*. Berkeley: University of California Press.

Barnes, S. H., M. Kaase, K. Allerbeck, F. Heunks, R. Inglehart, M.K. Jennings et al. (1979). *Political Action*. Beverly Hills: Sage.

Barro, R. J. (1997). *Determinants of Economic Growth*. Cambridge: MIT Press.

Bates, W. (2012). *Free to Flourish*. Kindle Version (B00APoF9HO).

Baumeister, R. F., E. J. Masicampo, & C. N. DeWall (2009). "Prosocial Benefits of Feeling Free." *Personality and Social Psychology Bulletin* 35: 260–68.

Beck, N. (2001). "Time-Series-Cross-Section Data." *Annual Review of Political Science* 4: 271–93.

Beck, N. & J. N. Katz (1995). "What to Do (and Not to Do) with Time-Series-Cross-Section Data in Comparative Politics." *American Political Science Review* 89: 634–47.

Beck, U. (2002). "Losing the Traditional: Individualization and 'Precarious Freedoms'." In U. Beck & E. Beck-Gernsheim (eds.), *Individualization*. London: Sage, pp. 1–21.

Becker, G. S. (1981). *A Treatise on the Family*. Cambridge, MA: Harvard University Press.

Becker, G.S. & R. J. Barro (1988). "A Reformulation of the Economic Theory of Fertility." *Quarterly Journal of Economics* 103: 1–25.

Beetham, D. (1999). *Democracy and Human Rights*. Cambridge, UK: Polity Press.

Beitz, C. E. (2009). *The Idea of Human Rights*. Oxford: Oxford University Press.

Bell, D. (1973). *The Coming of Postindustrial Society*. New York: Basic Books.

Bentley, J. H., H. F. Ziegler, & H. E. Streets-Salter (2010). *Traditions and Encounters: Volume II*. New York: McGraw-Hill.

Bentzen, J. S., N. Kaarsen, & A. M. Wingender (2012). "Irrigation and Autocracy." (University of Copenhagen, Department of Economics) *Discussion Paper* 12–06.

Berlin, I. (2006 [1957]). *Four Essays on Liberty*. Oxford: Oxford University Press.

Bernhagen, P. & M. Marsh (2007). "Voting and Protesting." *Democratization* 14: 44–72.

Bernhard, M. & E. Karakoc. (2007). "Civil Society and the Legacies of Dictatorship." *World Politics* 59: 539–67.

Bernstein, W. J. (2004). *The Birth of Plenty*. Seattle: McGraw Hill.

Birch, C. & J. B. Cobb Jr. (1981). *The Liberation of Life*. Cambridge: Cambridge University Press.

Blumberg, R. L. (2004). "Extending Lenski's Schema to Hold Up both Halves of the Sky." *Sociological Theory* 22: 278–91.

Bockstette, V., A. Chanda, & L. Putterman (2002). "States and Markets." *Journal of Economic Growth* 7: 347–69.

Boix, C. (2003). *Democracy and Redistribution*. New York: Cambridge University Press.

Boix, C. & S. L. Stokes (2003). "Endogenous Democratization." *World Politics* 55: 517–49.

Bollen, K. (1984). "Multiple Indicators: Internal Consistency of No Necessary Relationship." *Quality and Quantity* 18: 377–85.

Bollen, K. & P. Paxton (2000). "Subjective Measures of Liberal Democracy." *Comparative Political Studies* 33: 58–86.

Bollen, K. A. & R. W. Jackman (1985). "Political Democracy and the Size Distribution of Income." *American Sociological Review* 50: 438–57.

Boserup, E. (2011 [1970]). *Women's Role in Economic Development*. London: Earthscan.

Bowles, S. & H. Gintis (2011). *A Cooperative Species*. Princeton: Princeton University Press.

Boyd, R. & P. J. Richerson (2005). "How Microevolutionary Processes Give Rise to History." In R. Boyd & P. J. Richerson, *The Origin and Evolution of Cultures*. New York: Oxford University Press, pp. 287–309.

Bratton, M. & R. Mattes (2001). "Support for Democracy in Africa." *British Journal of Political Science* 31: 447–74.

Braudel, F. (1993). *A History of Civilizations*. London: Penguin Books.

Brettschneider, C. (2007). *Democratic Rights*. Princeton: Princeton University Press.

Brown, D. (1991). *Human Universals*. New York: McGraw Hill.

Bueno de Mesquita, B., F. M. Cherif, G. W. Downs, & A. Smith (2005). "Thinking Inside the Box: A Closer Look at Democracy and Human Rights." *International Studies Quarterly* 49: 439–458.

Bunce, V. J. & S. L. Wolchik (2010). "Defeating Dictators: Electoral Change and Stability in Competitive Authoritarian Regimes." *World Politics* 62: 43–86.

Cain, B., P. Egan, & S. Fabbrini (2003). "Towards More Open Democracies." In B. Cain, R. J. Dalton & S. E. Scarrow (eds.), *Democracy Transformed?* New York: Oxford University Press, pp. 115–39.

Canovan, M. (2006). "The People." In J. S. Dryzek, B. Honig & A. Phillips (eds.), *The Oxford Handbook of Political Theory*. Oxford: Oxford University Press, pp. 349–62.

Carey, P. (2004). *Data Protection*. New York: Oxford University Press.

Carter, A. (2012). *People Power and Political Change*. London: Routledge.

Castles, F. (ed.) (1993). *Families of Nations*. Brookfield: Dartmouth Publishing.

Cavalli-Sforza, L. L., P. Menozzi, & A. Piazza (1994).*The History and Geography of Human Genes*. Princeton: Princeton University Press.

Catterberg, G. (2003). "Evaluations, Referents of Support, and Political Action in New Democracies." *International Journal of Comparative Sociology* 44: 173–98.

Chafetz, J. S. (1988). *Feminist Sociology*. Itasca, IL: F. E. Peacock.

Chattoe, E. (2002). "Developing the Selectionist Paradigm in Sociology." *Sociology* 36: 817–33.

Chenoweth, E. & K.G. Cunningham (2013). "Understanding Nonviolent Resistance." *Journal of Peace Research* 50: 271–276.

Chiao, J. Y. & K. D. Blizinsky (2010). "Culture–gene Coevolution of Individualism–Collectivism and the Serotonin Transporter Gene." *Proceedings of the Royal Society* 277: 529–37.

Chirkov, V. I., R. M. Ryan, Y. Kim, & U. Kaplan (2003). "Differentiating Autonomy from Individualism and Independence." *Journal of Personality and Social Psychology* 84: 97–110.

Chirot, D. (1994). *How Societies Change*. Thousand Oaks, CA: Pine Forge.

Chomsky, N. (2000). *New Horizons in the Study of Language and Mind*. New York: Cambridge University Press.

Cingranelli, J. & D. L. Richards (1999). "Respect for Human Rights after the End of the Cold War." *Journal of Peace Research* 36: 511–34.

Cingranelli, J. & D. L. Richards (2010). *CIRI Dataset 2008* (online at: ciri.binghamton. edu/index.asp).

Clark, D. A. (2002). *Visions of Development*. Northampton, MA: Edward Elgar.

Clark, D. A. (2006). "Capability Approach." In D. A. Clark (ed.), *The Elgar Companion to Development Studies*. Cheltenham: Edward Elgar.

Clark, H. (2009). "Introduction." In H. Clark (ed.), *People Power: Unarmed Resistance and Global Solidarity*. London: Pluto Press, pp. 1–22.

Coleman, I. (2004). "The Payoff from Women's Rights." *Foreign Affairs* 83: 80–95.

Coleman, J. S. (1990). *Foundations of Social Theory*. Cambridge, MA: Harvard University Press.

Collier, D. & S. Levitsky (1997). "Democracies with Adjectives." *World Politics* 49: 430–51.

Coltman, T., T. M. Divenney, D. F. Midgley, & S. Venaik (2008). "Formative versus Reflective Measurement Models." *Journal of Business Research* 61: 1250–1262.

Conrad, C. R. & J. H. DeMeritt (2013). "Constrained by the Bank and the Ballot." *Journal of Peace Research* 50: 106–119.

Cronbach, L. & L. Furby (1970). "How Should We Measure Change – Or Should We?" *Psychological Bulletin* 105: 68–80.

Dahl, R. A. (1973). *Polyarchy* (1st ed. 1971). New Haven: Yale University Press.

Dahl, R. A. (1989). *Democracy and Its Critics*. New Haven: Yale University Press.

Dahl, R. A. (2000). *On Democracy*. New Haven: Yale University Press.

Dalai Lama (1999). "Buddhism, Asian Values, and Democracy." *Journal of Democracy* 10: 3–7.

Dalton, R. J. (1994). *The Green Rainbow*. New Haven: Yale University Press.

Dalton, R. J. (2004). *Democratic Challenges, Democratic Choices*. Oxford: Oxford University Press.

Dalton, R. J. (2006). *Citizen Politics*. Washington, DC: CQ Press.

Dalton, R.J. & C. Welzel (eds.) (2013). *The Civic Culture Transformed: From Allegiant to Assertive Citizens*. New York: Cambridge University Press, forthcoming.

Dalton, R.J., D.C. Shin, & W. Jou (2007). "Understanding Democracy." *Journal of Democracy* 18: 142–56.

Dalton, R.J., A. van Sickle, & S. Weldon (2010). "The Individual-Institutional Nexus of Protest Behavior." *British Journal of Political Science* 40: 51–73.

Davenport, C. (2005). "Introduction." In C. Davenport, H. Johnston & C. Mueller (eds.), *Repression and Mobilization*. Minneapolis: University of Minnesota Press.

Davenport, C. (2007). "State Repression and Political Order." *Annual Review of Political Science* 10: 1–23.

Davenport, C. & D.A. Armstrong (2004). "Democracy and the Violation of Human Rights." *American Journal of Political Science* 48: 538–554.

Davidson, R. & G.J. MacKinnon (1993). *Estimation and Inference in Econometrics*. Oxford: Oxford University Press.

Deci, E.L. & R.M. Ryan (2000). "The What and Why of Goal Pursuits. *Psychological Inquiry* 11: 227–68.

Dell, M., B.F. Jones, & B.A. Olken (2011). "Temperature Shocks and Economic Growth." (NBER Working Paper No. 14132), Cambridge, MA: National Bureau of Economic Research.

Delhey, J. (2009). "From Materialist to Postmaterialist Happiness ?" *World Values Research* 2: 30–54.

Delhey, J., K. Newton, & C. Welzel (2011). "How General is Trust in 'Most' People?" *American Sociological Review* 76: 786–807.

Denton, T. (2008). "Indexes of Validity and Reliability for Cross-Societal Measures." *Cross-Cultural Research* 42: 118–47.

Deschenes, O. & M. Greenstone (2007). "The Economic Impacts of Climate Change" *American Economic Review* 97: 354–385.

Diamantopoulos, A. & H.M. Winklhofer (2001). "Index Construction with Formative Indicators." *Journal of Marketing Research* 38: 269–77.

Diamond, J. (1997). *Guns, Germs, and Steel*. New York. W.W. Norton.

Diamond, J. (2005). *Collapse*. New York: Viking Press.

Diamond, L. (2002). "Thinking about Hybrid Regimes." *Journal of Democracy* 13: 21–35.

Diamond, L. (2008). *The Spirit of Democracy*. New York: Henry Holt.

Diamond, L. & A. Inkeles (1980). "Personal Development and National Development." In A. Szalai & F.M. Andrews (eds.), *The Quality of Life: Comparative Studies*. London: Sage, pp. 73–110.

Diener, E., R.E. Lucas, & C.N. Scollon (2006). "Beyond the Hedonic Treadmill." *American Psychologist* 61: 305–14.

Distin, K. (2011). *Cultural Evolution*. New York: Cambridge University Press.

Divale, W. (2004). "Codebook for the Standard Cross-Cultural Sample." *World Cultures* 14: 1–362.

Donnelly, J. (2003). *Universal Human Rights in Theory and Practice*. Ithaca: Cornell University Press.

Donnelly, J. (2006). "Human Rights." In J.S. Dryzek, B. Honig & A. Phillips (eds.), *The Oxford Handbook of Political Theory*. Oxford: Oxford University Press, pp. 601–20.

Doorenspleet, R. (2000). "Reassessing the Three Waves of Democratization." *World Politics* 52: 384–406.

Dreher, A., N. Gaston, & W. J. M. Martens (2008). *Measuring Globalisation*. New York: Springer.

Drucker, P. (1993). *Post-Capitalist Society*. New York: Harper Collins.

Dumont, L. (1986). *Essays on Individualism*. Chicago: University of Chicago Press.

Dunbar, R., C. Knight, & C. Power (1999). "An Evolutionary Approach to Human Culture." In R. Dunbar, C. Knight & C. Power (eds.), *The Evolution of Culture*. New Brunswick: Rutgers University Press, pp. 1–14.

Dunbar, R. & S. Shultz (2007a). "Evolution in the Social Brain." *Science* 7: 1344–1347.

Dunbar, R. & S. Shultz (2007b). "Understanding Primate Brain Evolution." *Philosophical Transactions of the Royal Society B: Biological Sciences* 362: 649–658.

Dunlap, R. E. (2008). "The Globalization of Environmental Concern and the Limits of the Postmaterialist Values Explanation." *The Sociological Quarterly* 49: 529–563.

Dunlap, R. E. & A. G. Mertig (1997). "Global Environmental Concern: An Anomaly for Postmaterialism." *Social Science Quarterly* 78: 24–29.

Durkheim, É. (1988 [1893]). *Über soziale Arbeitsteilung* [On Social Division of Labor]. Frankfurt a. M., Germany: Suhrkamp.

Dworkin, R. (1988). *The Theory and Practice of Autonomy*. Cambridge: Cambridge University Press.

Easterlin, R. (1995). "Will Raising the Incomes of All Raise the Happiness of All?" *Journal of Economic Behavior and Organization* 27: 35–48.

Easterlin, R. (2005). "Feeding the Illusion of Growth and Happiness." *Social Indicators Research* 74: 429–433.

Easterly, W. (2010). "Democratic Accountability in Development: The Double Standard." *Social Research* 77: 1075–1104.

Easterly, W., D. Comin, & E. Gong (2010). "Was the Wealth of Nations Determined in 1000 BC?" *American Economic Journal of Macroeconomics* 2: 65–97.

Easterly, W. & R. Levine (2003). "Tropics, Germs, and Crops." *Journal of Monetary Economics* 50: 3–39.

Easton, D. (1965). *A Systems Analysis of Political Life*. New York: Wiley.

Eckstein, H. (1966). *A Theory of Stable Democracy*. Princeton: Princeton University Press.

Eckstein, H. (1998). "Congruence Theory Explained." In H. Eckstein, F. J. Fleron, E. P Hoffmann & W. H. Reisinger (eds.), *Can Democracy Take Root in Post-Soviet Russia?*. Lanham, ML: Rowman & Littlefield, pp. 3–34.

Edwards, J. R. & R. P. Bagozzi (2000). "On the Nature and Direction of Relationships between Constructs and Measures." *Psychological Methods* 5: 155–74.

Ehrlich, P. R. (2000). *Human Natures*. Covelo, CA: Island Press.

Eisenstadt, S. N. (2003 [1988]). *The Great Revolutions and the Civilizations of Modernity*. Leiden: Brill.

Elias, N. (1984 [1939]). *The Civilizing Process II*. [German original: Der Zivilisationsprozess, Band 2]. Oxford: Basil Blackwell.

Elias, N. (2004 [1984]). "Knowledge and Power: An Interview by Peter Ludes." In Stehr, N. & V. Meja (eds.), *Society & Knowledge*. New Brunswick: Transaction, pp. 203–242.

Ember, C. R. & M. Ember (1998). "Cross-Cultural Research." In Bernard, H. R. (ed.), *Handbook of Methods in Cultural Anthropology*, Walnut Creek: Altamira, pp. 647–687.

Engerman, S. & K. L. Sokoloff (1997). "Factor Endowments, Institutions, and Differential Paths of Growth Among New World Economies." In S. H. Haber (ed.), *How Latin America Fell Behind*. Stanford: Stanford University Press, pp. 260–304.

Epp, C. R. (1998). *The Rights Revolution*. Chicago, IL: University of Chicago Press.

Estes, R. J. (1998). "Trends in World Social Development." *Journal of Developing Societies* 14: 11–39.

Estes, R. J. (2000a). "Social Development Trends in the Middle East." *Social Indicators Research* 50: 51–81.

Estes, R. J. (2000b). "European Social Development Trends." In J. Vogel (ed.), *Valfart and Ofard pa 90-Talet* [Good Times and hard Times During the 1990s]. Stockholm: Statistics Sweden, pp. 435–68.

Estes, R. J. (2010). "The World Social Situation." *Social Indicators Research* 98: 363–402.

Fails, M. D. & H. N. Pierce (2008). "Changing Mass Attitudes and Democratic Deepening." *Political Research Quarterly* 63: 174–87.

Fernandez-Armesto, F. (2002). *Civilizations*. New York: Simon & Schuster.

Fincher, C., R. Thornhill, D. R. Murray & M. Schaller (2008). "Pathogen Prevalence predicts Human Cross-cultural Variability in Individualism/Collectivism." *Proceedings of the Royal Society* 275: 1279–85.

Finer, S. E. (1999). *The History of Government* (3 vols.). Oxford: Oxford University Press.

Fischer, R. & D. Boer (2011): "What is More Important for National Wellbeing: Money or Autonomy?" *Journal of Personality and Social Psychology* 101: 164–184.

Flanagan, S. (1987). "Value Change in Industrial Society." *American Political Science Review* 81: 1303–19.

Flanagan, S. & A.-R. Lee (2001). "Value Change and Democratic Reform in Japan and Korea." *Comparative Political Studies* 33: 626–59.

Flanagan, S. & A.-R. Lee (2003). "The New Politics, Culture Wars, and the Authoritarian-Libertarian Value Change in Advanced Industrial Democracies." *Comparative Political Studies* 36: 235–70.

Flinn, M. & K. Coe (2007). "The Linked Red Queens of Human Cognition, Coalitions, and Culture." In S. W. Gangestad & J. A. Simpson (eds.), *The Evolution of Mind*. New York: Guilford Press, pp. 339–47.

Flinn, M., D. C. Geary, & C. W. Ward (2005). "Ecological Dominance, Social Competition, and Coalitionary Arms Races." *Evolution and Human Behavior* 26: 10–46.

Florida, R. (2002). *The Creative Class*. New York: Basic Books.

Fontaine, J. R. J., Y. H. Poortinga, L. Delbeke, & S. H. Schwartz (2008). "Structural Equivalence of the Values Domain Across Cultures." *Journal of Cross-Cultural Psychology* 39: 345–65.

Forgas J. P., K. D. Williams, & L. Wheeler (2001). *The Social Mind*. Cambridge: Cambridge University Press.

Foweraker, J. & T. Landman (1997). *Citizenship Rights and Social Movements*. Oxford: Oxford University Press.

Franck, T. M. (2001). *The Empowered Self*. New York: Oxford University Press.

Francisco, R. A. (1995). "The Relationship between Coercion and Protest." *The Journal of Conflict Resolution* 39: 263–82.

Francisco, R. A. (2005). "The Dictator's Dilemma." In C. Davenport, H. Johnston & C. Mueller (eds.), *Repression and Mobilization*. Minneapolis: University of Minnesota Press.

Freedom House (2012). *Freedom in the World*. New York: Freedom House (data downloadable at www.freedomhouse.org).

Freeman, M. D. (ed.) (2003). *Children's Rights*. Burlington, VT: Ashgate.

Frey, B. & A. Stutzer (2000). "Happiness Prospers in Democracy." *Journal of Happiness Studies* 1: 79–102.

Freymeyer, R. H. (2010). "A Cross-Cultural Investigation of Factors Influencing Environmental Actions." *Sociological Spectrum* 30: 185–195.

Freud, S. (2005 [1930]). *Civilization and Its Discontents* [German Original: *Das Unbehagen in der Kultur*]. New York: W. W. Norton.

Fukuyama, F. D. (1992). *The End of History and the Last Man*. New York: Free Press.

Fukuyama, F. D. (1995a). "Confucianism and Democracy." *Journal of Democracy* 6 (2): 20–33.

Fukuyama, F. D. (1995b). *Trust*. New York: Free Press.

Fukuyama, F. D. (2000). "Social Capital." In L. E. Harrison & S. P. Huntington (eds.), *Culture Matters*. New York: Basic Books, pp. 99–111.

Fukuyama, F. D. (2012). *The Origins of Political Order*. London: Profile Books.

Fung, A. (2003). "Associations and Democracy." *Annual Review of Sociology* 29: 515–39.

Furguson, N. (2011). *Civilization: The West and the Rest*. New York: Penguin Books.

Gächter, S., B. Herrmann & C. Thöni (2010). "Culture and Cooperation." *Philosophical Transactions of the Royal Society B*: Biological Sciences 365: 2651–61.

Galor, O. (2011). *Unified Growth Theory*. New York: Cambridge University Press.

Gallup, J. L. & J. Sachs (2000). "Agriculture, Climate, and Technology." *American Journal of Agricultural Economics* 82: 731–37.

Gallup, J. L., A. Mellinger, & J. Sachs (1999). "Geography and Economic Development." *International Regional Science Review* 22: 179–232.

Gallup, J. L., A. Mellinger, & J. Sachs (2010). "Geography Datasets." (http://hdl.handle. net/1902.1/14429%20UNF:5:SnYwMY387RxYcu3OxaSFgA), Murray Research Archive, V1-Version.

Gause, F. G. (2011). "Why Middle East Studies Missed the Arab Spring." *Foreign Affairs* 90: 81–86.

Gat, A. (2006). *War in Human Civilization*. New York: Oxford University Press.

Geary, D. C. (2007). "The Motivation to Control and the Evolution of General Intelligence." In S. W. Gangestad & J. A. Simpson (eds.), *The Evolution of Mind*. New York: Guilford Press, pp. 305–12.

Gelfand, M. J., D. P. S. Bhawuk, L. H. Nishii, & D. J. Bechtold (2004). "Individualism and Collectivism." In R. J. House et al. (eds.), *Culture, Leadership, and Organizations*. Thousand Oaks: Sage, pp. 437–512.

Gelfand, M., J.L. Raver, L. Nishii, L.M. Leslie, J. Lun & B.C. Lim et al. (2011). "Differences between Tight and Loose Cultures." *Science* 27: 1100–1104.

Gerring, J., P. Bond, W. T. Barndt, & C. Moreno (2005). "Democracy and Economic Growth." *World Politics* 57: 323–64.

Gibney, M., R. Wood, & L. Cornett (2008). "The Political Terror Scale." *Online Manuscript* (online at www.politicalterrorscale.org).

Gleditsch, K. S., P. Wallensteen, M. Eriksson, M. Sollenberg & H. Strand (2002). "Armed Conflict 1946–2001: A New Dataset." *Journal of Peace Research* 39: 615–37.

Gleditsch, K. S. & M. D. Ward (2006)."Diffusion and the International Context of Democratization." *International Organization* 60: 911–33.

Global Footprint Network (2012). "Footprint der Nationen" (online at http://www. footprintnetwork.org/de/index.php/GFN/page/footprint_for_nations)

Goertz, G. (2006). *Social Science Concepts*. Princeton: Princeton University Press.

Goklany, I. M. (2007). *The Improving State of the World*. Washington, DC: Cato Institute.

Goldstone, J. (2009). *Why Europe*. New York: McGraw Hill.

Graff Zivin, J. & M. J. Neidell (2010). "Temperature and the Allocation of Time" (NBER Working Paper No. 15717), Cambridge, MA: National Bureau of Economic Research.

Grayling, A. C. (2007). *Toward the Light of Liberty*. New York: Walker.

Greene, W. (2003). *Econometric Analysis*. Upper Saddle River: Prentice Hall.

Gugliemo, S., A. E. Monroe & B. F. Malle (2009). "At the Heart of Morality Lies Folk Psychology." *Inquiry* 52: 449–66.

Guinnane, T. W. (2008). "The Historical Fertility Transition and Theories of Long-Run Growth." (Center Discussion Paper No. 990), New Haven: Yale Economic Growth Center.

Gurr, T. R. (1970). *Why Men Rebel*. Princeton: Princeton University Press.

Habermas, J. (1996). *Between Facts and Norms*. Cambridge, UK: Polity Press.

Hadenius, A. & J. Teorell (2005). "Cultural and Economic Prerequisites of Democracy." *Studies in Comparative International Development* 39: 87–106.

Hagerty, M. & R. Veenhoven (2006). "Rising Happiness in Nations, 1946–2004." *Social Indicators Research* 79: 421–36.

Hajnal, J. (1982). "Two Kinds of Pre-Industrial Household Formation Systems." In R. Wall, J. Robin & P. Laslett (eds.), *Family Forms in Historic Europe*. Cambridge, UK: Cambridge University Press, pp. 65–104.

Hakim, C. (2003). *Models of the Family and Modern Society*. London: Ashgate.

Hall, J. A. (1989). "States and Societies." In Baechler, J., J. Hall & M. Mann (eds.), *Europe and the Rise of Capitalism*. Oxford: Basil Blackwell, pp. 20–38.

Haller, M., & M. Hadler (2004). "Happiness as an Expression of Freedom and Self-Determination." In W. Glatzer, S. von Below & M. Stoffregen (eds.), *Challenges for Quality of Life in the Contemporary World*. Dordrecht: Kluwer.

Hardin, R. (2002). *Trust and Trustworthiness*. New York: Russell Sage.

Harris, S. (2012). *Free Will*. New York: Free Press.

Harrison, G. W. (1987). "Stocks and Flows." *The New Palgrave Dictionary of Economics* (vol. 4). London: Palgrave, pp. 506–509.

Hartman, M. S. (2004). *The Household and the Making of History*. New York: Cambridge University Press.

Hatemi, P. K. & R. McDermott (2012). "The Political Psychology of Biology, Genetics, and Behavior." *Political Psychology* 33: 307–12.

Headey, B., R. Muffels & G. Wagner (2012). "Choices which Change Life Satisfaction." *Social Indicators Research* 106: 591–605.

Heitzmann, K., J. Hofbauer, S. Mackerle-Bixa & G. Strunk (2009). "Where There Is a Will, There Is a Way: Civic Participation and Social Inequality." *Journal of Civil Society* 5: 283–301.

Held, D. (1993). "Democracy: From City-States to a Cosmopolitan Order?" In D. Held (ed.), *Prospects for Democracy*. Cambridge, MA: Polity Press.

Held, D. (2006). *Models of Democracy*. Stanford: Stanford University Press.

Heylighen, F. & J. Bernheim (2000). "Global Progress I: Empirical Evidence for Ongoing Increase in Quality-of-Life." *Journal of Happiness Studies* 1: 323–49.

Hibbert, A. (2004). *Children's Rights*. North Mankato, MN: Sea-to-Sea Publications.

Higgins, T. E. (2005). "Value from Regulatory Fit." *American Psychological Society* 14: 209–13.

Higley, J. & M. Burton (2006). *Elite Foundations of Liberal Democracy*. Lanham: Rowman & Littlefield.

Hofstede, G. (1997). *Cultures and Organizations*. New York: McGraw Hill.

Hofstede, G. (2001 [1980]). *Culture's Consequences*. Beverly Hills, CA: Sage.

Holden, B. (1992). *Understanding Liberal Democracy*. New York: Harvester Wheatsheaf.

Homer-Dixon, T. (2000). *The Ingenuity Gap*. Toronto: Knopf.

Hudson, V., B. Ballif-Spanvill, M. Caprioli & C.F. Emmett (2012). *Sex and World Peace*. New York: Columbia University Press.

Human Security Report Project (2006). *The Human Security Report 2005* (online at www.humansecurityreport/info).

Huntington, S.P. (1984). "Will More Countries Become Democratic?" *Political Science Quarterly* 99: 193–218.

Huntington, S.P. (1991). *The Third Wave*. Norman: Oklahoma University Press.

Huntington, S.P. (1996). *The Clash of Civilizations and the Remaking of the World Order*. New York: Simon & Schuster.

Ibrahim, S.E. (2002). *Egypt, Islam, and Democracy*. Cairo: American University Press.

Ignatieff, M. (2000). *The Rights Revolution*. Toronto: House of Anansi Press.

Inglehart, R. (1977). *The Silent Revolution*. Princeton: Princeton University Press.

Inglehart, R. (1990). *Culture Shift in Advanced Industrial Societies*. Princeton: Princeton University Press.

Inglehart, R. (1995). "Public Support for Environmental Protection." *PS: Political Science and Politics* 28: 57–72.

Inglehart, R. (1997). *Modernization and Postmodernization*. Princeton: Princeton University Press.

Inglehart, R. (2003). "How Solid Is Mass Support for Democracy – And How Do We Measure It?" *PS: Political Science and Politics* 36: 51–7.

Inglehart, R. (2008). "Changing Values among Western Publics from 1970 to 2006." *West European Politics* 31: 130–146.

Inglehart, R. & P. Abramson (1999). "Measuring Postmaterialism." *The American Political Science Review* 93: 665–77.

Inglehart, R. & W.E. Baker (2000). "Modernization, Cultural Change, and the Persistence of Traditional Values." *American Sociological Review* 65: 19–51.

Inglehart, R. & G. Catterberg (2003). "Trends in Political Action." In R. Inglehart (ed.), *Islam, Gender, Culture, and Democracy*. Willowdale: de Sitter, pp. 77–93.

Inglehart, R., R. Foa, C. Peterson, & C. Welzel (2008). "Development, Freedom and Rising Happiness." *Perspectives on Psychological Science* 3: 264–85.

Inglehart, R. & P. Norris (2003). *Rising Tide*. New York: Cambridge University Press.

Inglehart, R., E. Ponarin, & C. Welzel (forthcoming). "Culture, Genes, and Political Choices" (unpublished manuscript).

Inglehart, R. & C. Welzel (2005). *Modernization, Cultural Change, and Democracy*. New York: Cambridge University Press.

Inkeles, A. & D. Smith (1974). *Becoming Modern*. Cambridge, MA: Harvard University Press.

International Gay and Lesbian Human Rights Commission (2010). *Country Reports* (online at http://www.iglhrc.org/content/information-country)

Ishay, M. R. (2008). *The History of Human Rights*. Berkeley: University of California Press.

Jackman, R. W. & R. A. Miller (1998). "Social Capital and Politics." *Annual Review of Political Science* 1: 47–73.

Jones, E. L. (1987). *The European Miracle*. New York: Cambridge University Press.

Kabeer, N. (1999). "Resources, Agency and Achievements." *Development and Change* 30: 435–464.

Kafka, T. (2005). *Gay Rights*. San Diego: Lucent Books.

Kagitcibasi, C. (1997). "Individualism and Collectivism." In J. W. Berry, M. H. Segall & C. Kagitcibasi (eds.), *Handbook of Cross-cultural Psychology* (vol. 3). Needham Heights: Allyn & Bacon, pp. 1–50.

Kagitcibasi, C. (2005). "Autonomy and Relatedness in Cultural Context." *Journal of Cross-Cultural Psychology* 36: 403–22.

Kalandadze, K. & M. A. Orenstein (2009). "Electoral Protests and Democratization beyond the Color Revolutions." *Comparative Political Studies* 42: 1403–1425.

Kaplan, H. S., M. Gurven, & J. B. Lancaster (2007). "Brain Evolution and the Human Adaptive Complex." In S. W. Gangestad & J. A. Simpson (eds.), *The Evolution of the Mind: Fundamental Questions and Controversies*. NY, Guilford Press, pp. 269–279.

Karatnycky, A. & P. Ackerman (2005). *How Freedom Is Won*. Washington, D.C.: Freedom House.

Kaufmann, D., A. Kraay, & M. Mastruzzi (2008). "Governance Matters V." *World Bank Policy Research Department Working Paper* No. 2195. Washington, D.C.: World Bank.

Keane, J. (2009). *The Life and Death of Democracy*. New York: Norton.

Keele, L. & N. J. Kelly (2006). "Dynamic Models for Dynamic Theories." *Political Analysis* 14: 186–205.

King, G., R. O. Keohane, & S. Verba (1994). *Designing Social Inquiry*. Princeton: Princeton University Press.

Kiyoshi, H. (1999). "Marriage Patterns and the Demographic System of Late Tokugawa Japan." *Japan Review* 11: 129–144

Klingemann, H. D. (1999). "Mapping Political Support in the 1990s." In P. Norris (ed.), *Critical Citizens*. New York: Oxford University Press.

Kluckhohn, C. (1951). "Value and Value Orientation in the Theory of Action." In T. Parsons & E. Shils (eds.), *Towards a General Theory of Action*. Cambridge, MA: Harvard University Press.

Kohlberg, L. (1971). "From 'Is' to 'Ought': How to Commit the Naturalistic Fallacy and Get Away with It in the Study of Moral Development." In T. Mischel (ed.), *Cognitive Development and Epistemology*. New York: Academic Press, pp. 151–284.

Kohlberg, L. (1981). *Essays on Moral Development*. San Francisco: Harper & Row.

Kohlberg, L., C. Levine & A. Hewer (1983). *Moral Stages*. Basel: Karger.

Krieckhaus, J. (2004). "The Regime Debate Revisited." *British Journal of Political Science* 34: 635–655.

Kriesi, H.-P. (2009). "Social Movements." In D. Caramani (ed.), *Comparative Politics*. Oxford: Oxford University Press.

Kuhle, M. (2011). "Ice Age Development Theory." In V. P. Singh, P. Singh & U. K. Haritashya (eds.), *Encyclopedia of Snow, Ice and Glaciers*. New York: Springer, pp. 576–581.

Kukathan, C. (2006). "Moral Universalism and Cultural Difference." In J. S. Dryzek, B. Honig & A. Phillips (eds.). *The Oxford Handbook of Political Theory*. Oxford: Oxford University Press, pp. 581–98.

Kuran, T. (1991). "Now Out of Never: The Element of Surprise in the East European Revolution of 1989." *World Politics* 44: 7–48.

Kuran, T. (2004). "Why the Middle East is Economically Underdeveloped." *Journal of Economic Perspectives* 18: 71–90.

Kymlicka, W. (1995). *Multicultural Citizenship*. Oxford: Oxford University Press.

Lal, D. (1998). *Unintended Consequences*. Boston: MIT Press.

Landes, D. S. (1998). *The Wealth and Poverty of Nations*. New York: W. W. Norton.

Landman, T. (2005). *Protecting Human Rights*. Washington, DC: Georgetown University Press.

Landman, T. (2006). *Studying Human Rights*. London: Routledge.

Laslett, P. (1989). "The European Family and Early Industrialization." In J. Baechler, J. Hall & M. Mann (eds.), *Europe and the Rise of Capitalism*. Oxford: Basil Blackwell, pp. 234–42.

Lasswell, H. (1951). *Democratic Character*. Glencoe, IL: Free Press.

Lax, J. R. & J. H Philipps (2012). "The Democratic Deficit." *American Journal of Political Science* 56: 148–166.

Lenzen, M. & S. A. Murray (2003). "The Ecological Footprint." *ISA Research Paper* 01–03. Sidney: University of Sidney.

Levine, D. (2001). *At the Dawn of Modernity*. Berkeley: University of California Press.

Levitsky, S. & L. A. Way (2002). "Elections Without Democracy." *Journal of Democracy* 13: 51–65.

Levitsky, S. & L. A. Way (2010). *Competitive Authoritarianism*. New York: Cambridge University Press.

Liker, J. K., S. Augustyniak, & G. J. Duncan (1985). "Panel Data and Models of Change." *Social Science Research* 14: 80–101.

Lipset, S. M. (1959). "Some Social Requisites of Democracy." *American Political Science Review* 53: 69–105.

Lipset, S. M. (1960). *Political Man*. Garden City: Doubleday.

Lipsey, R.G., K. Carlaw & C. Bekar (2005). "Historical Record on the Control of Family Size." In R.G. Lipsey, K. Carlaw & C. Bekar (eds.), *Economic Transformations: General Purpose Technologies and Long-Term Economic Growth*. New York: Oxford University Press, pp. 335–340.

Lomborg, B. (2001). *The Skeptical Environmentalist*. Cambridge, UK: Cambridge University Press.

Long, I. (2004). *Consumer Rights*. Dublin: Thomas Round Hall.

Lykken, D. (2000). *Happiness*. New York: St. Martin's Griffin.

Mackerle-Bixa, S., M. Meyer, & G. Strunk (2009). "Membership and Participation." *Journal of Civil Society* 5: 243–63.

Macpherson, C. B. (1977). *The Life and Times of Liberal Democracy*. Oxford: Oxford University Press.

Maddison, A. (2007). *Contours of the World Economy 1–2030*. Oxford: Oxford University Press.

Mahajan, G. (2011). *Accommodating Diversity*. New Delhi: Oxford University Press.

Mandela, N. (1994). *Long Walk to Freedom*. New York: Backbay Book.

Mann, M. (1986). The Sources of Social Power (vol. 1). New York: Cambridge University Press.

Markoff, J. (1996). *Waves of Democracy*. Thousands Oaks: Pine Forge Press.

Marshall, T. H. (1950). *Citizenship and Social Class and Other Essays*. Cambridge: Cambridge University Press.

Marshall, M. G. & K. Jaggers (2004). *Polity IV Project* (Data Users Manual). University of Maryland.

Maryanski, A. & J. H. Turner (1992). *The Social Cage*. Stanford: Stanford University Press.

Maslow, A. (1988 [1954]). *Motivation and Personality* (3rd ed.). New York: Harper & Row.

Masters, W. A. & K. D. Wiebe (2000). "Climate and Agricultural Productivity." Center for International Development. Cambridge, MA: Harvard University.

Matthews, G., I. J. Deary, & M. C. Whiteman (2003). *Personality Traits*. New York: Cambridge University Press.

Mattes, R. & M. Bratton (2007). "Learning about Democracy in Africa." *American Journal of Political Science* 51: 192–217.

McAdam, D., S. Tarrow, & C. Tilly (2003). *Dynamics of Contentious Action*. New York: Cambridge University Press.

McAnany, P. & N. Yoffee (2010). "Why We Question Collapse and Study Human Resilience, Ecological Vulnerability, and the Aftermath of Empire." In P. McAnany & N. Yoffee (eds.), *Questioning Collapse*. Cambridge: Cambridge University Press, pp. 1–17.

McCarthy, J. & M. Zald (1977). "Resource Mobilization and Social Movements." *American Journal of Sociology* 82: 1212–41.

McCallum, R. C. & M. W. Browne (1993). "The Use of Causal Indicators in Covariance Structural Models." *Psychological Bulletin* 114: 533–41.

McFaul, M. (2002). "The Fourth Wave of Democracy and Dictatorship." *World Politics* 54: 212–44.

McNeill, W. H. (1990). *The Rise of the West*. Chicago: University of Chicago Press.

Meadows, D. H., D. L. Meadows, J. Randers & W. W. Behrens (1972). *The Limits to Growth*. New York: Universe Books.

Meadows, D. H., J. Randers, & D. L. Meadows (2004). *Limits to Growth: The 30-Year Update*. White River Junction: Chelsea Green Publishing Company.

Merkel, W. (2004). "Embedded and Defective Democracies." *Democratization* 11: 33–58.

Mertus, J. (2007). "The Rejection of Human Rights Framing: LGBT Advocacy in the US." *Human Rights Quarterly* 29: 1036–64.

Meyer, D. (2004). "Protest and Political Opportunities." *Annual Review of Sociology* 30: 125–45.

Midlarsky, M. I & E. Midlarsky (1999). "Environmental Influences on Democracy." In Midlarsky, M. I. (ed.), *Inequality, Democracy, and Economic Development*. New York: Cambridge University Press.

Milbrath, L. (1984). *Environmentalists*. Buffalo, SUNY Press.

Miller, G. (2001). *The Mating Mind*. New York: Anchor Books.

Miller, T. & M. Kane (2001). "The Precision of Change Scores under Absolute and Relative Interpretations." *Applied Measurement in Education* 14: 307–327.

Mithen, S. (2007). "Did Farming arise from a Misapplication of Social Intelligence?" *Philosophical Transactions of the Royal Society B: Biological Sciences* 362: 705–718.

Modelski, G. (2003). World Cities: -3000 to 2000. Washington, D.C.: Faros.

Modelski, G. & P. Gardner (2002). "Democratization in Long Perspective Revisited." *Technological Forecasting and Social Change* 69: 359–76.

Moore, S. & J. L. Simon (2000). *It's Getting Better All the Time*. Washington, D.C.: Cato Institute.

Morales, L. & P. Geurts (2007). "Associational Involvement." In J. van Deth, J. R. Montero & A. Westholm (eds.), *Citizenship and Involvement in European Democracies*. London: Routledge, pp. 135–57.

Moran, D. D., M. Wackernagel, J.A. Kitzes, S.H. Goldfinger & A. Butaud (2008). "Measuring Sustainable Development – Nation by Nation." *Ecological Economics* 64: 470–74.

Moravcsik, A. (2000). "The Origin of Human Rights Regimes." *International Organization* 54: 217–52.

Morris, I. (2010). *Why the West Rules – For Now*. New York: W. W. Norton.

Moyn, S. (2010). *The Last Utopia: Human Rights in History*. Cambridge: Harvard University Press.

Muller, E. N. (1979). *Aggressive Political Participation*. Princeton: Princeton University Press.

Murdock, G. P. & D. White (1969). "The Standard Cross-Cultural Sample." *Ethnology* 8: 329–69.

Murray, D. R. & M. Schaller (2010). "Historical Prevalence of Infectious Diseases Within 230 Geopolitical Regions." *Journal of Cross-Cultural Psychology* 41: 99–108.

Nazaretyan, A. P. (2009). "Technology, Psychology, and Catastrophes: On the Evolution of Non-Violence in Human History." *Social Evolution & History* 8: 102–132.

Nolan, P. & G. Lenski (1999). *Human Societies*. New York: McGraw Hill.

Norris, P. (ed.) (1999). *Critical Citizens*. New York: Oxford University Press.

Norris, P. (2002). *Democratic Phoenix*. New York: Cambridge University Press.

Norris, P. (2011). *Democratic Deficits*. New York: Cambridge University Press.

North, D. C., D. J. Wallis & B. R. Weingast (2009). *Violence and Social Orders*. New York: Cambridge University Press.

Nussbaum, M. C. (2000). *Women and Human Development*. New York: Cambridge University Press.

Nussbaum, M. C. (2006). *Frontiers of Justice*. Cambridge, MA: Harvard University Press.

Nussbaum, M. C. & A. Sen (1993). *The Quality of Life*. Oxford: Clarendon Press.

O'Donnell, G. (2004). "Why Rule of Law Matters." *Journal of Democracy* 15: 5–19.

O'Donnell, G. & P. C. Schmitter (1986). *Transitions from Authoritarian Rule*. Baltimore: Johns Hopkins University Press.

Olsen, M. (1987 [1965]). *The Logic of Collective Action*. Boston: Harvard University Press.

Olsson, O. & D. Hibbs (2005). "Biogeography and Long-Run Economic Development." *European Economic Review* 49: 909–38.

Opp, K. D. (1990). "Postmaterialism, Collective Action, and Political Protest." *American Journal of Political Science* 34: 212–35.

Opp, K. D. (1994). "Repression and Revolutionary Action." *Rationality and Society* 6: 101–38.

Oppenheimer, S. (2004). *Out of Eden: The Peopling of the World*. London: Robinson.

Ostrom, E. (1990). *Governing the Commons*. New York: Cambridge University Press.

Ottaway, M. (2003). *Democracy Challenged*. Washington, D.C.: Carnegie Endowment for International Peace.

Page, B. I. & R. Y. Shapiro (1992). *The Rational Public*. Chicago: University of Chicago Press.

Parsons, T. (1964). "Evolutionary Universals in Society." *American Sociological Review* 29: 339–57.

Pascarella, E. T. & G. C. Wolniak (2004). "Change or Not to Change – Is There a Question: Response to Pike." *Journal of College Student Development* 45: 345–7.

Paxton, P. (2007). "Association Memberships and Generalized Trust." *Social Forces* 86: 47–76.

Peel, M. C., B. L. Finlayson & T. A. McMahon (2007). "Updated World Map of the Köppen–Geiger Climate Classification." *Hydrological Earth System Science* 11: 1636–1645.

Pegram, T. (2010). "Diffusion across Political Systems." *Human Rights Quarterly* 32: 729–760.

Petts, J. (2001). "Evaluating the Effectiveness of Deliberative Processes." *Journal of Environmental Planning and Management* 44: 207–26.

Philpott, D. (1995). "In Defense of Self-Determination." *Ethics* 105: 352–85.

Pike, G. R. (2004). "Lord's Paradox and the Assessment of Change During College." *Journal of College Student Development* 45: 348–53.

Pinker, S. (2002). *The Blank Slate*. New York: Penguin Books.

Pinker, S. (2011). *The Better Angels of Our Nature*. London: Allen Lane.

Ponting, C. (2007). *A New Green History of the World*. London: Vintage Books.

Popper, K. R. (1971 [1962]). *The Open Society and Its Enemies* (two volumes). Princeton: Princeton University Press.

Popper, K. R. (2009 [1987]). *Alles Leben ist Problemlösen: Über Erkenntnis, Geschichte und Politik [All Life is About Problem Solving: On Insight, History and Politics]*. München, Germany: Piper.

Powelson, J. P. (1997). *Centuries of Economic Endeavor*. Ann Arbor: University of Michigan Press.

Putnam, R. D. (with L. R. Nanetti) (1993). *Making Democracy Work*. Princeton: Princeton University Press.

Putnam, R. D. (2000). *Bowling Alone*. New York: Simon & Schuster.

Putterman, L. (2008). "Agriculture, Diffusion, and Development: Ripple Effects of the Neolithic Revolution." *Economica* 75: 729–48.

Quality of Governance Institute (2012). *The Quality of Governance Dataset*. Gothenburg (online at www.qog.se).

Qi, L. & D. C. Shin (2011). "How Mass Political Attitudes Affect Democratization." *International Political Science Review* 32: 245–262.

Quigley, C. (1979). *The Evolution of Civilizations*. Indianapolis: Liberty Press.

Rawls, J. (1971). *A Theory of Justice*. Boston: Harvard University Press.

Ridley, M. (2010). *The Rational Optimist*. New York: Harper Collins.

Riesman, D. (2001 [1961]). *The Lonely Crowd*. New Haven: Yale University Press.

Risse, T., S. Ropp, & K. Sikkink (2011). *From Commitment to Compliance*. Cambridge: Cambridge University Press.

Rohrschneider, R. (1990). "The Roots of Public Opinion Toward New Social Movements." *American Journal of Political Science* 34: 1–30.

Rohrschneider, R & M. Peffley (2003). "Democratization and Political Tolerance in Seventeen Countries." *Political Research Quarterly* 56: 243–57.

Rohrschneider, R., M. Peffley & M. Miles (2013). "Values and Environmental Activism." In R. J. Dalton & C. Welzel (eds.), *The Civic Culture Transformed: From Allegiant to Assertive Citizens*. New York: Cambridge University Press, forthcoming.

Rokeach, M. (1968). *Beliefs, Attitudes and Values*. San Francisco: Jossey-Bass.

Rokeach, M. (1973). *The Nature of Human Values*. New York: Free Press.

Roller, E. (2005). *The Performance of Democracy*. Oxford: Oxford University Press.

Romer, P. (1990). "Endogenous Technological Change." *Journal of Political Economy* 98: 71–102.

Roller, E. & B. Wessels (1996). "Contexts of Political Protests in Western Democracies." In F.D. Weil (ed.), *Research on Democracy and Society* (vol. 3). London: Sage, pp. 91–134.

Rose, R. (2009). "Democratic and Undemocratic States." In P. Bernhagen et al (eds.), *Democratization*. Oxford: Oxford University Press, pp. 10–23.

Rose, R. & D. C. Shin (2001). "Democratization Backward." *British Journal of Political Science* 31: 331–75.

Ross, M. L. (2001). "Does Oil Hinder Democracy ?" *World Politics* 53: 325–61.

Roux, V. (2010). "Technological Innovations and Development Trajectories." In M. J. O'Brian & S. J. Shennan (eds.), *Innovation in Cultural Systems*. Boston: MIT Press.

Rowlands, J. (1995). "Empowerment Examined." *Development in Practice* 5: 101–107.

Rubin, P. H. (2002). *Darwinian Politics: The Evolutionary Origin of Freedom*. Piscataway, NJ: Rutgers University Press.

Rudra, N. (2005). "Globalization and the Strengthening of Democracy in the Developing World." *American Journal of Political Science* 49: 704–30.

Rueschemeyer, D., E. H. Stephens, & J. D. Stephens (1992). *Capitalist Development and Democracy*. Chicago: University of Chicago Press.

Runciman, W. G. (1998). "The Selectionist Paradigm and Its Implications for Sociology." *Sociology* 32 (1): 163–88.

Rustow, D. A. (1970). "Transitions to Democracy." *Comparative Politics* 2: 337–63.

Ryan, R. M. & E. L. Deci (2000). "Self-Determination Theory and the Facilitation of Intrinsic Motivation, Social Development, and Well-Being." *American Psychologist* 55: 68–78.

Sachs, J. (2005). *The End of Poverty*. New York: Penguin Books.

Sartori, G. (1984). "Guidelines for Concept Analysis." In G. Sartori (ed.), *Social Science Concepts*. Beverly Hills: Sage, pp. 15–85.

Saward, M. (2006). "Democracy and Citizenship." In J. S. Dryzek, B. Honig & A. Phillips (eds.), *The Oxford Handbook of Political Theory*. Oxford: Oxford University Press, pp. 400–22.

Scarrow, S. E. (2001). "Direct Democracy and Institutional Design." *Comparative Political Studies* 34: 651–65.

Schedler, A. & R. Sarsfield (2006). "Democrats with Adjectives." *European Journal of Political Research* 46: 637–59.

Schmitt, D. P., J. Allik, R.R. McCrae, V. Benet-Martinez, L. Alcalay & L. Ault et al. (2012). "The Worldwide Distribution of Big-Five Personality Traits" (manuscript available online at: www.maryannefisher.com/wp-content/uploads/2011/01/Schmitt-JCCP.pdf).

Schock, K. (2005). *Unarmed Insurrections*. Minneapolis: University of Minnesota Press.

Schock, K. (2013). "The Practice and Study of Civil Resistance." *Journal of Peace Research* 50: 277–290.

Schumpeter, J. A. (2003 [1943]). *Capitalism, Socialism, and Democracy*. New York: Taylor & Francis.

Schwartz, B. (2004). "The Tyranny of Choice." *Scientific American*: 71–75.

Schwartz, S. H. (1992). "Universals in the Content and Structure of Values." In M. Zanna (ed.), *Advances in Experimental Social Psychology* (vol. 25). Orlando: Academic Press, pp. 1–65.

Schwartz, S. H. (2004). "Mapping and Interpreting Cultural Differences around the World." In Vinken, H., J. Soeters & P. Ester (eds.), *Comparing Cultures*. Leiden: Brill, pp. 43–73.

Schwartz, S. H. (2006). "A Theory of Cultural Value Orientations." *Comparative Sociology* 5: 137–82.

Schwartz, S. H. (2007). "Value Orientations." In R. Jowell, C. Roberts, R. Fitzgerald & G. Eva (eds.), *Measuring Attitudes Cross-Nationally*. London: Sage, pp. 161–93.

Schwartz, S. H. & K. Boehnke (2004). "Evaluating the Structure of Human Values with Confirmatory Factor Analysis." *Journal of Research in Personality* 38: 230–55.

Sen, A. (1999). *Development as Freedom*. New York: Alfred Knopf.

Shin, D. C. & R. F. Tusalem (2007). "The Cultural and Institutional Dynamics of Global Democratization." *Taiwan Journal of Democracy* 3: 1–28.

Sidanius, J., F. Pratto, & L. Bobo (1994). "Social Dominance Orientation and the Political Psychology of Gender." *Journal of Personality and Social Psychology* 67: 998–1011.

Sidanius, J., S. Levin, J. Lin, & F. Pratto (2000). "Social Dominance Orientation, Anti-Egalitarianism, and the Political Psychology of Gender." *European Journal of Social Psychology* 30: 41–67.

Simmel, G. (1984 [1908]). *Das Individuum und die Freiheit: Essays [The Individual and Freedom]*. Berlin, Germany: Duncker & Humblodt.

Simmons, B. (2009). *Mobilizing for Human Rights*. New York: Cambridge University Press.

Simon, J. L. (1996). *The Ultimate Resource 2*. Princeton: Princeton University Press.

Simon, J. L. (1998). "What Does the Future Hold?" In Simon, J. L. (ed.), *The State of Humanity*. Oxford: Blackwell, pp. 642–660

Smith, M. (2008). *Political Institutions and Lesbian and Gay Rights in the United States and Canada*. New York: Routledge.

Smith, G. & C. Wales (2000). "Citizens' Juries and Deliberative Democracy." *Political Studies* 48: 51–65.

Sniderman, P. (1975). *Personality and Democratic Politics*. Berkeley: University of California Press.

Snow, D., E. Vliegenhart, & C. Corrigal-Brown (2007). "Framing the French Riots." *Social Forces* 86: 386–416.

Solomon, S. (2011). *Water: The Epic Struggle for Wealth, Power, and Civilization*. New York: McMillan.

Sowell, T. (1996). *Migrations and Cultures: A World View*. New York: Basic Books.

Spier, F. (2010). *Big History and the Future of Humanity*. Malden, MA: Blackwell.

Srivastava, V.K. & D.E.A. Gilles (1987). *Seemingly Unrelated Regression Models*. New York: Marcel Dekker.

Starr, H. (1991). "Democratic Dominoes." *Journal of Conflict Resolution* 35: 356–381.

Stein M. B., M. D. Fallin, N. J. Schork, & J. Gelernter (2005). "COMT Polymorphisms and Anxiety-related Personality Traits." *Neuropsychopharmacology* 30: 2092–102.

Stimson, J. A. (1999). *Public Opinion in America*. Boulder, CO: Westview Press.

Stimson, J. A., M. B. MacKuen, & R. S. Erikson (2002). *The Macro Polity*. New York: Cambridge University Press.

Strom, S. H. (2003). *Women's Rights*. Westport: Greenwood Press.

Suh, E., E. Diener, S. Oishi, & H. C. Triandis (1998). "The Shifting Basis of Life Satisfaction Judgments across Cultures." *Journal of Personality and Social Psychology* 74: 482–493.

Sunder, M. (2003). "Piercing the Veil." *Yale Law Journal* 112: 1399–1472.

Tainter, J. A. (2007). *The Collapse of Complex Societies*. Cambridge: Cambridge University Press.

Tarrow, S. (1998). *Power in Movement*. New York: Cambridge University Press.

Teorell, J. (2010). *Determinants of Democratization*. New York: Cambridge University Press.

The Economist (2007). *The Economist Intelligence Unit's Democracy Index* (available online at http://www.economist.com/media/pdf/DEMOCRACY_INDEX_2007_v3.pdf).

Thompson, M. R. (2004). *Democratic Revolutions: Asia and Eastern Europe*. London: Routledge.

Thornhill, R., C. Fincher, & D. Aran (2008). "Parasites, Democratization, and the Liberalization of Values across Contemporary Countries." *Biological Reviews* 84: 113–131.

Tilly, C. (1997). *Coercion, States, and Capital*. New York: Cambridge University Press.

Tilly, C. (2007). *Democracy*. New York: Cambridge University Press.

Tilly, C. & L. J. Wood (2009). *Social Movements, 1768–2008*. New York: Paradigm.

Tocqueville, A. de (1994 [1837]). *Democracy in America*. London: Fontana Press.

Toennies, F. (1955 [1887]). *Community and Association*. London: Routledge and Kegan Paul.

Toffler, A. (1990). *Power Shift: Knowledge, Wealth and Violence at the Edge of the 21st Century*. New York: Bantham.

Toynbee, A. (1974 [1946]). *A Study of History* (6 volumes). New York: Oxford University Press.

Triandis, H. C. (1995). *Individualism and Collectivism*. Boulder, CO: Westview Press.

Turner, J. H. & A. Maryanski (2008). *On the Origin of Societies by Natural Selection*. Boulder: Paradigm Publishers.

Ulfelder, J. (2005). "Contentious Collective Action and the Breakdown of Authoritarian Regimes." *International Political Science Review* 26: 311–34.

UNIFEM (2000). "Chapter 2: Commitments to the Progress of the World's Women: Rights and Targets." *Progress of the World's Women*. UN Women Headquarters.

United Nations Development Program (2011). *Human Development Report*. New York: United Nations Press.

Ungar, M. (2000). "State Violence and Lesbian, Gay, Bisexual and Transgender Rights." *New Political Science* 22: 61–75.

Uslaner, E. M. (2002). *The Moral Foundations of Trust*. New York: Cambridge University Press.

Uslaner, E. M. (2004). "Trust, Civic Engagement and the Internet." *Political Communication* 21: 223–42.

Valea, E. (2010). "Salvation and Eternal Life in World Religions." *Comparative Religion* (online at www.comparativereligion.com/salvation.html).

Vanhanen, T. (1997). *Prospects of Democracy*. London: Routledge.

Vanhanen, T. (2003). *Democratization*. London: Routledge.

van der Meer, T. W. G., M. Grotenhuis, & P. L. H. Scheepers (2009). "Three Types of Voluntary Associations in Comparative Perspective." *Journal of Civil Society* 3: 227–41.

van de Vliert, E. (2008). *Climate, Affluence, and Culture.* New York: Cambridge University Press.

van Deth, J. (2006). *Citizenship and Involvement in European Democracies.* London: Routledge.

Veenhoven, R. (2000). "Freedom and Happiness." In E. Diener & E. Suh (eds.), *Subjective Well-being across Cultures.* Cambridge: MIT Press, pp. 257–88.

Veenhoven, R. (2010). "Life is Getting Better: Societal Evolution and Fit with Human Nature." *Social Indicators Research* 97: 105–22.

Verba, S., N. H. Nye, & J.-O. Kim (1978). *Participation and Political Equality.* Cambridge, UK: Cambridge University Press.

Verba, S., K. L. Schlozman, & H. E. Brady (1995). *Voice and Equality.* Cambridge, MA: Harvard University Press.

Verweij, M. & R. Pelizzo (2009). "Singapore: Does Authoritarianism Pay?" *Journal of Democracy* 20: 18–32.

Wackernagel, M. & W. Rees (1998). *Our Ecological Footprint.* Gabriola Island: New Society Publishers.

Walker, I., N. K. Wong, & K. Kretzschmar (2002). "Relative Deprivation and Attribution: From Grievance to Action." In I. Walker & H. J. Smith (eds.), *Relative Deprivation.* New York: Cambridge University Press, pp. 288–312.

Walter, L. (ed.) (2001). *Women's Rights.* Westport, CT: Greenwood Press.

Wang, C. (ed.) (2005). *One China – Many Paths.* London: Verso.

Warren, M. E. (2001). *Democracy and Association.* Princeton, NJ: Princeton University Press.

Weber, M. (1958 [1904]). *The Protestant Ethic and the Spirit of Capitalism.* New York: Charles Scribner's Sons.

Weischet, W. & C. N. Caviedes (1993). *The Persisting Ecological Constraints of Tropical Agriculture.* New York: Longman Scientific and Technical.

Weijnert, B. (2005). "Diffusion, Development, and Democracy, 1800–1999." *American Sociological Review* 70: 53–81.

Wellman, B. (1979). "The Community Question." *American Journal of Sociology* 84: 1201–31.

Wellman, B. (2001). "Computer Networks and Social Networks." *Science* 293: 2031–4.

Welzel, C. (1999). "The Development of Civil Societies: Civic Commitment and 'Collective Action Capacity' in 45 Nations," In A. Koryushkin & G. Meyer (ed.), *Communitarianism, Liberalism, and the Quest for Democracy.* St. Petersburg: St. Petersburg University Press, pp. 140–154.

Welzel, C. (2006). "Democratization as an Emancipative Process." *European Journal of Political Research* 45: 871–899.

Welzel, C. (2007a). "Are Levels of Democracy Influenced by Mass Attitudes?" *International Political Science Review* 28: 397–424.

Welzel, C. (2007b). "Individual Modernity," In R. J. Dalton & H.-D. Klingemann (eds.), *Oxford Handbook of Political Behavior.* New York: Oxford University Press, pp. 185–295.

Welzel, C. (2009). "Theories of Democratization." In Haerpfer, C., R. Inglehart, P. Bernhagen & C. Welzel (eds.), *Democratization.* Oxford: Oxford University Press, pp. 74–90.

Welzel, C. (2010). "How Selfish Are Self-Expression Values." *Journal of Cross-Cultural Psychology* 41: 152–74.

Welzel, C. (2011). "The Asian Values Thesis Revisited: Evidence from the World Values Surveys." *Japanese Journal of Political Science* 12: 1–31.

Welzel, C. (2012). "The Myth of Asian Exceptionalism." *Journal of Cross-Cultural Psychology* 43: 1039–1054.

Welzel, C. (2013). "Evolution, Empowerment and Emancipation: How Societies Ascend the Utility Ladder of Freedoms." *World Values Research* 6: 1–45.

Welzel, C. & R. J. Dalton (2013). "Conclusion: How Culture Affects Governance." In R. J. Dalton & C. Welzel (eds.), *The Civic Culture Transformed: From Allegiant to Assertive Citizens*. New York: Cambridge University Press, forthcoming.

Welzel, C. & F. Deutsch (2011). "Emancipative Values and Nonviolent Protest: The Importance of 'Ecological' Effects." *British Journal of Political Science* 42: 465–479.

Welzel, C. & R. Inglehart (2010). "Values, Agency, and Well-Being: A Human Development Model." *Social Indicators Research* 97: 43–63.

Welzel, C., R. Inglehart, & F. Deutsch (2005). "Social Capital, Voluntary Associations, and Collective Action." *Journal of Civil Society* 1: 121–46.

Welzel, C., R. Inglehart, & H.-D. Klingemann (2003). "The Theory of Human Development." *European Journal of Political Research* 42: 341–80.

Wichers, M., M. Aguilera, G. Kenis, L. Krabbendam, I. Myin-Germeys & N. Jacobs et al. (2008). "The catechol-O-methyl transferase Val[158]Met Polymorphism and Experience of Reward in the Flow of Daily Life." *Neuropsychopharmacology* 33: 3030–36.

Williams, A. (2006). "Liberty, Equality, and Property." In J. S. Dryzek, B. Honig & A. Phillips (eds.), *The Oxford Handbook of Political Theory*. Oxford: Oxford University Press, pp. 488–506.

Wilson, E. O. (2004). *On Human Nature*. Cambridge: Harvard University Press.

Wilson, S. (2009). "Horizontal and Vertical Compromise in Securing LGBT Rights." *Texas Journal of Women and the Law* 18: 125–46.

Wittfogel, K. (1957). *Oriental Despotism*. New Haven: Yale University Press.

Wong, D. (2006). *Natural Moralities*. Oxford: Oxford University Press.

Woodley, M. & E. Bell (2012). "Consanguinity as a Major Predictor of Levels of Democracy." *Journal of Cross-Cultural Psychology* 42: 1–18.

World Bank (2010). *World Development Indicators*. Washington, DC: World Bank.

Wright, R. (2004). *A Short History of Progress*. Toronto: House of Anansi Press.

Yale Center for Environmental Law and Policy (2012). "Environmental Performance Index" (online at http://epi.yale.edu/).

Yew, L. K. (1994). "Culture Is Destiny: An Interview with Fareed Zakaria." *Foreign Affairs* 73: 109–26.

Zavadskaya, M. & C. Welzel (2013). "Values, Repression and Subversion." *World Values Research* 6: 46–75.

Zellner, A. (1962). "An Efficient Method of Estimating Seemingly Unrelated Equations and Tests for Aggregation Bias." *Journal of the American Statistical Association* 57: 348–368.

Index

Made in the USA
Middletown, DE
26 October 2023

41408970R00263